WORKSHOPS IN COMPUTING
Series edited by C. J. van Rijsbergen

Also in this series

Formal Aspects of Measurement
Proceedings of the BCS-FACS Workshop on Formal Aspects of Measurement, South Bank University, London, 5 May 1991
Tim Denvir, Ros Herman and R.W. Whitty (Eds.)

AI and Cognitive Science '91
University College, Cork, 19–20 September 1991
Humphrey Sorensen (Ed.)

5th Refinement Workshop, Proceedings of the 5th Refinement Workshop, organised by BCS-FACS, London, 8–10 January 1992
Cliff B. Jones, Roger C. Shaw and Tim Denvir (Eds.)

Algebraic Methodology and Software Technology (AMAST'91)
Proceedings of the Second International Conference on Algebraic Methodology and Software Technology, Iowa City, USA, 22–25 May 1991
M. Nivat, C. Rattray, T. Rus and G. Scollo (Eds.)

ALPUK92, Proceedings of the 4th UK Conference on Logic Programming, London, 30 March–1 April 1992
Krysia Broda (Ed.)

Logic Program Synthesis and Transformation
Proceedings of LOPSTR 92, International Workshop on Logic Program Synthesis and Transformation, University of Manchester, 2–3 July 1992
Kung-Kiu Lau and Tim Clement (Eds.)

NAPAW 92, Proceedings of the First North American Process Algebra Workshop, Stony Brook, New York, USA, 28 August 1992
S. Purushothaman and Amy Zwarico (Eds.)

First International Workshop on Larch
Proceedings of the First International Workshop on Larch, Dedham, Massachusetts, USA, 13–15 July1992
Ursula Martin and Jeannette M. Wing (Eds.)

Persistent Object Systems
Proceedings of the Fifth International Workshop on Persistent Object Systems, San Miniato (Pisa), Italy, 1–4 September 1992
Antonio Albano and Ron Morrison (Eds.)

Formal Methods in Databases and Software Engineering, Proceedings of the Workshop on Formal Methods in Databases and Software Engineering, Montreal, Canada, 15–16 May 1992
V.S. Alagar, Laks V.S. Lakshmanan and F. Sadri (Eds.)

Modelling Database Dynamics
Selected Papers from the Fourth International Workshop on Foundations of Models and Languages for Data and Objects, Volkse, Germany, 19–22 October 1992
Udo W. Lipeck and Bernhard Thalheim (Eds.)

14th Information Retrieval Colloquium
Proceedings of the BCS 14th Information Retrieval Colloquium, University of Lancaster, 13–14 April 1992
Tony McEnery and Chris Paice (Eds.)

Functional Programming, Glasgow 1992
Proceedings of the 1992 Glasgow Workshop on Functional Programming, Ayr, Scotland, 6–8 July 1992
John Launchbury and Patrick Sansom (Eds.)

Z User Workshop, London 1992
Proceedings of the Seventh Annual Z User Meeting, London, 14–15 December 1992
J.P. Bowen and J.E. Nicholls (Eds.)

Interfaces to Database Systems (IDS92)
Proceedings of the First International Workshop on Interfaces to Database Systems, Glasgow, 1–3 July 1992
Richard Cooper (Ed.)

AI and Cognitive Science '92
University of Limerick, 10–11 September 1992
Kevin Ryan and Richard F.E. Sutcliffe (Eds.)

Theory and Formal Methods 1993
Proceedings of the First Imperial College Department of Computing Workshop on Theory and Formal Methods, Isle of Thorns Conference Centre, Chelwood Gate, Sussex, UK, 29–31 March 1993
Geoffrey Burn, Simon Gay and Mark Ryan (Eds.)

Algebraic Methodology and Software Technology (AMAST'93)
Proceedings of the Third International Conference on Algebraic Methodology and Software Technology, University of Twente, Enschede, The Netherlands, 21–25 June 1993
M. Nivat, C. Rattray, T. Rus and G. Scollo (Eds.)

Logic Program Synthesis and Transformation
Proceedings of LOPSTR 93, International Workshop on Logic Program Synthesis and Transformation, Louvain-la-Neuve, Belgium, 7–9 July 1993
Yves Deville (Ed.)

continued on back page...

Catriel Beeri, Atsushi Ohori and Dennis E. Shasha (Eds.)

Database Programming Languages (DBPL-4)

Proceedings of the Fourth International Workshop on Database Programming Languages – Object Models and Languages, Manhattan, New York City, USA, 30 August–1 September 1993

Springer-Verlag
Berlin Heidelberg GmbH

Catriel Beeri, PhD
Institute of Computer Science
The Hebrew University of Jerusalem
Givat-Ram, Jerusalem 91904, Israel

Atsushi Ohori, PhD
Research Institute for Mathematical Sciences
Kyoto University, Kitashirakawa, Sakyo-ku
Kyoto 606–01, Japan

Dennis E. Shasha, PhD
Department of Computer Science
Courant Institute of Mathematical Sciences
New York University, 251 Mercer Street
New York, NY 10012–1185, USA

ISBN 978-3-540-19853-6

British Library Cataloguing in Publication Data
Database Programming Languages. – 4th: Proceedings of the Fourth International Workshop on Database Programming Languages – Object Models and Languages, Manhattan, New York City, USA, 30 August–1 September 1993. – (Workshops in Computing Series)
I. Beeri, Catriel II. Series
005.13
ISBN 978-3-540-19853-6 ISBN 978-1-4471-3564-7 (eBook)
DOI 10.1007/978-1-4471-3564-7

Library of Congress Cataloging-in-Publication Data
International Workshop on Database Programming Languages (4th : 1993: New York, N.Y.)
Database programming languages (DBPL- 4) : proceedings of the Fourth International Workshop on Database on Database Programming Languages – Object Models and Languages, Manhattan, New York City, USA, 30 August–1 September 1993 / Catriel Beeri, Atsushi Ohori, Dennis E. Shasha (eds).
p. cm. – (Workshops in computing)
"Published in collaboration with the British Computer Society."
Includes bibliographical references and index.
ISBN 978-3-540-19853-6
1. Database management – Congresses. 2. Programming languages (Electronic computers) – Congresses. I. Beeri, C. (Catriel) II. Ohori, Atsushi, 1957– . III. Shasha, Dennis Elliot. IV. British Computer Society. V. Title. VI. Series.
QA76.9.D3I585 1993 93–45322
005.74–dc20 CIP

Typesetting: Camera ready by contributors

34/3830-543210 Printed on acid-free paper

Preface

The Fourth International Workshop on Database Programming Languages – Object Models and Languages (DBPL-4) took place in Manhattan, New York City, 30 August – 1 September 1993. The areas of interest and the format of DBPL-4 focused on the integration of programming languages, object models, type systems and database systems. As in the previous DBPL workshops, the setting was informal, allowing the participants to actively discuss and argue about the ideas presented in the talks. The comments and remarks made by the participants during and after the presentations were taken into account in the preparation of the final versions of the papers. The result, we believe, is a set of excellent papers.

The DBPL sequence is closely related to the sequence of International Workshops on Persistent Object Systems (POS), first started in 1985. While the DBPL workshops focus on language and model issues, the POS workshops have focused on implementation issues; thus the two sequences complement each other. Many researchers participate in both workshop series.

The eight sessions of the technical program of DBPL-4 were as follows:

1. Bulk types and their query languages (two sessions).
2. Object models and languages.
3. Data types with order.
4. Mechanisms to support persistence, reflection, and extensibility.
5. Query optimization and integrity constraints.
6. Logic-based models.
7. Implementation and performance issues.

Two invited talks helped to put into focus some important problems and expected future developments in the area:

- "Programming Languages and Data Models for Multimedia, and Authoring Issues, from the Telecommunications Perspective", by Al Aho from Bell Communication Research;
- "What do C++, SQL, and Hell Have in Common", by Tim Andrews from Ontos Corp.

DBPL-4 was co-chaired by Catriel Beeri, Atsushi Ohori, and Dennis Shasha. Jason Wang was the organizing chair. The Program Committee members were:

A. Albano (U. Pisa)	M. Atkinson (U. Glasgow)
C. Beeri (Hebrew U.)	V. Breazu-Tannen (U. Pennsylvania)
A. Dearle (U. Adelaide)	N. Gehani (AT&T)
A. Makinouchi (Kyusyu U.)	U. Lipeck (U. Hannover)
A. Ohori (Kyoto U.)	D. Shasha (New York U.)
E. Simon (INRIA)	S. Zdonik (Brown U.)

The organizers would like to gratefully acknowledge partial support provided to the workshop by NYU and NJIT. Many thanks also to Paris Kanellakis of Brown University for providing invaluable advice on organizing the workshop.

The following individuals helped in the review process of the papers:

Sonia Berman	Fred Brown	Peter Buneman
Richard Connor	Richard Cooper	Susan Davidson
Laurent Daynes	Henry Detmold	Alex Farkas
Michael Gertz	David Hulse	Gerhard Koschorreck
Anthony Kosky	Leonid Libkin	João Lopes
Michael Oudshoorn	Paul Philbrow	Dag Sjøberg
Susan Spence	Dan Suciu	Francis Vaughan
Ray Welland	Andrew Wendelborn	Limsoon Wong

Catriel Beeri, Atsushi Ohori, Dennis Shasha
DBPL-4 co-chairs

Contents

Invited Talk

Regular Papers

Invited Talk

Designing Linguistic Interfaces to an Object Database or What do C++, SQL, and Hell have in Common?

T. Andrews
Ontos Corp.
Burlington, MA 01801 USA

Introduction

I was asked to address a few interesting issues in this talk from the perspective of a practitioner making commercial products. What type of DBPL would you create if you could have anything? What did you create? What are some of your experiences in dealing with C++ and SQL as "de fact" standard languages for OOPL and database query? The joke in the title is one that has circulated amongst the technical community I've been in for years. It points out that "industry" seems to make the worst possible choices from a technical view: many would argue that the dominant relational and object products are not the most technically superior, and SQL became the dominant language in the relational database world, despite many clearly better ideas: Quel and E-Quel from Ingres, the Relational Model book produced by Michael Brodie et al, and so forth. Now SQL is the standard database interface even if your database is not relational!

Along similar lines the programming community has chosen C++ as the standard OOPL, despite more promising languages such as Smalltalk, CLOS, Prolog, Eiffel, etc. Today C++ is the standard language for object descriptions as well — most object databases (OODBs) use C++ as their type description language, and new standards, such as the IDL language from OMG, are spin-offs from C++. In each case we have chosen one of the "lowest level" languages in the field, and after all, you can't get much lower that hell itself.

It is indeed unfortunate that these standards prevail, but I believe it reflects a deeper, cultural problem: that of the paradigm shift. Kuhn wrote elegantly about the difficulty of changing perspectives even when individuals try to change. Software seems no different; it seems that part of the problem is the lack of guideposts until a new generation appears who aren't tied to the old guideposts. Programmers using SQL and C++ are doing better than the previous generation of COBOL and assembly language programmers. It seems difficult for the community to grasp that it is simply improving the "old way" and that there is a "new way" with dramatically better results. After all, there is not the critical mass of tangible successes using the "new way" so even if it is never adopted, who will miss it?

The Ideal Form

Against this backdrop, I will answer the questions posed at the beginning, the first of which dealt with the construction of an ideal DBPL. For me, this means a unifying framework between the programming and database environment, which, for me, means objects at the heart. In order to gain the benefits I want: a language that is terse, expressive, extensible, and reflexive, I am drawn towards an object approach. If I give up on any of these goals I lose a lot when trying to deal with DBMS issues. For example, if the language is not extensible, I cannot unify new concepts that arise after the DBMS is in use with those already in the system. And I want operators and behavioral extensions so that the entire language is under my control: the ability to add new data in an existing form with fixed behavior is not satisfying (my single biggest issue with the relational model).

If the language is not reflexive, i. e. self-describing, then I must add this meta- layer myself because I cannot rationally build a DBMS without it. A DBMS is inherently dynamic over time: I save things there and find them later. This is very generic behavior and so I want to define it once at a higher layer of abstraction. Relational systems often support this to some extent by maintaining catalogs as tables that can be queried via the standard mechanisms.

It is the combination of features together that results in the enormous benefits shown in Fig. 1 "Kay's Slope Theory", taken from [1]. It tries to capture the notion of elegance as opposed to function. C++ is capable of expressing any computation, and it is extensible, but it lacks parsimony. This one lack causes systems written in C++ to explode in size when complex problems are attacked: it is difficult to leverage previous efforts as effectively as in functional languages such as LISP or declarative languages such as Prolog or even (ugh) SQL.

SQL, on the other hand, lacks extensibility. This makes it very difficult to create new concepts and new forms to control their behavior. This prohibits layering abstractions, a crucial technique for managing large and complex systems, and foists the problem upon the programmer, who then has to deal with three worlds: the relational world of SQL, the structured world of the programming environment, and the passage between the two.

I will not attempt to outline syntactical solutions here. That is after all, the pervue of the research community. Syntax, while important, is not the issue. Ultimately I want the DBMS language to be the (virtual) hub for the semantics of my system. It should be able to support the descriptions of any of today's languages as shown in Fig. 2, and should more easily integrate with OOPL's.

Back to Reality

In the commercial world, any product wishing to compete as a system product in distributed environments must support C++ as a system programming language. In a sense, this makes the job simpler by eliminating the need to define a new language. On the other hand, it means one must find ways to make C++ a DBPL. This presents many challenges, a few of which I will outline here.

C++ is at its best as an application language. It lacks much in the environment to support system development involving large numbers of dynamically invoked modules. Names and namespace management are particularly vexing. C++ has a Byzantine algorithm for creating unique message names from member functions. This is crucial information for an object database managing these classes so that the appropriate member functions can be invoked. C++ also provides no central name directory, and consequently name conflicts are common when trying to combine class libraries. We have compensated for this by building an elaborate naming scheme with global naming services, directories, relative naming, and more within ONTOS DB.

These problems are really a derivative of the more general problem within C++: the lack of runtime type information. For example, given a database full of objects, how does one construct a C++ object in program memory? Without meta information, one must construct meta representations and store them in the database such that any object can be instantiated in memory. This is not trivial in C++ because there is no standard dispatch table, or vptr, initialization. Simply setting the vptr generally works, but this ignores the compiler, and if the compiler does it differently, nothing will work. On the other hand, the only other way to initialize the vptr is to call the object's C++ constructor, which must be compiled. This means compiling a constructor for every class which might be called. Neither solution is ideal, and both get worse as the size of the system increases.

There are also "land mines" that we have encountered that defy categorization. The worst came as a result of the following scenario. In one release of the product, our root class and our customer's class looked liked this (greatly simplified)...

```
class Ontos_Object {...
    print ();
};

class Customer_Object public Ontos_Object {...
    virtual print ();
};
```

In the next release the definitions were:

```
class Ontos_Object {...
    virtual print ();
};

class Customer_Object public Ontos_Object {...
    virtual print ();
};
```

Since our product, like most, is shipped as a library, our customer merely relinked (in systems supporting shared libraries, even this is unnecessary), and in fact most everything broke immediately. C++ gurus will recognize right away that the problem is that changing the declaration of print in Ontos_Object from "plain" to "virtual" added an entry to the vtbl of Ontos_Object and potentially changed the vtbl of all its successors. Without recompilation, the customer's compiled member function calls were sometimes pointing to the wrong place. I point this problem out because it was particularly insidious it two ways that are common to commercial C++ products. First, Ontos_Object::print was a private function whose definition was not shipped in the header files with the product, since it did not change the physical data structure of objects, and was not meant for customer use.

Worse yet, lots of things, but not everything, broke immediately with no obvious explanation for the customer or us. There was no obvious connection to the print member function since lots of other member functions also broke, and some others worked. It seemed random, and created quite a furor until we realized what had happened. Even after we realized it, we were not sure what we could do. We knew we could have prevented this because we had changed the definition, but what if we wanted to add a new virtual function to a base class? Then everyone who built anything from our system would have to recompile everything.

And Then There Was SQL

As if having to deal with C++ as an object definition and manipulation language wasn't bad enough, we were also obliged to support SQL, the accepted database language standard. As I pointed out in the Introduction, this is somewhat akin to recognizing the car as a major advance in transportation, and then demanding that the controls be stirrups and reins. It is particularly unfortunate that we must support SQL in specific as opposed to a relational calculus in general. But support it we do, and in fact we had the clever idea of expanding the semantics of the expressions possible in the terms rather than extending the syntax of the language itself. We simply generalized the types of the terms (e. g. the FROM clause can take any expression whose result is a collection of objects with comparison operations defined), and allowed full message sending to go on within terms.

The biggest limitation of SQL from an object viewpoint is the lack of any concept of identity. SQL is value-based, which makes predicate processing straightforward but forces the awkward value unification operator Join to be used for traversing relations. In my experience this is the most difficult aspect of query construction for practitioners. Most SQL expressions involve several joins to "navigate" the implicit structural model of the DBMS, and only one or two filter expressions. Users can readily construct the filter expressions, but have great difficulty with the joins, and the difficulty increases geometrically with the number of joins in a query. I do not agree with the general notion of the commercial object database community that joins mean "slow". The real difficulty is the lack of expressiveness of SQL due to the lack of identity as a primitive. We finessed this by extending the semantics of the dot notation to mean "traverse the object reference herei" rather than denote the attribute within the relation. This results in expressions like:

```
Select p.name
From Part p
Where p.specification.material.type = ''radioactive''
```

```
Select m.name
From Managers m
Where m.department.employees->cardinality() > 100
```

Note that the use of objects also improves another sore spot with existing relational implementations: the lack of abstract domains. Chris Date has long argued with some cogency that a relational implementation with good expression processing and abstract, user-defined domains is an object database. If one includes the notion of identity and the notion of message sending within domains then I agree. We do not have to worry in ONTOS about joining department id to employee weight because both are defined by their class as having different types and thus cannot be compared.

A Note About Standards

In the commercial world, standards are a dominant force. There are two primary kinds of standards, de facto and de jure, both of which are important to commercial vendors. SQL has moved from de facto to de jure, as has C++. Now objects are making their way through the standards process. I am not a big fan of standards as they exist. The idea is great: standardize on key elements to enable work at a higher level and assure customers of interoperability between products compliant with the standard. However, in the case of SQL, the standard was minimal, and large issues were left out. Vendors created proprietary solutions by extending the syntax or adding features, the most obvious being stored procedures.

In this environment the interoperability argument is specious since commercial developers must use the proprietary features of a product to create a practical application. The object community seems headed in the same direction. There is a group called ODMG (Object Database Management Group) developing a standard interface. It is a slight variant of C++ and again leaves many large issues untouched. The SQL committee is determined to snatch the object high ground with SQL-3. I can only assume that Codd, Date, and others cringe at the sight of it.

SQL-3 seems to be a leap backwards in many respects. It inserts procedural mechanics into the standard, which not only destroys the integrity of the calculus, it goes against the very grain of the declarative semantics that makes SQL interesting in the first place. It adds object "feature" in an ad hoc fashion; specifically its notion of inheritance is structural rather than behavioral. However, SQL-3 will almost certainly be the dominant object database standard, adding more credence to the title once again.

Final Words

I opened my talk by trying to exhort the researchers to continue their labors because they do have impact. I wanted to say something positive before I launched into my diatribe on the commercial realities! But it reflects the truth, and even if only a small percentage of the real power of research ideas makes it into commercial products, it is better than none. The work of Beeri, Cardelli,

Bunneman, Atkinson, Kay, Bobrow, etc. was a major influence on me and my colleagues in formulating our product ideas. The continuing work of today's research will have impact on tomorrow's commercial products, even as they support C++ and SQL-3.

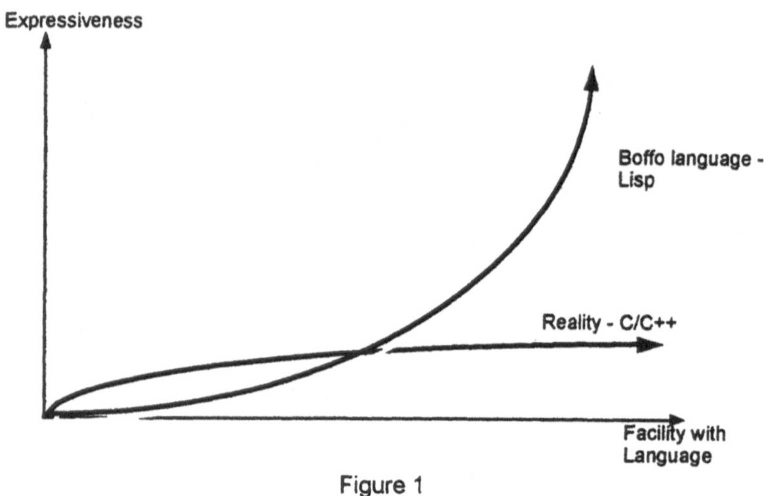

Figure 1

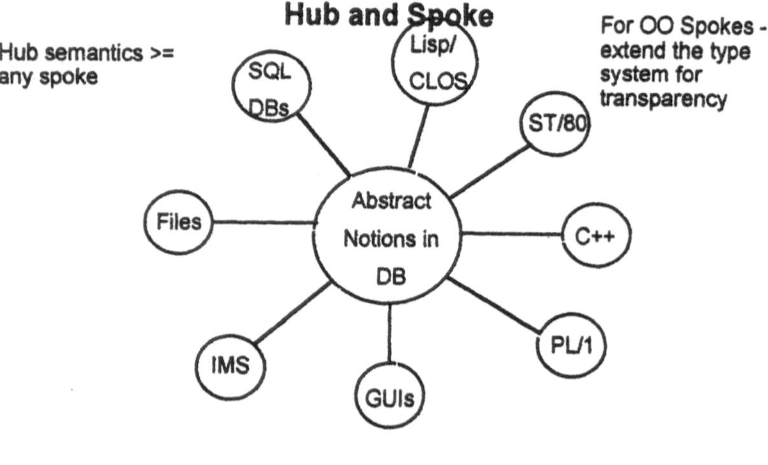

Figure 2

References

[1] Kay, Alan C. The Early History of Smalltalk. in *Proceedings of the History of Programming Languages*, ACM, New York, N.Y. 1992.

Regular Papers

Extensible Grammars for Language Specialization

Luca Cardelli Florian Matthes * Martín Abadi

Digital Equipment Corporation
Systems Research Center
130 Lytton Avenue
Palo Alto, CA 94301, USA

Abstract

A frequent dilemma in the design of a database programming language is the choice between a language with a rich set of tailored notations for schema definitions, query expressions, etc., and a small, simple core language. We address this dilemma by proposing extensible grammars, a syntax-definition formalism for incremental language extensions and restrictions based on an initial core language.

The translation of programs written in rich object languages into a small core language is defined via syntax-directed patterns. In contrast to macro-expansion and program-rewriting tools, our extensible grammars respect scoping rules. Therefore, we can introduce binding constructs while avoiding problems with unwanted name clashes.

We develop extensible grammars and illustrate their use by extending the lambda calculus with let-bindings, conditionals, and SQL-style query expressions. We then give a formal description of the underlying parsing, transformation, and substitution rules. Finally, we sketch how these rules are exploited in the implementation of a generic, extensible parser package.

1 Introduction

A frequent dilemma in the design of a database programming language is the choice between a user-friendly language with a rich set of tailored notations for schema definitions, query expressions, etc., and a small, conceptually simple core language. We address this dilemma by proposing extensible grammars, a syntax-definition formalism for incremental, problem-specific language extensions and restrictions based on an initial core language.

The translation of programs written in rich, user-friendly object languages into a small core language is defined via syntax-directed patterns. In contrast to traditional macro-expansion and program-rewriting tools, our extensible grammars respect scoping rules. Therefore, we can introduce new binding constructs like quantifiers, iterators, and type declarations, while avoiding problems with unwanted name clashes ("variable captures").

*The second author was supported by the European Commission, ESPRIT, EC/US-FIDE Collaborative Activity, 006:9829.

Syntax extensions provide syntactic sugar for common problem-specific abstractions. For example, embedded query notations like the relational calculus, the relational algebra, iteration statements, or set comprehensions can be introduced as abstractions defined from more primitive iteration constructs [OBBT89, BTBN91, Tri91, MS91]. Transactions can be introduced as stylized patterns for side-effect control and exception handling. Similarly, structured form definitions in user interface code can be represented as abstractions over low-level routines for data formatting, input, and validation. At the type level, data modeling constructs like classes, objects, and binary relationships can be viewed as syntactic sugar for more complex type expressions involving recursive types, record types, function types, or abstract data types [SSS+92, SSS88, PT93].

Syntax restrictions introduce intentional limitations on the expressiveness or orthogonality of a core language. The rationale behind restrictions is to facilitate meta-level reasoning and optimizations tailored to a particular application domain. While ad-hoc syntax restrictions are generally considered harmful in programming language design (from a pragmatic and a semantic perspective), they are common practice in database models and database languages. For example, many schema definition languages disallow nested declarations (nested sets, nested classes) or limit recursive declarations to top-level class or type definitions. Furthermore, user-defined types frequently do not have first-class status, e.g., they may not appear as arguments to collection-type constructors. Similarly, query languages typically impose restrictions to rule out side-effecting operations or calls to user-defined functions in selection and join predicates [SQL87]. Some query languages require static bindings to function identifiers (disallowing higher-order functions or dynamic method dispatch) [SFL83], and some disallow lambda abstractions within quantified expressions [BTBN91]. Finally, recursive queries or views are often subject to stratification constraints [Naq89].

The form of extensible grammars discussed in this paper was invented during the implementation of a polymorphically typed lambda calculus [Car93]. Here, we develop extensible grammars in a more general context and describe them in more detail. Section 2 gives a conceptual overview of the issues that must be addressed by a syntax-extension formalism. In section 3 we introduce extensible grammars by examples. An initial grammar for the lambda calculus is extended incrementally with new syntactic forms like let-bindings, conditionals, as well as algebraic and calculus-style query notations. In section 5 the static type rules for grammar definitions and the semantics of parsers generated from extensible grammars are defined. We also present a soundness result for the type system with respect to the evaluation semantics. The impact of these foundations on the implementation of an extensible parser module for the Tycoon database environment [Mat93] is highlighted in section 5. Finally, section 6 compares our concept of extensible grammars with other approaches to syntax extension.

2 Overview

The syntax extension formalism described in this paper assumes the scenario depicted in figure 1. Given the abstract syntax and the scoping structure of a target language *TL*, a new object language OL_0 can be defined by giving

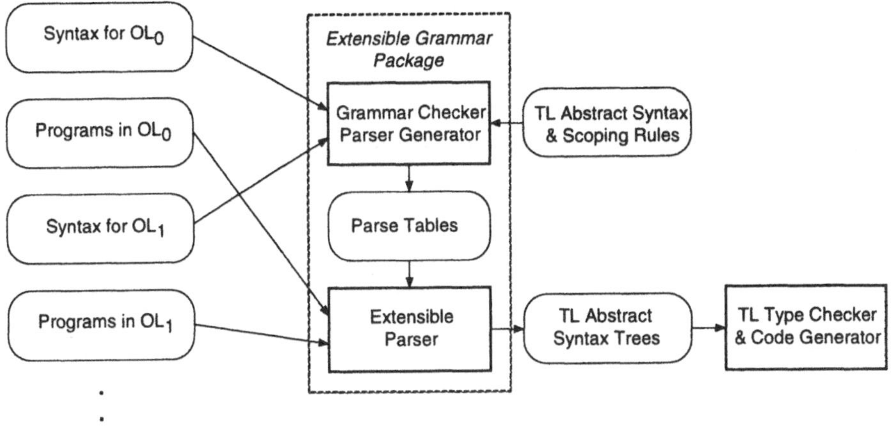

Figure 1: The syntax-extension scenario

its context-free grammar and the rewrite rules that map OL_0 terms into TL terms. The mapping also defines the scoping structure of OL_0. Our formalism is incremental since it allows also the definition of an object language OL_n by a translation (rewriting) into another object language OL_{n-1}.

For example, assuming TL to be a functional language, the object language OL_0 could have either a Lisp-like list notation or an Algol-like keyword-based notation:

```
(defn succ(x) (plus x 1))
function succ (x); begin return plus(x, 1); end succ;
```

Both syntactic forms translate into the same abstract syntax tree in the target language TL that is passed to the TL type checker and code generator:

```
Abs(x App(App(plus x) 1))
```

Section 3.1 gives a complete example of the target-language and the object-language definition for an untyped lambda calculus.

A simple example of an incremental syntax definition is the definition of a language with infix function application (OL_1) as an extension of a language with only prefix application (OL_0). The notation `A` $\Rightarrow$ `B` is used to indicate that the input `A` in an extended language is equivalent to the input `B` in a non-extended language:

```
function succ (x);                     function succ(x);
begin return x + 1 end succ;     =>    begin return plus(x,1) end succ;
```

In a database programming setting, OL_n could be a language with SQL-like query notations that is translated into a lambda calculus, OL_{n-1}, with primitive operations on a collection type (`nil, cons, iter`) [Tri91]:

```
select x.a           iter(X)(nil)(fun(x)fun(z)
from x in X    ⇒      if p(x) then cons(x.a)(z) else z)
where p(x)
```

Incremental grammar definitions are discussed in more detail in section 3.2 and 3.3. The definition of an SQL-like grammar in our formalism is given in section 3.4.

Extensible grammars require extensible parsers. That is, a parser cannot be generated once for a given target language, but has to be extended dynamically to handle programmer-defined object languages. New grammar definitions should be checked to avoid problems typical of macro definitions [KR77], such as grammar ambiguity, non-termination of macro expansion, and generation of illegal syntax trees. Our checking is performed already at grammar-definition time and includes standard grammar analysis [ASU87] to avoid the first two problems. To address the third problem, we develop a sorting discipline on productions (see section 4.1).

A more subtle source of difficulties associated with incremental grammar definition is the binding structure of the target language. The rewriting of object-language expressions into target-language expressions must be sensitive to the scoping rules of the target language and may require renaming operations to avoid name clashes ("variable captures"). A small example using C and the C preprocessor illustrates the issue in a familiar setting:

```
#define swap(x,y)  {int z; z = x; y = x; x = z;}
{int a, b;  swap(a,b);}    /* ok */
{int z, y;  swap(z,y);}    /* name clash */
```

The expansion of `swap(z, y)` leads to the program fragment `{int z; z = z; y = z; z = z}`, where the local declaration of `z` hides the variable `z` that is passed as an argument to the macro. Removing the curly brackets in the macro definition does not solve the problem but yields a name clash between two declarations of the variable `z` in the same scope.

A solution of the scoping issues associated with rewriting inside binding structures requires a formalization of the scoping rules of a specific target language. To adapt our grammar formalism easily to several target languages, we divide the scoping problem into a generic bookkeeping task for the extensible parser and a parameterized language-specific renaming operation. This conceptual division of labor is exploited in the implementation of the extensible grammar package to factor out target-language dependencies. Scoping problems are avoided by distinguishing between binding and applied identifier occurrences, and by renaming when name clashes between identifiers in input programs and in rewrite rules could occur. Note that this solution is not an option for a simple token-based preprocessor. Section 4.2 describes the parsing and renaming rules of our formalism (for initial as well as incremental grammar definitions). We are also able to prove that these dynamic parse rules are consistent with the static type rules given in section 4.1.

3 Grammar Definitions

In this section we introduce our extensible grammar formalism by examples. We start with a small initial grammar for an untyped lambda calculus that is extended incrementally to support database programming language constructs.

```
grammar
  simpleTerm:Term ==
   x=ide                              => mkTermVar(x)
  |"(" a=term ")"                     => a
  |"fun" "(" x=ide ")" a=term         => mkTermFun(x a)
  |"{" f=fields "}"                   => mkTermRcd(f)
  |a=pIde:Term                        => a

  fields:Fields ==
   x=ide "=" a=term f=fields          => mkFieldCons(x a f)
  |                                   => mkFieldNil()
  |f=pIde:Fields                      => f

  term:Term ==
   a=simpleTerm b=termIter(a)         => b

  termIter(a:Term):Term ==
   "(" b=term ")"                     => termIter(mkTermApp(a b))
  |"." x=ide                          => termIter(mkTermDot(a x))
  |                                   => a
end
```

Figure 2: Definition of a concrete syntax for the lambda calculus

3.1 Initial Grammar Definitions

This section explains how to define the abstract syntax and the scoping rules of a particular target language TL as well as the syntax for an initial object language OL_0 (see the oval boxes in figure 1). This information is validated by the grammar checker and then used to generate an initial parser for OL_0 programs.

We use an untyped lambda calculus with records as the target language for our examples. Given a set of identifiers x, the sets of terms (a, b) and fields (f) are recursively defined as follows:

$$a,\ b \ ::= \ x \mid \lambda x.a \mid a(b) \mid \{f\} \mid a.x$$
$$f \ ::= \ \emptyset \mid x{=}a\ f$$

The first step in the definition of an extensible grammar is to define the names of the *sorts* and the signatures of the *constructors* available for the construction of target-language terms. Our example uses the following target-language-specific sorts:

`Term`	terms of the lambda calculus
`Fields`	ordered associations between field names and terms

Since identifiers require particular attention during expression rewriting, there are three predefined sorts to distinguish the binding properties of identifiers:

`Binder`	identifiers appearing in binding positions
`Var`	identifiers appearing as variables inside the scope of a binder
`Label`	identifiers that are not subject to scoping

These sort names appear in the signatures of the term constructors for the lambda calculus:

```
mkTermVar(x:Var):Term
mkTermFun(x:Binder a:Term):Term
mkTermApp(a:Term b:Term):Term
mkTermRcd(f:Fields):Term
mkTermDot(a:Term x:Label)
mkFieldNil():Fields
mkFieldCons(x:Label a:Term f:Fields):Fields
```

Lambda abstractions (**mkTermFun**) introduce identifiers in binding positions, while other identifiers inside terms (**mkTermVar**) appear in non-binding positions. In our example, field labels (**mkTermDot, mkFieldCons**) are not subject to block-structured scoping rules and are therefore defined to be of sort **Label**. For the purpose of grammar definitions it is not necessary to present the binding rules of the target language in more detail.

Given a target-language description in terms of constructors and sorts, a context-free grammar is defined as a collection of productions that translate phrases in an input stream into terms of the target language. A concrete syntax for the lambda calculus with records is defined in figure 2. The notation used is explained in the rest of this section.

This grammar consists of four mutually recursive productions that define precedence of applications over abstractions and left-associativity of applications. Here are examples of input phrases parsed according to the root production **term**:

```
peter        mkTermVar(peter)
peter.age    mkTermDot(mkTermVar(peter) age)
fun(p)p(b)   mkTermFun(p mkTermApp(mkTermVar(p) mkTermVar(b)))
```

The result of parsing is a structured term of the target language. This term can be viewed as a tree in which the inner nodes correspond to term constructor applications and the leaves correspond to identifiers (or literals) extracted from the source text. A token sequence to which no production applies is rejected by the parser with an error message.

A grammar introduces a set of non-terminals (**simpleTerm**, **term**, ...) as identifiers for productions. Productions can be parameterized by terms of the target language (see, e.g., **termIter**). The signature of a non-terminal defines its parameter names and sorts as well as the sort of terms returned by the production.

Each production consists of $n \geq 1$ expression sequences separated from each other by a vertical bar (|). Each expression specifies an input syntax and a result expression (following the => symbol) to construct a term of the target language. Based on the token sequence encountered during parsing, one of the alternative expression sequences is selected and its corresponding result expression is evaluated in an environment that contains the actual parameter bindings and local bindings introduced on the left of the => symbol.

The input syntax accepted by an alternative is defined using the following notation:

"x"	accept the keyword **x**
ide	accept any non-keyword identifier
x	accept the input specified by the production identified by the non-terminal **x**
x(y)	accept the input specified by the parameterized production identified by the non-terminal **x** with the argument **y**
x=y	bind the term defined by **y** to a local variable **x**
pIde:S	accept a pattern variable of sort **S** (see section 3.3)

Each grammar determines a set of keywords reachable from productions of the grammar. The set of identifiers accepted by **ide** in a given grammar **g** excludes the keywords of **g**. Therefore, syntax extensions may introduce new keywords while syntax restrictions may change existing keywords into identifiers.

The binding structure of the concrete syntax is defined implicitly by passing identifier tokens from the input as arguments to term constructors. For example, the variable **x** in the grammar definition

```
"fun" "(" x=ide ")" a=term    => mkTermFun(x a)
```

appears in a **Binder** position of the term constructor **mkTermFun**. Therefore, it can be deduced that the variable **person** in the source text **fun(person)** ... appears in a binding position.

The recursive production **fields** in figure 2 generates right-associative syntax trees for field lists while the production **termIter** generates left-associative syntax trees for function applications. Because we use an LL(1) parser, left-associative grammars are handled in our grammar formalism by passing the syntax tree for the left context of a phrase as a production argument for the recursive invocation of a production (e.g., **a:Term** in production **termIter** in figure 2).

3.2 Incremental Grammar Definitions

This section explains how to define the syntax of a new object language OL_n as an extension or a restriction of an existing object language OL_{n-1}. Such a syntax redefinition is validated by the grammar checker and used to derive a parser for OL_n from an existing parser for OL_{n-1}.

A grammar defines a mapping from non-terminals (e.g., **simpleTerm**, **term**) to variables that are initialized with productions. Inside a production, each non-terminal denotes the production identified by its variable. Three incremental grammar operations are available: addition, extension, and update. The rationale behind these operations is to allow update and re-use of existing non-terminal definitions, preserving the recursive structure of the grammar.

A grammar addition (==) defines a mapping from a non-terminal to a newly created variable initialized with a production. For example, we could use the standard encoding of let bindings:

```
let x=a in b                        ⇒ (fun(x) b)(a)
```

to add the new non-terminal **topLevel**:

```
grammar
  topLevel:Term ==
   a=term                          => a
  |"let" x=ide "=" a=term
   "in" b=topLevel                 => mkTermApp(mkTermFun(x b) a)
end
```

The non-terminal **topLevel** is mapped to a newly created variable initialized with a production that accepts terms of the base language and (nested) let bindings at the top level, but not inside terms.

A grammar extension (|==) destructively updates the variable identified by a non-terminal with a new production. The new production extends the old production with additional alternatives. For example, to extend **simpleTerm**, we could write:

```
grammar
  simpleTerm:Term |==
   "unit"                          => mkTermRcd(mkFieldNil())
  |"let" x=ide "=" a=term
   "in" b=term                     => mkTermApp(mkTermFun(x b) a)
end
```

This grammar extension affects all productions referring to **term**, allowing **unit** and nested **let** bindings within terms.

A grammar update (:==) destructively updates the contents of a variable identified by a non-terminal with a new production that has the same signature, thereby affecting all productions referring to that non-terminal. For example, the definition of **term** could be updated as follows:

```
grammar
  term:Term :==
   x=ide                           => mkTermVar(x)
  |"(" a=term b=term ")"           => mkTermApp(a b)
  |"{" f=fields "}"                => mkTermRcd(f)
end
```

This redefinition affects all productions referring to **term** (**simpleTerm**, **fields**, **termIter**), thereby restricting the expressiveness of the original language by disallowing abstractions.

3.3 Pattern-based Action Definitions

In the previous section, abstract syntax trees produced by actions are specified with explicit constructor applications. In this section we introduce patterns which allow us to write grammars more conveniently by using the existing target language. For example, the syntax for **let** and **where** bindings could be written more clearly using a pattern:

```
grammar
  simpleTerm:Term |==
   "let" x=ide "=" a=term
   "in" b=term                    => term<<(fun(x) b)(a)>>
end
```

Inside the pattern `term<<(fun(x) b)(a)>>`, the variables **x**, **a**, and **b**, introduced on the left-hand side of the production, act as placeholders (pattern variables) of sort `Binder`, `Term`, and `Term`, respectively. A pattern `p<<s>>` in a grammar **g** is translated into constructor applications by parsing the input token stream **s** starting with the production **p**. For example, the pattern `term<<(fun(y) b)(a)>>` yields the nested constructor application `mkTermApp( mkTermFun(y b) a)` when the token stream **(fun(y) b)(a)** is parsed as a `term`.

The keyword **pIde** followed by a sort identifier is used in the initial grammar definition (see section 3.1) to indicates those positions in the input syntax where pattern identifiers may appear. Pattern variables of the sorts `Binder`, `Var`, and `Label` may appear also at those places in the input syntax where the keyword **ide** is used to accept identifier tokens of the appropriate sort.

Many pattern-based syntax extensions require the introduction of fresh identifiers, i.e., identifiers distinct from other identifiers appearing in `Binding` and `Var` positions, to avoid variable captures and name clashes. For example, the syntax for functional composition (**f * g**) could be defined as:

```
grammar
  termIter(a:Term):Term |==
   "*" b=term x=local      => termIter(term<<fun(x)a(b(x))>>)
end
```

The notation **x=local** guarantees that a fresh identifier is bound to **x** for every instantiation of this production during parsing. For example, **f*g*h** is expanded to **fun(x2)(f(fun(x1)g(h(x1))) (x2))**, and **x*y** is expanded to **fun(x1)(x(y(x1)))**, avoiding a variable capture of the input variable **x** by a binder introduced in the pattern.

Since grammar definitions can be interspersed with object-language expressions, it is desirable to allow patterns to contain variables that refer to global bindings. For example, the boolean constants true and false are sometimes represented by the following functions which, when applied to two arguments, return one of them:

```
let T = fun(x)fun(y)x
let F = fun(x)fun(y)y
```

In the scope of these definitions, the following grammar could be defined to replace the keywords **true** and **false** by the variables **T** and **F**, respectively.

```
grammar
  simpleTerm:Term |==
   "true"                        => term<<T>>
  |"false"                       => term<<F>>
  |"if" a=term "then" b=term
   "else" c=term                 => term<<a(b)(c)>>
end
```

During expansion of a pattern with free variables (T and F in the example above), unwanted variable captures must be avoided. For example, a naive macro expansion of the term **fun**(T) T(**true**) would yield the term **fun**(T) T(T) where the expansion of the keyword **true** is bound incorrectly. Therefore, free variables in extensible grammars are handled as follows: Each occurrence of a free variable x in a grammar definition is replaced by a fresh variable x'. During parsing, these modified patterns generate expansions that contain unbound variables (T' and F'). For example, T(**fun**(T) T(**true**)) is expanded to T(**fun**(T) T(T')). After the full input has been parsed, a target-language-specific renaming function is applied to the parsed term. It replaces the binder T and its bound variables by T'' and T' by T. The resulting term T(**fun**(T'') T''(T)) is then submitted to the type checker and code generator.

3.4 Further Examples: Query Notations

In this section we show how some typical database query notations can be viewed as mere "syntactic sugar" for the application of a single higher-order iterator function. The reduction of query notations into a single canonical iteration construct has been exploited in the literature to simplify the type checking of database programming languages [OBBT89], the code generation for query expressions [Tri91], and the verification of functional database programs [SS91, SSS88]. The following examples demonstrate that extensible grammars provide sufficient expressive power to define the syntax of typical database query languages as well as their translation into lambda calculus. This translation preserves the usual scoping rules defined for these query languages.

We assume the grammar extension for booleans defined above and the following global definitions that provide a standard encoding of the list constructors nil and cons and a list iterator iter:

```
let nil = fun(x)fun(n)fun(c) n
let cons = fun(hd)fun(tl)fun(n)fun(c) c(hd)(tl(n)(c))
let iter = fun(l)fun(n)fun(c) l(n)(c)
```

The syntax of a "list algebra" with selection, projection, and binary join can then be defined as follows:

```
grammar
  simpleTerm:Term |==
    "select" x=ide "in" a=term "where" b=term y=local
  => term<<iter(a)(nil)(fun(x)fun(y)if b then cons(x)(y) else y)>>
  | "project" x=ide "in" a=term "onto" f=fieldList(x) y=local
  => term<<iter(a)(nil)(fun(x)fun(y)cons({f})(y))>>
  | "join" x=ide "in" a=term "," y=ide "in" b=term
    "where" c=term x2=local y2=local
  => term<<iter(a)(nil)(fun(x)fun(x2)iter(b)(x2)(fun(y)fun(y2)
           if c then cons({fst=x snd=y})(y2)else y2))>>
  fieldList(x:Var):Fields ==
     y=ide "," f=fieldList(x)      => fields<<y=x.y f>>
  |                                => fields<<>>
end
```

For example, a selection expression with a variable identifier x, a range expression a, and a selection predicate b is translated into an iterative loop. This loop over a has x as its loop variable and starting with the empty list nil it adds those elements that satisfy the selection predicate b:

```
iter(a)(nil)(fun(x)fun(y)if b then cons(x)(y) else y)
```

In this expression, y is a fresh local variable which is bound during iteration to the result of the previous iteration step. This translation correctly captures the scoping rules for the list algebra, since the variable x is visible only in b and not in a. Furthermore, global identifiers are visible in a and b.

The parameterized production fieldList demonstrates how parameters may be used to distribute terms (in this case a variable identifier x) into multiple subterms. Using the extended grammar one can write, for example, the following queries that use global identifiers Persons, thirty, and equal:

```
select p in Persons where greater(p.age)(thirty)
project p in Persons onto name, age
join p in Persons, s in Students where equal(p.name)(s.name)
```

Furthermore, it is possible to nest queries and to parameterize queries:

```
fun(limit) select p in
    select p in Persons where greater(p.salary)(limit)
where greater(p.age)(thirty)
```

Note that the identifier p in the subquery will be correctly bound to the inner p in the generated lambda term.

Simulating SQL expressions is slightly more complicated, since SQL allows the repetition of range expressions to express selections, projections, and n-way joins using a uniform notation:

```
select target(x) from x in a where predicate(x)
select target(x)(y) from x in a, y in b where predicate(x)(y)
select target(x)(y)(z) from x in a, y in b, z in c
where predicate(x)(y)(z)
...
```

Therefore, the rewrite rules have to ensure that the target and the selection expressions appear in the scope of n ($n > 1$) **fun** binders in the generated lambda term. The following grammar uses a recursive, parameterized production rangeIter to achieve the desired rewriting:

```
grammar
  simpleTerm:Term |==
     "select" a=term "from" x=ide "in" b=term c=rangeIter(a)
  => term<<iter(b)(nil)(fun(x)c)>>
  rangeIter(a:Term):Term ==
     "," x=ide "in" b=term c=rangeIter(a) y=local
  => term<<fun(y)iter(b)(y)(fun(x)c)>>
    |"where" b=term y=local
  => term<<fun(y)if b then cons(a)(y) else y>>
end
```

For example, a two-way join would be expanded as follows:

```
select {x.a y.b}              iter(X)(nil)(fun(x)
from x in X, y in Y   ⇒        fun(z1) iter(Y)(z1)(fun(y)
where p(x.c)(y.c)                fun(z2) if p(x.c)(y.c) then
                                  cons({x.a y.b})(z2) else z2))
```

4 Formalizing Grammars and Parsers

In section 4.1 we describe the rules that are used in the grammar checker (see figure 1) to statically decide whether a sequence of grammar definitions and grammar extensions is well-formed. In section 4.2 we formalize the parse rules that define the mapping from an input stream into a constructed term of the target language. We also present a soundness result of the dynamic parse rules with respect to the static type rules of section 4.1 which guarantees that parsers derived from well-typed grammars return well-formed parse trees. This result is generalized in the full paper to parsers derived from incremental pattern-based grammar definitions.

4.1 Static Typing of Grammar Definitions

To describe the type rules for grammar definitions and extensions, we first define the relevant syntactic objects (sorts, signatures, productions, grammars, grammar sequences).

The syntax for term sorts B and signatures S is defined as follows:

$B ::=$	Unit | Var | Binder | Label	predefined term sorts
|	B^1 | ... | B^n	target-language-specific sorts ($n \geq 0$)
$S ::=$	$(B_1, \ldots, B_k)B$	production signatures ($k \geq 0$)

The abstract syntax of productions is slightly more orthogonal than the concrete syntax we have used in the examples. In particular, terminal productions like `ide(B)` or `"x"` may appear nested within constructor and production argument lists. Furthermore, the syntactic separation of productions into a binding sequence and a constructor application (to the right and left of the `=>`, respectively) is no longer enforced. For example, the production `x=ide => mkTermVar(x)` in the concrete syntax is translated into a simple sequential composition $x = \mathbf{ide}(\mathrm{Var})$ `mkTermVar`(x).

$p ::=$	**unit**	unit production
|	$"x"$	keyword token production
|	**ide**(B)	variable token production (of sort B)
|	**local**	fresh object-language variable
|	**global**(x)	global object-language variable
|	x	term variable
|	$p_1\ p_2$	sequential composition
|	$x = p_1\ p_2$	pattern variable binding
|	$p_1 \mid p_2$	choice
|	$x(p_1, \ldots, p_k)$	non-terminal application ($k \geq 0$)
|	$c_{(B_1,\ldots,B_k)B}(p_1, \ldots, p_k)$	sorted constructor application ($k \geq 0$)

The set of constructors $c_{(B_1,\ldots,B_k)B}$ with argument sorts B_i and result sort B contains the target-language-specific constructors (e.g., **mkTermVar, mkTermFun**).

A grammar consists of a list of non-terminal definitions that define a signature, a modification operator, and a production.

$g ::=$	$[]$	empty grammar
$\mid$	$g\ x : (x_1{:}B_1,\ldots,x_k{:}B_k)B\ a\ p$	non-terminal definition
$a ::=$	$==$	grammar addition
$\mid$	$:==$	grammar update
$\mid$	$\mid==$	grammar extension

Each grammar is defined in the scope of its preceding grammar definitions:

$gseq ::=$		empty grammar sequence
$\mid$	$gseq\ g$	grammar composition

A global environment E assigns signatures to non-terminals:

$E ::=$	$\oslash$	empty environment
$\mid$	$E, x : S$	non-terminal x has signature S

A local environment L assigns signatures to term variables:

$L ::=$	$\oslash$	empty environment
$\mid$	$L, x : B$	variable x has sort B

Environment concatenation is written as E, E'. The domain of an environment, denoted by $Dom(E)$, is the set of variables x defined in E. A variable name x may occur more than once in an environment. In this case, the type rules for variables retrieve the rightmost sort or signature assigned to x.

The static semantics of grammars involves the following judgements:

$E; L \vdash p : B$	production p has sort B assuming E and L
$E \vdash g :: E'$	grammar g defines signatures E' consistent with E
$E \vdash g$ **ok**	grammar g defines productions consistent with E
$\vdash gseq \Rightarrow E$	grammar sequence $gseq$ defines a final environment E

The structure of the sort rules for productions p resembles the structure of typing rules for terms in a simply-typed lambda calculus:

$$E; L \vdash \mathbf{unit} : \mathrm{Unit}$$

$$E; L \vdash \text{"}x\text{"} : \mathrm{Unit}$$

$$E; L \vdash \mathbf{ide}(B) : B$$

$$E; L \vdash \mathbf{local} : \mathrm{Binder}$$

$$E; L \vdash \mathbf{global}(x) : \mathrm{Var}$$

$$\frac{x \notin Dom(L')}{E; L, x : B, L' \vdash x : B}$$

$$\frac{E; L \vdash p_1 : B \qquad E; L \vdash p_2 : B'}{E; L \vdash p_1\ p_2 : B'}$$

$$\frac{E; L \vdash p_1 : B \qquad E; L, x : B \vdash p_2 : B'}{E; L \vdash x = p_1\ p_2 : B'}$$

$$\frac{E; L \vdash p_1 : B \qquad E; L \vdash p_2 : B}{E; L \vdash p_1 \mid p_2 : B}$$

$$\frac{E; L \vdash p_i : B_i \quad 1 \leq i \leq k}{E; L \vdash c_{(B_1,\ldots,B_k)B}(p_1,\ldots,p_k) : B}$$

$$\frac{E; L \vdash p_i : B_i \quad 1 \leq i \leq k \quad x \notin Dom(E')}{E, x : (B_1,\ldots,B_k)B, E'; L \vdash x(p_1,\ldots,p_k) : B}$$

Since non-terminal definitions can be recursive, the type checking of a grammar g is performed in two passes. A first pass ($E \vdash g :: E'$) collects the signatures E' of all non-terminals in g, verifies that each non-terminal is defined at most once in g, and asserts that all grammar updates ($x : S{:}{=}{=}p$) and grammar extensions ($x : S|{=}{=}p$) refer to non-terminals with matching signatures in the scope E of g:

$$E \vdash [] :: \oslash$$

$$\frac{E \vdash g :: E' \quad x \notin Dom(E')}{E \vdash g\ x : (x_1{:}B_1, \ldots, x_k{:}B_k)B == p\ ::\ E', x : (B_1, \ldots, B_k)B}$$

$$\frac{E \vdash g :: E' \quad x \notin Dom(E') \quad a \in \{:==, |==\} \quad E \vdash x : (B_1, \ldots, B_k)B}{E \vdash g\ x : (x_1{:}B_1, \ldots, x_k{:}B_k)B\ a\ p\ ::\ E', x : (B_1, \ldots, B_k)B}$$

In a second pass ($E \vdash g$ **ok**), the bodies p of all non-terminal definitions in g are checked to match their signatures in E. The rules for parameterized non-terminal definitions resemble the type rules for lambda abstractions:

$$E \vdash []\ \mathbf{ok}$$

$$\frac{E \vdash g\ \mathbf{ok} \quad E; \oslash, x_1 : B_1, \ldots, x_k : B_k \vdash p : B \quad a \in \{==, :==, |==\}}{E \vdash g\ x : (x_1{:}B_1, \ldots, x_k{:}B_k)B\ a\ p\ \mathbf{ok}}$$

A sequence of grammars is verified by performing the above two passes on each grammar in the sequence using the environment established by its preceding grammars:

$$\vdash \Rightarrow \oslash \qquad \frac{\vdash gseq \Rightarrow E \quad E \vdash g :: E' \quad E, E' \vdash g\ \mathbf{ok}}{\vdash gseq\ g\ \Rightarrow E, E'}$$

It is possible to derive a simple consistency-checking algorithm from these inference rules as follows: Starting with the proof goal $\vdash gseq \Rightarrow E'$, the inference rules have to be applied "backwards" (from the conclusions to the assumptions). Since for each syntactic construct there is exactly one applicable inference rule, the derivation either reaches the axioms (in time proportional to the size of the grammar) or gets stuck in a configuration where no inference rule can be applied. In the latter case the grammar sequence is rejected as ill-typed. In the next section we prove that parsers derived from well-typed grammars never generate ill-formed syntax trees.

4.2 Parsing and Term Construction

Each non-terminal x in a grammar serves a dual purpose. On the one hand, it determines how to parse an input token stream and how to construct a corresponding term of the target language. On the other hand, it defines how to transform a pattern (a token stream inside <<>> brackets) occurring in an incremental grammar definition into an equivalent production. In this section we describe the parsing of input token streams, while pattern parsing is described in the full paper.

For the purpose of parsing it is convenient to rewrite a grammar sequence $gseq$ into a single grammar g of the form $[], x_1 : S_1{=}{=}p_1, \ldots, x_k : S_k{=}{=}p_k$ ($k \geq 0$) such that $x_i \neq x_j$ for $i \neq j$. We use the notation:

$gseq \leadsto g$ grammar sequence $gseq$ normalizes to g

$$g; M \vdash \langle s, i\rangle\, \textbf{unit} \Rightarrow \langle s, i\rangle\, \textbf{unit}$$

$$g; M \vdash \langle x :: s, i\rangle\, "x" \Rightarrow \langle s, i\rangle\, \textbf{unit}$$

$$g; M \vdash \langle x :: s, i\rangle\, \textbf{ide}(B) \Rightarrow \langle s, i\rangle\, x_B \quad x \notin K(g) \quad B \in \{\text{Binder}, \text{Var}, \text{Label}\}$$

$$g; M \vdash \langle s, i\rangle\, \textbf{local} \Rightarrow \langle s, i+1\rangle\, x^{i}_{Binder}$$

$$g; M \vdash \langle s, i\rangle\, \textbf{global}(x) \Rightarrow \langle s, i\rangle\, x_{Var}$$

$$g; M, x = t, M' \vdash \langle s, i\rangle\, x \Rightarrow \langle s, i\rangle\, t \quad x \notin Dom(M')$$

$$g; M \vdash \langle s, i\rangle\, x \Rightarrow \langle s, i\rangle\, \textbf{wrong} \quad x \notin Dom(M)$$

$$\frac{g; M \vdash \langle s, i\rangle\, p_1 \Rightarrow \langle s', i'\rangle\, t \quad t \neq \textbf{wrong} \qquad g; M \vdash \langle s', i'\rangle\, p_2 \Rightarrow \langle s'', i''\rangle\, t'}{g; M \vdash \langle s, i\rangle\, p_1\ p_2 \Rightarrow \langle s'', i''\rangle\, t'} \qquad \frac{g; M \vdash \langle s, i\rangle\, p_1 \Rightarrow \langle s', i'\rangle\, \textbf{wrong}}{g; M \vdash \langle s, i\rangle\, p_1\ p_2 \Rightarrow \langle s'', i''\rangle\, \textbf{wrong}}$$

$$\frac{g; M \vdash \langle s, i\rangle\, p_1 \Rightarrow \langle s', i'\rangle\, t \quad t \neq \textbf{wrong} \qquad g; M, x = t \vdash \langle s', i'\rangle\, p_2 \Rightarrow \langle s'', i''\rangle\, t'}{g; M \vdash \langle s, i\rangle\, x = p_1\ p_2 \Rightarrow \langle s'', i''\rangle\, t'}$$

$$\frac{g; M \vdash \langle s, i\rangle\, p_1 \Rightarrow \langle s', i'\rangle\, \textbf{wrong}}{g; M \vdash \langle s, i\rangle\, x = p_1\ p_2 \Rightarrow \langle s', i'\rangle\, \textbf{wrong}}$$

$$\frac{g; M \vdash \langle s, i\rangle\, p_1 \Rightarrow \langle s', i'\rangle\, t}{g; M \vdash \langle s, i\rangle\, p_1 \mid p_2 \Rightarrow \langle s', i'\rangle\, t} \qquad \frac{g; M \vdash \langle s, i\rangle\, p_2 \Rightarrow \langle s', i'\rangle\, t}{g; M \vdash \langle s, i\rangle\, p_1 \mid p_2 \Rightarrow \langle s', i'\rangle\, t}$$

$$\frac{g; M \vdash \langle s_{j-1}, i_{j-1}\rangle\, p_j \Rightarrow \langle s_j, i_j\rangle\, t_j \quad 1 \leq j \leq k}{g; M \vdash \langle s_0, i_0\rangle\, c_{(B_1,\ldots,B_k)B}(p_1, \ldots, p_k) \Rightarrow \langle s_k, i_k\rangle\, c_{(B_1,\ldots,B_k)B}(t_1, \ldots, t_k)}$$

$$\frac{g; M \vdash \langle s_{j-1}, i_{j-1}\rangle\, p_j \Rightarrow \langle s_j, i_j\rangle\, t_j \quad 1 \leq j \leq k \qquad (x : (x_1{:}B_1, \ldots, x_k{:}B_k)B) {=}{=} p \in g \qquad g; \oslash\ x_1 = t_1\ \ldots\ x_k = t_k \vdash \langle s_k\rangle\, p \Rightarrow \langle s', i'\rangle\, t}{g; M \vdash \langle s_0, i_0\rangle\, x(p_1, \ldots, p_k) \Rightarrow \langle s', i'\rangle\, t}$$

$$\frac{g; M \vdash \langle s_{j-1}, i_{j-1}\rangle\, p_j \Rightarrow \langle s_j, i_j\rangle\, t_j \quad 1 \leq j \leq k \qquad (x : (x_1{:}B_1, \ldots, x_k{:}B_k)B {=}{=} p) \notin g \qquad g; \oslash\ x_1 = t_1\ \ldots\ x_k = t_k \vdash \langle s_k\rangle\, p \Rightarrow \langle s', i'\rangle\, t}{g; M \vdash \langle s_0, i_0\rangle\, x(p_1, \ldots, p_k) \Rightarrow \langle s', i'\rangle\, \textbf{wrong}}$$

Figure 3: Parse rules for terms

In this rewrite process, grammar updates ($x : S{:}{==}p$) and grammar extensions ($x : S|{==}p$) are eliminated by changing their corresponding original definitions ($x : S{==}p'$) into $x : S{==}p$ and $x : S{==}p \mid p'$, respectively. Name conflicts between grammar additions $x : S{==}\ p$ and $x : S'{==}p'$ ($p \neq p'$) in two grammars of *gseq* are resolved by consistently renaming one of the non-terminals to a fresh non-terminal x' within in its local scope. It is easy to see that normalization preserves typing, that is, if $gseq \rightsquigarrow g$ and $\vdash gseq \Rightarrow E$, then $\vdash g \Rightarrow E'$, where E' is equal to E up to duplicate elimination.

We use the following notation to describe how a production of a grammar g applied to an input stream constructs a term t of the target language:

$$g; M \vdash \langle s, i\rangle\, p \Rightarrow \langle s', i'\rangle\, t$$

It states that production p executed in environment $g; M$ starting in the initial configuration $\langle s, i\rangle$ returns a term t and a final configuration $\langle s', i'\rangle$. A dynamic environment M contains local term variable bindings. A configuration $\langle s, i\rangle$ consists of the input stream s and an integer counter i to generate unique fresh identifiers x_B^i distinct from user-defined identifiers of the form x_B.

The parsing rules are given in figure 3. These rules involve syntactic objects of the following categories:

$s ::=$			**input streams**
		$*$	empty input stream
	$\mid$	$x :: s$	identifier token
$b ::=$			**terms**
		unit	trivial term
	$\mid$	x_{Binder}	binder identifier
	$\mid$	x_{Var}	variable identifier
	$\mid$	x_{Label}	label identifier
	$\mid$	x_B^i	fresh identifier of sort B ($i \geq 0$)
			$B \in \{\text{Binder}, \text{Var}, \text{Label}\}$
	$\mid$	$c_{(B_1,\ldots,B_k)B}(b_1, \ldots, b_k)$	constructed term ($k \geq 0$)
$t ::=$			**parse results**
		b	term
	$\mid$	**wrong**	type error
$M ::=$			**dynamic environments**
		$\oslash$	empty environment
	$\mid$	$M, x = b$	term binding

An input stream is a sequence of identifiers, some of which may have been declared to be keywords (e.g., "`if`") in g. We use the notation $K(g)$ to denotes the set of keywords defined in productions of g. The parsing rules for terminals use $K(g)$ to distinguish between keywords and identifiers appearing in the input stream.

The sort of a term can be determined without reference to an environment:

$$\textbf{unit} : \text{Unit} \quad x_B : B \quad x_B^i : B \quad \frac{b_1 : B_1 \ldots b_k : B_k}{c_{(B_1,\ldots,B_k)B}(b_1, \ldots, b_k) : B}$$

A dynamic environment M is said to match a static environment L (written as $M \models L$) if its term bindings have names and sorts compatible with the names and sorts in L.

$$\oslash \models \oslash \qquad \frac{M \models L \quad b : B}{M, x = b \models L, x : B}$$

The following theorem relates the dynamic parse rules in figure 3 with the static type rules presented in section 4.1.

Theorem 1 *(parsing respects typing) For all g, E, L, p, M, s, s', i and i' such that*

1. $\oslash \vdash g :: E$
2. $\oslash \vdash g$ **ok**
3. $E; L \vdash p : B$
4. $M \models L$
5. $g; M \vdash \langle s, i \rangle\, p \Rightarrow \langle s', i' \rangle\, t$

$t : B$ holds.

The proof of this theorem can be found in the full paper. In particular, if a non-parameterized ($L = M = \oslash$) parser with result sort B for a root production p_0 defined in a type-correct grammar g consumes the full input stream s (returning the empty input stream $*$), the parse result t is guaranteed to be of sort B:

Corollary 1 *If*

- $\oslash \vdash g :: E$
- $\oslash \vdash g$ **ok**,
- $E; \oslash \vdash p_0 : B$, *and*
- $g; \oslash \vdash \langle s, 1 \rangle\, p_0 \Rightarrow \langle *, i' \rangle\, t$

then $t : B$ and $t \neq$ **wrong**.

5 An Extensible Parser Package

Extensible grammars as described in this paper were developed in the context of the Tycoon database programming environment [Mat93]. However, as sketched in figure 1, the extensible grammar package was implemented in a way that factors out all target-language dependencies (the base sorts B^i, the abstract syntax tree constructors $c_{(B_1,\ldots,B_k)B}$, and the renaming operation on abstract syntax trees) from the package implementation.

A token stream s is represented as an object with a local state and methods to inspect the current input token and to advance to the next input token.

A parser for terms of a sort B is represented as a function that takes a scanner object and returns a typed abstract syntax tree, modifying the state of the scanner object and a variable counter to generate fresh variable identifiers.

A grammar g_i is represented as an object of an abstract data type encapsulating information about the target language TL and the object language OL_i accepted by g_i. The implementor of a compiler for a language with an extensible grammar links the parser package into the compiler. A grammar for the target language at hand is generated via calls to the parser interface. Finally, a parser for this grammar is generated which in turn is used to parse actual program input.

The following steps have to be taken to generate the grammar g_0 and a parser for the initial object language OL_0. Each of these steps is implemented by a function call to the parser package that passes the grammar as an explicit argument.

1. Creation of an initial (empty) grammar g_0. Arguments to this operation provide information to the parser package about the tokens returned by the scanner and functions to create fresh identifiers. An initial grammar already contains the names of the builtin sorts Label, Var, and Binder.
2. Addition of named sorts to g_0. These sorts correspond to abstract-syntax-tree types in the target-language compiler. For each newly defined sort, an AST copy routine, an AST renaming routine, and a distinguished error value have to be supplied. The error value is generated by the parser package in case of parse errors.
3. Addition of named constructors to g_0. Constructors correspond to functions in the target-language compiler that take $k \geq 0$ typed abstract syntax trees and return an aggregated syntax tree. For each constructor, the list of its argument sorts and its result sort have to be specified.
4. Addition of a concrete syntax for grammar definitions to g_0. Target-language implementors can adopt either the concrete syntax used in this paper (**grammar** ... **end**) or they can define their own tailored syntax for the definition of productions p that match the abstract syntax given in section 4.1.
5. Generation of a parser for g_0. Parser generation involves the calculation of director sets to support efficient LL(1) parsing. Furthermore, variable and non-terminal references are resolved into direct table indices.
6. Parsing of a grammar extension g using the parser generated in the previous step. The grammar extension g defines the mapping from OL_0 terms to TL terms.
7. Extension of g_0 by g.
8. Generation of a parser for the extended g_0.

A parser for OL_i derived from a grammar g_i returns either a term of the target language proper, or an abstract syntax tree for an incremental syntax extension g_Δ. In the latter case the parser package is invoked to check the type correctness of g_Δ in the scope of the environment E_i established by the current grammar g_i. If this check succeeds, the extended grammar is obtained by normalizing the grammar sequence $g_i, g_\Delta \rightsquigarrow g_{i+1}$. Finally, a new parser is generated for g_{i+1}; this parser can then be used to parse further input in the extended language OL_{i+1}.

If the parsing result is a term t of the target language, the parser package also returns a list of variable renamings. These renamings have to be performed by the target-language compiler in t to establish bindings to global variable identifiers (see section 3.3).

6 Comparison with Related Work

Syntactic extensibility has been studied previously in the context of programming languages and theorem provers.

Linguistic reflection [SMM91, SSS+92, SSF92, Kir92] in persistent programming languages has been used to add high-level (query) notations to strongly-typed programming languages. These extensions are achieved by executing user-defined code at compile time to transform syntax trees returned from the parser prior to further processing by the type checker and code generator. Our approach differs from this work since we are able to guarantee the termination of compilation, even when our transformation operations are defined recursively. Furthermore, we are not aware of work in the context of linguistic reflection to handle correctly the problematic binding situations sketched in section 3.3.

Some non-persistent language implementations, like CAML and SML, integrate YACC or a similar parser generator that allows them to introduce new syntax [MR92]. If the new syntax is to be mixed with the old one, the new syntax must be quoted in some way. Instead, we can freely intermix new and old syntax without special quotations.

Hygienic macros [KFFD92, Koh86] have goals similar to those of our extensible grammars; these macros also work on the abstract syntax and avoid binding anomalies. However, these macros account only for explicit (parameterized) macro calls and not for more liberal keyword-based syntax extensions. Hygienic macros employ a multi-pass time-stamping algorithm to prevent variable capture; this algorithm is different from our one-pass renaming algorithm. Furthermore, we do not handle quotation and antiquotation in the style of Lisp.

Griffin [Gri88] has enumerated desirable properties of notational definitions and has studied their formalization. Unlike Griffin who translates notations to combinator form, we are able to handle variables bound to non-local binders in patterns. Moreover, while Griffin discusses abstract translations, we provide a specific grammar definition technique and an efficient parsing algorithm. Parsing is efficient because it is LL(1) and because it avoids the creation of intermediate parse trees, producing abstract syntax trees that do not require normalization.

Bove and Arbilla [BA92] discuss how to use explicit substitutions to implement syntax extensions. Theirs is an elegant idea that may be exploited in systems where the target compiler supports explicit substitutions. As in the previous case, their work does not describe a parsing algorithm, but presents an interesting theory.

7 Concluding Remarks

Extensible grammars avoid many of the problems associated with traditional macro-expansion or program-rewrite tools by sort constraints at grammar-definition time and by a careful handling of identifiers in binding constructs. Furthermore, since our work extends the well-understood parser technology by a small set of concepts, extensible parsers can be integrated with little overhead in today's compilation environments.

Traditional database programming languages have a bias towards a specific data model by providing built-in syntactic support tailored to the structures and operations of that data model. In a programming environment equipped with extensible grammars, such syntactic forms can be eliminated from the core language definition and can be introduced in application libraries shared by larger user communities.

References

[ASU87] A.V. Aho, R. Sethi, and J.D. Ullmann. *Compilers: Principles, Techniques and Tools.* Addison-Wesley, 1987.

[BA92] A. Bove and L. Arbilla. A Confluent Calculus of Macro Expansion and Evaluation. In *ACM Conference on Lisp and Functional Programming*, pages 278–287, 1992.

[BTBN91] V. Breazu-Tannen, P. Buneman, and S. Naqvi. Structural Recursion as a Query Language. In *Proceedings of the Third International Workshop on Database Programming Languages*, Nafplion, Greece, 1991. Morgan Kaufmann Publishers.

[Car93] L. Cardelli. An Implementation of $F_{<:}$. Report 97, Digital Equipment Corporation, Systems Research Center, 1993.

[Gri88] T. Griffin. Notational definition – A formal account. In *Proceedings Symposium on Logic in Computer Science*, pages 372–383, 1988.

[KFFD92] E. Kohlbecker, D.P. Friedman, M. Felleisen, and B. Duba. Hygienic macro expansion. In *ACM Conference on Lisp and Functional Programming*, 1992.

[Kir92] G.N.C. Kirby. Persistent Programming with Strongly Typed Linguistic Reflection. FIDE Technical Report Series FIDE/92/40, FIDE Project Coordinator, Department of Computing Sciences, University of Glasgow, 1992.

[Koh86] E.E. Kohlbecker. *Syntactic extensions in the programming language LISP.* PhD thesis, Indiana University, 1986.

[KR77] B.W. Kernighan and D.M. Ritchie. *The C Programming Language.* Prentice Hall, Englewood Cliffs, NJ, 1977.

[Mat93] F. Matthes. *Persistente Objektsysteme: Integrierte Datenbankentwicklung und Programmerstellung.* Springer-Verlag, 1993. (In German.)

[MR92] M. Mauny and D. Rauglaudre. Parsers in ML. In *ACM Conference on Lisp and Functional Programming*, 1992.

[MS91] F. Matthes and J.W. Schmidt. Bulk Types: Built-In or Add-On? In *Proceedings of the Third International Workshop on Database Programming Languages*, Nafplion, Greece, 1991. Morgan Kaufmann Publishers.

[Naq89] S.A. Naqvi. Stratification as a Design Principle in Logical Query Languages. In *Proceedings of the Second International Workshop on Database Programming Languages*, Salishan, Oregon, 1989.

[OBBT89] A. Ohori, P. Buneman, and V. Breazu-Tannen. Database Programming in Machiavelli – a Polymorphic Language with Static Type Inference. In *Proceedings of the ACM-SIGMOD International Conference on Management of Data, Portland, Oregon*, pages 46–57, 1989.

[PT93] B. Pierce and D. Turner. Object-Oriented Programming without Recursive Types. In *Proceedings of the 20th ACM Symposium on Principles of Programming Languages*, pages 299–312, 1993.

[SFL83] J.M. Smith, S. Fox, and T. Landers. ADAPLEX: Rationale and Reference Manual (2nd ed.). Technical report, Computer Corporation of America, Cambridge, Mass., 1983.

[SMM91] D. Stemple, R. Morrison, and Atkinson M. Type-safe Linguistic Reflection. In *Database Programming Languages: Bulk Types and Persistent Data*, pages 357–362, Nafplion, Greece, 1991. Morgan Kaufmann Publishers.

[SQL87] ISO. *Standard ISO 9075, Information processing systems - Database language SQL*, 1987.

[SS91] D. Stemple and T. Sheard. A Recursive Base for Database Programming Primitives. In *Proceedings of the Kiev East/West Workshop on Next Generation Database Technology*, volume 504 of *Lecture Notes in Computer Science*, 1991.

[SSF92] D. Stemple, T. Sheard, and L. Fegaras. Linguistic Reflection: A Bridge from Programming to Database Languages. In *Proc. HICSS, Hawaii*, pages 46–55, 1992.

[SSS88] D. Stemple, A. Socorro, and T. Sheard. Formalizing Objects for Databases using ADABTPL. In *Advances in Object-Oriented Database Systems*, pages 110–172, 1988.

[SSS+92] D. Stemple, R.B. Stanton, T. Sheard, P. Philbrow, R. Morrison, G.N.C. Kirby, L. Fegaras, R.L. Cooper, R.C.H. Connor, M.P. Atkinson, and S. Alagic. Type-Safe Linguistic Reflection: A Generator Technology. Research Report CS/92/6, Univ. of St. Andrews, Dept. of Comp. Science, 1992.

[Tri91] P. Trinder. Comprehensions, a Query Notation for DBPLs. In *Proceedings of the Third International Workshop on Database Programming Languages*, Nafplion, Greece, 1991. Morgan Kaufmann Publishers.

Linguistic Support for Persistent Modules and Capabilities

John Rosenberg
Department of Computer Science, University of Sydney
Sydney, Australia

Michael Hitchens
Department of Computing, University of Western Sydney
Sydney, Australia

Abstract

Over the last ten years considerable effort has been expended attempting to build systems which support orthogonal persistence. In a *persistent* system all data is created and manipulated in a uniform manner, regardless of how long it persists. A common approach in existing persistent systems is to structure the store in terms of procedures. This paper describes a new programming language which provides support for persistent modules and protection based on capabilities. It is shown how the module structure provides explicit support for sharing and simplifies the development of reusable components. The capability structure allows control over access to data and supports deletion of objects in a controlled manner.

1 Introduction

Over the last ten years considerable effort has been expended attempting to build systems which support orthogonal persistence. In a *persistent* system all data is created and manipulated in a uniform manner, regardless of how long it persists [4]. Thus the traditional distinction between short-term memory (variables, etc.) and long-term memory (files) found in conventional systems is removed. Arbitrary data structures which outlive the program may be created and programs may access data structures generated by other programs. *Orthogonal persistence* means that all data types may persist and that the mechanism for identifying persistent objects is independent of the type system.

The advantages of persistent systems include:

- a reduction in complexity because of the simplified model of the world involving only programming language constructs and no database/file system [17]
- potential reduction in code size and execution time because there is no need to write code to flatten and rebuild data structures for storage in files [4].

- since all data resides in the same store a single model of protection may be used. This is in contrast to the multi-level protection involving processes and files on conventional systems [20].

These advantages are not achieved without a cost. In particular persistent systems have a considerable impact on memory management, protection and distribution.

Most research groups working in this area have concentrated on producing persistent programming languages. These languages provide support for persistence as an integral component of the language semantics. The first language which supported orthogonal persistence was PS-algol [1] developed by the Universities of St Andrews and Glasgow. More recently the same group has produced a new language called Napier88 [19]. Napier88 supports a powerful polymorphic type system and abstract data types. Other languages which support persistence, but in a non-orthogonal manner include Pascal-R [29], DBPL [16], E [23] , Galileo [2] and the PGraphite language [11].

All of these programming languages are implemented above a conventional operating system (in most cases Unix). Little support is available from either the hardware or the operating system and the support environment for the language tends to be quite complex. Difficulties are encountered with efficiency and scalability. In addition protection is implemented using the type system of the programming language. While this is conceptually appealing, it does effectively prohibit the use of multiple languages operating on the same store.

The Persistent Systems Research Group at the University of Sydney has taken a different approach. We have concentrated on developing an appropriate hardware architecture and operating system environment. We have argued that it is unreasonable to expect conventional systems, which were designed to support the file system paradigm, to be a good base on which to develop persistent systems. This work has resulted in the development of the Monads architecture [12, 26] which has been implemented in a microcoded machine known as Monads-PC [27]. A second implementation, based on the SPARC processor with addressing extensions, is underway [21, 28].

The Monads architecture implies a computing model which is different from that supported by many other persistent systems. In particular it includes support for:

- persistent modules with procedural interfaces [14]
- a uniform protection mechanism based on *capabilities* [9]
- a process model in which processes are orthogonal to modules [26].

This model has been described in the literature and is summarised in section 2 below. Because of our concentration on architectural and system issues little work has been done on language support for the architecture. All of the existing software (which includes an operating system, editor, etc.) has been developed in a dialect of Pascal known as Pascal/M [25], except for the kernel which is written in a high-level assembly language [24]. This lack of proper language support has created a number of difficulties which include:

- misunderstanding of the architecture by other research groups because of the lack of a concrete syntax to describe operations
- inability to fully exploit the features available in the architecture
- lack of consistency in Pascal/M because of continual extension and modification

In the middle 1980s considerable work was performed on the design of a language called Leibniz [8, 13]. Leibniz was very ambitious, with support for bulk data types based on sets and sequences. For various reasons a fully operational Leibniz compiler was never produced. In this paper we take a more pragmatic approach and describe a language, known as MPL, which both complements and supports the Monads architecture, but is conceptually very simple. MPL highlights the facilities provided in the Monads architecture and makes them accessible to the programmer.

The language draws heavily from the authors' experience with Napier88 in terms of general structure and syntax. In particular the syntax for declarations, expressions and control statements is identical to Napier88. The reasons for this are quite straightforward and practical. First, our interests are in support for modules and capabilities; we see no reason to "re-invent the wheel". Second, we hope to be able to make use of the existing tools developed for Napier88, including parts of the compiler, and this is simplified if MPL has a similar style to Napier88. Finally we intend to build a first implementation of MPL above the Napier88 store and persistent abstract machine [6] which is designed to support a Napier88 style of language.

The key differences between Napier88 and MPL relate to the latter's support for modules and capabilities. In Napier88 the basic structuring tool is the procedure; procedures are first class data types and are used to generate persistent data. Conversely, in MPL, information-hiding modules with procedural interfaces are used to structure the store. They are first class data types and encapsulate persistent data. Access to modules is dynamically controlled by capabilities which are also first-class data types. The implications of this difference are discussed later in the paper. The aim of the exercise was to capture the essence of the architecture in a more or less minimal language. Therefore features such as support for bulk data types and inheritance have been excluded at this stage.

As we have progressed with the language design it has become clear that, although originally we envisaged MPL as being only suitable for the Monads architecture, it is clearly implementable in other environments. The language offers a different style of persistent computing and therefore there would be of value in providing implementations above other persistent stores.

This paper begins by reviewing the Monads programming model. This is followed by an example which shows how modules are represented in MPL and the model of persistence. We then discuss support for capabilities in MPL and describe the operations available for their manipulation and storage. The model of persistence in terms of reachability from multiple roots is then described. Finally we discuss some of the issues still under investigation.

2. The Model

MPL supports a global persistent address space. Every object (integer, structure, etc.) has a unique name in that address space. The address space is structured into regions which are called *modules* (strictly speaking, module instances). A module consists of some encapsulated data and a set of access procedures. This is similar to the notion of *objects* in object oriented systems, where the procedures would be the access methods. However, only procedures may appear on the interface in MPL, i.e. all modules are strictly information-hiding. Certain data types have pointer semantics and therefore it is possible to pass references between modules; hence the need for a global address space.

The notion of a concurrent activity is represented by a *process*. The state of a process is also held in the global address space and so processes are persistent. Processes are orthogonal to modules. A process requests a service from a module by calling one of the interface procedures. This is similar to a conventional procedure call in that parameters may be passed, possibly on a stack. The one major difference is that a change of protection domain occurs. That is, on entry to the called module all data of the calling module becomes inaccessible and the data of the called module becomes addressable.

During its life a process may call many different modules and may traverse through an arbitrary number of levels of inter-module call. It is possible for multiple processes to be executing in a single module at the same time. Synchronisation on access to data, if required, is the responsibility of the implementor of the module and appropriate primitives are provided in the language.

The memory model is designed to complement the computational model described above. For each module type there is a *module manager*. The module manager is effectively a constructor for *instances* of that module type. All instances created by a particular module manager share the same code, but have their own data. A module instance, in turn, may be used to construct a *handle* for the instance. A handle may then be used to make calls to the interface routines of the module. Module, instances and handles are first-class data types; they may be assigned, compared, passed as parameters and returned as the result of procedure calls.

The two levels of constructor are related to the model of persistence supported by MPL. There are three categories of data accessible to a module:

(i) *Instance* data is the encapsulated data which belongs to a module instance. All processes executing in a module instance share the same instance data. The root of the instance data of a module is created when the module instance is created. Instance data persists as long as it is reachable from this root.

(ii) *Local* data is data created on entry to a procedure of a module. It is private to the calling process and ceases to exist when the process exits the procedure. This is the equivalent of block structured data in languages such as Pascal.

(iii) *Handle* data[1] belongs to a particular use of a module instance by a process. Such a use of the module instance is represented by a module *handle*. The root of handle data is created when the handle is constructed. Handle data persists as long as it is reachable from this root.

This model can best be understood by considering an example. Suppose we wish to implement a module which will store a list of books held in a library. The instance data would consist of the list of books. Notice that it is possible to have multiple instances of the module for different libraries, each with its own list of books. The interface routines to such a module may require temporary variables (e.g. to act as a loop counters). These may be declared as local variables within a procedure and unique local variables will be used on each call to the routine.

The module may also have two procedures to enable scanning through books written by a particular author. The first routine takes as a parameter the key for a book and sets the current location. The second routine returns the details of the next book matching that key. In order to implement the second routine the procedure must remember its current position in the list of books. This current position pointer would be held in handle data. It is retained between calls to the module, but is private to a particular use of the module, represented by a module handle.

It is worth noting that other persistent languages (and conventional languages) also have a need for the equivalent of handle data. They implement this in one of three ways. The first is to pass in a status parameter on each call to the module. The code of the module updates the status parameter with the current position so that it can be passed in on the next call. This scheme allows the implementation of details of the module to escape and is therefore undesirable. The second scheme is to hold a list of the current position for each user of the module in the instance data. The caller is given an index into this list which is returned on each subsequent call. Such a scheme is used by operating systems such as Unix for access to files, i.e. a file number is returned. This scheme has two problems. First, the calling program has to be aware of the fact that the data is shared and to maintain the "call index". Second, there is a potential security problem since an unscrupulous user could deliberately use a different index and possibly affect the execution of another process.

The third scheme is employed by languages such as Napier88 which use generators to create instance and handle data. The library system described above would have a generator procedure which would create an instance of the library system. An interface procedure of the instance would generate a scan function which would have encapsulated within it the handle data holding the current position. Thus the same number of levels of generator are required. The difference is that these generators must be written explicitly in Napier88, but are implicit within the computational model of MPL.

---

[1] In previous papers we have used the term retained data instead of handle data.

There are two major advantages of this model for persistent systems construction. First, the explicit separation of instance data from handle data allows a well-defined model of sharing. Instances may be shared with private handle data for each use. This eliminates the need for the author of a module to provide explicit code to allow for sharing, or to protect the private data belonging to a user of an instance from another user of the instance. Of course, it is still necessary for the programmer to provide appropriate code to synchronize on access to the shared (instance) data. In addition, handles may be shared, providing shared access to both the instance and handle data. This is useful in cases where multiple modules require access to the one "use" of another instance, e.g. an error reporting module. All of this is possible in other systems, but only by the development of explicit code for each particular case.

The second advantage relates to the issue of support for multiple languages. The clean module structure with purely procedural interfaces simplifies communication between objects in different languages. Providing there is some agreement on a common set of types for parameters, modules developed in different languages may be combined to form applications.

Superimposed on the computational model described above is an access control mechanism based on capabilities [9]. In general a capability contains the name of an entity[2] and a specification of the access available. In MPL there are three categories of capability: module capabilities, instance capabilities and handle capabilities. These correspond to the entities described above. Capabilities are not used to access other objects (integers, structures, etc.). The overhead resulting from the use of capabilities for coarse grain objects is considered acceptable; however this would be unacceptable for fine grain objects. Each capability names the entity and lists the interfaces which may be called. A module, instance or handle may only be accessed if the program presents a capability which permits execution of the called procedure.

Capabilities are checked dynamically allowing access to entities to be revoked. In addition new capabilities with reduced access may be constructed. For example, in the case of the library system above it would be possible to produce a handle capability which only allowed sequential access to the library with no updates. Notice that these access rights are directly related to the semantic operations supported by the module and so it is possible to control access in terms of these operations, rather than machine operations such as read and write.

3. Modules and Persistence - An Example

Modules, instances and handles, as described above, are directly supported in MPL. A type corresponding to the library module mentioned above may be declared as shown in figure 1. The module has been generalised to allow an arbitrary search key to be associated with each book. The preceding declarations of the *book* structure and the *book_result* variant exactly follow the Napier88 syntax which is described in [19].

---

[2] We use the term entity to refer to a module, instance or handle.

The type definition indicates that *library* is a constructor which takes a single parameter of type integer (the maximum number of books to be held in the library) and produces an instance of the library module. The instance is, in turn, a constructor which takes a single boolean parameter (whether inserts change the current position) and returns a handle for the instance. The handle provides access to three interface procedures. The first, *insert_entry*, adds a new book and its corresponding key to the library. The second, *find*, searches for a book with the given key and sets the current position to this book. The final interface, *get_next*, returns the book at the current position and steps to the next book in key order.

```
type book is structure ( title, author, isbn : string; year : int )
type book_result is variant ( a_book : book; empty : null )

type library is module ( int ) ->
                    instance ( bool ) ->
                        handle
                            proc insert_entry ( string, book ) ->
bool
                            proc find ( string ) -> bool
                            proc get_next () -> book_result
                        end_handle
```

Figure 1: Declaration of a library module type

An implementation of this type is shown in figure 2. This implementation would be processed by the compiler which would produce a capability for the new module. The compiler is itself an interface procedure of a system defined module held in the store, although the first version will be a cross compiler. In its simplest form the type of the compile procedure may be considered to be:

```
proc compile ( source ) -> cap
```

That is, compile takes a representation of the source of a module and returns a result of type *cap*. Cap is a predefined type which is the infinite union of all capability types, i.e. the infinite union of all module, instance and handle capabilities. This is analogous to the type *any* in Napier88 [18]. Although not strictly necessary, the type cap makes it much easier to manage capabilities and to build the equivalent of directories [15]. Type cap is dynamically checked. In order to make use of a capability it is necessary to project the capability onto an actual type.

For example, suppose that the capability returned by the compiler for the library module is *c*. Then the following statement will cause a dynamic type check and will project *c* onto *lib_module* as type *library*:

```
let lib_module := use c as library
```

```
module ( max_books : int )
      rec type book_list is variant ( elem : structure (
        the_key : string; the_book : book; next : book_list ); tip : null )
      let the_library := book_list ( tip : nil )
      let book_count := 0

      instance ( set_current_on_insert : bool )
            let current_position := book_list ( tip : nil )

            handle
                  proc insert_entry ( key : string;  an_entry : book )
                        -> bool
                        if book_count >= max_books then
                              false
                        else  begin
                              the_library := book_list (
                                 elem : struct ( the_key := key;
                                 the_book := an_entry;
                                 next := the_library ) )
                              if set_current_on_insert do
                                    current_position := the_library
                              book_count := book_count + 1
                              true
                        end

                  proc find ( key : string ) -> bool
                  begin
                        ! searches list for the book and sets
                        ! current_position to its position in the list
                        ! or returns false
                        ................
                  end

                  proc get_next () -> book_result
                        if current_position is tip then
                              book_result ( empty : nil )
                        else  begin
                              let result := book_result (
                                 a_book : current_position'elem (
                                 the_book ))
                              current_position :=
                                 current_position'elem ( next )
                              result
                        end

            end_handle
```

Figure 2: An implementation of the library module

Notice that this check may result in failure if the type of *c* is not *library*. In this case an exception is raised. The exception mechanism supported by MPL is not described in this paper. The type check shown above is the only dynamic type check required. The rest of the code for creating an instance, creating a handle and calling interface procedures may be statically type checked, since they are all derived from *c*.

An instance of the library module, called *lib_instance*, may be created by:

```
let lib_instance := lib_module ( 10000 )
```

Additional instances of the library module may be created by subsequent calls to *lib_module*. Each instance will share the code of *lib_module* but will encapsulate its own instance data. Finally, a handle for *lib_instance* may be created using:

```
let lib_handle := lib_instance ( true )
```

Again, additional handles may be created by further calls to *lib_instance*. Each handle has its own private handle data, but shares the data of the creating instance. It is also possible for several processes to share the same handle and therefore share the handle data. This can be useful where, for example, a group of processes is to use the same current position within a module. The handle may be used to call interfaces of the instance as follows:

```
if lib_handle.find ( "key for a book") do
        let result := lib_handle.get_next ()
```

The key advantage of supporting both instance and handle data is that it provides a well-defined model of sharing. The model allows the construction of modules which allow processes to have access to both shared and private encapsulated data.

The above example has demonstrated how the model of modules is represented in MPL. In the following section we describe the capability model and show how capabilities may be used to control access to objects.

4. Capabilities

In the example above we have declared and used variables representing modules, instances and handles. Strictly speaking, these variables represent capabilities for these entities. A capability contains the name of an entity and access control information. The name uniquely identifies an entity and enables the entity to be unambiguously located. The access control information defines the operations which may be performed on the capability itself as well as on the corresponding entity.

An important feature of capabilities is that they are protected. Programs cannot create arbitrary capabilities, nor can they arbitrarily modify existing ones. Capabilities can only be created under system control and can only be modified in a well-defined manner. We envisage that this protection is implemented below the type system so that, even in a multilingual environment, it is not possible to gain access to data unless the owner of the data intends such access to occur. The only way in which access to a module may be obtained is by presentation of a valid capability. In this sense capabilities may be viewed as "keys" which unlock objects.

Capabilities are not a new idea. They have been used by several operating system and language designers as an access control mechanism [3, 22, 30]. They have proven to be a powerful and flexible access control mechanism which solve such problems as revocation of access and confinement [7].

It is important to distinguish between capabilities, which are a dynamic access control mechanism, and other static access control schemes. Jones and Liskov [10] described an access control mechanism which is closely related to capabilities, but requires the static specification of the access required to an object. This could then be statically checked at compile time. We reject this as being too inflexible. For example, consider the development of an editing system which allows both the examination and modification of data. It should be possible to invoke the editing system on an object to which we have read-only access. Providing we do not attempt to use any of the editing commands which involve modifying the object this should be allowed. Such an arrangement requires dynamic checks and can be supported by capabilities. In the Jones and Liskov scheme this would require the provision of two editing systems, one which statically specified at least read-only access and another which specified read-write access.

In MPL capabilities are represented by an implementation-defined structure. Capabilities have pointer semantics, in the same manner as structures and other aggregate types. Thus a variable of type *cap* (or of any module, instance or handle type) contains a pointer to a capability. This capability, in turn, contains the name of some entity (module, instance or handle). This is illustrated in figure 3.

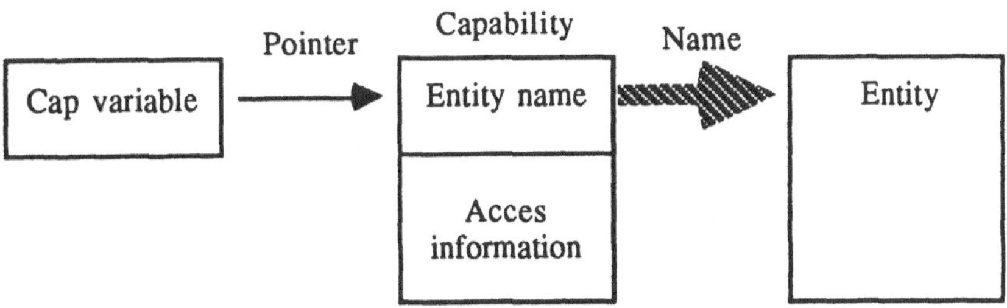

Figure 3: The semantics of capabilities

Note that the entity name is *not* a pointer. It is a value which will uniquely identify an entity. The difference is subtle, but important to the model. The issue is the lifetime of objects in a persistent system. Most existing persistent systems support persistence by reachability. That is, there is some notion of a root of persistence and as a long as an object is reachable (via a series of pointer de-references) it will continue to exist. A garbage collector is employed to periodically remove unreachable objects.

This approach is quite acceptable in a single-user environment. However, in a multi-user environment there are some difficulties. Consider an object created by one user and made accessible to another user by providing that user with a pointer to the object. The original user is now unable to delete the object unless it also possible to remove the other user's pointer. The ability to remove one's own objects seems reasonable and is certainly available in conventional systems. There is no reason to believe that it is not desirable in persistent systems.

It is precisely for this reason that we have distinguished between pointers and entity names. MPL still supports persistence by reachability. However, it also supports explicit deletion of modules, instances and handles. In order to allow for this it is necessary to distinguish between pointer references and references to entities. Whenever a capability is used to access an entity the name is validated to ensure that the entity still exists. Thus modules, instances and handles may be explicitly deleted when required. The ability to delete an entity is itself controlled by the access information in capabilities for the entity.

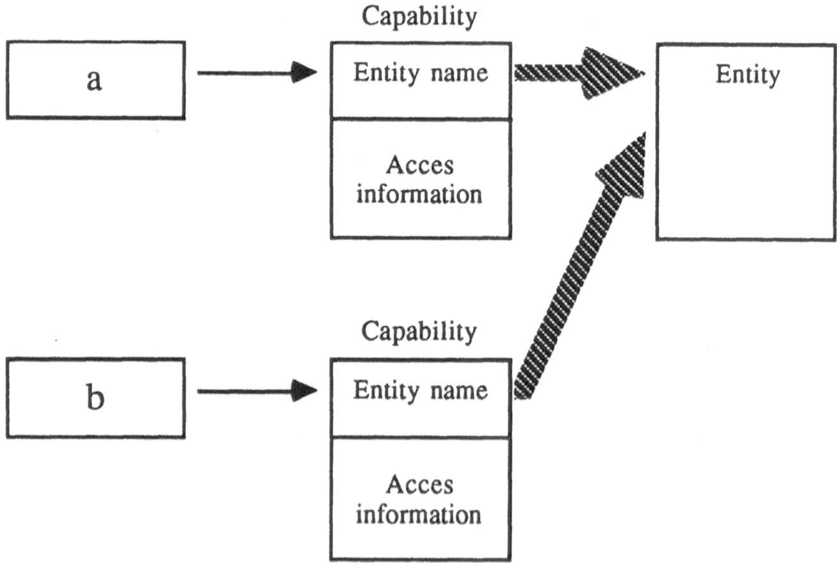

Figure 4: The **copy** operation

Capabilities are first-class data types in MPL. As such they may be assigned, compared, passed as parameters and returned as the result of procedures. In addition there are several special operations which may be performed on capabilities. The first of these is the copy operation.

Since capabilities are accessed using pointer semantics it is necessary to provide some other mechanism for producing a copy of a capability. Copying of the aggregate data types such as structures can be coded by the programmer as a procedure which copies the individual fields of the structure. Capabilities are protected and so the system must provide this facility as a built-in operation. A copy of the capability *a* may be produced, and a pointer to this copy assigned to a variable *b* by:

b := **copy** a

This operation is illustrated in figure 4. A new capability which contains the same entity name as the capability referenced by *a* and a copy of the access information is created and pointed to by *b*. The access information may later be individually modified for the capabilities pointed to by *a* and *b*. Notice that this is quite different from the statement:

b := a

which makes the variable *b* point at the same capability as *a*, as illustrated in figure 5.

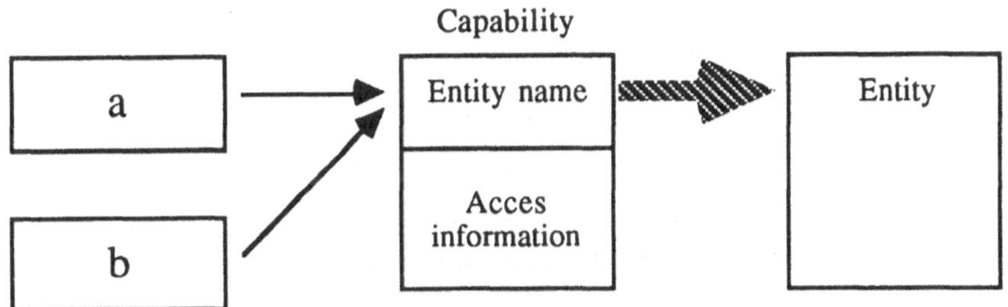

Figure 5: The assignment operation

An entity referenced by a capability may be destroyed using the *destroy* statement. For example, the statement:

destroy a

will destroy the entity referenced by the capability *a*. The use of any capability referring to the same entity as *a* will result in failure following the execution of this statement and an appropriate exception will be raised. Figure 6 illustrates the result of this operation on the structure shown in figure 5.

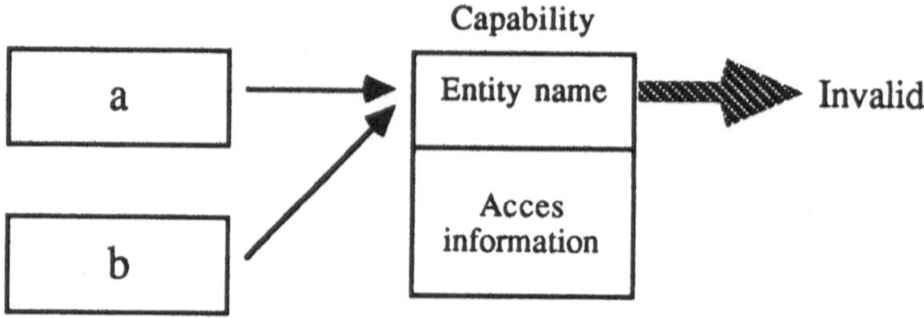

Figure 6: The **destroy** operation

MPL also provides statements for manipulating the access information. The access information may be considered to be a set of access rights. These access rights are divided into two groups. The first group, called capability rights, relate to the capability itself and the corresponding entity. There are three access rights in this group, *copy*, *disallow* and *destroy*. The *copy* right allows the holder of a capability to create a copy as described above. An attempt to perform the copy operation using a capability which does not include the *copy* access right will result in failure. The *disallow* right allows the holder to reduce the access permitted by the capability. The *destroy* right allows the holder of the capability to destroy the corresponding entity.

The second group of access rights, called interface rights, correspond to the interface procedures of the entity. There is one such right for each interface procedure. Thus for the library example given earlier there would be three access rights called *insert_entry*, *find* and *get_next*. For a handle, these rights indicate that the corresponding procedures may be called. For an instance, handles created using the instance will have the indicated access rights. For a module, all instances created using the module will have the indicated access rights.

The existence of one or more access rights may be tested in MPL using the **allows** clause. For example, the capability for the handle in the example above may be tested as follows:

if lib_handle **allows** insert_entry, find **then** ...

The body of the if statement will only be executed if the capability referenced by *lib_handle* has the *insert_entry* and *find* access rights.

The only modification to a capability which is allowed is to reduce the access. This is only permissible if the capability also has the *disallow* right. For example, the *insert_entry* right and the *copy* right could be removed from *lib_handle* by the statement:

in b **disallow** insert_entry, copy

Copy can be used in conjunction with disallow if it is desired to give a capability providing reduced access to some entity to another user. A new capability may be constructed and then the access available via this new capability may be reduced. For example, the following code will produce a new copy of *lib_handle* which only allows *find* and *get_next.*

```
let reduced_lib_handle := copy lib_handle
in reduced_lib_handle disallow insert_entry, copy, disallow, destroy
```

An advantage of producing a copy of the capability is that access may be revoked at a later stage. A pointer to the copy is maintained and the capability can be effectively invalidated at any time by the statement:

```
in reduced_lib_handle disallow all
```

As an example, this could be used in a student environment after the due date for an assignment to disallow any further access to data relating to the exercise.

The final facility provided is a standard procedure *access*, which will produce a string listing the access rights available using a capability. For example,

```
s := access(c)
```

will produce a string, *s*, which lists the access rights available using the capability referenced by *c*.

5. Persistence

MPL assumes a global persistent address space in which all objects reside. As we have discussed above, MPL supports persistence by reachability. The root of persistence is effectively a directory containing a map from strings to capabilities (i.e. entities of type *cap*). Any object reachable from one of these capabilities will persist. However, unlike other persistent systems there is not necessarily a single root of persistence. There may be many such roots; for example, one corresponding to each user of the system. These may be thought of as the equivalent of home directories. An arbitrary graph of directories may be constructed below these by inserting capabilities for additional directories into a home directory. A scheme for managing such an arrangement is described in [15].

A program may obtain a capability for the current root by calling the standard procedure *root* which has the type:

```
proc() -> cap
```

This structure allows us to confine users to their own regions of the store, but to allow access to required entities by providing copies of capabilities to these entities.

6. Other Issues

There are a number of issues related to MPL which are still under investigation. The first of these is coping with failure. Clearly operations can fail in MPL. For example, an attempt to access a destroyed entity or to obtain access not permitted by a capability will result in failure. We propose to provide an exception mechanism to handle such failures. The exact structure of this mechanism is currently being discussed. However, it will allow detection of the exception type and nesting of handlers.

A second issue we are still investigating is support for polymorphism. It is intended that MPL will support polymorphic modules. This is parametric polymorphism similar to that supported by Napier88 [5]. However, it can be extended to allow for polymorphic instances, handles and procedures. Thus in the example above the module definition could begin with

module [t] (max_books : **int**)

and all key fields could be declared to be of type *t* instead of string. This would allow the creation of instances of the library with different key types. In a similar fashion the handle constructor or any of the procedures could be parameterised. This appears to offer a powerful facility which can greatly improve genericity and is worthy of further consideration.

The third area still under discussion is support for concurrency. As we have described above, processes are orthogonal to modules in our model. We will require some basic synchronisation primitives and the ability to create and control processes. The exact structure for these facilities has not been decided.

7. Conclusions

In this paper we have described linguistic support for a model of computation based on modules and capabilities. The model provides explicit support for the construction of modules, instances and handles. The main differences between the model described and that supported by other persistent programming languages are:

- direct support for an implicit model of sharing via the module mechanism
- dynamic control over access using capabilities
- support for explicit deletion

We have shown that these features have several advantages for system developers. They remove the need to provide explicit code to support sharing and multi-user access to objects. They also allow full control over the lifetime of objects.

We are currently undertaking a prototype implementation of MPL. This implementation is being built above the Napier88 store and utilises many of the tools developed for that system. Capabilities are not physically protected but are be implemented as data structures within the store. This will allow us to develop some applications and evaluate the language. In the longer term we intend to produce a code generator for the Monads-PC system which provides full support for hardware protected capabilities.

Acknowledgments

The authors wish to express their gratitude to many people who have contributed towards the ideas presented in this paper. In particular we must thank Malcolm Atkinson, Peter Brössler, Richard Connor, Alan Dearle, Frans Henskens, Graham Kirby and Ron Morrison for their comments and many fruitful discussions. This work is supported by a grant from the Australian Research Council.

References

[1] "PS-algol Reference Manual - fourth edition", University of Glasgow and St Andrews, Persistent Programming Research Report 12/88, 1988.

[2] Albano, A., Cardelli, L. and Orsini, R. "Galileo: A Strongly Typed, Interactive Conceptual Language", *ACM Transactions on Database Systems*, 10(2), pp. 230-260, 1985.

[3] Alsberg, P. A. and Day, J. D. "A Principle for Resilient Sharing of Distributed Resource", *Proceedings of the Second International Conference on Software Engineering*, Los Angeles, 1976.

[4] Atkinson, M. P., Bailey, P., Chisholm, K. J., Cockshott, W. P. and Morrison, R. "An Approach to Persistent Programming", *The Computer Journal*, 26, 4, Nov., pp. 360-365, 1983.

[5] Bernstein, P. A., Shipman, D. W. and Rothnie, J. B. "Concurrency Control in a System for Distributed Databases (SDD-1)", *ACM Transactions on Database Systems*, vol. 5, pp. 18-51, 1980.

[6] Brown, A. L., Connor, R. C. H., Carrick, R., Dearle, A. and Morrison, R. "The Persistent Abstract Machine", Universities of Glasgow and St. Andrews, Persistent Programming Research Report PPRR-59-88, 1988.

[7] Eager, D. L. and Sevcik, K. C. "Achieving Robustness in Distributed Systems", *ACM Transactions on Database Systems*, vol. 8, ACM, pp. 354-381, 1983.

[8] Evered, M. "LEIBNIZ - A Language to Support Software Engineering", Dr.Ing. Thesis, Faculty of Informatics, Technical University of Darmstadt, 1985.

[9] Fabry, R. S. "Capability-Based Addressing", *Communications of the A.C.M.*, 17(7), pp. 403-412, 1974.

[10] Gifford, D. K. "Weighted Voting for Replicated Data", *Proceedings of the Seventh ACM Symposium on Operating Systems Principles*, ACM, pp. 150-161, 1979.

[11] Henskens, F. A. and Rosenberg, J. "Distributed Persistent Stores", *Microprocessors and Microsystems*, 17(3), Butterworth-Heinemann, Oxford, U.K., pp. 147-159, 1993.

[12] Keedy, J. L. and Rosenberg, J. "Support for Objects in the MONADS Architecture", *Proceedings of the International Workshop on Persistent Object Systems*, (ed J. Rosenberg and D. M. Koch), Springer-Verlag, 1989.

[13] Keedy, J. L. and Rosenberg, J. "Uniform Support for Collections of Objects in a Persistent Environment", *Proceedings of the 22nd Hawaii International Conference on System Sciences*, vol II, (ed B. D. Schriver), pp. 26-35, 1989.

[14] Keedy, J. L. and Vosseberg, K. "Persistent Protected Modules and Persistent Processes as the Basis for a More Secure Operating System", *Proceedings of the 25th Hawaii International Conference on Systems Sciences*, vol 1, IEEE, Hawaii, USA, pp. 747-756, 1992.

[15] Manzo, W. A. "Performance Evaluation of Checkpoint Rollback-Recovery Algorithms in Distributed Systems", Ph.D Thesis, University of Illinois, 1991.

[16] Matthes, F. and Schmidt, J. W. "The Type System of DBPL", *Proceedings of the Second International Workshop on Database Programming Languages*, Morgan Kaufmann, pp. 219-225, 1989.

[17] Morrison, R. and Atkinson, M. P. "Persistent Languages and Architectures", *Proceedings of the International Workshop on Computer Architectures to Support Security and Persistence of Information*, (ed J. Rosenberg and J. L. Keedy), Springer-Verlag and the British Computer Society, pp. 9-28, 1990.

[18] Morrison, R., Brown, A. L., Carrick, R., Connor, R., Dearle, A. and Atkinson, M. P. "The Napier Type System", *Persistent Object Systems - Proceedings of the Third International Workshop*, (ed J. Rosenberg and D. Koch), Springer-Verlag, pp. 3-18, 1989.

[19] Morrison, R., Brown, A. L., Conner, R. C. H. and Dearle, A. "Napier88 Reference Manual", Universities of Glasgow and St. Andrews, Persistent Programming Research Report PPRR-77-89, 1989.

[20] Morrison, R., Brown, A. L., Connor, R. C. H., Cutts, Q. I., Dearle, A., Kirby, G., Rosenberg, J. and Stemple, D. "Protection in Persistent Object Systems", *Proceedings of the International Workshop on Computer Architectures to Support Security and Persistence of Information*, Springer-Verlag, Bremen, Germany, pp. 48-66, 1990.

[21] Ng, T. P. "Checkpointing in a Virtual Shared Memory System", University of Illinois, Report No. UIUCDCS-R-91-1700, 1991.

[22] Pu, C., Noe, J. D. and Proudfoot, A. "Regeneration of Replicated Objects: A Technique and its Eden Implementation", *Proceedings of the Second International Conference on Data Engineering*, Los Angeles, pp. 175-187, 1986.

[23] Richardson, J. E. and Carey, M. J. "Implementing Persistence in E", *Proceedings of the Third International Workshop on Persistent Object Systems*, (ed J. Rosenberg and D. M. Koch), Springer-Verlag, pp. 175-199, 1989.

[24] Rosenberg, J. "MONADS-PC Assembler Manual", Department of Computer Science, University of Newcastle, Technical Report 3, 1987.

[25] Rosenberg, J. "Pascal/M - A Pascal Extension Supporting Orthogonal Persistence", Department of Computer Science, University of Newcastle, Technical Report 89/1, 1989.

[26] Rosenberg, J. "The MONADS Architecture - A Layered View", *Proceedings of the 4th International Workshop on Persistent Object Systems*, Morgan-Kaufmann, 1990.

[27] Rosenberg, J. and Abramson, D. A. "MONADS-PC: A Capability Based Workstation to Support Software Engineering", *Proc, 18th Hawaii International Conference on System Sciences*, pp. 515-522, 1985.

[28] Rosenberg, J., Koch, D. M. and Keedy, J. L. "A Massive Memory Supercomputer", *Proc. 22nd Hawaii International Conference on System Sciences*, vol 1, pp. 338-345, 1989.

[29] Schmidt, J. W. "Some High Level Language Constructs for Data of Type Relation", *ACM Transactions on Database Systems*, 2(3), pp. 247-261, 1977.

[30] Thomas, P. A. "A Majority Consensus Approach to Concurrency Control", *ACM Transactions on Database Systems*, vol. 4, ACM, pp. 180-209, 1979.

Octopus: A Reflective Language Mechanism for Object Manipulation

Alex Farkas

Department of Computer Science, University of Adelaide
Adelaide, Australia

Alan Dearle

Department of Computer Science, University of Adelaide
Adelaide, Australia

Abstract

A class of database programs exist which are required to operate over an infinite number of types; included in this class are object browsers and query tools. The types over which these programs operate cannot be enumerated statically. One solution to this problem is to provide a reflective language mechanism that permits the types of values to be abstracted over and the values manipulated in a type independent manner; this paper describes such a mechanism. The mechanism is called Octopus which is an acronym for Object Closure Transplantable to Other Persistent User Spaces. The essence of the technique is to allow values from the programming language value space to be *hoisted* up to a meta level and manipulated in ways which the programming language would not otherwise permit. When manipulation is complete they may be *dropped* back into the value space, provided that they still conform to the language's type system. An additional feature of this technique, as the name suggests, is the ability to isolate portions of closures, and copy them to other locations. Partial closures may be *rewired*, possibly in a different context, using the meta level interface supplied by Octopus.

1 Introduction

1.1 Background

In most programming languages, programs and data form directed graphs with nodes consisting of arbitrary values, such as program fragments (i.e. procedures), records and arrays. Scalars form the leaf nodes of the graphs: they may be referenced but do not themselves reference other values. Figure1.1.1 shows a conceptual view of such a graph in which the nodes represent values and the arcs represent bindings between values. In general, bindings have four components: a name, a value, a type, and an indication as to whether or not the value may be modified [17].

A database may be considered to be a collection of binding graphs such as the one shown above. Database applications consist of programs which construct or navigate these graphs, in most cases the types of the nodes over which the program will operate are statically known by the database application programmer. For example, the programmer of an airline booking system will know that the nodes consist of seats, flights, people etc. In this case the programmer may write a, possibly strongly typed, program to navigate the graph performing some computation which may modify the graph.

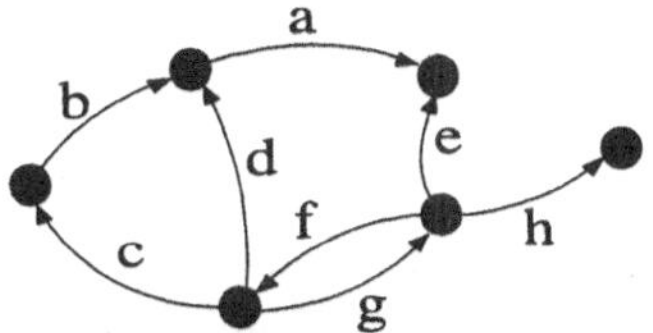

Figure 1.1.1: A conceptual view of programs and data structures.

Another class of database program exists in which the application programmer does not know the types of the data which may be encountered by the program. For example, consider an object browser that displays the contents of an arbitrary database to the user. Most programming languages permit an infinite number of types to be constructed, instances of which the browser may encounter. Clearly, in this case, some form of dynamic type checking must be provided. However, the problem is not entirely addressed by dynamic typing since the types of the values encountered by the browser cannot be textually enumerated.

One solution to these problems is to make use of some form of *linguistic reflection* [20]. Reflective systems permit their own structures to be altered from within. Using the notation of Stemple et al., programs are written in a representation of the language L called L_{rep} and have a universe of discourse, *Val*. For linguistic reflection to occur, L_{rep} must be a subset of *Val* or there must be a way of mapping a subset of *Val* into L_{rep}. Some mechanism must also be provided to map L_{rep} into *Val*; this is commonly provided by a function such as *eval* in Lisp.

Linguistic reflection has two basic forms: compile-time and dynamic. Both permit the construction of new program elements from within another program, the difference is when reflection is performed.

Compile-time linguistic reflection allows the language to manipulate semantically meaningful constructs within that language and cause the compiler to perform computation over these constructs. This allows the user to write generic code that could not otherwise be written. This technique is akin to having a macro processor for the host language which is context sensitive and has the ability to manipulate context. The reader is referred to [20] for more details of this important language mechanism.

When dynamic linguistic reflection is employed, new programs are constructed dynamically and introduced to the running program. For example, when the PS-algol [7] and Napier88 [15] browsers encounter a value of a type which has not previously been encountered, they construct, compile and execute a new program (procedure) to display the value. This new program is cached in the closure of the browser for future use. This technique requires two facilities in the programming language. Firstly, since the browser program can take any data type as a parameter, some dynamic type checking is required. This may be satisfied using a type such as *dynamic* in Quest [4], or *any* in Napier88 [18]. The second requirement is that the reflective part of the language has the ability to deliver the type of the value supplied to the browser. In Napier88 this is achieved through the use of a special function which delivers a representation of the type of a value encapsulated in an *any*. Making use of such reflective techniques can be expensive. For example, the construction of generic tools is complicated by the need to construct programs which have the ability to construct and compile further programs to deal with unknown types.

1.2 Octopus

This paper describes a new dynamic linguistically reflective mechanism called Octopus. This mechanism provides a dynamic infinite union type with a set of reflective operations. These operations may be used to manipulate values of any type without the expense of the dynamic techniques described above. In essence, Octopus provides a uniform abstract interface to values of any type, this facilitates a number of higher level activities, namely:

- construction of browsing tools,
- software debugging,
- querying over complex objects,
- evolution of programs and data, and
- distribution of complex object closures.

Octopus is an acronym for Object Closure Transplantable to Other Persistent User Spaces. The essence of the technique is to allow values from the programming language value space to be *hoisted* up to the meta level and manipulated in ways which the programming language would not otherwise permit. When manipulation is complete, they may be *dropped* back into the value space, provided that they still conform to the language's type system.

In the Octopus model, all values conceptually have special mappings, or *wiring diagrams*, associated with them which contain information about the bindings within those values. Wiring diagrams are normally inaccessible to programmers; however, a hoisting procedure may be called to convert a value into an Octopus. An Octopus may be thought of as a uniform viewing mechanism with which values of any type and their associated wiring diagrams may be viewed and manipulated using the same set of operations.

The Octopus model provides the ability to *cut* and *rewire* the bindings within a hoisted value. When a value from the value space is hoisted up to the meta level, all of its bindings are treated as hooks from the hoisted value to the bound values. A binding is cut by detaching the hook from the bound value, and is rewired by attaching the hook to another value of the same type; it is not possible to rewire values of an incompatible type. Neither is it possible to drop the hoisted value back into the value space until all bindings are correctly rewired.

The Octopus model facilitates the distribution of object closures by allowing partial closures to be exported to other persistent stores. Upon arrival, the Octopus may be rewired and dropped into the value space. The main advantage of this technique is that it removes the need to unnecessarily duplicate and transport values which may already be present at the destination. The model is targeted at persistent systems in which software components, such as window manager systems or compilers, are often common to many persistent stores. The model allows values to be detached from such common values and rewired to the equivalent values in another store.

This paper describes the Octopus model and a number of applications of the model. The language used to implement the model is the persistent programming language Napier88, and the applications are described in terms of simple Napier88 examples.

The paper is structured as follows: Section 2 describes the Octopus model, Sections 3, 4, 5 and 6 describe, in detail, some applications of the model, while Section 7 offers some conclusions.

2 The Octopus Model

Two special operations exist which allow a value to be hoisted to and dropped from an Octopus. Type declarations for the two operations are shown in Figure2.1.

```
coerceToOctopus    : proc( Value → Octopus )
coerceFromOctopus  : proc( Octopus → Value )
```

Figure 2.1: The Octopus hoist and drop operations.

The first operation, *coerceToOctopus*, hoists a value up into an Octopus. Using the notation of Stemple et al. this is a mapping from *Val* to L_{rep}. In the Octopus model, L_{rep} is a subset of *Val* and consequently the hoisted value is still part of the value space. The other operation, *coerceFromOctopus*, first checks to ensure that all bindings in the Octopus are resolved before extracting the encapsulated value. If any of the bindings are unresolved, the Octopus is returned unchanged. This operation maps from L_{rep} to *Val*.

The *coerceToOctopus* operation produces an Octopus which provides a view of the hoisted value. The operations provided by the Octopus act on the original value rather than a copy of the value, and, in particular, manipulation of the encapsulated value is performed in place. Similarly, the *coerceFromOctopus* operation causes the actual value encapsulated in the Octopus to be dropped into the language value space.

In the procedure signatures above, the value hoisted to and dropped from an Octopus has the type *Value*. Since values of any type may be represented as an Octopus, the type *Value* must be an infinite union type, and type checking must be performed dynamically. This functionality is delivered by Napier88 through the infinite union type, *any*, into which values of any type may be injected. Values encapsulated in an *any* are type compatible with each other even if the encapsulated values are of different types.

```
type Octopus is structure( getType    : proc( → TypeRep );
                           getSource  : proc( → Source ) ;
                           scan       : proc( proc( Binding ) ) )
```

Figure 2.2: The structure of an Octopus.

An Octopus is a set of three operations which allow the bindings within a value to be examined and manipulated. These operations are implemented as a package of functions contained in a structure; the hoisted value is encapsulated in the closure of these functions and the functions operate on the value's wiring diagram. The corresponding type declaration for an Octopus is shown in Figure2.2.

The *getType* operation returns a representation of the type of the value encapsulated in the Octopus. This representation is a value in the programming language space and may not be used as a denotation for a type. A complete set of selector, constructor, equivalence and iterator functions are provided by the Napier88 system that operate on this representation [5]. Thus, using these functions, the programmer can obtain any required information about the type.

The *getSource* operation returns a representation of the source code for the value. If the value is a procedure, this source code is similar to the hyper-program model of source code described in [9], [13] and [14]. If the value encapsulated in an Octopus is not a procedure, then *getSource* returns a representation of the value which is suitable for use in hyper-programs. The model of source representation is the topic of related research and will not be discussed further in this paper.

A *scan* procedure is provided to iterate over the bindings contained in an Octopus; *scan* takes as its single parameter a programmer specified procedure which is iteratively applied to each binding in the Octopus. The specified procedure may perform an arbitrary computation on a binding; for example, the procedure may be used to display a binding's value. Bindings are also represented as a package of functions, and are described below.

2.1 Bindings

```
type Binding is structure( cut      : proc( → bool );
                           add      : proc( Value → bool );
                           get      : proc( → Value );
                           resolved : proc( → bool );
                           getType  : proc( → TypeRep );
                           getName  : proc( → string ) )
```

Figure 2.1.1: The representation of a binding.

Each binding is represented by six operations, as shown by the corresponding type declaration in Figure2.1.1. The operations on bindings behave as follows:

cut When applied, this operation causes the associated binding to be dissolved. As described in the introduction, the process of cutting a binding is simply a meta level indication that the binding is no longer resolved. Cut bindings may still be accessed via direct bindings to the naked value.

add The add operation allows an unresolved binding to be rewired, or resolved, using the given value. The operation fails if the binding is already resolved or if the supplied value is of the wrong type.

get When applied, *get* returns the current value of the binding. If the binding is unresolved, a fail value is returned.

resolved This operation returns *true* if the binding is in a resolved state and *false* otherwise.

getType This operation returns a representation of the type of the corresponding bound value.

getName This returns the name of the bound value.

```
let scanner = proc( b : Binding )
begin
        writeString( b( getName )() )
        if EqualType( INT, b( getType )() ) then
           writeString( " : int'n" )
        else if EqualType( STRING, b( getType )() ) then
           writeString( " : string'n" )
        else    writeString( " : unknown type'n" )
end

type example is structure( a : int ; b : string ; c : bool )
let myrecord = example( 1,"hello",true )

let olly = coerceToOctopus( myrecord )
olly( scan )( scanner )
```

Figure 2.1.2: A program to display the type of a value.

```
a : int
b : string
c : unknown type
```

Figure 2.1.3: Output of the program shown in Figure 2.1.2.

A simple example of the use of the Octopus operations is shown in Figure2.1.2 which displays the types of the fields of the record denoted by *myrecord*. The output of this program is shown in Figure2.1.3. The procedure *scanner* displays the name and type of a binding; this procedure is iteratively applied to each binding in the Octopus *olly* using the *scan* operation. This is achieved by obtaining the type of each binding using the *getType* operation of the binding and checking for type representation equality using the *EqualType* operation provided by the Napier88 system. As presented in this example, *scanner* only has knowledge of two types, integer and string. However a more sophisticated version of this procedure could be written using the *getType* operation provided by Octopuses to display the type of an arbitrary value.

3 Viewing

A common activity in persistent programming and database environments is browsing. Object browsers such as those described in [7], [9] and [15] are used for debugging data structures and applications, for viewing values and for discovering reusable components in the object repository [3]. This is achieved by allowing arbitrary data structures to be examined and by displaying graphical representations of values in the form of menus connected by arrows. Thus, the values and the relationships between objects may be graphically displayed.

As described above, some persistent object browsers generate and compile code on demand at run-time. This technique can be expensive due to construction and compilation overheads. Browsers which avoid this overhead have been constructed by making use of *magic* functions. Magic functions allow the programmer to perform operations below programming language type system level. Typical of these operations are assignment, the construction of new values and the ability to obtain type information. These functions are not generally available to the Napier88 programmer since they fundamentally compromise the type system of the programming language.

The Octopus model simplifies the construction of browsing tools by removing the need to compile new browsing routines, whilst retaining the security offered by the type system of the language.

As the Octopus model provides a uniform interface to values, the code for interrogating values becomes more succinct and generic than using the programming language alone. For example, consider the program in Figure3.1.1 which presents the user with menus for browsing an arbitrary object closure.

The program shows the declaration of a procedure called *browse* which takes as its parameter an Octopus. The procedure first creates an empty menu by calling a procedure called *createMenu*. Next, a procedure called *makeMenuEntry* is declared which, when applied to a binding, causes an entry for the binding to be inserted into the menu. Each menu entry consists of two parts: a name that is displayed to the user and a procedure which is executed when the entry is selected. An entry is inserted into the menu as follows: firstly, the name of the bound value is obtained using *getName*. Next, the procedure to be executed, *action*, is declared, which extracts the bound value using *get* and injects it into an Octopus before passing it to a recursive call of the browser. Finally, the bound value name and *action* are inserted into the menu.

```
rec let browse = proc( octopus : Octopus )
begin
        !** create new, empty menu
        let menu = createMenu()

        !** procedure to add a binding to a menu
        let makeMenuEntry = proc( b : Binding )
        begin
                !** get name of bound value
                let entry = b( getName )()

                !** the procedure to call when this menu entry is selected
                let action = proc(); browse( coerceToOctopus( b( get )() ) )

                !** add binding to menu
                menu( addEntry )( entry,action )
        end

        octopus( scan )( makeMenuEntry )
        menu( display )()
end
```

Figure 3.1.1: A simple menu-style browser.

The menu to represent the value is constructed by applying the *scan* operation of the Octopus with the *makeMenuEntry* procedure as a parameter. The *scan* operation applies *makeMenuEntry* to each binding in the Octopus and causes an entry for each binding to be placed in the menu. This menu is then displayed on the screen by calling the menu *display* procedure. When a menu entry is selected by the user, the appropriate action procedure is called which causes the browser to be recursively applied to the corresponding bound value.

The browser in Figure3.1.1 is able to traverse all values in the value space due to the uniform interface provided by Octopuses. Thus, the amount of code required to construct the browser is reduced, and the need to dynamically adapt to values whose types have not been encountered previously by the browser is removed.

4 Querying Complex Objects

In the previous section, it was shown that the Octopus model may be used to provide a uniform view of values. The techniques used to browse an object closure may be applied in order to perform a query over an arbitrarily complex object closure. For example, suppose all of the bindings with the name *balance*, of type integer and with value greater than 100 within a particular closure are required. In a language such as SQL [12], dedicated to performing database operations, this may be achieved by a query such as the one shown below.

```
select object from database
where object.balance > 100

let resultList = createList()
let visitedList = createList()

rec let query = proc( octopus : Octopus )
if ~visitedAlready( octopus ) do
begin
    !** The function to be passed to scan.
    let check = proc( b : binding )
    begin
        if b( getName )() = "balance" and
           isType( b( getType )(),INT ) then
        begin
           project b( get )() as i onto
              int      :  if i > 100 do
                          addToResultList( octopus )
              default  :  {}
        end
        else
           query( coerceToOctopus( b( get )() ) )
    end
    !** Query body
    addToVisitedList( octopus )
    octopus( scan )( check )
end
```

Figure 4.1: Querying an object closure.

In a programming language such as Napier88 this kind of query could be written in one of two ways. Firstly, if the types of the values over which the query was to be performed were known, a statically typed program could be written. This program could not be used on data structures of any other type since it has type information, such as field labels, encoded into it. Parametric polymorphism yields no extra power: a polymorphic query function could be written but it would be required to be parameterised by selector functions for each field of each type, and there may be an unbounded number of these. However, a more general purpose program could be written which dynamically examined the types of the values to which it was applied. In order to cater for an unbounded number of types, this program would be required to use the reflective techniques described earlier.

In all of the above cases not all the values in a closure may be accessed. Those values encapsulated in procedures and abstract data types remain hidden. Using Octopus, it is possible to construct a program which performs a query over an arbitrarily typed set of values. Furthermore the Octopus mechanism permits all the values, encapsulated or otherwise, within a closure to be examined. This ability is somewhat controversial and is discussed in the conclusions. The program shown in Figure4.1 illustrates how a database query such as the one shown above may be implemented using the Octopus mechanism.

The first two lines of the program create two empty lists. The first list, *resultList*, is used to collect all Octopuses within an object closure which contain a binding to a value with name *balance*, of type integer and with magnitude greater than 100. The second, *visitedList*, is used to record those Octopuses in the closure which have already been visited by the query.

If a given Octopus has not been visited, the *query* procedure adds it to the visited list and then examines its bindings by supplying a procedure to the Octopus's *scan* operation. The procedure *check* examines the bound value, and if it has the name *balance*, is of type integer with a magnitude greater than 100, the Octopus containing this binding is inserted into the *resultList*. Otherwise, the bound value is converted into an Octopus and supplied to the *query* procedure. In this manner, a depth first query of the object closure is performed.

4.1 High level query abstractions

The selection criteria of the query shown in Figure4.1 is domain specific, it only finds integer values called *balance* whose values are greater than 100. It is possible to abstract over the *query* procedure by allowing the selection criteria to be passed to the query as a parameter.

To illustrate this, consider the query shown in Figure4.1.1. A procedure called *Find* is declared, which takes a selection predicate as one of its parameters. Octopuses associated with bindings which satisfy the predicate are collected and returned.

The procedure *Find*, is one of a number of high level abstractions over Octopuses. Figure4.1.2 contains a list of other operators we have found to be useful. *Find* has already been described, *Apply* applies the procedure *action* to every binding in the closure. *CondApply* is an extension of *Apply* that applies the procedure *action* to those bindings which satisfy *pred*. The last operator, *Fold*, is polymorphic, and applies the function *map* to all bindings in the closure. Each call of *map* returns a value which is supplied to the collector procedure *collect*. The result of the final call to *collect* is returned by *Fold*. Each of the previous operations may be constructed in terms of *Fold*, but are implemented separately as an optimisation. It is the subject of current research to find a useful set of such operations which may be used to implement a number of tasks such as the ones described in this paper.

```
let visitedList = createList()

rec let Find = proc(   octopus : Octopus ;
                       select : proc( Binding → bool ) → OctopusList )
if ~visitedAlready( octopus ) do
begin
    let resultList = createList()
    !** The function to be passed to scan.
    let check = proc( b : binding )
    begin
         if  select( b ) then
             addToResultList( octopus )
         else
             concat(  resultList,
                      Find( coerceToOctopus( b( get )() ),
                         select,action ) )
    end
    !** Find body
    addToVisitedList( octopus )
    octopus( scan )( check )
    resultList
end
```

Figure 4.1.1: A general querying procedure to return a list of Octopuses.

```
Find      :  proc(   octopus : Octopus ;
                     pred : proc( Binding → bool ) → OctopusList )

Apply     :  proc(   octopus : Octopus ; action : proc( Binding ) )

CondApply:  proc(   octopus : Octopus ; pred : proc( Binding → bool ) ;
                     action : proc( Binding ) )

Fold      :  proc[ t,l ](  octopus : Octopus ; map : proc( Binding → t ) ;
                           collect : proc( t, l → l ) → l )
```

Figure 4.1.2: High level operators.

It has been shown that the Octopus mechanism may be used to implement arbitrary queries over the value space. The approach is to provide some low level, yet powerful, operations on top of which queries may be implemented. In this way, many query languages and paradigms may be provided by a single database environment. This is in contrast to other database programming languages such as Galileo [1] and DBPL [16] which provide a fixed set of higher level query operations as intrinsic features of the language.

One of the drawbacks of this approach is that there is less opportunity for optimisation: each Octopus provides a uniform interface to an arbitrary value, so optimisations which are dependent on the type of a value are impossible to make. Furthermore, the fact that procedures passed to the operations have unknown side effects makes optimisation almost impossible.

Lastly, the composition of various library routines makes no allowances for the possible algebraic optimisations of a query which may exist. This opportunity may be regained by constructing query languages which are translated into operations in terms of Octopuses.

5 Evolution of Programs and Data

The technique of programming enabled by Octopuses may also be used to support program and data evolution. Data and programs may be evolved from one form into another by cutting old components and wiring in new ones. To illustrate this, consider a database of parts [2] with the type shown in Figure5.1.

```
type Part is structure( name     : string ;
                        number   : int ;
                        describe : proc() )
```

Figure 5.1: Type of data held in parts database.

Each part in the database is represented by a record of three components: a name, a unique number and a procedure which, when applied, displays a description of that part. Each instance of *Part* is bound, via the name *describe*, to the same procedure, *display*, which is encapsulated within *describe*. To clarify, a constructor function for parts is shown in Figure5.2 below.

```
let display = proc( s : string ); !** a procedure to display a string

let createPart = proc( name,description : string ; number : int → Part )
      !** Return a new record. Part is used as a constructor here.
      Part( name,                               !** name
            number,                             !** number
            proc(); display( description ) )    !** describe
```

Figure 5.2: The *Part* constructor function.

Suppose that a parts database has been populated with parts created using the *createPart* function, and that the *display* function has been found to be erroneous or inefficient. In order for the parts database to make use of a new display function, all instances of *Part* bound to *display* need to be located and updated.

Using the Octopus model, a *Part* record may be hoisted into an Octopus, the binding to the old *display* procedure cut and a binding to the new *display* procedure established. This process is illustrated by the program in Figure5.3.

In this program, a predicate, *select*, is declared which examines a binding to see if it has the name *display* and if the associated value is a procedure which takes a single string as a parameter. Next, an update procedure, *updateDisplay*, is declared which causes bindings to the old *display* procedure to be updated. It achieves this by cutting the original binding and attaching the *newDisplay* procedure. Finally, the program locates and updates all values in the parts database which are bound to the *display* procedure using the *CondApply* operator described earlier.

```
let newDisplay = proc( s : string ); ... !** a new display procedure.

!** Define the selection criteria.
let select = proc( b : Binding → bool )
        b( getName )() = "display" and
        EqualType( b( getType )(),typeRep( "proc( string )" ) )

!** Update the binding.
let updateDisplay = proc( b : Binding )
begin
        !** First, cut the binding to the old display procedure.
        let ok := b( cut )()
        !** Next, bind in the new display procedure.
        ok := b( add )( newDisplay )
end

!** Update all components which are bound to display.
CondApply( coerceToOctopus( partsDB ),select,updateDisplay )
```

Figure 5.3: Evolving the parts database.

6 Distribution of Complex Object Closures

The task of copying arbitrary object closures from one persistent store to another is complex since, in practice, object closures tend to span all (or a large proportion) of the objects in an object store. One way of tackling this problem is to permit parts of an object closure to be isolated, by cutting a number of bindings, so that the object closure can be partially copied and rewired in another context. This was the original motivation for the Octopus model and the task from which its name derives.

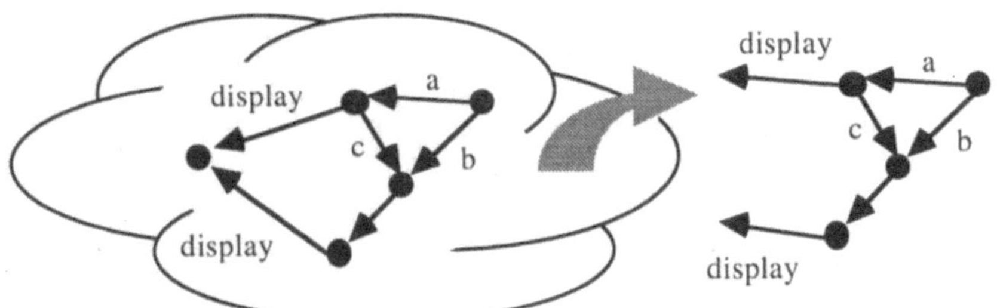

Figure 6.1: Distributing the parts database.

To illustrate this technique, suppose that the parts database is to be installed in another persistent store. Various components of the database are bound to the *display* procedure, and this *display* procedure is common to all persistent stores. In order to avoid unnecessary copying, the application is converted into an Octopus, and the bindings to *display* are cut. The resulting Octopus is then transmitted to a destination persistent store and rewired. Figure6.1 shows a simplified, conceptual view of this process.

When the transmission is complete, the database may not be dropped back into the value space until the closure is wired to the necessary components, i.e.

the unresolved *display* bindings must be rewired to the *display* procedure in the new persistent store. Once the rewiring is complete, the installed version of the parts database has the same state as the original database.

Rewiring may be achieved using a program sent to the other store along with the closure to be rewired. This program is equivalent to an installation script in the Macintosh environment [11]. Figure6.2 shows an installation procedure which may be transmitted to the destination persistent store in order to automatically rewire and reinstall the parts database.

The *rewire* procedure is constructed in a similar way to the procedure in Figure5.3, used to evolve the parts database. Firstly, a selection procedure, *select*, is declared, followed by a computation which locates the *display* procedure in the destination persistent store. A procedure, *rebind,* is declared which binds the procedure *localDisplay* to the closure. *CondApply* is used to establish the rebinding process. Finally, the Octopus is dropped back into the programming language value space and placed in the persistent store.

To allow transmission, two operations *exportOctopus* and *importOctopus* are provided. The mode of transmission may be a remote procedure call such as the one described in [8], or simply the placement of the partial closure in a file.

```
let rewire = proc( octopus : Octopus )
begin
     !** Define the selection criteria.
     let select = proc( b : Binding → bool )
          b( getName )() = "display" ...

     !** Locate the display procedure in the destination persistent store.
     let localDisplay = ...

     let rebind = proc( b : Binding )
     begin
          let ok = b( add )( localDisplay )
          if ~ok do error( ... )
     end

     !** Rewire all components which are bound to display.
     CondApply( octopus,select,rebind )

     !** Place parts database in new store.
     in PS() let application = coerceFromOctopus( octopus )
end
```

Figure 6.2: A procedure to rewire and install the parts database.

7 Conclusions

The Octopus model has been implemented in Napier88. In the process of implementing the model, the architecture of the Napier88 system was modified in a number of ways to provide support for some of the features of Octopuses.

The primary changes were to make use of boxed representations [19] for values and to combine this with the idea of flat static environments [6]. These changes, whilst not affecting the language itself, allowed the cut and rewire operations of Octopuses to be implemented as described in this paper. One of the additional benefits of this architecture is an improvement in storage utilisation, by decreasing the number of retained objects within closures. However, the price paid is an additional dereference on values which would have remained unboxed in the original Napier88 architecture. A more detailed description of this architecture is the topic of another paper.

In the current prototype of the system described in this paper, the source code obtained from an Octopus is a linear textual representation. Our intention is to extend the source code representation to support the features offered by hyper-programming [13, 14]. In addition, by allowing partially resolved hyper-programs to exist, a method of template programming [10] may be developed. These techniques appear to be complementary to the ideas presented in this paper.

In this paper a mechanism which provides a uniform abstract interface to values of any type has been presented. The Octopus approach is to provide a few simple, but powerful reflective mechanisms in the language and to use these to construct higher level tools. These relatively simple mechanisms provide enough power to allow many reflective applications to be written which previously required much heavier weight mechanisms, such as the use of a compiler at run-time, or unsafe language mechanisms. In particular, it has been shown how the Octopus mechanism may be used to browse and query graphs of values of arbitrary data types.

Perhaps the most controversial aspect of Octopus is the ability to examine bindings encapsulated within functions, procedures and abstract data types. This undoubtably breaks the encapsulation and information hiding associated with these language constructs. This raises a philosophical argument as to whether this information should be available to (meta) language mechanisms. Two arguments favour this approach, one is the fact that this mechanism permits programs to be written that could not otherwise be written. The other is the fact that the protection and encapsulation afforded by these mechanisms is not compromised unless the reflective constructs are used. No doubt we will be judged in the fullness of time.

Acknowledgments

This work is supported in part by the Defence Science and Technology Organisation of Australia through their assistance in the PIPE project, and by the Australian Research Council.

References

1. Albano, A., Cardelli, L. and Orsini, R. "Galileo: A Strongly Typed, Interactive Conceptual Language", ACM Transactions on Database Systems, vol 10, 2, pp. 230-260, 1985.
2. Atkinson, M. P. "Malcolm's Famous Parts Example", Personal Communication, 1887.
3. Bachman, C. W. "The Programmer as Navigator", Turing Award Lecture, *in Communications of the ACM*, vol 16, 11, pp. 653-658, 1973.
4. Cardelli, L. "Typeful Programming", Research Report 45, DIGITAL Systems Research Center, 1989.

5. Connor, R. C. H., Brown, A. L., Cutts, Q. I., Dearle, A., Morrison, R. and Rosenberg, J. "Type Equivalence Checking in Persistent Object Systems", *in Proceedings of the 4th International Workshop on Persistent Object Systems*, Morgan-Kaufmann, Martha's Vineyard, Massachusetts, pp. 151-164, 1990.

6. Davie, A. J. T. and McNally, D. J. "PCASE - A Persistent Lazy Version of an SECD Machine", Research Report, University of St. Andrews, CS/92/7, 1992.

7. Dearle, A. and Brown, A. L. "Safe Browsing in a Strongly Typed Persistent Environment", *The Computer Journal*, vol 31, 6, pp. 540-545, 1988.

8. Dearle, A., Rosenberg, J. and Vaughan, F. "A Remote Execution Mechanism for Distributed Homogeneous Stable Stores", *in Proceedings of the Third International Workshop on Database Programming Languages*, Morgan Kauffman, pp. 125-138, 1991.

9. Farkas, A. M., Dearle, A., Kirby, G., Cutts, Q., Morrison, R. and Connor, R. "Persistent Program Construction through Browsing and User Gesture with some Typing", *in Proceedings of the Fifth International Workshop on Persistent Object Systems*, Pisa, pp. 376-393, 1992.

10. Futatsugi, K., Goguen, J., Meseguer, J. and Okada, K. "Parameterized Programming in OBJ2", *in Proceedings of the Ninth International Conference of Software Engineering*, pp. 51-60, 1987.

11. Apple Computer Inc., "Inside Macintosh", Addison-Wesley, 1986.

12. American National Standards Institute, "Database Language SQL", New York, 1986.

13. Kirby, G. N. C. "Reflection and Hyper-Programming in Persistent Programming Systems", Ph.D. Thesis, University of St. Andrews, 1993.

14. Kirby, G. N. C., Connor, R. C. H., Cutts, Q. I., Dearle, A., Farkas, A. and Morrison, R. "Persistent Hyper-Programs", *in Proceedings of the Fifth International Workshop on Persistent Object Systems*, Pisa, pp. 86-106, 1992.

15. Kirby, G. N. C. and Dearle, A. "An Adaptive Browser for Napier88", Research Report, University of St. Andrews, 90/16, 1990.

16. Matthes, F. and Schmidt, J. "The Type System of DBPL", *in Proceedings of the 2nd International Workshop on Database Programming Languages*, Oregon, pp. 219-225, 1989.

17. Morrison, R., Atkinson, M. P., Brown, A. L. and Dearle, A. "On the Classification of Binding Mechanisms", *Information Processing Letters*, vol 34, 2, pp. 51-55, 1990.

18. Morrison, R., Brown, A. L., Connor, R. and Dearle, A. "The Napier88 Reference Manual", University of St. Andrews, PPRR-77-89, 1989.

19. Peyton-Jones, S. "The implementation of functional languages", Prentice-Hall, 1987.

20. Stemple, D., Stanton, R. B., Sheard, T., Philbrow, P., Morrison, R., Kirby, G., Fegaras, L., Cooper, R. L., Connor, R. C. H., Atkinson, M. P. and Alagic, S. "Type-Safe Linguistic Reflection: A Generator Technology", ESPRIT BRA Project 3070 FIDE Technical Report, FIDE/92/49, 1991.

Calculi for Bags and their Complexity *

Stéphane Grumbach
I.N.R.I.A., Rocquencourt BP 105, 78153 Le Chesnay, France
email: Stephane.Grumbach@inria.fr

Tova Milo
Dept. of Computer Science, U. of Toronto, Ontario M5S 1A4, Canada,
email: milo@db.toronto.edu

Yoram Kornatzky
Dept. of Math. and CS, Ben-Gurion U., Beer-Sheba 84105, Israel,
email: yoramk@bengus.bgu.ac.il

Abstract

In this paper, we propose calculi to express queries over bags (i.e. multisets), and study their complexity. We show that the calculus for bags is undecidable in general. Nevertheless, simple syntactic restrictions on the calculus result in computable languages. We provide here two restricted calculi with bounded complexity, and show that the restrictions are minimal. Indeed, any looser restriction leads to non computable queries.

1 Introduction

The standard approach to database modeling assumes that database relations are sets, or in other words that no duplicates are allowed. In practice, many systems relax this restriction [MD86, Fea87, HM81, CDV88], often to save the cost of duplicate elimination. Moreover, in practical query languages (e.g., SQL), some operations (e.g. aggregate functions such as COUNT, AVG) depend on the presence of duplicates.

Recently, much effort has been made to develop suitable languages for manipulating bags. Algebras were developed by extending the relational algebra [KG85, DGK82, Alb91, GM93, LW93]. The optimization problem for bag languages was studied in [Mum90, CV93], and shown to be drastically different from the optimization problem for set languages. The expressive power of algebras for bags was investigated in [GM93]. It turns out that the bag algebra is more powerful than the relational algebra, but is still rather limited. In particular it was proved that the algebra for flat (non nested) bags is strictly included in LOGSPACE.

There are several techniques to increase the expressive power of a query language, such as adding new primitive operations, adding control constructs (such as a fixpoint operator), allowing nested structures (nested relations) with

*Work supported in part by the Esprit Project BRA FIDE 2. Part of this work was done while authors visited each other.

corresponding algebraic operations (powerset, nest, unnest), using a calculus with higher order quantification, etc.

All the above extensions were considered for languages manipulating sets, and shown to be closely related. In particular it was shown that the complex object algebra (algebra for nested sets) and the calculus with quantification over sets have the same expressive power [AB87]. It has also been shown in [GV91b], that a fixpoint operator can be added to the language to get exact expressive power results with respect to complexity classes of queries.

The impact on the complexity of both (i) the addition of numerous algebraic operations on bags, and (ii) the nesting of bags was studied in [GM93]. It was shown that both directions have an impact on the expressive power of the bag algebra. The expressive power gained was shown to be significantly different than that obtained in the case of *sets*. (For two levels of nesting, the algebra expresses the set of hyper-exponential queries, and adding a fixed point leads to Turing completeness.)

In this paper we investigate another option, namely calculi with quantification over bags. We propose calculi, for relations over bags, which include algebraic operations over the bags. Our aim is to demonstrate how the use of quantification over bags affects the expressive power and the complexity of queries. In particular, we consider the interaction between the operations used for handling bags and the complexity. To this end, we extend the traditional notion of *active domain*, and consider quantifiers that range over bags (vs. sets in the classical case) constructed from constants in the database. Note that unlike the case of sets, the active domain may be infinite.

Not surprisingly, it turns out that introducing quantification over such infinite domain may cause queries not to be computable. Nevertheless, simple restrictions on the operations used for manipulating bags result in computable languages, even in the presence of unbounded quantification. We identify two sets of algebraic operations, such that the calculi restricted to these sets become decidable. We present upper bounds on the complexity of the resulting languages. We also show that the restrictions are minimal. Indeed, looser restrictions on the set of operations lead to non computable queries.

The quantifiers in the restricted languages range over unnested bags. We prove that quantification over nested bags lead to undecidability even with very restricted sets of operations. Therefore, the decidable languages we propose are maximal in a very strong sense.

The proof techniques used in the paper are specific. In particular, the proofs of the upper bounds for the restricted languages are based on reduction to weak arithmetics, such as Presburger arithmetic [FR74, FR79]. This subject is related more generally to the decidability of second-order theories [Rab77, Gur85].

The results presented here signal out, again, the difference between languages for sets and languages for bags. While, for sets, quantification over sets (in the calculus) and nesting (in the algebra) result in computable languages with the same expressive power, this is not the case for languages for bags.

The paper is organized as follows. In the next section, we present the algebra for bags. The calculus is defined in Section 3, and shown to be undecidable. Section 4 is devoted to decidable languages. In Section 5 we show that the languages can not be extended while preserving decidability. Finally, conclusions are presented in the last section.

2 Preliminaries

In the following we present an algebra for bag manipulation, BALG, which is a natural extension of the relational algebra. The algebra is identical to that of [GM93] except for some "syntactic sugar", which makes the presentation easier in this paper. The calculus presented in the next section use the following operators to define and manipulate bags.

We assume the existence of an atomic type U, whose domain is an infinite set of constants. We consider tuples of any arity k, $U^k = [U, ..., U]$. A bag is a (homogeneous) collection of tuples that may contain duplicates. If U^k is a tuple type, then $\{\!\{U^k\}\!\}$ is a *bag* type[1], whose domain is the set of bags of tuples of type U^k. We say that a tuple *n-belongs* to a bag if it belongs to that bag and has exactly n occurrences.

We start by presenting the algebra operators. Let B and B' be bags of type $\{\!\{t\}\!\}$ (unless stated otherwise). Let $o, o_1, \ldots, o_k$ be objects of types $t, t_1, \ldots, t_k$ respectively.

Basic bag operations

- *Additive union,* $\uplus$: $B \uplus B'$ is a bag of type $\{\!\{t\}\!\}$, such that o n-belongs to $B \uplus B'$ iff o p-belongs to B and q-belongs to B' and $n = p + q$.
- *Subtraction,* $-$: $B - B'$ is a bag of type $\{\!\{t\}\!\}$, such that o n-belongs to $B - B'$ iff o p-belongs to B and q-belongs to B' and $n = sup(0, p - q)$.
- *Maximal union,* $\bigcup$: $B \bigcup B'$ is a bag of type $\{\!\{t\}\!\}$, such that o n-belongs to $B \bigcup B'$ iff o p-belongs to B and q-belongs to B' and $n = sup(p, q)$.
- *Intersection,* $\bigcap$: $B \bigcap B'$ is a bag of type $\{\!\{t\}\!\}$, such that o n-belongs to $B \bigcap B'$ iff o p-belongs to B and q-belongs to B' and $n = inf(p, q)$.

Constructive operations[2]

- *Tupling,* τ : $\tau(o_1, \ldots, o_k) = [o_1, \ldots, o_k]$ is a k-ary tuple, containing o_i in its ith attribute.
- *Bagging,* β : if $o_1, \ldots, o_k$ are objects of the same type t, then $\beta(o_1, \ldots, o_k) = \{\!\{o_1, \ldots, o_k\}\!\}$ is a bag of type $\{\!\{t\}\!\}$, containing $o_1, \ldots, o_k$. An object o may appear several times in the sequence $o_1, \ldots, o_k$. o n-belongs to $\beta(o_1, \ldots, o_k)$ if it has exactly n occurrences.
- *Cartesian product,* $\times$: if B and B' are bags containing tuples of arity k and k' respectively, then $B \times B'$ is a bag containing tuples of arity $k + k'$, such that $o = [a_1, \ldots, a_k, a_{k+1}, \ldots, a_{k+k'}]$ n-belongs to $B \times B'$ iff $o_1 = [a_1, \ldots, a_k]$ p-belongs to B, $o_2 = [a_{k+1}, \ldots, a_{k+k'}]$ q-belongs to B' and $n = p \times q$.

---

[1]Note that we consider here only non-nested bags. Nested bags will be considered in Section 5.

[2]For each k, there is one operation τ and one operation β.

Filters

- *Selection*, σ_φ: if B is a bag containing tuples of arity k, then $\sigma_\varphi(B)$ is also a bag containing k-ary tuples. The selection criteria φ is an expression of the form $i = j$ (where $i, j \in \{1, \ldots, k\}$ are the indices of the attributes), or $i = c$ (where i is an index and c is an object of corresponding type). o n-belongs to $\sigma_{i=j}(B)$ iff $o.i = o.j$, and o n-belongs to B. o n-belongs to $\sigma_{i=c}(B)$ iff $o.i = c$, and o n-belongs to B.
- *Projection*[3], $\pi_{i_1,\ldots,i_m}$: If $o = [o_1, \ldots, o_k]$ is a k-ary tuple, and for every j, $i_j \in \{1, \ldots, k\}$, then $\pi_{i_1,\ldots,i_m}(o) = [o_{i_1}, \ldots, o_{i_m}]$.
  If B is a bag containing tuples of arity k, and for every j, $i_j \in \{1, \ldots, k\}$, then $\pi_{i_1,\ldots,i_m}(B)$ is a bag of m-ary tuples, constructed by applying $\pi_{i_1,\ldots,i_m}$ on all the members of B. An object o n-belongs to $\pi_{i_1,\ldots,i_m}(B)$ iff for some l there exist exactly l different tuples $o_1, \ldots, o_l$, such that for every $j \in \{1, \ldots, l\}$, $\pi_{i_1,\ldots,i_m}(o_j) = o$, o_j n_j-belongs to B, and $n = n_1 + n_2 + \ldots + n_l$.
- *Duplicate elimination*, ϵ : $\epsilon(B)$ is a bag containing exactly one occurrence of each object of B. More formally, an object o 1-belongs to $\epsilon(B)$ iff o p-belongs to B for some $p > 0$.

The bag algebra is very similar to the relational algebra. The operations $-, \cap, \cup, \times, \sigma$, when applied to bags where each element occurs at most once, behave exactly as the corresponding relational operations. For π, if it is followed by duplicate elimination, then the result is the same as for the corresponding relational projection.

Some of the dependencies between the different operations were studied in [Alb91]. The results were extended in [GM93]. In particular, it was shown that $\cap$ and $\cup$ can be expressed by $\uplus$ and $-$, and that $\uplus$ can be expressed using $\pi, \times, \beta$ and $\cup$. We shall further consider this subject bellow.

3 Calculus for Bags

In this section, we introduce **BagCalc**, a typed extension of the first-order calculus for relations over bags, in the spirit of extensions for complex objects [HS88, GV91b].

It is important to note that we consider relations over bags — that is, non first normal form relations containing bags of tuples of atomic constants — and not *multi-relations* of bags. The highest type level is therefore a set.

As mentioned in the previous section, the *types* we consider are of the following form: an atomic type U, whose domain is an infinite set of constants; tuples of any arity k, $U^k = [U, ..., U]$; and *bags* of tuples of any arity k, $\{\!\{U^k\}\!\}$.

The *alphabet* contains the *operations* of the algebra BALG, namely, $\uplus$, $-$, $\cup$, $\cap$, τ, β, $\times$, σ, π, and ϵ. The alphabet also includes typed *equality* predicates, $=$, for all types.

Terms consist of the following: (i) typed variables, (we shall usually omit the type notation when it can be inferred from the context), (ii) well-typed expressions in BALG using constants and variables.

[3]There is overloading on the name of the operator π which applies both on tuples and on bags of tuples.

Atomic formulas are typed expressions of the form $t_1 = t_2$ (where t_1, t_2 are terms with the obvious type compatibility restrictions), and $R(t)$, (where R is a relation name, and t a term).

Formulas are constructed as usual using the logical connectives $\wedge, \vee, \neg, \rightarrow$ and typed quantifications $\forall x : T$ and $\exists x : T$. Well-formed formulas are defined with the obvious restrictions.

Finally, a *query* from an input schema $\mathbf{R} = \{R_1, ..., R_n\}$ to an output schema containing one relation, $\mathbf{S} = \{S\}$, is an expression of the form:

$$\{x : T \mid \varphi(x)\},$$

where φ is a formula whose relations are in the input schema, and containing one free variable x.

The semantics is defined as the *active domain semantics*, and the definition is very similar to the one used for nested relations. Let $D \subset U$ be a finite set of constants. The *active domain* of type T with respect to D, denoted by $dom(T, D)$, contains all the objects of type T that can be constructed from constants in D. Note that unlike in the set case, the active domain can be infinite (using one constant, one can construct infinitely many bags). Consider a formula φ over a database schema $\mathbf{R}$ and let $\mathbf{I}$ be an instance of $\mathbf{R}$. Let $D_{I,\varphi}$ be the set of atomic constants occurring in I or in φ. In the evaluation of φ on $\mathbf{I}$, each variable of type T in φ ranges over $dom(T, D_{I,\varphi})$. The *satisfaction* of a sentence by an instance $\mathbf{I}$ is defined as follows.

- $\mathbf{I} \models t_1 = t_2$, where t_1 and t_2 are ground terms, if t_1 and t_2 denote the same object. If t_1,t_2 are bags, this implies that they not only contain the same objects but also have the same number of occurrences for each object.
- $\mathbf{I} \models R(t)$, where R is a relation in $\mathbf{I}$ and t is a ground term, if t belongs to the extension of R in $\mathbf{I}$.
- $\mathbf{I} \models \exists x : T\ \varphi(x)$ if there exists an element a in $dom(T, D_{I,\varphi})$ such that $\mathbf{I} \models \varphi(a)$.
- $\mathbf{I} \models \forall x : T\ \varphi(x)$ if for every object a in $dom(T, D_{I,\varphi})$, $\mathbf{I} \models \varphi(a)$.

The definition of the satisfaction is the usual Tarskian semantics for logical connectives.

Note that bag containment ($\subseteq$) and membership ($\in$) predicates can easily be expressed in the calculus using operations in BALG and the equality predicate. We use the symbols $\subseteq$ and $\in$ in the following, to simplify the presentation.

In the following, we study the decidability of **BagCalc**. We prove that the calculus is undecidable. In other words, the set of valid sentences in **BagCalc** is not recursive. The undecidability is due to the fact that the cartesian product on bags allows to simulate the multiplication on integers and therefore the full arithmetic.

Theorem 3.1 **BagCalc** is undecidable.

Proof : (sketch) The proof is based on an encoding of the multiplicative arithmetic into the language. By Gödel incompleteness theorem, the theory of natural numbers with addition and multiplication $\mathcal{N} = \langle N, +, \times, =, \leq, 0, 1\rangle$ is undecidable. We define the theory $\mathcal{B} = \langle \mathcal{B}_a, \uplus, \times, =, \subseteq, \emptyset, \{\!\{a\}\!\}\rangle$ of the bags over only one constant a. There is an obvious correspondence between formulas in the arithmetic and formulas over bags of a single constant. For each formula $\varphi_\mathcal{N}$ over the integers, there is a formula $\varphi_\mathcal{B}$ over bags, such that: $\mathcal{N} \models \varphi_\mathcal{N}$ iff $\mathcal{B} \models \varphi_\mathcal{B}$. This proves the undecidability of **BagCalc** as soon as there is at least one constant in the domain. □

Theorem 3.1 admits the following corollary on queries. The *membership problem* is the problem of testing if an object belongs to the output of a query on a given input.

Corollary 3.2 The membership problem in **BagCalc** is undecidable.

Proof : It is easy to verify that it is undecidable if a belongs to the answer of a query of the form $Q = \{x | x = a \wedge \varphi_\mathcal{B}\}$. □

Restrictions on the algebraic operations allowed on the bags, lead to decidable languages. We consider such restricted languages next.

4 Complexity

We consider in this section restricted calculi, and study their complexity. The proof technique we use is based on quantifier elimination and reduction to the decidability of restricted arithmetics such as the Presburger arithmetic. For a good survey of the complexity of logical theories, see [FR79].

We denote a restricted version of **BagCalc**, when some BALG operator, θ, is not allowed in the formulas, by $\mathbf{BagCalc}_\theta$. We start by investigating the language $\mathbf{BagCalc}_\times$, i.e. **BagCalc** without the cartesian product operation. We show that this restricted language is decidable. Moreover, we give an upper bound on the complexity of queries in $\mathbf{BagCalc}_\times$. Note that we consider the data complexity of the language, i.e. the complexity of evaluating the membership problem w.r.t the size of the input.

Theorem 4.1 The data complexity of $\mathbf{BagCalc}_\times$ is in double exponential space.

The above theorem deals with a calculus that has all the algebraic operations, but the cartesian product. It is also possible to leave the cartesian product operator in the language, and still have a decidable language with some other restrictions. Let $\mathbf{BagCalc}_{\uplus,-,\cup,\cap,\pi}$ be the calculus without the operations $\uplus, -, \cup, \cap$, and π.

Theorem 4.2 The data complexity of $\mathbf{BagCalc}_{\uplus,-,\cup,\cap,\pi}$ is in triple exponential space.

To prove the above two theorems, we use a systematic reduction of **BagCalc** formulas to arithmetic formulas over integers. The reduction is based on replacing formulas over bags by formulas over the number of occurrences of each individual tuple.

The next example illustrates the way a formula over bags can be represented by a formula over integers. The formal encoding is presented afterwards.

Example 4.1 Consider the formula:

$$\forall x' : \{\!\{U\}\!\}\ \forall x'' : \{\!\{U\}\!\}\ \exists x : \{\!\{U^2\}\!\}\ \forall t : U^2\ \exists t' : U\ \exists t'' : U$$
$$(t \in x \Leftrightarrow (t' \in x' \wedge t'' \in x'' \wedge t = [t', t'']))$$

stating that for every two bags x', x'' containing constants, there exists a bag of 2-ary tuples x constructed from the constants in x', x''. The first (second) attribute of each tuple is taken from the bag x' (x''). Another way to state the above property is to say that if the number of occurrences of a tuple in the bag x is positive, then the number of occurrences of its first attribute in x' is positive, and so is the number of occurrences of its second attribute in x''.

Assume that the domain contains only two constants, $D = \{a, b\}$. According to the active domain semantics, this means that x can contain tuples of the form $[a, a], [a, b], [b, a]$ or $[b, b]$. The number of $[a, a]$ in x is positive iff the number of a's in x' and x'' is positive. The number of $[a, b]$ is positive iff the number of a's in x' is positive and the number of b's in x'' is positive, etc. We encode each bag in terms of the number of occurrences of its members, and rephrase the above formula over bags and tuples as a formula over the integers as follows:

$$\forall x'_a\ \forall x'_b\ \forall x''_a\ \forall x''_b\ \exists x_{[a,a]}\ \exists x_{[a,b]}\ \exists x_{[b,a]}\ \exists x_{[b,b]}$$
$$\bigwedge_{s,t \in \{a,b\}} (x_{[s,t]} \geq 1 \Leftrightarrow (x'_s \geq 1 \wedge x''_t \geq 1)).$$

The variables x'_a, x'_b, x''_a, and x''_b represent the number of occurrences of a's and b's in x' and x'', respectively. Similarly, the variables $x_{[a,a]}, x_{[a,b]}, x_{[b,a]}$, and $x_{[b,b]}$ represent the number of occurrences of the tuples $[a, a], [a, b], [b, a]$, and $[b, b]$ in x. It is easy to see that this rephrased formula is valid over the integers iff the original formula is valid for bags.

We next present the encoding from formulas over bags to formulas over integers. We first explain how, given a tuple $\overline{a}$, and a term t, in **BagCalc**, one can construct an arithmetic term t' that represents the number of occurrences of $\overline{a}$ in t.

Definition 4.1 Let t be a term in **BagCalc**, where the only variables in t are of bag type[4]. Let $\overline{a}$ be a k-ary tuple, and assume that the type of t is either U^k, or $\{\!\{U^k\}\!\}$. The **restriction** of t to $\overline{a}$, denoted by $t\downarrow_{\overline{a}}$, is defined as follows:

[4]Other variables of atomic or tuple types will be removed during the encoding. See Definition 4.3.

1. If X is a variable of bag type, then $X \downarrow_{\overline{a}}$ is a new variable $X_{\overline{a}}$ of type *integer*.

2. $\tau(e_1, \ldots, e_k) \downarrow_{\overline{a}} = [e_1, \ldots, e_k] \downarrow_{\overline{a}} \begin{array}{ll} = 1 & \text{if } [e_1, \ldots, e_k] = \overline{a}, \\ = 0 & \text{otherwise.} \end{array}$

3. If e is a constant (of atomic type), then $e \downarrow_{\overline{a}} = [e] \downarrow_{\overline{a}}$.

4. $\beta(e_1, \ldots, e_k) \downarrow_{\overline{a}} = n$, where n is the number of occurrences of $\overline{a}$ among $e_1, \ldots, e_k$.

5. $(A \uplus B) \downarrow_{\overline{a}} = A \downarrow_{\overline{a}} + B \downarrow_{\overline{a}}$.

6. $(A - B) \downarrow_{\overline{a}} = A \downarrow_{\overline{a}} - B \downarrow_{\overline{a}}$.

7. $(A \cup B) \downarrow_{\overline{a}} = max(A \downarrow_{\overline{a}}, B \downarrow_{\overline{a}})$.

8. $(A \cap B) \downarrow_{\overline{a}} = min(A \downarrow_{\overline{a}}, B \downarrow_{\overline{a}})$.

9. $(A \times B) \downarrow_{\overline{a}} = A \downarrow_{\overline{b}} \times B \downarrow_{\overline{c}}$, where $\overline{b} = \pi_{1,\ldots,i}(\overline{a})$, $\overline{c} = \pi_{i+1,\ldots,k}(\overline{a})$, $arity(\overline{b}) = arity(A) = i$, and $arity(\overline{c}) = arity(B) = (k - i)$[5].

10. $(\pi_{i_1,\ldots,i_k} A) \downarrow_{\overline{a}} = \Sigma_{\overline{b}} (A \downarrow_{\overline{b}})$, where $\overline{b}$ ranges over all tuples in the active domain such that $\pi_{i_1,\ldots,i_k}(\overline{b}) = \overline{a}$.

11. $(\sigma_\psi A) \downarrow_{\overline{a}} = A \downarrow_{\overline{a}}$ if $\psi(\overline{a})$ holds, and 0 otherwise.

12. $(\epsilon(A)) \downarrow_{\overline{a}} = min(1, A \downarrow_{\overline{a}})$.

We next define the encoding of an atomic formula in **BagCalc** to a formula over the integers. The idea is that two bag terms are equal iff each object has the same number of occurrences in both bags.

Definition 4.2 Let t_1 and t_2 be terms in **BagCalc** containing only variables of bag type. Assume that the type of both terms is either U^k or $\{\!\{U^k\}\!\}$. Let D be a set of constants (including all the constants appearing in t_1 and t_2). The **integer version** of the atomic formula $t_1 = t_2$, with respect to D, is a formula over the integers, denoted by $(t_1 = t_2) \downarrow_D$, and defined as follows:

$$(t_1 = t_2) \downarrow_D \;=\; \bigwedge_{\overline{a} \in D^k} (t_1 \downarrow_{\overline{a}} = t_2 \downarrow_{\overline{a}}).$$

The following proposition follows from the definition.

Proposition 4.3 For every two **BagCalc** terms t_1, t_2 and every set of constants D including all the constants appearing in t_1 and t_2, $(t_1 = t_2)$ holds iff $(t_1 = t_2) \downarrow_D$ holds.

[5]The symbol "×" on the left hand side of the equation denotes cartesian product, and the one on the right hand side denotes multiplication.

Remark: Consider the membership predicate $\in$. Let X be a variable of bag type, and let $\overline{a}$ be some tuple. The formula $\overline{a} \in X$ can be expressed in **BagCalc** as $\{\!\{\overline{a}\}\!\} \cap X = \{\!\{\overline{a}\}\!\}$. The integer version of this equation is:

$$\bigwedge_{\overline{b} \in D^k} min(\{\!\{\overline{a}\}\!\} \downarrow_{\overline{b}}, X \downarrow_{\overline{b}}) = \{\!\{\overline{a}\}\!\} \downarrow_{\overline{b}},$$

which when evaluated, is equivalent to:

$$(\ min(1, X_{\overline{a}}) = 1\ )\ \wedge\ \bigwedge_{\overline{b} \neq \overline{a}} (\ min(0, X_{\overline{b}}) = 0\ ),$$

which is equivalent to $X_{\overline{a}} \geq 1$. Thus, the integer version of $\overline{a} \in X$ is $X_{\overline{a}} \geq 1$. This is rather intuitive, $\overline{a}$ belongs to the bag X, iff it occurs in X at least once. □

We can now define the encoding of a general formula φ over bags to a formula over integers. The idea is to replace φ by formulas "speaking" about every specific tuple of constants. So instead of considering bags, we consider integers representing the number of occurrences of each tuple.

Definition 4.3 Let φ be a well-formed **BagCalc** formula in prenex form, with no relation symbols. Let D be the set of all constants appearing in φ. The *integer-version* of φ, denoted by φ_{int}, is a formula over the integers, constructed as follows[6]:

1. Replace each universal (existential) quantifier on variable x of bag type, by a sequence of universal (existential) quantifiers on variables of integer type, one variable $x_{\overline{a}}$ for every tuple $\overline{a}$ in D^k.

   For example, $\forall x : \{\!\{U^k\}\!\}$ is replaced by $\forall x_{[a_1,\ldots,a_1]}, \ldots, \forall x_{[a_n,\ldots,a_n]}$, if $D = \{a_1, \ldots, a_n\}$.

2. Replace each universal (existential) quantifier of atomic/k-ary tuple type, by a conjunction (disjunction) over all the constants/tuples in D/D^k, where each occurrence of the variable x in the conjunction (disjunction) is replaced by the corresponding constant/tuple in D/D^k.

   For example, $\forall x : U^k \varphi(x)$ is replaced by:

   $$\bigwedge_{\overline{a} \in D^k} \varphi(\overline{a}).$$

3. Replace every atomic formula $(t_1 = t_2)$ by its integer version $(t_1 = t_2) \downarrow_D$.

In the next example, we consider again the formula of Example 4.1. Note that the membership predicate is used as an abbreviation (see remark above).

[6]Note that the formulas in intermediate steps belong neither to the bag nor to the integer calculus.

Example 4.2 After step (1.), the formula obtained is:

$$\forall x'_a\,\forall x'_b\,\forall x''_a\,\forall x''_b\,\exists x_{[a,a]}\,\exists x_{[a,b]}\,\exists x_{[b,a]}\,\exists x_{[b,b]}\,\forall t\!:\!U^2\,\exists t'\!:\!U\,\exists t''\!:\!U$$
$$(t \in x \Leftrightarrow (t' \in x' \wedge t'' \in x'' \wedge t = [t',t''])).$$

After step (2.), the formula is as follows:

$$\forall x'_a\,\forall x'_b\,\forall x''_a\,\forall x''_b\,\exists x_{[a,a]}\,\exists x_{[a,b]}\,\exists x_{[b,a]}\,\exists x_{[b,b]}$$
$$\bigwedge_{[s,t]\in\{a,b\}^2}\ \bigvee_{p\in\{a,b\}}\ \bigvee_{q\in\{a,b\}} (([s,t] \in x \Leftrightarrow (p \in x' \wedge q \in x'' \wedge [s,t] = [p,q]))).$$

To clarify the presentation, we simplify the above formula before applying step 3. Note that the simplification is not essential for the translation process. It is simply used for convenience reasons. After simplification (only the conjunct satisfying $[s,t] = [p,q]$ are distinguished) the formula has the following form:

$$\forall x'_a\,\forall x'_b\,\forall x''_a\,\forall x''_b\,\exists x_{[a,a]}\,\exists x_{[a,b]}\,\exists x_{[b,a]}\,\exists x_{[b,b]}$$
$$(([a,a] \in x \Leftrightarrow (a \in x' \wedge a \in x'' \wedge [a,a] = [a,a]))\wedge$$
$$(([a,b] \in x \Leftrightarrow (a \in x' \wedge b \in x'' \wedge [a,b] = [a,b]))\wedge$$
$$(([b,a] \in x \Leftrightarrow (b \in x' \wedge a \in x'' \wedge [b,a] = [b,a]))\wedge$$
$$(([b,b] \in x \Leftrightarrow (b \in x' \wedge b \in x'' \wedge [b,b] = [b,b])).$$

After step (3.) (and some more simplification) the formula reduces to:

$$\forall x'_a\,\forall x'_b\,\forall x''_a\,\forall x''_b\,\exists x_{[a,a]}\,\exists x_{[a,b]}\,\exists x_{[b,a]}\,\exists x_{[b,b]}$$
$$\bigwedge_{s,t\in\{a,b\}} (x_{[s,t]} \geq 1 \Leftrightarrow (x'_s \geq 1 \wedge x''_t \geq 1)).$$

The following proposition shows that a formula in **BagCalc** and its integer version are closely related.

Proposition 4.4 Let φ be a formula in **BagCalc** without relation symbols, and assume $|\varphi| = n$. The integer version of φ, φ_{int}, is of size polynomial in n, and φ holds iff φ_{int} holds.

The proof is based on a careful examination of the encoding process.

We next use the close relationship between **BagCalc** formulas and arithmetic formulas over integers, to investigate restricted versions of **BagCalc**. In particular, we use the encoding to prove Theorems 4.1 and 4.2 presented at the beginning of this section. The two results are based on the following classical theorems.

Theorem 4.5 [Pre29] The theory of integers under addition $\mathcal{Z}^+ = \langle Z, +, =, \leq, 0, 1\rangle$, known as the Presburger arithmetic, is decidable in double exponential space.

Theorem 4.6 [Sko30] The theory of natural numbers under multiplication $\mathcal{N}^{\times} = \langle N, \times, =, 0, 1\rangle$, is decidable in triple exponential space.

We first consider Theorem 4.1, whose proof is based on the following proposition.

Proposition 4.7 Let φ be a formula in $\mathbf{BagCalc}_{\times}$, without relation symbols, where $|\varphi| = n$. Then, there exists a formula ψ in the Presburger arithmetic, with size polynomial in n, such that ψ holds iff φ holds.

Proof : Let φ_{int} be the *integer-version* of φ. From Proposition 4.4, it follows that φ_{int} is of size polynomial in n, and that φ holds iff φ_{int} holds. It is easy to see that φ_{int} is equivalent to a formula ψ in the Presburger arithmetic. Indeed, the operations $-$, *min* and *max* are easily simulated by $+$ with some more variables. The sum expressions Σ (corresponding to the projections in φ) can be replaced by explicit sum $A\downarrow_{\bar{b}_1} + \ldots + A\downarrow_{\bar{b}_l}$ of all the tuples $\bar{b}_i$ in the active domain. Finally, we add the restriction $x \geq 0$ for each variable x in the formula (the integers manipulated are cardinals). Since we do not have relation names, the number of tuples in the active domain is polynomial in the size of the formula. Thus ψ is of size polynomial in n. □

We can now prove Theorem 4.1. We restate the theorem below.

Theorem 4.1 : The data complexity of $\mathbf{BagCalc}_{\times}$ is in double exponential space.

Proof : Assume that φ is a formula in $\mathbf{BagCalc}_{\times}$ over a schema $\mathbf{R}$ with maximal arity k. Consider an input $\mathbf{I}$ over $\mathbf{R}$ such that $|\mathbf{I}| = n$. We first replace every occurrence of a relation symbol R_i in φ by the disjunction of possible values for the tuples in R_i. We denote the new formula without relation symbols by φ_I. Clearly, $|\varphi_I| \leq cn^k$, for some constant c. Thus, the size of φ_I is not more than polynomial in n.

Next, we replace the formula over bags φ_I by a formula ψ_I in the Presburger arithmetic, as done in Proposition 4.7. Note that the size of ψ is polynomial in the size of φ_I, and therefore polynomial in the size of the input.

The upper bound for the complexity of formulas in the Persburger arithmetic is DSPACE($2^{2^{a^n}}$) for some constant a, where n is the size of the formula (See Theorem 4.5). Since the size of ψ is polynomial in the size of the input, the space complexity of queries in $\mathbf{BagCalc}_{\times}$ is not more than double exponential in the size of the input. □

Theorem 4.2 is proved using a similar technique. We restate the theorem below.

Theorem 4.2 : The data complexity of $\mathbf{BagCalc}_{\uplus,-,\cup,\cap,\pi}$ is in triple exponential space.

Proof : Consider a formula φ in $\mathbf{BagCalc}_{\uplus,-,\cup,\cap,\pi}$. It is easy to see that the formula obtained using the encoding technique presented in the previous section contains only the arithmetic operation $\times$ (generated while translating cartesian product), and expressions of the forms $min(1,x)$ (generated while encoding duplicate elimination). Note that $y = min(1,x)$ is equivalent to: $(y = 0 \vee y = 1) \wedge (y = 0 \Leftrightarrow x = 0)$. Therefore the resulting formula is a formula of the theory of natural numbers under multiplication, and has triple exponential space complexity (See Theorem 4.6). □

5 Extensions

In this section, we show that the decidable languages presented above are maximal in two different ways. First, we prove that both $\mathbf{BagCalc}_{\times}$ and $\mathbf{BagCalc}_{\uplus,-,\cup,\cap,\pi}$ cannot be augmented with any algebraic operation while still preserving decidability. We next consider the nesting of bags. The quantifiers in the restricted languages range over unnested bags. We prove that quantification over nested bags lead to undecidability even with very restricted sets of operations. Therefore, looser restrictions on the languages lead to non computable queries.

Proposition 5.1 .

1. The operations $\uplus, -, \cup, \cap, \pi$ cannot be expressed in $\mathbf{BagCalc}_{\uplus,-,\cup,\cap,\pi}$. Moreover if any of them is added to the language, it becomes undecidable.

2. Inclusion of bags ($\subseteq$) cannot be expressed in $\mathbf{BagCalc}_{\uplus,-,\cup,\cap,\pi}$. Moreover, if it is added to the language, it becomes undecidable.

Proof: We prove the proposition by showing that adding any of the operations $\uplus, \cup, \cap, -, \pi$, or the predicate $\subseteq$ to the language, enables expressing formulas in the theory of natural numbers with multiplication and addition, or multiplication and order, which are both known to be undecidable [FR79]. The encoding of a formula in number theory to a formula over bags is done as in theorem 3.1. We only show here how linear order and addition can be expressed using $\uplus, \cup, \cap, -, \pi$, and $\subseteq$. Let i_1, i_2, i_3 be three integers, and let b_1, b_2, b_3 be bags containing i_1, i_2 and i_3 occurrences (resp.) of some constant a. The expression $i_1 \leq i_2$ can be expressed by any of the following formulas: $b_1 \cap b_2 = b_1$; or $b_1 \cup b_2 = b_2$; or $b_1 - b_2 = \{\!\{\}\!\}$; or $b_1 \subseteq b_2$. The expression $i_1 + i_2 = i_3$ can be expressed by the formulas: $b_1 \uplus b_2 = b_3$; or:

$$\exists x \ \ (\epsilon(x) = \{\!\{[a,c],[b,c]\}\!\}) \ \wedge \ (\pi_1(\sigma_{x.1=a}(x)) = \pi_2(b_1 \times \{\!\{[a]\}\!\})) \wedge$$

$$(\pi_2(x) = \pi_2(b_3 \times \{\!\{[c]\}\!\}))) \ \wedge \ (\pi_1(\sigma_{x.1=b}(x)) = \pi_2(b_2 \times \{\!\{[b]\}\!\})). \ \square$$

Remark: Note that membership ($\in$) can be expressed in both $\mathbf{BagCalc}_{\times}$ and $\mathbf{BagCalc}_{\uplus,-,\cup,\cap,\pi}$. Thus there is no point in adding it to the languages. Also note that adding $\times$ to $\mathbf{BagCalc}_{\times}$ result in an undecidable language (Theorem 3.1). Thus both languages cannot be extended with any of the algebraic operation or logical predicates of **BagCalc** while still preserving decidability.

So far we considered quantifiers over variables of type U^k and $\{\!\{U^k\}\!\}$. We next consider quantification over nested bags, i.e. bags of tuples were each attribute can also be a bag. We call the extended language **BagCalc**^{i}, where i denotes the level of bag nesting. The algebra operators are adjusted (typed) accordingly. The language **BagCalc** considered above allows only one level of bags, thus corresponds to **BagCalc**^{1}. It turns out that increasing the bag nesting results in undecidability even for extremely restricted set of operations.

Theorem 5.2 The calculus **BagCalc**^{2} with no algebraic operations, and with only equality and membership testing predicates, is Turing complete.

Proof : (sketch) The encoding of the Turing machine is fairly simple. The first level of bags $\{\!\{U\}\!\}$ is used to encode as many indices as needed for the time and space of the machine. The second level of bags stores tuples of the form: $[c, t, v, s]$, where c and t denote bags encoding respectively the indices for the cell of the tape and the time; v is the content of the cell c at time t; and s is the state if the head is on cell c at time t, and another symbol otherwise. The formula states that there is a bag (with 4-ary tuples of the above structure) containing the initial content of the tape and which is closed under the transitions of the machine. □

It follows that the restrictions on the decidable language presented in this work can not be relaxed while preserving decidability.

6 Conclusion

We presented calculi for bags and proved that a general calculus for bags is undecidable. Nevertheless, simple syntactic restrictions on the calculus result in computable languages.

Note that bags can be used to simulate integers. Therefore, the results presented in this paper can be used to study query languages for first normal form relations with arithmetic functions formally.

We present above two restricted calculi, **BagCalc**$_\times$ and **BagCalc**$_{\uplus,-,\cup,\cap,\pi}$, and prove upper bound complexity results. We also show that the restrictions on the languages are minimal, and that looser restrictions lead to non computable queries. Nevertheless, the real expressive power of these languages is still rather unclear. It is open if they are complete with respect to some complexity class.

It would also be interesting to know how the languages compare with languages for complex objects restricted to relational input and output [HS88, HS89, GV91b, GV91a]. For example, the complexity of algebra queries for complex objects restricted to types with three levels of sets nesting is also in double exponential space. Its relationship with **BagCalc**$_\times$ seems to be a difficult question.

Acknowledgments: The authors wish to thank Yuri Gurevich for technical remarks.

References

[AB87] S. Abiteboul and C. Beeri. On the power of languages for the manipulation of complex objects. In *Proc. Int. Workshop on Theory and Applications of Nested Relations and Complex Objects (extended abstract)*, Darmstadt, 1987. INRIA research report n 846.

[Alb91] J. Albert. Algebraic properties of bag data types. In *Proc. 17th Int'l Conf. on Very Large Data Bases*, pages 211–219, 1991.

[BTS91] V. Breazu-Tannen and R. Subrahmanyam. Logical and computational aspects of programming with sets/bags/lists. In *Proc. 18th Int. Col. on Automata, Languages and Programming*, 1991.

[CDV88] M. Carrey, D. DeWitt, and S. Vandenberg. A data model an query language for exodus. In *Proc. ACM SIGMOD 1988 Int'l Conf. on Managment of Data, Chicago, IL*, 1988.

[CV93] S. Chaudhuri and M. Vardi. Optimization of real conjunctive queries. In *Proc. 12th ACM Symp. on Principles of Database Systems*, Washington, May 1993.

[DGK82] U. Dayal, N. Goodman, and R.H. Katz. An extended relational algebra with control over duplicate elimination. In *Proc. ACM Symp. on Principles of Database Systems, Los Angeles, CA,*, 1982.

[Fea87] D.H. Fishman and et al. Iris: An object oriented database managment system. In *ACM Trans. Office Information Systems, 5:1*, 1987.

[FR74] M.J. Fischer and M.O. Rabin. Super-exponential complexity of Presburger arithmetic. In *Proc. AMS Symp. on Complexity of real computation process*, volume VII, 1974.

[FR79] J. Ferrante and C.W. Rackoff. *The computational complexity of logical theories*, volume 718 of *Lecture Notes in Mathematics*. Springer, 1979.

[GM93] S. Grumbach and T. Milo. Towards tractable algebras for bag. In *Proc. 12th ACM Symp. on Principles of Database Systems*, Washington, May 1993.

[Gur85] Y. Gurevich. *Model Theoretic Logics*, chapter Monadic Second-Order Theories, pages 479–506. Springer-Verlag, 1985.

[GV91a] S. Grumbach and V. Vianu. Expressiveness and complexity of restricted languages for complex objects. In *Proc. 3rd Int. Workshop on database programming languages*, Nafplion, Aug. 1991.

[GV91b] S. Grumbach and V. Vianu. Tractable query languages for complex object databases. In *Proc. 10th ACM Symp. on Principles of Database Systems*, pages 315–327, Boulder, May 1991.

[HM81] M. Hammer and D. Mcleaod. Database Description with SDM: a Semantic Database Model. *ACM trans. on Database Systems 6,3*, 1981.

[HS88] R. Hull and J. Su. On the expressive power of database queries with intermediate types. In *Proc. 7th ACM Symp. on Principles of Database Systems*, 1988.

[HS89] R. Hull and J. Su. Untyped Sets, Invention and Computable Queries. In *Proc. 8th ACM Symp. on Principles of Database Systems*, 1989.

[KG85] A. Klausner and N. Goodman. Multirelations semantics and languages. In *Proc. 11th Intl. Conf. on Very Large Databases, Stockholm, Sweden*, 1985.

[LW93] L. Libkin and L. Wong.. Some Properties of Languages for Bags. In *Proc. 4th Intl. Workshop on Database Programming Languages, NYC*, 1993.

[MD86] F. Manola and U. Dayal. Pdm: An objected-oriented data model. In *Proc. Intl. Workshop on Object Oriented Database Systems, Asilomor,CA*, 1986.

[Mum90] I.S. Mumick. et al. The magic of duplicates and aggregates. In *Proc. 16th Intl. Conf. on Very Large Databases, Brisbane, Australia*, 1990.

[Pre29] M. Presburger. über die Vollständigkeit eines gewissen systems der arithmetik ganzer zahlen, in welchem die addition als einzige operation hervortritt. In *Comptes rendus du premier Congrès des Mathématiciens des Pays Slaves*, pages 92–101, Warszawa, 1929.

[Rab77] M. Rabin. *Handbook of Mathematical Logic*, chapter Decidable Theories, pages 595–629. North-Holland, 1977.

[Sko30] T. Skolem. über einige satzfunktionen in der arithmetik. *Skrifter Norske Vid. Akad. Oslo I. Klasse*, 7, 1930.

Bulk Data Types, A Theoretical Approach *

Catriel Beeri, Paula Ta-Shma
Institute of Computer Science
The Hebrew University of Jerusalem
Israel
{beeri,paula}@cs.huji.ac.il

Abstract

The treatment of bulk data types (BDTs) is a fundamental issue in database programming languages. A uniform, formal, treatment of BDTs is still lacking. We present a formal definition of bulk data types, based on parameterized algebraic specifications. We then define appropriate relationships between bulk types, and show that BDTs together with such relationships form a category with sets as the terminal object. We consider how to apply structural recursion (using a function called *pump*) to all bulk types, and show how equationally constrained BDTs imply similar constraints on the arguments to *pump*.

1 Introduction

Bulk data types (BDTs) are container types with finite type definitions, and arbitrarily large instances. A container type collects elements of some other type. Thus *integer* is not a container type. Tuples (of fixed arity), sets and trees have finite descriptions, but only the last two have arbitrarily large instances.

Most databases and database programming languages emphasize relations, i.e., sets of tuples. However, because of the simplicity of the relational model, it is unsuitable for the representation of data in many applications. In the last decade, generalizations of this model (with associated query languages) have been proposed, such as *nested relation* and *complex object* models that still use the set type constructor, but allow the set and tuple constructors to be arbitrarily interleaved. Some systems go further, and allow other container types, such as bags (multisets), and lists (sequences). O_2 provides lists and sets, and its query language enables them to be queried in a similar manner [3]. However, this approach is still limited, because it only supports a small fixed set of built-in bulk types, which may not cater for many applications. Also, if the built-in approach is adopted, the large investment of source code in BDT implementation is hard-wired into the system and is not available for re-use by its other aspects [12].

An alternative approach, that has attracted a lot of interest recently, is that of having an *extensible* type system, so that users can define new BDTs to suit their needs. If this approach is to be feasible, efficient implementation

*Based on P. Ta-Shma's M.Sc. thesis. Work partially supported by a grant from GIF — the German Israeli Foundation for Scientific Research and Development

techniques, declarative query languages and optimization strategies must be developed and specialized for new bulk types. Moreover, a uniform approach to the above issues for a class of bulk types is needed. To attain these goals, we need to have a formal view of BDTs as a family, with properties shared by all members, and well-defined relationships between different members.

Recent research has provided promising results in some of these directions. *Maps* [1] provide an implementation technique and are included in a query language for a class of bulk types. *Monad comprehensions* [16, 15] generalize set and list comprehensions [17] to form a query language over a class of bulk types. Hull and Su [11] deal with complexity theoretic properties of some BDTs. However, none of these approaches deals with the full spectrum of BDTs that we consider. Beeri and Kornatzky [5] consider optimization for a large class of BDTs, although our treatment of bulk types is more uniform and general.

In this paper we provide a formal definition which we feel captures the intuitive notion of bulk data type, and perform an initial investigation of some properties of this family of types. We base our framework on the *algebraic specifications* approach [20], which is well known for its treatment of abstract data types. Abstraction is necessary to model BDTs such as sets and bags. To model container types, it is natural to consider *parameterized* specifications, where the parameter describes the requirements (if any) that an element type must satisfy (e.g., sets are often required to have equality over the member type). We use the *initial algebra* approach [10, 9] for the semantics of specifications.

This paper proceeds as follows. Section 2 defines bulk data types, section 3 considers relationships between BDTs, and section 4 shows that BDTs together with such relationships form a category. Section 5 considers some applications of our theory, and section 6 presents our conclusions.

2 What is a Bulk Data Type ?

We view a *bulk data type* as a type constructor, that is, as a type defined by a parameterized specification with two parts: a parameter specification which defines a set of *minimum* requirements for parameter types, and a target specification which defines the "container" type itself. Both parts may import fixed, predefined specifications. For example, if predicates are required, we need to import *bool*. We take the standard initial algebra semantics for fixed specifications, and loose semantics for the parameter specification [20, 9]. We assume a single parameter, called **data**. Throughout, we assume that actual parameters are **data**-algebras. The formal semantics of parameterized specifications, and the restrictions that guarantee that they are well-defined are discussed in [9].

2.1 Constructors

In general, a specification uses operations, and the relationships between elements constructed by operations are determined by (Horn clause) equations. A subset of the operations (of the target) is a **set of constructors** if, for any parameter algebra, every element of the target algebra can be expressed using only the constructors. For example, although a specification of lists may define many operations, nil and insert (also called cons) suffice as a set of constructors.

A **B-specification** is a parameterized specification for which a minimal set of constructors has been designated. All other operations are called *functions*.

We require B-specifications to *protect* the specifications they import, including parameters. Briefly, this means the following. A specification has a model, say, the initial algebra. When a specification S is used in a specification T, then S is actually a subspecification of T. The part of the initial algebra of T that corresponds to S should be isomorphic to the initial algebra of S. If that is not the case, we say that the protection of S has been violated. One case is when the additional equations in T force additional equalities on terms of S, not derivable from S; another case is when there are additional terms for a sort of S in the T-algebra. In either case, violation of protection can be seen as an inconsistency in how S is used in T. For further details see [9]. We also expect the presence of functions and the equations defining them to have no effect on the sorts being defined by the B-specification. That is, given a B-specification with constructors only, the addition of function definitions should protect the sorts in the algebra; the only effect is the addition of operations. Indeed, if this is not the case, then the equations that involve only the constructors do not imply all the equalities on the terms. We regard such a specification as ill-presented.

Terms composed of constructors only (using **data**-elements) are called **data terms**. The set of all such data terms for a B-specification $\bar{B}$ with parameter A is denoted by $DT_{\bar{B}(A)}$. $\equiv$ denotes the equivalence relation between terms deduced from the equations.
In the sequel we assume that $\bar{B}$ is a B-specification, and A is a parameter for $\bar{B}$. For brevity, parameter specifications are usually described informally in the sequel.

Example 2.1
We present a B-specification ADJLISTS for *adjacency lists*. The parameter specification *data* is given by

<u>data</u> = <u>bool</u> +
sorts : data
opns : eq : data, data $\rightarrow$ bool
eqns : x,y,z $\in$ data
eq(x,y) = true :- eq(y,x) = true
eq(x,z) = true :- eq(x,y) = true, eq(y,z) = true
eq(x,x) = true

Note that *bool* is imported. All actual parameters must have a predicate *eq* which is an equivalence relation.

The target specification is given by

<u>ADJLISTS</u> =
import : <u>data</u>, <u>bool</u>
sorts : list
cons : nil : $\rightarrow$ list, insert : data, list $\rightarrow$ list
func : member : data, list $\rightarrow$ bool
eqns : $x, y \in$ data L $\in$ list
insert(x,insert(x,L)) = insert(x,L)
member(x,nil) = false
member(x,insert(y,L)) = eq(x, y) $\vee$ member(x,L)

We assume that *bool* has the predicate ∨ (disjunction). The constructors are nil and insert. *member* is a function which returns *true* if a data element belongs to a list. This type describes lists where adjacent duplicates are removed. □

2.2 Large Types

Bulk data types should have arbitrarily large instances. We define an operator, the *contents* operator, which returns the set of data elements appearing in a term. For each data term t of $DT_{\bar{B}(A)}$, **C**(t) is the set of elements of A that appear in t.

Definition 2.2 *A B-specification $\bar{B}$ is* **large** *if there exists a parameter A for $\bar{B}$ such that for any natural number n, there exists a term $t \in DT_{\bar{B}(A)}$ with $|\mathbf{C}(t)| > n$*

This concept applies to the type constructor. Thus *set* is large: even though there are only a finite number of sets of characters, there exist arbitrarily large sets of integers. [1] It is easy to see that the ADJLIST type is large. A simple graph-theoretic characterization of large types is given in [14].

2.3 Conservativity

Although being large is a necessary property of bulk types, it is not a sufficient condition. Consider the following example.

Example 2.3
We add the equation insert(x,L) = L to ADJLISTS, to obtain NOLISTS. In NOLISTS the elements are ignored - the insertion of a new element into a nolist results in the original nolist. NOLISTS is large, since it admits arbitrarily large terms, although they are all equivalent to nil. Consequently, it is impossible to define a function over the NOLIST algebra whose results depend on the elements of a nolist. For example, consider the *member* function. We have *member*(5,insert(5,nil)) equals *true*, *member*(5,nil) equals *false*, but these two can be proven equal. Thus, *true* and *false* have been coalesced, and therefore the protection of *bool* has been violated. Although NOLISTS is large, even a simple membership function is not available over it, and therefore it is unreasonable to call it a bulk data type. □

Definition 2.4 *A B-specification $\bar{B}$ is* **conservative** [2] *if for all parameters A, and for all $t, t' \in DT_{\bar{B}(A)}$, $t \equiv t'$ implies $\mathbf{C}(t) = \mathbf{C}(t')$.*

This means that any two data terms in the same equivalence class of $\bar{B}(A)$ have the same contents, so **C** can be defined over the equivalence classes of $\bar{B}(A)$, and is actually defined for all terms including those which are not data terms. Whereas largeness of a type depends on its constructors, conservativity depends on its equations. Clearly, ADJLISTS is conservative but NOLISTS is not.

---

[1]Note that parameter specifications of large types must admit infinite algebras. See [14].
[2]conservativity here is not related to *conservative extension* in logic.

Note that we must choose the constructors judiciously. Including an operation *delete*, which removes the first element of a list term, as a list constructor would prevent lists from being conservative. The application of constructors should not decrease the contents of the terms they are applied to. See also [19].

In order to query instances of bulk data types, we require, at least, the availability of certain basic functions commonly associated with sets, such as membership. A reasonable membership function cannot be defined over any non-conservative B-specification without violating protection.

Theorem 2.5 *Conservativity is co-recursively enumerable, but not recursive.*

Proof (sketch) : Co-recursive enumerability follows from the fact that the set of ground equations derivable from a specification is recursively enumerable [9]. For the other direction, we modify a specification for combinatory logic (see [20]) by identifying data terms with different contents if combinatory logic terms are determined equal. In this way, conservativity is reduced to the inequality of terms in combinatory logic. This is known not to be recursive. ◇

Despite this pessimistic general result, we can still expect to find sufficient conditions that guarantee conservativity. One simple condition is that variables of any type and expressions of type **data** appearing in an equation between data terms, should appear on both sides of the equality.

We say that a B-specification defines a *bulk data type* if it is large and conservative.

3 BDT Morphisms

In this section we consider bulk data types having the same parameter specification SPEC and the same imported sorts. Given types $\bar{B}$ and $\bar{B}'$, we define a *bulk morphism* from $\bar{B}$ to $\bar{B}'$ as a family of mappings, one from $\bar{B}(A)$ to $\bar{B}'(A)$ for each parameter A, such that each mapping satisfies some constraints, and the family as a whole also satisfies constraints.

3.1 b-morphisms

Definition 3.1 *A* **b-morphism** h^A *from* $\bar{B}(A)$ *to* $\bar{B}'(A)$ *is a pair of functions* (h_F, h^A_{DT})*, such that:*

function mapping: h_F *maps the functions of* $\bar{B}'$ *to the functions of* $\bar{B}$

element mapping: h^A_{DT} *maps data terms of* $\bar{B}(A)$ *to data terms of* $\bar{B}'(A)$*, and elements of imported sorts (including* A*) to themselves*

b-morphism criterion : *For all functions* f *of* $\bar{B}'$ *and data terms* $t_1, \ldots, t_n$ *of* $\bar{B}$
$f(h^A_{DT}(t_1), \ldots, h^A_{DT}(t_n)) = h^A_{DT}(h_F(f)(t_1, \ldots, t_n))$

The function mapping associates functions of $\bar{B}'$ with functions of $\bar{B}$ that play an analogous role, according to the b-morphism criterion. This criterion states that functions related by h_F should give results related by h^A_{DT} if the inputs are related by h^A_{DT}. f and $h_F(f)$ must have the same arity.

The element mapping describes how data terms, and in particular constructors, of the two B-specifications are related. The separation into constructors and functions allows b-morphisms between types that are constructed differently. The constructors of $\bar{B}$ and $\bar{B}'$ can have different arities, and need not correspond exactly. The definition of b-morphism was inspired by the binding morphisms in [6]. Most of the theory developed here remains valid if h_F maps in the opposite direction, or even if it is a many-to-many relationship.

Example 3.2
The following is an example of a b-morphism from lists of integers to binary trees of integers. The parameter is required to have 0 and +, so *int* is suitable.

LIST =
import : data
sorts : list
cons : nil : $\rightarrow$ list, insert : data, list $\rightarrow$ list
func : total : list $\rightarrow$ data
eqns : $x \in$ data, L $\in$ list, total(nil) = 0, total(insert(x,L)) = x + total(L)

total calculates the sum of the elements in a list.

BINTREE =
import : data
sorts : bintree
cons : empty : $\rightarrow$ bintree, leaf : data $\rightarrow$ bintree,
node : bintree, bintree $\rightarrow$ bintree
func : sum : bintree $\rightarrow$ data
eqns: $x, y \in$ bintree, $d \in$ data
sum(empty) = 0, sum(leaf(d)) = d,
sum(node(x, y)) = sum(x) + sum(y)

sum calculates the sum of the elements in the leaves of the tree.
We define a b-morphism from LIST(int) to BINTREE(int) :

1. h_F(sum) = total

2. For $i \in int$, L $\in$ list, $h_{DT}^{int}(i) = i$, h_{DT}^{int}(nil) = empty, h_{DT}^{int}(insert(i,L)) = node(leaf(i),h_{DT}^{int}(L))
h_{DT}^{int} maps each list to a "right-handed" tree - the left child of each node in such a tree is a leaf.

3. For $i \in int$ we have $h_{DT}^{int}(i) = i$. Therefore to prove the b-morphism criterion it suffices to show that for all list data terms m, sum($h_{DT}^{int}(m)$) = total(m). This is done by an easy inductive argument.

□

3.2 B-morphisms

Let $\mathcal{A}$ denote the class of all actual parameters (SPEC-algebras), and let H_{DT} denote a class $\{h_{DT}^{A} : \bar{B}(A) \rightarrow \bar{B}'(A) | A \in \mathcal{A}\}$. In the sequel, if we say H_{DT} has a certain property, it means all of its members have this property.

Definition 3.3 *A* **B-morphism** *$H = (h_F, H_{DT}) : \bar{B} \rightarrow \bar{B}'$ is a family of b-morphisms from $\bar{B}$ to $\bar{B}'$ one for each member of H_{DT} such that H_{DT} forms a natural transformation. (Note: h_F is shared by all the b-morphisms.)*

The semantics of parameterized specifications can be described as free functors, and natural transformations are morphisms between functors. Parameter specifications SPEC define the operations that must be present in all actual parameters. A SPEC-homomorphism between any two actual parameters preserves these operations. Natural transformations can be explained as follows: For SPEC-algebras A and A' and a SPEC-homomorphism $\pi : A \rightarrow A'$, we extend π to $\pi_{\bar{B}} : \bar{B}(A) \rightarrow \bar{B}(A')$

1. For $a \in A$, $\pi_{\bar{B}}(a) = \pi(a)$
2. For c, a constant symbol of $\bar{B}$, $\pi_{\bar{B}}(c) = c$
3. For k, an n-ary constructor or function of $\bar{B}$, $\pi_{\bar{B}}(k(x_1, \ldots, x_n)) = k(\pi_{\bar{B}}(x_1), \ldots, \pi_{\bar{B}}(x_n))$

$\pi_{\bar{B}}$ replaces occurrences of elements $a \in A$ in terms of $\bar{B}(A)$ by $\pi(a)$.

Lemma 3.4 *$\pi_{\bar{B}}$ is well defined, i.e., for each t in $\bar{B}(A)$, there is a unique value for $\pi_{\bar{B}}(t)$*

Proof: It is obvious that $\pi_{\bar{B}}$ is defined for each term constructed of constants of A, using the constructors of $\bar{B}$. Any two terms t_1, t_2 in $\bar{B}(A)$ which are equivalent can be shown to be so using the equations of $\bar{B}$ and those of SPEC. Since π is a SPEC-homomorphism, all equations which are true of $a_1, a_2 \in A$ are also true of $\pi(a_1), \pi(a_2) \in A'$. Therefore, $\pi_{\bar{B}}(t_1)$ and $\pi_{\bar{B}}(t_2)$ can be shown equivalent using the same equations. Thus, $\pi_{\bar{B}}$ defines a unique value for each equivalence class of terms of $\bar{B}(A)$.

Definition 3.5 *$H_{DT} : \bar{B} \rightarrow \bar{B}'$ is a* **natural transformation** *if for all $A, A' \in \mathcal{A}$, and for all SPEC-homomorphisms $\pi : A \rightarrow A'$,*

$$\pi_{\bar{B}'} \circ h^{A}_{DT} = h^{A'}_{DT} \circ \pi_{\bar{B}}$$

This is the same as saying that the following diagram is commutative. Intuitively, we want B-morphisms to be natural transformations because this guarantees they act in a uniform way over all suitable actual parameters, giving similar results for similar inputs.

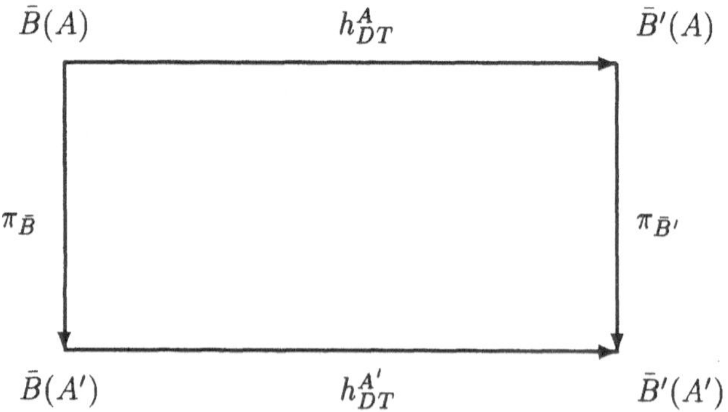

It may seem that defining a b-morphism for each A and then proving the above properties is a difficult task. However, the practical approach is to provide a uniform definition, from which a definition for each A is automatically derived. This can be done by using equations, as in example 3.2 , to define the element mapping in H_{DT}. Even in this case, it is still necessary to prove that the equations **define a function family**, that is, for each $A \in \mathcal{A}$ there *exists* a *unique* function h^A_{DT} which satisfies them. The responsibility of providing such a proof lies with the user who supplies the equations. A common approach is to use a recursive definition. The user must ensure that the recursion is **well-behaved** in the sense that computing the value for the function on a term involves only computing it on subterms, and that there exist 'exit' equations. This approach to defining functions and techniques for proving that a definition is well-behaved are well known, and are not discussed here. For this special, but practically important case, we have:

Theorem 3.6 *If H_{DT} defines a function family and is defined by well-behaved recursion, then it forms a natural transformation.*

Proof : To prove the theorem, we need to verify the commutativity of the diagram above. That is, for each A, A', each $\pi : A \longrightarrow A'$, and each t in $\bar{B}(A)$, we want to show, abstracting out some notation, that $\pi(h_{DT}(t)) = h_{DT}(\pi(t))$. In other words, we want to show that π commutes with h_{DT}, or that π can be 'pushed through' h_{DT}. For simplicity, relying on Lemma 3.4, we write π rather than $\pi_{\bar{B}}$ or $\pi_{\bar{B}'}$.

To prove the above we need, in particular, to reason about $h^A_{DT}(t)$ and $h^{A'}_{DT}(t)$. Each t in $\bar{B}(A)$ can be expressed (possibly in more than one way) as a term built from elements of A, using the constructors of $\bar{B}$, such that the term matches the left side of at least one of the equations defining H_{DT}. For otherwise, $h^A_{DT}(t)$ is not defined, and the equations do not define a function family. To prove the theorem, it suffices to prove the claim for terms (rather than values of $\bar{B}(A)$) that match the left side of some equation. Before doing that, let us consider the form and meaning of equations.

Assume that the equations defining H_{DT} are defined using a function symbol h, and let $h(\mathcal{L}) = \mathcal{R}$, be an equation. First, we note that both $\mathcal{L}$ and $\mathcal{R}$ use variables ranging over both *data* and *data*-terms. For example, the equation above that defines the mapping from LIST to BINTREE for terms of the form $insert(d, L)$ uses a *data*-variable d, and a *data*-list variable L. The meaning of an equation is determined by the implicit universal quantification: For each substitution that maps *data* variables to A and *data*-term variables to $\bar{B}(A)$, the two sides are equal. Note that each variable that appears in $\mathcal{R}$ must appear in $\mathcal{L}$; otherwise, assuming sorts with more than one element, this extra variable can assume different values for a fixed substitution for the variables of $\mathcal{L}$, and the equation does not satisfy the conditions of the theorem. Another point to note is that $\mathcal{R}$ in general may contain not only operations (including constants) of $\bar{B}'$, but also occurrences of h applied to subterms of $\mathcal{L}$, operations of $\bar{B}$ not in the scope of h, and occurrences of operations of the parameter SPEC. For example, in a mapping from LIST to BINTREE $\mathcal{R}$ might have the form **if** $member(x, L)$ **then**$\ldots h(L_1)$ **else** $\ldots node(\ldots h(L_2))$, in which *member* is a function of LIST that occurs outside the scope of an occurrence of h. If $member(x, L)$ is replaced by $EQ(x, y)$, we have an occurrence of a function of SPEC. Anyway, the value of $\mathcal{R}$ is in $\bar{B}'(A)$, as required.

The claim we prove is that for each left side of an equation, $\mathcal{L}$, and each substitution θ, $\pi(h(\mathcal{L}\theta)) = h(\pi(\mathcal{L}\theta))$. The proof uses induction on the size of terms. That is, for a given $\mathcal{L}\theta$, we prove the claim assuming that for each subterm M (of $\mathcal{L}$), $\pi(h(M\theta)) = h(\pi(M\theta))$ holds.

Let us fix a substitution θ. The values of all expressions below are under this substitution. Now, since $h(\mathcal{L}) = \mathcal{R}$, the path to the right from $\mathcal{L}$ leads to $\mathcal{R}$, and going down yields $\pi(\mathcal{R})$. Being a $SPEC$-morphism, π commutes with operations of SPEC, and by definition it also commutes with operations of $\bar{B}$ and $\bar{B}'$, so it can be pushed inside occurrences of such operations. However, we may obtain subexpressions of the form $\pi(h(M))$. In such as case, by the assumption that we have a well-behaved recursion, M is a subterm of $\mathcal{L}$. By induction hypothesis, the commutativity of the diagram holds for $M\theta$, so this can be replaced by $h(\pi(M))$. Thus, we can push π inside all the way until it applies to leaves of the expression $\mathcal{R}$. Note that if $\mathcal{L}$ is a constant of $\bar{B}$, then it has no subterm M, so there is no need to use the induction hypothesis. In this special case, the equation is one of the exit equations, and the proof goes through without using any induction hypothesis.

Walking down from $\mathcal{L}$, we obtain $\pi(\mathcal{L})$. Here also π can be pushed inside, to the level of the leaves. Now, this can be viewed as an instance of $\mathcal{L}$, obtained by replacing each variable v by another 'variable' $\pi(v)$, of the same sort (*data* or *data*-term). Using the same equation, we obtain the instance of $\mathcal{R}$ in which each variable v has been replaced by $\pi(v)$. This is precisely what we obtained by going the right-then-down path, so obviously the two paths lead to the same values under θ and the proof is complete.

Remark: In the proof above, we evaluate $\mathcal{R}$, which contains operations of $SPEC$, $\bar{B}, \bar{B}'$. Formally, the evaluation takes place in the algebra $(\bar{B} \oplus \bar{B}')(A)$ that contains both $\bar{B}(A)$ and $\bar{B}'(A)$ as subalgebras, in which the sorts and operations of A and all imported specifications appear once, and the sorts and operations of $\bar{B}$ and $\bar{B}'$ are disjoint. Also, h is interpreted as the function h^A_{DT}. Finally, by Lemma 3.4, π defines a morphism from $(\bar{B}\oplus\bar{B}')(A)$ to $(\bar{B}\oplus\bar{B}')(A')$, so terms with occurrences of π can be evaluated, for a substitution θ, in this algebra.

Example 3.7
We continue example 3.2 by showing that the morphism defined there is in fact a B-morphism. Indeed, the recursion is well-behaved. It is easy to see that every list term matches precisely one of the left sides of the first or second equations that define h^{int}_{DT}, and uniqueness follows. Existence follows since LIST has no equations. □

3.3 Bulk-morphisms

Bulk-morphisms are contents preserving B-morphisms between bulk data types. Let $\bar{B}$ and $\bar{B}'$ be BDTs. In the following we assume H_{DT} is defined by a set of eqyaions, hence we can use the notation $H_{DT}(t)$, for a term t.

Definition 3.8 *A bulk-morphism is a B-morphism $H : \bar{B} \to \bar{B}'$ such that for all $t \in DT_{\bar{B}}$, $\mathbf{C}(H_{DT}(t)) = \mathbf{C}(t)$.*

It is easy to show that the image of a bulk-morphism is large. Since $\bar{B}'$ is a BDT, the image is also conservative. So we have

$$H_{DT}(t) \equiv H_{DT}(t') \Rightarrow \mathbf{C}(t) = \mathbf{C}(t') \qquad (1)$$

Thus any two equivalence classes of $\bar{B}$ which are merged by H_{DT} must have the same contents.

Example 3.9
We continue example 3.7 . Recall that H_{DT} maps lists to right-handed trees, and we show that it is a bulk-morphism.

basis : $\mathbf{C}(H_{DT}(\mathsf{nil})) = \mathbf{C}(\mathsf{empty}) = \emptyset = \mathbf{C}(\mathsf{nil})$

induction : Assume for a list m, we prove for $\mathsf{insert}(d, m)$, where $d \in$ **data**.
$\mathbf{C}(H_{DT}(\mathsf{insert}(d,m))) = \mathbf{C}(\mathsf{node}(\mathsf{leaf}(d), H_{DT}(m))) = \{d\} \cup \mathbf{C}(H_{DT}(m))$
$= \{d\} \cup \mathbf{C}(m) = \mathbf{C}(\mathsf{insert}(d,m))$

□

4 Category Theoretical Structure

In this section we show that by taking bulk data types with the same parameter specification $SPEC$ as *objects*, and bulk-morphisms between them as *morphisms*, we obtain a category, denoted $\mathcal{B}_{SPEC}$. Set[3], the bulk data type representing sets, is the terminal object in this category.

4.1 Bulk Data Types Form a Category

See [4] for background on category theory.

Definition 4.1 *b-morphisms are composable if they are over the same parameter and the source of one is the target of the other. The* **composition** *of b-morphisms $(h_F, h^A_{DT}) \circ (h'_F, h'^A_{DT})$ is defined as $(h'_F \circ h_F, h^A_{DT} \circ h'^A_{DT})$. The composition of bulk-morphisms $(h_F, H_{DT}) \circ (h'_F, H'_{DT})$ is defined as the family of compositions of their b-morphisms. The* **identity** *bulk-morphism $id_{\bar{B}} = (id_F, Id_{DT})$ where id_F and $Id_{DT} = \{id^A_{DT} | A \in \mathcal{A}\}$ denote identity mappings on function symbols and data terms of $\bar{B}$ respectively.*

It is easy to see that for any $\bar{B}$, $Id_{\bar{B}}$ is a bulk-morphism. In the sequel, $J = (j_F, J_{DT})$ and $K = (k_F, K_{DT})$ are bulk-morphisms such that K is composable with J. J^A denotes the b-morphism (j_F, j^A_{DT}), and similarly for K^A.

Lemma 4.2 *The composition of bulk-morphisms is a bulk-morphism.*

Proof : We show that $K \circ J$ is a bulk-morphism.

b-morphism : Since J^A and K^A satisfy the b-morphism criterion, we have for n-ary functions f, f'

1. $f(k^A_{DT}(t_1), \ldots, k^A_{DT}(t_n)) \equiv k^A_{DT}(k_F(f)(t_1, \ldots, t_n))$
2. $f'(j^A_{DT}(t_1), \ldots, j^A_{DT}(t_n)) \equiv j^A_{DT}(j_F(f')(t_1, \ldots, t_n))$

[3]In category theory Set is often used with a different meaning.

Therefore,

$$f(k^A_{DT} \circ j^A_{DT}(t_1), \ldots, k^A_{DT} \circ j^A_{DT}(t_n)) \equiv_1$$
$$k^A_{DT}(k_F(f)(j^A_{DT}(t_1), \ldots, j^A_{DT}(t_n))) \equiv_2$$
$$k^A_{DT} \circ j^A_{DT}(j_F \circ k_F(f)(t_1, \ldots, t_n))$$

So $K^A \circ J^A$ satisfies the b-morphism criterion.

B-morphism : The composition of natural transformations is a natural transformation [4].

bulk-morphism : Contents preservation is immediate.

Lemma 4.3 *The composition of bulk-morphisms is associative.*

Bulk-morphisms are essentially tuples of functions, and the composition of functions is associative.

Lemma 4.4 *For every bulk-morphism $H : \bar{B} \rightarrow \bar{B}'$ the following holds*

$$H \circ Id_{\bar{B}} = H = Id_{\bar{B}'} \circ H$$

Theorem 4.5 *Bulk data type specifications and bulk-morphisms form a category.*

Proof : This follows directly from lemmas 4.2, 4.3 and 4.4.

We denote the category of all bulk data types with parameter specification SPEC and the bulk-morphisms between them by $\mathcal{B}_{SPEC}$.

4.2 Set is Terminal

In this section we show that for each parameter SPEC, sets are terminal in $\mathcal{B}_{SPEC}$.

Definition 4.6 *A bulk data type $\bar{B}$ is* **terminal** *in $\mathcal{B}_{SPEC}$ if there exists a unique bulk-morphism from every BDT in $\mathcal{B}_{SPEC}$ to $\bar{B}$.*

Terminal objects are unique (upto isomorphism).

Recall equation 1 for bulk-morphisms. Consider a bulk-morphism such that the following holds

$$\mathbf{C}(t) = \mathbf{C}(t') \Rightarrow H_{DT}(t) \equiv H_{DT}(t')$$

All equivalence classes with the same answer for **C** would be coalesced under such a mapping (this is the most we can do while ensuring the mapping is contents preserving). Such a mapping would be unique if there was exactly one equivalence class in the target with given contents. **Set** with no functions satisfies this requirement. This is not surprising as the contents operator has been defined to return sets.

Example 4.7
Set can be obtained in many ways; in particular, it can be obtained from BINTREE (example 3.2) by adding the equations:

$$\begin{aligned}
&\mathsf{node}(x,\mathsf{empty}) = x && (1)\\
&\mathsf{node}(\mathsf{empty},x) = x && (2)\\
&\mathsf{node}(\mathsf{node}(x,y),z) = \mathsf{node}(x,\mathsf{node}(y,z)) && (3)\\
&\mathsf{node}(x,y) = \mathsf{node}(y,x) && (4)\\
&\mathsf{node}(x,x) = x && (5)
\end{aligned}$$

This specification for sets is well known. empty is the empty set, leaf is the singleton set constructor, and node is set union. The equations allow us to convert a tree to a "right-handed" tree (3), to eliminate null left children (2), so we have a list, then to bring identical elements to adjacent positions (3) and (4), then eliminate duplicates (3) and (5). Set_{SPEC} is Set with parameter SPEC.

□

For any bulk data type $\bar{B}$ we can define a bulk-morphism toSet : $\bar{B} \rightarrow$ Set as follows:

1. for all constructors $k :\rightarrow T$, add the equation
   $\mathsf{toSet}(k) = \mathsf{empty}$

2. for all constructors $k : T_1, \ldots, T_n \rightarrow T$ add the equation
   $t_1 \in T_1, \ldots, t_n \in T_n$,
   $\mathsf{toSet}(k(t_1, \ldots, t_n)) = \mathsf{node}(\mathsf{S}(t_1), \ldots \mathsf{node}(\mathsf{S}(t_n), \mathsf{empty}) \ldots)$
   where
   $$\mathsf{S}(t_i) = \begin{cases} \mathsf{leaf}(t_i) & \text{if } t_i \in \textbf{data} \\ \mathsf{toSet}(t_i) & \text{otherwise} \end{cases}$$

Lemma 4.8 *For any bulk data type $\bar{B}$,* toSet : $\bar{B} \rightarrow$ Set *is a bulk-morphism.*

Theorem 4.9 *For all parameter specifications SPEC,* Set_{SPEC} *is terminal in* $\mathcal{B}_{SPEC}$.

Proof : It remains to show the uniqueness of toSet. Since a bulk-morphism must be contents preserving, data terms of $\bar{B}$ must be mapped to the set having the same contents. There is only one such set in Set. ◇

5 Applications

5.1 Using Equations to Generate Bulk-Morphisms

As in example 4.7, one way to create a new bulk type is to add equations to an existing one. Such equations should not violate conservativity or the protection of imported sorts, and equations satisfying these constraints are said to be *conservative* and *consistent* respectively. Conservative and consistent equations can be said to generate a bulk-morphism between the old and new bulk data types. The data mapping can be defined as the identity function since both types have the same constructors, and similarly for the function mapping. It is straight forward to show that this forms a bulk-morphism.

Example 5.1
Recall the *member* function of examples 2.1 (ADJLIST) and 2.3 (NOLIST).

Since *member* returns a boolean value, it has the potential of violating the protection of *bool*. This happens, for example, in NOLIST, because *member* returns different results for lists which are equivalent. In this case we say that the NOLIST equation insert(x,L) = L is not consistent with *member*. (Moreover, it is not conservative). We can be sure that protection of *bool* is *not* violated in ADJLIST, by showing that for all $d, x \in$ **data**, $L \in$ adjlist

$$member(d, \mathsf{insert}(x, \mathsf{insert}(x, L))) = member(d, \mathsf{insert}(x, L))$$

This suffices, because it deals with the only equation identifying adjlist data terms [4]. *member* is therefore guaranteed to return the same result for equivalent adjlists, and we say that *member* is *well defined* over ADJLIST. Since this ADJLIST equation is also conservative, it can be viewed as generating a bulk-morphism from lists (with *member*) to ADJLIST. □

5.2 Pump

Many database programming languages provide an aggregate generating operation, to be used with sets, such as the *pump* of FAD [2] and the *hom* of Machiavelli [13]. We now discuss such an operation, that we also call *pump*, that can be used over many bulk data types, and is closely related to *structural recursion* [7, 8]. We start with a definition for *pump* over binary trees (example 3.2).

$$\begin{aligned} pump(e,l,n)(\mathsf{empty}) &= e \\ pump(e,l,n)(\mathsf{leaf}(x)) &= l(x) \\ pump(e,l,n)(\mathsf{node}(x,y)) &= n(pump(e,l,n)(x), pump(e,l,n)(y)) \end{aligned}$$

n denotes a binary function, l is a unary function which is applied to data at the leaves of the tree before aggregation is performed, and e is a constant denoting the value of *pump* over empty data collections. For example, sum = $pump(0, id, +)$. If e has type β, l has type $\alpha \to \beta$, and n has type $\beta \times \beta \to \beta$, then $pump(e, l, n)$ has type $BINTREE(\alpha) \to \beta$.

In order to ensure that *pump* is well-defined over sets, for instance, we need to show that the five equations presented in example 4.7 are consistent with it. For the first equation we need

$$pump(e, l, n)(\mathsf{node}(x, \mathsf{empty})) \equiv pump(e, l, n)(x)$$

which is equivalent to

$$n(pump(e, l, n)(x), e) = pump(e, l, n)(x)$$

Setting $y = pump(e, l, n)(x)$, we must have $n(y, e) = y$, which holds ift e is a right unit of n (right null elimination). Similarly for the other equations, we need $y = n(y, e)$ (left null elimination), $n(n(x, y), z) = n(x, n(y, z))$ (associativity), $n(x, y) = n(y, x)$ (commutativity), and $n(x, x) = x$ (idempotence, duplicate elimination).

We can show, using induction on the structure of BINTREE, that we can apply *pump* to a binary tree data term by replacing all occurrences of empty

[4] *member* must also return the same result for *identical* adjlists.

by e, leaf by l, and node by n, then evaluating the tree. Thus, for any equation L = R over data terms of BINTREE, if we carry out such a replacement we get an equation in terms of e, l and n. This equation has to be satisfied if $pump(e, l, n)$ over the resulting BDT is to be well-defined.

Equations leading to laws such as null elimination, associativity, commutativity, and idempotence are commonly used to produce bulk types such as lists, bags and sets. Putting things in a more general framework shows that new properties and different combinations of the above properties can generate more unusual bulk types.

Example 5.2
Adding the equation $\mathsf{node}(x, y) = \mathsf{node}(y, x)$ to binary trees gives unordered binary trees. Over such trees we can pump a binary function which is commutative but not associative, such as the 'binary average' function $\mathsf{av}(x, y) = \frac{x+y}{2}$. □

5.3 Unary Pump

Lists, bags and sets can be defined using constructors empty, single and union, or using insert and nil [8]. We have seen a representation of sets obtained from binary trees by adding equations; it is known that the a representation using $\emptyset$ and *insert* can be similarly obtained from lists. The *pump* defined above for binary trees can be 'inherited' by types obtained by adding equations, provided the binary function satisfies the associated conditions. The same applies to types obtained from lists, which can be viewed as unary trees. Let us call the 'unary' pump *ipump*. Lists are defined as in example 3.2 , and the equations for *ipump* are:

$$ipump(e, n)(\mathsf{nil}) = e$$
$$ipump(e, n)(\mathsf{insert}(x,\mathrm{L})) = n(x, ipump(e, n)(\mathrm{L}))$$

If e has type β and n has type $\alpha \times \beta \rightarrow \beta$, then $ipump(e, n)$ has type $LIST(\alpha) \rightarrow \beta$.

If we add to BINTREE only equation (3) of example 4.7, we obtain lists. Thus, when *pump* is specialized to lists, the binary function needs to be associative. In contrast, *ipump* does not require its binary function to be associative over lists since it predefines the order of evaluation to be right associative. We could obtain the result of *ipump* on a list by converting it to a right-handed binary tree and then applying *pump*. This suggests that we could obtain other, equally suitable definitions for *ipump*. For example, we could define lists, as was done in [18], to insert elements at the right end giving an insert constructor with signature insert : list, data → list. In this case, *ipump* would predefine the order of evaluation to be left associative.

If n is associative, then using *pump* over lists gives more room for optimization than does *ipump*. If n is not associative, then *pump* over trees could generate many aggregate functions (corresponding to the the tree structures for the list), whereas *ipump* generates only one such function for a given list type. *pump* is therefore more flexible. For these reasons, *pump* seems superior to *ipump*, when it can be used.

Bags can be defined by adding the equation

$$\mathsf{insert}(x, \mathsf{insert}(y, B)) = \mathsf{insert}(y, \mathsf{insert}(x, B))$$

to lists. For *ipump* to be well defined over bags we must have $n(x, n(y, e)) = n(y, n(x, e))$. If e is a right unit of n, that is $n(x, e) = x$ [5] we need to have $n(x, y) = n(y, x)$, which means n must be commutative. It must also be associative, since we must have

$$n(x, n(y, n(z, e))) = n(z, n(x, n(y, e))) \Rightarrow n(x, n(y, z)) = n(z, n(x, y))$$

$$\Rightarrow n(x, n(y, z)) = n(n(x, y), z) \quad \text{(by commutativity)}$$

More 'exotic' types can be similarly defined.

Example 5.3
For $n \geq 2$ we define n-bags to be bags with at most $n - 1$ copies of each element. Note that 2-bags are therefore sets, and in 3-bags each element can appear 0,1 or 2 times. We obtain 3-bags by adding the following equations to LIST (example 3.2).

> $x, y \in$ data, B $\in$ list
> insert(x,insert(y,B)) = insert(y,insert(x,B))
> insert(x,insert(x,insert(x,B))) = insert(x,B)

By a theorem of Fermat we have $x^p \equiv x \pmod{p}$, for all integers x and all prime numbers p. Multiplication modulo p is also associative and commutative, and it has 1 as a right (and left) unit. Therefore for p prime, we can pump multiplication modulo p in p-bags, and 1 is a suitable base element ($e = 1$, $i = * \bmod 3$). Denote *ipump*(1,$*$ mod 3) as *product*$_3$. Then in 3-bags we have

$$2 \equiv product_3(\{2, 5, 7, 2, 5, 5\}) \equiv product_3(\{2, 2, 5, 7\}) \equiv 2$$

If multiplication modulo 3 is expensive relative to the cost of *triplicate elimination*, then the right hand side is cheaper to compute. □

5.4 Pump for all BDTs

We generalize *pump* for use over every bulk data type. Let $\mathcal{V}$ be a function which associates the type variable α with the sort *data*, and the type variable β with the sort of $\bar{B}(data)$. For a bulk type $\bar{B}$ with n constructors $K_1, \ldots, K_n$ we define $pump(k_1, \ldots, k_n) : \bar{B}(\alpha) \rightarrow \beta$ as follows

1. For constant constructors $K_i : \rightarrow T$, $pump(k_1, \ldots, k_n)(K_i) = k_i$
   k_i has type $\mathcal{V}(T)$.

2. For m-ary constructors $K_i : T_1, \ldots, T_m \rightarrow T$,
   and for $t_1 \in T_1, \ldots, t_m \in T_m$
   $$pump(k_1, \ldots, k_n)(K_i(t_1, \ldots, t_m)) = k_i(\mathsf{P}(k_1, \ldots, k_n)(t_1), \ldots, \mathsf{P}(k_1, \ldots, k_n)(t_m))$$
   where
   $$\mathsf{P}(k_1, \ldots, k_n)(t_j) = \begin{cases} t_j & \text{if } t_j \in \textbf{data} \\ pump(k_1, \ldots, k_n)(t_j) & \text{otherwise} \end{cases}$$
   k_i has type $\mathcal{V}(T_1) \times \ldots \times \mathcal{V}(T_m) \rightarrow \mathcal{V}(T)$

[5] A reasonable requirement, meaning that the presence of nil has no effect on the outcome of *pump*.

This generalizes *pump* and *ipump*. For *pump*, K_1 = empty, K_2 = leaf, K_3 = node, $k_1 = e$, $k_2 = l$, $k_3 = n$, $\mathcal{V}(\mathbf{data}) = \alpha$, and $\mathcal{V}(\text{bintree}) = \beta$. For *ipump*, K_1 = nil, K_2 = insert, $k_1 = e$, $k_2 = n$, $\mathcal{V}(\mathbf{data}) = \alpha$, and $\mathcal{V}(\text{list}) = \beta$.

In summary, we have shown that the concept of *pump* is applicable, in principle, to all bulk types. We have also shown that relationships between types, such as those obtained by adding equations, imply similar constraints on the functions that can be used in *pump* operations.

6 Conclusions

In this paper we have presented a theoretical framework describing bulk data types and the relationships between them, and have shown that BDTs form a category with sets as the terminal object. We have also applied structural recursion to all BDTs, and have explored the connection between equationally constrained BDTs, and the constraints that structural recursion must satisfy. Bulk types have been subject to much attention recently, and we hope that this research will help provide a formal basis for this subject. Until now, database systems support only small fixed sets of BDTs efficiently. A better understanding of the properties BDTs have in common could form the basis of DBPLs supporting both a wider range of built-in BDTs, and user defined BDTs.

Acknowledgements

Thanks to Guido Moerkotte, Giuseppe Castagna, and Sophie Cluet for their helpful comments.

References

[1] M. Atkinson, P. Richard, P. Trinder. Bulk Types for Large Scale Programming, *Proceedings of the Kiev East/West Workshop on Next Generation Database Technology*, LNCS Volume 504, April 1991.

[2] F. Bancilhon, T. Briggs, S. Khoshafian, P. Valduriez. FAD, A Powerful and Simple Database Language, *Proceedings of the Thirteenth International Conference on Very Large Data Bases*, Brighton, 1987.

[3] F. Bancilhon, S. Cluet, C. Delobel A Query Language for the O_2 Object-Oriented Database System, *Proceedings of the Second International Workshop on Database Programming Languages*, Oregon, June 1989.

[4] M. Barr, C. Wells. *Category Theory for Computing Science.* Prentice Hall International Series in Computer Science, UK, 1990.

[5] C. Beeri, Y. Kornatzky. Algebraic Optimization of Object-Oriented Query Languages, *Proceedings of the Third International Conference on Database Theory*, LNCS 470, France, 1990.

[6] C. Beeri, T. Milo. Subtyping in OODB's. *Tenth Symposium on Principles of Database Systems*, Denver, Colorado, May 1991.

[7] V. Breazu-Tannen, P. Buneman, S. Naqvi. Structural Recursion as a Query Language, *Proceedings of the Third International Workshop on Database Programming Languages*, 1991.

[8] V. Breazu-Tannen, R. Subrahmanyam. Logical and Computational Aspects of Programming with Sets/Bags/Lists, *International Colloquium on Automata, Languages and Programming*, LNCS 510, 1991.

[9] H. Ehrig, B. Mahr. *Fundamentals of Algebraic Specifications I, Equations and Initial Semantics*, EATCS Monographs on Theoretical Computer Science 6, Springer-Verlag, Berlin, 1985.

[10] J. Goguen, J. Thatcher, E. Wagner. An Initial Algebra Approach to The Specification, Correctness and Implementation of Abstract Data Types. *Current Trends in Programming Methodology* volume 4. Raymond T. Yeh (ed) 1978, pp 80-150.

[11] R. Hull, J. Su. On Bulk Data Type Constructors and Manipulation Primitives : A Framework for Analyzing Expressive Power and Complexity *Proceedings of the Second Workshop on Database Programming Languages*, 1989.

[12] F. Matthes, J. Schmidt. Bulk Types : Built-In or Add-On ? *Proceedings of the Third International Workshop on Database Programming Languages*, 1991.

[13] A. Ohori, P. Buneman, V. Breazu-Tannen. Database Programming in Machiavelli - a Polymorphic Language with Static Type Inference, *Proceedings of the ACM SIGMOD International Conference on Management of Data*, Portland, Oregon, June 1989.

[14] P. Ross (now P. Ta-Shma). Bulk Data Types - A Theoretical Approach, Masters Thesis, The Hebrew University of Jerusalem, September 1992.

[15] P. Trinder. Comprehensions, a Query Notation for DBPLs, *Proceedings of the Third International Workshop on Database Programming Languages*, 1991.

[16] P. Wadler. Comprehending Monads. *ACM Conference on Lisp and Functional Programming*, Nice, June 1990.

[17] P. Wadler. List Comprehensions, in S. Peyton Jones, *The Implementation of Functional Programming Languages*, Prentice Hall, 1987.

[18] P. Wadler. Views : A way for pattern matching to cohabit with data abstraction. *Proceedings of Principles of Programming Languages 1987*.

[19] D. Watt, P. Trinder. Towards a Theory of Bulk Types. FIDE Technical Report FIDE/91/26.

[20] M. Wirsig. Algebraic Specification in: J. Van Leeuwen, ed., *Handbook of Theoretical Computer Science, Vol. B*, Elsevier, Amsterdam 1990 pp 675 - 788.

Some Properties of Query Languages for Bags

Leonid Libkin* Limsoon Wong†

Department of Computer and Information Science
University of Pennsylvania, Philadelphia, PA 19104-6389, USA
email: {|libkin, limsoon|}@saul.cis.upenn.edu

Abstract

In this paper we study the expressive power of query languages for nested bags. We define the ambient bag language by generalizing the constructs of the relational language of Breazu-Tannen, Buneman and Wong, which is known to have precisely the power of the nested relational algebra. Relative strength of additional polynomial constructs is studied, and the ambient language endowed with the strongest combination of those constructs is chosen as a candidate for the basic bag language, which is called $\mathcal{BQL}$ (Bag Query Language). We prove that achieveing the power of $\mathcal{BQL}$ in the relational language amounts to adding simple arithmetic to the latter. We show that $\mathcal{BQL}$ has shortcomings of the relational algebra: it can not express recursive queries. In particular, parity test is not definable in $\mathcal{BQL}$. We consider augmenting $\mathcal{BQL}$ with powerbag and structural recursion to overcome this deficiency. In contrast to the relational case, where powerset and structural recursion are equivalent, the latter is stronger than the former for bags. We discuss problems with using structural recursion and suggest a new bounded loop construct which works uniformly for bags, sets and lists. It has the power of structural recursion and does not require any preconditions to be verified. We find relational languages equivalent to $\mathcal{BQL}$ with powerbag and structural recursion/bounded loop. Finally, we discuss orderings on bags for rigorous treatment of partial information.

1 Summary

Sets and bags are closely related structures. While sets have been studied intensively by the theoretical database community, bags have not received the same amount of attention. However, real implementations frequently use bags as the underlying data model. For example, the "select distinct" construct and the "select average of column" construct of SQL can be better explained if bags instead of sets are used. In an earlier paper [5], Breazu-Tannen, Buneman, and Wong defined a language based on monads [20, 29] and structural recursion [3] for querying sets. In section 2 of this report, the same syntax is given a bag-theoretic semantics. We use this language as our ambient bag language

*Supported in part by NSF Grant IRI-90-04137 and AT&T Doctoral Fellowship.

†Supported in part by NSF Grant IRI-90-04137 and ARO Grant DAAL03-89-C-0031-PRIME.

and study its properties. Due to space limitations, we give only sketches of some of the proofs. Full proofs can be found in [18].

The ambient bag language is inadequate in expressive power as it stands; for example, it can not express duplicate elimination. In section 3, additional primitives are proposed and their relative strength with respect to the ambient language is fully investigated. The primitive *unique* which eliminates duplicates from a bag is shown to be independent of the other primitives. A similar result was obtained by Van den Bussche and Paredaens in the setting of pure object oriented databases [8]. The primitive *monus* which subtracts one bag from another is proved to be the strongest amongst the remaining primitives. This result was independently obtained by Albert [2]. However, his investigation on relative strength is not as complete as this report. As a consequence, we regard the ambient language augmented with *monus* and *unique* as our basic bag language. This language will be called $\mathcal{BQL}$ (Bag Query Language).

The relationship between bag and set queries is studied in Section 4. It is shown that the class of set functions computed by the ambient bag language endowed with equality on base types, an emptiness test, and *unique*, is precisely the class of functions computed by the nested relational language of [5]. Furthermore, if equality at all types is available, then the former strictly includes the latter. Grumbach and Milo also examined the relationship between sets and bags [9]. However they considered set functions on relations whose height of set nesting is at most 2. No such limit is imposed in this report.

The relationship between sets and bags can be examined from a different perspective. In the remainder of section 4, we investigate augmenting the set language of [5] to endow it with precisely the expressive power of our basic bag language $\mathcal{BQL}$. This is achieved by adding natural numbers, multiplication, subtraction, and a summation construct to the nested relational language. This also illustrates the natural relationship between bags and numbers.

In section 5, we use the connection to nested relational language established in section 4 to prove several fundamental properties of $\mathcal{BQL}$. In particular, the inexpressibility of properties (such as parity test) on natural numbers that are simultaneously infinite and co-infinite.

Breazu-Tannen, Buneman, and Wong proved that the power of structural recursion on sets can be obtained by adding a powerset operator to their language [5]. However, this result is contingent upon the restriction that every type has a finite domain. In section 6, the powerbag primitive of Grumbach and Milo [9] is contrasted with structural recursion on bags. In particular, the latter is shown to be strictly more expressive than the former. Although a powerbag primitive increases expressive power considerably, it is difficult to express algorithms that are efficient. While structural recursion does not have this deficiency, it requires the satisfaction of certain preconditions that cannot be automatically verified [4]. In section 6, a bounded loop construct which does not require the verification of any precondition is introduced. It is shown to be equivalent in expressive power to structural recursion over sets, bags, as well as lists. This confirms the intuition that structural recursion is just a special case of bounded loop. Furthermore, in contrast to the powerbag primitive which gives us all elementary functions [9], structural recursion gives us all primitive recursive functions. Also in section 6 we show that nonpolynomial operations on bags are more powerful than their set analogs, and find the primitive that precisely fills the gap.

Finally, in section 7, we show how to extend the approach of Buneman, Jung and Ohori [6] and Libkin [16] that uses certain partial orders to give semantics of databases with partial information to bags. We extend the idea of Libkin and Wong [18] of defining an ordering whose meaning is "being more partial". Such an ordering is fully characterized for bags, and we demonstrate an efficient algorithm to test it.

Related work. The semantic aspects of programming with collections using structural recursion were studied by Breazu-Tannen and Subrahmanyam in [4]. In particular, they showed that certain preconditions have to be satisfied for structural recursion to be well defined. Breazu-Tannen, Buneman and Naqvi brought out the connection between structural recursion and database query languages [3]. Breazu-Tannen, Buneman and Wong avoided the need of checking preconditions by placing a simple syntactic restriction on structural recursion [5]. The language so restricted has several equivalent formulations, one of them being $\mathcal{NRC}$ [5, 30]. This language is equivalent to the algebra of Abiteboul and Beeri [1] without the powerset operator.

Then Wong [30] proved that the language has the conservative extension property at all input/output heights. That is, the expressive power of the language is independent of the height of set nesting in the intermediate data. Then Libkin and Wong [19] showed that in the presence of very simple arithmetic operators conservativity can be extended uniformly to all input/output heights for languages augmented with bounded fixpoint operator, transitive closure, powerset and many other operators.

In [17] Libkin and Wong extended the use of the language $\mathcal{NRC}$ for querying or-sets. Grumbach and Milo [9] applied the algebra of Abiteboul and Beeri to bags. In particular, they investigated the relationship between set and bag languages restricted to certain input/output heights and the expressive power of bag languages with respect to the level of bag nesting. The basic bag language proposed in this report ($\mathcal{BQL}$) is precisely the language of Grumbach and Milo without the powerbag operator. Vickers [28] studied refinements of bags which are a more general concept than the ordering we introduce in this paper. In particular, our ordering can be expressed as a refinement, but there exist certain refinements of bags which lead to counterintuitive results when applied in the study of partial information.

The expressive power of Datalog under set and bag semantics was compared in [21]. In particular, an example of query was given that can not be expressed under the former but can be expressed under the latter. In [27] Saraiya shows that Datalog can be simulated with structural recursion on sets, preserving the PTIME complexity, by using as an intermediate step the loop operator described in section 6.2, and proving in the process that loop can be simulated by structural recursion (half of theorem 6.3 below). Several complexity-theoretic results for program properties and transformations can then be obtained by recourse to known results for Datalog.

2 The ambient nested bag language

The nested relational language proposed by Breazu-Tannen, Buneman, Wong [5] is denoted by $\mathcal{NRL}$ here. We now define an ambient bag query language $\mathcal{NBL}$. It is obtained by replacing the set constructs in $\mathcal{NRL}$ by the corresponding bag constructs. The language has two presentations – algebraic, called $\mathcal{NBA}$, and calculus style, called $\mathcal{NBC}$ – which are equivalent in terms of expressive power.

Types. The types in $\mathcal{NBL}$ are either complex object types or are function types $s \to t$ where s and t are complex object types. These types are the same as those of $\mathcal{NRL}$ except that bags $\{\!|s|\!\}$ instead of sets $\{s\}$ are used. The grammar for complex object types is given below.

$$s ::= b \mid unit \mid s \times s \mid \{\!|s|\!\}$$

A complex object type denotes a set of objects. *unit* is a special base type having exactly one element which we denote by (). $s \times t$ is the set of pairs whose first component is from s and whose second component is from t. $\{\!|s|\!\}$ are finite bags containing elements of type s. A bag is different from a set in that it is sensitive to the number of times an element occurs in it while a set is not. Finally, b are base types to be specified.

Expressions. The expressions of $\mathcal{NBA}$ and $\mathcal{NBC}$ are given in figure 1. The type superscripts are usually omitted as they can be inferred [13, 23]. The semantics of these constructs is similar to the semantics of $\mathcal{NRL}$ except duplicates are not eliminated. Semantics of $\mathcal{NBA}$ constructs is as follows. Kc is the constant function that produces the constant c. id is the identity function. $g \circ h$ is the composition of functions g and h; that is, $(g \circ h)(d) = g(h(d))$. The bang ! produces () on all inputs. π_1 and π_2 are the two projections on pairs. $\langle g, h\rangle$ is pair formation; that is, $\langle g, h\rangle(d) = (g(d), h(d))$. $K\{\!|\,|\!\}$ produces the empty bag. $\uplus$ is the additive bag union. b_η forms singleton bags: $b\_\eta(x) = \{\!|x|\!\}$. b_μ flattens a bag of bags: $b\_\mu\{\!|B_1, \ldots, B_n|\!\} = B_1 \uplus \ldots \uplus B_n$. $b\_map(f)$ applies f to every item in the input bag. Function b_ρ_2 is used for interaction between bags and pairs: $b\_\rho_2(x, y)$ pairs x with every item in the bag y. For example, $b\_\rho_2(1, \{\!|1, 2|\!\})$ returns $\{\!|(1, 1), (1, 2)|\!\}$.

Semantics of the $\mathcal{NBC}$ constructs which differ from $\mathcal{NBA}$ constructs is as follows. $\{\!|\,|\!\}$ is the empty bag. $\{\!|e|\!\}$ is the singleton bag containing e. $\biguplus\{\!|e_1 \mid x \in e_2|\!\}$ is the bag obtained by first applying the function $\lambda x.e_1$ to each item in the bag e_2 and then taking the bag union of the results. For example, $\biguplus\{\!|\{\!|x, x+1|\!\} \mid x \in \{\!|1, 2, 3|\!\}|\!\}$ evaluates to $\{\!|1, 2, 2, 3, 3, 4|\!\}$.

Proposition 2.1 *The languages $\mathcal{NBA}$ and $\mathcal{NBC}$ have the same expressive power.* □

Therefore, we normally work with the component that is most convenient.

3 Relative strength of bag operators

Breazu-Tannen, Buneman, and Wong [5] added equality test eq_s for all types s to $\mathcal{NRL}$. They showed that the presence of equality tests elevates $\mathcal{NRL}$ from a language that merely has structural manipulation capability to a full-fledged nested relational language. The question of what primitives to add to $\mathcal{NBL}$ to make it a useful nested bag language should now be considered.

Unlike languages for sets for which we have a well-established yardstick, very little is known about bags. Due to this lack of an adequate guideline, a large number of primitives are considered. Let us first fix some meta notations. A bag is just an *unordered* collection of items. $count(d, B)$ is defined to be

EXPRESSIONS OF $\mathcal{NBA}$

Category with Products

$$\frac{}{Kc : unit \to b} \quad \frac{}{id^s : s \to s} \quad \frac{h : r \to s \quad g : s \to t}{g \circ h : r \to t} \quad \frac{}{!^s : s \to unit}$$

$$\frac{}{\pi_1^{s,t} : s \times t \to s} \quad \frac{}{\pi_2^{s,t} : s \times t \to t} \quad \frac{g : r \to s \quad h : r \to t}{\langle g, h \rangle : r \to s \times t}$$

Bag Monad

$$\frac{}{b\_\eta^s : s \to \{\!|s|\!\}} \quad \frac{}{b\_\mu^s : \{\!|\{\!|s|\!\}|\!\} \to \{\!|s|\!\}}$$

$$\frac{f : s \to t}{b\_map(f) : \{\!|s|\!\} \to \{\!|t|\!\}} \quad \frac{}{K\{\!||\!\}^s : unit \to \{\!|s|\!\}}$$

$$\frac{}{\uplus^s : \{\!|s|\!\} \times \{\!|s|\!\} \to \{\!|s|\!\}} \quad \frac{}{b\_\rho_2^{s,t} : s \times \{\!|t|\!\} \to \{\!|s \times t|\!\}}$$

EXPRESSIONS OF $\mathcal{NBC}$

Lambda Calculus and Products

$$\frac{}{c : b} \quad \frac{}{x^s : s} \quad \frac{e : t}{\lambda x^s.e : s \to t} \quad \frac{e_1 : s \to t \quad e_2 : s}{e_1\ e_2 : t}$$

$$\frac{}{() : unit} \quad \frac{e : s \times t}{\pi_1\ e : s \quad \pi_2\ e : t} \quad \frac{e_1 : s \quad e_2 : t}{(e_1, e_2) : s \times t}$$

Bag Monad

$$\frac{}{\{\!||\!\}^s : \{\!|s|\!\}} \quad \frac{e : s}{\{\!|e|\!\} : \{\!|s|\!\}} \quad \frac{e_1 : \{\!|s|\!\} \quad e_2 : \{\!|s|\!\}}{e_1 \uplus e_2 : \{\!|s|\!\}}$$

$$\frac{e_1 : \{\!|t|\!\} \quad e_2 : \{\!|s|\!\}}{\biguplus \{\!|e_1 \mid x^s \in e_2|\!\} : \{\!|t|\!\}}$$

Figure 1: Syntax of $\mathcal{NBL}$

the number of times the object d occurs as an element in the bag B. The bag operations to be considered are listed below.

- $monus : \{\!|s|\!\} \times \{\!|s|\!\} \to \{\!|s|\!\}$. $monus(B_1, B_2)$ evaluates to a B such that for every $d : s$, $count(d, B) = count(d, B_1) - count(d, B_2)$ if $count(d, B_1) > count(d, B_2)$; and $count(d, B) = 0$ otherwise.
- $max : \{\!|s|\!\} \times \{\!|s|\!\} \to \{\!|s|\!\}$. $max(B_1, B_2)$ evaluates to a B such that for every $d : s$, $count(d, B) = \max(count(d, B_1), count(d, B_2))$.
- $min : \{\!|s|\!\} \times \{\!|s|\!\} \to \{\!|s|\!\}$. $min(B_1, B_2)$ evaluates to a B such that for every $d : s$, $count(d, B) = \min(count(d, B_1), count(d, B_2))$.
- $eq : s \times s \to \{\!|unit|\!\}$. $eq(d_1, d_2) = \{\!|()|\!\}$ if $d_1 = d_2$; it evaluates to $\{\!||\!\}$ otherwise. That is, we are simulating booleans as a bag of type $\{\!|unit|\!\}$. True is represented by the singleton bag $\{\!|()|\!\}$ and False is represented by the empty bag $\{\!||\!\}$.
- $member : s \times \{\!|s|\!\} \to \{\!|unit|\!\}$. $member(d, B) = \{\!|()|\!\}$ if $count(d, B) > 0$; it evaluates to $\{\!||\!\}$ otherwise.
- $subbag : \{\!|s|\!\} \times \{\!|s|\!\} \to \{\!|unit|\!\}$. $subbag(B_1, B_2) = \{\!|()|\!\}$ if for every $d : s$, $count(d, B_1) \leq count(d, B_2)$; it evaluates to $\{\!||\!\}$ otherwise.
- $unique : \{\!|s|\!\} \to \{\!|s|\!\}$. $unique(B)$ eliminates duplicates from B. That is, for every $d : s$, $count(d, B) > 0$ if and only if $count(d, unique(B)) = 1$.

Each of these operators has polynomial time complexity with respect to size of input. Hence every function definable in $\mathcal{NBL}$(*monus*, *max*, *min*, *eq*, *member*, *subbag*, *unique*), where we have explicitly listed the additional primitives in brackets, has polynomial time and space complexity with respect to the size of input.

The expressive power of these primitives relative to $\mathcal{NBL}$ is compared here. In contrast to $\mathcal{NRL}$, where all nonmonotonic primitives are interdefinable [5], these bag primitives differ considerably in expressive power. As a consequence of the theorem below, $\mathcal{NBL}$(*monus*, *unique*) can be considered as the most powerful candidate for a standard bag query language. We denote $\mathcal{NBL}$(*monus*, *unique*) by $\mathcal{BQL}$.

Theorem 3.1 *monus can express all primitives other than unique. unique is independent of the rest of the primitives. min is equivalent to subbag and can express both max and eq. member and eq are interdefinable and both are independent of max.* □

The results of theorem 3.1 can be visualized in the following diagram.

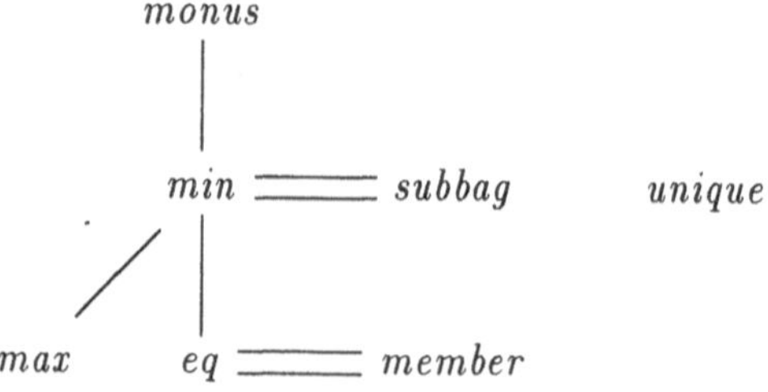

The independence of *unique* was also proved by Van den Bussche and Paredaens [8] and the fact that *monus* is the strongest amongst the remaining primitives was also showed by Albert [2]. However, their comparison was incomplete. For example, the incomparability of *max* and *eq* was not reported. In contrast, the results presented in this section can be put together in theorem 3.1 which completely and strictly summarizes the relative strength of these primitives.

4 Relationship between bags and sets

In this section, we study the relationship between bags and sets from two perspectives. First, we find a bag language whose set theoretic expressive power is that of $\mathcal{NRL}(eq)$. Then we consider endowing $\mathcal{NRL}(eq)$ with new primitives that would give it precisely the expressive power of the basic bag language $\mathcal{BQL}$.

4.1 Set-theoretic expressive power of bag languages

Several fragments of our nested bag language are compared with the nested relational language $\mathcal{NRL}(eq)$. This can be regarded as an attempt to understand the "set theoretic" expressive power of these bag languages. In order to compare bags and sets, two technical devices are required for conversions between bags and sets. We use the following constructs for this purpose:

$$\frac{f : s \rightarrow t}{bs\_map(f) : \{\!|s|\!\} \rightarrow \{t\}} \qquad \frac{f : s \rightarrow t}{sb\_map(f) : \{s\} \rightarrow \{\!|t|\!\}}$$

The semantics is as follows. $bs\_map(f)(R)$ applies f to every item in the bag R and then puts the results into a set. For example, $bs\_map(\lambda x.1+x)\{\!|1,2,3,1,4|\!\}$ returns the set $\{2,3,4,5\}$. $sb\_map(f)(R)$ applies f to every item in the set R and then puts the results into a bag. For example, $sb\_map(\lambda x.4)\{1,2,3\}$ returns the bag $\{\!|4,4,4|\!\}$.

Let s be a complex object type not involving bags. Then $to\_bag(s)$ is a complex object type obtained by converting all set brackets in s to bag brackets. Every object o of type s is converted to an object $to\_bag_s(o)$ of type $to\_bag(s)$. Conversely, let s be a complex object type not involving sets. Then $from\_bag(s)$ is a complex object type obtained by converting all bag brackets in s to set brackets. Every object o of type s is converted to an object $from\_bag_s(o)$ of type $from\_bag(s)$. The conversion operations are given inductively below.

$$\begin{aligned} &to\_bag_{unit} := \lambda x.x \\ &to\_bag_{s\times t} := \lambda x.(to\_bag_s(\pi_1\ x), to\_bag_t(\pi_2\ x)) \\ &to\_bag_{\{s\}} := sb\_map(to\_bag_s) \end{aligned}$$

$$\begin{aligned} &from\_bag_{unit} := \lambda x.x \\ &from\_bag_{s\times t} := \lambda x.(from\_bag_s(\pi_1\ x), from\_bag_t(\pi_2\ x)) \\ &from\_bag_{\{\!|s|\!\}} := bs\_map(from\_bag_s) \end{aligned}$$

Define $\mathcal{SET}(\Gamma)$ to be the class of functions $f : s \rightarrow t$ where s and t are complex object types not involving bags and Γ is a list of primitives such that there is f' :

$to\_bag(s) \rightarrow to\_bag(t)$ definable in $\mathcal{NBL}(\Gamma)$ and the diagram below commutes.

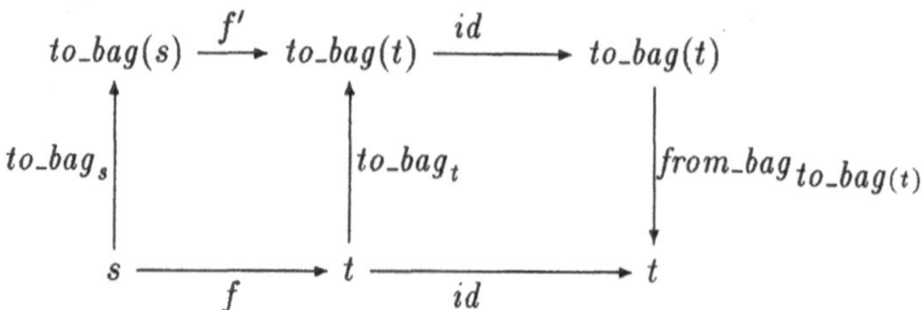

Let eq_b be equality test restricted to base types. Let $empty : \{\!|unit|\!\} \rightarrow \{\!|unit|\!\}$ be a primitive such that it returns the bag $\{\!|()|\!\}$ when applied to the empty bag and returns the empty bag otherwise. Then

Theorem 4.1 *1.* $\mathcal{SET}(unique, eq_b, empty) = \mathcal{NRL}(eq)$.

2. $\mathcal{NRL}(eq) \subsetneq \mathcal{SET}(unique, eq)$

3. $\mathcal{NRL}(eq)$ *and* $\mathcal{SET}(monus)$ *are incomparable.* □

The class $\mathcal{SET}(\Gamma)$ is precisely the class of "set theoretic" functions expressible in $\mathcal{NBL}(\Gamma)$. Thus, the above results say that $\mathcal{NBL}(unique, eq_b, empty)$ is *conservative* over $\mathcal{NRL}(eq)$ in the sense that it has precisely the same set theoretic expressive power. On the other hand, $\mathcal{NBL}(unique, eq)$ is a true extension over the set language. However, the presence of *unique* is in a technical sense essential for a bag language to be an extension of a set language.

4.2 A set language equivalent to $\mathcal{BQL}$

It was shown earlier that $\mathcal{BQL} = \mathcal{NBL}(monus, unique)$ is the most powerful amongst the bag languages considered so far. From the foregoing discussion, this bag language is a true extension of $\mathcal{NRL}(eq)$. In this subsection, the relationship between sets and bags is studied from a different perspective. In particular, the *precise* amount of extra power $\mathcal{BQL}$ possesses over $\mathcal{NRL}(eq)$ is determined.

Let us endow $\mathcal{NRL}(eq)$ with natural numbers $\mathbb{N}$ together with multiplication, subtraction, and summation as defined below.

- $\cdot : \mathbb{N} \times \mathbb{N} \rightarrow \mathbb{N}$. The semantics of $\cdot$ is multiplication of natural numbers.
- $\dot{-} : \mathbb{N} \times \mathbb{N} \rightarrow \mathbb{N}$ (sometimes called *modified subtraction*). The semantics is as follows:

$$n \dot{-} m = \begin{cases} n - m & \text{if } n - m \geq 0 \\ 0 & \text{if } n - m < 0 \end{cases}$$

- $\sum g : \{s\} \rightarrow \mathbb{N}$ where $g : s \rightarrow \mathbb{N}$. The semantics is as follows: $\sum g \; \{o_1, \ldots, o_n\} = g(o_1) + \ldots + g(o_n)$.

In the sequel, the notaion $\mathcal{L} \simeq \mathcal{L}'$ means that two languages $\mathcal{L}$ and $\mathcal{L}'$ have the same expressive power. If $\mathcal{L}$ and $\mathcal{L}'$ have different type systems, this requires translations from one type system to another. In the following result, this is achieved by treating bags as sets of pairs element–number of occurrences.

Theorem 4.2 $\mathcal{BQL} \simeq \mathcal{NRL}(\mathbb{N}, \Sigma, \cdot, \dot{-}, eq)$. □

In summary, we have the following exact characterization of the relative strength between the basic bag language and the relational language of Breazu-Tannen, Buneman, and Wong: $\mathcal{NRL}(\mathbb{N}, \sum, \cdot, \dot{-}, eq) \simeq \mathcal{BQL}$ and $\mathcal{NRL}(eq) = \mathcal{SET}(unique,\ eq_b,\ empty)$. Klug [15] and Ozsoyoglu, Ozsoyoglu, and Matos [24] had to introduce aggregate functions by repeating them for every column position of a relation. That is, $aggregate_1$ is for column one, $aggregate_2$ is for column two, etc. Klausner and Goodman used a notion of hiding to explain the nature of aggregate functions in relational query languages [14]. In addition to projections, they introduced hiding operators that "hide" columns of a relation. Aggregate functions are then applied to the column that is left exposed. Hiding is different from projection. Let $R := \{(1,2),(1,3)\}$. Then projecting out column two on R gives $\{1\}$ while hiding column two on R gives $\{(1,[2]),(1,[3])\}$, where $[\cdot]$ signifies hidden values. The use of hiding to retain duplicates (since sets have no duplicate by definition) is a little clumsy. It is better to use bags. The $\sum$ primitive can be used to implement aggregate functions and should be seen as a generalization of their approaches.

5 Relationship between bags and numbers

As seen earlier, natural numbers are present in our nested bag language as objects of type $\{\!|unit|\!\}$, which we now write as $\mathbb{N}$. In this section, the relationship between bags and numbers is investigated in more detail. The equivalence between $\mathcal{BQL}$ and $\mathcal{NRL}(\mathbb{N}, \sum, \cdot, \dot{-}, eq)$ allows us to establish the following fundamental result.

Theorem 5.1 *Let $\mathcal{U}$ be a property of natural numbers. That is, $\mathcal{U} \subseteq \mathbb{N}$. Then membership in $\mathcal{U}$ can be expressed in $\mathcal{BQL}$ iff either $\mathcal{U}$ or $\mathbb{N} - \mathcal{U}$ is finite.*

Proof sketch: Assume there is an infinite and co-infinite property $\mathcal{U}$ of natural numbers that is expressible in $\mathcal{BQL}$. Then by theorem 4.2 a function $f : \mathbb{N} \to \mathbb{N}$ such that $f(n) = 1$ for $n \in \mathcal{U}$ and $f(n) = 0$ for $n \notin \mathcal{U}$ is expressible in $\mathcal{NRL}(\mathbb{N}, \Sigma, \cdot, \dot{-}, eq)$. In [19] we proved that expressions of $\mathcal{NRL}(\mathbb{N}, \Sigma, \cdot, \dot{-}, eq)$ are independent of the height of the intermediate data. Careful analysis of functions of type $\mathbb{N} \to \mathbb{N}$ that do not involve set constructs shows that they coincide with polynomials almost everywhere and hence can not have infinitely many roots, without being zero almost everywhere. □

It is well known that the traditional relational languages cannot express parity test [7]. By the result of [30], it cannot be expressed in $\mathcal{NRL}(eq)$. It follows from the theorem we just proved that it remains inexpressible even in the greatly enhanced $\mathcal{NRL}(\mathbb{N}, \Sigma, \cdot, +, \dot{-}, eq)$ and hence not expressible in $\mathcal{BQL}$. From this many other inexpressibility results follow.

Corollary 5.2 *None of the following functions is expressible in $\mathcal{BQL}$:*

- *parity test;*
- *division by a constant;*
- *bounded summation;*
- *bounded product;*
- *gen* $: \mathbb{N} \to \{\!|\mathbb{N}|\!\}$ *given by* $gen(n) = \{\!|0, 1, \ldots, n|\!\}$. □

Therefore, the arithmetic of our basic bag query language is very limited. In fact, its arithmetic power can be characterized. A unary function $f : \mathbb{N} \rightarrow \mathbb{N}$ is said to be *almost polynomial* if there exists a polynomial function $g : \mathbb{N} \rightarrow \mathbb{N}$ (that is, a function built from its argument and constants by using addition, subtraction and multiplication) and a number n such that $f(x) = g(x)$ for any $x \geq n$ (that is, f is g in all but finitely many points). The class of almost polynomial functions is denoted by $\mathcal{P}^{\approx}$.

Proposition 5.3 *$\mathcal{P}^{\approx}$ is the class of unary arithmetic functions expressible in $\mathcal{BQL}$.* □

6 Power operators, bounded loop and structural recursion

Abiteboul and Beeri [1] suggested *powerset* as a new primitive for $\mathcal{NRL}(eq)$ to increase its expressive power. For instance, both parity test and transitive closure become expressible in $\mathcal{NRL}(eq, powerset)$. On the other hand, Breazu-Tannen, Buneman, and Naqvi [3] introduced structural recursion as an alternative means for increasing the horsepower of query languages.

It was shown in [5] that endowing $\mathcal{NRL}(eq)$ with a structural recursion primitive, which we denote by *s_sri*, or with the *powerset* operator yields languages that are equi-expressive. However, this is contingent upon the contrived restriction that the domain of each type is finite. Since every type has finite domain, this result has an important consequence. Suppose the domain of type $\{s\}$ has cardinality n. Then every use of *powerset* on an input of type $\{s\}$ can be safely replaced by a function that computes all subsets of a set having at most n elements. Such a function is easily definable in $\mathcal{NRL}(eq)$. Therefore, $\mathcal{NRL}(eq) \simeq \mathcal{NRL}(eq, s\_sri) \simeq \mathcal{NRL}(eq, powerset)$, if all types have finite domains. Hence the extra power of *s_sri* and *powerset* has effect only when there are types whose domains are infinite. Types such as natural numbers proved to be important in the earlier part of this report. Therefore, the relationship of structural recursion and power operators should be re-examined.

The syntax for the structural recursion construct on sets is

$$\frac{i : s \times t \rightarrow t \quad e : t}{s\_sri(i, e) : \{s\} \rightarrow t}$$

The semantics is $s\_sri(i, e)\{o_1, \ldots, o_n\} = i(o_1, i(o_2, i(\ldots, i(o_n, e)\ldots)))$, provided i satisfies certain preconditions [4]. In particular, it is commutative: $i(a, i(b, X)) = i(b, i(a, X))$ and idempotent: $i(a, i(a, X)) = i(a, X)$. *s_sri* is undefined otherwise. Breazu-Tannen, Buneman, and Naqvi [3] proved that efficient algorithms for computing functions such as transitive closure can be expressed using structural recursion. While structural recursion gives rise to efficient algorithms, its well-definedness precondition cannot be automatically checked by a compiler [4]. Therefore this approach is not completely satisfactory.

The *powerset* operator is always well defined. Unfortunately, algorithms expressed using *powerset* are often unintuitive and inefficient. For example, to find transitive closure of a binary relation $R : \{s \times s\}$, one finds the domain of R by taking union of first and second projections of R, takes powerset of cartesian product of the domain with itself and then selects all elements from this powerset which are transitive and contain R. Intersection of those elements is the transitive closure of R.

To the best of our knowledge, the problem of expressing a polynomial time transitive closure algorithm in $\mathcal{NRL}(eq, powerset)$ is still open. We do not advocate the elimination of every expensive operations from query languages. However, we believe that expressive power should not be achieved using expensive primitives. That is, if a function can be expressed using a polynomial time algorithm in some languages, then one should not be forced to define it using an exponential time algorithm. For this reason, *powerset* is not a good candidate for increasing expressive power.

This section has three main objectives. First, we endow $\mathcal{BQL}$ with the bag analogs of the powerset and structural recursion operators and we show that the former is strictly less expressive than the latter. Second, we suggest an efficient bounded loop primitive which captures the power of structural recursion but does not require any preconditions. Finally, we show that bag nonpolynomial operators are strictly more expressive than their set analogs, and we show that the analog of the *gen* primitive on sets fills the gap.

6.1 Powerset, powerbag and structural recursion

Grumbach and Milo [9], following Abiteboul and Beeri [1], introduced the *powerbag* operator into their nested bag language. The semantics of *powerbag* is the function that produces a bag of all subbags of the input bag. For example, $powerbag\{\!|1,1,2|\!\} = \{\!|\{\!||\!\}, \{\!|1|\!\}, \{\!|1|\!\}, \{\!|2|\!\}, \{\!|1,1|\!\}, \{\!|1,2|\!\}, \{\!|1,2|\!\}, \{\!|1,1,2|\!\}|\!\}$. They also defined the *powerset* operator on bags as *unique* ∘ *powerbag*. For example, $powerset\{\!|1,1,2|\!\}$ is $\{\!|\{\!||\!\}, \{\!|1|\!\}, \{\!|2|\!\}, \{\!|1,1|\!\}, \{\!|1,2|\!\}, \{\!|1,1,2|\!\}|\!\}$. We do not consider *powerset* on bags further because of the following result.

Proposition 6.1 $\mathcal{BQL}(powerbag) \simeq \mathcal{BQL}(powerset)$.

Proof sketch. Suppose a bag B is given; then another bag B' can be constructed such that for any $a \in B$, B' contains a pair $(a, \{\!|a,\ldots,a|\!\})$ where the cardinality of the second component is $count(a, B)$. Let $B'' = unique(B')$; then B'' can be computed by $\mathcal{BQL}$. Now observe that changing the second component of every pair to its *powerset* and then $b\_map(b\_\rho_2)$ followed by flattening will give us a bag where each element $a \in B$ will be given a unique label. Now applying *powerset* to this bag followed by elimination of labels produces $powerbag(B)$. □

Structural recursion on bags is defined using the construct

$$\frac{e : t \quad i : s \times t \to t}{b\_sri(i, e) : \{\!|s|\!\} \to t}$$

It is required that i satisfy the commutativity precondition: $i(a, i(b, X)) = i(b, i(a, X))$, which can not be automatically verified [4]. Its semantics is similar to the semantics of s_sri. We want to show that it is strictly stronger than *powerbag*.

Theorem 6.2 $\mathcal{BQL}(powerbag) \subsetneq \mathcal{BQL}(b\_sri)$.

Proof sketch. First, *powerbag* can be expressed using *b_sri*, cf. [3]. Then it can be shown that any function in $\mathcal{BQL}$(*powerbag*) produces outputs whose sizes are bounded by an elementary function on the size of the input, but in $\mathcal{BQL}$(*b_sri*) it is possible to define a function that on the input of size n produces the output of the hyperexponential size (where the height of the stack of powers depends on n) and hence can not be bounded by an elementary function. □

As an illustration of theorem 6.2, we characterize precisely the classes of arithmetic functions that both languages express. It also gives an alternative proof of theorem 6.2.

Theorem 6.3 *a) The class of functions* $f : \mathbb{N} \times \ldots \times \mathbb{N} \to \mathbb{N}$ *definable in* $\mathcal{BQL}$(*b_sri*) *coincides with the class of primitive recursive functions.*
b) The class of functions $f : \mathbb{N} \times \ldots \times \mathbb{N} \to \mathbb{N}$ *definable in* $\mathcal{BQL}$(*powerbag*) *coincides with the class of Kalmar-elementary functions.* □

Similar results for other languages for bags or sets with built-in natural numbers were proved in [9, 12].

6.2 Bounded loop and structural recursion

As mentioned earlier, *powerbag* is not a good primitive for increasing the power of the language. It is not polynomial time and compels a programmer to use clumsy solutions for problems that can be easily solved in polynomial time. In addition, *powerbag* is weaker than structural recursion. On the other hand, *b_sri* is efficient [3] but its well definedness precondition can not be verified by a compiler [4]. In this section, we present a bounded loop construct

$$\frac{f : s \to s}{loop^t(f) : \{\!|t|\!\} \times s \to s}$$

Its semantics is as follows: $loop(f)(\{\!|o_1, \ldots, o_n|\!\}, o) = f(\ldots f(o) \ldots)$ where f is applied n times to o.

The bounded loop construct is more satisfactory as a primitive than *powerbag* and *b_sri* for several reasons. First, in contrast to *powerbag*, efficient algorithms for transitive closure, division, etc. can be described using it. For example, given $R : \{\!|s \times s|\!\}$, let $f_R : \{\!|s \times s|\!\} \to \{\!|s \times s|\!\}$ be the function whose semantics is $f_R(R') = R \circ R'$. Let $dom(R)$ be the domain of R. Then $loop(f_R)(dom(R), R)$ is the transitive closure of R. Second, it is very similar to the for-next-loop construct of familiar programming languages such as Pascal and Fortran. Third, in contrast to *b_sri*, it has no preconditions to be satisfied. Lastly, it has the same power as *b_sri*.

Theorem 6.4 (see also [27]) $\mathcal{BQL}(loop) \simeq \mathcal{BQL}$(*b_sri*).

Proof sketch. For one inclusion, observe that $loop(f)(n, e) = b\_sri(f \circ \pi_2, e)(n)$. For the reverse inclusion, given an input bag B, first generate all possible permutations of B (that is, all possible rank assignments to elements of B). It can be done in $\mathcal{BQL}(loop)$. Then, using *loop*, simulate *b_sri* for each rank assignment, assuming the ranks tell us the order in which elements are processed. Having done so, apply ***unique*** to the result. Hence, any function of type $s \to \{\!|t_1|\!\} \times \ldots \times \{\!|t_k|\!\}$ that is definable in $\mathcal{BQL}$(*b_sri*) is also definable in

$\mathcal{BQL}(loop)$. If one of the types is not under the scope of the bag brackets, then in that position a singleton will be produced. □

Therefore replacing structural recursion by bounded loop eliminates the need for verifying any precondition. If the i in $b\_sri(i,e)$ is not commutative, the translation used in the proof simply produces a bag containing all possible outcomes of applying $b\_sri(i,e)$, depending on how elements of the input are enumerated. If i is commutative, then such a bag has one element which is *the* result of applying $b\_sri(i,e)$. Hence b_sri is really an optimized bounded loop obtained by exploiting the knowledge that i is commutative. Furthermore, *loop* coincides with structural recursion over sets, bags, and (with appropriately chosen primitives) lists. The implementation of $b\_sri(i,e)$ using the bounded loop construct given in the proof of theorem 6.4 has exponential complexity but the source of inefficiency is in computing all permutations in order to return all possible outcomes. If we are allowed to pick a particular order of application of i in $b\_sri(i,e)$, then more efficient implementations are possible (see the full paper [18]).

Theorem 6.4 also sheds some light on theorem 6.3 a). It is known that functions computable by a language that has an assignment statement and *for n do S* are precisely the primitive recursive functions [22]. It was also proved by Robinson and Gladstone that the primitive recursive functions are built from the initial functions by composition and iteration: $f(n,\vec{x}) = g^{(n)}(\vec{x})$, see [22]. Now we proved that the power of the structural recursion is precisely the power of the bounded loop, which is in essence the $for - do$ iteration or the iteration schema of Robinson and Gladstone. This is the intuitive reason why the class of functions definable by the structural recursion on bags coincides with the class of the primitive recursive functions.

6.3 Power operators and structural recursion on sets and bags

We have introduced power operators and structural recursion for sets and bags. In section 4.2 we also demonstrated how a set language can be extended to capture the power of our basic bag language: $\mathcal{BQL} \simeq \mathcal{NRL}(\mathbf{N}, \Sigma, \cdot, \dot{-}, eq)$. Under the translations of theorem 4.2, $n : \mathbf{N}$ is carried to a bag of n units: $\{\!|(),\ldots,()|\!\}$. Consider the following primitive in the set language (cf. corollary 5.2):

$$gen : \mathbf{N} \rightarrow \{\mathbf{N}\}, \qquad gen(n) = \{0, 1, \ldots, n\}$$

Under translations of theorem 4.2, it corresponds to the bag language primitive that takes a bag of n units and returns bag of bags containing i units for each $i = 0, 1, \ldots, n$. In other words, it is $powerset^{unit} = unique \circ powerbag^{unit}$ Observe that it remains a polynomial operation.

Having made this observation, we can formulate the first result of the section.

Theorem 6.5 *a)* $\mathcal{NRL}(\mathbf{N}, \Sigma, \cdot, \dot{-}, eq, powerset) \subsetneq \mathcal{BQL}(powerbag)$;
b) $\mathcal{NRL}(\mathbf{N}, \Sigma, \cdot, \dot{-}, eq, s\_sri) \subsetneq \mathcal{BQL}(b\_sri)$.

Proof sketch. Inclusion easily follows from theorem 4.2. To demonstrate strictness, observe that $powerset^{unit}$ is definable in both $\mathcal{BQL}(powerbag)$ and

$\mathcal{BQL}(b\_sri)$. Hence, in view of theorem 6.2, it is enough to show that *gen* is not expressible in $\mathcal{NRL}(\mathbb{N}, \Sigma, \cdot, \dot{-}, eq, s\_sri)$. Define the size of an object as follows: size of an object of a base type is 1 and size of a pair or a set is sum of the sizes of the components. Then, it is possible to show that for any function f definable in $\mathcal{NRL}(\mathbb{N}, \Sigma, \cdot, \dot{-}, eq, s\_sri)$ there exists a primitive recursive function φ_f such that, if $f(i) = o$ and sizes of i and o are s_i and s_o, then $s_o \leq \varphi_f(s_i)$. Now assume that *gen* is definable. Let $n = \varphi_{gen}(1)$. Then $n + 1 = size(gen(n + 1)) \leq \varphi_{gen}(size(n + 1)) = n$. This contradiction shows that *gen* is not definable. □

Now we have a problem of filling the gap between set and bag languages with power operators or structural recursion. It turns out that the *gen* primitive is sufficiently powerful to do the job. The following result is proved by extending translations of theorem 4.2.

Theorem 6.6 *a)* $\mathcal{NRL}(\mathbb{N}, \Sigma, \cdot, \dot{-}, eq, powerset, gen) \simeq \mathcal{BQL}(powerbag)$; *b)* $\mathcal{NRL}(\mathbb{N}, \Sigma, \cdot, \dot{-}, eq, s\_sri, gen) \simeq \mathcal{BQL}(b\_sri)$. □

As another illustration of the power of the *gen* primitive, we show that it allows us to simplify the *loop* construct without considerably losing expressiveness of the language. We simplify the *loop* construct by defining $iter(f) : \{\!|unit|\!\} \to \{\!|unit|\!\}$ where $f : \{\!|unit|\!\} \to \{\!|unit|\!\}$ as $iter(f)(n) = f(f(\ldots(f(\{\!|\,|\!\}))\ldots))$ where f is applied n times.

Corollary 6.7 $\mathcal{BQL}(iter, powerset^{unit})$ *expresses all unary primitive recursive functions.* □

7 Orderings on bags

In the previous sections we have concentrated on comparing expressive power of set and bag languages. In this section we study another important problem where sets and bags differ considerably, that is, semantics of partial information.

We follow the idea of Buneman, Jung and Ohori [6] and Libkin [16], where databases were considered as subsets of certain partially ordered sets in order to provide rigorous mathematical treatment of partial information. The intuitive meaning of the ordering is "being more partial". In [6, 16] only sets were considered. A rather intuitive approach to defining the orderings was adopted in [6, 16], and later in Libkin and Wong [17] that approach was justified. However, it is not immediately clear how to generalize any of the orderings of [6, 16, 17] to bags, and hence additional study is needed. In this section we use techniques of [17] to define an ordering for *bags*. Even though the ordering appears somewhat awkward, we demonstrate an effective algorithm to test whether two bags are comparable.

As in [11, 6, 16], we assume that partiality can be expressed by means of a partial order on database objects. That is, $a \leq b$ expresses the fact that a is more partial than b or b is more informative than a. It was mentioned in [6] that many models of partial information can be captured by this very general scheme. This approach is also suitable for databases *without* partial information. In such a case, values of base types are totally unordered.

It is usually assumed that orders on the base types are given. For example, if base type is $\mathbf{N}_\perp$ whose values are natural numbers or null ($\perp$), the usual ordering is $\perp \le n$ for any $n \in \mathbf{N}$ and any two distinct natural numbers are not comparable, see Gunter [10]. The ordering is then extended to pairs in the usual way. That is, $(x, y) \le (x', y')$ iff $x \le_1 x'$ and $y \le_2 y'$. However, if one wants to extend the ordering to subsets of an ordered set, many possibilities arise. In [17] we tried to define an ordering by saying that a set X is less informative than a set Y if there is a sequence of simple updates, each leading to a more informative set. Dealing with sets, we defined the primitive updates as follows: $X \rightarrowtail (X - \{a\}) \cup X'$ where $a \le b$ for any $b \in X'$. Notice that if $a \notin X$, this is equivalent to augmenting X by X'.

To extend this idea to bags, recall that having a bag rather than a set means that each element of a bag represents an object and if there are many occurrences of some element, then at the moment certain objects are indistinguishable. This justifies the following definition. We say that a bag B_2 is more informative than a bag B_1 if B_2 can be obtained from B_1 by a sequence of updates of the following form: (1) an element a is removed from B_1 and is replaced by an element b such that b is more informative than a, or (2) an element b is added to the bag B_1. Formally, let $\langle D, \le \rangle$ be a partially ordered set. Let $\mathcal{P}^b_{\text{fin}}(D)$ be the set of all finite bags whose elements are in D. Then, for $B_1, B_2 \in \mathcal{P}^b_{\text{fin}}(D)$, $B_1 \rightsquigarrow B_2$ iff $B_2 = (B_1\, monus \{\!|a|\!\}) \uplus \{\!|b|\!\}$ where $a \le b$ or $B_2 = B_1 \uplus \{\!|b|\!\}$. The transitive-reflexive closure of $\rightsquigarrow$ is denoted by $\trianglelefteq$. That is, we say that B_1 is *less informative* than B_2 if $B_1 \trianglelefteq B_2$.

As proved in [17], the ordering on *sets* obtained as the transitive-reflexive closure of $\rightarrowtail$ coincides with the *lower powerdomain ordering* [10] defined as

$$X \le^{\flat} Y \text{ iff } \forall x \in X.\ \exists y \in Y.\ x \le y$$

A similar construction can be used to characterize $\trianglelefteq$. Let $\mathbf{N}^{\shortparallel}$ denote the totally unordered poset whose elements are natural numbers (the superscript is used to distinguish it from $\mathbf{N}$ which in this paper denotes natural numbers with the usual ordering). For a finite bag B and an injective map $\phi : B \to \mathbf{N}^{\shortparallel}$, which is sometimes called *labeling*, by $\phi(B)$ we denote the set $\{(b, \phi(b)) \mid b \in B\}$. In other words, ϕ assigns a unique label to each element of a bag. If $B \in \mathcal{P}^b_{\text{fin}}(D)$, the ordering on pairs (b, n) where $b \in B$ and $n \in \mathbf{N}^{\shortparallel}$ is the usual pair ordering; that is, $(b, n) \le (b', n')$ iff $b \le b'$ and $n = n'$.

Proposition 7.1 *The binary relation $\trianglelefteq$ on bags is a partial order. Given two bags B_1, B_2, $B_1 \trianglelefteq B_2$ iff there exist labelings ϕ and ψ on B_1 and B_2 respectively such that $\phi(B_1) \le^{\flat} \psi(B_2)$.* □

The lower powerdomain ordering $\le^{\flat}$ of sets can be effectively verified. Indeed, if two sets are given, there is an $O(n^2)$ time complexity algorithm to check if they are comparable. The description of $\trianglelefteq$ given above seems to be somewhat awkward algorithmically. However, it is not much harder to test for.

Proposition 7.2 *There exists an $O(n^{5/2})$ time complexity algorithm that, given two bags B_1 and B_2 in $\mathcal{P}^b_{\text{fin}}(D)$, returns* true *if $B_1 \trianglelefteq B_2$ and* false *otherwise.*

Proof sketch. The problem is reduced to finding a maximal matching in a certain bipartite graph whose size in linear in the sum of the sizes of the two given bags. Hence, it can be solved by the Hopcroft-Karp algorithm in $O(n^{5/2})$. □

There is a big difference between orders on sets and bags. While $X \leq^{\flat} Y$ does not say anything about cardinality of X and Y, $B_1 \trianglelefteq B_2$ implies that the cardinality of B_1 is less than or equal to the cardinality of B_2. This reflects our point of view that having a bag rather than a set stored in a database means that each element of a bag represents an object and having two or more occurrences of the same elements means that at the moment some objects are indistinguishable. Therefore, the cardinality can not be reduced in the process of obtaining more information.

8 Conclusion and further work

Many results on bags are presented in this report. A large combination of primitives have been investigated and the relative strength is determined. The relationship between bags and sets has been studied from two different perspectives. First, various bag languages are compared with a standard nested relational language to understand their set-theoretic expressive power. Second, the extra expressive power of bags is characterized accurately. The relationship between bags and natural numbers is studied. In particular, we show that properties that are simultaneously infinite and co-infinite are inexpressible. Finally, the relationship between structural recursion and the powerbag operator has been re-examined. The former is shown to be stronger than the latter. Then we introduce the bounded loop construct that captures the power of structural recursion but has the advantage of not requiring verification of any precondition. Moreover, we prove that structural recursion gives us all primitive recursive functions.

There are several conjectures we have not yet proved. Does adding *gen* give us precisely lower elementary functions [26]? Are functions such as testing whether a graph is a tree or testing connectivity or transitive closure expressible in the set language equivalent to $\mathcal{BQL}$? What is the expressive power of this set language augmented by transitive closure? We know, for example, that test for balanced binary trees can be expressed in this language, but can it express bounded fixpoint? When augmented with *gen*, how powerful is it?

Breazu-Tannen, Buneman and Wong [5], Libkin and Wong [17], and this paper studied the use of monads and structural recursion for querying sets, or-sets and bags respectively. We hope to extend this methodology to other collection types such as lists, arrays, etc.

Acknowledgements. Peter Buneman gave us the initial inspiration and provided many helpful suggestions. We also thank Val Breazu-Tannen, Jean Gallier, Dan Suciu, Bennet Vance, Steve Vickers and Scott Weinstein for valuable comments and suggestions.

References

[1] S. Abiteboul and C. Beeri. On the power of languages for the manipulation of complex objects. In *Proc. Int. Workshop on Theory and Applications of Nested Relations and Complex Objects*, Darmstadt, 1988.

[2] J. Albert. Algebraic properties of bag data types. In *VLDB 91*, pages 211–219.

[3] V. Breazu-Tannen, P. Buneman, and S. Naqvi. Structural recursion as a query language. In *DBPL 91*, pages 9–19.

[4] V. Breazu-Tannen and R. Subrahmanyam. Logical and computational aspects of programming with sets/bags/lists. In *LNCS 510: ICALP 91*, pages 60–75.

[5] V. Breazu-Tannen, P. Buneman, and L. Wong. Naturally embedded query languages. In *ICDT 92*, pages 140–154.

[6] P. Buneman, A. Ohori, and A. Jung. Using powerdomains to generalize relational databases. *Theoretical Computer Science*, 91:23–55, 1991.

[7] A. Chandra and D. Harel. Structure and complexity of relational queries. *JCSS*, 25:99–128, 1982.

[8] J. Van den Bussche and J. Paredaens. The expressive power of structured values in pure OODB. Technical Report 90-23, University of Antwerp, 1990. Extended abstract in *PODS 91*.

[9] S. Grumbach and T. Milo. Towards tractable algebras for bags. In *PODS 93*, pages 49–60.

[10] C. A. Gunter. *Semantics of Programming Languages: Structures and Techniques*. The MIT Press, 1992.

[11] T. Imielinski and W. Lipski. Incomplete information in relational databases. *Journal of the ACM*, 31:761–791, 1984.

[12] N. Immerman, S. Patnaik and D. Stemple, The expressiveness of a family of finite set languages, in *Proceedings of the 10th Symposium on Principles of Database Systems*, 1991, pages 37–52.

[13] L. A. Jategaonkar and J. C. Mitchell. ML with extended pattern matching and subtypes. In *Proceedings of ACM Conference on LISP and Functional Programming*, pages 198–211, Snowbird, Utah, July 1988.

[14] A. Klausner and N. Goodman. Multirelations: semantics and languages. In *VLDB 85*, pages 251–258.

[15] A. Klug. Equivalence of relational algebra and relational calculus query languages having aggregate functions. *J. ACM*, 29(3):699–717, 1982.

[16] L. Libkin. A relational algebra for complex objects based on partial information. In J. Demetrovics and B. Thalheim editors, *LNCS 495: Proceedings of Symposium on Mathematical Fundamentals of Database Systems, Rostock, May 1991*, pages 36–41. Springer-Verlag, 1991.

[17] L. Libkin and L. Wong. Semantic representations and query languages for or-sets. In *PODS 93*, Washington, D. C., May 1993, pages 37–48. Full paper available as UPenn Technical Report MS-CIS-92-88.

[18] L. Libkin and L. Wong. Query languages for bags, Technical Report MS-CIS-93-36, University of Pennsylvania, 1993.

[19] L. Libkin and L. Wong. Aggregate functions, conservative extension, and linear orders. This volume.

[20] E. Moggi. Notions of computation and monads. *Information and Computation*, 93:55–92, 1991.

[21] I. S. Mumick and O. Shmueli, How expressive is stratified aggregation, submitted.

[22] P. Odifreddi. *Classical Recursion Theory*. North Holland, 1989.

[23] A. Ohori, P. Buneman, and V. Breazu-Tannen. Database programming in Machiavelli: a polymorphic language with static type inference. In *SIGMOD 89*, pages 46–57.

[24] G. Ozsoyoglu, Z. M. Ozsoyoglu, and V. Matos. Extending relational algebra and relational calculus with set-valued attributes and aggregate functions. *ACM TODS*, 12(4):566–592, 1987.

[25] J. Paredaens and D. Van Gucht. Converting nested relational algebra expressions into flat algebra expressions. *ACM Transaction on Database Systems*, 17(1):65–93, 1992.

[26] H. E. Rose. *Subrecursion: Functions and Hierarchies*. Clarendon Press, Oxford, 1984.

[27] Y. Saraiya, Fixpoints and optimizations in a language based on structural recursion on sets, Manuscript, December 1992.

[28] S. Vickers. Geometric theories and databases. In P. Johnstone and A. Pitts, editors, *Applications of Categories in Computer Science*, volume 177 of *London Mathematical Society Lecture Notes*, pages 288–314. Cambridge University Press, 1992.

[29] P. Wadler. Comprehending monads. In *Proceedings of ACM Conference on Lisp and Functional Programming*, Nice, June 1990.

[30] L. Wong. Normal forms and conservative properties for query languages over collection types. In *PODS 93*, pages 26–36, Washington, D. C., May 1993. Full paper available as UPenn Technical Report MS-CIS-92-59.

Ordered Types in the AQUA Data Model*

Bharathi Subramanian
Brown University
Providence, RI, USA

Stanley B. Zdonik
Brown University
Providence, RI, USA

Theodore W. Leung
Brown University
Providence, RI, USA

Scott L. Vandenberg†
University of Massachusetts
Amherst, MA, USA

Abstract

We present a query algebra that supports ordering among the data elements. Order is defined as a relationship between various data elements of an instance. This relationship can be a total or partial order among the elements or among equivalence classes where each equivalence class consists of one or more elements. In terms of data structures, ordered types can be viewed as graphs, trees, or lists.

Lately there has been a lot of interest in bulk types like lists, trees, and graphs that are not supported by traditional data models and query algebras. This interest is fueled by the fact that much of the data in the scientific domain is inherently ordered. Therefore, scientific applications that involve genome sequences, satellite data, scientific data, etc. require database support for ordered data structures like lists, trees, and graphs. In this paper, we discuss an extension to the AQUA query algebra to handle ordered types and their operators. We show how these operators can fit into a framework for query optimization.

1 Introduction

There are many applications [3,4,8] in which ordered types are required. Scientific applications have a need to store ordered types such as time-series data and genome sequences, and textual databases store information that is structured as a tree. These applications store huge volumes of data and must locate information from these structures very efficiently.

Query languages and algebras support declarative retrieval from a database. They are based on a set of high-level operations over collections of objects. These operations hide the looping structure that would be present in an algorithm that executes them. By and large, these operations have been confined to manipulations of sets. While there has been some recent work on extending query languages to other bulk types like sequences [5,10], additional research is needed.

---

*Partial support for this work was provided by the Advanced Research Projects Agency under contract N00014-91-J-4052 ARPA order 8225, and contract DAAB-07-91-C-Q518 under subcontract F41100.

†Current address: Computer Science Dept., Siena College, Loudonville, NY 12211

This paper presents an extension to the AQUA (A QUery Algebra) query algebra [9] to include ordered types like graphs, lists, and trees. N-dimensional arrays are a topic for future work. We begin by defining algebraic operations over graphs. Graphs are used as the fundamental building block out of which the operations for the other types are derived. Sequences and trees are viewed as specialized graphs. Duplicates are introduced into these graph structures through a notion of a *cell* type.

We could argue that graphs and trees could be viewed as nested list structures, but the onus of maintaining the structure is placed on the user. For example in a tree structure, the user has to prevent two nodes from pointing to the same "child" list. Also, viewing trees and graphs as types in their own right allows us to utilize their specialized properties for query optimization and gives us more flexibility in defining operations over them. This distinction might also help in other related areas like specialized storage structures to speed access and specialized index structures for querying.

This paper focuses on an algebraic approach to queries over ordered types. An order is represented by a graph. Such an order can be restricted further to produce a tree (i.e., a partial order) or a list (i.e., a total order).

A goal of this work has been to define the operators on all the bulk types so that they are consistent with each other. The operations on a more specific version of a bulk type must follow from the operations on a more general version. For example, *Select* for a tree must be the same as *Select* for a graph when the tree is viewed as a graph. A graph with an empty edge set is essentially a set. Thus, this kind of degenerate graph must behave in all ways like a set. Identities that apply to sets must apply to graphs with no edges as well.

In several cases, an operation on an ordered type will not return an object of the starting type. We do not view this as a violation of the closure property. In our view, closure should require that an operation will return an object of a type within the model. For example, a **select** over a tree is not guaranteed to produce another tree; however, it will always produce a list of trees which is a perfectly good type in the model. Such a result can be composed with other operators for that type.

This paper first briefly introduces the AQUA data model. Next, it examines some related work, and then describes our approach to ordered types. This is followed by a discussion of the specific operators that we support for graphs, trees, and lists. We close with a few examples of how these operators are used and some suggestions for future research.

2 AQUA Model

The AQUA query algebra [9] is based on an object-oriented data model. All objects have identity, and these identities allow us to distinguish between objects using identity-based equalities.

Equality is essential to the definition of operators like union, intersection and other comparison-based operators. The default equality is identity, similar to that for unordered bulk types like sets and multisets. In the case of sets and multisets, other notions of equality are handled by providing the special operators **group** (which creates equivalence classes based on a given equality) and **choose** (which picks a member of each class nondeterministically). For ordered types, the notion of other equalities is simulated by using these equality-specific set operators on the node and the edge sets.

2.1 Constructing Types

One of the primary goals of the algebra and the model has been to support a large number of bulk types in a uniform manner. A type constructor is a metatype which defines a family of types. The *Set* type constructor defines the family of types that includes *Set[Int], Set[Department]*, etc. New types are created by instantiating the metatype *Set[T : Type]* with a specific type, like *Int* or *Department*.

AQUA provides the following type constructors: *sets, multisets, tuples, unions, functions, cells, lists, graphs,* and *trees*. The algebra also supports the *abs* constructor that allows creation of new abstract types. The *operators* of the AQUA algebra are a subset of the methods on the AQUA type constructors and include operations like **select**, **join**, and **union**.

2.2 Duplicates

All the ordered types are defined as a set of nodes N, and a set of edges E. However, as in the case of multisets, there are cases when there is a need to allow duplicates. Duplicate nodes could be handled in a manner similar to multisets but that would not allow for distinction between edges of two identical nodes. Thus, we introduce the concept of a cell. A cell can be thought of as a *wrapper* around an object that allows us to distinguish between two nodes containing the same object. With cells, we could have the same object represented as two different nodes, as the identity of the cells provides the uniqueness.

3 Related Work

Much of the previous work with ordering deals with order as in sequences or arrays. Beeri and Kornatzky [1] discuss trees in their paper. However, there is no known work with directed acyclic graphs or graphs, in the domain of database applications.

Beeri and Kornatzky propose an object-oriented query processing paradigm where the objects are built of primitive objects, an explicit object identity type constructor, and bulk type constructors. Then operations and optimizations are presented, which apply to any bulk type constructor definable in their paradigm. In this approach, lists, arrays, and trees can all be defined, and a subset of the useful operations on such structures is described in the paper. These operations include a "pump" function, which is similar to AQUA's **fold** operation. Since the operations described in [1] are intended to be applicable to any bulk type, not just to lists and trees, they are too general for our purposes – we wish to distinguish between ordered and unordered types, and provide a richer set of operations. Furthermore, many of the operations listed in [1] are not described precisely, and their existence is assumed. Here we remove that assumption. Graphs are not discussed in [1], and it is not clear how (or if) they would fit into the paradigm presented there.

A = [cat crow mouse sparrow dog robin parrot]

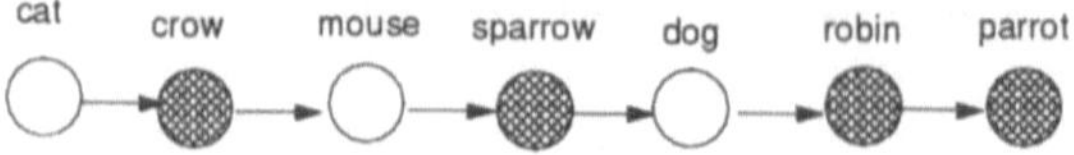

1. Select (A , birds) = [crow], [sparrow], [robin parrot]

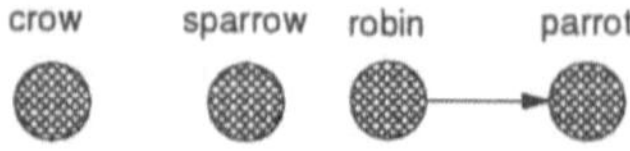

Lists treated as graphs

2. Select (A, birds) = [crow sparrow robin parrot]

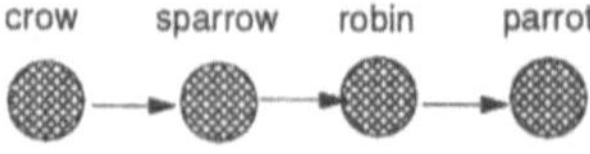

Assuming transitive "Next" relationships for lists

Figure 1: Select for Lists

MDM [10] talks about a query algebra to support lists in an object-oriented data model. Operators from a discrete, linear-time temporal logic provide the basis for the algebra. The salient feature of the algebra is the extension of the predicate language to allow position-dependent queries, which adds a lot more flexibility to the kind of queries that can be posed to the database. Union and difference are similar to the corresponding operators in EXTRA/EXCESS [12]. However, the MDM algebra does not provide for operations on trees or graphs.

The NST algebra [6] is specifically designed for structured office documents and is an extension of relational algebra. The data model is based on nested sequences of tuples. It tries to maintain the order of the input lists whenever possible, with a higher preference for the order of the first input list. For example, in union, elements are concatenated and duplicates from the second list are eliminated. As a result, most of the operators are not commutative. Duplicates are allowed in lists, however union and intersection eliminate duplicates from the result set. A tree-like structure in a document (paragraphs under sections) is handled by treating it as a nested sequence of sequences.

Rs-operations [5] are sequence operations that are based on pattern matching. Along with these operations, sequence logic (SL), which is a first-order logic, is also introduced. Ginsburg and Wang define a set of powerful operations based on regular expressions, which act as a kind of template for the operation. However, the paper does not mention how these operations can be extended to trees. Also, the authors do not specify how these operations fit into a query optimization scheme.

The EXTRA/EXCESS system [12] contains an array type constructor; arrays can be fixed- or variable-length and can contain entities of any EXTRA type. The elements of an array are accessed using their array indices, but there is no ability to traverse from one element to another in these arrays. Operators are provided for extraction of elements and subarrays, for creating and concatenating arrays, and for applying a function to all elements of an array. The system provides no support for lists, trees, or graphs, and multidimensional arrays are constructed as arrays of arrays. Thus the arrays of EXTRA/EXCESS bear more resemblance to AQUA's N-dimensional arrays (which will be discussed in a future paper) than to the structures described in this paper.

4 Ordered Types

In this section, we describe *ordered* bulk types and the operations on them. Order in our setting is a mechanism to specify a "precedes" or "follows" relationship between pairs of elements. In its most general form, this kind of relationship can be represented as a graph, where elements are represented as nodes of the graph and edges between elements represent explicit precedence relationships. "Precede" is an antisymmetric relation, i.e. if a precedes b and b precedes a, then a and b are equivalent. As a parallel, strongly-connected components in graphs (a strongly connected component is one in which all nodes are reachable from each other) could be viewed as an equivalence class. In a sense, all nodes in the strongly-connected component are reachable from the same set of nodes in the graph and are equivalent for reachability queries.

Graphs form the basis for our definition of ordered types. Lists and trees are specialized forms of graphs. Besides the obvious restriction that the underlying structure be a tree (or a list), we impose an additional constraint of transitivity. In other words, if there is a directed path $a_0, a_1, \cdots, a_n$ in the tree (list), we assume that there is an implicit edge between a_0 and a_n. Note that these implicit edges are not actually present in the tree structure. To see why this transitivity assumption is *natural* when viewing lists, consider selecting birds from a list of animals A = [cat crow mouse sparrow dog robin parrot] (Figure 1). Treating list A as a graph would give us a set of graphs instead of a list [1]. Most of us would expect the select to return [crow sparrow robin parrot].

However, note that the edges between crow and sparrow & sparrow and robin did not exist in the original list though they are there in the *expected* result. The implicit assumption here is that the relationship between the elements is transitive. A similar example can be used to show that transitivity is a natural assumption for trees as well. Note that the ***transitivity*** property ensures that the resultant type is the same as the input type (Lists $\mapsto$ Lists and Trees $\mapsto$ Trees or a set of Trees). As a result of this property, the behavior of the operators for graphs is slightly different than that for lists and trees.

Sets in the AQUA model are at the other end of the spectrum; they can be viewed as the most *unordered* form of graphs, as sets can be represented as graphs with empty edge sets. We explore this connection in greater detail in section 5.4.

4.1 Graphs

Graphs are defined as a set V of nodes, and a set E of directed edges between the nodes. An edge is defined as a pair of nodes and the direction of the edge

[1] Assuming we ignore the typing issues for the moment.

is from the first node to the second.

The type constructor for graphs is defined as *Graph[T]*, which constructs a graph type consisting of objects of type T as the nodes. Edges in the graph are tuples consisting of a pairs of nodes of type T. As mentioned earlier, this definition does not allow duplicate objects as nodes. Duplicates are handled by using a graph of type *Graph[Cell[T]]*. Since this is used later, while defining type conversion operators on trees and lists, we use the term "cell-graphs" to refer to such graphs. Graphs, like sets and multisets, do not participate in sub-typing.

4.2 Trees and Lists

Trees and lists are also defined as a set V of nodes, and a set (or a list in the case of ordered trees) E of directed edges between the nodes. However, the underlying structure of a tree (list) instance must be a tree (or a list). Assuming edges are directed away from the root, this implies that a tree must have one node with no incoming edges and all other nodes must have a single parent (or incoming edge). For a list, there must be one node with no incoming edge and a node with no outgoing edge (except for the empty list). All other nodes in a list must have one incoming edge and one outgoing edge.

The AQUA model supports two kinds of trees, *ordered-* and *unordered-trees*. Ordered-trees are trees where there is an order between the children of a node and unordered-trees assume that there is no explicit order between the children. Ordered-trees are defined as a set V of nodes and a list E of directed edges (as opposed to a set of directed edges for unordered-trees). The relative ordering among the edges from the parent node to the child node in the list E determines the order of the children nodes.

A tree (or list) of type T consists of nodes of type *Cell[T]* and the edges between these nodes. The node typing is different from that of graphs, where the nodes are of type T. We do this since it allows us to handle duplicates in a consistent manner. Duplicates in trees and lists present a problem when dealing with operators that could possibly map two or more nodes of the original tree onto the same object. In such a scenario, preserving all the associated edges might violate the tree (or list) structure. As a result, we adopt the "cell" structure to avoid duplicate nodes.

The type constructor for trees is defined as *Tree[T]*, which is a tree type consisting of nodes of the same type *Cell[T]* and edges between these nodes. The type constructor for lists is similar, *List[T]* is a list type consisting of nodes of type *Cell[T]* and their associated edges. Lists and trees do not participate in subtyping.

5 Operators

In this section, we describe in detail the various operations on graphs, trees and lists. The functionality of most operators is similar across all the ordered types. The syntax of the operations is similar to that used in AQUA[9], and is based on lambda calculus.

Predicates are functions with *boolean* return type, and are composed using AQUA's built-in operators and its term language (which is based on lambda calculus). Predicates are passed as parameters to operators like **select**.

Cells have two operators: **Cell**(a) creates a cell containing a. **Cell_content**(c) returns the object contained in cell c.

5.1 Graphs

In this subsection we describe the operators on graphs. Table 1 details all the operator definitions. We now describe some of the notation used in the table. The input graphs are $G = (V_G, E_G)$ and $H = (V_H, E_H)$ and the output graph is $R = (V_R, E_R)$. Individual nodes are denoted by lowercase letters, with the graph name as a subscript (for example, u_G, v_G, x_G). Predicates are indicated by p and f represents a function.

The primary query operators are **select**, **apply**, **union**, and **intersect**. Both **union** and **intersect** use the default equality for unioning (or intersecting) the node and edge sets. **Im_ancestor** and **im_descendant** are the traversal operators. The algebra also defines other *support* operators like **nodes** and **edges** along with *update* operators like **add_node**, **add_edge**, and **delete_edge**. The algebra also has *conversion* operators to convert from a graph (of the appropriate structure) to a tree or a list.

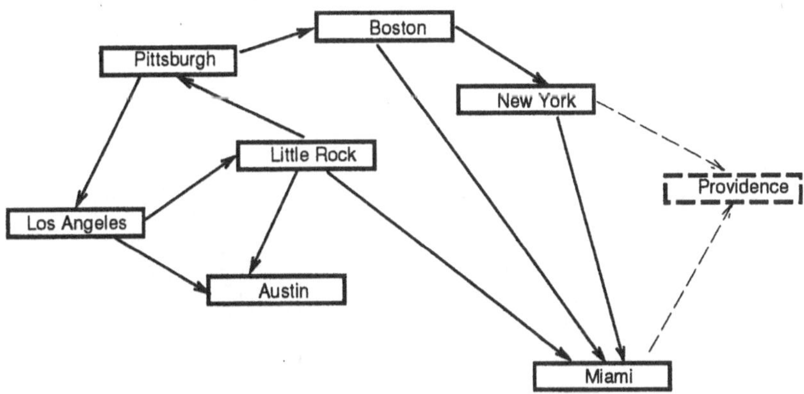

Figure 2: Flight graph for *Airline*1

As an example, consider an airline company, Airline1. They have a large number of airports out of which they operate, with flights connecting them (figure 2). In our graph, the nodes represent the airports and the edges represent the flights between the airports. The nodes are assumed to have more details about the airports, besides their city names.

type *Airport* = *abs*(*Tuple*[*city* : *String*, ...]
  city(*Airport*) → *String*;
  ⋮
)

type *Airline* = *Graph*[*Airport*]

Definitions		
$\mathbf{select}(p)(G)$	=	$(V_R = \{v_R \mid p(v_G)\},\ E_R = \{(u_R, v_R) \mid ((u_R, v_R) \in E_G) \wedge p(u_R) \wedge p(v_R)\})$
$\mathbf{apply}(f)(G)$	=	$(V_R = \{f(v_G)\},\ E_R = \{(f(u_G), f(v_G)) \mid (u_G, v_G) \in E_G\})$
$\mathbf{union}(G, H)$	=	$(V_R = \mathbf{union}(V_G, V_H),\ E_R = \mathbf{union}(E_G, E_H))$
$\mathbf{intersect}(G, H)$	=	$(V_R = \mathbf{intersect}(V_G, V_H),\ E_R = \mathbf{intersect}(E_G, E_H))$
$\mathbf{im\_ancestor}(x_G)(G)$	=	$\{v_G \mid (v_G, x_G) \in E_G\}$
$\mathbf{im\_descendant}(x_G)(G)$	=	$\{v_G \mid (x_G, v_G) \in E_G\}$
$\mathbf{sources}(G)$	=	$\{v_G \mid (x_G, v_G) \notin E_G\}$
$\mathbf{sinks}(G)$	=	$\{v_G \mid (v_G, x_G) \notin E_G\}$
$\mathbf{nodes}(G)$	=	V_G
$\mathbf{edges}(G)$	=	E_G
$\mathbf{graph}(x)$	=	$(V_R = \{x\},\ E_R = \emptyset)$
$\mathbf{t\_closure}(G)$	=	$(V_G,\ E_R = \{(u_G, v_G) \mid connected(u_G, v_G)\}$ where $((u_G, v_G) \in E_G) \vee (u_G = v_G) \Rightarrow connected(u_G, v_G)$ and $((u_G, m_G), (n_G, v_G) \in E_G) \wedge (connected(m_G, n_G))$ $\Rightarrow connected(u_G, v_G))$
$\mathbf{append}(u_G, v_H)(G, H)$	=	$(V_R = \mathbf{union}(V_G, V_H),\ E_R = \mathbf{union}(\{(u_G, v_H)\}, \mathbf{union}(E_G, E_H)))$
$\mathbf{add\_node}(x)(G)$	=	$(V_R = \mathbf{union}(V_G, \{x\}),\ E_G)$
$\mathbf{delete\_node}(x_G)(G)$	=	$(V_R = \mathbf{diff}(V_G, \{x_G\}),\ E_R = \mathbf{diff}(E_G, \mathbf{union}(\{(u_G, x_G)\}, \{(x_G, v_G)\})))$
$\mathbf{add\_edges}(S)(G)$	=	$(V_G,\ E_R = \mathbf{union}(E_G, \{(u_G, v_G) \mid ((u_G, v_G) \in S) \wedge (u_G, v_G \in V_G)\})$
$\mathbf{delete\_edges}(S)(G)$	=	$(V_G,\ E_R = \mathbf{diff}(E_G, S))$
$\mathbf{replace\_node}(x_G, y)(G)$	=	$\mathbf{add\_edges}(A)(\mathbf{add\_node}(y)(\mathbf{delete\_node}(x_G)(G)))$ where $A = \mathbf{union}(\{(y, v_G) \mid (x_G, v_G) \in E_G\}, \{(u_G, y) \mid (u_G, x_G) \in E_G\})$

Table 1: Graph Operators

Our query is to find all the places that have a direct flight to Boston, either by *Airline*1 or *Airline*2. The basic query is to get all the **im_ancestors** of the node *Boston* in the combined airline map, *TwoAirlines*. The combined airline map is obtained by unioning the maps of *Airline*1 and *Airline*2.

TwoAirlines = **union**(*Airline*1, *Airline*2)

DirectToBoston = **im_ancestor**(**choose**(**nodes**(**select**($\lambda(n)\, n.city = Boston$)
(*TwoAirlines*))))
(*TwoAirlines*)

5.2 Trees

In this section, we briefly describe the operators on trees. Most of the tree operators have been derived from the corresponding graph operators, so in the following paragraphs we shall highlight the differences between the corresponding graph and tree operators. We discuss the operators for ordered-trees below; operators for unordered-trees follow logically from the ordered-tree operators. Therefore, for the sake of simplicity we use the short-form "tree" to refer to ordered-trees. Also, in all our examples we assume that all edges are directed away from the root of the tree.

The basic tree operators in AQUA are: **select** (p) (T), **apply** (f) (T), **sub_select** (r) (T), **PT** (T), **all_desc** (r) (T), **all_anc** (r) (T), **sources** (T), **sinks** (T), **nodes** (T), **edges** (T), **e_edges** (T), **im_ancestor** (x)(T), **im_descendant** (x) (T), **tree** (x), and **find_path** (x) (T). The update operators are: **append** (*from_node*, *sibling*) (T_1, T_2), **add_node** (x, *parent*, *sibling*) (T), **delete_node** (x) (T), **replace_node** (x, y) (T), and a number of *conversion* operators to go from a tree to a graph or a list.

Note that some functions are defined only on graphs: **union**, **intersect**, **t_closure**, **add_edges** and **delete_edges**. This is mainly because the result of these operations will not be a tree (the resultant structure will be a graph). However, the functionality of the operators can be obtained by converting the input trees to graphs and applying the corresponding graph operators. For example, **union** on two trees with common nodes might produce a graph due to unioning the edge sets of the common nodes from the two input trees. This operation however, can be performed by "converting" trees to graphs.

The main differences between the other tree operators and their corresponding graph operators are:

- The children of a node in a tree are ordered. As a result, the operators return a list of nodes or sub-trees instead of a set. For example, **sources**(T), **sinks**(T), **im_ancestor**(x)(T), and **im_descendant**(x)(T) are similar to the corresponding graph operators, except that the result is a list of nodes. So, **source** returns a singleton list consisting of the root of the tree, **sinks** returns a list consisting of all the leaves of the tree, **im_ancestor** returns a list containing the parent of the given node in the tree and **im_descendant** returns a list of all the children of the given node, in order.
- The edges of a tree are transitive. Therefore, **edges** operator returns a list containing all the edges of the tree – this includes the edges that

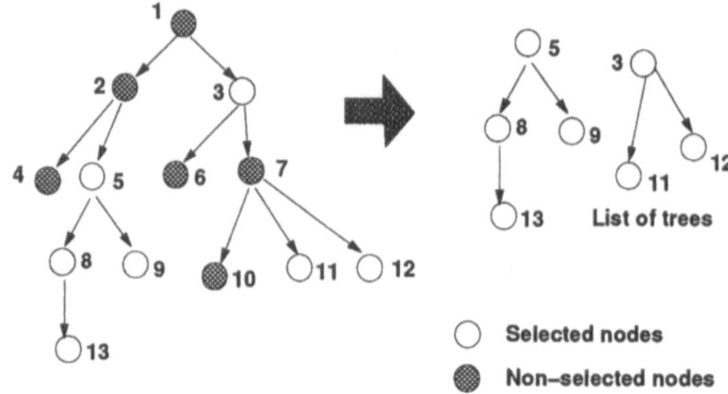

Figure 3: Select on a tree

were explicitly added to the tree and the edges that were "created" due to the transitive property of the edges. The **e_edges** operator, in contrast, returns a list containing only the edges that were explicitly added to the tree. For example, **edges** on the tree rooted at 5 (figure 3) would return $[\{5,8\},\{5,9\},\{8,13\},\{5,13\}]$ and **e_edges** would return $[\{5,8\},\{5,9\},\{8,13\}]$. This property also influences any operator that "deletes" nodes (**select** and **delete_node**). Deletion of a node causes an implicit edge, i.e. an edge created due to transitivity, to become an explicit edge which can be loosely thought of as the edges used to draw the tree. So, if we just look at explicit edges, a deletion causes addition of new edges (from the list of all edges) between the the parent and the children nodes of the deleted node (Figure 4).

Select$(p)(T)$ selects a list of sub-trees of tree T, based on the nodes that satisfy predicate p. All the edges between selected nodes from the input tree are present in the resultant graph. Any new edges "created" due to the transitivity relationship between the nodes are also added in the resultant tree (Figure 3). The ordering in the resultant list is based on the *relative* ordering of the roots of each tree in the list. For example, in figure 3, the tree with node 5 as the root comes "before" the tree rooted at node 3, in spite of the difference in levels. The ordering is mainly based on position – if sub-tree A is to the left of sub-tree B (assuming ordering is from left to right), then A is followed by B in the resultant list. It is a kind of depth-first ordering. The sub-trees in the list are ordered based on the relative order in which the respective roots of the sub-trees are visited in a depth-first traversal.

- For certain operators, there are certain constraints on their behavior, as the result has to be a tree. For example, **add_node** adds a node and an edge connecting the node to the tree (at the specified point).

  In the case of **append**, the *to_node* is always the root of the second tree, hence it is not a parameter to the operator. **Append** (*from_node*, *sibling*) (T_1, T_2) appends tree T_1 to tree T_2, as a child of the *from_node*, after the sub-tree rooted at *sibling* (which is also a child of the

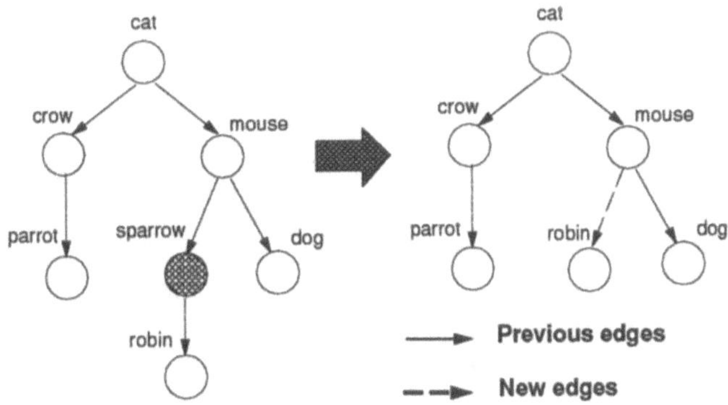

Figure 4: Deletion in a tree

from_node). If *sibling* is not specified, the tree T_2 is added as the first child of the *from_node*.

- Trees of type T are composed of cells that contain objects of type T. As a result, most function applications deal with the contained-object instead of the cell. So, as in the case of **apply** on a graph, **apply** on trees transforms the "contained-object" based on the parameter function f.

  Apply$(f)(T)$ applies the function f to the "content" of each cell (node) of the tree to transform the existing object into a new object. The edge-set remains the same. This ensures that the basic structure of the tree is not modified. The resultant tree is built of new cells that contain the transformed objects (Figure 5).

Other operators that are specific to trees are: **Tree**(x) creates a tree that consists of node x. **Find_path**$(x)(T)$ returns a list of nodes encountered on the path from the root of the tree T to the node x. The last node of the resultant list is x, and the first node is the root of the tree. **Sub_select**$(r)(T)$ returns a set of all sub-trees of tree T that match the pattern r. The **PT**(T) operator (powertree) takes as input a tree T and returns a set of all sub-trees of T. This operator is somewhat similar in spirit to the power-set operator for sets and is used primarily for defining other more specific operators. For example, **sub_select** can be expressed as:

$$\textbf{sub\_select}(r)(T) = \textbf{set\_select}(\lambda(x)\ x \in \mathcal{L}(r))(\textbf{PT}(T))$$

PT generates a set of all subtrees of T and **set_select** (**select** over a set) selects those subtrees that are in the tree language defined by the tree regular expression r ($\mathcal{L}(r)$). **All_desc**$(r)(T)$ and **all_anc**$(r)(T)$ are specialized cases of the **PT** operator that extract all maximal subtrees of T that start (**all_desc**) or end (**all_anc**) with the pattern r. Specification of the match pattern r is discussed in detail in subsection 6.2.

Replace_node and **nodes** are similar to the corresponding operators in graphs. The only difference is due to typing of the input and the output. For example, **nodes** on a tree returns a set containing all the nodes of the tree,

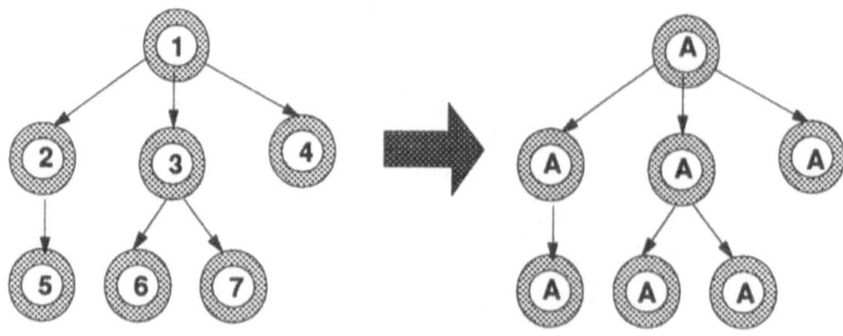

Figure 5: **Apply**$(\lambda(x)\, A)(T)$

similar to **nodes** for graphs. However, the tree-nodes are cells unlike graph-nodes which are objects.

5.3 Lists

In this section, we discuss operations on lists. These operators are almost identical to the corresponding operators on trees, except for the input and output types which are lists instead of trees, and the absence of the "sibling" parameter. Any kind of add operation in trees requires a *sibling* parameter, that specifies the node after which the new node/sub-tree must be added. This is needed for trees as the children of a node are ordered. In the case of a list however, since there is only one child for every node, this parameter is unnecessary.

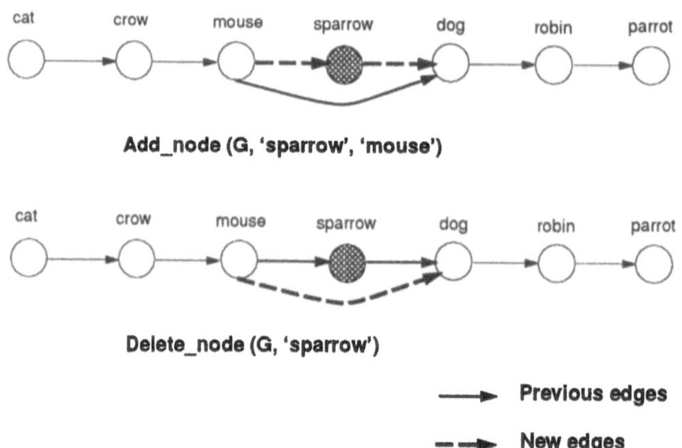

Figure 6: Add_node and Delete_node on a list

Select (p) (L), **apply** (f) (L), **sub_select** (r) (L), **PL** (L) (similar to **PT**), **all_suffix** (r) (L) (similar to **all_desc**), **all_prefix** (r) (L) (similar to **all_anc**), **nodes** (L), **edges** (L), **e_edges** (L), **add_node** (x, y) (L), **replace_node** (x, y) (L), **delete_node** (x) (L), and the *conversion* operators are similar to the corresponding unordered tree operators. List predicates are discussed in greater detail in subsection 6.1. **Add_node** in a tree does not involve deletion of any existing edges, however, in the case of lists adding a node in the middle of the list might result in deletion of an edge and addition of up to two edges (Figure 6). **Source**(L), **sink**(L), **im_ancestor** (x) (L), **im_descendant**(x)(L) are also similar to their equivalent graph operators but they return a single node for lists instead of a list of nodes as in trees. **Append**(L_1, L_2) is similar to **append** in trees and graphs, but the *from_node* is always the last node of list L_1 and the *to_node* is the first node of list L_2. This results in a concatenation of the two input lists.

There are list operators that do not have corresponding tree operators. **List**(x) creates a list with a single element x. **Sort**(f)(L) sorts list L based on the comparator function f. f is a transitive function that given any two elements (a, b) from the list L, returns *less-than* if a should appear before b in the result list, *greater-than* if a should appear after b in the result list and *equal-to* if a and b are "equal" based on the function f.

5.4 Sets as graphs

The AQUA model supports various bulk types, among them sets and graphs. Sets can be viewed as graphs with an empty edge set. With this view, all the operators for graphs neatly transform into the corresponding operators for sets. For example, **union** and **intersection** on graphs with empty edge sets are similar to these operations on sets. Similarly, **apply** and **select** behave the same way for graphs with an empty edge set, as with sets. This makes the addition of ordered types into the model seamless and consistent with the other bulk types.

6 Predicates

Ordered bulk types, unlike sets and multisets, have the notion of "position" of the constituent objects. This opens up possibilities of having a more powerful predicate language. The remainder of this section describes a richer set of predicate formers for lists and trees.

This investigation was motivated by the observation that query optimization is facilitated by identities that allow us to break a predicate into pieces, some of which can be evaluated cheaply. These pieces must be composable to produce the original query. We give examples of this type of decomposition in the context of our pattern-based predicate languages.

6.1 List Predicates

In this subsection we discuss order-based predicates for lists. These predicates are based on regular expressions (for describing match patterns) and lambda calculus. However, we do envisage a more user-friendly interface that would translate user-defined queries to algebra queries based on regular expressions.

We use the standard notations for specifying regular expressions – "(" and ")" are used for specifying precedence, | for disjunction (union), * for Kleene star, $\circ$ for concatenation, ^ to mark the beginning of the list, and $ to mark the end of the list. We use ab as a shorthand for $a \circ b$, which stands for list

a concatenated with list b. As an example, consider the regular expression $R = (ab)^* \mid a^+$, defined over strings of characters. R defines a language that contains strings formed by either repeating the pattern ab zero or more times or by repeating a one or more times. Instances of strings in this language are $\emptyset$, aaa, ab, $abab$. $\emptyset$ denotes the null string and $+$ is similar to the Kleene star and the language defined by x^* is the language defined by $x^+ \mid \emptyset$, for any regular expression x. We can also specify wild cards (or *don't cares*) by using the symbol ?, which acts as a placeholder for one symbol. ?* matches zero or more symbols; so $?^*a$ matches all strings ending in a. We also use the terms string and sequence to signify a list composed of immutable characters.

To illustrate the use of these predicates, consider a sample query that finds all sub-sequences of a sequence that match a particular pattern $a?t?^*tg$. Such a query could potentially find use in a genome sequence database, where we are searching for a particular protein sequence or a gene. The above query would translate to **sub_select**$(a?t?^*tg)(L)$ in the query algebra. **Sub_select** selects all substrings of the list L that match the input pattern. So, if $L = [acctcggagtccccacttg]$, then **sub_select**$(a?t?^*tg)(L)$ would return set $\{[agtccccacttg], [acttg]\}$, containing the two sub-sequences that match the regular expression $a?t?^*tg$.

This query can also be expressed in terms of other operators like **PL**, **all_suffix**, and **all_prefix** (subsection 5.3). This provides the query optimizer with numerous options for rewriting the query, depending on the cost-effectiveness of the resultant query. The **PL** operator returns a set of all the possible sublists of the input list. **All_suffix** and **all_prefix** are specialized forms of the **PL** operator. They return maximal substrings (i.e. the portion of the list from a given point till one of the ends) starting with the pattern or ending with the pattern respectively, for each occurrence of the pattern. These two operators are very useful for establishing the position(s) of the pattern in the list as they are always anchored at one of the end-points. For example,

$$\begin{aligned} \mathbf{PL}([abc]) &= \{[a],[b],[c],[ab],[bc],[abc]\} \\ \mathbf{all\_suffix}([e?g])([abcdefghidefgh]) &= \{[efghidefgh],[efgh]\} \\ \mathbf{all\_prefix}([ef])([abcdefghidefgh]) &= \{[abcdef],[abcdefghidef]\} \end{aligned}$$

In the next few paragraphs we illustrate some possible query transformations using the **sub_select**$(a?t?^*tg)(L)$ query as an example.

One possible way of expressing the same query in terms of **PL** is:

$$\mathbf{set\_select}(\lambda(l)\, l \in \mathcal{L}(a?t?^*tg))(\mathbf{PL}(L))$$

PL(L) returns all the possible substrings of L. We then use the **select** operator over sets (aliased to **set_select** to avoid any ambiguity) and the list predicate to pick the sub-sequences that match the pattern.

Now suppose we already have an index on all the positions of the symbol a in the sequence L. We could then rewrite the query to take advantage of this information in the following manner:

$$\mathbf{apply}(\lambda(l)\, \mathbf{all\_prefix}(\hat{\ }a?t?^*tg)(l))(\mathbf{all\_suffix}(a)(L))$$

All_suffix takes advantage of the index on the input list L and can therefore be computed very quickly. Also, the result reduces the positions we need to check for a match. So, to obtain the final result we need to check if the lists (in the set of lists obtained by the **all_suffix** operation) start with (denoted by ^) the pattern $\hat{}a?t?^*tg$, using the **all_prefix** operator. **All_prefix** extracts the sub-sequences that are in the language defined by the regular expression $\hat{}a?t?^*tg$. Similarly, if we had an index on tg, we could rewrite the query as:

$$\textbf{apply}(\lambda(l)\,\textbf{all\_suffix}(a?t?^*tg\$)(l))(\textbf{all\_prefix}(tg)(L))$$

In a similar manner, we can rewrite the query to take advantage of indices on both a and tg.

$$\begin{array}{l}\textbf{set\_select}(\lambda(s)\,s \in \mathcal{L}(\hat{}a?t?^*tg\$)) \\ \qquad (\textbf{apply}(\lambda(l)\,\textbf{all\_suffix}(a)(l))(\textbf{all\_prefix}(tg)(L)))\end{array}$$

A slightly more complex strategy can be used if we only have an index for occurrences of t in L. Assume that the list L is split into two lists L_1 and L_2 such that $L_1L_2 = L$ and L_2 starts with t (using the index). So, for each such split we have to check if the query below is non-empty and in such a case, return the matching sublist.

$$\textbf{set\_select}(\lambda(l)\,l \in \mathcal{L}(?^*a?))(L_1) \wedge \textbf{set\_select}(\lambda(l)\,l \in \mathcal{L}(t?^*tg?^*))(L_2)$$

Another interesting case is querying over a set of lists S to check if a particular pattern $a?t?^*tg$ exists in any of the lists. This can be expressed as:

$$\textbf{set\_select}(\lambda(l)\,l \in \mathcal{L}(?^*a?t?^*tg?^*))(S)$$

As in the earlier examples, we can use any indices for query rewrites. If we have an index into the set S indicating the lists that contain the symbol t (or any sub-string of the match pattern), we could rewrite the above query as:

$$\textbf{set\_select}(\lambda(l)\,l \in \mathcal{L}(?^*a?t?^*tg?^*))\;(\textbf{set\_select}(\lambda(s)\,s \in \mathcal{L}(?^*t?^*))(S))$$

The first **set_select** uses the index and as a result reduces the input size for the second **set_select**. We could also use multiple indices in the same way:

$$\begin{array}{l}\textbf{set\_select}(\lambda(l)\,l \in \mathcal{L}(?^*a?t?^*tg?^*)) \\ \qquad (\textbf{set\_select}(\lambda(s)\,s \in \mathcal{L}(?^*t?^*))(S) \cap \\ \qquad \textbf{set\_select}(\lambda(s)\,s \in \mathcal{L}(?^*g?^*))(S))\end{array}$$

6.2 Tree Predicates

Recall that the standard **select** operator is defined to return a set of nodes based on the properties of the contents of those nodes. The **sub_select** operator returns all subtrees of a tree that satisfy a certain property. In other words, **sub_select** takes connectivity and structure into account while **select** does not.

Consider the query "retrieve all the portions of this family tree in which somebody named a is an ancestor of somebody named b". In this case we are searching for any subtree which matches the predicate "somebody named a is an ancestor of somebody named b". In the case of lists, similar conditions can be stated using regular expressions. To extend the standard regular expression notation to trees, we build on the results of [2,11]. The basic notation is the same as that of regular expressions: * for Kleene closure, | for union (disjunction), and $a \circ b$ for "a concatenated with b" (we use ab as a shorthand for $a \circ b$). The only fundamental difference is in the meaning of the concatenation operator. In a regular expression, which always represents a string (i.e., a total ordering), ab simply means that b follows immediately after a. However, a node in a tree may have more than one successor (child).

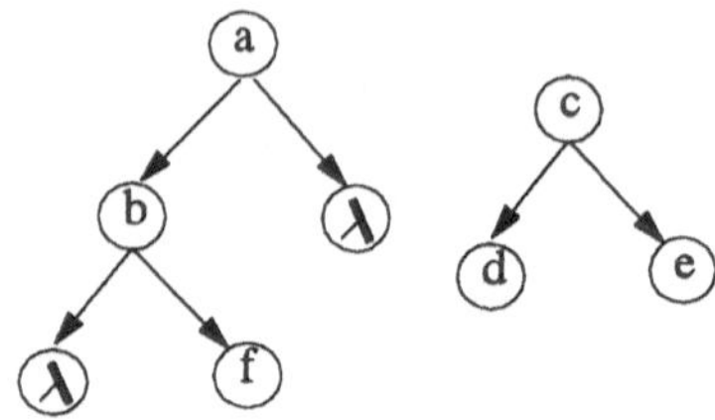

Figure 7: Multiple concatenation points

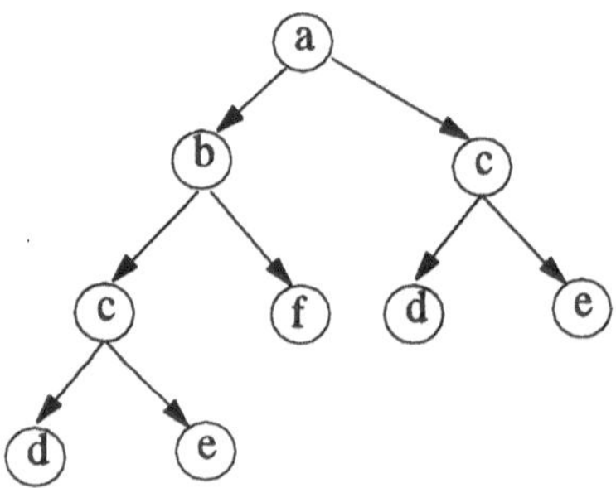

Figure 8: Result of figure 7

To introduce our notation, we must remember that there is a clear distinction between terms that represent trees and terms that represent patterns, just as there is a difference between a regular expression and an actual string. For example, consider the string "*abacdeb*" and the regular expression "b^*de". The regular expression matches the substring "*bacde*" of the first string. As a simple example of our notation, consider the tree (not pattern) represented by "$a\,(b\,c)$". This is a tree with "a" at the root, "b" at the left child, and "c" at the right child. In our notation for trees, a node is followed by "(" then by its children, then by ")". This corresponds to a preorder listing of the nodes. We do not consider unordered trees in this section, although most of the ideas apply there as well.

As another example, consider the tree term T = "$a\,(b\,(d\,e)\,c\,(f\,g))$", representing a full binary tree with three levels. The notation for tree *patterns* extends the simple tree notation in a manner similar to the extension made to strings by regular expressions. In what follows, it should be clear from the context whether a tree or a pattern is being described by a particular term. As a simple example, consider the *pattern* represented by the term "$a\,(b\,c)$". It matches a *subtree* of T which is represented by the term "$a(bc)$". Note that just as in the matching of substrings to regular expressions, we are not interested in what *follows* the matching subtree in T. We are only interested in finding the matching subtree, just as in the above regular expression example we noted that the matching substring is "*bacde*", not "*bacdeb*". The **sub_select** operator is defined to return the matching subtrees, not what follows them (see examples below).

To represent concatenation in a pattern, we use a special symbol to indicate the *concatenation points* – the points in the expression where the second term is to be appended to the first. We first illustrate this graphically and then describe the algebraic notation. In figure 7 we have two trees. The special symbol λ indicates a concatenation point and must appear at the leaves. The concatenation of the left and right trees in figure 7 gives the result in figure 8. Note that λ appears twice in the left tree. The meaning of the concatenation point is that all occurrences of the concatenation point are to be replaced with the tree on the right, giving the result in figure 8.

The union operation on tree patterns is no different from its regular expression counterpart. The Kleene operator * is based on the concatenation of one pattern onto itself, any number of times. Thus it also needs to make use of the notion of concatenation points. As an example, consider a tree with three nodes, a at the root, b at the left child, and λ at the right child, and call it T. Then some of the elements of T^* are shown in figure 9.

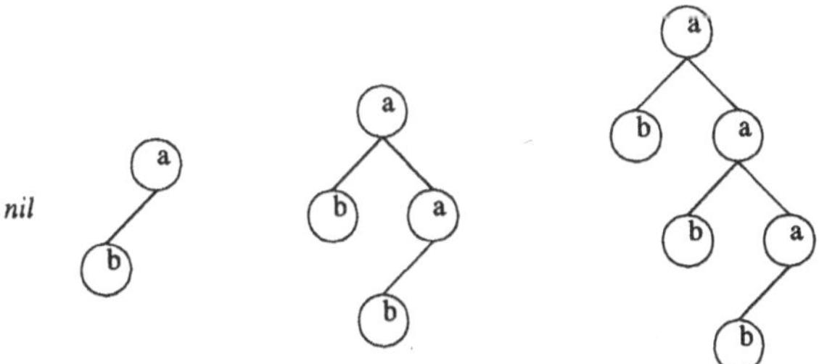

Figure 9: Part of a Kleene closure

We now describe the syntax that will enable us to express these patterns inside an algebraic query. The basic idea is that any concatenation, including one engendered by *, must be given one or more instances of λ as concatenation points. As an example, the concatenation of the trees of figure 7 is described as follows in our syntax, where square brackets are used for grouping:

$$[[a\,(b\,(\lambda\ f\,)\,\lambda)]\ [c\,(d\ e\,)]]$$

Only a node together with all of its children may be the subject of concatenation or *. The trees in figure 9 are a subset of

$$[a\,(b\,\lambda\,)]^*$$

Let us examine a more complicated example of concatenation. Consider the following pattern:

$$[[a\,(\lambda\ \lambda\,)]\ [\,[c|d]\,(e\ f)]]$$

Formally, the result of a concatenation is defined as the set of all trees formed by replacing every λ in every tree matching the first pattern with a tree matching the second pattern. Not every λ need be replaced by the same tree from the second set, but every λ must be replaced by one of them. Figure 10 shows two of the four trees that satisfy the previous pattern.

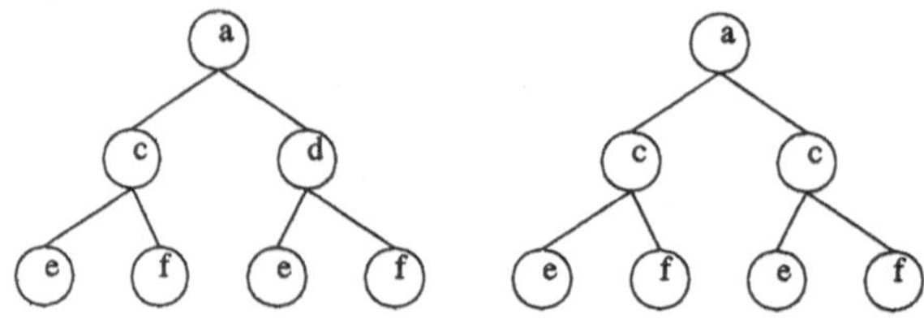

Figure 10: Two concatenations of $[a(\lambda\ \lambda)]\ [[c \mid d](e\ f)]$

The symbol ? indicates that the contents of a node can be anything. Thus a pattern with any value at the root and the values b and c as the left and right children, and no other nodes, would be expressed as

$$[?\ (b\ c\ )]$$

This ? symbol, however, stands only for any possible *contents* of a node, not for any possible subtree. In other words, ? represents a tree with one node, whose contents are unknown. An important special case of tree patterns are those in which we are only interested in the structure of the tree [7], not in the contents of the nodes. The ? symbol makes such patterns easy to express in our notation. To represent the most general tree pattern, which will match any tree at all, we need an analog to the "?*" of regular expressions. We define the symbol $T?$ to stand for any binary tree as follows:

$$T? = [?(\lambda\ \lambda)]^*$$

Now we present some examples of queries that select from some tree T all subtrees matching a given pattern. Recall that **sub_select** returns exactly the subtree(s) matching the pattern, and does not return descendants of those subtrees. As a realistic application, consider a relational query optimizer which represents queries as trees. All operators are unary or binary, and to simplify the presentation we will ignore additional parameters. Given some query tree Q, the following AQUA algebra expression returns all subtrees of Q representing a join whose left input is also a join:

$$\textbf{sub\_select}(join\ (join\ ?))(Q)$$

We do not specify the children of the inputs to the first join because this query is intended to return only the portion of the tree with this structure, not any of its children.

Now consider a query to retrieve all subtrees of Q representing a join whose left input contains a selection somewhere in it:

$$\textbf{sub\_select}(join\ ([[?\ [(\lambda\ ?) \mid (?\ \lambda)]]^*\ select]\ ?))(Q)$$

The disjunction ensures that any subtree containing a selection will match the pattern. Intuitively, it ensures that any number of left and right "turns" leading to a selection will qualify.

In these examples we have been assuming very simple node contents – immutable strings. However, the syntax easily accommodates arbitrarily complex node contents. Any algebraic expression which evaluates to something of the appropriate type can be used to specify the contents of a node inside a tree pattern. It would also be possible to define an extended version of **sub_select** which takes an additional parameter indicating an algebraic expression to be applied to each node. The result of this expression, rather than the actual node, could then be matched against the pattern.

The **sub_select** operator can clearly find all occurrences of any tree pattern inside any tree. However, there are other ways of expressing the same queries. We now use the **PT** and **all_desc** operators to define alternative ways of expressing some queries.

The **PT** (powertree) operator takes a tree T and returns all subtrees of T. The definition of "subtree" is analogous to the definition of "substring". **All_desc** (r) (T) retrieves all subtrees of T which *start with* the pattern r and include all descendants of that occurrence of r.

One motivation for the **all_desc** operator can be illustrated by the following example. Consider the tree T of figure 11 and the query:

$$\textbf{sub\_select}(e\ (a\ b))(T)$$

This query can be rewritten using **all_desc** as follows:

$$\textbf{collapse}(\textbf{apply}(\lambda(s)\ \textbf{sub\_select}(e\ (a\ b))(s))\ (\textbf{all\_desc}(e)(T)))$$

This version of the query first finds all subtrees of T whose root contains simply "e" and whose descendants go as far down T as possible. The query then finds all subtrees of each of these subtrees that have "a" and "b" as the children of "e".

This query might be "cheaper" when we have an index that will return all nodes containing "e". In that case, the **all_desc** operation makes direct use of the index to compute its result. The **sub_select** operations, in this case, will only be examining subtrees with the proper root node. Assuming the situation of figure 11, in which there may be thousands of nodes in the outlined region R, none of which contain "e", the processing time for the query is potentially orders of magnitude faster than in the initial version. Note that the rewriting used above does not always result in a more efficient execution of the query, even if an index is used. For example, if "e" occurred many times in the same large subtree, many copies of parts of that subtree would be returned, resulting in a potentially longer search than with the original **sub_select** query.

Suppose now that we have available an index which provides fast access to all nodes containing "e" that also have "a" as their first child. A similar rewriting of the query can facilitate the use of such an index:

$$\textbf{collapse}(\textbf{apply}(\lambda(s)\ \textbf{sub\_select}(e\ (a\ b))(s))\ (\textbf{all\_desc}(e\ (a\ ?))(T)))$$

In this case, the index is even more restrictive, leaving even less work for the expensive (**sub_select**) portion of the query.

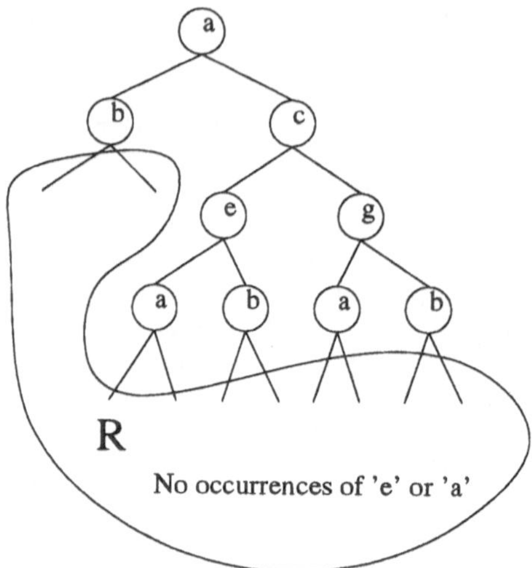

Figure 11: A large tree

AQUA also provides an **all_anc** operator, which travels up the tree in the way that **all_desc** travels down the tree. In other words, **all_anc** (r) (T) will retrieve a set containing all occurrences of r in T alongwith their paths from the root to r. We omit a complete description of **all_anc** here due to space limitations.

7 Conclusions and Future Work

This paper has described the support for ordered bulk data types provided by the AQUA data model and algebra. The primary ordered bulk type is a graph, from which we derive trees and lists by imposing constraints on the edge set. Uniqueness of tree and list nodes is enforced using the *Cell* type constructor. Important aspects of AQUA's ordered bulk type support are the consistency of operators and semantics among the various ordered types and the close relationship between graphs and sets, resulting in a very uniform data model.

We have further described a simple predicate language for lists and trees that supports queries that depend on order. This formalism is based on regular expressions, but could be extended to more expressive pattern languages such as context-free grammars.

Current and future research includes investigation of additional operators on ordered bulk types (e.g. LFP, as described in [9]) and implementation techniques for indexing over ordered bulk types. We are presently looking at ways to extend our tree pattern language to work with DAGs. Indexable ordered types in AQUA (such as N-dimensional arrays) will be discussed in a future paper.

Acknowledgments

We would like to thank Catriel Beeri, Gail Mitchell, Arnold Rosenberg, and Sairam Subramanian for useful discussions.

References

[1] Catriel Beeri and Yoram Kornatzky, "Algebraic Optimization of Object-Oriented Query Languages," *Proceedings of the International Conference on Database Theory* (1990), 72–83.

[2] John Doner, "Tree Acceptors and Some of their Applications," *Journal of Computer and System Sciences* 4 (1970), 406–451.

[3] James C. French, Anita K. Jones, and John L. Pfaltz, "Summary of the Final Report of the NSF Workshop on Scientific Database Mgmt.," *SIGMOD Record* 19 (1990), 32–40.

[4] Karen A. Frenkel, "The Human Genome Project and Informatics," *Communications of the ACM* 34 (1991), 41–51.

[5] Seymour Ginsburg and Xiaoyang Wang, "Pattern Matching by Rs-Operations: Towards a Unified Approach to Querying Sequenced Data," *Proceedings of the 11th ACM Principles of Database Systems* (1992), 293–300.

[6] Ralf Harmut Güting, Roberto Zicari, and David M. Choy, "An Algebra for Structured Office Documents," *ACM Transactions on Office Information Systems* 7 (1989), 123–157.

[7] R. Karp, R. Miller, and A. Rosenberg, "Rapid Identification of Repeated Patterns in Strings, Trees, and Arrays," *Proc. 4th Annual ACM Symposium on Theory of Computing* (1972), 125–136.

[8] Eric S. Lander, Robert Langridge, and Damien M. Saccocio, "Mapping and Interpreting Biological Information," *Communications of the ACM* 34 (1991), 33–39.

[9] Theodore W. Leung, Gail Mitchell, Bharathi Subramanian, Bennet Vance, Scott L. Vandenberg, and Stanley B. Zdonik, "The AQUA Data Model and Algebra," *Proc. 4th Intl. Workshop on Database Programming Languages* (1993).

[10] Joel Richardson, "Supporting Lists in a Data Model (A Timely Approach)," *Proceedings of the 18th VLDB Conference* (1992).

[11] J. W. Thatcher and J. B. Wright, "Generalized Finite Automata Theory with an Application to a Decision Problem of Second-Order Logic," *Mathematical Systems Theory* 2 (1968), 57–81.

[12] Scott L. Vandenberg and David J. DeWitt, "Algebraic Support for Complex Objects with Arrays, Identity, and Inheritance," *SIGMOD Proceedings* (1991), 158–167.

A Functional Object Database Language

Christian Laasch, Marc H. Scholl
Faculty of Computer Science, Databases and Information Systems
University of Ulm, D 89069 Ulm, Germany
e-mail: {laasch, scholl}@informatik.uni-ulm.de

Abstract

The language BCOOL is formally defined using a denotational semantics approach. BCOOL is a functional object database language with a very flexible, yet strong and statically checked, type system. Its main source of flexibility is its support for object evolution, that is, dynamic type changes of existing objects. Originally, BCOOL was used as a formal basis for a more traditional (relational algebra-style) database language, COOL. In this paper, though, BCOOL is presented on its own. The purpose being to compare with other functional languages and discuss the virtues and limitations that BCOOL and these functional languages have w.r.t. each other in terms of (i) the above-mentioned flexibility in the type system, which we consider essential for *objects* and (ii) the orthogonality of the language.

1 Introduction

COOL is an object database query language developed in the COCOON project [20, 21]. In a nutshell, COOL is an object-flavored extension of a (nested) relational algebra. The object flavor is established by the inclusion of concepts such as abstract object types, functions (methods), type hierarchies, and classes. The effects of the algebraic query operators are pretty similar to their relational counterparts, except for the fact that they have to take into account that they now work with objects with an identity (which led to the notion of object-preserving queries) and with a much richer type/class system that requires typing (and classification) of query results. Informal presentations of COCOON and the COOL language have been given earlier [19, 21]. A formalization of COCOON and COOL using BCOOL was developed in [20].

In this paper, we discuss the functional object language BCOOL in detail. We present the formal semantics of query and update operations using a denotational approach. In contrast to [17] and [10], which also propose operations for object evolution, we also analyze the impact of dynamic type changes on the type system. Further, we compare our approach with functional database languages. While these typically offer more flexibility w.r.t. orthogonality and genericity of the type system, BCOOL provides objects and object evolution (i.e., dynamic type changes). Adding any of these extra capabilities to the other language, brings them close together. We show how this can be achieved and what the consequences are.

For this purpose, BCOOL serves as a formal basis for the integration of functional (database) languages supporting polymorphism, static type inferencing, and orthogonality (e.g., as in Machiavelli [16] or FAD [5]) with object-oriented data models including objects with subtyping and flexible update facilities (e.g., as in Iris [27], Melampus [17], or COCOON [12]). The key objectives are:

- an extension of the relational algebra to an object query language. We started from relational algebra in order to preserve the potential for and knowledge on query optimization.
- static type-checking that allows for early error detection and reduction of run-time effort.
- update operations that allow object evolution such that objects are not only added to and removed from collections ("classes"), but can also change their types dynamically.
- extensibility of the set of type constructors such that the model can be tailored to requirements of new applications.

In this paper, the main focus is on the type system; we define subtyping and the impact of object evolution on static-type checking. After introducing the syntax in Section 2, we define the semantics of types, the type inference rules for expressions, and the impact of object evolution operations in Section 3. We formalize the model by using a denotational semantics approach [24], in which the semantics of language elements (i.e., types, expressions, and updates) are defined by "denotation functions" that return elements of the "semantic domain". In Section 4 we further analyze the commonalities and differences between object database and pure functional languages by discussing extensions of both that narrow the gap between them. On the one hand, we sketch how to extend BCOOL to become fully orthogonal and include genericity, on the other hand, we discuss the integration of objects with their respective operations into Machiavelli as one well-known functional (database) language.

2 BCOOL Model: Concepts and Syntax

Initially, BCOOL was developed as a formal model for the definition of COOL, which has a number of concepts, such as predicative specification of collections (called classes) that can be derived from more basic constructs provided in BCOOL. Hereinafter we will focus on the essentials of the formal language BCOOL and sometimes use the more syntactically sugared COOL syntax for illustration only.

BCOOL consists of only the few following concepts, which can also be found in (almost) all object-oriented models:

Types can be basic or constructed. *Basic types* describe (pairwise) disjoint sets of instances. Besides concrete (or *printable* [11]) types describing **data**, or values, (such as integers, boolean, strings), there is a basic type denoting **objects**, on which *object types* can be defined by subtyping (see below). Objects are fully encapsulated. They can be used and manipulated only by means of their interface, a set of functions. *Constructed types* can be specified using the build-in type constructors set ({ }) and function (→).[1]

Types serve several purposes: (i) they represent a "repository" of possible values (this will be called the *domain* of the type below, an intensional notion of type); (ii) they are used by the compiler for type checking (i.e., assuring that only "(type) valid" expressions are ever executed. For example, we would not allow to compute the square root of a string. Finally, (iii) types are often also used as containers (collections) for those values of that type, which are currently "in use" in the database (an extensional notion). Notice that we do *not* use this aspect of types in general, but only for *object* types (where this will be called the "active domain" of the type).

Subtyping is used to describe (sub)-sets of objects with common interfaces, such that type-checking becomes more meaningful. The COOL definition of a subtype consists of three parts: a set of supertypes, a set of local functions, and (possibly) a type name. Any instance of the subtype is also an instance of its supertypes (*substitutability*), and all functions defined on the supertypes are applicable to the instances of the subtype (*inheritance of the interface*), in addition to the locally defined functions.

As a running example let us consider persons and employees defined by the COOL definitions:

type *Pers* **isa** *Object* = *name* : **string**,
age : **integer**,
children : **set of** *Pers*;
type *Empl* **isa** *Pers* = *sal* : **integer**,
manager : *Mngr*;
type *Mngr* **isa** *Empl* = *budget* : **integer**;

The functions *name, age,* and the set-valued function *children* are applicable to instances of *Pers*, which is a subtype of the predefined type *Object*, which has no user-defined functions. Because *Empl* is a subtype of *Pers*, the functions of *Pers* are inherited by *Empl*, such that *name, age, children, sal,* and *manager* can be applied to *Empl*'s instances. Similarly, the function *budget* can be applied to managers (the instances of *Mngr*) in addition to the *Empl*'s functions. [2]

On the (formal) BCOOL level, however, we omit the names of object types. Instead, object types are identified by the set of applicable functions. Syntactically, *Pers* is referred to as $[name, age, children]$ and *Empl* as $[name, age, children, sal]$. Thus, the syntax of BCOOL type expressions can be described by the following list:

$$
\begin{array}{rll}
\tau = & (\tau) & /*\ \text{types}\ */ \\
 & \mid \beta_{Int} & /*\ \text{INTEGER}\ */ \\
 & \mid \beta_{Bool} & /*\ \text{BOOLEAN}\ */ \\
 & \vdots & \\
 & \mid \beta_{Object} & /*\ \text{Objects}\ */ \\
 & \mid [f_1, ..., f_n] & /*\ \text{object types}\ */ \\
 & \mid \{\tau\} & /*\ \text{set types}\ */ \\
 & \mid \beta_{Object} \rightarrow \tau & /*\ \text{function types}\ */
\end{array}
$$

[1] In Sec. 4 we discuss how to integrate additional type constructors.

[2] Range restrictions of functions within subtypes are regarded as different functions by unique function names that are prefixed by the COOL type name similar to C++.

Functions (denoted by the meta-variable f) are described by a unique name and a signature. We can distinguish retrieval (stored or computed) and update functions. Generic update operations can only be used for stored retrieval functions, which are uniform abstractions of "attributes" and "relationships" of classical data models. Direct updates of computed functions require type-specific methods, whereas indirect updates (i.e., updates to values used in the derivation) are automatically propagated.

Because of the desired flexibility (e.g., in case of projections), the domain of a function is not the COOL type on which the function is defined, but the (usually unnamed) object type on whose instances only the function itself is applicable. For example, the function *name* might typically be introduced in a type $Pers = [name, age, children]$. Formally, however, we use "$[name] \rightarrow$ **string**" as the signature of *name*. The reason for this is the semantics of object types, which allows to apply the *name* function not only to persons, but also, more generally, to objects that are contained in the active domain of the type $[name]$. Thus, it becomes possible that, e.g., the *children* function can be hidden by projecting only the *name* and *age* of persons. In other words, the substitutability of typed expressions is adapted to unnamed typed, such that not only specializations of types can be created, but also generalizations. Consequently, object types are arranged into a lattice (see Sec. 3.1).

Variables (denoted by x) are used as temporary names ("handles") for instances of any type (e.g., data values, objects, sets, or functions). They have to be declared with their type in the database language, for compile-time type checking.

Query Language. The query language on objects is an extension of a (nested) relational algebra [18] with *object-preserving* semantics. It contains a selection (**select**), a projection (**project**), and the set operations ($\cup$, $\cap$). Instead of join we use a macro mechanism known from functional languages (**let**) that allows to define additional (virtual) functions mapping objects onto their join partners. An informal presentation and rationale for this query language was given in [21]. Additionally, we provide the following constructors for building expressions and make use of the standard operations for integers (e.g., + and −), boolean (e.g., $\wedge$, $\vee$, and $\neg$), and comparisons (e.g., =) that are not mentioned here any further:

e	=	$(\ e\ )$	/* expressions */
		$\mid c$	/* constants */
		$\mid x$	/* variables */
		$\mid$ **new** ()	/* creating objects */
		$\mid$ **adom** $([f_1, ..., f_n])$	/* active domains */
		$\mid \lambda x : \tau .\ e$	/* function expression */
		$\mid f\ (e)$	/* function applications */
		$\mid \{\ e\ \}$	/* sets */
		$\mid$ **pick** (e)	/* pick one element of a set */
		$\mid e_1 \in e_2$	/* test for set-membership */
		$\mid e \cup e$	/* unions */
		$\mid e \cap e$	/* intersections */
		$\mid$ **select** $[\lambda x.e]\ (e)$	/* selections */
		$\mid$ **project** $[f_1, ..., f_n]\ (e)$	/* projections */
		$\mid$ **let** $f = e$ **in** e **end**	/* joins */

Update Operations. In order to change the state of a database, assignments (:= and **set**) are provided to set the values of variables and functions. Additional operations allow for object evolution: objects can be created, deleted, and can change their types dynamically.

$u =$ (u) /* updates */
| $x := e$ /* setting variables */
| **set** $[f := e](e)$ /* setting function values */
| **new** () /* creating objects */
| **gain** $[f_1, ..., f_n](e)$ /* adding functions to objects */
| **lose** $[f_1, ..., f_n](e)$ /* removing functions from objects */
| **destroy** (e) /* deleting objects */

The motivation for dynamic type changes is the longevity of objects. In contrast to programs, where data are valid only until the end of program, information stored in databases is usually valid over a couple of years, such that the "role" of objects might change. For example, if an object created with the type *Pers* is hired by a company, the type of this object must be changed to the type *Empl* in order to make functions *sal* and *manager* applicable, while still talking about the identical object. In case that this employee is fired, the functions that are applicable to employees, but not to persons, must not be applied anymore; i.e., the instance relationship between the object and the type *Empl* has to be removed.

However, there is a problem in combining dynamic type changes with (static) type-checking. Considering the above example, let us assume that the variable p of type *Pers* denotes a person that is to be hired. Of course, using p in **set** $[sal := \ldots](p)$ should cause a type error, because the *sal* function is not defined on the type *Pers*. Instead, we would use the COOL operation **gain** $[Empl](p)$ that makes the person instance of the type *Empl* such that the salary can be assigned. Notice, however, that we have to cope with undefined function values, if there is no mechanism for default values associated with type changes. In this paper, we only point out where and how to integrate such a mechanism, but leave the actual integration as future work.

As usual in object models, more complex updates can be performed by methods as combinations of the above operations. Again, we do not propose a full method language here, but only employ the two most basic constructs: besides sequencing, the iterator **apply_to_all** provides set-oriented application of update sequences with deterministic semantics [13]:

$u =$ u ; u /* composition of updates */
| **apply_to_all** $[u](e)$ /* set-oriented application of updates */

3 Semantics of BCOOL

In the denotational approach, the semantics of a language is defined by (higher order) functions [24]. A "semantic domain" represents interpreted constructs used as the "denotation" (semantics) of syntactic constructs. For each syntactic construct, such as constants, expressions and statements, a function is given that maps syntax to semantics. In particular, for updates the target of this denotation function is again a function (from an old to a new state).

- The state function σ represents the current database state. It captures the following information: (i) the current instances for each object type (the active domains), (ii) the values of all possible function applications (F denotes the set of functions defined in the schema below), and (iii) the values of all variables (X denotes the set of variables defined in the schema, which is a superset of F, because functions are regarded as variables over function types).

- The typing function A is used to represent the type declarations of variables and functions: for example, $A(x)$ returns the type expression τ for a variable declaration **var** $x : \tau$.

- The domain function $[\![\ ]\!]$ returns the semantics (the domains) of type expressions τ (see Sec. 3.1).

- The expression function $E[\![\ ]\!]$ returns the value of expressions in the current state σ (see Sec. 3.2).

- The update function $U[\![\ ]\!]$ turns the state functions for update expressions (see Sec. 3.3).

3.1 Semantics of Type Expressions, Subtyping

The semantic domain of values is defined by the following recursive domain equations:

$$\mathcal{V} = \mathcal{B}_{Bool} \cup \mathcal{B}_{Int} \cup \mathcal{B}_{String} \cup \mathcal{B}_{Object} \cup \mathcal{F} \cup \mathcal{S}$$
$$\mathcal{B}_{Bool} = \{\bot_{Bool}, true, false\},$$
$$\mathcal{B}_{Int} = \{\bot_{Int}, 0, 1, -1, 2 ...\},$$
$$\mathcal{B}_{String} = \{\bot_{String}, "a", "A", ...\},$$
$\mathcal{B}_{Object}$ contains countably infinite objects,
$$\mathcal{F} = \mathcal{B}_{Object} \rightarrow_{fin} \mathcal{V},$$
$$\mathcal{S} = P_{fin}(\mathcal{V}).$$

$\mathcal{B}_i$ are domains of basic values (e.g., boolean and integer). $\mathcal{F}$ denotes the domain of finite mappings from $\mathcal{B}_{Object}$ to $\mathcal{V}$, and $\mathcal{S}$ all finite powersets over $\mathcal{V}$. The type specific bottom elements ($\bot_i$) denote undefined values. In order to improve readability we omit the type information and use $\bot$ instead.

In general, equality must be defined for types on which sets are constructed (e.g., for testing set-membership). Because the equality for function types is undecidable in general, the domains of function types are restricted to objects. The equality on these restricted functions would be still undecidable, because the domain $\mathcal{B}_{Object}$ is infinite. However, since all instances of functions that can ever occur in any database state are restricted to the *active domains* of the corresponding object types (which are *finite* sets), all functions can be regarded as finite sets of pairs, such that equality is decidable. Hence, we do not need to separate types with equality from those without equality, which would be necessary otherwise.

3.1.1 Basic and Constructed Types

Except for object types, our semantics of types and subtyping is quite usual and follows [3, 4, 14]: i.e., the denotations of basic types are given by the following equations:

Definition Semantic Domain:

$$[\![\beta_i]\!] = \mathcal{B}_i, \text{ in case that } \mathcal{B}_i \text{ is a summand of } \mathcal{V}$$
$$[\![\{\ \tau\ \}]\!] = \{x \in \mathcal{S} \mid x \subseteq [\![\tau]\!]\} \in \mathcal{V}$$
$$[\![\tau_1 \rightarrow \tau_2]\!] = \{f \in \mathcal{F} \mid x \in [\![\tau_1]\!] \Longrightarrow f(x) \in [\![\tau_2]\!]\} \in \mathcal{V}.$$

The subtype relationship ($\preceq$) is based on set inclusion: i.e., if a type is defined as a subtype of another, then every instance of the subtype is also an instance of its supertype (which allows *substitutability*): $\tau_1 \preceq \tau_2 \Longrightarrow [\![\tau_1]\!] \subseteq [\![\tau_2]\!]$. This leads to the following inference rules for constructed types:[3]

Definition Subtyping:

$$[\text{SETS}]\ \frac{\tau_1 \preceq \tau_2}{\{\tau_1\} \preceq \{\tau_2\}} \qquad [\text{FUNS}]\ \frac{\tau_1^{dom} \preceq \tau_2^{dom},\ \tau_2^{rng} \preceq \tau_1^{rng}}{\tau_2^{dom} \rightarrow \tau_2^{rng} \preceq \tau_1^{dom} \rightarrow \tau_1^{rng}}$$

3.1.2 Object Types

Let us now focus on the semantics of object types. In Section 3.1 we argued to use the basic type $\mathcal{B}_{Object}$ as the domain of all functions, such that function signatures are homogeneous. Then, however, type-checking is less meaningful, because each function may be applied to any object. The more specific function domains are, the more errors are detected at compile-time. Therefore, we use subtypes $[f_1, ..., f_n]$ of $\mathcal{B}_{Object}$. In particular, there is a object type $[f_1, ..., f_n]$ for any subset of F that contains the functions defined in a database schema. In order to get concise type inference rules in Section 3.2, the object types are arranged to a lattice. Intuitively, applications of the function f on instances of $[f_1, ..., f_n]$ pass static type-checking, iff f is contained in $\{f_1, ..., f_n\}$.

Nonetheless, the *semantic domains* of all object types are the same, in order to allow for object evolution, such that objects can gain and lose instance relationships dynamically.

In contrast to instances of data types like integers, objects can be created and deleted. That is, it is not possible to refer to arbitrary instances of object types, rather only to those that have been created and not yet deleted. Therefore, the domains of object types (denoted by $[\![[f_1, ..., f_n]]\!]$) have to be distinguished from the *active domains* (denoted by $\sigma([f_1, ..., f_n])$) that contain the instances of these types in the current state σ.

Thus, we use the state function in order to refer to active domains already in this section, though its definition is given in Section 3.3 by the semantics of operations that manipulate the active domain. This is done, because the notion of active domains is not only important for the restriction of function types (as discussed above), but also for the definition of subtyping on object types. Notice that only the active domains of the type without functions ($[\,]$) and the types with only one function ($[f_i]$) are explicitly maintained. The other

[3]The horizontal bar corresponds to logical implication. Notice the antimonotonicity (contra-variance) in [FUNS], which is needed for the set-inclusion semantics of the subtype relationship.

active domains (of types with more functions $[f_i, f_j, \ldots]$) are derived from the former according to the type lattice (see below).

There are two requirements for the definition of the active domains:

- the active domain has to be a subset of the domain in any state: [4] $\sigma([f_1, \ldots, f_n]) \subset [\![[f_1, \ldots, f_n]]\!]$.
- the subtype relationship has to capture the substitutability of objects: $[f_1, \ldots, f_n] \preceq [f'_1, \ldots, f'_m] \implies \sigma([f_1, \ldots, f_n]) \subseteq \sigma([f'_1, \ldots, f'_m])$

The second requirement adapts the usual notion for subtyping to object types, which implies a subset relationship on the respective domains (see above). In particular, this adaptation is important, because the domains of object types have to be the same in order to allow for object evolution.

After this motivation of object types, let us now define the semantic domains and subtyping for object types.

Definition Semantic Domains:

$[\![[f_1, \ldots, f_n]]\!] = [\![[\,]]\!] = B_{Object}$, for $\{f_1, \ldots, f_n\} \subseteq F$.

The subtype relationship between object types is defined on the superset relationship between their function sets, as follows:[5]

Definition Subtyping:

$[f_1, \ldots, f_n] \preceq [f'_1, \ldots, f'_m] \iff \{f_1, \ldots, f_n\} \supseteq \{f'_1, \ldots, f'_m\}$.

In order to make type-inference more concise, object types are arranged in a lattice:

Definition Object Type Lattice:

The set of object types forms a lattice, where the subtype relationship is the partial order. The least upper bound ($\sqcup$), and the greatest lower bound ($\sqcap$) are defined as follows:

$$\begin{aligned}
[f_1, \ldots, f_n] \sqcup [f'_1, \ldots, f'_m] &= [f''_1, \ldots, f''_l], \\
\text{where } \{f''_1, \ldots, f''_l\} &= \{f_1, \ldots, f_n\} \cap \{f'_1, \ldots, f'_m\}. \\
[f_1, \ldots, f_n] \sqcap [f'_1, \ldots, f'_m] &= [f''_1, \ldots, f''_l], \\
\text{where } \{f''_1, \ldots, f''_l\} &= \{f_1, \ldots, f_n\} \cup \{f'_1, \ldots, f'_m\}.
\end{aligned}$$

Finally, let us define the active domains of object types containing more than one function dependent on the types with exactly one function. (The active domains of object types with none or one function are defined in Section 3.3).

Definition Active Domains $[f_1, \ldots, f_n]$ (for $n \geq 2$):

$$\sigma([f_1, \ldots, f_n]) = \bigcap_{f \in \{f_1, \ldots, f_n\}} \sigma([f]).$$

Notice that this definition guarantees the subset relationship between the active domains of a subtype and its supertypes (see the second requirement for active domains above), because of the superset relationship between their function sets:

$$[f_1, \ldots, f_n] \preceq [f'_1, \ldots, f'_m] \implies \{f_1, \ldots, f_n\} \supseteq \{f'_1, \ldots, f'_m\}$$
$$\implies \sigma([f_1, \ldots, f_n]) \subseteq \sigma([f'_1, \ldots, f'_m]).$$

[4] Because all active domains are finite sets, the subset relationship is always proper.

[5] Notice that this definition captures inheritance of interfaces in the usual way.

3.2 Semantics of Expressions

In this section, we define the type inference rules and the semantics of expressions. First, expressions are reduced to syntactically correct ones by type inference rules. Secondly, the semantics of expressions is defined by the denotation function E, that returns the value $E[\![e]\!]_\sigma$, which is an element of a component of the semantic domain $\mathcal{V}$, by evaluating the expression e in the current state σ.

In order to improve readability, we often simplify the notation of type inference rules by omitting the assertions of variable declarations (included in the typing function A) and subtyping information, which are part of the premisses. Similarly, we simplify the semantic denotations by leaving out preconditions and result types that are covered by type inference rules, and omit the current state σ in cases where it is only used as an input parameter of the function E. Additionally, we use the domains instead of the active domains in the denotations. Notice, however, that the semantics of update operations guarantees that values are restricted to the active domains.[6]

Constants and Variables:

$$c :: \tau \qquad\qquad E[\![c]\!] = C, \text{ where } C \text{ is a constant} \in [\![\tau]\!].$$

$$\frac{A(x) = \tau}{x :: \tau} \qquad\qquad E[\![x]\!]_\sigma = \sigma(x) \in [\![\tau]\!].$$

New creates new objects. That is, the application of the operation **new** yields an object that does not yet occur in the current state of the database. Formally, the "invention" of objects is non-deterministic, such that $E[\![\ ]\!]$ is a mapping rather than a function (as claimed above). This non-determinism could be eliminated, for example, by assuming an order on objects (such that **new** yields the "smallest" not yet created object). However, since the object identities are not visible on the BCOOL level, we do not need to care about different states that are isomorphic up to renaming object identities (see the notion of O-isomorphisms in [2]). Therefore, we take the freedom to allow the non-deterministic invention of object identities: This is certainly desirable on the implementation level, furthermore it allows **new** operations to be executed in parallel within an **apply_to_all** statement [13].

$$\mathbf{new}\,() :: \beta_{Object} \qquad\qquad E[\![\mathbf{new}\,()]\!]_\sigma = o \ \mathbf{with}\ o \in [\![[\,]]\!] \wedge o \notin \sigma([\,]).$$

Active domains of object types are returned by the operation **adom**:

$$\frac{[f_1, \ldots, f_n] \preceq \beta_{Object}}{\mathbf{adom}\,([f_1, \ldots, f_n]) :: \{[f_1, \ldots, f_n]\}} \qquad E[\![\mathbf{adom}\,([f_1, \ldots, f_n])]\!]_\sigma = \sigma([f_1, \ldots, f_n]).$$

Lambda abstractions define functions on the active domains of object types, where $\sigma' = \sigma\{v/x\}$ denotes the substitution of v for x, i.e., it is identical to σ except that $\sigma'(x) = v$. This form of abstractions does not cause problems w.r.t. to the equality test on functions, because the free variable x is restricted to the active domain of the respective object type. Thus, functions can be regarded as

[6] In particular, this is also true for values constructed on object types such as sets of persons.

finite sets of pairs[7]. The type inference rule means that $e :: \tau_2$ can be inferred under the assumption that x is a variable of the object type τ_1:

$$\frac{A(x) = \tau_1, \tau_1 \preceq \beta_{Object} \vdash e :: \tau_2}{\lambda x : \tau_1.e :: \tau_1 \rightarrow \tau_2} \quad E[\![\lambda x : \tau_1.e]\!]_\sigma = \{\langle v, E[\![e_{\{v/x\}}]\!]\rangle \mid v \in \sigma(\tau_1)\}.$$

Function applications return the function value if defined. Notice that there is no difference whether a tuple with the null value ($\perp$) as second component is included in the set of function tuples or not:

$$\frac{f :: \tau_1 \rightarrow \tau_2,\ e :: \tau_1}{f(e) :: \tau_2} \qquad E[\![f\ (e)]\!] = \begin{cases} v & \text{if } \langle E[\![e]\!], v\rangle \in E[\![f]\!], \\ \perp & \text{otherwise.} \end{cases}$$

Sets can be constructed by including an expression in braces:

$$\frac{e :: \tau}{\{e\} :: \{\tau\}} \qquad E[\![\{\ e\ \}]\!] = \{E[\![e]\!]\}.$$

Pick is used to deconstruct sets, i.e., to get rid of the braces in case of singleton sets. Notice that **pick** is not deterministic in case of sets with more than one element. In order to avoid a non-deterministic semantics in case that the set contains more than one object, we could restrict the applicability (which, however, can only be checked at run-time) or assume an order on objects (see above).

$$\frac{e :: \{\tau\}}{\mathbf{pick}\,(e) :: \tau} \qquad E[\![\mathbf{pick}\,(e)]\!] = \begin{cases} v \in E[\![e]\!] & \text{if } E[\![e]\!] \neq \emptyset, \\ \perp & \text{otherwise.} \end{cases}$$

Set membership can be tested by the predicate $\in$:

$$\frac{e_1 :: \tau, e_2 :: \{\tau\}}{e_1 \in e_2 :: \mathbf{bool}} \qquad E[\![e_1 \in e_2]\!] = \begin{cases} \mathit{true} & \text{if } E[\![e_1]\!] \in E[\![e_2]\!], \\ \mathit{false} & \text{otherwise.} \end{cases}$$

Unions of two sets result in a set that is associated to the least upper bound of the element types:

$$\frac{e_1 :: \{[f_1, ..., f_n]\},\ e_2 :: \{[f'_1, ..., f'_m]\}}{e_1 \cup e_2 :: \{[f_1, ..., f_n] \sqcup [f'_1, ..., f'_m]\}} \qquad E[\![e_1 \cup e_2]\!] = E[\![e_1]\!] \cup E[\![e_2]\!].$$

Intersections of two sets are related to the greatest lower bound of the element types:

$$\frac{e_1 :: \{[f_1, ..., f_n]\},\ e_2 :: \{[f'_1, ..., f'_m]\}}{e_1 \cap e_2 :: \{[f_1, ..., f_n] \sqcap [f'_1, ..., f'_m]\}} \qquad E[\![e_1 \cap e_2]\!] = E[\![e_1]\!] \cap E[\![e_2]\!].$$

Selections are used to specify subsets of e_2 according to the predicate $\lambda x.e_1$. Notice that this is a restricted case of lambda abstractions, because the free variable x, which may occur in e_1, ranges over the elements in e_2: [8]

[7] One might argue that functions are total, because they yield the $\perp$ value except for a finite set of arguments. Notice, however, that there is no means to refer to instances of β_{Object} that are not contained in the active domain.

[8] Notice that differences between sets can be expressed by a selection predicate that checks whether an object is not contained in a set.

$$\frac{\lambda x : \tau.e_1 :: \tau \rightarrow \mathbf{bool}, e_2 :: \{\tau\}}{\mathbf{select}[\lambda x.e_1](e_2) :: \{\tau\}} \quad E[\![\mathbf{select}[\lambda x.e_1](e_2)]\!] = \{v \in E[\![e_2]\!] \mid E[\![e_{1\{v/x\}}]\!]\}.$$

Projections restrict the interfaces of set elements as in the relational algebra (see also transformational filters in [1]). In contrast to projections in [9, 23, 25] that generate objects or values, **project** is defined with object preserving semantics [21]. Therefore, it can be used for hiding information, similar to assignments of instances to variables of a supertype:

$$\frac{e :: \{[f_1', ..., f_m']\},\ [f_1', ..., f_m'] \preceq [f_1, ..., f_n]}{\mathbf{project}\,[f_1, ..., f_n]\,(e) :: \{[f_1, ..., f_n]\}} \quad E[\![\mathbf{project}\,[f_1, ..., f_n]\,(e)]\!] = E[\![e]\!].$$

Qualified Expressions allow for a macro mechanism, such that the expression e_2 can be substituted in e_1 by f. In particular, this macro mechanism can be used, for example, to express joins by virtual functions:[9]

$$\frac{e_2 :: \tau_2, A(f) = \tau_2 \vdash e_1 :: \tau_1}{\mathbf{let}\ f = e_2\ \mathbf{in}\ e_1\ \mathbf{end} :: \tau_1} \quad E[\![\mathbf{let}\ f = e_2\ \mathbf{in}\ e_1\ \mathbf{end}\,]\!]_\sigma = E[\![e_{1\{e_2/f\}}]\!].$$

Usually, operations of an algebra are orthogonal to each other, such that non of them can be defined by the others. However, up to now the operation **project** can be defined by other operations as follows:

$$\mathbf{project}\,[f_1, ..., f_n](e) \equiv \mathbf{select}\,[\lambda x.x \in e](\mathbf{adom}\,([f_1, ..., f_n]))$$

The reason for this lack of orthogonality is that casting the interface of objects has been bundled together with set-orientation. The extension of the relational algebra with object types (that are arranged in a lattice) needs active domains. These can be used together with operations like $\cap$ and $\cup$ that are defined with respect to the type lattice. Therefore type inference is more powerful than in relational algebra, in which set operations require the same schema on the input relations. That is, the problem originates from the extension of the relational algebra, in which operations are defined on sets, because of the potential for optimization. However, if not only sets but also other type constructors are integrated into the model, **project** is decoupled from sets, such that it only casts the type of a single object (see Sec. 4.1).

Examples: Finally, let us illustrate how joins can be expressed in BCOOL by the following two examples. In the first example, we are looking for employees that are managed by their parents. In order to improve readability, we use COOL type names (such as *Empl*) instead of the respective BCOOL function sets ($[name, age, children, sal, manager]$). In the relational algebra this query would involve the join operation (if the schema fulfills at least third normal form). However, in object algebras composition of functions can be explored:

$$\mathbf{select}\,[\lambda x.x \in children(manager(x))](\mathbf{adom}\,(Empl)).$$

In the second example we make use of a virtual function for a more complex join.[10] All employees that have the same manager as x are collected in the

[9] The type inference rule means that $e_1 :: \tau_1$ can be inferred under the assumption that f is a variable of type τ_2.

[10] See [21] for a discussion of different alternatives for joins: symmetric tuple/object generating; asymmetric as functions.

function *colleagues*, whose scope is limited by the **let** operation. If we are interested in all employees who have at least one colleague, the virtual function *colleagues* can be used in the subsequent selection:

$$\textbf{let}\ colleagues = \lambda x : [manager].\ \textbf{select}\ [\lambda y.\ manager(y) = manager(x) \wedge x \neq y](\textbf{adom}\ (Empl))$$
$$\textbf{in}\ \textbf{select}\ [\lambda x.\ colleagues(x) \neq \emptyset](\textbf{adom}\ (Empl))\ \textbf{end}.$$

3.3 Semantics of Update Operations

Update operations are defined by a function U that maps the old state σ onto the new one: $U[\![\, upd\text{-}op \,]\!]_\sigma$. The definitions require that certain typing restrictions are fulfilled, which are notated as preconditions. Since these preconditions can be verified by the static type-checker already at compile-time, only update statements that fulfill the restrictions are executed. In the COCOON model the semantics of update operations is defined w.r.t. model inherent constraints (e.g., sub-/typing, class membership, and class predicates) [12]. That is, applying an update operation to a consistent database state returns a consistent state. Similarly, the update operations of BCOOL are defined w.r.t. typing and subtyping constraints. For example, if an object is deleted, "dangling references" are avoided, and removing or adding instance relationships is propagated to subtypes or supertypes, respectively.

Assignment. Variables can be bound to new values by an assignment (:=). The new state is the same as the old one for all variables, types, and functions except for the variable x. The precondition ensures the substitutability of x's value (ϕ ranges over variables, functions, and object types):

Precondition: $x \in X$ and $e :: \tau$ and $\tau \preceq A(x)$.

$$U[\![\, x := e \,]\!]_\sigma(\phi) = \begin{cases} E[\![\, e \,]\!]_\sigma & \text{if } \phi = x, \\ \sigma(\phi) & \text{otherwise.} \end{cases}$$

Partial Assignments. Function values can be changed by partial assignments (**set**) for a single argument:

Precondition: $f :: [f] \rightarrow \tau_r$ and $e' :: \tau'$ and $\tau' \preceq [f]$ and $e :: \tau$ and $\tau \preceq \tau_r$.

$$U[\![\, \textbf{set}\ [f := e](e') \,]\!]_\sigma(\phi) = \begin{cases} f' & \text{if } \phi = f, \\ \sigma(\phi) & \text{otherwise,} \end{cases}$$

$$\textbf{with}\ f'(\psi) = \begin{cases} E[\![\, e \,]\!]_\sigma & \text{if } \psi = e', \\ \sigma(f)(\psi) & \text{otherwise.} \end{cases}$$

The **set** operation only affects the value of the function f. It is substituted by a new function value f' that differs from f only for the argument designated by the expression e', for which the result is e.

In the following, we define the semantics of update operations that manipulate the active domains of object types. The existence of objects can be manipulated by **new** and **destroy**, and is captured by the membership in the set $\sigma([\,])$, which is the active domain of the most general object type. The active domains of object types including a single function are manipulated by the operations **gain** and **lose**.[11]

[11] The active domains of types with more than one function have been defined in Sec. 3.1.

New. The creation of an object by **new** () instantiates the top element of the object type lattice (β_{Object}) with a new object. That is, the active domain of this type is extended by the object that is the return value of the operation:[12]

$$U[\![\mathbf{new}\,()]\!]_\sigma(\phi) = \begin{cases} \sigma(\phi) \cup \{E[\![\mathbf{new}\,()]\!]_\sigma\} & \text{if } \phi = \beta_{Object} \\ \sigma(\phi) & \text{otherwise.} \end{cases}$$

Gain. An existing object can be made instance of additional object types by the operation **gain** $[f_1, ..., f_n](e)$ that makes each function in $[f_1, ..., f_n]$ applicable to the object e:[13]

Precondition: e :: $\tau'$and $\tau' \preceq \beta_{Object}$ and $\{f_1, ..., f_n\} \subseteq F$.

$$U[\![\mathbf{gain}\,[f_1, ..., f_n](e)]\!]_\sigma(\phi) = \begin{cases} \sigma(\phi) \cup \{E[\![e]\!]_\sigma\} & \text{if } \phi = [f] \wedge f \in \{f_1, ..., f_n\} \\ \sigma(\phi) & \text{otherwise.} \end{cases}$$

That is, the object becomes instance of the active domains $\sigma([f])$ for all f in $\{f_1, ..., f_n\}$, which propagates to object types with more than one function according to the definition in Sec. 3.1. In other words, if the type $[f_1', ..., f_m']$ has been the least upper bound of all types the object has been instance of, then the object becomes instance of $[f_1, ..., f_n] \sqcap [f_1', ..., f_m']$ and all its supertypes.

Example: Let us consider a person object denoted by the variable p that is of type *Pers*[14]. The person p can be made instance of the type *Empl* by the following **gain** operation that makes the functions *sal* and *manager* applicable to p:

gain $[sal, manager](p)$

Up to now the function values $sal(p)$ and $manager(p)$ are undefined ($\perp$). However, a mechanism for providing default values could be integrated here very easily by a corresponding extension of syntax. Later on the employee might become a manager in a similar way.

Lose. In contrast to the **gain** operation, instance relationships can be deleted by **lose**. The effect of **lose** $[f_1, ..., f_n](e)$ is that all functions in $\{f_1, ..., f_n\}$ are no longer applicable to the object denoted by e.

Precondition: e :: τ' and $\tau' \preceq \beta_{Object}$ and $[f_1, ..., f_n] \preceq \beta_{Object}$.

$$U[\![\mathbf{lose}\,[f_1, ..., f_n](e)]\!]_\sigma(\phi) = \begin{cases} \sigma(\phi) \setminus \{E[\![e]\!]_\sigma\} & \text{if } \phi = [f] \wedge f \in \{f_1, ..., f_n\} \\ \sigma(\phi) & \text{if } \phi = [f] \wedge f \notin \{f_1, ..., f_n\} \\ nv(\sigma(\phi), A(\phi)) & \text{otherwise.} \end{cases}$$

Thus, the state after an operation **lose** $[f_1, ..., f_n](e)$ can be derived in two steps. First, the object denoted by the expression e is excluded from the active

[12] Notice that $E[\![\mathbf{new}()]\!]_\sigma$ denotes the return value of the operation (which is the newly created object) whereas $U[\![\mathbf{new}()]\!]_\sigma$ denotes the intermediate state after the evaluation of $E[\![\mathbf{new}()]\!]_\sigma$ and before the execution of the statement in which **new**() is used.

[13] In contrast to **new**, the operation **gain** is defined as a statement that does not return a value. However, one can define a macro **gain'** that returns the input object with the new type by the following definition: **gain'**$[f_1, ..., f_n](e) \equiv$ **pick** (**select** $[\lambda x.x = e]$(**adom** $([f_1, ..., f_n])$)).

[14] Again we use the COOL type names instead of the respective function sets in order to improve readability.

domains of the types $[f_i]$ $(i = 1, ..., n)$; see the first case). This automatically propagates to the other object types.

The second step of the definition refers the occurrences of the object within values of variables, sets, and functions. Due to strong typing we have, for example, to exclude that the function f_i is applied to the object e, which might be the value of a variable. In general, this constraint is assured by removing each occurrence of the object denoted by e from variables, sets and functions, if these are related to a type that contains at least one function in $\{f_1, ..., f_n\}$. Therefore, the values of all variables (and functions) are recursively derived from the new active domains by the function nv.

The function nv is applied to an old value v and its type τ and returns the new value $nv(v, \tau)$. The new value is different form the old one only if the old one would not fulfill the type constraints. Therefore, the function is defined as follows:

$$nv(v,\tau) = \begin{cases} \bot & \text{if } \tau \preceq \beta_{Object} \\ & \wedge\, v \notin U[\![\mathbf{lose}\,[f_1,...,f_n](e)]\!]_\sigma(\tau) \\ \bigcup\limits_{v' \in v} nv(v',\tau') & \text{if } \tau = \{\tau'\} \\ \{\langle x, nv(v',\tau_2)\rangle \mid \langle x, v'\rangle \in v \,\wedge & \text{if } \tau = \tau_1 \rightarrow \tau_2 \\ \quad x \in U[\![\mathbf{lose}\,[f_1,...,f_n](e)]\!]_\sigma(\tau_1)\} & \\ v & \text{otherwise.} \end{cases}$$

The idea of the derivation is to use the structure of types in order to reduce the problem of specifying the new value of sets and functions to easier cases. In the first case, the old value, which is not element of the type τ anymore, is replaced by the null value ($\bot$). This case together with the last case, in which all remains the same, are the anchors of the derivation. If the old value is a set (the second case), the derivation is evaluated for each element of this set recursively. The return value of the set is constructed by the union over all elements[15]. Similarly, the value of each function is also checked recursively (the third case).

Notice that the **lose** operation and the deletion of objects have a strong impact on constructed values. Without objects, instances of constructed types such as sets and functions are regarded as values that can not be created or deleted [6]. However, if object types are used to construct sets of functions, the constructed domains become dynamic as well, since the existence of constructed values depends on the active domains of object types.

Example: Assume the variable declarations

p ::	$Pers$;
e ::	$Empl$;
mgr ::	$Mngr$;
$jones\_pers$ ::	$\{Pers\}$;
$jones\_empls$ ::	$\{Empl\}$;

and a state in which an object named "Jones", which is manager of an employee denoted by e. After the following assignments, the variables p and mgr denote the same object Jones, which is also contained in both set variables $jones\_pers$ and $jones\_empls$:

[15] The union ignores null values as elements, i.e., $S \cup \{\bot\} = S$.

$$
\begin{array}{ll}
jones\_pers := & \textbf{select}\,[name = \text{“}Jones\text{”}](\textbf{adom}\,(Pers));\\
jones\_empls := & \textbf{select}\,[name = \text{“}Jones\text{”}](\textbf{adom}\,(Empl));\\
p := & manager(e);\\
mgr := & manager(e);
\end{array}
$$

If Jones retires or is fired, the functions associated to the type *Empl* and its subtypes must not applied to him/her anymore. This can be achieved by the operation

lose $[sal, manager, budget](p)$

that removes Jones from the respective active domains. The propagation to variables, sets, and functions leads to the state in which Jones is still contained in *jones_pers*, but is removed from *jones_empls* (because of the type declaration that would allow to apply e.g., the *sal* function to elements of *jones_empls*). Similarly, the variable p still denotes Jones, whereas mgr is undefined as well as the function application $manager(e)$.

Destroy. In contrast to **lose**, the **destroy** operation has an effect on the existence of objects. The operation **destroy** (e) removes e from the active domains of all object types, which propagates to variables, sets, and functions:

Precondition: $e :: \tau'$ and $\tau' \preceq \beta_{Object}$.

$$U[\![\,\textbf{destroy}\ (e)\,]\!]_\sigma(\phi) = \begin{cases} \sigma(\phi) \setminus \{E[\![\,e\,]\!]_\sigma\} & \text{if } \phi = [f] \wedge f \in F \text{ or } \phi = \beta_{Object} \\ nv(\sigma(\phi), A(\phi)) & \text{otherwise.} \end{cases}$$

Notice that the semantics of these operations is defined with respect to the requirements for active domains in Sec. 3.1. That is, **new** and **gain** are defined such that the subset relationship between active domains and their respective domain is valid. The definitions of **lose** and **destroy** guarantee that no “dangling references” occur. That is, the procedure nv “removes invalid objects from values”. Therefore the state only contains objects that are elements in active domains. Finally, the subset relationship between subtypes and their supertypes is guaranteed by the definition of active domains for object types with more than one function (in Sec. 3.1) together with the definitions in **gain** and **destroy**.

4 Relationship to functional models

In this section we discuss the similarities between object algebras (such as BCOOL) and functional models (such as ML [15], and Machiavelli [7, 16]). On the one hand they have enough in common that a combination of both is possible; on the other hand the challenge is whether the advantages of either model can be preserved in the integration. We show (i) how to add full orthogonality and genericity to BCOOL and (ii) discuss how to extend Machiavelli by the concept of objects, which is more than just a reference.

4.1 Extending Object Query Languages by Orthogonality and Genericity

Up to now most operations of object query algebras (including BCOOL) center around sets. This has been done in order to take advantage of the optimization capabilities that arise from descriptive set-oriented queries and have already been used in relational systems. However, since many applications need other type constructors than sets (such as lists, tuples, and arrays), these constructors should also be integrated into object data models. Moreover, instead of a fixed collection of constructors, the variety of constructors should be extensible.

Therefore, let us discuss as a first extension, how BCOOL can be extended such that type constructors or generic types can be defined. That is, in this paper we omit other extensions of BCOOL, e.g., extensions of the algebra towards a programming language by providing operations such as loop and conditional instruction.

In the previous sections, we have concentrated on sets. Therefore, some of the proposed query operations are not orthogonal w.r.t. to type constructors other than sets. That is, operations that work on sets of objects have to be separated into elementary operations associated to type constructors from operations on objects, for example. This is similar to the separation of update operations into the **apply_to_all** iterator [13] and a few elementary update operations defined in the previous section. The iterator is used to apply sequences of elementary update operations to all elements of a set deterministically.

Consequently, the BCOOL set-oriented query operations **project** should be redefined to work on single objects (denoted by ′) such that they can be used not only within sets:

$$\frac{e :: [f'_1, ..., f'_m]}{\mathbf{project}' \, [f_1, ..., f_n] \; (e) :: [f_1, ..., f_n]} \qquad E[\![\, \mathbf{project}' \, [f_1, ..., f_n] \; (e) \,]\!] = E[\![\, e \,]\!]$$

Then, if a set-iterator **map** is provided (akin to *hom* in Machiavelli [7], *replace* [1] or *pump* in FAD [5]), the previous set-oriented operations can, for example, be derived as [16]:

$$\mathbf{project} \, [f_1, ..., f_n](S) \;\equiv\; \mathbf{map}[\mathbf{project}' \, [f_1, ..., f_n](e)](e : S).$$

Now we can easily extend BCOOL to work on lists of objects. After defining the constructors and deconstructors of lists, as well as an iterator on lists (for example, **lmap**), a projection on lists can be defined by the combination of **project′** and **lmap**. Similarly we can add subtyping rules for lists (akin to [SETS] and [FUNS] in Sec. 3.1) if necessary.

In general, the inclusion of a new type constructor requires the specification of subtyping rules and operations on the types' instances (including constructors and deconstructors). Notice that there are no update operations on instances of constructed types, because—as values—they are not created, updated, or deleted explicitly, but are rather constructed from components. However, if the type variable of constructors can be instantiated by object types, a mapping is required how constructed values "including" an object are mapped onto another value, if this object is deleted (similar to the mapping for sets and functions in the definition of the **lose** operation in Sec. 3.3).

Notice that the gain of orthogonality does not necessarily decrease performance, if we use overriding in the implementations. For example, efficient implementations of the relational algebra or any object algebra could be used

---

[16] Similarly, **select** can be defined by an iterator such as *hom*, if an **if-then-else** construct is provided in the model.

for the all instances of sets of tuples (sets of objects), respectively. Thus, the system can still make use of the optimization techniques provided for standard database models.

Another lack of orthogonality is the restriction that functions can only be defined on object types. In an orthogonal type system, one would expect that any type can serve as function domain. This extension, however, causes problems, since equality of functions is undecidable in general. Then, constructing sets over function types has to be prohibited, because the test for set-membership requires the equality test on the elements. A possible solution is the separation of types with an without equality known from functional languages (e.g., ML, Machiavelli), which could easily be employed in BCOOL.

4.2 Integrating objects in functional data models

One important objective in functional languages is to be purely descriptive and avoid imperative statements. Therefore, no explicit update operations are provided in purely functional languages (e.g., Miranda [26]). Consequently, sharing is also no important issue, because it becomes relevant only through updates. Nevertheless, there are also functional languages in which references are provided in order to express sharing with a rudimentary update capability (e.g., ML [15] or its derivative Machiavelli [7]).

Before discussing the lacks of modeling objects by references, let us briefly illustrate the concepts that are essential for this modeling. In Machiavelli, references are used as pointers to typed data items with the following three generic operations: creating new references (**new**), de-referencing ("!"), and assignments (":="). In contrast to Cardelli and Wegner's type system, in which values might be instances of multiple types [8], values in Machiavelli are instances of *one unique* type. However, kinds are provided to describe sets of types with common properties, such that type-checking in fact refers to kinds. That is, all instances of the subtypes of *Pers* are regarded as instances of a set of types that is described by the kind that allows the application of the *Pers* functions. Therefore, the semantics of subtyping is captured by kinds.

However, because references have not been considered when the type system has been extended to kinds, the following problems arise, if references are used to model objects:

- An object might be instance of different types (that are usually related by the subtype relationship). Therefore, references to the same object with different types must be provided. This can be done either by using the most specific type in the declaration of the referenced type or by using different references for different records that describe the properties of the same object. In the first approach, the bottom type of the type lattice is required in order to allow for object evolution. The second approach is similar to "object specialization" [22], in which the same real world entity is represented by several objects. There, the problem is, that the system has to keep track, which references belong to the same object. If the real world object is deleted, this has to be propagated to all references; the substitutability might require that a reference must be mapped onto another; and equality of references to objects needs more than comparing two object identities. That is, the advantages of objects according to sharing and substitutability are lost.

- Considering the longevity and dynamics of persistent objects, object evolution becomes necessary. Machiavelli has no explicit means to delete objects, nor operations to add or remove objects to or from the active domain of types. Notice, however, that the lack of operations for object evolution is not particular to functional models, similar deficiencies are found in most object-oriented programming languages.

Therefore, let us discuss how objects could be integrated into Machiavelli akin to BCOOL objects. The general idea is to consider objects as references to kinded records. The extension of references to kinds of records simplifies substitutability and subtyping. The more powerful update facility results from adjusting Machiavelli's type constructor **ref**.

In more detail, the following two kinding rules are added to those in [7], such that the kind assignment $\mathcal{K}$ that maps types to kinds can be adapted to object types and their respective subtyping:

$$\mathcal{K} \vdash t :: \mathbf{ref}'([\![l_1 : \tau_1, ..., l_n : \tau_n]\!]) \quad \text{if } t \in domain(\mathcal{K}), \mathcal{K}(t) = \mathbf{ref}'([\![l_1 : \tau_1, ..., l_n : \tau_n, ...]\!])$$

$$\mathcal{K} \vdash \mathbf{ref}'([l_1 : \tau_1, ..., l_n : \tau_n, ...]) :: \mathbf{ref}'([\![l_1 : \tau_1, ..., l_n : \tau_n]\!])$$

Machiavelli's type constructor **ref** can be changed to **ref**$'$ as follows: the generic operation **new** is adopted from BCOOL, such that it returns a newly created instance of $\mathbf{ref}'([\![\ ]\!])$. The operation for dereferencing is either adopted from Machiavelli, or dereferencing is done implicitly, if the dot operation is applied (which corresponds to BCOOL's function application). Similarly, assignments can be specific to components of objects (such as Machiavelli's *modify*) or common to all designators including variables and functions.

However, a fundamental consequence of using objects or references is that domains become dynamic. Without objects there is no need to separate the active domain from the domain, and no instances of any type could be created or deleted. Further, the domains of types that are constructed using objects become dynamic as well. However, it is not possible to invent an instance of a constructed type. That is, the domains of constructed types are static with respect to the active domains of their component types. Notice, however, that deletions cause problems: for example, a transformation is needed that maps a set containing object o to a set without o, if o is deleted. Therefore, we have to keep track of the active domains, similar to BCOOL. Then we can provide additional operations for **ref**$'$ that allow for the evolution of objects:

- The semantics of **gain** $[l : \tau](e)$ is to remove e from its current type $\mathbf{ref}'([l_1 : \tau_1, ..., l_n : \tau_n])$ and add it to the type $\mathbf{ref}'([l : \tau, l_1 : \tau_1, ..., l_n : \tau_n])$.

- The semantics of **lose** $[l](e)$ is defined conversely. The object e is removed from its current type $\mathbf{ref}'([l : \tau, l_1 : \tau_1, ..., l_n : \tau_n])$ and added to the "supertype" $\mathbf{ref}'([l_1 : \tau_1, ..., l_n : \tau_n])$ that does not contain the component l.

5 Summary

The intended contribution of this paper is twofold: First, we proposed generic update operations for an object-oriented model that cope with object sharing and typing constraints of variables and functions, and allow to dynamically change the types of objects. Secondly, we discussed how functional models and object models could be combined such that object models gain flexibility by more orthogonality and functional models are extended by objects and their corresponding update operations.

Acknowledgements. We thank the referees, especially Limsoon Wong and Leonid Libkin, for their remarks on an earlier version of this paper.

References

[1] S. Abiteboul and C. Beeri. On the power of languages for the manipulation of complex objects. Technical Report 846, INRIA, Paris, May 1988.

[2] S. Abiteboul and P.C. Kanellakis. Object identity as a query language primitive. In *Proc. ACM SIGMOD Conf. on Management of Data*, pages 159–173, Portland, June 1989. ACM, New York.

[3] H. Balsters and C. C. de Vreeze. A semantic of object-oriented sets. In *Proc. of 3rd Intl. Workshop on Database Programming Languages*, pages 187–200, Nafplion, Greece, August 1991.

[4] H. Balsters and M. M. Fokkinga. Subtyping can have simple semantics. *Theoretical Computer Science*, 87:81–96, 1991.

[5] F. Bancilhon, T. Briggs, S. Khoshafian, and P. Valduriez. FAD, a powerful and simple database language. In *Proc. Int. Conf. on Very Large Databases*, pages 97–105, Brighton, September 1987.

[6] C. Beeri. Formal models for object-oriented databases. In W. Kim, J.-M. Nicolas, and S. Nishio, editors, *Proc. 1st Int'l Conf. on Deductive and Object-Oriented Databases*, pages 370–395, Kyoto, December 1989. North-Holland. Revised version appeared in "Data & Knowledge Engineering", Vol. 5, North-Holland.

[7] P. Buneman and A. Ohori. Polymorphism and type inference in database programming. *ACM Transactions on Database Systems*, 1993. to appear.

[8] L. Cardelli and P. Wegner. On understanding types, data abstraction, and polymorphism. *ACM Computing Surveys*, 17(4):471–522, December 1985.

[9] K.C. Davis and L.M.L. Delcambre. A denotational approach to object-oriented query language definition. In *Proc. Int'l. Workshop on Specifications of Database Systems*, Glasgow, Scotland, June 1991. Workshops in Computing, Springer.

[10] D.H. Fishman, J. Annevelink, D. Beech, E. Chow, T. Connors, J.W. Davis, W. Hasan, C.G. Hoch, W. Kent, S. Leichner, P. Lyngbaek, B. Mahbod, M.A. Neimat, T. Risch, M.C. Shan, and W.K. Wilkinson. Overview of the iris dbms. In W. Kim and F.H. Lochovsky, editors, *Object-Oriented Concepts, Databases, and Applications*, chapter 10, pages 371–394. ACM Press, Addison-Wesley, New York, 1989.

[11] R. Hull and R. King. Semantic database modeling: Survey, applications, and research issues. *ACM Computing Surveys*, 19(3):201–260, September 1987.

[12] C. Laasch and M.H. Scholl. Generic update operations keeping object-oriented databases consistent. In *Proc. of 2. GI Workshop Information Systems and Artificial Intelligence*, pages 40–55, Ulm, Germany, February 1992. IFB 303, Springer Verlag, Heidelberg.

[13] C. Laasch and M.H. Scholl. Deterministic semantics of set-oriented update sequences. In *Proc. of the IEEE Conf. on Data Engineering*, pages 4–13, Vienna, Austria, April 1993.

[14] M.V. Mannino, I.J. Choi, and D.S. Batory. The object-oriented functional data language. *IEEE Transactions on Software Engineering*, 16(11):1258–1272, November 1990.

[15] R. Milner, M. Tofte, and R. Harper. *The Definition of Standard ML*. The MIT Press, Cambridge, Mass, 1990.

[16] A. Ohori, P. Buneman, and B. Breazu-Tannen. Database programming in Machiavelli a polymorphic language with static type inference. In *Proc. ACM SIGMOD Conf. on Management of Data*, pages 46–57, Portland, OR, May-June 1989.

[17] J. Richardson and P. Schwarz. Aspects: Extending objects to support multiple, independent roles. In *Proc. ACM SIGMOD Conf. on Management of Data*, pages 298–307, Denver, CO, May 1991.

[18] H.-J. Schek and M. H. Scholl. The relational model with relation-valued attributes. *Information Systems*, 11(2):137–147, jun 1986.

[19] M. H. Scholl, C. Laasch, and M. Tresch. Updatable views in object-oriented databases. In C. Delobel, M. Kifer, and Y. Masunaga, editors, *Proc. Int. Conf. on Deductive and Object-Oriented Databases (DOOD)*, pages 189–207, Munich, Germany, December 1991. LNCS 566, Springer Verlag, Heidelberg.

[20] M.H. Scholl, C. Laasch, C. Rich, H.-J. Schek, and M. Tresch. The COCOON object model. Technical Report 193, ETH Zürich, Dept. of Computer Science, 1992.

[21] M.H. Scholl and H.-J. Schek. A relational object model. In S. Abiteboul and P.C. Kanellakis, editors, *ICDT '90 - Proc. Int'l. Conf. on Database Theory*, pages 89–105, Paris, December 1990. LNCS 470, Springer Verlag, Heidelberg.

[22] E. Sciore. Object specialization. *ACM Trans. on Information Systems*, 7:103–122, April 1989.

[23] G.M. Shaw and S.B. Zdonik. A query algebra for object-oriented databases. In *Proc. of the IEEE Conf. on Data Engineering*, pages 154–162, Los Angelos, CA, February 1990.

[24] J. E. Stoy. *The Scott-Strachey Approach to Programming Language Theory*. The MIT Press, Cambridge (Mass.), 1977.

[25] D.D. Straube and M.T. Özsu. Queries and query processing in object-oriented databases. *ACM Transactions on Office Information Systems*, 8(4):387–430, October 1990.

[26] D.A. Turner. Miranda: A non-strict functional language with polymorphic types. In *Proc. IFIP Int'l Conf. on Functional Programming Languages and Computer Architecture*, Nancy, France, September 1985. LNCS 201, Springer.

[27] K. Wilkinson, P. Lyngbaek, and W. Hasan. The Iris architecture and implementation. *IEEE Trans. on Knowledge and Data Engineering*, 2(1):63–75, March 1990. Special Issue on Prototype Systems.

The AQUA Data Model and Algebra*

Theodore W. Leung
Brown University
Providence, USA

Gail Mitchell[†]
Brown University
Providence, USA

Bharathi Subramanian
Brown University
Providence, USA

Bennet Vance
Oregon Graduate Institute
of Science & Technology
Oregon, USA

Scott L. Vandenberg[‡]
University of Mass. at Amherst
Amherst, USA

Stanley B. Zdonik
Brown University
Providence, USA

Abstract

This paper describes a new object-oriented model and query algebra that will be used as an input language for the query optimizers that are being built as a part of the EREQ project. The model adopts a uniform view of objects and values and separates syntactic, semantic, and implementation concerns. The algebra addresses issues of type-defined equality and duplicate elimination as well as extensions to bulk types other than sets.

1 Introduction

Recently, a great deal of work has been done on the topic of object-oriented query algebras [29, 24, 12] and the modeling of bulk types [4, 27, 21]. These proposals, as well as those of other researchers on the topic, have explored some of the fundamental issues and provided the starting point for the work reported here. AQUA (A QUery Algebra) is the result of a joint effort among researchers who have participated in the design of previous algebras [28, 32, 33].

AQUA has been designed to address a number of detailed modeling issues that we believe needed further work, but the overarching goal for this work has been the design of an algebra that would serve as the input to a broad class of query optimizers. In this way, it could be used as a de facto standard in the construction of object-oriented query optimizers. It would serve as the target language for user-level query languages. Any user language for which there was a translator to AQUA could then be processed by any of the optimizers that are designed for AQUA. Thus, AQUA is an intermediate language between the user's query and the query optimizer.

*This research is sponsored by the Advanced Research Projects Agency under ARPA order No. 18 and administered by U.S. Army Research Laboratory under contract DAAB-07-91-C-Q518. Bennet Vance is supported in part by NSF Grant IRI 91 18360.

[†] Current address: GTE Laboratories Incorporated, Waltham, MA, 02254

[‡] Current address: Computer Science Dept., Siena College, Loudonville, NY 12211

AQUA and the data model on which it is based are strongly typed and are designed to deal correctly and uniformly with abstract types. It should be kept in mind that although we often talk about tuples in this context, they are abstractions as well and are not the stored representation of the objects.

AQUA is closed in the sense that all of its operators return objects that are defined in the model. It should also be pointed out that although AQUA supports updates through the use of methods, we do not discuss this here.

Any query language or algebra must be embedded in some data model. We have attempted to provide a simple model that would be general enough to cover the modeling concepts in other object-oriented models. We have adopted a model in which everything is an object in the sense that it has a well-defined interface and can be referenced from other objects, yet, we also support value-based semantics as described later in this paper.

AQUA has been designed to be very general. We have purposely included a rich set of operators that could directly simulate the operators in other proposals. AQUA is not a minimal set of operators. Redundancy allows us to more easily accommodate many query languages, and, at the same time, allows us to have a powerful and varied set of optimization strategies. Operator redundancy supports optimization by making query rewrites possible.

Another goal of our work has been to support many different bulk types in a uniform manner. We have designed AQUA in such a way that it will not preclude additional bulk types like lists or arrays. The AQUA design also addresses the problems introduced by type-specific equalities by providing special functions that deal with equivalence classes and duplicate elimination in a bulk type object based on some equality specific to the element type. The presentation in this paper covers two bulk types, sets and multisets. The discussion of more complex, ordered types is beyond the scope of this paper [31].

Some of the operators that one would expect to find in any algebra appear in AQUA as well. They have, however, been generalized to deal with many data models and many possible bulk types. For example, our **join** operator (see Table 4) takes the standard three arguments - the two input sets or multisets and a matching predicate. It also takes an extra argument which is a function of two inputs that combines every pair of objects from the two input sets that satisfy the matching predicate. This can cover **joins** that produce sets of pairs or **joins** that behave like **semi-joins**, for example. If the two input sets were sets of lists, it could combine the two elements by concatenation, thereby producing a set of lists.

AQUA is currently being used as the input language for two prototype extensible optimizers, Epoq at Brown University [23] and Revelation at OGI [11]. It appears to give us the power that we need for expressing complex queries while, at the same time, it seems to cover the functionality of all the query algebras of which we are aware.

2 Related Work

One of the primary goals of AQUA is to provide a model general enough to simulate the constructs of any object-oriented data model (and most value-oriented models), no matter what choices it makes with respect to certain features (bulk types, encapsulation, identity versus value, notions of equality, inheritance, and operations (up to a point)). Other models have claimed similar goals, but not necessarily in all these areas at once, and our mechanisms for achieving these goals differ substantially from those of our predecessors. Many of the specific constructs of AQUA were inspired by or drawn from the EXTRA/EXCESS system [33], ENCORE/EQUAL [28], and Revelation [32].

AQUA is intended to support large numbers of bulk types and to do so in a flexible, uniform way, such that the addition of other bulk types later on will be straightforward. [6] proposes a meta-level algebra for collections of complex objects with identity and also includes some transformation rules for optimization. This algebra, however, does not correspond to a specific data model but rather to a higher-level notion of collections of objects. Its operations and rules are templates that are intended to be "instantiated" in actual systems according to certain parameters of the specific data model being implemented. Thus it takes a different approach to generality than does AQUA. It also does not support several of the constructs of AQUA (including grouping and immutable semantics). EXTRA/EXCESS [33] also attempts to support a large number of bulk types, but does not explicitly provide sets (they are provided only by eliminating duplicates from multisets). The inclusion of a union type is not new (see [19]), but we provide it with a clean algebraic interface using both **tagcase** and **typecase** constructs to be fully general. The importance of being flexible about the addition of new bulk types has been established (see [21]); the modularity of the AQUA approach facilitates this to an extent by following a rationale similar to that of Rozen and Shasha (see [27]) in several respects.

In attempting to support both values and objects, some systems (e.g. EXCESS [33]) choose to support only values in the type system and to model objects by using explicit identifiers. Other systems (e.g. Smalltalk and ORION [13, 5]) choose to support only objects in the type system and to model values as a special case of objects. IQL (see [1]) defines two separate languages, one enforcing object identity and one not supporting it at all. Our characterization of the distinction between "objects" and "values" as the difference between entities (objects) with mutable and immutable semantics provides a much cleaner formalism, and was partially inspired by systems such as Larch [14]. By cleanly separating the notions of type (a syntactic concept) and semantics we provide a model that treats both values and objects as first-class citizens and has a simpler type system. We are not aware of another model that takes this approach, nor of one that takes the clearly-separated, 3-level view of an object that we do (type, semantics, and implementation; see Section 3.1). Buneman and Ohori (see [8]) exhibit a similar philosophy, though, in their distinction between a *kind* and a *type*.

C++ [30] has a notion of "const" that is similar to our notion of "immutable", but in C++ this notion is part of the type system, and thus causes a variety of problems that motivated us to separate type and semantics. Eiffel [22] makes a distinction between reference and copy semantics, but not between mutable and immutable semantics. Unlike ILOG (see [15]) and others, we avoid explicit identifiers in the model, viewing them as an implementation concern, and reflecting the distinctions between objects and values by using varying semantics (see Section 3.3).

It has been pointed out by Atkinson et al. (see [4]) that in object-oriented systems, a type may supply its own method for testing equality. This capability, however, introduces problems such as what is the meaning of operators like set union that depend on equality for their own semantics. The AQUA approach to enforcing a notion of equality among the elements of a set seems to be without precedent because in many cases there is no need for any notion of equality other than object identity but it still allows the (non-deterministic) creation of sets whose members are determined by an arbitrary equivalence relation. Many models (e.g. MDM [25]) do not have this flexibility.

Most "pure" object-oriented models ([13, 20], and others) provide and enforce encapsulation of data types. In AQUA our notion of type is more general: not everything is forced to be of an encapsulated, abstract data type whose only interface is that provided by the definer of the type. But AQUA does support such types, and does so using the "abstraction" type constructor, allowing any database object to be described using a single uniform type system. This is similar to the ADT concept provided by Postgres [26], but more general in the sense that any type definable in the AQUA type system can be abstracted into a true encapsulated type, and an abstraction in AQUA is a first-class citizen of the type system – the abstraction constructor has the same status as any other constructor. The distinction is that an object of an abstraction type has only the user-defined methods as an interface, while an object of (for example) a set type has an interface consisting of union, difference, etc. This is similar to Postgres's notion of user-defined Postquel functions and the functions and procedures of EXCESS [9], but in those systems, the ability to define functions allows one to add operations to an existing, non-encapsulated type (i.e., encapsulation is not enforced in those systems but is in AQUA). AQUA can, of course, emulate these features of Postgres and EXCESS. The use of a type constructor to represent abstraction enables all objects in an AQUA database to exist in one seamless type system. Our approach is similar to that of [3], but in their model not everything is an object, so their equivalent to our abstraction constructor must enforce many more of the facets of "objectness" than must ours.

Several of our operators resemble operators of ENCORE/EQUAL, EXTRA/EXCESS, and Revelation. See Section 5 for detailed descriptions of the operators. **Fold** comes directly from Revelation, but we have adapted it for use with both sets and multisets, as it is basically a form of structural recursion ([7]). **Apply** is similar to mapping-style operators of other models; it is closely related to the SET_APPLY operation of EXCESS. Our **nest** and **unnest** operations are generalizations of those defined in ENCORE/EQUAL, and the **group** and **set** operations are also found in EXCESS. **Dup_elim** for both sets and multisets (as we've defined it) and **convert** appear to be original to this model, with **dup_elim** being by far the more interesting. AQUA's **dup_elim** can be thought of as a generalization of other duplicate elimination operators (e.g. that of ENCORE/EQUAL [28]). Our binary **join** operation is similar to the n-ary **image** operator of MDM [25], but differs from it in that we separate the join predicate from the function to be applied to matching pairs; the idea of this is to enhance optimization by making certain queries (e.g. equijoins) easier to recognize. A set-theoretic **choose** operator appears in the algebras of Osborne and MDM (see [24, 25]). Non-determinism is also present in [2], which describes a *witness* operator which operates in a logical (rather than an algebraic) setting and creates a set of possible interpretations of a formula, resulting in non-determinism. Also, the decision to make the boolean operators (**and**, **or**, and **not**) full-fledged algebra operators, rather than constructs available only in certain parts of the language (e.g. predicates), as in the relational algebra, EXCESS, and Straube's algebra (see [33, 29]), adds to the flexibility of the algebra. Finally, the type parameter to **union**, **difference**, and **intersection** is similar to that used in EXCESS.

3 The AQUA Data Model

The AQUA data model is founded on the notions of strong typing and abstract data types. In the AQUA data model, an object has a type, and its state is accessed and modified via a well defined set of interface functions. The *state* of an object is a mapping from AQUA objects to *mathematical values*. All AQUA objects are unique, and this uniqueness can be detected by the user. AQUA objects have identity, and can be distinguished using equality that is based on identity. We do not specify the implementation of identity, to prevent a fixation on object identifiers. The most important point is that objects are unique, and that given two objects, we can determine whether or not they are the same object.

Everything that is stored in an AQUA database is an object. Database objects can have global names which facilitate access to the corresponding object. This approach allows the model to have a uniform flavor. The expressive power of the model is not crippled by this uniformity, as we shall see below.

The uniformity of the data model allows us to easily and consistently define algebraic operators over collections of objects and values.

3.1 A Three Tiered Object Model

A common view of types is that they are a description of various aspects of the meaning or behavior of that type. In the AQUA type system, we have separated the notion of "syntactic" type from the notion of "semantic" type. Types are a syntactic property of names. Each type has an associated non-empty set of semantics, each of which provides a description of meaning and behavior that objects of the type can have. Every type provides a set of interface functions, since everything in AQUA is an object. The interface presented by the type is a set of signatures for the interface functions. The meaning and implementation of the interface functions is determined by the semantics and implemention of a given instance of the type.

An AQUA *type* is defined recursively:

$\mathcal{B} = \{integer, float, boolean, string\}$
(the set of base types)

(name, hier, C($m_1 : t_1, ..., m_n : t_n$))
m_i is a name, t_1, ..., t_n are types or objects, and C is a type constructor.

The *hier* symbol represents the set of immediate supertypes of the type being defined. The data model supports subtyping via the notion of substitutability. Since our types are syntactic, substitutability is also syntactic. We use the symbols $\sqsubseteq$ and $\sqsupseteq$ to indicate subtype and supertype relationships between types. Functions have types, although our notation (described below) only allows the instantiation of particular functions. The name equivalence rule is used for determining the equality of two AQUA types.

The *semantics* of a type might loosely be thought of as a Larch [14] specification, which axiomatically describes properties of the operations on a type. The particular language used for describing semantics is a topic of our current research.

Specifying semantics separately from types allows different instances of the same type to have different behaviors. For example, making this distinction aids us in our goal of viewing all entities as abstract data types by moving the traditional distinction between objects and values into the semantics layer. This is discussed in more detail below. At present, we define two possible semantics, mutable and immutable. Objects with mutable semantics may update their state, while objects with immutable semantics may not.

Another example of the use of semantics is the declaration that certain operations are commutative. A query optimizer could then make use of such information when optimizing a query. The semantics describing commutativity for deques might be written as $notEmpty(q) \Rightarrow enque(deque(q), x) = deque(enque(q, x))$. Commutativity axioms for sets might include: $\mathbf{select}(p2)(\mathbf{select}(p1)(s)) = \mathbf{select}(p1)(\mathbf{select}(p2)(s))$ or $\mathbf{join}(p, f)(A, B) = \mathbf{join}(p, f)(B, A)$, provided p and f are commutative. See Section 5.1 for a complete description of the AQUA **join** operator).

Each semantics of a type may have multiple *implementations*, resulting in the third tier of our three tiered type system. An implementation is a description of how an instance of a type with a particular semantics is to be implemented (in terms of data structures and algorithms). The specification of implementation allows the database or a user to select the most desirable implementation at any point in the lifetime of the object. Thus, an object really is an instance of a particular implementation of a particular semantics of a type. A result of our approach is that type can be determined statically (at compile-time), but semantics and implementation can only be determined at run time.

3.2 Constructing Types

A type constructor is a meta type which defines a family of types. The *Set* type constructor defines the family of types that includes *Set[Person]*, *Set[Department]*, etc. New types are created by instantiating the meta type with a specific type, like *Person* or *Department*.

The interface of a new type is determined by the particular type constructor and its parameters. AQUA types with user-defined interfaces may also be defined using a special "*abs*traction" type constructor, defined below. All types defined using the *abs*traction constructor must provide their own **new** operation for creating objects of that type. The *operators* of the AQUA algebra are the methods on the AQUA type constructors.

We define the following standard type constructors; *Set[T]* – a collection of unique entities of the same type; *Multiset[T]* – a bag of entities of the same type (i.e. an entity may appear more than once in a multiset); $Tuple[l_1 : T_1, \ldots, l_n : T_n]$ – a fixed-length list of labeled entities of (possibly) different types; $Union[l_1 : T_1, \ldots, l_n : T_n]$ – a tagged union, similar to that found in many programming languages; *Function*$[T_1, \ldots, T_n, T_r]$ – a named list of types, the last of which is the output type of the function (the others being the input types); $Abs[f_1 : T_{f_1}, \ldots, f_n : T_{f_2}]$ – abstraction. An abstraction is a new abstract data type and has a collection of named functions, which form the interface of the abstraction. (We leave the representation of the abstraction to the implementation and do not discuss it here); *N-dimensional array[T](n,l)* – an n-dimensional collection of entities of the same type; individual entities can be accessed directly. The parameter l is a list of n dimensions; at most one of the dimensions may be of variable length; *List[T]* – a sequence of entities of the same type; *Tree[T]* – a tree whose nodes all contain entities of the same specified type; and *Graph[T]* – a graph whose nodes all contain entities of the same specified type. Lists, trees, and graphs are not discussed further here; see [31] for a complete description of them. N-dimensional arrays are a subject of our future research.

*Abs*tractions, *tuples* and *unions* are subtypeable. Functions are subtypeable using the standard contravariance rule. *Sets* and *multisets* are not subtypeable. As a reminder, the principle of substitutability states that a subtype may be used anywhere its supertype may be used. If we allowed sets to be subtypeable, then given a variable *zoo* with type *Set*[*Animal*],and $Dog \sqsubseteq Animal$, then we could assign *zoo* an object of type *Set*[*Dog*], and then we could also incorrectly insert the elephant Dumbo, an animal, into *zoo*, a *Set*[*Dog*]. A similar argument shows that multisets are not subtypeable.

3.3 Our Approach to Values

Mutable and immutable semantics are the key to incorporating the traditional notions of object and value into the AQUA model. In the discussion that follows, we use object to refer the the traditional notion of object, and use AQUA object to refer to objects as they appear in AQUA. There are (so far) two possible semantics for AQUA objects, mutable and immutable. Other semantics can be defined, and AQUA objects may have any semantics that has been defined in the system and is applicable to that type.

AQUA supports the traditional notion of values via immutable semantics for objects. If an AQUA object is immutable, its contents can never change, and it becomes impossible to detect whether or not it is being shared — it takes on the role of a value. The AQUA base types only support immutable semantics. Traditionally, objects are used to achieve sharing, and values are used to prevent sharing.

The type system will allow an immutable AQUA object to be assigned to a variable referencing a mutable AQUA object. Variables only have a type, not a semantics. For example, semantics allow us to create a single type, say *Person*, which has mutable and immutable semantics. We can then create a mutable *Person* and an immutable *Person*, and use either one where a *Person* is required. The behavior of the program depends on whether or not the *Person* is mutable or immutable at the time that the code is executed. As discussed in the next section, this allows us to have type compatible *Person* "objects" and *Person* "values".

3.4 Examples

We will use the following schema definitions to show the use of the abstraction type constructor, and to set the stage for some sample queries described later. The examples use the abstraction constructor to specify the interface of of the abstract data type, and show a name implementation specification to describe the representation of the abstract type. A *Company* is an abstract data type which uses a tuple as its representation, and which supplies a set of methods to access and update its name and address. *Person* is similar, but it also has an Employer field which is of type *Company*. We also have a set of *Company* objects, $Companies = Set[Company]$ and a set of *Person* objects, $Persons = Set[Person]$. No semantics is presented since our language for defining semantics is incomplete.

type Company =
  abs($name(Company) -> String;$
    $change\_name(Company, String);$
    $address(Company) -> String;$
    $change\_address(Company, String);$
)

Implementation CompanyA for Company =
  $Tuple[name : string, address : string]$

type Person =
  abs($name(Person) -> String;$
    $address(Person) -> String;$
    $employer(Person) -> Company;$
)

Implementation PersonA for Person =
  $Tuple[name : string, address : string,$
      $employer : Company]$

4 The AQUA Approach to Algebra Design

In this section, we discuss some of the design issues related to the AQUA algebra, including the syntax of terms, the use of type parameters, and the treatment of equality.

4.1 Syntax

Expressions in the algebra are represented by *terms*. A term is either: a variable, constant or function symbol, a *lambda abstraction* of the form $\lambda(x_1 : T_1, x_2 : T_2, \cdots, x_n : T_n)t : R$, or an *application*, $t_0(t_1 : T_1, \cdots, t_k : T_k)(t_{k+1} : T_{k+1}, \cdots, t_n : T_n) : R$, where $t_0, t_1, \ldots, t_n$ are terms and t_0 must have a function type. A lambda abstraction can be given a name. For example, the term $Names =$ **apply**($\lambda(p)$**invoke**$(name)(p))(Persons)$ is a named term returning a set containing the names of each person in a set of Persons. **Apply** (defined in table 1), **invoke** and *name* are function symbols, p is a variable, and $\lambda(p)$**invoke**$(name)(p)$ is a lambda abstraction.

We note that *predicates* must be functions with *boolean* return type. Predicates are composed using AQUA's built-in operators and its term language, which is based on lambda calculus. They are normally passed as parameters to operators like **select**, **join**, **exists**, and **forall**. All queries result in the creation of a new AQUA object as the result. For example, the query discussed in the previous paragraph would result in a *new* set containing the names of each person in a set of Persons.

Some of the AQUA operations are parameterized by an equality, a type, a function, a name, or some combination of these. In the next subsections we describe type parameters and equalities, before actually describing the operations in Section 5.

We adopt some conventions and notations for defining the operators. A and B are used to refer to the input sets or multisets; R is used to denote the output set/multiset or the result set/multiset; a is used to represent an element of the input set or multiset A; f, g and h are used to represent functions; id represents the default equality (identity); and p represents a predicate. T indicates the result type of an operator. Tuples are represented by $<>$, L is a tuple field name, and a/L means the tuple value a minus the field labeled L. Other notations will be defined as needed.

4.2 Type Parameters

The parameterized type constructors, and subtyping requirements for types, are designed to support static type-checking. One choice that was made to assist in this support is to explicitly give a result type as a parameter to some of the algebraic operations.

Many of the operations in our algebra construct instances of new types as their result. In such cases, inferring the result type is not easy in an algebra that allows multiple supertypes and union types. In order to resolve this difficulty and provide flexibility, the algebra takes the result type as an input parameter for operators in which we may not always have a unique supertype when combining inputs of compatible (but not identical) types. For example, consider the union of a set of oranges and a set of lemons. The type of the result can be either a set of "fruits" or a set of "good sources of Vitamin C" (Figure 1). To resolve this, the user has to specify the type of the result.

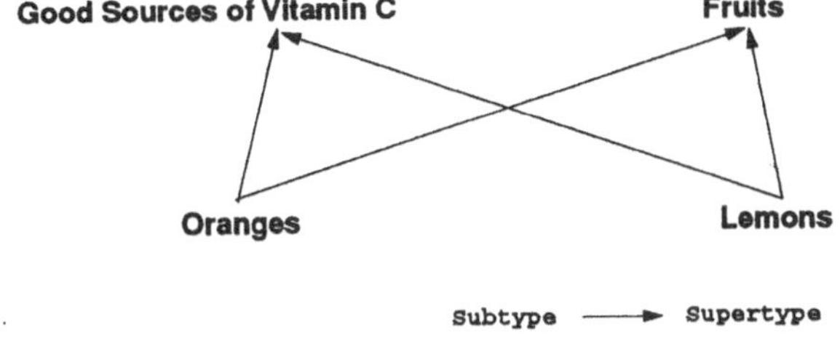

Figure 1: Result type for **union** with multiple supertypes

4.3 Equality

Some types may have more than one useful notion of equality. The default equality for every type is identity. The built-in primitive types (*integer*, *float*, *boolean* and *string*) have the standard definitions for equality. Meaningful user-defined equalities should induce an equivalence relation over all the instances of that type.

Equality is essential to the definition of some operators, including **union**, **intersection**, **difference**, **membership**, **LFP** (least fixed point), and **nest** for sets, and **union**, **additive_union**, **intersection** and **difference** for multisets. These operators take a user defined equality as parameter. This equality is used to eliminate duplicates in the result.

The set **union** and **LFP** operations display the following useful property. If the result of, say, a **union** operator is used as input to another operator, then it is not necessary to eliminate duplicates when the **union** is computed. Instead, the subsequent operator(s) assume responsibility for eliminating duplicates. In this case identity should be supplied as the equality parameter for the **union**. In the case where **union** or **LFP** is the outermost operator, or the case where an existing set is viewed through a different (other than the one that created it) equality, the **dup_elim** operator is used to eliminate duplicates according to a user specified equality. This operator takes an equality (in the form of a binary predicate) as a parameter, and eliminates duplicates under that equality. Any object that is a duplicate under identity is a duplicate under the user equality, but not vice versa.

Dup_elim can be defined in terms of two other operators, **group** and **choose**. If *eq* is a binary predicate, and S is a set,

$$\begin{aligned}\mathbf{dup\_elim}(eq)(A) = \mathbf{apply}(&\mathbf{choose} \circ snd) \\ &(\mathbf{group}(\lambda(a)\mathbf{Immutable}(\\ &\qquad \mathbf{select}(\lambda(b)eq(a,b))(A))(A)))\end{aligned}$$

The **Group**$(f)(S)$ operator groups the elements of set S into equivalence classes by using the f parameter, returning a set of tuples whose first field is the result of applying f to a member of an equivalence class and whose second field is the set of instances in the equivalence class. In the definition of **dup_elim**, this produces a set of tuples with two field, each of which is a set of elements which is equivalent to an element a of A. This set of tuples is supposed to represent the set of equivalence classes induced by the equality *eq* to **dup_elim**. There is a small problem. The result of a **select** is always a new set object. This means that there will be tuples which have first elements which are not identical, but would be the same values. The second elements of such tuples would be immutable objects (values) according to the definition of **group**. Such tuples should be considered duplicates and one should be removed, but the non-identical first fields prevent the elimination of the tuples. **Immutable**(x) is a semantics cast, which forces the expression x to have immutable (value) semantics. Applying **Immutable** to the result of the **select** forces the set values to be created. Now **group** will be able to eliminate duplicate tuples representing a single equivalence class. To obtain the final result, we pick one element from each equivalence class to serve as a representative for that class. This is accomplished by extracting the second field of each tuple (using the *snd*

Definitions		
apply$(f)(A)$	$=$	$\{f(a) \mid a \in A\}$
select$(p)(A)$	$=$	$\{a \mid a \in A, p(a)\}$
exists$(p)(A)$	$=$	$\exists a \in A.p(a)$
forall$(p)(A)$	$=$	$\forall a \in A.p(a)$
mem$(a, eq)(A)$	$=$	$\exists x \in A.eq(a, x)$
fold$(u, f, \oplus)(A)$	$=$	$\begin{cases} u, & A = \emptyset \\ \bigoplus_{a \in A} f(a), & A \neq \emptyset \end{cases}$

Table 1: Unary Set Iterators

function), and the using the **Choose** operator to nondeterministically select on element of the resulting set. The **dup_elim**ed set has no duplicates with respect to the new equality, thus it also has no duplicates according to identity. See Tables 1 and 4 for definitions of **apply**, **choose**, **group**, and **select**.

For many queries, this approach allows any equality to be used at any point during query processing without compromising our notion of "set". The operators remain defined in the abstract and we are assured that they can handle any kind of equality that may arise, including anything the writer of a query might wish to pass in as a parameter.

Consider the union of two sets A = $\{(1, a), (2, b)\}$ and B = $\{(2, a), (2, b)\}$. Assume we want A union B using a notion of equality that says two elements are equal if their fields are pairwise equal, so that the $(2, b)$ in A and the $(2, b)$ in B are equal. The result will then have three elements: $\{(1, a), (2, b), (2, a)\}$.

Now suppose we want A union B using a notion of equality that says two elements are equal if their second fields are equal. The $(1, a)$ in A and the $(2, a)$ in B are also equal. The required result is then $\{(1, a), (2, b)\}$ or $\{(2, a), (2, b)\}$. Either result is correct since the equality only examines the second element of each tuple. $(5, a)$ could legally be in the result, but is disallowed by our definition of **dup_elim** – it was not in the set before **dup_elim** was applied.

5 The Operators

In this section we describe the operations defined on the different types. Some of these operators can be expressed in terms of some others, leading to many redundancies in the operator set. They have been retained partly because they permit some expressions to be written with greater conciseness and clarity than would otherwise be possible, and partly because they lend themselves to specialized implementations and optimizations that can be more efficient than those of a more general operator.

5.1 Set Operators

This subsection describes the set operators in our algebra. Most of these operators are derived from similar operators in the literature [9, 28, 32] and exceptions are noted as they arise. It is our combination and utilization of them, in

Definitions		
union$(eq, T)(A, B)$	=	**dup_elim**$(eq)(\{x \mid (x \in A \; or \; x \in B)\})$
intersect$(eq, T)(A, B)$	=	**dup_elim**$(eq)(\{x \mid (x \in A \; or \; x \in B) \; and$ (**mem**$(x, eq)(A)$ *and* **mem**$(x, eq)(B))\})$
diff$(eq, T)(A, B)$	=	**dup_elim**$(eq)(\{x \mid x \in A$ $and \; \neg($**mem**$(x, eq)(B))\})$

Table 2: Binary Set Operators

Definition		
LFP(eq, f)	=	**dup_elim**$(eq)(\bigcup_{i=0}^{\infty}(f^i(\{\})))$

Table 3: Least Fixed Point Operator

Definitions		
set(a)	=	$\{a\}$
choose(A)	=	some $a \in A$
group$(f)(A)$	=	$\{(f(a), eqclass(a)) \mid a \in A\}$, where $eqclass(a) =$ $\{a' \mid a' \in A, f(a) = f(a')\}$
dup_elim$(eq)(A)$	=	$R \subseteq A \; s.t. \; \forall x, y \in R, eq(x, y) \Rightarrow id(x, y)$, and $\forall x \in A, \exists y \in R \; s.t. \; eq(x, y)$
nest$(eq, L)(A)$	=	$\{$**tup_concat**$(a/L, < L : \{b.L \mid b \in A \; and$ $eq_t(a/L, b/L)\} >) \mid a \in A\}$
unnest$(L)(A)$	=	$\{$**tup_concat**$(a/L, < L : s >) \mid a \in A \; and$ $s \in a.L\}$
convert(A)	=	$\{* \, x \mid x \in A \, *\}$

Table 4: Set Restructuring Operators

Definitions		
join$(p, f)(A, B)$	=	$\{f(a, b) \mid a \in A, b \in B, p(a, b)\}$
tup_join$(p)(A, B)$	=	**join**$(p,$ **tup_concat**$)(A, B)$
outer_join$(p, f, g, h, T)(A, B)$	=	$\{f(a, b) \mid a \in A, b \in B, p(a, b)\}$ $\cup \{g(a) \mid a \in A, \forall b \in B. \neg p(a, b)\}$ $\cup \{h(b) \mid b \in B, \forall a \in A. \neg p(a, b)\}$

Table 5: Join Operators

addition to the original operators, that makes this approach more flexible than previous ones.

A list of all the operators for sets and a brief definition for each of them, is given in tables 1 through 5. Table 1 lists the unary set operators, table 2 deals with the binary set operators, table 3 defines the least fixed point (**LFP**) operator, table 4 describes the set restructuring operators, and table 5 lists the various join operators. In the rest of the subsection, we expand upon issues about some of the operators of the algebra.

The **fold** operator is a powerful operator – $\mathbf{fold}(u, f, \oplus)(A)$ reduces set A to a single value by applying f to each element and iteratively combining the results with a dyadic operator $\oplus$. u is the result of **fold** on the empty set. For example, **set_collapse** can be implemented using **fold**, the identity function, and the **union** operator (using the default equality).

$$\mathbf{fold}(\{\}, \lambda(x)x, \mathbf{union}(id))(\{\{1,2\},\{2,3,4\},\{5\}\}) = \{1,2,3,4,5\}$$

Operators **exists**, **forall** and **mem** return a *boolean* value and can be used as predicate formers. **Nest** and **unnest** have been defined in table 4 using a single tuple field name L. However, this definition can be easily extended to a list of field names. In such a case, a/L refers to the tuple value a minus the fields in the list L and $a.L$ is the concatenation of all the values of the fields in list L. To compare the equality of a pair of tuples minus the field L, we use the equality eq_t, which does a pairwise comparison of the contents of each field using the equality eq.

The binary set operators, **union**, **intersection** and **difference** are the familiar set-theoretic operations; however our definitions are complicated by considerations of typing. When two sets are combined using a binary set operator, it is not necessary that they have the same type. As in EXCESS [9], these operators take an extra argument that specifies the type of the result, as discussed in subsection 4.2. The result type of **union** has to be a supertype of the types of the input sets. However, in **intersection** the result type can either be a supertype of both input types or be one of the input types. In the case of **difference**, the result type has to either be the type of the first input set or one of its supertypes.

To briefly illustrate some of the set operators, consider a query that finds all of the people who live in the same city in which they work and groups them based on the name of this city. This is done by using the employer field of a *Person* object. We use $A.B$ as a shorthand for **invoke** (A, B), which invokes method B on object A.

$$\begin{aligned}&LiveWhereWorkPeople =\\&\quad \mathbf{select}(\lambda(x)x.address = x.employer.address)(Persons)\end{aligned}$$

Next, we use **group** to group the people in *LiveWhereWorkPeople* by the city in which they live.

$$\mathbf{group}(\lambda(x)x.address)(LiveWhereWorkPeople)$$

The result consists of a set of ordered pairs (*city*, *people*) where *city* is the name of a city in which at least one person both lives and works and *people* is

Definitions		
multiset(a)	=	$\{* a *\}$
convert(A)	=	$\{ x \| x \in A \}$
dup_elim(eq)(A)	=	**convert**(**dup_elim**(eq)(**convert**A))

Table 6: Multiset Restructuring Operators

a set of *Person* objects all of whom live and work in *city*.

The various **join** operators deserve special mention due to their generality. **Join** takes a function as a parameter, thus allowing the user to define a "combining" function. The other **join** operators are similar generalizations involving a predicate and a function. Note that the union used in the definition of **outer_join** is the set **union**, using the default equality. The resultant type T of the **outer_join** must be a supertype of the result types of functions f, g and h, to allow unioning the results of the functions. Left and right outer joins can be expressed in terms of **outer_join** with the appropriate interpretation of *null* values. Familiar join operators like **natural_join**, **equijoin**, **semijoin** and **antijoin** are not primitives in the algebra, but they can be expressed easily in terms of the included join operators.

The **LFP** operator [17] is defined in table 3. The function f is of type $T \rightarrow T$, where T is a set type. The notation f^i is equivalent to $f(f^{i-1})$. The **union** for LFP uses the equality parameter for **LFP** as its equality parameter, and its type parameter, T, must be the input/result type of f. We also make the restriction that f be "monotonic" in the sense that $A \subseteq B \Rightarrow f(A) \subseteq f(B)$.

5.2 Multiset Operators

Multisets support nearly all the same operations as sets, with very similar semantics in most cases. The difference between a multiset and a set is that a multiset may contain multiple occurrences of the same element. The notation used to denote multisets is $\{* e_1, e_2, \cdots, e_n *\}$, where e_i are the elements of the multiset. A multiset former is similar to a set former, so the multiset former $\{* x | x \in M \ and \ x > 1 *\}$ is read as "the multiset of items x, such that each occurrence of x in M is greater than one". We define the *cardinality of an element* of a multiset as the number of occurrences of that element in the multiset. The notation $|A|_a$ means "the cardinality of a in multiset A". Similarly, the notation $|A|_{eq(a)}$ means "the cardinality of elements "equal" to a (where equality is determined by the equality operator, *eq*) in multiset A". We will also speak of the *cardinality of a multiset* $|A|$, meaning its total element count, tallying duplicates as many times as they occur. *Multiset*[T] denotes a multiset containing objects of type T.

Most multiset operators are quite similar to the corresponding set operators, except for the fact that the input and output types are multisets instead of sets. Most of the formal definitions in tables 1, 3, 4, and 5 hold for multisets too.

The exceptions are **multiset**, **dup_elim**, **convert**, defined in table 6; and **union**, **additive_union**, **intersection** and **difference** which are defined in table 7.

In the binary operators on multisets, we find the greatest departure from the corresponding set operators. All the binary operators are based on the

Definitions		
union$(eq,T)(A,B)$	=	$R : Multiset[T]$ such that $\forall x : T$, $\|R\|_{eq(x)} = \max(\|A\|_{eq(x)}, \|B\|_{eq(x)})$ Also, $x \in R \Rightarrow (x \in A)$ *or* $(x \in B)$
additive_union$(eq,T)(A,B)$	=	$R : Multiset[T]$ such that $\forall x : T$, $\|R\|_{eq(x)} = \|A\|_{eq(x)} + \|B\|_{eq(x)}$ Also, $x \in R \Rightarrow (x \in A)$ *or* $(x \in B)$
intersect$(eq,T)(A,B)$	=	$R : Multiset[T]$ such that $\forall x : T$, $\|R\|_{eq(x)} = \min(\|A\|_{eq(x)}, \|B\|_{eq(x)})$ Also, $x \in R \Rightarrow (x \in A)$ *or* $(x \in B)$
diff$(eq,T)(A,B)$	=	$R : Multiset[T]$ such that $\forall x : T$, $\|R\|_{eq(x)} = \max(0, \|A\|_{eq(x)} - \|B\|_{eq(x)})$ Also, $x \in R \Rightarrow (x \in A)$ *or* $(x \in B)$

Table 7: Binary Multiset Operators

cardinality of the elements in the two input sets (table 7). For example, **union** in a multiset is,

$$\textbf{union}\,(id, Int)(\{*\,1,1,2\,*\},\{*\,1,2,2\,*\}) = \{*\,1,1,2,2\,*\}$$

However, regarding the typing of the arguments and the result, binary multiset operators are similar to the set operators. We also define **additive_union** for multisets.

5.3 Other Type Operators

Besides sets and multisets, the algebra supports a host of other types. The union type along with its constructor allows creation of discriminated unions. The operations defined for the type are **union**, **tagcase** and **typecase**. **Union** (U, tag, e) creates an instance of union type U and initializes its contents to be entity e with tag tag. Both **tagcase** (e) and **typecase** (e) selectively execute a set of terms based either on the tag or the type of the union instance e.

Function types represent functions, which take some number of typed parameters and return a single typed result. Instances of function types are created by the use of typed lambda expressions. These instances cannot be tested for equality, since it is impossible to compare two functions.

Tuples are records with named fields, with the familiar operators for instance creation (**tuple**), concatenation (**tup_concat**), and field selection (**select_field** or infix "."). Sufficient care is taken to avoid duplicate field names in **tup_concat**.

Boolean is actually a type rather than a constructor. Booleans are used to represent truth values for conditionals and are provided as the result of comparisons and quantifiers (the set operators **exists** and **forall**). Operations on booleans are **and**, **or**, and **not**.

Abstract data types are composite types whose elements are accessed only via a set of functions, which are called the interface. The functions are accessed via the **invoke**(I, f) operator which invokes f on instance I.

Type	Operators
Set	Set, Choose, Union, Fold, LFP
Multiset	Multiset, Choose, Additive_Union, Fold, LFP
Union	Make_union, Tagcase, Typecase
Tuple	Tuple, Select_field
Boolean	And, Not
Abs	New, Invoke

Table 8: Primitive AQUA Operators

5.4 Primitive Operators

Table 8 provides a minimal set of *primitive* operators[1] for each type. All non-primitive operators can be defined in terms of the primitive operators for the type. For example, **mem** for a set can be defined in terms of **fold**:

$$\textbf{mem}(eq, a)(A) = \textbf{fold}(false,\ \lambda(x)eq(x,a),\ \textbf{or})(A)$$

Similarly, **select** can also be expressed in terms of **fold**:

$$\textbf{select}(p)(A) = \textbf{fold}(\{\ \},\ \lambda(x)\text{if } p(x) \text{ then } \textbf{set}(x) \text{ else } \{\ \},\ \textbf{union}(id, T))(A)$$

Dup_elim can also be expressed using **fold** with **set** and **union** (using identity as the union equality). Indeed, most operations (e.g., **union**, **intersect** and **diff** with equality parameters, **apply**, **group**) can be defined with those three primitive operations.

6 Conclusions

This paper has briefly summarized the AQUA data model and algebra. It is proposed as the input language for object-oriented query optimizers. It has been designed to cover the functionality of many existing query languages, and to provide the maximum potential for optimization. As a result, the set of operators is purposefully not minimal. We have illustrated its use with a few simple examples.

The AQUA data model embodies a uniform approach to objects and values. Values are simply immutable objects. They are objects in all other respects. They have an abstract interface, and they possess an identity that can be used to refer to them.

A type describes syntactic properties of objects and their methods. Semantic properties of a type are supplied by an axiomatic specification, called its *semantics*, that is separated from the type definition (i.e., syntax). Immutability is an example of something that would be specified in the semantics. A given type can be associated with multiple semantics, and each of these semantics can be implemented in many ways. Currently we provide a default mechanism for determining the semantics of objects that are results of algebraic queries and we provide a mechanism for overriding this default.

---

[1]The primitive set union in the table uses identity for equality

This paper has discussed algebraic operators for the *Set* and the *Multiset* types. We also propose an extension to AQUA to include algebraic operators for other bulk types such as *List*, *Tree*, and *Graph* [31].

Acknowledgements

Thanks to: Catriel Beeri, DARPA, Leo Fegaras, David Maier, Scott Meyers, and Hagit Shatkay.

References

[1] S. Abiteboul and P. Kanellakis. Object identity as a query language primitive. In James Clifford, Bruce Lindsay, and David Maier, editors, *Proceedings of the SIGMOD International Conference on Management of Data*. ACM Press, Portland, Oregon, June 1989.

[2] S. Abiteboul, E. Simon, and V. Vianu. Non-deterministic languages to express deterministic transformations. In *Proceedings of the Ninth ACM SIGACT/SIGMOD Symposium on Principles of Database Systems*, Nashville, Tennesee, April 1990.

[3] Antonio Albano, Giorgio Ghelli, and Renzo Orsini. Objects for a database programming language. In Kanellakis and Schmidt [18], pages 236–253.

[4] M. P. Atkinson, C. Lecluse, P. Philbrow, and P. Richard. Design issues in a map language. In Kanellakis and Schmidt [18], pages 20–32.

[5] Jay Banerjee, Hong-Tai Chou, Jorge F. Garza, Won Kim, Darrell Woelk, Nat Ballou, and Hyoung-Joo Kim. Data model issues for object-oriented applications. *ACM Transactions on Office Information Systems*, 5(1):3–26, January 1987.

[6] Catriel Beeri and Yoram Kornatzky. Algebraic optimization of object-oriented query languages. In S. Abiteboul and P. C. Kanellakis, editors, *Proceedings of the Third International Conference on Database Theory*, pages 72–88, Paris, France, December 1990.

[7] Val Breazu-Tannen, Peter Buneman, and Shamim Naqvi. Structural recursion as a query language. In Kanellakis and Schmidt [18], pages 9–19.

[8] Peter Buneman and Atsushi Ohori. A type system that reconciles classes and extents. In Kanellakis and Schmidt [18], pages 191–202.

[9] M. Carey, D. DeWitt, and S. Vandenberg. A data model and query language for EXODUS. In Haran Boral and Per ake Larson, editors, *Proceedings of the SIGMOD International Conference on Management of Data*, pages 413–423, Chicago, Illinois, June 1988.

[10] A. Chandra. Theory of database queries. In *Proc. Conf. on Principles of Database Systems*, pages 1–9, 1988.

[11] Scott Daniels, Goetz Graefe, Thomas Keller, David Maier, Duri Schmidt, and Bennet Vance. Query Optimization in Revelation, an Overview. *IEEE Data Engineering Bulletin*, 14(2):58–62, June 1991.

[12] Umeshwar Dayal, Frank Manola, Alejandro Buchmann, Upen Chakravarthy, David Goldhirsch, Sandra Heiler, Jack Orenstein, and Arnon Rosenthal. Simplifying complex objects: The PROBE approach to modelling and querying them. In Stanley B. Zdonik and David Maier, editors, *Readings in Object-Oriented Database Systems*, pages 390–399. Morgan Kaufmann Publishers, Inc., Los Altos, California, 1990.

[13] Adele Goldberg and David Robson. *Smalltalk-80: The Language and its Implementation*. Addison-Wesley, Reading, MA, 1983.

[14] John V. Guttag, James J. Horning, and Jeanette M. Wing. The Larch family of specification languages. *IEEE Software*, 2(5):24–36, September 1985.

[15] Hull and Yoshikawa. ILOG: Declarative creation and manipulation of object identifiers. In Dennis McLeod, Ron Sacks-Davis, and Hans Schek, editors, *Proceedings of the 16th International Conference on Very Large Data Bases*. Morgan Kaufmann Publishers, Inc., Brisbane, Australia, August 1990.

[16] IEEE. *Proceedings of the Sixth International Conference on Data Engineering*, Los Angeles, California, February 1990. IEEE Computer Society Press.

[17] Paris Kanellakis. Elements of relational database theory. In J. van Leeuwen, editor, *Handbook of Theoretical Computer Science*, volume 2, chapter 17, pages 1073–1144. Elsevier Science Publishers B.V., Amsterdam, 1990.

[18] Paris Kanellakis and Joachim W. Schmidt, editors. *Bulk Types & Persistent Data: The Third International Workshop on Database Programming Languages*, Nafplion, Greece, August 1991. Morgan Kaufmann Publishers, Inc.

[19] G. M. Kuper. *The Logical Data Model: A New Approach to Database Logic*. Ph.D. thesis, Dept. of Computer Science, Stanford University,, Stanford, CA, Sept 1985.

[20] David Maier, Jacob Stein, Allen Otis, and Alan Purdy. Development of an object-oriented DBMS. In Norman Meyrowitz, editor, *Proceedings of the Conference on Object-oriented Programming Systems, Languages and Applications*, pages 472–482, Portland, Oregon, September-October 1986.

[21] Florian Matthes and Joachim W. Schmidt. Bulk types: Built-in or add-on? In Kanellakis and Schmidt [18], pages 33–53.

[22] Bertrand Meyer. *Object-Oriented Software Construction*. Prentice-Hall, Englewood Cliffs, New Jersey, 1988.

[23] Gail Mitchell, Stanley B. Zdonik, and Umeshwar Dayal. An Architecture for Query Processing in Persistent Object Stores. In *Proceedings of the Hawaii International Conference on System Sciences*, volume II, pages 787–798, January 1992.

[24] S. Osborn. Identity, equality, and query optimization. In K. Dittrich, editor, *Advances in Object-Oriented Database Systems*. Berlin, Germany, 1988.

[25] Joel Richardson and Peter Schwarz. MDM: An object-oriented data model. In Kanellakis and Schmidt [18], pages 86–95.

[26] L. Rowe and M. Stonebraker. The POSTGRES data model. In *Proceedings of the Thirteenth Very Large Databases Conference*. Morgan Kaufmann Publishers, Inc., 1987.

[27] Steve Rozen and Dennis Shasha. Rationale and design of Bulk. In Kanellakis and Schmidt [18], pages 71–85.

[28] Gail M. Shaw and Stanley B. Zdonik. A query algebra for object-oriented databases. In *Proceedings of the Sixth International Conference on Data Engineering* [16], pages 152–162.

[29] David D. Straube and M. Tamer Ozsu. Queries and query processing in object-oriented database systems. *ACM Transactions on Office Information Systems*, 8(4), Oct 1990.

[30] B. Stroustrup. *The C++ Programming Language*. Addison-Wesley Publishing Company, Reading, Massachusetts, second edition, 1992.

[31] Bharathi Subramanian, Stanley B. Zdonik, Theodore W. Leung, and Scott L. Vandenberg. Ordered types in the AQUA data model. In *Proceedings of the Fourth International Workshop on Database Programming Languages*, New York, New York, August 1993. Springer Verlag.

[32] B. Vance. Towards an object-oriented query algebra. Tech. Report CS/E91-008, Dept. of Computer Science and Eng., Oregon Graduate Institute, Beaverton, OR, January 1992.

[33] S. Vandenberg and D. DeWitt. Algebraic support for complex objects with arrays, identity, and inheritance. In James Clifford and Roger King, editors, *Proceedings of the SIGMOD International Conference on Management of Data*, pages 158–167, Denver, Colorado, May 1991.

An Abstract Object-Oriented Query Execution Language

Bennet Vance
Oregon Graduate Institute of Science & Technology
Portland, Oregon, USA

Abstract
What is an appropriate generalization of relational *join* to object-oriented query algebras? No satisfactory answer has yet been given; the difficulty of the question prompts us to address a different, though related question: What are appropriate abstractions for expressing object-oriented query execution plans? Our answer takes the form of a *language* that can serve as the interface between an optimizer and an execution engine. Our query execution language is designed to express arbitrary object-oriented queries, and to couch them in terms of efficient algorithms—such as join algorithms—when possible. By carefully choosing our query execution abstractions, we are able to optimize join-like queries in ways that had been inaccessible at the algebraic level. Yet the optimizations we achieve have an "algebraic flavor." Indeed, the execution language may be thought of as a kind of low-level algebra; moreover, through its data abstraction facilities it may be extended with new types and operators in such a way that it acquires the functionality of a higher-level algebra. Our language thus creates a framework in which both the inputs and outputs of an optimizer can be expressed, and their semantics compared.

1 Introduction

1.1 Overview

In pursuing efficient object-oriented query processing strategies, it is logical to take relational technology as a model and starting point. An idealized picture of the phases of relational query processing appears in Figure 1. In the first phase, a user query written in an SQL-like language is translated into an expression in the relational algebra. In the second phase—the optimization phase—this algebraic expression may be rewritten to an alternative expression (equivalent in meaning, but less costly to evaluate) before finally being translated into a *query plan* (or query *execution* plan). Finally, in the third phase, the query plan is executed against the database.

If we wish to adapt the relational technology to object-oriented queries, we must make adjustments to the picture in Figure 1. For one thing, the relational algebra is no longer adequate. What takes its place? Surely the analogue of the relational algebra would have to be the *object-oriented algebra*; indeed, several object-oriented algebras have been proposed. But it is premature to speak of *the* object-oriented algebra. While various algebras are starting to converge in their expression of select-like and project-like operators, there is no such convergence in the offing for join-like operators, much less for multidimensional array operators.

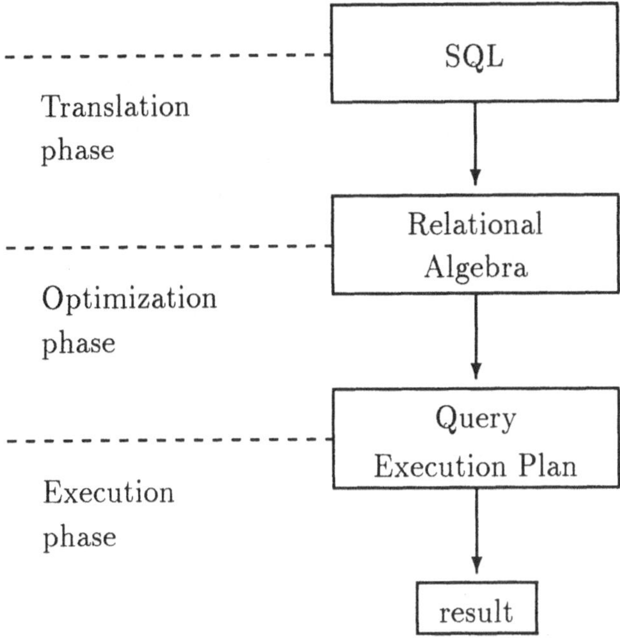

Figure 1: Phases of Relational Query Processing

What about the query execution plan language? The mechanisms used to encode query plans are perhaps not generally thought of as constituting a language; they are treated more as implementation internals of a query processing system. But it may be profitable to develop abstractions of those mechanisms so that they *can* be regarded as constituting a language. Doing so not only clarifies the interface between the optimization and execution phases of query processing, but also (as we shall see) points the way to optimization strategies that might otherwise have remained obscure.

This paper presents the preliminary design of the REVELATION Abstract Execution Algorithm Language (REXALL). REXALL is, first and foremost, an object-oriented functional language. But since the objective of the language is to support efficient query evaluation, the core language is augmented with built-in mechanisms for carrying out operations on collection types. These mechanisms are abstractions of familiar techniques in the evaluation of relational queries.

1.2 Motivation

1.2.1 Benefits of a Query Execution Language

A formal query execution language such as REXALL offers benefits on several planes:

- By nailing down the interface between the optimizer and execution engine, such a language promotes genuinely modular construction of these query processing components. Existing query processing systems are insufficiently modular to allow mixing and matching of optimizers and execution engines.

- Without a precise way of describing query plans and assigning a semantics to them, it is impossible to verify that a given plan has a semantics that is faithful to the algebraic expression from which it derives. Hence it is impossible to prove that an optimizer behaves correctly in the sense of preserving semantics of queries. The REXALL notation is amenable to denotational description; furthermore, it is extensible in such a way that it can express higher-level algebraic expressions as well as execution plans, and thus it provides a single framework in which to compare the semantics of expressions at different levels of abstraction.

- In transforming algebraic expressions into execution plans, current optimizers rely on *ad hoc* annotations such as *physical properties* as a crutch to get some of the details right. However, the physical property of sort order is needed only because optimizers fail to maintain a precise semantic relationship between algebraic expressions and execution plans. If transformation rules were expressed so as to preserve semantics, some of the physical property constraints could be absorbed into the transformation rules themselves, simplifying the optimizer specification.

- A well-crafted query execution language will have interesting algebraic properties that can serve as the basis for novel optimizations.

The last point deserves further comment.

Query algebra expressions contain *logical* operators such as **`select`**, **`project`**, and **`join`**, whereas execution plans contain *physical* operators such as **`filter`**, **`hash_join`**, and **`merge_join`**. Reflecting this distinction, execution plans are sometimes referred to as *physical algebra* expressions. This terminology suggests that execution plans are recognized as having an algebraic character; yet current practice makes no allowance for optimizations based on the algebraic properties of physical operators. For example, rule files accepted by the Volcano Optimizer Generator [20] may contain logical-to-logical and logical-to-physical transformations, but not physical-to-physical transformations.

Presumably the reason for shunning physical-to-physical transformations is that whenever possible, it is preferable to transform an expression at the logical level. For example, **`join`**, **`hash_join`**, and **`merge_join`** are all commutative. But by reordering join arguments exclusively at the logical level, one need only consider a single commutativity law for the logical operator **`join`**, rather than a multiplicity of laws for **`hash_join`**, **`merge_join`**, and perhaps other physical join implementations that a system might support.

In other instances, a logical rule has no physical counterpart. Consider the logical rule

$$R \cup S \Rightarrow S \cup R,$$

which expresses the commutativity of set union. At the physical level, sets are typically represented as ordered sequences (i.e., *lists*), and the union of two sets could be obtained by concatenating their representations (call these $\bar{R}$ and $\bar{S}$) and then removing duplicates (here ++ denotes list concatenation):

$$R \cup S \Rightarrow \texttt{dup\_elim}(\bar{R} +\!\!+ \bar{S})$$

But the physical rule that would then express commutativity of set union,

$$\texttt{dup\_elim}(\bar{R} +\!\!+ \bar{S}) \Rightarrow \texttt{dup\_elim}(\bar{S} +\!\!+ \bar{R}),$$

is unsound, since the left- and right-hand sides yield different lists in general.

However, it is a mistake to conclude from these examples that all transformations should be carried out at the logical level. There are also *physical* transformations that have no *logical* counterpart. For example, when joining two relations on attribute A and then *grouping* the result by attribute A, it is possible to combine the two operations into one: A variant of merge join can accomplish both the logical join and the subsequent grouping in a single physical operation. But as yet we have no notation for expressing this variant of merge join, and consequently no algebraic formulation of this plainly valuable transformation.

The foregoing observations raise several questions: Can all interesting transformations on physical operators be expressed as algebraic laws? Are there useful transformations that have so far gone unnoticed? Are there unifying principles that underlie seemingly different transformations? We can begin to answer these questions only if we can say, with some precision, what the physical operators are.

1.2.2 The Object-Oriented Join Problem

The relational operators `select`, `union`, `set_difference`, and `cross_product` generalize easily to arbitrary sets, bags, and lists. But recent work in query algebras has gone beyond merely generalizing the relational operators to new, non-relational contexts. The analysis by Breazu-Tannen, Buneman, and Naqvi [6] is particularly clear in bringing out the underlying patterns of computation that relate these different operators to one another. Given set union as a primitive, the other operators may be seen as instances of a single reduction operator Φ. Moreover, some compositions of relational operators, such as a `project` of a `select`, can be expressed as a *single* application of Φ. Interestingly, the physical operator `filter` used by the Volcano system [19] to implement `select` and `project` is closely related to the algebraic abstraction Φ, and indeed is capable of performing both selection and projection in one step. It is perhaps paradoxical that the low-level physical operator `filter` should bear such a strong similarity to the high-level, abstract operator Φ; but the intent of both operators is to capture a computational idiom that arises in query processing, and seen in this light, the parallel between them is not surprising.

In devising a generalized form of relational join suitable for an object-oriented algebra, one might hope to capture a computational idiom embodied by some physical algorithm that implements join. If the parallel were as strong as in the case of Φ and `filter`, the generalized join should be able to express other operations that can be implemented with the same physical algorithm, such as intersection, difference, grouping, and duplicate elimination. More than that, one would expect that the generalized operator would obey algebraic laws relating these different operations; for example, the possibility of combining two such operations into a single physical operation ought to be expressible as a law involving our hypothetical generalized join operator.

Unfortunately, it is difficult to generalize join at all, much less to devise an operator with the characteristics we have just described. One of the properties of relational join that contributes to the effectiveness of algebraic optimization is its associativity; but when it is generalized in a straightforward way to accept arguments that are sets of arbitrary objects, and not necessarily sets of *tuples*, associativity is lost. The `Ojoin` operator of the ENCORE algebra [35] overcomes this difficulty by behaving differently depending on whether both, one, or neither of its operands are sets of tuples. The definition is so constructed that `Ojoin` is associative, but its nonuniformity disrupts the orthogonality of the algebra, and complicates its semantics. Yet no better solution has been offered.

A further difficulty in the generalization of join resides in the predicates by which join operators are parameterized. The applicability of efficient join algorithms to relational equijoins is assured by the simple predicate structure of relational queries. When richer predicates are allowed, as is usual in object-oriented algebras, it is no longer clear that these efficient algorithms apply, and consequently it is unclear whether a join operator still has value.

In the present work we evade these problems by focusing on the physical level, paying little attention to the logical algebraic level. We proceed on the assumption that whatever logical algebra one ultimately comes up with, it will include one or more operators that should map into efficient join algorithms. Thus our execution language includes an abstraction of a physical hash-join algorithm; we shall show both how it can be used to express a variety of logical operations, and how it can facilitate low-level transformations of queries.

1.2.3 A Sample Query

To illustrate the kind of optimization made possible by our hash-join abstraction, we shall consider the expression $\mathtt{sum}(A \cap B) - \mathtt{sum}(A - B)$. Here A and B are assumed to be large sets of integers, **sum** sums a set of integers, and the two occurrences of $-$ denote, respectively, integer subtraction and set difference. Not much can be done to optimize this expression in the framework of existing algebras.

Yet we know that the computation of $(A \cap B)$ and that of $(A - B)$ will *each* involve something akin to a hash join of A and B. That being the case, should it not be possible to compute both $(A \cap B)$ and $(A - B)$ with a *single* hash join? It not only *should be* possible, but it *is* possible, and later on we will see how it may be done. The query at hand, $\mathtt{sum}(A \cap B) - \mathtt{sum}(A - B)$, is not known to be of great practical import; but it usefully demonstrates the efficacy of our approach in exposing transformations that at first glance would appear to be beyond the reach of algebraic optimization.

1.3 Goals and Organization

If it is to realize the benefits cited in the previous section, a query execution language should possess at least the following characteristics:

- Simplicity. Simplicity is particularly desirable for the purpose of giving the language a rigorous semantics and for reasoning about it formally. But a simple execution language is desirable also from the perspective of implementing an optimizer or an execution engine with the execution language as its interface.
- Expressiveness. As an intermediate language in query processing, it must be able to express user queries. Specifically, for the REVELATION project [27], it must be able to express any construct in the REVELATION user language [15] without undue contortion.
- Amenability to efficient execution—with particular emphasis on bulk operations, which are at the heart of query processing.
- Amenability to transformation through simple algebraic laws. Possession of this trait largely accounts for the relational algebra's success as a vehicle for query optimization.

As is typical with design criteria, there are tensions among these goals, and no single compromise is obviously "right." Our own compromise will emphasize simplicity somewhat more, and efficiency somewhat less, than if we were designing a query execution language for commercial purposes.

The language REXALL is intended to meet the stated goals. Following a brief survey of related work, we proceed as follows: In section 3, we sketch the REXALL core language, which captures the essential functionality of the REVELATION user language. Section 4 presents two of the built-in operators with which the core language will be augmented so that REXALL can provide access to efficient algorithms for bulk operations. Section 5 describes the mechanism by which the inputs and outputs of different bulk operations are tied together. Section 6 summarizes, and mentions future work.

2 Related Work

The present work is a synthesis of previous work that comes principally from two areas. The first of these areas is programming language theory, and in particular, the theory of object-oriented programming. Cardelli, Mitchell, and Bruce, among others, have studied miniature languages that attempt to capture the essence of object-orientedness with a minimum of extraneous baggage [7, 8, 11, 12, 13, 30]. In the process, these and other researchers have explored type systems that integrate the parametric polymorphism familiar to functional programmers with the inclusion polymorphism of object-oriented programming [14, 10, 1].

The second area we draw on is relational query processing technology [21, 29], and especially our experience with the Volcano query execution engine [19, 23, 18]. The idea of using concurrency to construct DAGs of iterators appeared long ago in the EXPRESS system [36]. Similar notions are found in the literature on concurrent evaluation of functional programs; the reader is referred to the text by Kelly [24], which provides further references. However, the concurrent evaluation networks in the present work are more closely related to Reppy's work [33] on lightweight threads and channels in Standard ML. Note that lazy evaluation is essential to the execution of the networks described by Kelly, whereas Reppy's threads execute within a call-by-value language.

Although our topic here is not query algebras per se, several papers on object-oriented query algebras, and on general operators over bulk types, deserve mention as motivating influences on the present work [3, 4, 6, 32, 35, 37, 38, 39, 40]. Also deserving mention are several previous papers in which an intermediate language of some kind is proposed to assist in optimizing and efficiently executing queries [9, 16, 26]. However, the languages discussed in those papers bear little if any resemblance to the language presented here.

3 The REXALL Core Language

The language REXALL consists of two quite distinct components: a *core language*, and a collection of built-in primitives for carrying out bulk processing operations. One way to think of the division between these components is by analogy to other languages such as C; in such an analogy, the REXALL core language corresponds to the C language itself, while the REXALL built-in primitives correspond to the C library. Another, rather different way to think about the structure of REXALL is to compare it to the relational algebra. Expressions in the relational algebra consist not only of relational operators and names of relations, but also of *predicates* that parameterize selection and join operations. (They also contain *attribute lists* that parameterize projection operations.) The syntax used to express predicates may be thought of as a *predicate language* that is embedded within the relational algebra. In REXALL, the core language plays the role of the predicate language in the relational algebra. That is, the core language provides the means for expressing predicates and other phrases that parameterize the built-in bulk processing operations. In this sense, REXALL has very much the flavor of an object-oriented query algebra. Indeed, though we call REXALL an execution language and use it as such, it may also be thought of as a kind of low-level query algebra, in which the built-in operators and data types have direct physical realizations.

But comparison with the relational algebra also reveals important contrasts. While the predicate language of the relational algebra has limited expressive power, the predicate languages of object-oriented algebras tend to be much more expressive, reflecting the greater complexity of the data they manipulate. In the case of REXALL, the core language is sufficiently general and expressive that it may serve as a query language in its own right, without any reliance at all on the bulk processing primitives. The reason for augmenting the core language with bulk processing primitives is not to add expressive power, but simply to increase efficiency and conciseness—with the added benefit that bulk operations lend themselves to high-level optimizing transformations. Note how different the relational algebra is in this regard: the operators of the relational algebra are its essence, and without them it could express nothing.

When we optimize a REVELATION user query, we will translate the query into an expression in the REXALL core language. Since we want that expression to execute efficiently, we will seek to make use of appropriate bulk processing operations wherever possible. But in the worst case, we will simply end up with an expression in the core language that reflects the original user query. Thus, the paramount requirement of the core language is that it be able to express arbitrary user queries.

The purpose of this section is to give a sense of what the core language looks like, and how its expressions are constructed. In a nutshell, the core language is a λ-calculus extended with object-oriented features; some details and examples follow below.[1] It may seem at first peculiar that the core language is a general-purpose language that has nothing in particular to do with databases. But on reflection one may come to feel that it is entirely appropriate—where feasible—to avoid making a distinction between general-purpose computations and database computations.

3.1 Objects and Values

Because there are different conventions on the usage of the terms *object* and *value*, we begin by clarifying our own usage. We use *value* much as it is used in the functional programming literature, as an all-embracing term for the elements of computational domains; thus, a value may be a Boolean, a string, a tuple, a function, or—in our usage—an *object*. An object is a value that *understands messages*.[2] (What it means to understand a message will become clearer as we proceed.) Thus, in the following, an *object type* is simply the type of a particular variety of values.

A frequent convention regarding "objects" is that they possess "object identity," and that any two objects created separately, even if behaviorally identical, are distinguishable. However, there is no reason why this property of objects must necessarily be lumped together with the property of understanding messages. We prefer to separate these notions. Our objects all understand messages, but they may or may not possess "object identity"; as a rule, they do not.

3.2 Data Types

Syntactically, the simplest types in REXALL are such types as `string` or `bool` or `int`. These types may be thought of as *base types*, although they are actually *predefined object types*. Exactly two things may be done with an object: it may be passed as an argument to a function, or it may be sent a message. An object of type `int`, for example, may be sent the messages $+$, $-$, or $>$, as well as other messages representing arithmetic and comparison operators. Examples of message-passing constructs will be given in the following.

We also have predefined *type constructors*, such as `List`. Constructors are not themselves types, but may be applied to type arguments, using a bracket notation, to construct new types. Thus, `List[int]` and `List[List[int]]` are types, and have the expected meanings: a list of integers, and a list of lists of integers.

[1] The notations (and ideas) that appear in the core language derive chiefly from $F_{<:}$ [12], **fun** [13], and Standard ML [28]. See also the functional programming text by Bird and Wadler [5].

[2] It is not merely to be facetious that we note a perverse reading of this definition: *Every* value is an object, since every value understands zero or more messages. In fact we may usefully view every value type as also being an object type; that view allows function types to participate in the same type hierarchy as other object types.

The type constructors for tuples and functions have special syntax. By a *tuple* we mean an ordered, unlabeled tuple, such as a pair of integers, which we denote (`int`, `int`). (The topic of *labeled* records is omitted from this paper.) Our function types resemble those of other functional languages. Thus, a function conforms to type $\tau_1 \rightarrow \tau_2$ if and only if it accepts an argument conforming to type τ_1, and yields a result conforming to type τ_2.

In contrast to many functional languages, REXALL requires that quantification of parametrically polymorphic functions be explicit. For example, consider the function **select** which, given a predicate and a list, selects those elements of the list that satisfy the predicate. If the list elements have type α, then the predicate should have type ($\alpha\rightarrow$**bool**), and a plausible curried typing for the selection function as a whole would be ($\alpha\rightarrow$**bool**)$\rightarrow$**List**[α]$\rightarrow$**List**[α]; that is, given a predicate on α's and a list of α's, it returns a new list of α's. But a REXALL type may not contain free occurrences of a type variable such as α. To bind the α's, the type of **select** must be given as

$$\forall[\alpha]\ (\alpha\rightarrow\mathtt{bool})\rightarrow\mathtt{List}[\alpha]\rightarrow\mathtt{List}[\alpha].$$

Intuitively, this typing may be read as saying that for *any* type α, **select** will accept a predicate of type ($\alpha\rightarrow$**bool**) and a list of type **List**[α], and return a new list of type **List**[α]. Further discussion of quantified types may be found in the survey on types, data abstraction, and polymorphism by Cardelli and Wegner [13]. Other, more fundamental issues in the typing of functional languages, including currying, are presented nicely in the text by Bird and Wadler [5].

This cursory account of the REXALL type system has skipped over many significant aspects of it, notably subtyping and bounded quantification. But while those aspects of the type system are integral to the conception of REXALL as an object-oriented execution language, we need not trouble ourselves with them here, as they do not come into play in the remainder of this paper.

3.3 Value Expressions

The simplest value expressions or *terms* in REXALL are constants, e.g., numeric and string constants, and identifiers such as x or **EmptySet** or **select**. An identifier denotes the value it is bound to; it may be bound to a value through a local binding, as described in the following, or it may have a predefined or persistent binding. However, we shall not discuss the mechanism by which persistent bindings are created.

The next simplest expressions are tuple constructors. For example, if E_1 and E_2 are value expressions, then the pair constructor (E_1, E_2) denotes the pair of values denoted by E_1 and E_2; thus, if x is bound to 3, then the expression $(x, 5)$ denotes the pair of integers $(3, 5)$.

In most functional languages, function application is denoted by juxtaposition; that is, $f\ x$ denotes the application of f to x. This convention is followed by REXALL as well, but in REXALL the function argument is required to be surrounded by parentheses. Accordingly, the expression $f(x)$ denotes the application of f to x, where f and x may themselves be complex expressions. Evaluation order is eager; that is, the expressions f and x are completely evaluated first, and only then is the function denoted by f applied to the value denoted by x.

New functions are created through λ-abstraction. For example,

$$\lambda(x : \mathtt{int})\ \mathtt{max}(x, 3)$$

is the function which returns either its argument, or 3, whichever is larger. (We assume here that **max** is a predefined function that returns the maximum of its two arguments.) Note that the formal parameter x is *local* to the body of the abstraction; occurrences of x outside the abstraction body must refer to some different x. When the abstraction is applied to an argument, the variable x is *bound* to that argument inside the abstraction body. Unlike function abstractions in many functional languages, our abstractions *require* that a type be specified for the formal parameter; the expression $\lambda(x)\ \mathtt{max}(x, 3)$ would not be legitimate.

It is convenient in some situations to use a **let** construct to create local bindings for one or more variables. If the expression v has type τ, then the expression **let** $x = v$ **in** E is equivalent to $(\lambda(x : \tau)\ E)(v)$; that is, the value of the expression as a whole is obtained by evaluating E with x bound to the value of v. Similarly, **let** $(x, y) = (v, w)$ **in** E is equivalent to $(\lambda(x : \tau_1, y : \tau_2)\ )(v, w)$ when v and w have types τ_1 and τ_2, respectively.

In addition to functions whose arguments are *values*, REXALL provides for *second-order* functions whose arguments are *types*. For example, the function **select** discussed above had type

$$\forall[\alpha]\ (\alpha \rightarrow \mathtt{bool}) \rightarrow \mathtt{List}[\alpha] \rightarrow \mathtt{List}[\alpha].$$

To supply a binding for the type variable α, **select** would have to be applied to a type before it could be given any other arguments. Thus, one might select the positive integers from a list ℓ of integers by writing

$$\mathtt{select}[\mathtt{int}](\lambda(x : \mathtt{int})\ x > 0)(\ell).$$

An argument in square brackets, such as [**int**] in this example, is a type argument. The argument $\lambda(x : \mathtt{int})\ x > 0$ is a predicate function of type **int→bool**. (The abstraction body $x > 0$ involves message sending, which will be explained presently.) To create a new function that takes a type as an argument, one would use a *second-order abstraction*; however, we will not discuss such abstractions here. For further elucidation of second-order functions, the reader is again referred to the survey by Cardelli and Wegner [13].

Probably the least familiar notation in REXALL, at least for functional programmers, is the notation for sending messages. Messages without arguments are straightforward. Imagine that there is a message **empty**, understood by lists, that tells whether a list is the empty list. Then if ℓ denotes a list, the construct ℓ **empty** denotes a Boolean value, **true** if ℓ is empty and **false** otherwise. In this simple case, the notation for message sending is simple juxtaposition, as in Smalltalk [17]. Message-sending constructs in REXALL can be distinguished from function applications by virtue of the fact that a message will not be surrounded by parentheses. Thus, ℓ **empty** is a message-sending expression, whereas ℓ(**empty**) is a function application—albeit an illegal one, since a list is not a function.

Now integers, as we have noted, understand such messages as +, −, and >, but these messages have arguments. We may send the message + to the integer i by using juxtaposition as before; thus, we may write $i+$. But this expression is incomplete, in a sense; what it denotes is a *function* which, when applied to an argument j, will yield the sum of i and j. In other words, the sum of i and j may be written as $(i+)(j)$, or, equivalently, as $i + (j)$, since message sending and function application associate to the left, rendering the first pair of parentheses unnecessary. However, the notation $i + (j)$ is still awkward, so we adopt the convention that $i + j$ means the same thing: that is, it means, "Send the message + to i, and apply the resultant function to j."

3.4 Data Abstraction

The REXALL core language has a data abstraction facility for creating new abstract data types. There are two aspects to this facility: in the syntax of types, there is a construct for defining new object types, and in the syntax of terms, there is a corresponding construct for forming new objects of a given object type. However, the specifics of these provisions in REXALL need not concern us here. More important is the concept that the behavior of an abstract data type may be defined by declaring a *representation* for objects of that type, together with *methods* that implement operations on those objects through manipulations of the objects' representations. Such a concept of data abstraction appears in the programming language CLU [25]; it also appears in object-oriented languages such as Smalltalk [17], in which the notion of a *representation* is replaced by *instance variables*, which serve the same purpose.

The REXALL data abstraction facility is important for expressing constructs of the user-level language. But it also turns out to play a pivotal role in establishing a semantic relationship between query execution plans and higher-level query algebra expressions. The importance of data abstraction in relating expressions on different levels may best be conveyed through an example.

Consider the data type `Bag`, and imagine defining it as an abstract data type with a representation and some collection of abstract operations. A likely choice for the representation would be a `List`. Now one of the basic dyadic operations on bags is additive union (usually denoted $\uplus$), and this operation on bags could be straightforwardly defined to concatenate the list representations of the two bags being combined, and then to convert the resultant list into a new bag abstraction. Other operations on bags could be handled similarly.

However, there is something missing from the bag abstraction just described. Bags as we have defined them behave no differently from lists, but we know that bags should have some properties that lists do not have; for example, additive union on bags is commutative, whereas list concatenation is not. One way of obtaining the desired algebraic properties for the bag abstraction is simply to *assert* those properties; however, taking that approach does not advance the cause of establishing a semantic link between algebraic expressions and execution plans. On the contrary, asserting out of the blue that an abstract data type possesses particular algebraic properties can wreak semantic havoc. If A and B are bags, and if $\bar{A}$ and $\bar{B}$ are the representations of those bags as lists, we would like to be able to say that the execution plan $\bar{A} +\!\!+ \bar{B}$ preserves the semantics of the algebraic expression $A \uplus B$. Similarly, the plan $\bar{B} +\!\!+ \bar{A}$ ought to be semantically faithful to the expression $B \uplus A$. But now we face a dilemma, for if $\uplus$ is commutative, then $A \uplus B$ must be semantically equivalent to $B \uplus A$; but the semantics of these expressions, we have agreed, are captured respectively by $\bar{A} +\!\!+ \bar{B}$ and by $\bar{B} +\!\!+ \bar{A}$, and hence we are forced to conclude that the last two expressions are semantically equivalent, which is patent nonsense.

The source of the difficulty is that while $\bar{A} ++ \bar{B}$ is a valid implementation for $A \uplus B$, it is not the *only* valid implementation. We may not semantically equate the abstract operation $A \uplus B$ with some particular implementation, but rather we must equate the abstract operation with the *set of all possible valid implementations* for the given representation. To assist us in this objective, REXALL provides several nondeterministic choice operators; the one that will help us with bag semantics is called the *disorder* operator, and is written as ξ. The disorder operator takes a list as its argument, and arbitrarily permutes the elements of that list. Thus, applying ξ to the list $[1,2,3]$ could yield any of the lists $[1,2,3]$, $[1,3,2]$, $[2,1,3]$, $[2,3,1]$, $[3,1,2]$, or $[3,2,1]$—we cannot say which one.

Armed with the disorder operator, we may amend the definition of additive union for bags. We shall now say that $A \uplus B$ is implemented by $\xi(\bar{A} ++ \bar{B})$, which by leaving the order of the result indeterminate, effectively allows multiple implementations of the operation. Now, since an arbitrary permutation of $\bar{A} ++ \bar{B}$ may equally well be viewed as an arbitrary permutation of $\bar{B} ++ \bar{A}$, we have the equivalence

$$\xi(\bar{A} ++ \bar{B}) \equiv \xi(\bar{B} ++ \bar{A}).$$

It then follows that $A \uplus B \equiv B \uplus A$; this algebraic law is now a provable *consequence* of the definition of the bag abstraction, and not just some wishful postulate.

In future papers we will go into the disorder operator and related matters in more depth. The objective of the brief discussion here has been to illustrate how we are able to express operations on abstract data types, and to give them the correct semantics, even though we have not built those data types into our language. As a result, REXALL can function as a high-level query algebra, provided we supply appropriate definitions for the data types we wish the algebra to manipulate. Yet at heart REXALL is a low-level language. The built-in bulk processing primitives, as described in section 4, address just a single bulk type—lists. It is through the language's extensibility that they indirectly support other bulk types as well.

3.5 Efficiency

We have emphasized the fact that we intend to obtain efficiency in query processing through the bulk processing primitives, and that in the design of the core language itself we are more concerned with expressiveness. However, there are also efficiency considerations that enter into the design of the core language. When a core language expression parameterizes a bulk operation, often that expression will be executed repeatedly, perhaps once for each element of a large collection. Gross inefficiencies in the execution of such an expression would therefore be unacceptable. We also need to be concerned with the sizes of the physical data representations used by the core language. Inefficiencies in the representations of small objects will be magnified when many such objects are aggregated together into large objects.

Some of the provisions of the core language that directly address efficiency issues are as follows. Access to machine arithmetic is provided through integer and real constants and through built-in mechanisms for operating on them.

Similarly, character strings are given primitive support. Language constructs for tupling and discriminated unions permit these types of objects to be compactly represented and rapidly manipulated. Run-time integrity checks are avoided by virtue of the language's strong static typing. The idea behind these provisions is to put the language roughly in the same league as Standard ML [28] with respect to the quality of code that can be generated from it.[3] With current compiler technology [2], one should expect to obtain code that runs possibly an order of magnitude slower than C code with the same functionality. While such a level of performance is hardly ideal, it is adequate for the purposes of a research language.

3.6 Summary

We have discussed a handful of essential aspects of the REXALL core language. Many details have been omitted, among them the typing of messages, subtyping, the mechanics of object formation, and the construction of recursive and mutually recursive functions.

But the main points of this section have been conceptual. The core language may be thought of as a predicate language for parameterizing bulk operations, but it also serves as a general-purpose query language that can express arbitrary user queries. One of the facilities it includes to that end is a data abstraction mechanism, which plays a dual role in that it also provides the means to extend the low-level execution language to a high-level algebra.

In addition to these conceptual observations, we have given some explanation of the technical details of core language constructs. Those constructs will appear again when we present examples of the parameterization of bulk operations in the following section.

4 Bulk Processing Abstractions in REXALL

Built-in operators in REXALL provide efficient support for the collection-oriented operations that are at the heart of query processing. These built-in operators may be thought of as abstractions of such execution algorithms as file scan, hash join, merge join, and so on. Both in the interest of keeping the number of abstractions manageable, and in the interest of making them flexible, we place as little operator-specific functionality as possible in the abstractions themselves, instead allowing them to be specialized to particular operators through function parameters. In the following we describe two of our bulk processing abstractions.

4.1 Aggregation

One of the most straightforward operations on collection types is aggregation—the computation of sums, averages, membership, quantified predicates, and so

[3]Note that existing implementations of Standard ML tend to make heavy use of indirection (i.e., *boxed* values) when constructing complex data structures. It is possible, and in database applications almost certainly desirable, to reduce this reliance on indirection. The cost in doing so is that it may become necessary for a compiler to create multiple versions of polymorphic functions [31].

on. Rather than providing separate abstractions for each such aggregation operator, we have a single abstraction, **accum**, with several parameters. The parameter of greatest interest here is a *function* that is applied once for each element of the collection being aggregated. This function must accept three arguments: the running "total" so far, the next collection element to be aggregated, and a *continuation*, about which we will say more below. Thus, to sum a collection of integers, we would provide the aggregation parameter

$$\text{INTSUM} = \lambda(\mathit{total} : \texttt{int}, \mathit{element} : \texttt{int}, \mathit{kdone} : \texttt{Cont[int]})\ \mathit{total} + \mathit{element},$$

where `Cont` is the type constructor for continuations. Then in carrying out a summation, the REXALL aggregation mechanism would repeatedly invoke INTSUM, passing it a running total, a collection element, and a continuation as arguments. On each invocation, the body of INTSUM would add the given *element* to the running *total* and return a new running total; that new total would become the first argument to INTSUM on the next iteration. In this example, the continuation argument *kdone* is not used.

The continuation argument is useful in situations where it may not be necessary to examine all elements of a collection to determine the result of the aggregation. Consider existential quantification of a predicate: to implement this aggregate, we would want to examine the elements of a collection until we found one that satisfied the predicate—and then immediately return `true` without examining further elements. Invoking an aggregation function's continuation argument allows the aggregation to be shortcut in just this way.

4.2 Hash Join

We now move on to a more complicated abstraction—our abstraction of hash join. A variety of logical operations, including joins, intersections, differences, groupings, and duplicate eliminations, can all be performed by a hash-join algorithm. A successful abstraction of hash join will retain that versatility.

4.2.1 Conception

Recall the way in which hash join implements a relational equijoin. The two relations to be joined are referred to as the *build* input and the *probe* input, respectively. The algorithm first constructs a hash table containing the elements of the build input, using its join attribute as the hash key. Then for each element in the probe input, the hash table is consulted to find the elements of the build input whose join attribute matches that of the given probe element; pairs of matching build and probe elements are combined and emitted as result elements. In an ordinary equijoin, that is the end of the algorithm. However, in a left outer join, there is an additional, final step: the hash-table elements that were never probed (i.e., that matched no probe elements) are padded with nulls and emitted as result elements.

Let us develop an abstraction of this algorithm in two stages. Consider first what is needed to perform the equijoin $R \bowtie_{r.A=s.B} S$:

1. Given a tuple from R, the algorithm needs to be able to extract its A attribute. Accordingly, we will parameterize our abstraction with a projection function p_1 for computing the value of the join attribute.

2. Similarly, a second projection function p_2 will be needed to extract the join attribute B from tuples of S.

3. When a tuple of R and a tuple of S match on their join attribute, the algorithm must combine the two matching tuples to produce a result tuple. Let f be the function that performs this combining operation.

Thus, we might initially conceive of parameterizing our hash-join abstraction as **equijoin**$(p_1, p_2, f)(R, S)$. The algorithm would then be responsible for maintaining hash tables and so on, but would not have to concern itself with the structure of the R-tuples, S-tuples, or result tuples—those details would be encapsulated in the join parameters. Indeed, as far as the algorithm is concerned, it is not even necessary that the elements of R, S, and the result be *tuples*; they could be objects of any type.

However, this initial conception of a join abstraction is not sufficiently general to express outer joins, grouping operations, and the like. Without in any way changing the underlying algorithm, we may devise a more general abstraction **match** with the following parameterization:

1. As before, we need a "projection" function p_1 that may be applied to elements of the build input. But it is a matter of indifference to the join algorithm whether this function is actually a *projection*. Virtually any function will do, so long as its codomain is a hashable type (e.g., a number, a string, or a tuple of hashable types). If a is an element of the build input, then the algorithm will use $p_1(a)$ as the hash key for a when inserting it into the hash table.

2. We also need a generalized "projection" function p_2 applicable to elements of the probe input. A given build and probe element will be considered to match if they agree on their generalized projections, i.e., if they agree on their hash keys.

3. Again, we need a way to combine matching build and probe elements. But in the course of constructing the hash table, the hash-join algorithm will have grouped together the build elements according to their hash keys. Probing the hash table using the hash key of a probe element will turn up an entire *group* of build elements with the same hash key. If we combine matching build and probe elements one pair at a time, we discard that grouping information.

   Therefore, as our third parameter, let us specify a function that combines each probe element with a *group* of matching build elements to yield a *group* of result elements. These groups will be represented as lists; thus, for our third parameter we want a function of type $(\texttt{List}[\alpha], \beta) \rightarrow \texttt{List}[\gamma]$, where α and β are the element types of the build and probe inputs, respectively, and γ is the element type of the result. The **match** operator will concatenate all the lists produced by this function, and so yield a final result.

4. There may be build elements that match no probe elements, or probe elements that match no build elements. In a simple join, these non-matching elements are discarded, but in an outer join (for example) they must be preserved.

We already have the means for handling non-matching *probe* elements, for we may regard such a probe element as one that matches *zero* build elements; in other words, it will be combined with an empty group of build elements using **match**'s third parameter discussed above. An appropriate combining function would then produce zero result elements for an ordinary join, and one or more result elements for a right outer join.

To accommodate non-matching *build* elements, we add a fourth parameter to **match**. For each group of build elements that were never probed, this fourth parameter must produce a group of result elements. Because no probe elements are involved in this case, the result values must be computed from the build values alone, as when null padding is used to fill out records in a left outer join. Thus, for our fourth parameter we would like a function of type $\mathtt{List}[\alpha] \rightarrow \mathtt{List}[\delta]$, where once again α is the element type of the build input.

But what is δ? A crucial detail of our abstraction is that to maximize generality, we assume that the third and fourth parameters contribute to *two different* result lists, rather than both contributing to a single result list. Thus γ is the element type of the result list for matches, and δ is the element type of the result list for non-matches. If the results for both matches and non-matches belong together in a single list, as in the case of a left outer join, we may always take γ and δ to be the same, and concatenate the two lists produced by **match**.

Note that the inputs and outputs of our hash-join abstraction are *lists*; in other words, they are ordered collections. However, the hash-join algorithm scrambles the build input in a way that is, for all practical purposes, unpredictable. For example, if we parameterize **match** to perform duplicate elimination, then the result of eliminating duplicates from $[1, 2, 2, 3, 1, 2, 1]$ could be $[1, 2, 3]$, or $[1, 3, 2]$, or $[2, 1, 3]$, etc., depending on implementation details of the hash join. An abstraction of the algorithm should hide such details; would we not be better off viewing the inputs and outputs as *bags*? Possibly so, but our intent is to reflect the reality that the inputs and outputs are ordered, whether we like it or not. We cope with the unpredictability of the order by expressing the semantics of the hash-join operator in terms of the disorder operator described in section 3.4.

4.2.2 Examples

As an example of the use of **match**, consider first the problem of eliminating duplicates from a list of integers. This operation has only one input list and one output list, so we will have to supply a dummy list as one of the inputs to **match**, and ignore one of the outputs. Specifically, we will supply an *empty* list as the probe input. As a result, none of the build values will match any probe values; they may match one another, however, and will be grouped together accordingly in the construction of the hash table. Then to eliminate duplicates among the build values, the following parameterization of **match** will serve:

$$\text{DUP\_ELIM\_PARAMS} = (\mathbf{id[int]},\ \ \ldots,\ \ \ldots,\ \ \lambda(\ell : \mathbf{List[int]})\ \mathbf{singleton(head(}\ell\mathbf{))}\ )$$

The second and third parameters are irrelevant since there will be no probe values—these function parameters must still be supplied, but they will never be invoked. For the first parameter, we supply the identity function on integers, since two integers should be considered duplicates of one another exactly when they are equal. The fourth parameter specifies what to do with a group ℓ of duplicate integers. We take one of them—the head of the list ℓ—and make a singleton list containing that integer. Then **match** will concatenate those singleton lists to produce a list of unique integers.

As a second example, observe that if **match** is truly more general than **equijoin**, then it ought to be able to express any operation that **equijoin** can. Indeed it can. For any parameterization (p_1, p_2, f) of **equijoin** as described above, the same operation can be achieved by **match** with the parameterization

$$\text{EQUIJOIN\_PARAMS} = (p_1,\ p_2,\ \lambda(\ell : \mathtt{List}[\alpha], b : \beta)\ \mathtt{map}[\alpha][\gamma]\ (\lambda(a : \alpha)\ f(a, b))\ \ell,\ \lambda(\ell)\ \emptyset),$$

where α and β are the element types of the build and probe elements, respectively, and $\emptyset$ denotes an empty list. The third parameter accepts a group ℓ of build elements and a probe element b, and for each build element a in ℓ, computes the value $f(a, b)$, just as **equijoin** would have done.[4] The fourth parameter is a function that ignores its argument and always returns an empty list, since when joining we are not interested in groups of build elements that have no matching probe element. The result of **match**, so parameterized, is a pair of lists—the first being the same list that would have been obtained with **equijoin**, and the second being an empty list.

Next let us consider the use of **match** to implement the intersection of two sets of integers (represented as lists):

$$\text{INTERSECT\_PARAMS} = (\mathtt{id}[\mathtt{int}],\quad \mathtt{id}[\mathtt{int}],\quad \lambda(\ell : \mathtt{List}[\mathtt{int}], b : \mathtt{int})\ \ell,\ \lambda(\ell : \mathtt{List}[\mathtt{int}])\ \emptyset)$$

The given "projection" functions are both the identity, since two integers should match just when they are equal as integers. In the case of a match, we know the list of build values matching the probe value will be a singleton list, because the build input, coming from a set, contains no duplicates. We may therefore pass the contents of this singleton list on as output—that is accomplished by the parameter $\lambda(\ell : \mathtt{List}[\mathtt{int}], b : \mathtt{int})\ \ell$. On the other hand, in the case that a (singleton) list of build values is not matched by a probe value, we specify in the fourth parameter that no output is to be produced. Consequently, given inputs A and B, this parameterization of **match** yields a pair of lists $(A \cap B, \emptyset)$.

In an analogous way, as a fourth example we may use the following parameters to **match** to implement set difference of two sets of integers:

$$\text{DIFFERENCE\_PARAMS} = (\mathtt{id}[\mathtt{int}],\quad \mathtt{id}[\mathtt{int}],\quad \lambda(\ell : \mathtt{List}[\mathtt{int}], b : \mathtt{int})\ \emptyset,\ \mathtt{id}[\mathtt{List}[\mathtt{int}]])$$

In this instance, if a list of build values has a matching probe value, we do not wish to include those build values in the result; hence our third parameter

[4] The function **map**, well-known to functional programmers, applies a function to each element of a list. For example, omitting type annotations, we may apply $\mathtt{map}(\lambda(x)\ x + 1)$ to the list $[1, 5, 7]$ to obtain $[2, 6, 8]$.

yields an empty list. On the other hand, in the case that a (singleton) list of build values is not matched by a probe value, we wish to include that list in the result, and hence specify the identity function as the fourth parameter. With this parameterization, **match** on inputs A and B will yield the pair $(\emptyset, A - B)$.

The important point for what follows is that because the match and non-match outputs are kept separate, we may splice together the parameters for intersection and difference to obtain a parameterization of **match** that computes both results at once:

$$\text{SPLICED\_PARAMS} = (\mathtt{id[int]},\quad \mathtt{id[int]},\quad \lambda(\ell : \mathtt{List[int]}, b : \mathtt{int})\ \ell,\ \mathtt{id[List[int]]}).$$

Conceptually, we may think of the result of a **match** with this parameterization, and with inputs A and B, as being the pair $(A \cap B, A - B)$. But while this conceptualization is useful for understanding the semantics of **match**, the realization of **match**, as we shall see, is somewhat more involved.

5 Concurrent Subexpressions

In the preceding section, we glossed over the question of how to specify the inputs of bulk operators, and how to collect their outputs. We turn to those questions now.

5.1 Wiring Together an Execution Network

Figure 2 gives a graphical representation of a query execution strategy for the sample query **sum**$(A \cap B)$ − **sum**$(A - B)$ mentioned in the introduction. The idea is that the elements of set A come streaming up the arrow labeled chA, one at a time, into the rectangle labeled "hash join"; the elements of set B also stream into the "hash join" box. The machinery inside that box compares the two incoming streams and computes, one at a time, the elements of $A \cap B$ and $A - B$. The elements of those result sets are sent streaming up the arrows labeled chY and chN, respectively. Each of these two arrows terminates at a rounded box labeled "aggregate" that sums up the elements it receives. The sums are then combined to yield the query result.

We shall refer to the rectangles as *iterators*, to the rounded boxes as *accumulators*, and to the arrows connecting them as *channels*. A network of iterators is created by means of *iterator abstractions* such as **match**, described above. In addition to its function parameters, **match** takes a pair of incoming channels as arguments, and yields a pair of outgoing channels as its result. The full typing of **match** is

$$\forall[\alpha]\ \forall[\beta]\ \forall[\gamma]\ \forall[\delta]\ \forall[\rho]\quad (\alpha \to \rho,\ \ \beta \to \rho,\ \ (\mathtt{List}[\alpha], \beta) \to \mathtt{List}[\gamma],\ \mathtt{List}[\alpha] \to \mathtt{List}[\delta]) \to (\mathtt{Channel}[\alpha], \mathtt{Channel}[\beta]) \to (\mathtt{Channel}[\gamma], \mathtt{Channel}[\delta]),$$

where α, β, γ, and δ are as before, and ρ is the type that the generalized "projection" functions map onto (thus, ρ becomes the type of the join attribute in a join). Thus, the full complement of arguments to **match**, curried in groups, consists of five types (the element types of the four channels, plus the generalized "join attribute type"); four function parameters as already discussed; and the

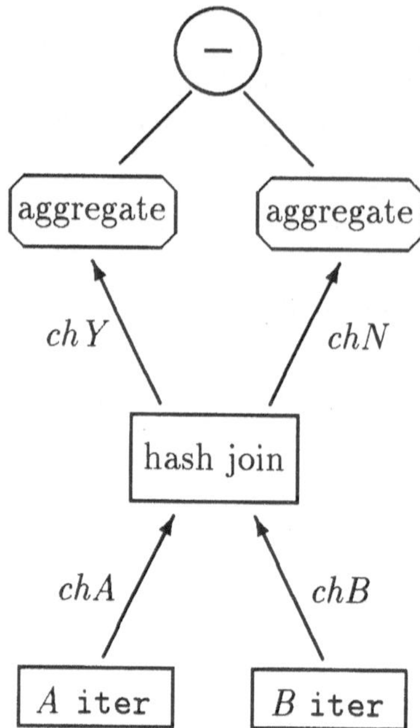

Figure 2: A Query Execution Network

two input channels. But this type signature does not quite tell the whole story. A latent effect of invoking **match**—invisible from its typing—is to create the iterator that will consume data from the incoming channels and produce data on the outgoing channels. Note, though, that creation of the iterator does not in itself cause any data to be consumed; it merely sets the stage for subsequent computation by building part of the execution network.

At the bottom of the network in Figure 2 we find iterators that consume no input. Such iterators are created through a built-in provision of the list objects that represent our sets; a list object may be sent an **iter** message to yield an output channel, and as a latent effect, to create an iterator that will ultimately produce the elements of the list on that channel.

The aggregation nodes near the top of the network are created by *accumulator abstractions*, which, like iterator abstractions, take one or more channels as arguments, but unlike iterator abstractions, yield ordinary values as their results, rather than yielding new channels. The accumulator abstraction we use here, **accum**, has type

$$\forall[\varepsilon]\ \forall[\sigma]\quad ((\sigma,\varepsilon,\mathbf{Cont}[\sigma])\rightarrow\sigma,\ \ \sigma)\rightarrow\mathbf{Channel}[\varepsilon]\rightarrow\sigma.$$

Here ε is the type of the elements being aggregated, and σ is the result type of the aggregation. The parameter of type $(\sigma,\varepsilon,\mathbf{Cont}[\sigma])\rightarrow\sigma$ represents the aggregation function discussed above, and the parameter of type σ represents the initial value of the "total."

Putting these facilities together, we may write the expression

$$\begin{array}{l}\textbf{let } (chA, chB) = (A\ \texttt{iter}, B\ \texttt{iter}) \\ \textbf{in let } (chY, chN) = \texttt{match[int][int][int][int][int]} \\ \qquad\qquad\qquad\qquad (\text{SPLICED\_PARAMS})(chA, chB) \\ \textbf{in } (\texttt{accum[int][int]}(\text{INTSUM}, 0)(chY)) - \\ \qquad\qquad\qquad\qquad (\texttt{accum[int][int]}(\text{INTSUM}, 0)(chN))\end{array}$$

to construct the network depicted in Figure 2. Evaluation of the final clause containing the accumulators activates the network; each iterator executes as a separate lightweight thread, and the final clause (including both accumulators) executes as an additional thread. The result of the final clause becomes the result of the whole expression.

5.2 Trade-offs of Concurrency

The fact that it is possible to structure the computation of the expression $\texttt{sum}(A \cap B) - \texttt{sum}(A - B)$ in the manner described above does not necessarily mean that it is *desirable* to do so. There is some overhead associated with executing multiple concurrent threads, although that is likely to be minor in comparison with the savings obtained by performing one hash join rather than two. More important is the risk—if not in the example at hand, then in other, more complicated examples—that the concurrent threads will compete for buffer space and slow each other down to the point where a more serialized strategy would perform better, even if it had to do more work.

However, the point of our example is not to argue that any one way of structuring a computation is best. The point is rather to illustrate that using REXALL as a target language presents an optimizer with choices that would be unavailable if our target language either

- offered less flexible bulk processing abstractions, or
- did not support concurrent execution of iterators as separate threads.

As with any potential transformation of a query, a transformation that trades computational effort against buffer usage may or may not be judged by the optimizer to be beneficial in a given context.

It is even conceivable that we may eventually want to provide different versions of `match` geared toward maximizing performance under different circumstances. For example, a variant with typing

$$\begin{array}{r}\forall[\alpha]\ \forall[\beta]\ \forall[\gamma]\ \forall[\delta]\ \forall[\rho]\ \ (\alpha\to\rho,\ \beta\to\rho,\ (\texttt{Channel}[\alpha], \beta)\to\texttt{Channel}[\gamma], \\ \texttt{Channel}[\alpha]\to\texttt{Channel}[\delta])\to \\ (\texttt{Channel}[\alpha], \texttt{Channel}[\beta])\to(\texttt{Channel}[\gamma], \texttt{Channel}[\delta]),\end{array}$$

would permit a greater degree of concurrency in some computations, though at a cost in overhead that would offset its gains in other, simpler computations.

It should be noted that concurrent threads of execution are potentially beneficial whenever an expression contains common subexpressions that yield lengthy output sequences, not just when a special two-output operator such as `match` is involved. If a lengthy output sequence is not concurrently consumed at all its points of use, it must either be retained in buffers for later use, or paged out to disk. But if it is retained in buffers, it increases pressure on other data to go out to disk. Either way, then, one is threatened with unnecessary I/O activity. On the other hand, concurrent execution of the consumer expressions does not guarantee that the extra I/O will be avoided; depending on the buffer requirements of the consumers themselves, avoiding the I/O at the producer may simply push it off on the consumers.

6 Conclusions and Future Work

We have sketched the preliminary design of REXALL, an abstract query execution language. This language can express arbitrary queries in the REVELATION user query language, and provides the means for them to execute efficiently. It is *abstract* in the sense that it provides access to query execution algorithms through a fairly high-level interface that is not tied to any particular implementation; yet we believe this interface is not so high-level as to preclude cost estimation on prospective query execution plans. REXALL is abstract in another sense as well: it distills the essential functionality of the user query language and leaves behind the complications that attend practical usability. Thus, by hiding both language details and implementation details, it provides a narrow interface between the earlier phases of query processing and the final execution phase.

Defining such an interface is worthwhile in itself, in that it facilitates modular construction of a query processing system. Moreover, it provides a notation in which to assign a semantics to query plans, without which formal correctness proofs of optimizers are not possible. But REXALL is also useful as a conceptual tool. By focusing our attention on the functional essence of query execution algorithms, it has enabled us to find optimizations that had previously eluded us.

In the future, we intend to develop a complete, formal definition of REXALL, and to test its viability in an actual implementation (currently only a crude prototype of the language is implemented). On a theoretical level, several treacherous details need to be addressed; above all, REXALL's type system needs to be examined more closely. It is based on careful work by others, but we have adapted it to our own needs; that it remains well-behaved is by no means a foregone conclusion.

Ultimately we intend to build a quasi-algebraic layer (or series of layers) on top of REXALL. This bottom-up approach will help us keep the goal of optimization in focus: to generate efficient plans. In ascending to higher layers, we would like to strip away some of the details of the execution language (or rather, to relegate them to black-box status) while retaining the ability to express useful transformations.

Acknowledgments

Thanks are due to Judy Cushing, Scott Daniels, Leo Fegaras, Goetz Graefe, Dave Maier, and the reviewers for valuable discussions, comments and suggestions. This research was supported in part by the Advanced Research Projects

Agency, ARPA order number 18, monitored by the U.S. Army Research Laboratory under contract DAAB-07-91-C-Q518, and by NSF Grant IRI 91 18360.

References

[1] R. M. Amadio and L. Cardelli. Subtyping recursive types. SRC Report #62, Digital Equipment Corporation, Aug. 1990.

[2] A. W. Appel. *Compiling with Continuations.* Cambridge University Press, 1992.

[3] M. Atkinson, P. Richard, and P. Trinder. Bulk types for large scale programming. In Schmidt and Stogny [34], pages 228–250.

[4] C. Beeri and Y. Kornatzky. Algebraic optimization of object-oriented query languages. In S. Abiteboul and P. C. Kanellakis, editors, *Proceedings of the Third International Conference on Database Theory*, volume 470 of *Lecture Notes in Computer Science*, pages 72–88. Springer-Verlag, Dec. 1990.

[5] R. Bird and P. Wadler. *Introduction to Functional Programming.* Prentice Hall, 1988.

[6] V. Breazu-Tannen, P. Buneman, and S. Naqvi. Structural recursion as a query language. In Kanellakis and Schmidt [22], pages 9–19.

[7] K. B. Bruce. A paradigmatic object-oriented programming language: Design, static typing and semantics. Technical Report CS-92-01, Williams College, Jan. 1992.

[8] K. B. Bruce. Safe type checking in a statically-typed object-oriented programming language. In *Conference Record of the Twentieth Annual ACM SIGPLAN-SIGACT Symposium on Principles of Programming Languages*, pages 285–298, Charleston, South Carolina, Jan. 1993.

[9] P. Buneman, R. E. Frankel, and R. Nikhil. An implementation technique for database query languages. *ACM Trans. Database Syst.*, 7(2):164–186, June 1982.

[10] P. Canning, W. Cook, W. Hill, and W. Olthoff. F-bounded polymorphism for object-oriented programming. In *The Fourth International Conference on Functional Programming Languages and Computer Architecture*, pages 273–280, Imperial College, London, Sept. 1989.

[11] L. Cardelli. A pure calculus of subtyping, and applications (outline). In Kanellakis and Schmidt [22], pages 185–187.

[12] L. Cardelli, S. Martini, J. C. Mitchell, and A. Scedrov. An extension of system F with subtyping. In T. Ito and A. R. Meyer, editors, *Theoretical Aspects of Computer Software*, volume 526 of *Lecture Notes in Computer Science*, pages 750–770, Sendai, Japan, Sept. 1991. Springer-Verlag.

[13] L. Cardelli and P. Wegner. On understanding types, data abstraction, and polymorphism. *ACM Comput. Surv.*, 17(4), Dec. 1985.

[14] S. Danforth and C. Tomlinson. Type theories and object-oriented programming. *ACM Comput. Surv.*, 20(1), Mar. 1988.

[15] S. D. Daniels. Speaking in tongues: The language of Revelation. Technical Report CS/E 91-007, Oregon Graduate Institute of Science & Technology, May 1990.

[16] J. C. Freytag and N. Goodman. Rule-based translation of relational queries into iterative programs. In C. Zaniolo, editor, *Proceedings of SIGMOD '86 International Conference on Management of Data*, pages 206–214, Washington, D.C., May 1986.

[17] A. Goldberg. *Smalltalk-80, The Interactive Programming Environment.* Addison-Wesley, 1984.

[18] G. Graefe. Query evaluation techniques for large databases. *ACM Comput. Surv.*, 25(2), June 1993.

[19] G. Graefe. Volcano, an extensible and parallel dataflow query processing system. *IEEE Transactions on Knowledge and Data Engineering*, 5(5), Oct. 1993. To appear.

[20] G. Graefe and W. J. McKenna. The volcano optimizer generator: Extensibility and efficient search. In *Proceedings of the IEEE Conference on Data Engineering*, pages 209–218, Vienna, Austria, Apr. 1993.

[21] M. Jarke and J. Koch. Query optimization in database systems. *ACM Comput. Surv.*, 16(2):111–152, June 1984.

[22] P. Kanellakis and J. W. Schmidt, editors. *Database Programming Languages: Bulk Types & Persistent Data, The Third International Workshop*, Nafplion, Greece, Aug. 1991. Morgan Kaufmann.

[23] T. Keller and G. Graefe. The one-to-one match operator of the Volcano query processing system. Technical Report CS/E 89-009, Oregon Graduate Institute of Science & Technology, June 1989.

[24] P. Kelly. *Functional Programming for Loosely-coupled Multiprocessors.* The MIT Press, 1989.

[25] B. Liskov, A. Snyder, R. Atkinson, and C. Schaffert. Abstraction mechanisms in CLU. *Commun. ACM*, 20(8):564–576, 1977.

[26] R. A. Lorie and J. F. Nilsson. An access specification language for a relational data base system. Computer Science Research Report RJ2218(30171), IBM Research Laboratory, San Jose, California, Apr. 1978.

[27] D. Maier, S. Daniels, G. Graefe, T. Keller, W. McKenna, and B. Vance. Challenges for query processing in object-oriented databases. In J. C. Freytag, D. Maier, and G. Vossen, editors, *Query Processing for Advanced Database Systems*, pages 337–380. Morgan Kaufmann, 1993.

[28] R. Milner, M. Tofte, and R. Harper. *The Definition of Standard ML*. The MIT Press, 1990.

[29] P. Mishra and M. H. Eich. Join processing in relational databases. *ACM Comput. Surv.*, 24(1):63–113, Mar. 1992.

[30] J. C. Mitchell, F. Honsell, and K. Fisher. A lambda calculus of objects and method specialization. In *1993 IEEE Symposium on Logic in Computer Science*, June 1993.

[31] R. Morrison, A. Dearle, R. C. H. Connor, and A. L. Brown. An ad hoc approach to the implementation of polymorphism. *ACM Trans. Prog. Lang. Syst.*, 13(3):342–371, July 1991.

[32] D. S. Parker, E. Simon, and P. Valduriez. SVP – a model capturing sets, streams, and parallelism. In L.-Y. Yuan, editor, *Proceedings of the 18th International Conference on Very Large Data Bases*, pages 115–126, Vancouver, Canada, Aug. 1992. Morgan Kaufmann.

[33] J. H. Reppy. CML: A higher-order concurrent language. In *Proceedings of the ACM SIGPLAN '91 Conference on Programming Language Design and Implementation*, pages 293–305, Toronto, Ontario, Canada, June 1991.

[34] J. W. Schmidt and A. A. Stogny, editors. *Next Generation Information System Technology*, volume 504 of *Lecture Notes in Computer Science*, Kiev, USSR, Oct. 1990. First International East/West Database Workshop, Springer-Verlag.

[35] G. M. Shaw and S. B. Zdonik. An object-oriented query algebra. In R. Hull, R. Morrison, and D. Stemple, editors, *Proceedings of the Second International Workshop on Database Programming Languages*, pages 103–112, Salishan Lodge, Gleneden Beach, Oregon, June 1989. Morgan Kaufmann.

[36] N. C. Shu, B. C. Housel, R. W. Taylor, S. P. Ghosh, and V. Y. Lum. EXPRESS: A data EXtraction, Processing, and REStructuring System. *ACM Trans. Database Syst.*, 2(2):134–174, June 1977.

[37] D. Stemple and T. Sheard. A recursive base for database programming primitives. In Schmidt and Stogny [34], pages 311–332.

[38] B. Vance. Towards an object-oriented query algebra. Technical Report CS/E 91-008, Oregon Graduate Institute of Science & Technology, Jan. 1992.

[39] S. L. Vandenberg and D. J. DeWitt. Algebraic support for complex objects with arrays, identity, and inheritance. In J. Clifford and R. King, editors, *Proceedings of the 1991 ACM SIGMOD International Conference on Management of Data*, pages 158–157, Denver, Colorado, June 1991.

[40] D. A. Watt and P. Trinder. Towards a theory of bulk types. Technical Report FIDE/91/26, FIDE, 1991.

Efficient Optimization of Iterative Queries

Leonidas Fegaras
Department of Computer Science and Engineering
Oregon Graduate Institute of Science & Technology
Portland, OR 97291-1000.
fegaras@cse.ogi.edu

Abstract

This paper presents a new query algebra based on *fold* iterations that facilitates database implementation. An algebraic normalization algorithm is introduced that reduces any program expressed in this algebra to a canonical form that generates no intermediate data structures and has no more nested iterations than the initial program. Given any inductive data type, our system can automatically synthesize the definition of the fold operator that traverses instances of this type, and, more importantly, it can produce the necessary transformations for optimizing expressions involving this fold operator.

Database implementation in our framework is controlled by user-defined mappings from abstract types to physical structures. The optimizer uses this information to translate abstract programs and queries into concrete algorithms that conform to the type transformation. Database query optimization can be viewed as a search over the reduced space of all canonical forms which are equivalent to the query after type transformation and normalization. The optimization space can be expanded to capture semantic information expressed as integrity constraints attached to types. This information may include specifications of materialized views and of alternative access paths.

The contribution of this paper is twofold. First, a new efficient algebraic optimization algorithm is introduced, based on loop fusion and partial evaluation, that normalizes a large class of queries over a wide spectrum of bulk data structures. Second, an effective query optimizer is described that searches the limited space of equivalent canonical forms for optimal programs, using additional semantic information to generate more alternatives.

1 Introduction

Database systems based on the relational model offer a high degree of data independence. In these systems the semantics of abstract data structures and their operations can be significantly independent of their implementations. This separation of specification from implementation offers many opportunities for optimization which would otherwise be lost if abstract operations were expressed by a detailed algorithm. For example, queries in the relational model are expressed declaratively, without any concern about efficiency, relying on the query optimizer to select the best evaluation plan among a variety of available access plans and algorithms [13].

Modern database applications require more advanced data structures and more expressive operations than those provided by the relational model. If complex storage structures are mapped into relational tables then semantic information is often lost. For example, information about object interconnection needs to be reconstructed in object queries by using joins, if object hierarchies are mapped into flat tables. This lost information offers more opportunities for optimization when stated explicitly in the schema description, as it would if the model supported these complex data structures directly.

In addition, ordered bulk data structures, such as lists, trees, and arrays, cannot be captured directly in relational tables as they are by definition unordered. This implicit ordering information must be captured explicitly or it may introduce inconsistencies in the resulting programs. On the other hand, if sets are represented as ordered sequences then the optimizer may miss opportunities for optimization. For example, using a commutative union (in a set based implementation) may allow a more efficient translation than using an noncommutative append (in a list based implementation).

These observations can be generalized: when a system is underspecified inconsistencies may be introduced in its translation, while when a system is overspecified optimization opportunities are lost. A specification framework must have enough modeling power to directly capture all semantic information of the system being specified. That way, the program optimizer can use semantic information directly to make intelligent decisions. Consequently, restrictions on data values, such as integrity constraints attached to the database state, should be provided explicitly as part of the schema, so that they may be used to generate alternatives during optimization [15].

There have been many proposals for query algebras that are more expressive than the relational algebra. Much research into these designs has been guided by the belief that the more the expressiveness (functionality) of a language the more difficult the program optimization task becomes. This paper will demonstrate that this belief is not necessarily true by presenting a query algebra that is both expressive enough to capture most polynomial time functions and still facilitates optimization. We believe that the infeasibility of optimization is controlled not by reducing the expressiveness of the language, but by reducing the number of possible program schemes that compute a function. The search for an optimal solution is more efficient if there is a smaller number of program schemes to consider. A provision must be taken, though, that most candidates for optimal solution are always within this search space. Therefore, there is a tension that needs to be resolved: the more programs schemes considered the better optimized are the resulting programs, but the more optimization time spent. In our approach program schemes that cannot be optimal under any circumstances will not be considered. By using an algebraic method that improves programs independently of the database state, we reduce the search space size by avoiding states that correspond to suboptimal programs.

The reduced number of program schemes is achieved by requiring that all structure traversals are expressed in terms of a very small number of stereotyped generic recursion schemes. We have only one traversal mechanism in our algebra: the *fold* operation [14, 8, 7]. Given any inductive data type (e.g. tuple, set, list, tree, boolean, and integer) our system is capable of automatically synthesizing the definition of the fold operator that traverses instances of this type. If some simple, easily recognizable, syntactic restrictions to this algebra are imposed, then some very nice properties result. For example, any operation expressed in this algebra can always be reduced, by a very simple and efficient algorithm, to a canonical form. We call this algorithm the *normalization algorithm*. This canonical form is, in a way, optimal, since it does not generate any intermediate data structures, (which might be generated when function calls are nested, passing intermediate results from one to another). It also has no more nested iterations than the program before the normalization. Note that elimination of intermediate data structures does not necessarily imply optimality. In fact, when we have a duplicate computation it is more efficient to pull out this computation, assign its intermediate result to a variable, and use the value of this variable instead of performing the computation twice. Fortunately, this type of program improvement can be done at any stage either before or after program normalization. We therefore choose to ignore it at this phase.

The normalization algorithm is both a loop fusion method [16, 4] that merges two cascaded iterations[1] into one, and an online partial evaluator [5] that specializes programs with respect to their static input. Based upon a generic *promotion theorem*, the algorithm is aided by the explicit inductive structure of folds rather than searching for implicit structure in an analysis phase, as is done in most program transformation systems [6].

The normalization algorithm devotes the same effort to all traversals, independent of the data structures they traverse. In our model there are no primitive types, such as integers or booleans; all types are user-defined data structures. Therefore, all primitive operations, such as integer addition and boolean conjunction, are computed using fold traversals. In this way all data types and the operations upon them are treated uniformly. Some researchers in the database community believe that a query optimizer should not spend time optimizing non-bulk operations, such as integer and boolean operations, since bulk operations involve heavy I/O use which is considerably slower than the CPU calculations. We believe that this argument is not necessarily true for two reasons. First, non-bulk operations may be mixed with bulk operations, as in a nested SQL statement where a selection predicate contains another SQL statement. Second, rewriting a non-bulk operation may reveal a new transformation for a bulk operation which could otherwise be unavailable. For example, transforming a join predicate into disjunctive normal form may trigger new join transformations.

The normalization algorithm can be used for algebraic optimization in both the abstract and physical layers. In fact, it generalizes many algebraic optimization algorithms found in database literature [10, 1]. In addition, loop fusion can effectively capture most stream-based pipelining techniques used in relational query evaluation for propagating values a tuple-at-a-time instead of a table-at-a-time between relational operations (this is achieved by fusing the loops of two nested relational operations into one loop). This ability to fuse loops serves as an additional argument for defining relational operators, such as the relational join, not as opaque abstractions that satisfy some properties, but as abstractions with an explicit predefined control structure. That way the control of an operator can be fused with the control of another operator resulting one more efficient program. Our fold operator can be seen as an al-

[1]That is, a loop that iterates over the result of another loop, such as two piped filters, not a nested loop in an imperative language.

gebraic formulation of a pipe. The difference is that, in our framework, pipes are constructed during optimization time, not during evaluation time. Thus we avoid the usual overhead of pipe synchronization.

Given a canonical form in our algebra computing a function f, it is easy to discover all other equivalent canonical forms. That is, all canonical forms that compute the same function f. In fact, the canonical forms that are equivalent to f are those that are derived mainly by commutativity laws (since associative forms in our algebra have the same canonical form). Our optimizer considers only the canonical forms equivalent to the one derived by applying the normalization algorithm to the original program that represents a query. Non-canonical programs are not considered at all. This is desirable since they can all be reduced to a more efficient canonical form from this class. This restricts the search for the best evaluation plan to a small, finite, class of programs that contains very few suboptimal programs. Note that by specifying a join as a nested fold, for example, we have not restricted its implementation to nested-loop join, because the optimizer can always discover algorithms, such as the sort-merge join, that have the same functionality as this nested fold but possibly different implementations. Therefore, we gain all the optimization opportunities of a highly declarative algebra in a framework of a more operational language that completely automates algebraic optimization. Furthermore, semantic information, such as integrity constraints, can also be reduced to canonical form and then be used to expand the search space of alternatives, offering different access paths for evaluating the same program. We have reduced the search space by eliminating suboptimal goals, but we have also expanded it by adding more alternatives that correspond to additional semantic information.

One important component of our algebraic query optimizer is *type transformation* [9]. In this framework we specify how an abstract data type is mapped into a concrete type (a data structure in the physical layer) by providing an *abstraction function*. This function, expressed in canonical form, maps any structure of the concrete type into a value of the abstract type. It is in general a many-to-one function. For example, a set can be implemented as an ordered sequence, such as a list, where the abstraction function inserts each element of the list into an initially empty set. Integrity constraints in the physical layer specify materialized views and access paths, such as a secondary indices. Integrity constraints in the logical layer represent conceptual views that may or may not be materialized, depending on the abstraction function and the storage structure they are mapped to. The abstraction functions and the integrity constraints in both the logical and physical layers form the necessary theory that specifies the database implementation. The query optimizer will use this transformation theory to derive efficient algorithms that compute queries as well as to verify the resulting translation.

The physical layer consists of a finite number of prespecified concrete primitives. In our translation framework these concrete primitives are assigned a *behavior* expressed in canonical form. The actual implementation of a concrete operation, such as the implementation for B-tree-find, may be many pages of C code, but its actual behavior can be described by few lines of canonical program. We will assume that the behavior of a concrete primitive is consistent with its implementation without any attempt to prove it. Each concrete primitive is also assigned a cost function that estimates its cost from the cost parameters of its input values, such as set cardinalities. The goal of the optimizer is to find a composition of concrete primitives such that the composition of their associated behaviors is equal to the canonical program that represents the initial query after type transformation. Furthermore, this composition must have the best cost among all such compositions with the same functionality. We call this algorithm the *fold optimization algorithm.* It is in a sense the inverse of the normalization algorithm, which reduces compositions to canonical form. The optimization algorithm is a search-based algorithm that searches the limited space of canonical forms. It takes into account semantic information, expressed as integrity constraints, to widen the search space, producing alternative access paths and algorithms.

2 Definitions

In this section we define the fold operator for a family of inductively defined algebraic data type. We will analyze sets and set folds in Section 4. There are no primitive types in our model, because integers, booleans and strings are defined in the same way as any bulk data type. This is desirable since we want all operations over any data type to be treated uniformly, in a context of a simple universal optimization algorithm. Our fold operator is similar to, but more expressive than, the *pump* operator [1] and the *structural recursion* operator [3]. The difference is that our system can derive the fold definition for most data types automatically by examining the type details.

The type definitions considered in this section are the simple sums-of-product types defined by using recursive equations of the form:

$$\begin{array}{rcl} T(\alpha_1,\ldots,\alpha_p) & = & C_1(s_{1,1}:t_{1,1},\ldots,s_{1,m_1}:t_{1,m_1}) \\ & & \mid \;\ldots \\ & & \mid \; C_n(s_{n,1}:t_{n,1},\ldots,s_{n,m_n}:t_{n,m_n}) \end{array}$$

where $\alpha_1,\ldots,\alpha_p$ denote type variables, the C_i are unique names of value constructor functions (we use the convention that the first letter of a constructor name is always in uppercase), $s_{i,j}$ are names of selector functions, $t_{i,j}$ are either type variables (in the set $\alpha_1,\ldots,\alpha_p$) or the type $T(\alpha_1,\ldots,\alpha_p)$ itself. For example, the following are simple sums-of-products type definitions:

$$\begin{array}{rcl} \text{boolean} & = & \text{False} \mid \text{True} \\ \text{prod}(\alpha,\beta) & = & \text{Pair}(\text{fst}:\alpha,\text{snd}:\beta) \\ \text{list}(\alpha) & = & \text{Nil} \mid \text{Cons}(\text{hd}:\alpha,\text{tail}:\text{list}(\alpha)) \\ \text{nat} & = & \text{Zero} \mid \text{Succ}(\text{pred}:\text{nat}) \\ \text{tree}(\alpha) & = & \text{Tip}(\text{info}:\alpha) \mid \text{Node}(\text{left}:\text{tree}(\alpha),\text{right}:\text{tree}(\alpha)) \\ \text{person} & = & \text{Make\_person}(\text{name}:\text{string},\text{ssn}:\text{nat},\text{address}:\text{string}) \\ & & \text{where string} = \text{list}(\text{nat}) \end{array}$$

Before expressing the general definition of the fold operator for any sums-of-products type, we give the definition of the *list* fold as an example. If a function $g:\text{list}(\alpha)\rightarrow\beta$ is defined by the following recursive equations:

$$\begin{array}{rcl} g(\text{Nil}) & = & f_n() \\ g(\text{Cons}(a,l)) & = & f_c(a,g(l)) \end{array}$$

for some functions f_n and f_c, then g is a list fold: $g = \text{fold}^{list}(f_n, f_c)$. Consider for example the length of a list computed by the following equations:

$$\begin{aligned}\text{length}(\text{Nil}) &= \text{Zero}\\ \text{length}(\text{Cons}(a,l)) &= \text{Succ}(\text{length}(l))\end{aligned}$$

In this case, $f_n() = \text{Zero} \Rightarrow f_n = \lambda().\text{Zero}$ and $f_c(a,r) = \text{Succ}(r) \Rightarrow f_c = \lambda(a,r).\text{Succ}(r)$[2]. Therefore,

$$\text{length}(x) = \text{fold}^{list}(\lambda().\text{Zero}, \lambda(a,r).\text{Succ}(r))\ x$$

Note that f_c in $\text{fold}^{list}(f_n, f_c)$ has the form $\lambda(a,r).e$, which is a lambda abstraction that has two parameters: a, bound to the current head of the list and r, bound to the recursively transformed tail of the list. That is, if the output type of the *list* fold is β then the type of r is also β.

In general, the fold operation over a sums-of-products type will use a pattern of recursion related to the pattern of recursion in the type definition. This recursion pattern is captured by the functor E. Functor E, like functors in category theory, satisfies $E(\text{id}) = \text{id}$ and $E(g) \circ E(h) = E(g \circ h)$, where g and h are functions, $\circ$ is function composition, and id is the identity function (i.e. $\text{id}(x) = x$). These properties can be easily verified for our definition below.

Definition 1 (The Functor E) *Associated with each constructor C_i of type $(t_{i,1}, \ldots, t_{i,m_i}) \rightarrow T(\alpha_1, \ldots, \alpha_p)$ is a monadic functor:*

$$E_i^T(f) = \lambda(x_{i,1}, \ldots, x_{i,m_i}).(K(x_{i,1}), \ldots, K(x_{i,m_i}))$$

where the bound variables $x_{i,j}$ have type $t_{i,j}$ and $K(x_{i,j})$ is either $f(x_{i,j})$, if $t_{i,j} = T(\alpha_1, \ldots, \alpha_p)$, or $x_{i,j}$, otherwise.

For example, for type *list*: $E_{Nil}^{list}(f) = \lambda().()$ and $E_{Cons}^{list}(f) = \lambda(x,y).(x, f(y))$.

With this notation it is now possible to describe the *fold* operator for any simple sums-of-products type.

Definition 2 (Fold) *The fold function over $T(\alpha_1 \ldots \alpha_p)$ is defined by the following set of recursive equations, one for each constructor C_i of T:*

$$\text{fold}^T(\overline{f}) \circ C_i = f_i \circ E_i^T(\text{fold}^T(\overline{f}))$$

where $\overline{f} = (f_1, \ldots, f_n)$.

For example, the *list* fold is defined recursively by the following two equations (in applicative form):

$$\begin{aligned}\text{fold}^{list}(f_n, f_c)\,\text{Nil} &= f_n()\\ \text{fold}^{list}(f_n, f_c)\,\text{Cons}(a,l) &= f_c(a, \text{fold}^{list}(f_n, f_c)\,l)\end{aligned}$$

The *nat* fold is defined as:

$$\begin{aligned}\text{fold}^{nat}(f_z, f_s)\,\text{Zero} &= f_z()\\ \text{fold}^{nat}(f_z, f_s)\,\text{Succ}(i) &= f_s(\text{fold}^{nat}(f_z, f_s)\,i)\end{aligned}$$

[2] $\lambda(x_1, \ldots, x_n).e$ is a lambda abstraction, expressed as $\lambda x_1.\ldots.\lambda x_n.e$ in lambda calculus, and $(e_1, \ldots, e_n)$ constructs a tuple of n values. Application $f(e_1, \ldots, e_n)$ can be seen as the application of the unary function f to the tuple $(e_1, \ldots, e_n)$.

The *tree* fold is defined as:

$$\begin{aligned}\text{fold}^{tree}(f_t, f_n)\,\text{Tip}(a) &= f_t(a)\\ \text{fold}^{tree}(f_t, f_n)\,\text{Node}(l, r) &= f_n(\text{fold}^{tree}(f_t, f_n)\,l, \text{fold}^{tree}(f_t, f_n)\,r)\end{aligned}$$

The *boolean* fold is defined as:

$$\begin{aligned}\text{fold}^{boolean}(f_f, f_t)\,\text{False} &= f_f()\\ \text{fold}^{boolean}(f_f, f_t)\,\text{True} &= f_t()\end{aligned}$$

Note that $\text{fold}^{boolean}(f_f, f_t)\,x \equiv \textbf{if}\,x\,\textbf{then}\,f_t()\,\textbf{else}\,f_f()$.

We call each f_i in $\overline{f}$ an *accumulating function.* Note that if each $f_i = C_i$ then $\text{fold}^T(\overline{f}) = \text{id}$.

The following are some examples of computations that can be defined using fold functions:

$$\begin{aligned}
\text{append}(x, y) &= \text{fold}^{list}(\lambda().y, \lambda(a, r).\text{Cons}(a, r))\;x\\
\text{map}(x, f) &= \text{fold}^{list}(\lambda().\text{Nil}, \lambda(a, r).\text{Cons}(f(a), r))\;x\\
\text{sum}(x) &= \text{fold}^{list}(\lambda().\text{Zero}, \lambda(a, r).a + r)\;x\\
\text{reverse}(x) &= \text{fold}^{list}(\lambda().\text{Nil}, \lambda(a, r).\text{append}(r, \text{Cons}(a, \text{Nil})))\;x\\
x + y &= \text{fold}^{nat}(\lambda().y, \lambda(r).\text{Succ}(r))\;x\\
x \times y &= \text{fold}^{nat}(\lambda().\text{Zero}, \lambda(r).y + r)\;x\\
\text{even}(x) &= \text{fold}^{nat}(\lambda().\text{True}, \lambda(r).\text{not}(r))\;x\\
x \wedge y &= \text{fold}^{boolean}(\lambda().\text{False}, \lambda().y)\;x\\
\text{if } x \text{ then } y \text{ else } z &= \text{fold}^{boolean}(\lambda().z, \lambda().y)\;x\\
\text{flat}(x) &= \text{fold}^{tree}(\lambda(i).\text{Cons}(i, \text{Nil}), \lambda(l, r).\text{append}(l, r))\;x\\
p.\text{address} &= \text{fold}^{person}(\lambda(n, s, a).a)\;p
\end{aligned}$$

The general law which applies to all fold functions is called the *promotion theorem*. We will use this theorem as a major component of our automated transformation algorithm, called the *normalization algorithm*. The promotion theorem states that the composition of any function g with some fold is another fold whose accumulating functions are related to the accumulating functions of the original fold by fixed equations. The normalization algorithm will describe how these new accumulating functions can be calculated. The promotion theorem for folds has appeared in the literature using various notations [11, 12]:

Theorem 1 (The Fold Promotion Theorem)

$$\forall i : \phi_i \circ E_i^T(g) = g \circ f_i \;\Rightarrow\; g \circ \text{fold}^T(\overline{f}) = \text{fold}^T(\overline{\phi})$$

Proof: Let $\eta = g \circ \text{fold}^T(\overline{f})$ and C_i a constructor of T. Then $\eta \circ C_i = g \circ \text{fold}^T(\overline{f}) \circ C_i = g \circ f_i \circ E_i^T(\text{fold}^T(\overline{f})) = \phi_i \circ E_i^T(g) \circ E_i^T(\text{fold}^T(\overline{f})) = \phi_i \circ E_i^T(g \circ \text{fold}^T(\overline{f})) = \phi_i \circ E_i^T(\eta)$. Therefore, $\eta \circ C_i = \phi_i \circ E_i^T(\eta)$, which shows that η has a form of a fold with accumulating functions $\overline{\phi}$ (by Definition 2). Thus $\eta = \text{fold}^T(\overline{\phi})$. □

For example, the fold promotion theorem for *list* is:

$$\frac{\begin{aligned}\phi_n() &= g(f_n())\\ \phi_c(a, g(r)) &= g(f_c(a, r))\end{aligned}}{g(\text{fold}^{list}(f_n, f_c)\,x) = \text{fold}^{list}(\phi_n, \phi_c)\,x}$$

For example, the boolean promotion theorem is:

$$g \circ \text{fold}^{boolean}(f_f, f_t) \;=\; \text{fold}^{boolean}(g \circ f_f, g \circ f_t)$$

The normalization algorithm which is based on the promotion theorems is described in detail in Section 3.2. Here we give an example of using the list promotion theorem for normalizing programs. We will improve filter(filter(x,p), q), where filter(x,p) returns the list of all elements in the list x that satisfy the predicate p:

$$\text{filter}(x,p) \;=\; \text{fold}^{list}(\lambda().\text{Nil}, \lambda(a,r).\textbf{if}\, p(a)\,\textbf{then}\,\text{Cons}(a,r)\,\textbf{else}\, r)\; x$$

We need to find some $\text{fold}^{list}(\phi_n, \phi_c)\, x = \text{filter}(\text{filter}(x,p),q)$. We apply the *list* promotion theorem with $g(x) = \text{filter}(x,q)$ and $\text{fold}^{list}(f_n, f_c)\, x = \text{filter}(x,p)$:

1) $\phi_n() \;=\; g(f_n()) \;=\; \text{filter}(f_n(),q) \;=\; \text{filter}(\text{Nil},q) \;=\; \text{Nil}$

2) $\phi_c(a, \text{filter}(r,q)) \;=\; g(f_c(a,r)) \;=\; \text{filter}(f_c(a,r),q)$
   $=\; \text{filter}(\textbf{if}\, p(a)\,\textbf{then}\,\text{Cons}(a,r)\,\textbf{else}\, r, q)$
   $=\; \textbf{if}\, p(a)\,\textbf{then}\,\text{filter}(\text{Cons}(a,r),q)\,\textbf{else}\,\text{filter}(r,q)$
   by the boolean promotion theorem
   $=\; \textbf{if}\, p(a)\,\textbf{then}\,(\textbf{if}\, q(a)\,\textbf{then}\,\text{Cons}(a,\text{filter}(r,q))\,\textbf{else}\,\text{filter}(r,q))$
   $\textbf{else}\,\text{filter}(r,q)$
   by the filter definition
   $\Rightarrow\; \phi_c(a,u) \;=\; \textbf{if}\, p(a)\,\textbf{then}\,(\textbf{if}\, q(a)\,\textbf{then}\,\text{Cons}(a,u)\,\textbf{else}\, u)\,\textbf{else}\, u$
   where filter(r,q) *was generalized to* u

Therefore, the composition filter(filter(x,p), q) is:

$$\text{fold}^{list}(\lambda().\text{Nil}, \lambda(a,u).\textbf{if}\, p(a)\,\textbf{then}\,(\textbf{if}\, q(a)\,\textbf{then}\,\text{Cons}(a,u)\,\textbf{else}\, u)\,\textbf{else}\, u)\; x$$

which is equal to $\text{filter}(x, \lambda(a).p(a) \wedge q(a))$.

The following corollary says that there is a unique way of expressing a function as a fold [12]. It is used for testing the functional equality of two folds:

Corollary 1 (Uniqueness Property)

$$\forall i:\; g \circ C_i = \phi_i \circ E_i^T(g) \;\;\Leftrightarrow\;\; g = \text{fold}^T(\overline{\phi})$$

3 Normalization of Expressions with Folds

The normalization algorithm presented in this section is a reduction algorithm that improves any program which is expressed only in terms of folds. This algorithm reduces any fold applied to another fold into a fold applied to a variable. Since every fold builds a data structure, improved programs will build fewer intermediate data structures.

Program normalization is accomplished by pushing the outer fold into the accumulating functions of the inner fold, as is directed by the promotion theorem. This is a generalization of loop fusion to arbitrary types because the outer fold will be pushed inside the inner one until it is eliminated by the generalizations introduced by the normalization algorithm.

3.1 The Term Language

In the following definitions we assume that programs are well-typed.

Definition 3 (The Term Language) *A* program *in the term language has the form* $\lambda(x_1, \ldots, x_n).\tau$*, where each* x_i *is a variable and* τ *is a term. Each term has one of the following forms:*

- variable: x, *bound in some outer lambda abstraction;*
- construction: $C(\tau_1, \ldots, \tau_n)$, *where* C *is a constructor and each* τ_i *is a term;*
- fold: $\text{fold}^T(f_1, \ldots, f_n)\,\tau$, *where* τ *is a term and each* f_i *has the form* $\lambda(x_1, \ldots, x_m).\tau_i$*, where* τ_i *is a term and each* x_j *is a variable.*

Definition 4 (Accumulative Result Variable) *Each accumulating function* f_i *in a fold in the term language has the form* $\lambda(x_1, \ldots, x_m).\tau$*, where the types of the bound variables* $x_1, \ldots, x_m$ *are associated with the types* $t_1, \ldots, t_m$ *in the domain of the corresponding constructor* C_i*. Each bound variable* x_j *whose associated type* t_j *is the recursive type* T *is an* accumulative result variable.

For example, in $\text{append}(x, y) = \text{fold}^{list}(\lambda().y, \lambda(a, r).\text{Cons}(a, r))\; x$, variable r is an accumulative result variable.

Definition 5 (Safe Program) *A program in the term language is safe if it does not contain terms* $\text{fold}^T(\overline{f})\,t$*, where* t *contains a reference to an accumulative result variable which is bound in an outer lambda abstraction.*

This basically says that the partial results of iterations (i.e. the values of the accumulative result variables) are black boxes (they cannot be traversed).

For example, reverse(x), defined in Section 2, is computed by

$$\text{fold}^{list}(\lambda().\text{Nil}, \lambda(a, r).\text{fold}^{list}(\lambda().\text{Cons}(a, \text{Nil}), \lambda(b, s).\text{Cons}(b, s))\; r)\; x$$

is not safe, since the inner fold (that computes append(r, Cons(a, Nil))) is over r, an accumulative result variable.

Definition 6 (Canonical Terms) *A canonical term is a term in which*

- *all folds in the term are over variables;*
- *none of these variables are accumulative result variables.*

Note that a canonical term is a safe term that does not produce any intermediate results. We will show that if a program in our term language is safe then it can be transformed into a canonical program by the normalization algorithm.

Even though the restriction that the intermediate results of recursion (i.e. the values of accumulative result variables) are not allowed to be traversed limits the expressiveness of safe programs, there are many useful programs that are still expressible. In fact, in [2], a language that poses a similar restriction was proved to capture all polynomial-time programs[3].

---

[3]Our language cannot be exactly PTIME since we have a decision algorithm for equalities (see Section 5) and it is well-known that function equality is undecidable for this class.

3.2 The Normalization Algorithm

Before expressing the normalization algorithm in detail, we give one simple example that illustrates how it works. We will improve length(append(x, y)), where:

$$\begin{array}{lcl} \text{length}(x) & = & \text{fold}^{list}(\lambda().\text{Zero}, \lambda(a,r).\text{Succ}(r))\,x \\ \text{append}(x,y) & = & \text{fold}^{list}(f_n, f_c)\,x \quad \text{where} \left\{ \begin{array}{lcl} f_n & = & \lambda().y \\ f_c & = & \lambda(a,r).\text{Cons}(a,r) \end{array} \right. \end{array}$$

We need to find some $\text{fold}^{list}(\phi_n, \phi_c)\,x$ equivalent to length(append(x, y)). We apply the *list* promotion theorem with $g =$ length:

$$\begin{array}{lcl} \phi_n() & = & \text{length}(f_n()) \;=\; \text{length}(y) \\ \phi_c(a, \text{length}(r)) & = & \text{length}(f_c(a,r)) \\ & = & \text{length}(\text{Cons}(a,r)) \\ & = & \text{Succ}(\text{length}(r)) \quad \textit{by length definition} \\ & \Rightarrow & \phi_c(a,u) \;=\; \text{Succ}(u) \\ & & \textit{where } \text{length}(r) \textit{ was generalized to } u \end{array}$$

Therefore, the composition length(append(x, y)) is:

$$\text{fold}^{list}(\lambda().\text{length}(y), \lambda(a,u).\text{Succ}(u))\,x$$

Note that the intermediate list structure append(x, y) is no longer produced.

The normalization algorithm is a meaning preserving transformation from a term to another term. It uses a parameter ρ which is a partial function from terms to variables. In our notation, $\rho[g/r]$ extends ρ with the mapping from g to r. Function ρ keeps all bindings, such as length$(r)/u$ in the previous example, to be used for eliminating all calls to g from the premise of the promotion theorem, that is, from $\phi_i \circ E_i^T(g) = g \circ f_i$, thus calculating an expression for the accumulating function ϕ_i. This is called the *generalization phase*. This generalization derives the fixpoint of the composition given the fixpoints of the components. We will prove that such a generalization is always possible for all safe terms.

The normalization algorithm consists of the following parts:

- *Generalization:* If the normalization algorithm derives a term mapped in ρ to some variable v, then this term is replaced by v.

- *Application to a Construction:* From the fold definition:

  $$\text{fold}^T(\overline{f})(C_i(\overline{u})) \;=\; f_i(E_i^T(\text{fold}^T(\overline{f}))(\overline{u}))$$

  For example, for length $=$ $\text{fold}^{list}(\lambda().\text{Zero}, \lambda(a,r).\text{Succ}(r))$:

  $$\text{length}(\text{Cons}(a,l)) \;=\; \text{Succ}(\text{length}(l))$$

- *Fold Promotion:* If the term is a composition $g(\text{fold}^T(\overline{f})\,x)$, where g is a fold, then the fold promotion theorem is applied to derive the term

$\text{fold}^T(\overline{\phi})\,x$, where, for all i, ϕ_i is computed by recursively improving the equation:

$$\phi_i(r_1, \ldots, r_{m_i}) \;=\; g(f_i(x_1, \ldots, x_{m_i}))$$

where all x_i and r_i are new variables. In each case, ρ is extended with the mappings from terms in $(E_i(g)(x_1, \ldots, x_{m_i}))$ to variables $r_1, \ldots, r_{m_i}$. For example, from the fold promotion theorem for lists we have:

$$g(\text{fold}^{list}(f_n, f_c)\,x) \;=\; \text{fold}^{list}(\phi_n, \phi_c)\,x$$

where

$$\begin{array}{lcl} \phi_n() & = & g(f_n()) \\ \phi_c(r_1, r_2) & = & g(f_c(x_1, x_2)) \quad \text{with } \rho[x_1/r_1,\; g(x_2)/r_2] \end{array}$$

For example, the following improves plus(length(x), length(y)), where

$$\text{plus}(x, y) \;=\; \text{fold}^{nat}(\lambda().y,\, \lambda(r).\text{Succ}(r))\,x$$

Let plus(length(x), length(y)) $=$ $\text{fold}^{list}(\phi_n, \phi_c)\,x$. We apply the promotion theorem for *list* with

$$\begin{array}{lcl} g(z) & = & \text{plus}(\text{length}(y), z) \\ & = & \text{fold}^{nat}(\lambda().\text{fold}^{list}(\lambda().\text{Zero}, \lambda(a, r).\text{Succ}(r))\,y, \\ & & \qquad \lambda(r).\text{Succ}(r))\,z \\ \text{fold}^{list}(f_n, f_c)\,x & = & \text{length}(x) \\ & = & \text{fold}^{list}(\lambda().\text{Zero}, \lambda(a, r).\text{Succ}(r))\,x \end{array}$$

to compose $g(\text{length}(x)) = \text{fold}^{list}(\phi_n, \phi_c)\,x$:

$$\begin{array}{lcll} \phi_n() & = & g(f_n()) & \\ & = & g(\text{Zero}) & \\ & = & \text{fold}^{list}(\lambda().\text{Zero}, \lambda(a, r).\text{Succ}(r))\,y & \\ \phi_c(r_1, r_2) & = & g(f_c(x_1, x_2)) & (\textit{where } \rho = [x_1/r_1,\; g(x_2)/r_2]) \\ & = & g(\text{Succ}(x_2)) & \\ & = & \text{Succ}(g(x_2)) & (\textit{application of } g \textit{ to a constructor}) \\ & = & \text{Succ}(r_2) & (g(x_2) \textit{ was generalized to } r_2) \end{array}$$

Therefore, plus(length(x), length(y)) is:

$$\begin{array}{l} \text{fold}^{list}(\lambda().\text{fold}^{list}(\lambda().\text{Zero}, \lambda(a, r).\text{Succ}(r))\,y, \\ \qquad \lambda(r_1, r_2).\text{Succ}(r_2))\,x \end{array}$$

which is equal to length(append(x, y)) (presented in the beginning of this subsection).

Theorem 2 (Correctness of the Normalization Algorithm) *The normalization algorithm transforms any safe term into a canonical form.*

Proof: We can see from the definitions of the term language and canonical forms that folds of the form $g(t) = \text{fold}^T(\overline{f})\,t$ need to be rewritten into folds over variables. If t is a construction, then we apply the application-to-a-construction rule. In that case the fold g is pushed inside to only those components of the construction that have recursive type. If t is a fold, then g is pushed into the accumulators of the inner fold, as is directed by the fold promotion theorem, and some new mappings are attached to ρ. After recursively applying the normalization algorithm only terms of the form $g(x)$, where x is a variable, remain. If x is an accumulative result variable, then, from the way ρ was extended during promotion, $g(x)$ is always bound in ρ to some new variable r. This is the generalization phase of the algorithm. If x is not an accumulative result variable, then $g(x)$ remains as is. Therefore, all folds in the resulting term are over non-accumulative result variables. It is necessary to prove that after fold promotion there remain no references of the old accumulative result variables other than those generalized by ρ. This is true only when g is a safe fold, that is, when the term t does not contain accumulative result variables. □

Note that the composition of two or more canonical terms is a safe term and, therefore, it can be reduced to canonical form. This makes our canonical term language closed under composition.

The normalization algorithm can be implemented very efficiently. Whenever we apply the promotion theorem we annotate each function g (the left part of the application) with a new number. Then, instead of inserting $g(x_i)/r_i$ in ρ, for some variables x_i and r_i, we can insert the triple of this number with x_i and r_i. Then the generalization phase is performed by checking if the current term $f(x)$ was annotated by a number already in ρ. That way, the complexity of the normalization algorithm is $\mathcal{O}(n \log n)$, where n is the size of the resulting canonical term (since a list of numbers can be searched in $\mathcal{O}(\log n)$). The size of the resulting term, though, can be exponential to the size of the initial term, such as in the case a fold is applied to a deeply nested construction[4]. This is a problem that all partial evaluators face.

The normalization algorithm can capture most stream-based pipelining techniques found in relational query optimization. These techniques model database operations as threads that propagate tuples or partitions of tuples to each other, instead of materializing intermediate relations. This can be achieved in our framework by fusing the loops of the nested relational operators into one loop using the normalization algorithm. Our method, though, is algebraic, fully automated, and it can be performed at any level and for any data structure. Note that the cases that we are forced to materialize results during pipelining, are the cases that require some special operators, such as the sort operator before a sort-merge join. These operations reflect the non-improvable terms in our algebra. Our work states this condition explicitly as a syntactic restrictions to program schemes.

[4]This does not contradict with the fact that the resulting programs are always more efficient than the initial, since folds are lazily evaluated, that is, only one accumulator function is evaluated each time.

4 Finite Sets

Finite sets cannot be captured as regular sums-of-products types since they must satisfy some special properties, such as, being independent of the order in which elements are inserted. All the type constructors described so far form free algebras, in which there is a unique way of constructing an instance of a type. Sets are very important abstractions in database specification as they offer high degree of data independence. They are also important in database implementation because operations on sets have more alternative translations than the operations on free algebra types, therefore they offer more opportunities for optimization, yielding more efficient programs. In spite of that, sets must not be considered as data structures suitable for all cases, as systems based on the relational model do. If there is some additional information on a collection, such as an order of some kind, then an ordered data structure may be more suitable than sets. Furthermore, if there is some dependency between two sets, then a hierarchical structure, such as sets of sets, may be more natural for expressing programs over these structures. The latter case does not imply that these structures can not be actually implemented as flat tables. As we will see in Section 7, abstract modeling can be effectively separated from implementation details. Therefore, the abstract specification of a program should capture as much as possible the semantic information of the problem domain and ignore implementation issues. The program optimizer must be able to use this semantic information to make intelligent decisions.

Finite sets are expressed as instances of a special built-in type $\text{set}(\alpha)$. The set type has two constructors: Emptyset that returns an empty set and $\text{Insert}(e, s)$ that constructs a new set by inserting the element e into the set s. (The type of Insert is $\alpha \times \text{set}(\alpha) \rightarrow \text{set}(\alpha)$.) Note that $\text{Insert}(a, \text{Insert}(b, s)) = \text{Insert}(b, \text{Insert}(a, s))$ and that if e is already in s then $\text{Insert}(e, s) = s$. The selector function $\text{split}(s)$ is a non-deterministic function that splits the non-empty input set s into an element and a set. It returns a pair that contains an arbitrary element of s and the set equal to s with this chosen element removed. That is, if $(a, r) = \text{split}(s)$ then $a \notin r$ and $\{a\} \cup r = s$.

A function suitable for traversing sets is set fold (similar to list fold):

Definition 7 (Set Fold) *The set fold* $\text{fold}^{set}(f_e, f_s)$ *is defined by the following recursive equation:*

$$\text{fold}^{set}(f_e, f_s)\, s \;=\; \begin{cases} \textbf{if } s = \text{Emptyset } \textbf{then } f_e() \\ \textbf{else let } (a, r) = \text{split}(s) \textbf{ in } f_s(a, \text{fold}^{set}(f_e, f_s)\, r) \end{cases}$$

For example,

$$\begin{aligned} \text{emptyp}(x) &= \text{fold}^{set}(\lambda().\text{True}, \lambda(a, r).\text{False})\; x \\ \text{union}(x, y) &= \text{fold}^{set}(\lambda().y, \lambda(a, r).\text{Insert}(a, r))\; x \\ \text{member}(e, x) &= \text{fold}^{set}(\lambda().\text{False}, \lambda(a, r).(a = e)\;\textbf{or}\; r)\; x \\ \text{restrict}(s, f) &= \text{fold}^{set}(\lambda().\text{Emptyset}, \\ &\qquad\qquad \lambda(a, r).\textbf{if } f(a)\;\textbf{then}\;\text{Insert}(a, r)\;\textbf{else}\; r)\; s \end{aligned}$$

Set equality of two sets x and y is computed by the following:

$$\text{set\_equal}(x, y) \;=\; \begin{cases} \text{fold}^{set}(\lambda().\text{fold}^{set}(\lambda().\text{True}, \\ \qquad\qquad\qquad \lambda(b, s).\text{member}(b, x)\;\textbf{and}\; s)\; y, \\ \qquad \lambda(a, r).\text{member}(a, y)\;\textbf{and}\; r)\; x \end{cases}$$

Another example is the generic join join($x, y, match, concat$) (it is generic enough to have selection and projection embedded in its input functions):

$$\begin{aligned}&\text{fold}^{set}(\lambda().\text{Emptyset}\\&\qquad\lambda(a,r).\text{fold}^{set}(\lambda().r, \lambda(b,s).\textbf{if } match(a,b)\\&\qquad\qquad\qquad\qquad\qquad\qquad\qquad\textbf{then } \text{Insert}(concat(a,b),s)\\&\qquad\qquad\qquad\qquad\qquad\qquad\qquad\textbf{else } s)\, y)\, x\end{aligned}$$

join($x, y, match, concat$) takes every combination of elements a and b from the sets x and y, checks whether these elements satisfy the *match* predicate, and if so it returns a new element by applying the *concat* function to form a new element of the result set. An example call to this join retrieves all employees working in the CSE department (this is a semijoin):

join(employees, departments,
  λ(emp,dept).(emp.dno=dept.dno **and** dept.name="CSE"),
  λ(emp,dept).emp)

A sufficient condition for a set fold being order-independent is f_s being both commutative and idempotent [3]:

Definition 8 (Commutative-idempotent function)
A function f is commutative-idempotent if:

$$\begin{array}{llll}\forall m\,\forall n\,\forall s: & f(m,f(n,s)) & = & f(n,f(m,s)) & \textbf{(commutativity)}\\ \forall n\,\forall s: & f(n,f(n,s)) & = & f(n,s) & \textbf{(idempotence)}\end{array}$$

For example, Insert is commutative-idempotent, while Cons is not.

The commutativity and the idempotence property of a function f can be verified by the equality decision algorithm described in Section 5.

Theorem 3 *If a function f_s is commutative-idempotent then*

$$\text{fold}^{set}(f_e, f_s)\,(\text{Insert}(a,s)) = f_s(a, \text{fold}^{set}(f_e,f_s)\,s)$$

Proof: If s = Emptyset then $\text{fold}^{set}(f_e, f_s)\,(\text{Insert}(a, \text{Emptyset})) = f_s(a, f_e)$ which is true (because $\text{split}(\text{Insert}(a, \text{Emptyset})) = (a, \text{Emptyset})$). If $a \in s$ then $\text{Insert}(a,s) = s$ and $f_s(a, \text{fold}^{set}(f_e,f_s)\,s) = \text{fold}^{set}(f_e,f_s)\,s$ (idempotence property). Otherwise, let $(b,r) = \text{split}(\text{Insert}(a,s))$. We assume that the theorem is true for $m = s - \{a,b\}$: $\text{fold}^{set}(f_e,f_s)\,(\text{Insert}(e,m)) = f_s(e, \text{fold}^{set}(f_e,f_s)\,m)$. Then $\text{fold}^{set}(f_e,f_s)\,(\text{Insert}(a,s)) = f_s(b, \text{fold}^{set}(f_e,f_s)\,r)$ $= f_s(b, \text{fold}^{set}(f_e,f_s)\,\text{Insert}(a,m)) = f_s(b, f_s(a, \text{fold}^{set}(f_e,f_s)\,m))$ (hypothesis) $= f_s(a, f_s(b, \text{fold}^{set}(f_e,f_s)\,m))$ (commutativity property) $= f_s(a, \text{fold}^{set}(f_e,f_s)\,s)$ (hypothesis). □

Theorem 4 (The Promotion Theorem for Set Folds)

$$\frac{\begin{array}{lcl}\phi_e() & = & g(f_e())\\ \phi_s(a,g(r)) & = & g(f_s(a,r))\end{array}}{g(\text{fold}^{set}(f_e,f_s)\,x) = \text{fold}^{set}(\phi_e,\phi_s)\,x}$$

and if f_s is commutative-idempotent then so is ϕ_s.

Proof: For x = Emptyset the theorem is true, since $\phi_e() = g(f_e())$. Otherwise, let $(a, r) = \text{split}(x)$. We assume that the theorem is true for $x = r$. Then we have $g(\text{fold}^{set}(f_e, f_s)\, x) = g(f_s(a, \text{fold}^{set}(f_e, f_s)\, r)) = \phi_s(a, g(\text{fold}^{set}(f_e, f_s)\, r))$ $= \phi_s(a, \text{fold}^{set}(\phi_e, \phi_s)\, r) = \text{fold}^{set}(\phi_e, \phi_s)\, x$. In addition, $\phi_s(a, \phi_s(b, g(r))) =$ $\phi_s(a, g(f_s(b, r))) = g(f_s(a, f_s(b, r)))$. Let f_s be a commutative-idempotent function. Then $\phi_s(a, \phi_s(a, g(r))) = g(f_s(a, f_s(a, r))) = g(f_s(a, r)) = \phi_s(a, g(r))$ and $\phi_s(a, \phi_s(b, g(r))) = g(f_s(a, f_s(b, r))) = g(f_s(b, f_s(a, r))) = \phi_s(b, \phi_s(a, g(r)))$. Therefore, ϕ_s is commutative-idempotent too. □

The normalization algorithm does not need any extensions to handle set folds, since the application-to-a-construction rule can be used as is for sets and the fold promotion theorem for sets is exactly like any fold promotion theorem in the free algebra. The condition f_s being an commutative-idempotent can be seen as an additional condition for a set fold being safe. The normalization algorithm can now improve any safe program that involves sets, lists, trees, tuples, integers, booleans etc.

The normalization algorithm captures many types of algebraic transformations already in use in relational algebra. For example, the following query:

```
restrict(join(employees, departments,
              λ(emp,dept).(emp.dno=dept.dno),
              λ(emp,dept).(emp,dept)),
         λ(emp,dept).dept.name="CSE")
```

is reduced by the normalization algorithm into a canonical form which is equivalent to:

```
join(employees, departments,
     λ(emp,dept).(emp.dno=dept.dno and dept.name="CSE"),
     λ(emp,dept).(emp,dept))
```

that is, the selection was pushed inside the join. Note that, if you have a good index to evaluate the join and if the result of the join is very small, it might be preferable not to push the selection inside the join. But there is some information missing in the above query. Our normalization algorithm always improves programs if these programs are evaluated as folds *directly*. That is, when select and join in our example are evaluated naively as loops. We will see in Section 7 that normalization should happen after type transformation. If there is an index available in the physical representation of the join inputs then this information will appear as part of the transformed query. That way path selection can be integrated neatly with algebraic optimization.

As another example, consider the following nested SQL query:

```
select * from d departments
where d.name="CSE"
      and exists( select * from e employees
                  where e.dno=d.dno and e.age>65 )
```

This query can be computed by the following safe program:

```
restrict(departments,
         λ(d).d.name="CSE"
              and (not emptyp(restrict(employees,
                                        λ(e).e.dno=d.dno and e.age>65))))
```

which is normalized into the following canonical form:

$$\begin{array}{l} \text{fold}^{set}(\lambda().\text{Emptyset}, \\ \quad \lambda(d,r).\textbf{if}\ d.\text{name} = \text{"CSE"} \\ \qquad \textbf{then}\ \text{fold}^{set}(\lambda().r, \\ \qquad\qquad \lambda(e,s).\textbf{if}\ e.\text{dno} = d.\text{dno} \\ \qquad\qquad\quad \textbf{then}\,\textbf{if}\ e.\text{age} > 65\ \textbf{then}\ \text{Insert}(e,s)\ \textbf{else}\ s \\ \qquad\qquad\quad \textbf{else}\ s) \\ \qquad\qquad \text{employees} \\ \qquad \textbf{else}\ r) \\ \quad \text{departments} \end{array}$$

5 Testing Functional Equalities

The following algorithm tests whether any two canonical terms compute the same function. It is based on the uniqueness property that says that there is a unique way for expressing a function as a fold. Given any two canonical programs $\lambda\overline{x}.t_1(\overline{x})$ and $\lambda\overline{y}.t_2(\overline{y})$ in our term language (i.e. t_1 and t_2 are canonical terms), $\mathcal{E}(t_1(\overline{x}), t_2(\overline{x}))$ returns true if and only if $t_1(\overline{x}) = t_2(\overline{x})$ for any input $\overline{x}$. $\mathcal{E}(x, y)$ is computed by the following rules:

$$\begin{array}{llcll} 1 & \mathcal{E}(x,x) & \longrightarrow & \textbf{true} & \\ 2 & \mathcal{E}(x,y) & \longrightarrow & \textbf{false} & \text{if } x \neq y \\ 3 & \mathcal{E}(C_k(\overline{u}), C_k(\overline{w})) & \longrightarrow & \bigwedge_i \mathcal{E}(u_i, w_i) & \\ 4 & \mathcal{E}(C_k(\overline{u}), C_m(\overline{w})) & \longrightarrow & \textbf{false} & \text{if } k \neq m \\ 5 & \mathcal{E}(\text{fold}^T(\overline{f})\,x, \text{fold}^T(\overline{g})\,x) & \longrightarrow & \bigwedge_i \mathcal{E}(f_i(\overline{y}), g_i(\overline{y})) & \\ 6 & \mathcal{E}(g(x), \text{fold}^T(\overline{f})\,x) & \longrightarrow & \bigwedge_i \mathcal{E}(g(C_i(\overline{y})), f_i(E_i^T(g)\,\overline{y})) & \\ 7 & \mathcal{E}(\text{fold}^T(\overline{f})\,x, g(x)) & \longrightarrow & \bigwedge_i \mathcal{E}(f_i(E_i^T(g)\,\overline{y}), g(C_i(\overline{y}))) & \end{array}$$

where $\overline{y}$ in Rules 5, 6, and 7 are new variable names. All rules are evaluated in sequence and only the first applicable rule is used. The last two rules come from the uniqueness property. They require that both terms $g(C_i(\overline{y}))$ and $f_i(E_i^T(g)\,\overline{y})$ are improved before they are passed to the equality checker $\mathcal{E}$. This implies that this algorithm can decide functional equalities only for safe terms. Rule 5 is used as the bottom case for Rules 6 and 7.

For example, $\mathcal{E}(\text{plus}(y,x), \text{plus}(x,y)) = \mathcal{E}(\text{fold}^{nat}(\lambda().x, \lambda(r).\text{Succ}(r))y,$ $\text{fold}^{nat}(\lambda().y, \lambda(r).\text{Succ}(r))x)$. We apply the uniqueness property for $g(x) = \text{fold}^{nat}(\lambda().x, \lambda(r).\text{Succ}(r))\,y$:

$$\begin{array}{ll} x = \text{Zero}: & \mathcal{E}(g(\text{Zero}), y) = \mathcal{E}(\text{fold}^{nat}(\lambda().\text{Zero}, \lambda(r).\text{Succ}(r))y, y) \\ & \qquad = \textbf{true} \\ x = \text{Succ}(i): & \mathcal{E}(g(\text{Succ}(i)), \text{Succ}(g(i))) \\ & \quad = \mathcal{E}(\text{fold}^{nat}(\lambda().\text{Succ}(i), \lambda(r).\text{Succ}(r))y, \text{Succ}(g(i))) \end{array}$$

we apply the uniqueness property again with $f(y) = \text{Succ}(g(i))$:

$$\begin{array}{ll} y = \text{Zero}: & \mathcal{E}(f(\text{Zero}), \text{Succ}(i)) = \mathcal{E}(\text{Succ}(i), \text{Succ}(i)) \\ & \qquad = \mathcal{E}(i,i) = \textbf{true} \\ y = \text{Succ}(j): & \mathcal{E}(f(\text{Succ}(j)), \text{Succ}(f(j))) = \mathcal{E}(\text{Succ}(f(j)), \text{Succ}(f(j))) \\ & \qquad = \mathcal{E}(f(j), f(j)) = \textbf{true} \end{array}$$

Therefore, $\mathcal{E}(\text{plus}(y,x), \text{plus}(x,y))$ is true.

Set equality is different than structural equality for sums-of-products types. Testing whether two expressions e_1 and e_2 of type *set* are equal is equivalent to testing whether set_equal(e_1, e_2) is equal to the term True.

Each canonical form specifies an equivalence class of safe programs that are reduced to this form by the normalization algorithm. In fact, there may be infinite number of such programs in a class. For example, $x+y$, $x+(y+0)$, $x+(y+0+0)$ etc. compute the same function and they are all reduced to the same canonical form $x+y$. The equivalence class of all canonical programs that compute the same function f is called the *canonical extension* of f. From the uniqueness property and by using case analysis we can prove that for any function f that can be expressed as a canonical program, the canonical extension is finite. The optimization of function f is a search over the finite space of the canonical extension of f. This process will be explained in detail in Section 8.

6 Program Synthesis

The program synthesis algorithm described in this section is a pattern matching algorithm. It is based on the equality tester for canonical programs, as it is described in Section 5. We use here the term program synthesis in its wider context of constructing programs, not in its usual narrow form of producing programs given the input/output specification of the programs.

A *canonical pattern* is a canonical program in which some of its variables are annotated as pattern variables. A pattern variable with name x is represented as $\#x$, in order to be distinguished from regular term variables. For example,

$$\text{Cons}(\#x, \text{fold}(\lambda().\text{Nil}, \lambda(a,r).\#y)\ z)$$

is a canonical pattern with pattern variables $\#x$ and $\#y$.

A substitution list ρ is either **fail** or a partial binding from pattern variables to canonical programs. We denote $\rho[x/g]$ the extension of ρ with the binding from the pattern variable $\#x$ to the canonical program g, $\rho[x]$ is the value of $\#x$ in ρ, and $\rho(f)$ is a canonical pattern that results after replacing all pattern variables in f that occur in ρ by their bindings. A canonical pattern f is equal to a canonical program g under the substitution ρ if $\rho(f)$ does not contain any pattern variables and $\mathcal{E}(\rho(f), g) = \textbf{true}$.

A canonical pattern f matches a canonical program g under a substitution ρ, denoted as $[f \equiv g]\,\rho$, if there is a substitution ρ' such that $\mathcal{E}(\rho'(\rho(f)), g) = \textbf{true}$. The algorithm in Figure 1 implements $[f \equiv g]\,\rho$. Rules 2 through 8 are very similar to the rules for $\mathcal{E}(f,g)$, as they are described in Section 5. The only difference is that instead of collecting all test results using the *and* operator, we accumulate all substitution lists, starting with ρ, as it is dictated by the $\mathcal{A}_i$ accumulation function:

$$\mathcal{A}_i(\ f_i\ )\,\rho \;=\; f_n(f_{n-1}(\cdots f_2(f_1(\rho))))$$

For example, $\mathcal{A}_i(\ [u_i \equiv w_i]\ )\,\rho$ in Rule 4 is:

$$[u_n \equiv w_n]\,([u_{n-1} \equiv w_{n-1}]\ldots([u_1 \equiv w_2]\,([u_1 \equiv w_1]\,\rho)))$$

Rules 9 through 12 involve pattern variables. Rule 9 is straightforward. Rule 10 is similar to Rule 6. It serves as a bottom case for Rules 11 and 12. If Rule 10

$$
\begin{array}{lcll}
[e \equiv u]\,\textbf{fail} & \longrightarrow & \textbf{fail} & \textbf{1} \\
[x \equiv x]\,\rho & \longrightarrow & \rho & \textbf{2} \\
[x \equiv y]\,\rho & \longrightarrow & \textbf{fail} \qquad \text{if } x \neq y & \textbf{3} \\
[C_k(\overline{u}) \equiv C_k(\overline{w})]\,\rho & \longrightarrow & \mathcal{A}_i(\,[u_i \equiv w_i]\,)\,\rho & \textbf{4} \\
[C_k(\overline{u}) \equiv C_m(\overline{w})]\,\rho & \longrightarrow & \textbf{fail} \qquad \text{if } k \neq m & \textbf{5} \\
[\text{fold}^T(\overline{f})\,x \equiv \text{fold}^T(\overline{g})\,x]\,\rho & \longrightarrow & \mathcal{A}_i(\,[f_i(\overline{z_i}) \equiv g_i(\overline{z_i})]\,)\,\rho & \textbf{6} \\
[g(x) \equiv \text{fold}^T(\overline{f})\,x] & \longrightarrow & \mathcal{A}_i(\,[g(C_i(\overline{z_i})) \equiv f_i(E_i^T(g)\,\overline{z_i})]\,)\,\rho & \textbf{7} \\
[\text{fold}^T(\overline{f})\,x \equiv g(x)] & \longrightarrow & \mathcal{A}_i(\,[f_i(E_i^T(g)\,\overline{z_i}) \equiv g(C_i(\overline{z_i}))]\,)\,\rho & \textbf{8} \\
 & & & \\
[\#f \equiv g]\,\rho & \longrightarrow & \rho[f/g] & \textbf{9} \\
[\text{fold}^T(\overline{g})\,\#f \equiv \text{fold}^T(\overline{\phi})\,x]\,\rho & \longrightarrow & [\text{fold}^T(\overline{g})\,x \equiv \text{fold}^T(\overline{\phi})\,x]\,(\rho[f/x]) & \textbf{10} \\
[\text{fold}^S(\overline{g})\,\#f \equiv \text{fold}^T(\overline{\phi})\,x]\,\rho & \longrightarrow & \rho'[f/\text{fold}^T(\lambda\overline{z_1}.\rho'[f_1],\ldots,\lambda\overline{z_n}.\rho'[f_n])\,x] & \textbf{11} \\
 & & \text{where } \rho' = \mathcal{A}_i(\,[\text{fold}^S(\overline{g})\,\#f_i \equiv & \\
 & & \qquad\qquad \phi_i(E_i^S(\text{fold}^S(\overline{g}))\,\overline{z_i})]\,)\,\rho & \\
[\text{fold}^S(\overline{g})\,\#f \equiv \phi]\,\rho & \longrightarrow & \rho'[f/C_k(\rho'[f_1],\ldots,\rho'[f_n])] & \textbf{12} \\
 & & \text{where } C_k \text{ is any constructor of } S \text{ and} & \\
 & & \rho' = [g_k(E_k^S(\text{fold}^S(\overline{g}))\,(\#f_1,\ldots,\#f_n)) \equiv \phi]\,\rho &
\end{array}
$$

Figure 1: The Program Synthesis Algorithm

is invoked then neither of Rules 11 or 12 can be invoked. Rule 11 comes from the promotion theorem with $g = \text{fold}(\overline{g})$. Rule 12 tests every constructor C_k of type S to see if it gives an acceptable solution for $\#f$. Rules 11 and 12 may overlap. This may result to more than one solution to a pattern matching. All these rules can be used as rewrite rules in a rule-base system. The search engine of this rule-base system should test each alternative until it finds one that does not fail. This search can be guided by cost functions and heuristics for synthesising the best solutions. Rule 12 may lead into an infinite recursion as in the following example:

$$[\text{fold}^{list}(\lambda().\text{Nil}, \lambda(a,r).\text{Cons}(a,r))\,\#f \equiv x]$$

This has the solution $f = \text{Cons}(\#f_1, \text{Cons}(\#f_2, \ldots))$ (infinite times). Fortunately, the search engine can detect such infinite loops by keeping each triple $(\text{fold}^S(\overline{g}),\ \phi,\ C_k)$ in Rule 12 in a stack and abort Rule 12 if it is invoked twice for the same triple.

For example, suppose that we want to synthesize f in

$$[\text{length}(\#f) \equiv \text{plus}(\text{length}(x), \text{length}(y))]$$

where $\text{length}(x) = \text{fold}^{list}(\lambda().\text{Zero}, \lambda(a,r).\text{Succ}(r))\,x$. After normalizing the right part of the previous equation we get:

$$[\text{length}(\#f) \equiv \text{fold}^{nat}(\lambda().\text{length}(y), \lambda(r).\text{Succ}(r))\,x]$$

We will try first $f = \text{fold}^{list}(\lambda().\#f_1, \lambda(a,r).\#f_2)\,x$ (from Rule 11). Then we get the following two equations:

$$[\text{length}(\#f_1) \equiv \text{length}(y)] \quad \text{and} \quad [\text{length}(\#f_2) \equiv \text{Succ}(\text{length}(r))]$$

The first equation gives $f_1 = y$ (from Rule 11). To solve the second equation we try first $f_2 = \text{Nil}$ (from Rule 12) which fails. Then we try $f_2 = \text{Cons}(f_3, f_4)$ that gives:

$$[\text{Succ}(\text{length}(\#f_4)) \equiv \text{Succ}(\text{length}(r))]$$

After using Rules 4 and 10 we get $f_4 = r$. Therefore,

$$f = \text{fold}^{list}(\lambda().y, \lambda(a,r).\text{Cons}(\#f_3, r))\, x$$

Variable f_3 was not bound to any term since it was eliminated during normalization. This means that it is universally quantified and can be bound to any canonical term. If $f_3 = a$ then f is list append.

7 Mapping Logical to Physical Operations

One of the goals of this work is to achieve a high degree of data independence, that is, a separation between the abstract model and the implementation details. That way the model designer does not have to worry about program efficiency and space utilization, but only to be concerned with expressing correct specification. In addition, this separation may offer more opportunities for optimization. One effective mechanism for separating the model from implementation is *type transformation* [9]. In this framework each abstract data type in the abstract program is mapped into a storage structure by an *abstraction function*.

Definition 9 (Abstraction Function) *Let T be an abstract type and S the type of a concrete storage structure. An abstraction function is a unary function $\mathcal{R}_S^T$ of type $S \to T$ expressed in canonical form.*

For example, if $T = set$ and $S = list$ then one possible $\mathcal{R}_{list}^{set}$ is:

$$\mathcal{R}_{list}^{set} = \text{fold}^{list}(\lambda().\text{Emptyset}, \lambda(a,r).\text{Insert}(a,r))$$

The abstraction function is in general a many-to-one function, that is, an abstract type may be mapped into many different storage structures. For example, a set can be mapped into a list of any order. Having the optimizer select the order is an additional source for optimization. Functions $\mathcal{R}_S^T$ can be provided in a form of an extensible system library. A mapping from an abstract type T to a concrete type S may have more than one abstraction functions $\mathcal{R}_S^T$. The database implementor is responsible for selecting the right storage structures to map the abstract types as well as the abstraction functions that specify this mapping. This implementation phase is performed after the specification phase. The optimizer will use this information to derive a translation that satisfies both the abstract specification and the mapping transformations. This is achieved by the following theory (derived from the type transformation diagram that commutes):

Definition 10 (Function Implementation) *Let f be an abstract function of type $T_1 \times \cdots \times T_n \to T_0$ and for $0 \leq i \leq n$, r_i is an abstraction function $\mathcal{R}_{S_i}^{T_i}$. Then a function F of type $S_1 \times \cdots \times S_n \to S_0$ is an implementation of f iff:*

$$r_0 \circ F = f \circ (r_1 \times \cdots \times r_n)$$

For example, let sets be mapped into lists by the function $\mathcal{R}_{list}^{set}$ described above. Then UNION (of type *list* × *list* → *list*) is the implementation of union (of type *set* × *set* → *set*) iff:

$$\mathcal{R}_{list}^{set} \circ \text{UNION} \;=\; \text{union} \circ (\mathcal{R}_{list}^{set} \times \mathcal{R}_{list}^{set})$$

that is, for all x and y:

$$\mathcal{R}_{list}^{set}(\text{UNION}(x,y)) \;=\; \text{union}(\mathcal{R}_{list}^{set}(x), \mathcal{R}_{list}^{set}(y))$$

For example, one solution for UNION that satisfies this equation is list append. Note that append maintains all duplicated elements while union does not. This is consistent with our type transformation since the result of append will be mapped by $\mathcal{R}_{list}^{set}$ into a set. If we want the output of UNION to reflect the output of union then we better use an isomorphic mapping for the output type of union.

The homomorphic equation $r_0 \circ F \;=\; f \circ (r_1 \times \cdots \times r_n)$ can be solved in two ways. We can select a detailed implementation of the output type T_0 of f by specifying the inverse abstraction function r_0^{-1} from T_0 to S_0. Then

$$F \;=\; r_0^{-1} \circ f \circ (r_1 \times \cdots \times r_n)$$

This implies that the mapping from T_0 to S_0 is specified as an isomorphism. This solution could miss some valid optimizations, especially in the case of sets. A more general solution is to use the program synthesis algorithm as it is described in Section 6. In that case, F is derived by the following pattern matching:

$$[r_0(\#F) \equiv f(r_1(x_1), \ldots, r_n(x_n))]\,\rho$$

Note that in both cases F is expressed in terms of concrete primitives only when it is normalized, such as UNION is expressed in list primitives exclusively. This can be proved by induction[5]: if F is a variable then the statement is true; if it is a construction $C(t_1, \ldots, t_n)$ then none of the parameters of C returns an abstract object since C is a constructor of a concrete type which by definition does not refer to any abstract type; if it is a fold $\text{fold}^T(\overline{f})\,x$ that returns a concrete type then all f_i return concrete types.

The type transformation model can also be used for translating virtual view updates. Each such view can be captured as a many-to-one function v from the abstract database type T to the view type S. Suppose that we perform an update u over this view, that is, u is a function from S to S. The view update problem is to find a database update U that transforms the database state in such a way that the view of the new database state is identical to the original view after the application of u. That is $v \circ U \;=\; u \circ v$. As before, the solution for U can be derived from $[v(\#U) \equiv u(v(db))]$.

Another application of type transformation is database restructuring after schema and/or implementation evolution. Schema evolution from a database type T to a database type T' can be captured as a function c of type $T' \to T$. If the abstraction function that implements the abstract database type T as the storage structure S was r, then this function should change to r' (of type $S' \to T'$) to reflect the schema changes. The function R that restructures

[5] We assume that there are no types in common between the abstract and concrete types.

the database state satisfies the equation $c \circ r' \circ R = r$, which can also be solved by using the synthesis algorithm. Note that the resulting solution for R may have uninstantiated variables. This indicates that there are values in the new database state that need to be filled, such as, in the case of a tuple extended with new components. Schema evolution can be performed in small parts by specifying how some components of the database type change. The compiler should be able to accumulate these pieces of information and use them to synthesize the functions c and r' from r. A convenient tool for performing this task is compile-time reflection [7].

8 Decomposition into Concrete Primitives

Suppose that a query is normalized into the following canonical form:

$$\text{fold}^{list}(\lambda().\text{fold}^{list}(\lambda().\text{Zero}, \lambda(a,r).\text{Succ}(r))\, y, \lambda(a,r).\text{Succ}(r))\, x$$

and there are the following abstractions in the physical layer:

$$\begin{array}{lcl} \text{append}(x,y) & = & \text{fold}^{list}(\lambda().y, \lambda(a,r).\text{Cons}(a,r))\, x \\ \text{length}(x) & = & \text{fold}^{list}(\lambda().\text{Zero}, \lambda(a,r).\text{Succ}(r))\, x \\ \text{plus}(x,y) & = & \text{fold}^{nat}(\lambda().y, \lambda(r).\text{Succ}(r))\, x \end{array}$$

then this canonical form can be expressed either as length(append(x, y)) or as plus(length(x), length(y)). If the cost of plus is 1, the cost of length is the size of its input, and the cost of append is the size of its first input, then clearly the latter choice is better than the first. The following analysis automates this process of mapping canonical forms into compositions of concrete primitives.

Definition 11 (Concrete Layer) *The concrete layer consists of a set $\mathcal{CL}$ of quadruples* (name, behavior, implementation, cost) *where name is the name of a concrete abstraction, behavior is the canonical program that specifies the behavior of this abstraction, implementation is the actual implementation of this abstraction in a possibly non-applicative reference-based language, and cost is the cost function that manipulates a user-defined cost data structure.*

The cost data structure is typically a tuple that contains the necessary components for computing cost values. Cost values satisfy a user-supplied partial order. Each component of a quadruple p from $\mathcal{CL}$, such as name, can be accessed as p[name].

The following algorithm, called the *fold optimization algorithm*, transforms a canonical form f into a composition of concrete primitives. It is invoked as $\mathcal{G}\, f\, \rho$. It returns the set of all possible compositions of concrete names from $\mathcal{CL}$ whose resulting canonical form is equal to f. This algorithm uses set comprehensions to derive all permutations.

$$\begin{array}{lll} \mathbf{1}\ \ \mathcal{G}\, f\, \textbf{fail} & = & \emptyset \\ \mathbf{2}\ \ \mathcal{G}\, v\, \rho & = & \{\, v \,\} \qquad \textit{(if } v \textit{ is a variable)} \\ \mathbf{3}\ \ \mathcal{G}\, C(f_1,\ldots,f_n)\, \rho & = & \{\, C(\phi_1,\ldots,\phi_n) \,/\, \forall i : \phi_i \leftarrow \mathcal{G}\, f_i\, \rho \,\} \\ \mathbf{4}\ \ \mathcal{G}\, f\, \rho & = & \{\, a[\text{name}](\phi_1,\ldots,\phi_n) \,/\, a \leftarrow \mathcal{CL}, \\ & & \qquad \rho' = [a[\text{behavior}](\#f_1,\ldots.\#f_n) \equiv f]\, \rho, \\ & & \qquad \forall i : \phi_i \leftarrow \mathcal{G}\,(\rho'[f_i])\, \rho' \,\} \end{array}$$

Rules 1 and 2 are straightforward. Rule 3 says that if f is a construction $C(f_1, \ldots, f_n)$ then we return $C(\phi_1, \ldots, \phi_n)$, where each ϕ_i is derived by calling this algorithm recursively for each component f_i. The last rule uses the synthesis algorithm to transform f into a call to the concrete operation a. The parameters ϕ_i of this call can be derived by using the program synthesis algorithm and can be transformed by using the fold optimization algorithm recursively. Rule 4 is evaluated when f is either a construction or a fold. The efficiency of this algorithm can be improved in many ways. First, this algorithm can be implemented as a search-based algorithm guided by a[cost]. The cost of a variable is derived from statistical information while the cost of a single construction is 'unit', which is a user-supplied constant. (A complete framework for specifying database statistics and for assigning costs to all variables in a canonical program is proposed in [7].) Estimating costs for canonical programs is easier than for non-canonical programs, since the former do not materialize intermediate results and, therefore, they do not require selectivity estimations. Second, we do not need to check all concrete abstractions a in $\mathcal{CL}$, since we can use type information to discriminate them.

9 Specifying Semantic Information as Type Restrictions

Each type is associated with a set of values, the instances of the type, that share common properties, such as common operations. We can restrict the set of instances of a type T further by using the **where** type constructor:

$$T' \;=\; T\ \mathbf{where}(x)\ p(x)$$

This defines a new type T' whose instances are all the instances x of type T that satisfy the predicate $p(x)$, where p is a canonical term of type $T \rightarrow$ boolean.

The following are examples of restrictions:

$$\begin{array}{lcl} \mathrm{range1} & = & \mathrm{nat}\ \mathbf{where}(x)\ x \geq 10\ \mathbf{and}\ x \leq 20 \\ \mathrm{nset}(\alpha) & = & \mathrm{set}(\alpha)\ \mathbf{where}(x)\ x \neq \mathrm{Emptyset} \\ \mathrm{slist}(\alpha) & = & \mathrm{Msl}(\mathrm{info} : \mathrm{list}(\alpha), \mathrm{size} : \mathrm{nat})\ \mathbf{where}(x)\ x.\mathrm{size} = \mathrm{length}(x.\mathrm{info}) \end{array}$$

The last example keeps the length of a list as redundant information attached to the list. Redundant information is very important to optimization as it offers alternative methods of execution to choose from that may have different costs. For example, it is cheaper to access x.size from the slist x to derive the length of x than it is to compute length(x.info).

In addition to type parameters, type definitions can be parameterized by values that are used in the where clauses of these type definitions. This is called a *parameterized restriction*:

$$T'[x_1 : t_1, \ldots, x_n : t_n] \;=\; T\ \mathbf{where}(x)\ p(x, x_1, \ldots, x_n)$$

This defines a new type T' whose instances are all instances x of the type T that satisfy the predicate $p(x, x_1, \ldots, x_n)$. That is, this restriction is parameterized and it is instantiated whenever the parameters x_i are instantiated to values during compile time. For example:

$$
\begin{aligned}
&\text{bounded}(\alpha)[low : \alpha, high : \alpha, f : (\alpha, \alpha) \rightarrow \text{boolean}] \\
&\qquad\qquad\qquad\qquad = \alpha \ \mathbf{where}(x)\ f(low, x) \ \mathbf{and}\ f(x, high) \\
&\text{range}[low : \text{nat}, high : \text{nat}] \ = \ \text{bounded}(\text{nat})[low, high, \leq] \\
&\text{range1} \ = \ \text{range}[10, 20] \\
&\text{ordered\_list}(\alpha)[f : (\alpha, \alpha) \rightarrow \text{boolean}] \ = \ \text{list}(\alpha) \ \mathbf{where}(x)\ \text{ordered}(x, f) \\
&\text{keyed\_set}(\alpha, \beta)[f : (\alpha) \rightarrow \beta] \\
&\qquad\qquad\qquad = \text{set}(\alpha) \ \mathbf{where}(x)\ \text{card}(x) = \text{card}(\text{image}(f)\, x) \\
&\text{persons} \ = \ \text{keyed\_set}(\text{person}, \text{nat})[\lambda p.(p.\text{ssn})]
\end{aligned}
$$

where ordered(x, f) is true if list x is ordered by the function f, card is set cardinality, and image$(f) = \text{fold}^{set}(\lambda().\text{Emptyset}, \lambda(a, r).\text{Insert}(f(a), r))$.

Instances of a restricted type should obey all restrictions propagated to this type. The following algorithm derives the predicate $\mathcal{I}\{T\}$ which all instances of a type T need to satisfy, by accumulating all restrictions from all types referred by T:

Definition 12 (Accumulated Restriction) *Each type T is associated with an accumulated restriction $\mathcal{I}\{T\}$ defined by the following inductive equations:*

$$
\begin{aligned}
\mathcal{I}\{T(t_1, \ldots, t_n)\}\, x \quad &= \quad \text{fold}^T(\ldots, \lambda\overline{x}. \textstyle\bigwedge \overline{x}, \ldots) \\
&\qquad\qquad (\text{map}^T(\mathcal{I}\{t_1\}, \ldots, \mathcal{I}\{t_n\})\, x) \\
\mathcal{I}\{T \ \mathbf{where}(x)\ f(x)\}\, x \quad &= \quad \mathcal{I}\{T\}x \ \mathbf{and}\ f(x) \\
\mathcal{I}\{T\}\, x \quad &= \quad \mathbf{true} \qquad\qquad \textit{(otherwise)}
\end{aligned}
$$

that is, each value x of type T must satisfy $\mathcal{I}\{T\}x$.

Here map^T maps any parametric type $T(\alpha_1, \ldots, \alpha_n)$ into $T(\beta_1, \ldots, \beta_n)$, thus it requires n functions, one for each type variable. In the first equation, fold^T accumulates all results from map^T using the $\wedge$ (**and**) operator.

For example, for the type T defined as:

$$T \ = \ \text{list}(\text{range}[0, 5]) \ \mathbf{where}(x)\ \text{length}(x) \leq 10$$

$\mathcal{I}\{T\}\, x$ is:

$$\text{fold}^{list}(\lambda().\mathbf{true}, \lambda(a, r).0 \leq a \ \mathbf{and}\ a \leq 5 \ \mathbf{and}\ r)\, x \ \mathbf{and}\ \text{length}(x) \leq 10$$

Type checking in the presence of type restrictions requires theorem proving capabilities. For example, $f(g(x))$, where $f : T \rightarrow \alpha$ and $g : \beta \rightarrow T'$, is type correct if type T is compatible (unifiable) with T' when all type restrictions are removed, and if $\mathcal{I}\{T'\}\, y \Rightarrow \mathcal{I}\{T\}\, y$ is true. This property is very useful for discriminating incompatible compositions of abstractions during decomposition into concrete primitives (Section 8). For example, the type signatures for sort and merge are:

fun sort (x : list(α), f : $\alpha \times \alpha \rightarrow$ boolean) $\rightarrow$ ordered_list$(\alpha)[f]$

fun merge (x : ordered_list$(\alpha)[f]$, y : ordered_list$(\alpha)[f]$, f : $\alpha \times \alpha \rightarrow$ boolean)
$\rightarrow$ ordered_list$(\alpha)[f]$

For example, merge(sort(x, f), sort(y, f), f) is type correct while merge(x, y, f) is not, where x and y are unordered lists.

Type restrictions must be used during type transformation to derive consistent implementations. Furthermore, they may yield additional alternatives for function implementations, such as in the case of redundancy constraints. That way, path selection can be performed during algebraic optimization, since alternative paths are specified by redundancy constraints attached to storage structures.

For example, suppose that a set(person) is mapped into

$$\begin{aligned} T \;=\; & \text{pair}(\text{ordered\_list}(\text{person})[\lambda(x,y).x.\text{ssn} \leq y.\text{ssn}], \\ & \quad \text{ordered\_list}(\text{person})[\lambda(x,y).x.\text{name} \leq y.\text{name}]) \\ & \textbf{where}(x)\; \mathcal{R}_{list}^{set}(x.\text{fst}) = \mathcal{R}_{list}^{set}(x.\text{snd}) \end{aligned}$$

using the abstraction function $r = \lambda x.\mathcal{R}_{list}^{set}(x.\text{fst})$. That is, a set of persons is mapped into two lists (that represent indices): one ordered by the ssn of persons and the other by the name of persons. Accessing a person can be achieved by accessing either of these two access paths. The optimizer should be able to select the access with the lowest cost.

Each abstract type T_i is mapped into a concrete type S_i by an abstraction function $r_i = \mathcal{R}_{S_i}^{T_i}$. All type restrictions involving either T_i or S_i must be used when deriving a function implementation F of f:

$$\bigwedge_i (\mathcal{I}\{S_i\}x_i \;\textbf{and}\; \mathcal{I}\{T_i\}r_i(x_i)) \;\Rightarrow\; r_0(F(x_1,\ldots,x_n)) = f(r_1(x_1),\ldots,r_n(x_n))$$

where $(x \Rightarrow y) \;=\; \text{fold}^{boolean}(\lambda().\text{True}, \lambda().y)\, x$.

Type restrictions can be used to control program synthesis (Section 6). In particular, redundancy constraints, such as the one in the slist example, can expand the search space of the program synthesizer. Suppose that we want to synthesize f such that $[g(\#f) \equiv \phi(x_1,\ldots,x_n)]\,\rho \neq \textbf{fail}$. Each variable x_i of type T_i must obey the $\mathcal{I}\{T_i\}$ predicate:

$$\bigwedge_i \mathcal{I}\{T_i\}x_i \;\Rightarrow\; ([g(\#f) \equiv \phi(x_1,\ldots,x_n)]\,\rho \neq \textbf{fail})$$

The solution for f can be derived from the following:

$$[g(\#f) \equiv \phi(\textbf{if}\, \mathcal{I}\{T_1\}x_1 \,\textbf{then}\, x_1 \,\textbf{else}\, \Box, \ldots, \textbf{if}\, \mathcal{I}\{T_n\}x_n \,\textbf{then}\, x_n \,\textbf{else}\, \Box)]\,\rho$$

This indicates that if x_i does not satisfy $\mathcal{I}\{T_i\}x_i$ then the ith parameter of ϕ is set to $\Box$ (a distinct canonical term). The program synthesiser must be extended to include the rule $[f \equiv \Box]\,\rho = \textbf{fail}$, that is, pattern matching fails if one of the integrity constraints is not satisfied. When $\Box$ is composed with a canonical term f during program improvement, the result is $\Box$, i.e. $\Box \circ f = f \circ \Box = \Box$. Therefore, the right part of the equation for $g(\#f)$ can be normalized to a canonical form that can be used by the program synthesizer to derive a solution for f.

10 Conclusion

We have presented a new query algebra based on a small number of primitives that facilitates query optimization. This algebra is expressive enough to capture a wide range of database operations over an extensible number of bulk data structures. Its simplicity and uniformity make it a perfect target for a rich functional database programming language.

Algebraic optimization can only be effective if it is combined with information about physical implementation, such as available access paths and algorithms. Our framework integrates implementation specifications with algebraic optimization in such a way that program normalization always improves efficiency independently of the database state. Cost estimates and database statistics can be used by the optimizer in a later phase to search the space of equivalent normalized physical programs, which are derived from the initial query after type transformation and normalization. Our optimizer is an extensible, general-purpose, optimizer that does not make a-priori assumptions about the underlying physical structures and algorithms. It would be interesting to compare the performance of such a powerful system with a special-purpose optimizer, such as the one for Ingres SQL. Special-purpose optimizers contain many shortcuts, especially when it comes to storage mapping, since they assume a fixed model for storage structures and algorithms. Therefore, such optimizers may be more efficient but less extensible.

In the future, we intend to design a user-friendly query language which can be translated directly into the fold algebra. Comprehensions are not adequate for this purpose since they are less expressive than folds. We would like also to define suitable fold operations for other data structures that cannot be captured as sums-of-products types. In particular, arrays are very interesting and challenging since they support random accesses.

Acknowledgements: The author is grateful to Sophie Cluet, Scott Daniels, Dave Maier, Eliot Moss, Sushant Patnaik, Tim Sheard, David Stemple, Jianwen Su, and Bennet Vance for helpful comments on the paper. This work is currently supported by the Advanced Research Project Agency, ARPA order number 018, monitored by the US Army Research Laboratory under contract DAAB07-91-C-Q518.

References

[1] C. Beeri and Y. Kornatzky. Algebraic Optimization of Object-Oriented Query Languages. In *International Conference on Database Theory, Paris, France*, pp 72–88. Springer-Verlag, December 1990. LNCS 470.

[2] S. Bellantoni and S. Cook. A new Recursion-Theoretic Characterization of the Polynomial Time. In *Proceedings of the 24th Annual ACM Symposium on Theory of Computing, Victoria, B.C.*, pp 283–293, May 1992.

[3] V. Breazu-Tannen, P. Buneman, and S. Naqvi. Structural Recursion as a Query Language. In *Proceedings of the Third International Workshop on Database Programming Languages: Bulk Types and Persistent Data, Nafplion, Greece*, pp 9–19. Morgan Kaufmann Publishers, August 1991.

[4] W. Chin. Safe Fusion of Functional Expressions. *Proceedings of the ACM Symposium on Lisp and Functional Programming, San Francisco, California*, pp 11–20, June 1992.

[5] C. Consel and O. Danvy. Tutorial Notes on Partial Evaluation. In *Proceedings of the Twentieth ACM Symposium on Principles of Programming Languages, Charleston, South Carolina*, pp 493–501, January 1993.

[6] J. Darlington and R. Burstall. A System which Automatically Improves Programs. *Acta Informatica*, 6(1):41–60, 1976.

[7] L. Fegaras. *A Transformational Approach to Database System Implementation.* PhD thesis, Department of Computer Science, University of Massachusetts, Amherst, February 1993. Also appeared as CMPSCI Technical Report 92-68.

[8] L. Fegaras, T. Sheard, and D. Stemple. Uniform Traversal Combinators: Definition, Use and Properties. In *Proceedings of the 11th International Conference on Automated Deduction (CADE-11), Saratoga Springs, New York*, pp 148–162. Springer-Verlag, June 1992. LNCS 607.

[9] L. Fegaras and D. Stemple. Using Type Transformation in Database System Implementation. In *Proceedings of the Third International Workshop on Database Programming Languages: Bulk Types and Persistent Data, Nafplion, Greece*, pp 337–353. Morgan Kaufmann Publishers, August 1991.

[10] J. C. Freytag and N. Goodman. On the Translation of Relational Queries into Iterative Programs. *ACM Transactions on Database Systems*, 14(1):1–27, March 1989.

[11] G. Malcolm. Homomorphisms and Promotability. In *Mathematics of Program Construction*, pp 335–347. Springer-Verlag, June 1989. LNCS 375.

[12] E. Meijer, M. Fokkinga, and R. Paterson. Functional Programming with Bananas, Lenses, Envelopes and Barbed Wire. In *Proceedings of the 5th ACM Conference on Functional Programming Languages and Computer Architecture, Cambridge, MA*, pp 124–144, August 1991. LNCS 523.

[13] P. Selinger, M. Astrahan, D. Chamberlin, R. Lorie, and T. Price. Access Path Selection in a Relational Database Management System. *Proceedings of the ACM-SIGMOD International Conference on Management of Data, Boston, Massachusetts*, pp 23–34, May 1979.

[14] T. Sheard and L. Fegaras. A Fold for All Seasons. *Sixth Conference on Functional Programming Languages and Computer Architecture, Copenhagen, Denmark*, pp 233–242, June 1993.

[15] S. Shenoy and Z. Ozsoyoglu. Design and Implementation of a Semantic Query Optimizer. *ACM Transactions on Knowledge and Data Engineering*, 1(3):344–361, September 1989.

[16] P. Wadler. Deforestation: Transforming Programs to Eliminate Trees. *Proceedings of the 2nd European Symposium on Programming, Nancy, France*, pp 344–358, March 1988. LNCS 300.

Nested Queries in Object Bases

Sophie Cluet
INRIA, Domaine de Voluceau
78153 Le Chesnay Cedex FRANCE

Guido Moerkotte
Fakultät für Informatik, Universität Karlsruhe
D–7500 Karlsruhe Germany

Abstract

Many declarative query languages for object-oriented databases allow nested subqueries. This paper contains the first (to our knowledge) proposal to optimize them. A two-phase approach is used to optimize nested queries in the object-oriented context. The first phase—called *dependency-based optimization*—transforms queries at the query language level in order to treat common subexpressions and independent subqueries more efficiently. The transformed queries are translated to nested algebraic expressions. These entail nested loop evaluation which may be very inefficient. Hence, the second phase *unnests* nested algebraic expressions to allow for more efficient evaluation.

1 Introduction

Many declarative query languages for object-oriented database management systems have been proposed in the last few years (e.g. [3, 5, 2, 18, 14]). To express complex conditions, access nested structure, or produce nested results, an essential feature found in these languages is the nesting of queries, i.e., the embedding of a query into another query.

The optimization of object-oriented (oo) queries has been intensively studied using algebraic rewriting [4, 7, 23, 24, 25] or rewriting of path expressions [7, 13, 14]. However, in spite of the importance of nested queries, we do not know of any research on their optimization. Nested queries in the oo context are usually translated into nested algebraic expressions which are evaluated through rather inefficient nested loops.

To a lesser extent, relational query languages also feature nested queries and their optimization has been considered in that contex. However, nested queries in the object-oriented context raise specific problems which have never been addressed before. The purpose of the present paper is to fill this gap. On one hand, we adapt some optimizing techniques from the relational context. On the other hand, we introduce novel techniques more directly related to the oo perspective.

The optimization of nested queries in the oo context should clearly use the vast body of knowledge on optimizing nested relational queries. Departing from the evaluation of nested SQL queries through nested loops [1], Kim proposed transforming SQL nested queries at the SQL level [19]. The leading tread behind the proposed transformations is to convert nested queries into joins so that a standard optimizer can work efficiently. However, there exist some major differences between nested queries and joins that are, as stated in [12], the creation of duplicates and the way empty tables are handled. Indeed, these differences are at the bottom of most of the bugs subsequently detected in the original algorithms [10, 17, 6, 8, 11, 12]. To solve them and among other techniques, [8, 11] introduced outer-joins. While these algebraic operators are a nice solution to some of the above problems, they raise new issues. If a sequence of join operations can easily be reordered, joins and outer-joins do not commute that easily and one has to find new ways of dealing with multi-layered nested queries [8, 20, 22]. Finally, a unifying framework for different unnesting strategies was proposed in [21].

There exist some significant differences between nested queries in the oo and the relational context. First, the result of an oo nested query is not always flat. Second, nested queries in the relational context were restricted to occur in the selection clause and, to a limited extent, in the range clause (nested constant blocks when querying views). In the oo context, nested queries may appear in any clause: the result clause (typically **select**, or **retrieve**), the range clause (typically **from** or **range**), and the selection clause (typically **where**). This implies that we have to consider queries that do not match any of the types introduced for classifying nested relational queries [19]. Third, nested queries in the oo context do not always correspond to algebraic operations (e.g., method calls, path expressions), and we have to find an appropriate treatment for these nested expressions as well. While the above considerations seem to complicate the issues, there also exists one essential difference that will somehow simplify the problem: set-valued attributes can be represented explicitly. In particular, a consequence is that there is no need to introduce *null* values to represent unnested empty sets.

As mentioned above, some relational techniques are easily adapted to the oo context. For instance, the whole idea of using joins and outer-joins for unnesting nested queries will be successfully applied throughout the paper. However, the differences between the two models lead us to consider new optimization techniques. We propose a two-phase optimization. The first phase addresses a new challenge related to the third difference stated above. During this phase we apply *dependency-based optimization* which transforms queries by factoring out constant or locally constant nested queries as well as common subexpressions. Although not new in the oo context [7, 14, 16], this factorization is essential for finding a good evaluation strategy. Then, the resulting queries are translated in a straightforward manner into the nested algebra. The algebra we use is an extension of the GOM algebra [15, 16] and features some nice properties most oo algebras lack (e.g., associativity of join operations). The second phase—called *algebraic optimization*—exploits new opportunities brought by the possibility to represent non-atomic attributes. More specifically, the applied algebraic equivalences will make extensive use of a new powerful grouping operation. We will see that the problems implied by the first and second differences stated above are solved by a combination of the two phases.

The paper is organized as follows. The next section introduces the model and the language we will be using thorough the paper. Section 3 summarizes the dependency based optimization mainly by means of an example. Section 4 introduces the algebra. The algebraic equivalences used to unnest nested algebraic expressions are presented in Section 5 and applied to some representative nested queries. Section 6 concludes the paper.

2 Preliminaries

The data model we are working on is similar to the O_2[9], GOM [14] or Exodus [5] model. It features objects that have an identity, that are manipulated through user-defined methods, whose structures are complex and that belong to classes that may be refined into subclasses. Each class has an extent which is a set containing all the objects belonging to the class. The model also features complex values with no identity, that are manipulated by standard operators and do not belong to classes. Hence, there are no extents for them.

A toy schema defined on this data model is given below. It will be used in the sequel of the paper.

A Database Schema	
Class Emp: tuple	(name: tuple(first_name: string, last_name: string), address: tuple(num: string, street: string, city: string), sales: set(Sale), dept: Dept, age: integer, children: set(tuple(name: string, age: integer)))
Method BestSales():	set(Sale)
Class Manager: tuple inherits Emp	(manages: set(Dept))
Class Sale: tuple	(description: set(tuple(item: Item, qty: integer)) date: tuple(day: integer, month: integer, year: integer), emp: Emp)
Method amount():	integer
Class Item: tuple	(code: string, description: string price: real)
Class Dept: tuple	(LocatedIn: Store, items: set(Item) emps: set(Emp), manager: Manager)
Class Store: tuple	(name: string, city: string,

The schema consists of classes, each of which has an extent, a type and some methods (although they do not always appear in the description). The type describes the structure of these objects and the methods their behaviour. Class *Manager* is a subclass of class *Emp*, i.e. it inherits its structure and methods, and the objects of Class *Manager* are contained in the extent of Class *Emp*. Class *Manager* has an added attribute which consists of a set of objects of Class *Dept*. Although this is not compulsory, all classes are of a tuple type. Attributes are either atomic values (e.g., *age*), or objects (e.g., *dept*) or what we refer to as complex values (e.g., *name*).

Throughout the paper we will use the O_2SQL language [2] for the examples. However, the techniques that we present are not restricted to this language and can easily be applied to other languages as well. The O_2SQL language is functional. It is defined by a set of basic functions/queries and a way of building new ones through composition and iterators. There exist basic functions for querying persistent roots (e.g., *Company* is a query that returns the set of objects of Class *Company*), atomic values (e.g., arithmetical operations, comparison operations), tuple values (selection of an attribute), set values (e.g., flatten, avg) and objects (method calls). O_2SQL may directly access the values of the objects (violating encapsulation) when used interactively. The basic functions may be combined in any way, the only limitation being a correct typing. A function that expects an argument of a tuple type, for example, cannot be invoked with an argument of a set type. O_2SQL features several iterators: *select-from-where*, *exists*, *forall*, *group-by* and *sort*. In this paper, we will only consider the first.

As stated above, a method can be invoked inside a query. This raises many optimization issues (cost model, code optimization, side effects) that, to our knowledge, are still unsolved. Our goal here is not to study them. We do not present a cost model, do not study method code optimization and consider only methods without side effects. Thus, for us, a method is very much like a stored attribute.

3 Dependency-Based Optimization

In the relational context, a nested query is one containing a block nested inside. In the object-oriented context, things are different. Operations inside a block may be method calls, long path expressions, set operations on attributes, etc. Hence, we have to consider the optimization of nested expressions—which are also queries by definition—that are not blocks. We illustrate this with the following example:

```
select  tuple(name:emp.name,
              sale:emp_sale.description,
              month: emp_sale.date.month)
from    emp in Employee,
        emp_sale in Sale
where   emp_sale in emp.BestSales() and
        emp_sale.amount() > avg(select  sale.amount()
                                from    sale in Sale
                                where   sale.date.month =
                                          emp_sale.date.month)
```

The method call to *BestSales* is used in the join predicate. We consider this as a nested query. A good optimization will push it out of the join operation so that it won't be evaluated more than necessary. The *emp_sale.date.month* path expression in the nested block is also a nested query that should be pushed out of (i) its nesting block and (ii) the join performed in the higher level block.

In this paper, we consider two kinds of optimization of nested queries that are complementary. One is based on dependencies (treated in this section) and the other on algebraic equivalences (cf. Section 5). We will also take advantage of the dependency-based optimization to perform some common subexpression factorization (e.g., the path expression *emp_sale.date.month* in the previous example).

The dependency optimization is performed at the O_2SQL level. This kind of optimization, although vital, is simple enough and requires mainly one traversal of the syntax tree of the query. Since it had been presented elsewhere [7], we will not detail it. Let us just say that the algorithm consists in splitting every operation. The splitting allows us to consider every possible subexpressions that can be factorized. In this paper, we will not split everywhere but only when necessary in order to demonstrate the major points. We now present the transformed above O_2SQL query and comment on it. More examples can be found in Section 5.

```
select  tuple(name:en, sale:esd, month: esdm)
from    emp in Employee,
        emp_sale in ebs
where   esa > as
define  n = emp.name,
        esd = emp_sale.description,
        esdm = emp_sale.date.month,
        ebs = emp.BestSales(),
        esa = emp_sale.amount(),
        as = avg(select  sa
                 from    sale in Sale
                 where   sdm = esdm
                 define  sa = sale.amount()
                         sdm = sale.date.month
```

The transformed query features a new **define** clause in each block. It is used to introduce variables representing expressions dependent only on its owner block. Note that the outer block **define** clause contains a variable for the *emp_sale.date.month* that is referenced twice (common subexpressions factorization): once in the inner block (constant subexpression factorization) and once in the outer block. During the translation to the algebra, we make use of the variable dependencies in order to push simple operations as far in as possible; especially before join operations are applied.

4 The Algebra

The core of the algebra consists of the following operators that are all defined on set values[1]: union ($\cup$), intersection ($\cap$), difference ($\setminus$), selection (σ), join($\bowtie$), left outer join ($\exists\!\bowtie$), mapping (χ), d-join ($< \cdot >$), grouping (Γ). Except for d-join and grouping, these operators are rather standard. The d-join operation is used for performing a join between two sets, the second one being dependent on the first. It is left-associative and will be applied in post order. This operator can be used for unnesting and is, in many cases, equivalent to a join between two sets with a membership predicate [23]. We introduced it in order to cope with the values of types that do not have extension (i.e. there exist no sets on

[1] Lists and Bags will be considered in another paper.

which a join could be applied). The grouping operator will make use of the fact that in the object-oriented context attributes can be set-valued. As we will see, this is useful for both unnesting nested queries and producing nested results.

Before defining the algebraic operators, we introduce some notations used in the sequel:

- We denote the type τ of an expression e by $e :: \tau$.
- The function $\mathcal{A}$ is defined as follows:
  $\mathcal{A}(e) = \{a_1, \ldots, a_n\}$ if
  $e :: \{[a_1 : \tau_1, \ldots, a_n : \tau_n]\}$ or $e :: [a_1 : \tau_1, \ldots, a_n : \tau_n]$
- $\mathcal{F}(e)$ denotes the set of all free variables of e.
- In order not to be explicit about the parameters of an expression, i.e., avoiding the λ notation, we introduce the following conventions:
  - For an expression e with free variables $\mathcal{F}(e) = \{a_1, \ldots, a_n\}$ and a tuple t with $\mathcal{F}(e) \subseteq \mathcal{A}(t)$ we define:
    $e(t) = e[a_1 \leftarrow t.a_1, \ldots, a_n \leftarrow t.a_n]$.
    Similarily, we define $e(t_1, t_2)$ for binary operations. Note that the attribute names of t_1 and t_2 should be distinct in order to avoid name conflicts.
  - For an expression e with only one free variable x, we define:
    $e(t) = e[x \leftarrow t]$.
- The symbol $\circ$ denotes function concatenation and (as a special case) tuple concatenation.
- Application of a function f to an argument e is denoted by either regular (e.g., $f(e)$) or dot (e.g., $e.f$) notation.
- As an abbreviation for a predicate $a_1\theta b_1, \ldots, a_n\theta b_n$ we often use $A\theta B$ if $A = \{a_1, \ldots, a_n\}$ and $B = \{b_1, \ldots, b_n\}$.
- $\overline{A}(e)$ is used for denoting $\mathcal{A}(e) \setminus A$. When e is clear from the context, we use $\overline{A}$ as a shorthand.

We now define the operators needed in the sequel. Let $\mathcal{E}$ be the valuation of an expression. Then

$$\begin{aligned}
\mathcal{E}(\chi_{e_2}(e_1)) &= \{\mathcal{E}(e_2(x)) | x \in \mathcal{E}(e_1)\} \\
\mathcal{E}(\chi_{a:e_2}(e_1)) &= \{y \circ [a : \mathcal{E}(e_2(y))] | y \in \mathcal{E}(e_1)\} \\
\mathcal{E}(\sigma_p(e)) &= \{x | x \in \mathcal{E}(e), \mathcal{E}(p(x))\} \\
\mathcal{E}(e_1 \bowtie_p e_2) &= \{y \circ x | y \in \mathcal{E}(e_1), x \in \mathcal{E}(e_2), p(y, x)\} \\
\mathcal{E}(e_1 ⟕_p^{g=c} e_2) &= \{y \circ x | y \in \mathcal{E}(e_1), x \in \mathcal{E}(e_2), p(y, x)\} \cup \\
&\quad \{y \circ z | y \in \mathcal{E}(e_1), \neg \exists x \in \mathcal{E}(e_2)\ p(y, x), \\
&\quad \mathcal{A}(z) = \mathcal{A}(e_2), g \in \mathcal{A}(e_2), \\
&\quad z.g = \mathcal{E}(c), \forall a \in \mathcal{A}(e_2)\ a \neq g \succ z.a = NULL\} \\
\mathcal{E}(e_1 < e_2 >) &= \{y \circ x | y \in \mathcal{E}(e_1), x \in \mathcal{E}(e_2(y))\}
\end{aligned}$$

$$\begin{aligned}
\mathcal{E}(\Gamma_{g;A\theta;f}(e)) &= \{y.[A] \circ [g:G] | y \in \mathcal{E}(e), \\
&\quad G = f(\{x | x \in \mathcal{E}(e), x.[A]\theta y.[A]\}\} \\
\mathcal{E}(flatten(e)) &= \{y | x \in \mathcal{E}(e), y \in x\} \\
\mathcal{E}(max_{g;m;a\theta;f}(e)) &= [m : max(\{x.a | x \in \mathcal{E}(e)\}), \\
&\qquad g : f(\{x | x \in \mathcal{E}(e), x.a\theta m\})]
\end{aligned}$$

Note that, apart from the χ and *flatten* operations, all these operations are defined on sets of tuples. This guarantees some nice properties among which is the associativity of the join operations. Note also that the operators may take complex expressions in their subscript, therefore allowing nested algebraic expressions.

The $\chi_{a:e'}(e)$ operation actually is a shorthand for mapping with tuple concatenation. The Γ, *flatten* and *max* operations are mainly needed for optimization purposes, as we will see in the sequel, but do not add power to the algebra. Note that a *min* operation similar to the *max* operation can easily be defined. Sometimes the χ operation is equivalent to a simple projection or renaming. In that case, we will use π instead of χ.

In the sequel we will use the following abbreviations: $\Gamma_{g;A;f}$ for $\Gamma_{g;A=;f}$, $\Gamma_{g;A}$ for $\Gamma_{g;A;id}$, $\bowtie$ for $\bowtie_{true}$, and $e[a]$ for $\chi_{[a:x]}(e)$.

The algebra is defined on sets whereas most OODBMS also manipulate lists and bags. We believe that our approach can easily be extended by considering lists as set of tuples with an added positional attribute and bags as sets of tuples with an added key attribute.

5 Algebraic Optimization

In this section we use representative example queries to present some original unnesting algebraic rewritings of nested queries. We are not concerned with other rewritings (e.g., using joins to evaluate path expressions, evaluating disjunctive predicates through union operation, etc.) although the algebra supports them. For each query, we show the result of the source level transformation, the algebraic translation and the rewriting.

Nested Blocks Within the Select Clause

Nested queries in the select clause appear when a nested result is required. The O_2SQL query we chose to illustrate this case is the following:

```
select  tuple(dept: d,
              emps: select  e
                    from    e in Emp
                    where   e.dept = d)
from    d in Dept
```

After the dependency based optimization:

```
select   tuple(dept: d, emps: des)
from     d in Dept
define   des = select  e
               from    e in Emp
               where   ed = d
               define  ed = e.dept)
```

Translating this expression into the algebra yields

$$q \equiv \chi_{[dept:d,emps:des]}(\chi_{des:e_2}(Dept[d]))$$
$$e_2 \equiv \chi_e(\sigma_{ed=d}(\chi_{ed:e.dept}(Emp[e])))$$

The e_2 nested algebraic expression represents the nested block. A block with one variable in the from clause is translated by (i) a map operation for constructing tuples whose single attribute represents the variable (e.g., $Dept[d]$), (ii) a map operation for evaluating the expressions depending on the block (e.g., $\chi_{des:e_2}$), (iii) a selection when needed (e.g., $\sigma_{ed=d}$) and finally (iv) a map operation for building the final result (e.g., $\chi_{[dept:d,emps:des]}$). Of course all the tuple constructions implied by this translation do not have to be performed (e.g., $Dept[d]$ can be interpreted as a scan on *Dept* with variable d). Further, $\sigma_{ed=d}(\chi_{ed:e.dept}(Emp[e]))$ can be processed by a single physical operation or an index scan.

The problem with this direct translation is that there is just one underlying evaluation plan for nested expressions which corresponds to a nested loop. As shown in [19], this kind of evaluation can be very inefficient. Indeed, in this example, it implies several scans on the *Emp* extension. The idea to solve this problem is to unnest the expression by performing a grouping on the nested expression followed by a left outer-join. We use an outer-join in order to consider empty nested sets that would be lost by a simple join operation. The main reason for favoring the grouping/outer-join combination is the possibility of several interesting implementations for this combination where the straightforward nested loop evaluation is only one of them. Another good reason is the reordering possibilities it offers in case of a more complex query (i.e., more levels of nesting) [8, 20, 22, 21]. Hence, we apply the following equivalence which allows to unnest nested χ operations:

$$\chi_{g:f(\sigma_{A_1=A_2}(e_2))}(e_1)) \quad = \quad \pi_{\overline{A_2}}(e_1 ⟕_{A_1=A_2}^{g=f(\emptyset)}(\Gamma_{g;A_2;f}(e_2))))$$
$$\text{if } A_i \subseteq \mathcal{A}(e_i),\ \mathcal{F}(e_2) \cap \mathcal{A}(e_1) = \emptyset,$$
$$A_1 \cap A_2 = \emptyset, g \notin \mathcal{A}(e_1) \cup \mathcal{A}(e_2)$$

The superscript $g = f(\emptyset)$ is the default value given when there is no element in the result of the group operation which satisfies $A_1 = A_2$ for a given element of e_1.

Applying this equivalence to our example query yields:

$$q \equiv \chi_{[dept:d,emps:des]}e_3$$
$$e_3 \equiv \pi_{\overline{\{e,ed\}}}(Dept[d] ⟕_{d=ed}^{des=\emptyset}(\Gamma_{des;ed;\chi_e}(\chi_{ed:e.dept}Emp[e])))$$

With this expression, many evaluation plans can be considered. For instance, the grouping can be evaluated using a sort operation, or, if there exists an index, by a simple index scan. Note that if we know that every department has at least one employee, we can skip the outer-join operation. Indeed, in this specific example, it is used solely to generate empty sets of employees related to departments having no employee.

Nested Aggregated Block Within the Select Clause

Nested aggregated queries differ from the previous ones by the fact that, even though a grouping is required, the result will not be nested. To illustrate this case, we chose an example in which we rely on some semantic information to derive the fact that inner and outer queries have a common range. This is a rather common case when aggregate functions are involved. The next query is:

```
select tuple(age:e1.age,
             nb:count(select s
                      from   e2 in Emp
                             s in e2.sales
                      where  e2.age ≤ e1.age))
from   e1 in Emp
```

It is transformed in the following way:

```
select tuple(age:e1a, nb:cs)
from   e1 in Emp
define e1a = e1.age,
       cs =  count(select s
                   from   e2 in Emp
                          s in e2.sales
                   where  e2a ≤ e1a
                   define e2a = e2.age)
```

and in the algebra

$$
\begin{aligned}
q &\equiv \chi_{[age:e1a,nb:cs]}(\chi_{cs:e_2}(e_1)) \\
e_1 &\equiv \chi_{e1a:e1.age}(Emp[e1]) \\
e_2 &\equiv count(\chi_s(\sigma_{e2a \leq e1a}(e_2'))) \\
e_2' &\equiv (\chi_{e2a:e2.age}Emp[e2]) < e2.sales[s] >
\end{aligned}
$$

The nested block represented by e_2 and e_2' features two variables in the from clause. This is translated by a d-join operation. Note that, in this block, we used informations on variable dependencies during the translation process to push the map operation on *Emp* before the d-join operation.

The main difference between this query and the previous one lies in the fact that $\leq$ is used for comparison instead of "=". The resulting problem is that values occurring in e_1 might show up several times for one value of e_2.

Assume for a moment that every employee has at least one sale. Then, we may use advantageously the fact that one variable (e2) of the inner block ranges over the same set (all the employees) than the variable of the outer block (e1). Hence, we have:

$$\begin{array}{rcl} \chi_{g:f(\sigma_{A_1 \theta A_2}(e_2))}(e_1)) & = & \pi_{A1:A2}(\Gamma_{g;\theta A_2;f}(e_2)) \\ & & if\ A_i \subseteq \mathcal{A}(e_i), \\ & & \quad \mathcal{F}(e_2) \cap \mathcal{A}(e_1) = \emptyset, \\ & & \quad e_1 = \pi_{A_1:A_2}(e_2)\ \ (implies\ A_1 = \mathcal{A}(e_1)) \\ & & \quad g \notin \mathcal{A}(e_1) \cup \mathcal{A}(e_2) \end{array}$$

By applying this equivalence to our example query, we get:

$$q \equiv \chi_{[age:e1a,nb:cs]}(\pi_{e1a:e2a}\Gamma_{cs;age\leq;count\circ\chi_s}(e_2'))$$

Note that the Γ operation can be efficiently implemented by first sorting the argument on its *age* values. If the argument is already sorted, e.g., due to an index scan, the Γ operation can be evaluated in linear time during a single scan of e_2, if f is linear.

Nested Queries With Flatten

Nested queries with flatten are commonly used in order to flatten some nested attributes. To discuss this case, consider the following example query:

```
flatten(select
            select tuple(name:c.name,age:c.age)
            from   c in e.children
            where  c.age < 18)
        from e in Emp)
```

whose transformation gives:

```
flatten(select  g
        from    e in Emp
        define  ec = e.children
                g = select tuple(name:n,age:a)
                    from   c in ec
                    where  a < 18
                    define n = c.name
                           a = c.age )
```

The standard translation is

$$\begin{array}{rcl} q & \equiv & flatten(\chi_g(\chi_{g:e_2}(\chi_{ec:e.children}(Emp[e])))) \\ e_2 & \equiv & \chi_{[name:n,age:a]}(\sigma_{a<18}(\chi_{a:c.age,n:c.name}(ec[c]))) \end{array}$$

In order to push the flatten operation inside, we have to eliminate the redundant tuple extension for the attribute g:

$$\begin{aligned} q &\equiv flatten(\chi_{e_2}(\chi_{ec:e.children}(Emp[e]))) \\ e_2 &\equiv \chi_{[name:n,age:a]}(\sigma_{a<18}(\chi_{a:c.age,n:c.name}(ec[c]))) \end{aligned}$$

Now, we know that for linear $f : \{\tau\} \to \{\tau'\}$ that

$$flatten(\chi_f(e)) = f(flatten(e))$$

Hence,

$$\begin{aligned} q &\equiv \chi_{[name:n,age:a]}(flatten(\chi_{e_2'})(\chi_{ec:e.children} Emp[e])) \\ e_2' &\equiv \sigma_{a<18}(\chi_{a:c.age,n:c.name}(ec[c])) \\ q &\equiv \chi_{[name:n,age:a]}(\sigma_{a<18}(flatten(\chi_{e_2''}(\chi_{ec:e.children} Emp[e])))) \\ e_2'' &\equiv \chi_{age:c.age,n:c.name}(ec[c]) \\ q &\equiv \chi_{[name:n,age:a]}(\sigma_{a<18}(\chi_{a:c.age,n:c.name} \\ &\qquad (flatten(\chi_{ec[c]}(\chi_{ec:e.children} Emp[e]))))) \\ &\equiv \chi_{[name:n,age:a]}(\sigma_{a<18}(\chi_{a:c.age,n:c.name} \\ &\qquad (flatten(\chi_{e.children[c]}(Emp[e]))))) \\ &\equiv \chi_{[name:n,age:a]}(\sigma_{a<18}(\chi_{a:c.age,n:c.name} \\ &\qquad (flatten(\chi_{children[c]}(Emp))))) \\ &\equiv \sigma_{age<18}(\chi_{[name:n,age:a]}(\chi_{[a:age,n:name]} \\ &\qquad (flatten(\chi_{children}(Emp))))) \\ &\equiv \sigma_{age<18}(\chi_{[name:name,age:age]}(flatten(\chi_{children}(Emp)))) \end{aligned}$$

where redundant tuple constructions where eliminated in the last steps. Note that the flatten operation is now applied on stored data. If there exists an appropriate index it can be evaluated very efficiently.

5.1 Nested Block Within the From Clause

As we will see, nested blocks in the from clause do not require nested algebraic expressions. They are queries whose original algebraic translation features operations pushed before a join (or d-join). Note that this kind of queries also occur in the relational context when views are queried. However, we do not know of any relational work where they are treated as simply as they should. The example is the following:

```
select  e
from    d in select  d
             from    d in Dept
             where   d.locatedIn.city
                     == "Paris",
        e in Emp
where   e.dept == d
```

The transformed query is:

```
define DD = select  dd
            from    dd in Dept
            where   dl == "Paris"
            define  dl = dd.locatedIn.city
       select  e
       from    d in DD,
               e in Emp
       where   ed == d
       define  ed = e.dept
```

The translation results in

$$\begin{aligned}
q &\equiv \chi_e(\sigma_{ed=d}(\chi_{ed:e.dept}(e_1))) \\
e_1 &\equiv (DD[d] < Emp[d] >) \\
DD &\equiv \chi_{dd}(\sigma_{dl=\text{"}Paris\text{"}}(\chi_{dl:dd.locatedIn.city}(Dept[dd]))) \\
e_1 &\equiv (\pi_d(\sigma_{dl=\text{"}Paris\text{"}}(\chi_{dl:d.locatedIn.city}(Dept[d])))) < Emp[e] > \\
&\equiv (\pi_d(\sigma_{dl=\text{"}Paris\text{"}}(\chi_{dl:d.locatedIn.city}(Dept[d])))) \bowtie (Emp[e])
\end{aligned}$$

The two transformations result from the variable binding convention and renaming, as well as the equivalence of d-join and join in case the inner argument of the d-join does not depend on the outer argument:

$$\begin{aligned}
e_1 < e_2 > \quad &= \quad e_1 \bowtie e_2 \\
&\quad\;\; \text{if } \mathcal{F}(e_2) \cap \mathcal{A}(e_1) = \emptyset
\end{aligned}$$

Note that the join is in fact a cross product.

We proceed with our example by pushing $\chi_{ed:e.dept}$ inside and transforming the crossproduct into a join

$$\begin{aligned}
e_2 &\equiv \pi_d(\sigma_{dl=\text{"}Paris\text{"}}(\chi_{dl:dd.locatedIn.city}(Dept[d]))) \\
e_3 &\equiv \chi_{ed:e.dept}(Emp[e]) \\
q &\equiv \chi_e(\sigma_{d=ed}(e_2 \bowtie e_3)) \\
&\equiv \chi_e(e_2 \bowtie_{d=ed} e_3)
\end{aligned}$$

where the last join actually is a semi-join which can be efficiently processed.

Aggregated Nested Block Within the Where Clause

Aggregated nested blocks also occur in the relational context. We treat them in similar manner although we rely on set attributes to avoid dealing with null values. Let us consider the following query:

```
select  d
from    d in Dept
where   count(select  e
              from    e in Emp
```

```
                where  e.dept == d)
        > 10
```

The transformed query is:

```
select  d
from    d in Dept
where   c > 10
define  c = count(select  e
                  from    e in Emp
                  where   ed == d
                  define  ed = e.dept)
```

The rewriting is similar to the already discussed case of nesting in the where clause with no aggregates applied:

$$q \equiv \chi_d(\sigma_{c>10}(\chi_{c:e_2}(Dept[d])))$$
$$e_2 \equiv count(\chi_e(\sigma_{d=ed}(\chi_{ed:e.dept}(Emp[e]))))$$
$$q \equiv \chi_d(\sigma_{c>10}(Dept[d] ⟕^{c=0}_{d=ed}(\Gamma_{c;ed;count \circ \chi_c}(\chi_{ed:e.dept}(Emp[e])))))$$

In case the outerjoin is followed by a selection which evaluates to false for the default value, the outer join can be replaced by a join. Thus we have:

$$q \equiv \chi_d(\sigma_{c>10}(Dept[d] \bowtie_{d=ed} (\Gamma_{c;ed;count \circ \chi_c}(\chi_{ed:e.dept}(Emp[e])))))$$

Furthermore, as in the first example, we may rely on semantics knowledge to skip the join operation. Indeed, if we know that all departments have at least one employee (i.e., we will access all departments from the Emp extent) and since all the information in the left argument of the equation is already present in the right argument (since $d == ed$) we may rewrite the query in the following way:

$$q \equiv \chi_{ed}(\sigma_{c>10}(\Gamma_{c;ed;count \circ \chi_c}(\chi_{ed:e.dept}(Emp[e]))))$$

Special Cases for Min and Max

There exist special cases where selections based on aggregates can be treated more efficiently. We will show that with the following query with two levels of nesting and a *max* function applied:

```
select tuple(name: e.name,
       bestSales: (select  s
                   from    s in e.sales
                   where   s.amount() =
                           max(select  s.amount()
                               from    s in e.sales)))
from   e in Emp
```

The transformed query is:

```
select tuple(name: en, bestSales: bs)
from   e in Emp
define en = e.name
       es = e.sales
       m = max(select  tv
               from    t in es
               define  tv = t.amount())
       bs = select  s
            from    s in es
            where   sv = m
            define  sv = s.amount()
```

Note that the dependency-based optimization already took one level of nesting off. The translation to the algebra yields:

$$\begin{aligned} q &\equiv \chi_{[name:en,bestSales:bs]}(\chi_{bs:e_2}(\chi_{m:e_1}(\chi_{en:e.name,es:e.sales}(Emp[e])))) \\ e_1 &\equiv max(\chi_{tv}(\chi_{tv:t.amount()}(es[t]))) \\ e_2 &\equiv \chi_s(\sigma_{sv=m}(\chi_{sv:s.amount()}(es[s]))) \end{aligned}$$

Here, we may apply the following equivalence:

$$\chi_{g:f(\sigma_{a=m}(e_1))}(\chi_{m:max(e_2)}(e)) = \chi_{\circ(max_{g;m;a;f}(e_1))}(e) \quad \text{if } e_1 = \pi_a(e_2)$$

We remind that the $max_{g;m;a;f}(e)$ operation returns a tuple containing (i) an attribute m representing the maximum value for the attribute a in the set e and (ii) an attribute g representing the result of f applied to the set of elements of e whose attribute a is equal to m. The above equivalence applied to the query yields:

$$\begin{aligned} q \equiv\ & \chi_{[name:en,bestSales:bs]}(\chi_{\circ(max_{bs;m;sv;\chi_s}(\chi_{sv:s.amount()}(es[s])))} \\ & (\chi_{en:e.name,es:e.sales}(Emp[e]))) \end{aligned}$$

Note that the max function can be computed in a single scan (linear time) for $max_{g;m;a;f}$ if f is linear.

Also note that an equivalent treatment for min can be applied. Furthermore, although the equivalence we used can easily be adapted to the relational context, we are not aware of any such optimization.

6 Conclusion

In this paper, we showed that much could be done for the optimization of nested queries in the object-oriented context. We have proposed a two-phase optimization. The first phase transformed a nested query at the source level in order to treat common subexpressions and those not dependent on the current block more efficiently. After the translation of the transformed queries to the nested algebra, the second phase used algebraic equations in order to unnest nested algebraic expressions. This opened the road for more efficient evaluations.

We are now working on a classification of oo nested queries. The main goal behind this classification is to help the optimizer in choosing the appropriate equivalences. Furthermore, it will help to better see the analogies and differences between relational and oo nested queries, thus allowing each world to benefit from the other. Our current studies also concern multi-layered nested queries among which more efficient treatment of special cases of tree queries (in the spirit of [20]).

The topics for further research can be divided into two classes. The first class is concerned with implementation. To this class belong the extension of existing cost models and search strategies to the nested algebra. The second class contains topics involved in extending the current approach in order to incorporate bags and lists on the data model side as well as quantifiers on the query language side. Also, we consider using inverse functions for optimizing nested queries.

Acknowledgements: The authors thank Serge Abiteboul and Victor Vianu for many valuable comments on a first draft of the paper.

References

[1] M. M. Astrahan and D. D. Chamberlin. Implementation of a structured English query language. *Communications of the ACM*, 18(10):580–588, 1975.

[2] F. Bancilhon, S. Cluet, and C. Delobel. A query language for the o_2 object-oriented database system. In *DBPL II*, Salishan Lodge, Oregan, 1989.

[3] D. Beech. A foundation for evolution from relational to object databases. In *EDBT*, 1988.

[4] C. Beeri and Y. Kornatzky. Algebraic optimization of object-oriented query languages. In *Proc. Int. Conf. on Database Theory (ICDT)*, pages 72–88, 1990.

[5] M. Carey, D. DeWitt, and S. Vandenberg. A data model and query language for EXODUS. In *Proc. of the ACM SIGMOD Conf. on Management of Data*, pages 413–423, 1988.

[6] S. Ceri and G. Gottlob. Translating SQL into relational algebra: Optimization, semantics and equivalence of SQL queries. *IEEE Trans. on Software Eng.*, pages 324–345, 1985.

[7] S. Cluet and C. Delobel. A general framework for the optimization of object-oriented queries. In *Proc. of the ACM SIGMOD Conf. on Management of Data*, pages 383–392, 1992.

[8] U. Dayal. Of nests and trees: A unified approach to processing queries that contain nested subqueries, aggregates, and quantifiers. In *VLDB*, pages 197–208, 1987.

[9] O. Deux. The story of o2. *IEEE Transaction on Knowledge and Data Engineering*, 2(1), March 1989.

[10] G. Lohman et al. Optimization of nested queries in a distributed relational database. In *Proc. Int. Conf. on Very Large Data Bases (VLDB)*, 1984.

[11] R. Ganski and H. Wong. Optimization of nested SQL queries revisited. In *Proc. of the ACM SIGMOD Conf. on Management of Data*, pages 23–33, 1987.

[12] W. Hasan and H. Pirahesh. Query rewrite optimization in starburst. Research Report RJ6367, IBM, 1988.

[13] P. Jenq, D. Woelk, W. Kim, and W. Lee. Query processing in distributed ORION. In *Proc. Int. Conf. on Extended Database Technology (EDBT)*, Venice, 1990.

[14] A. Kemper and G. Moerkotte. Advanced query processing in object bases using access support relations. In *Proc. Int. Conf. on Very Large Data Bases*, pages 294–305, 1990.

[15] A. Kemper and G. Moerkotte. Query optimization in object bases: Exploiting relational techniques. In *Proc. Dagstuhl Workshop on Query Optimization (J.-C. Freytag, D. M aier und G. Vossen (eds.))*. Morgan-Kaufman, to appear 1993.

[16] A. Kemper, G. Moerkotte, and K. Peithner. A blackboard architecture for query optimization in object bases. Informatik-Fachberichte 92-31, RWTH Aachen, 5100 Aachen, Germany, 1992.

[17] W. Kiessling. SQL-like and Quel-like correlation queries with aggregates revisited. ERL/UCB Memo 84/75, University of Berkeley, 1984.

[18] W. Kim. A model of queries for object-oriented database. In *Proc. Int. Conf. on Very Large Data Bases (VLDB)*, 1989.

[19] W. Kim. On optimizing an SQL-like nested query. *ACM Trans. on Database Systems*, 7(3):443–469, Sep 82.

[20] M. Muralikrishna. Optimization and dataflow algorithms for nested tree queries. In *Proc. Int. Conf. on Very Large Data Bases (VLDB)*, 1989.

[21] M. Muralikrishna. Improved unnesting algorithms for join aggregate SQL queries. In *Proc. Int. Conf. on Very Large Data Bases (VLDB)*, pages 91–102, 1992.

[22] A. Rosenthal and C. Galindo-Legaria. Query graphs, implementing trees, and freely-reorderable outerjoins. In *Proc. of the ACM SIGMOD Conf. on Management of Data*, pages 291–299, 1990.

[23] G.M. Shaw and S.B. Zdonik. A query algebra for object-oriented databases. In *Proc. IEEE Conference on Data Engineering*, pages 154–162, 1990.

[24] D. Straube and T. Özsu. Queries and query processing in object-oriented database systems. *ACM Trans. on Information Systems*, 8(4):387–430, 1990.

[25] S. L. Vandenberg and D. DeWitt. Algebraic support for complex objects with arrays, identity, and inheritance. In *Proc. of the ACM SIGMOD Conf. on Management of Data*, pages 158–167, 1991.

Thémis: a database programming language with integrity constraints

Véronique Benzaken
Université de Paris I - Sorbonne
12 place du Panthéon 75005 Paris, France email: benzaken@lri.lri.fr

Anne Doucet
Université de Paris XI - Orsay (LRI, Bat 490)
91405 Orsay, France email: anne@lri.lri.fr

Abstract

This paper is concerned with the problem of efficiently checking of integrity constraints in data base programming languages supporting subtyping and class hierarchies. More specifically, we consider two different problems: (1) statically reduce the number of constraints to be checked, and (2) generate an efficient run time checker. Using simple strategies, one can significantly improve the efficiency of the verification. We show how to reduce the number of constraints to be checked by characterising the portions of the database that are concerned by the constraints and involved in a transaction. We also show how to generate efficient algorithms for checking a large class of constraints. We show how all the techniques presented took great advantage of the underlying type system which provide a significant help both in solving (1) and (2). Last the current status of the Thémis prototype is presented.

1 Introduction

Efforts on database programming languages have mainly been devoted to the definition of elaborated type systems and persistence mechanisms for those languages. In particular, the problems of polymorphism, static typing and inference, and object identity were the main topics of [HMS89]. On the other hand, database programming languages are in general not able to express integrity constraints in a global and declarative way although some interesting works are done in the context of object-oriented databases [Mar91].

On the contrary, extended relational systems take integrity constraints and views into consideration, mainly in the relational way [Sto75, GM79, WSK83]. Those systems are mainly relational systems in which relations attributes domains are not necessarily atomic but can be constructed using abstract types. The associated query language can also be extended to manipulate these user defined types instances. However, extended relational systems are not integrated in the sense of database programming languages. In these systems, relations are a very special kind of data type that cannot be used orthogonally to the others. In most systems, sets cannot be constructed independently of relations, and the query languages are not integrated within the language used to define the new attributes domains.

In the deductive database field, the problem of integrity constraint checking has been fully investigated [HI85, BM86, KSS87, BDM88]. A first technique consists in determining without accessing the database whether a transaction may violate an integrity constraint. Such a technique relies on theorem proving mechanism [SS89]. A second approach assumes transactions to be provided with the *atomicity* property and consists in restricting the constraints to be enforced and in avoiding to retest the portion of the database that was consistent before the transaction [Sto75, Nic79].

Although the methods proposed in this paper rely on the same ideas, we would like to emphasize the benefits gained when relying on a type system in order to cope with object-oriented complexity.

We consider two different problems: (1) statically reduce the number of constraints to be checked, and (2) generate an efficient run time checker. Of course, in the general case the problem is very complicate and finding an optimal solution to (1), for instance, is undecidable. What we want to show is that, using simple strategies, we can significantly improve the efficiency of the verification. In this paper, we shall suppose that transactions can neither be nested nor call other transactions or functions, and that constraint specification does not involve method calls, in order to avoid interprocedural analysis. This general case will be the topic of a forthcoming study.

Our main goal is to fully exploit the type information in order to simplify constraint violation detection and to speed up constraint checking. Not only classes are partially ordered according to an inheritance hierachy but we also have to face the problem of constraint checking in an environment that allows updates to be propagated among several distinct paths among objects. A first part of the paper consists in using simple compilation techniques to statically determine which constraints might be violated by a transaction. The originality of this static analysis is that it captures the notion of inheritance and of subtyping. A second contribution consists, given a transaction and a constraint, in generating a checking algorithm which will operate on the smallest portion of the database involved by the transaction. Unlike in deductive databases, objects are much more structured and they can be accessed through several different paths in the database. We show how to significantly reduce the number of checking operations to be performed, relying on the underlying typing information.

The paper is organized as follows. In Section 2, we give an overview of the Thémis schema definition language and show how to define integrity constraints in this context. In section 3, we use simple compilation techniques to statically determine which constraints might be violated by a transaction, thus reducing the number of constraints to be checked. We propose in Section 4 to generate integrity constraints checking algorithms. These algorithms are shown to significantly improve naive checking methods. In Section 5, we describe the current implementation of the Thémis prototype. It allows to validate our work. Section 6 contains some concluding remarks.

2 Overview of the Thémis Schema Definition Language

We describe here the Thémis language and give several examples that will be used in the remainder of the paper.

2.1 Types

We consider a framework in which all database manipulations are strongly and statically typed. Types can be atomic types like **integer**, **string** or **boolean**. Types can also be concrete structures like tuple and set types:

```
[name: string, children: { string }]
{ Person }, { integer }
```

Subtyping of concrete types is structural and inferred following the classical rules of Cardelli [Car84]. We have, for instance:

```
[name: string, age: integer] ≺ [name: string]
{ [name: string, age: integer] } ≺ { [name: string] }
```

Concrete type instances are *non shared*, *non mutable* values. Abstract types have a name and a list of features which model attributes and operations, as follows:

```
type Person is abstract [
    name: string,
    age: integer,
    children: { Person },
    spouse: Person,
    licences: { string } ]
    changeAge(integer), /* an operation */
end

type Vehicle is abstract [
    type: string,
    agev: integer,
    colour: string,
    number: integer,
    owner: Person ]
end
```

The definition of the Person type states that a person has a name, an age, a set of children, a spouse and is equipped with an operation to update the age feature. Instances of an abstract type are "objects" in the sense that they have an identity which is independent of the value of their features (name, age, etc.). Instances of an abstract type are *mutable* and *shared* values. Subtyping of abstract types is explicit as shown in the following example:

```
type Plane subtype of Vehicle is abstract [
    capacity: integer ]
end
```

This definition states that the abstract type Plane is a subtype the abstract type Vehicle and the capacity feature is specific to planes.

2.2 Names and Classes

Types are used to describe the components of a database. The database can be seen as a graph of interconnected objets and values. The roots of this graph are names defined at the schema level:

let aSetofInts : { **integer** } := { 1, 2, 3 }
let Licences : { **string** } := { "truck", "car", "bike" }

The **let** keyword defines a new name with an associated type and binds an initial value to it. The value can be updated as for any variable.

The notion of class is an extensional notion which is not captured by the type definitions. A class represents a collection of objects of one type (abstract or not) and is characterised by a name and the type of its elements as follows:

class Persons **of type** Person
class Vehicles **of type** Vehicle
class Drivers **of type** [`driver`: Person, `car`: Vehicle]

Class names are special kinds of identifiers as they can be considered as set value names but classes can be organised in a subclass hierarchy. We can write, for example:

class Planes **subclass of** Vehicles **of type** Plane
class BadDrivers **subclass of** Drivers

The class Planes is declared as a subclass of the class Vehicles. Its associated type is Plane. The semantics of the subclass relationship is the set inclusion [LR89]. For instance, the class Planes is a subset of the class Vehicles.

2.3 Transactions

In our framework, transactions are provided with the atomicity property. In this paper, we suppose that transactions do not call other transactions.

We list the operations performed by a transaction. The set $\mathcal{B}$ of elementary statements is defined as follows:

$e_1 := e_2$
$e_1.\mathbf{a} := e_2$
insert e_1 **into** e_2 where e_2 denotes a class name
drop e_1 **from** e_2 where e_2 denotes a class name

The set $\mathcal{I}$ of transactions is recursively defined as follows:

$\forall$ s $\in \mathcal{B}$, s$\in \mathcal{I}$
$\forall$ s_1, $s_2 \in \mathcal{I}$, s_1; $s_2 \in \mathcal{I}$
$\forall$ s_1, $s_2 \in \mathcal{I}$, **if** (b) s_1 **else** $s_2 \in \mathcal{I}$
$\forall$ s $\in \mathcal{I}$, **for** (o $\in$ x) **when** (b) s $\in \mathcal{I}$

The following are examples of transactions:

```
let T1 = trans(t, c: string, p: Person, a, n: integer)
            insert Vehicle[type: t, agev: a, colour: c, number: n, owner: p]
            into Vehicles
/* this transaction inserts a new vehicle in the class Vehicles */

let T2 = trans(p1, p2: Person):
            p1.spouse := p2;
            p2.spouse := p1;
/* this transaction performs a marriage between two persons */
let T3 = trans()
            for p in Persons when (today = p.birthday)
                print("Happy Birthday ", p.name);
                p.age := p.age + 1
/* this transaction updates the age of all Persons born on the current day */
```

2.4 Integrity Constraints

In our framework, integrity constraints are well-typed boolean expressions built using the names and classes of the schema and general operators. More formally, terms are defined as follows:

- Constants (true, false, nil) are terms.
- Each variable x is a term.
- Let t be a term, let **a** be an attribute (and not an operation), t.**a** is a term.
- Let t_1 and t_2 be two terms, let θ be an arithmetical operator (+, -, *, ÷), $t_1\ \theta\ t_2$ is a term.

An integrity constraint, A, is an expression of the form:

$$A = Q_{x_1 \in S_1}, .., Q_{x_k \in S_k} M(x_1, .., x_k)$$

where Q ∈ {∀, ∃}, S_j is a set-structured expression and where $M(x_1, .., x_k)$ is a quantifier free formula. More precisely, formulas M are defined as follows:

- Let θ be a comparator $(=, \neq, <, >, \leq, \geq)$, let x and y be two terms, x θ y is an atomic formula,
- Each atomic formula is a formula,
- Let M and M' be two formulas, M ∧ M', M ∨ M', ¬ M et (M) are formulas.

Expression $Q_{x_1 \in S_1}, .., Q_{x_k \in S_k}$ is usually referred as the constraint *prefix* while M denotes the constraint *matrix*.

The equality operator can be applied on values of any type. The other comparators can be applied to numbers and sets.

While such expressions could also be built over tuple methods extraction, we first restrict our analysis to simple (non computable) field extraction.

The following are examples of constraints that can be constructed in our framework. They will be used as running examples in Sections 3 and 4.

(A_1) $\forall$ p $\in$ Persons, $\forall$ v $\in$ Vehicles,
(v.**name** $\neq$ "Ferrari" $\vee$ v.**owner** $\neq$ p) $\vee$ p.**age** ≥ 40

This constraint expresses that every Ferrari is owned by an instance of Persons older than 40.

(A_2) $\forall$ p $\in$ Persons, $\forall$ c $\in$ p.**children**, p.**age** $>$ c.**age**

This constraint expresses that every children must be younger than his (her) parents.

(A_3) $\forall$ d $\in$ Drivers, d.**driver.age** ≥ 18
(A_4) $\forall$ p $\in$ Persons, p.**age** $\leq 130 \wedge$ p.**age** ≥ 0;

Constraints A_3 and A_4 are range constraints. The reader should notice that it is different from a domain restriction in a type specification. A domain restriction is valid for every instance of a type and does not depend on the collection to which this instance belongs. A range constraint is local to a class (here Drivers and Persons) and does not mean for instance that *every* instance of the type [**driver**: Person, **car**: Vehicle] has to satisfy this restriction. This is one example of what cannot be expressed only by means of type systems.

(A_5) $\forall$ d $\in$ Drivers,
d.**car.type** $\neq$ "truck" $\vee$ "truck-licence" $\in$ d.**driver.licences**
(A_6) $\forall$ c $\in$ Vehicles, $\exists$ d $\in$ Drivers, d.**car** $=$ c $\wedge$ c.**agev** $=$ d.**driver.age**
(A_7) $\forall$ p $\in$ Persons, p.**spouse.spouse** $=$ p $\vee$ p.**spouse** $=$ **nil**;

Constraint A_5 expresses that every truck driver must have the corresponding licence. The dummy constraint A_6 expresses that for every vehicle there always exists a driver having the same age than the vehicle he drives. Finally the last constraint expresses that every person is either the spouse of his/her spouse or is not married.

In the Thémis language, those constraints are expressed in the following way:

let (A_1) := **constraint forall** p **in** Persons, **forall** v **in** Vehicles,
(v.**name** $\neq$ "Ferrari" **or** v.**owner** $\neq$ p) **or** p.**age** ≥ 40
let (A_2) := **constraint forall** p **in** Persons, **forall** c **in** p.**children**,
p.**age** $>$ c.**age**
let (A_3) := **constraint forall** d **in** Drivers, d.**driver.age** ≥ 18
let (A_4) := **constraint forall** p **in** Persons, p.**age** ≤ 130 **and** p.**age** ≥ 0;
let (A_5) := **constraint forall** d **in** Drivers,
d.**car.type** $\neq$ "truck"
or "truck-licence" **in** d.**driver.licences**
let (A_6) := **constraint forall** c **in** Vehicles, **exists** d **in** Drivers,
d.**car** $=$ c **and** c.**agev** $=$ d.**driver.age**
let (A_7) := **constraint forall** p **in** Persons,
p.**spouse.spouse** $=$ p **or** p.**spouse** $=$ **nil**;

3 Static Anaysis of a Thémis Schema

In order to avoid checking unnecessary constraints, we want to be able to statically characterise the integrity constraints that *may be* violated by a given transaction. As the problem of determining if a transaction will certainly violate a constraint is undecidable (because this depends on input data), we are only looking for the set of constraints which might be violated, and we give a necessary condition to detect this situation.

In order to characterise this superset of constraints, for a given transaction, we shall consider the parts of the database that are dealt with in a given constraint and/or involved in a given transaction. In the following subsections, we thus define *syntactical analysis* of constraints and transactions.

Such analysis consist, informally, in a set of *paths* in the database. A path starts from a schema name or a type name, which can be followed by one or several attribute names. For example, if the path "Person.**age**" is in the analysis of a constraint, this means that the constraint refers to the age of an object of type Person. If the same path is in the analysis of a transaction, this means that this transaction may update the age of a Person. Therefore, the transaction may violate the given constraint, and it will be checked at the end of the transaction.

One of the characteristics of this static analysis is the use we make of the underlying type system. As we said before, abstract types instances are mutable and shared values, whereas concrete types instances are non shared non mutable values. This concept of mutability and sharing is crucial when dealing with constraints checking. Indeed, an object may be referred to by several other objets and, as a consequence, updated through different database paths. The only information that can be statically manipulated for those objects is their type.

3.1 Static analysis of constraints

A constraint has the following generic form:

$A = Q\ x_1 \in S_1, \ldots, Q\ x_k \in S_k\ M(x_1, \ldots, x_k)$

where Q denotes a quantifier ($\forall$ or $\exists$), the S_j's are set expressions, and $M(x_1, \ldots, x_k)$ is a boolean expression with the x_j's as free variables.

As we said before, the analysis of a constraint is a set of paths in the database. For a constraint A, we shall note $\Upsilon(A)$ its analysis. The set of paths $\Upsilon(A)$ is recursively constructed as follows:

$\Upsilon(\text{expl}\ \theta\ \text{exp2}) = \Upsilon(\text{expl}) \cup \Upsilon(\text{exp2})$,
where θ denotes any comparator;
$\Upsilon(\text{<S>}) = \text{<S>}$, if S is a schema name and not a class name;
$= \bigcup_{C_i \leq S} \{C_i\}$ (the set of all subclasses of <S>, including itself, if <S> is a class name.)
$\Upsilon(\text{exp.}\mathbf{a}) = \bigcup_{t.\mathbf{a} \leq type(exp)} \{C_i\} \cup \Upsilon(\text{exp})$, if type(exp) is an abstract type (type() is a function which given an expression returns its corresponding type);
$= \Upsilon(\text{exp})$ otherwise.
$\Upsilon(x) = \Upsilon(S)$, where x represents a quantified variable in the constraint ranging over the set expression S;

Υ(M $\wedge$ M') = Υ(M) $\cup$ Υ(M'), where M, M' are two quantifier free formulas;
Υ(M $\vee$ M') = Υ(M) $\cup$ Υ(M'), where M, M' are two quantifier free formulas;
Υ($\neg$ M) = Υ(M);
Υ((M)) = Υ(M);

The construction of "Υ(exp.**a**)" deserves some comments. Such an expression can be either the extraction of a *tuple field (non mutable non shared value)*, or the extraction of an *object feature (mutable and shared value)*. If the type of the expression is an *abstract type*, this means that the corresponding value is an object that can be shared. Every update of an object of the same type may violate the constraint. For tuples that are not shared nor mutable, the expression "exp.**a**" may change only if the expression "exp" changes.

The analysis for the constraint examples are listed in Figure 1. BadDrivers appears in the analysis of constraints A_3, A_5, and A_6 because it is a *subclass* of Drivers. The same is true for Planes.

Constraint	Analysis
A_1	Person.**age**, Persons, Vehicle.**name**, Vehicle.**owner**, Vehicles, Planes, Plane.**name**, Plane.**owner**
A_2	Person.**age**, Person.**children**, Persons
A_3	Drivers, BadDrivers, Person.**age**
A_4	Persons, Person.**age**
A_5	Drivers, BadDrivers, Person.**licences**, Vehicle.**type**, Plane.**type**
A_6	Vehicles, Planes, Drivers, BadDrivers, Person.**age**, Vehicle.**agev**, Plane.**agev**
A_7	Persons, Person.**spouse**

Figure 1: Static analysis of constraints

The analysis of the constraint A_2 is made of three paths. This means that there are three ways to violate this constraint: we can modify the class Persons (add a new person in it for example) or we can either modify the age or the set of children of a given person.

For the constraint A_5, we obtain five paths. The first two paths express that a modification of the class Drivers (or BadDrivers) may violate the constraint. The following path expresses that the constraint may also be violated if the feature **licenses** of a Person is updated. The last two paths express that a constraint be be violated if the feature **type** of both Vehicle or Plane is modified. This takes the subtyping into account.

3.2 Static Analysis of Transactions

In this subsection, we propose a similar analysis of the transactions that can be run on the database. Our goal is to build, for every transaction T, the set ψ(T) of all paths involved in the transaction. Such paths lead to data that the transaction might modify.

In this paper, we suppose that transactions do not call other transactions or functions, so we shall do no interprocedural analysis. The analysis ψ of a transaction is then defined as follows:

$\psi(s_1 ; s_2) = \psi(s_1) \cup \psi(s_2)$;
$\psi($**if** (b) s_1 **else** $s_2) = \psi(s_1) \cup \psi(s_2)$;
$\psi($**for** (o **in** x) **when** (b) s$) = \psi(s)$;
$\psi(e_1 := e_2) = \Upsilon(e_1)$;
$\psi(\langle S \rangle) = \langle S \rangle$, if S is a schema name and not a class name;
= the set of all subclasses of <S>, including itself, if <S> is a class name.
$\psi($**insert** e_1 **into** $e_2) = \Upsilon(e_2)$;
$\psi($**drop** e_1 **from** $e_2) = \Upsilon(e_2)$;

This definition means that the analysis of a transaction is the union of the analysis of all the elementary statements involved in it. For an assignment operation like "$e_1 := en_2$", the data that can be modified is the data corresponding to the expression e_1, and it is analysed by $\Upsilon(e_1)$. We examplify this definition with the examples of transactions above.

Transaction	Analysis
T_1	Vehicles, Planes
T_2	Person.**spouse**
T_3	Persons, Person.**age**

Figure 2: Analysis of transactions

We have analysed both transactions and constraints as a set of paths into the database that are used by the constraint or involved in the transaction. The detection of the constraints which may be violated by a given transaction is then very simple, as stated by the following property:

Property 1 Let T be a transaction and A be a constraint; the transaction T may violate the constraint A only if $\Upsilon(A) \cap \psi(T)$ is non empty.

If we use this property on the running examples, we obtain the table shown in Figure 3.

Transaction	Constraints
T_1	A_1, A_6
T_2	A_7
T_3	A_1, A_2, A_3, A_4, A_6, A_7

Figure 3: Constraints hit by a transaction

4 Enforcement Tests Generation

4.1 Restriction of the constraint language

Incremental checking is not possible for every constraint. Existential quantifiers, for example, cannot be simply incrementally checked as illustrated by the following example:

exist x **in** aSet, Pred(x)

If a transaction removes an element α from aSet and Pred(α) is true, then there is no simple and cheap way to ensure that there is still another element that satisfies the predicate. In the remaining of this section, we shall thus consider only universally quantified and conjunctive constraints.

4.2 Constraint checking

The problem of efficiently checking a constraint at the end of a transaction consists in finding the minimal set of objects involved in the process of checking. Then, the constraint will be checked only on this set which guarantees that data consistency is ensured at the end of checking. However, this set is unfortunately not always reachable at run time. In order to illustrate this we use the following three constraints A_6, A_7 and A_2:

(A_6) $\forall$ p $\in$ Persons, p.**age** $\leq 130 \wedge$ p.**age** ≥ 0;
(A_7) $\forall$ p $\in$ Persons, p.**spouse.spouse** = p $\vee$ p.**spouse** = **nil**;
(A_2) $\forall$ p $\in$ Persons, $\forall$ c $\in$ p.**children**, p.**age** > c.**age**

together with the two transactions T_2 and T_3.

```
let T2 = trans(p1, p2: Person):
         p1.spouse := p2;
         p2.spouse := p1;
         /* this transaction performs a marriage between two persons */
let T3 = trans()
         for p in Persons when (today = p.birthday)
             print("Happy Birthday ", p.name);
             p.age := p.age + 1
         /* this transaction updates the age of all Persons born
         on the current day */
```

If we consider T_3, for the first constraint, we just have to collect the identifiers of every person whose age is modified. The objects collected by this process correspond to the ideal relevant set of objects on which A_6 has to be checked.

For the second constraint, when executing transaction T_2, the ideal relevant set is not so easy to obtain. This set consists of the identifiers of p_1 and p_2 as well as the identifiers of p_1.**spouse** and p_2.**spouse** *before* the assignment. Indeed, we need to know the former spouses of p_1 and p_2, because the constraint A_7 will certainly be violated for them. Of course, collecting those identifiers requires the checker manager to be provided with some kind of "intelligence".

For the third constraint, when executing T_3, we have no means to collect the parents of a child whose age has been modified, because we don't have backward pointers nor indices.

As a consequence, we will not attempt to obtain the ideal set of relevant objects. At the same time, we will not assume the existence of special access structures like indexes or backward pointers. We rather address the problem of finding an efficient checking algorithm which can be applied to all constraints. For constraints such as A_6, the algorithm will operate on the ideal relevant set of objects; for other constraints, we shall show that the checking algorithm improves the trivial approach which consists in performing a whole scan on the populations involved in the constraints.

Let T be a transaction, let A be a constraint. We are looking for an algorithm satisfying the following properties:

- The evaluation of this algorithm at the end of the transaction ensures that the constraint A is still satisfied.
- The evaluation of this algorithm is more efficient than the direct evaluation of A.

At execution time, the only objects which can be collected are those instances of abstract data types whose attributes relevant with respect to the constraints have been modified. It may be the case that such a set of objects exactly matches the ideal relevant set, as for constraint A_6. But in general, the set obtained at execution time only intersects the relevant set, as for constraint A_7 et A_2. Therefore, we propose to generate checking algorithms which allow to test the constraint on the whole set of relevant objects, thus ensuring the database consistency. As a consequence, we will have to perform some additional work, in order to get these objects.

In order to define these algorithms, let us introduce the following definitions.

Definition 1 Δ^{C}

Given a class C, we posit Δ^{C} the set of instances of class C which have been created by a transaction.

□

Definition 2 $\Gamma_{\mathbf{a}}^{\tau(x)}$

Given an iteration variable x of type τ(x) and an attribute **a** of x, we posit $\Gamma_{\mathbf{a}}^{\tau(x)}$ the set of instances of the abstract type τ(x), which attribute **a** has been modified by a given transaction.

□

This set represents information on the updates that a transaction has made on the database. The constraints considered here have the following generic form:

$$\forall x_1 \in \mathtt{C}_1, \forall x_{1,1} \in x_1.\mathtt{p}_{1,1}, \ldots, \forall x_{1,n_1} \in x_1.\mathtt{p}_{1,n_1},$$

$$\forall x_2 \in \mathtt{C}_2, \forall x_{2,1} \in x_2.\mathtt{p}_{2,1}, \ldots, \forall x_{2,n_2} \in x_2.\mathtt{p}_{2,n_2}, \ldots,$$

$$\forall x_k \in \mathtt{C}_k, \ldots, \forall x_{k,n_k} \in x_k.\mathtt{p}_{k,n_k}, \mathtt{M}(x_1, x_{1,1}, \ldots, x_k, \ldots, x_{k,n_k})$$

where the $\mathrm{p}_{i,j}$ denote prefix paths.

Let x be a variable ranging over class C_i, and let $y_1, \ldots, y_n$ be variables ranging respectively over $x.p_1, \ldots, x.p_n$, where p_i denotes a prefix path leading to a set structured component of x. In the following, we show how to generate enforcement tests.

For each class C_i, we generate the following enforcement test:

$\forall x \in \Delta^{C_i}$
    check [$\forall x_1 \in C_1, \ldots, \forall x_{i+1} \in C_{i+1}, \ldots,$
    $M(x_1, \ldots, x, \ldots, x_{i+1}, \ldots)$]

For each path $x.a_1 \ldots a_k$ (either in the prefix or in the matrix), we generate:

$\forall x \in C_i$
    $\forall y \in \Gamma_{a_1}^{\tau(x)}$, if $y = x$,
    check [$\forall x_1 \in C_1, \ldots, \forall x_{i+1} \in C_{i+1}, \ldots,$
    $M(x_1, \ldots, x, \ldots, x_{i+1}, \ldots)$]
    ...
    $\forall y \in \Gamma_{a_k}^{\tau(x.a_1 \ldots a_{k-1})}$, if $y = x \ldots a_{k-1}$,
    check [$\forall x_1 \in C_1, \ldots, \forall x_{i+1} \in C_{i+1}, \ldots,$
    $M(x_1, \ldots, x, \ldots, x_{i+1}, \ldots)$]

For each path $y_i.b_1 \ldots b_l$ in the matrix (where y_i ranges in $x.p_i$), we generate

$\forall x \in C_i$
    $\forall y \in x.p_i$
        $\forall z \in \Gamma_{b_1}^{\tau(y)}$, if $z = y$,
        check [$\forall x_1 \in C_1, \ldots, \forall x_{i+1} \in C_{i+1}, \ldots,$
        $M(x_1, \ldots, x, \ldots, y, \ldots, x_{i+1}, \ldots)$]
        ...
        $\forall z \in \Gamma_{b_1}^{\tau(y \ldots b_{l-1})}$, if $z = y \ldots b_{l-1}$,
        check [$\forall x_1 \in C_1, \ldots, \forall x_{i+1} \in C_{i+1}, \ldots,$
        $M(x_1, \ldots, x, \ldots, y, \ldots, x_{i+1}, \ldots)$]

For a given constraint A, the enforcement test generation consists in generating the above tests for each class C_i involved in the constraint prefix. Let us illustrate this on the following constraints.

(A_6) ∀ p ∈ Persons, p.**age** ≤ 130 ∧ p.**age** ≥ 0;
(A_7) ∀ p ∈ Persons, p.**spouse.spouse** = p ∨ p.**spouse** = **nil**;
(A_2) ∀ p ∈ Persons, ∀ c ∈ p.**children**, p.**age** > c.**age**
(A_1) ∀ p ∈ Persons, ∀ v ∈ Vehicles, (v.**name** ≠ "Ferrari" ∨ v.**owner** ≠ p) ∨
    p.**age** ≥ 40

For the constraint A_6, the checking algorithm is

$\forall$ x $\in \Delta^{\mathbf{Persons}}$, check ($A_6$(x))
$\forall$ x $\in$ Persons
  $\forall$ y $\in \Gamma^{\mathbf{Person}}_{\mathbf{age}}$, if y = x, check($A_6$(x))

This can be rewritten as following:

$\forall$ x $\in \Delta^{\mathbf{Persons}}$, check ($A_6$(x))
$\forall$ x $\in$ Persons $\cap\ \Gamma^{\mathbf{Person}}_{\mathbf{age}}$, check ($A_6$(x))

In this case, the set $\Gamma^{\mathbf{Person}}_{\mathbf{age}}$ actually represents the relevant set of objects on which the constraint has to be checked. Indeed, this algorithm leads to check the constraint on the set $\Gamma^{\mathbf{Person}}_{\mathbf{age}}$ testing for each element if it belongs to the class Persons. We thus perform as many check operations as the minimal algorithm does. Note that the trivial algorithm would have performed as many checks as the number of elements in the class Persons.

For the constraint A_7, the checking algorithm is

$\forall$ x $\in \Delta^{\mathbf{Persons}}$, check ($A_7$(x))
$\forall$ x $\in$ Persons
  $\forall$ y $\in \Gamma^{\mathbf{Person}}_{\mathbf{spouse}}$,
    if y = x, check(A_7(y))
  $\forall$ y $\in \Gamma^{\mathbf{Person}}_{\mathbf{spouse}}$,
    if y = x.spouse, check(A_7(y))

For this algorithm, we have to scan the whole class Persons and test whether an element of $\Gamma^{\mathbf{Person}}_{\mathbf{spouse}}$ corresponds to the spouse attribute of a given instance of Persons.

For the constraint A_2, the checking algorithm is

$\forall$ x $\in \Delta^{\mathbf{Persons}}$, check ($A_2$(x))
$\forall$ x $\in$ Persons
  $\forall$ y $\in \Gamma^{\mathbf{Person}}_{\mathbf{age}}$,
    if y = x, check(A_2(y))
  $\forall$ y $\in \Gamma^{\mathbf{Person}}_{\mathbf{children}}$,
    if y = x, check(A_2(x,y))
  $\forall$ y $\in$ x.children
    $\forall$ z $\in \Gamma^{\mathbf{Person}}_{\mathbf{age}}$,
    if z = y, check(A_2(x,y))

This algorithm iterates over three sets: Persons, $\Gamma^{\mathbf{Person}}_{\mathbf{age}}$ and $\Gamma^{\mathbf{Person}}_{\mathbf{children}}$. For each element x of Persons whose age has been modified, we have to check the constraint. For each element x of Persons, if the age of one of his/her children has been modified, we have to check whether the constraint is still valid. Last, for each element of Persons whose set of children has been modified, we also have to check the constraint.

Finally, for the constraint A_1, the checking algorithm is

$$
\begin{array}{l}
\forall\, x \in \Delta^{\texttt{Persons}},\ \text{check}\ (A_1(x))\\
\forall\, x \in \text{Persons}\\
\quad \forall\, y \in \Gamma^{\texttt{Person}}_{\texttt{age}},\\
\qquad \text{if } y = x,\ \text{check}(A_1(y))\\
\forall\, x \in \Delta^{\texttt{Vehicles}},\ \text{check}\ (A_1(x))\\
\forall\, x \in \text{Vehicles}\\
\quad \forall\, y \in \Gamma^{\texttt{Vehicle}}_{\texttt{name}},\\
\qquad \text{if } y = x,\ \text{check}(A_1(y))\\
\quad \forall\, y \in \Gamma^{\texttt{Vehicle}}_{\texttt{owner}},\\
\qquad \text{if } y = x\ \text{check}(A_1(y))
\end{array}
$$

This algorithm can be rewritten as follows:

$$
\begin{array}{l}
\forall\, x \in \Delta^{\texttt{Persons}},\ \text{check}\ (A_1(x))\\
\forall\, x \in \text{Persons} \cap \Gamma^{\texttt{Person}}_{\texttt{age}},\\
\qquad \text{check}(A_1(x))\\
\forall\, x \in \Delta^{\texttt{Vehicles}},\ \text{check}\ (A_1(x))\\
\forall\, x \in \text{Vehicles} \cap (\Gamma^{\texttt{Vehicle}}_{\texttt{name}} \cup \Gamma^{\texttt{Vehicle}}_{\texttt{owner}}\\
\qquad \text{check}(A_1(x))
\end{array}
$$

This last example deserves some comments: checking A_1 means that we check A_1 with respect to all the elements in either Vehicles or Persons. Therefore some tests are redundant. When checking the set of Persons whose age has been modified, we will consider all Vehicles and particularly those Vehicles whose name or owner attribute has been updated. In the second phase of the algorithm, we shall test the constraint for all updated Vehicles with respect to all Persons including those whose age has been modified. In order to avoid such redundant tests, we refine this algorithm in the following way. We saw on the previous examples (for the constraints A_6 and A_1) that the checking algorithms could be rewritten in an optimized form. Such an optimisation can only take place for the algorithms containing no navigation in the type structures. For example, it is not possible to optimise in this way the algorithm generated for the constraint A_2, because y has to range over `x.children`.

We now give a general optimized version of this class of algorithms.

$$
\begin{array}{l}
\forall x \in C_1 \cap (\cup \Gamma_1)\\
\quad \text{check}\ [\ \forall x_2 \in C_2, \ldots, \forall x_k \in C_k, \ldots,\\
\qquad M(x, \ldots, x_2, \ldots, x_k, \ldots)]\\
\quad \ldots\\
\forall x \in C_i \cap (\cup \Gamma_i)\\
\quad \text{check}\ [\ \forall x_1 \in C_1 - (C_1 \cap (\cup \Gamma_1)), \ldots,\\
\qquad \forall x_{i-1} \in C_{i-1} - (C_{i-1} \cap (\cup \Gamma_{i-1})), \ldots,\\
\qquad \forall x_{i+1} \in C_{i+1}, \ldots,\\
\qquad M(x_1, \ldots, x_2, \ldots, x, \ldots, x_k, \ldots)]\\
\quad \ldots\\
\forall x \in C_k \cap (\cup \Gamma_k)\\
\quad \text{check}\ [\ \forall x_1 \in C_1 - (C_1 \cap (\cup \Gamma_1)), \ldots,\\
\qquad \forall x_i \in C_i - (C_i \cap (\cup \Gamma_i)), \ldots,\\
\qquad \forall x_{k-1} \in C_{k-1} - (C_{k-1} \cap (\cup \Gamma_{k-1})),\\
\qquad M(x_1, \ldots, x_2, \ldots, x, \ldots)]
\end{array}
$$

The union of Γ_i denotes the set of all instances of an abstract type whose attributes relevant to a given constraint have been updated. Such an optimised version prevents from testing more than one time the same constraint on the same objects.

5 Implementation

This section describes the implementation of a first prototype for the Thémis language. Thémis is implemented on top of the O_2 system, using a preprocessing approach. The preprocessor O_2integrity takes a schema written in Thémis and produces an O_2 schema and a set of O_2 executables programs which allow to instanciate the constraints while preserving the inclusion semantics. O_2integrity is written in C^{++} and uses *lex* and *yacc*.

5.1 Mapping between Thémis and O_2

In this section, we describe the mapping between the Thémis language and O_2.

5.1.1 Atomic types

Thémis	O_2
int	integer
string	string
boolean	boolean
-	real
-	bits

5.1.2 Type Constructors

In the O_2 language, it is possible to define complex objects and values by using various constructors, as in Thémis.

Thémis	O_2
$[a_1{:}t_1,..,a_n{:}t_n]$	tuple$(a_1{:}t_1,..,a_n{:}t_n)$
$\{t_1\}$	set(t_1)
(t_1)	list(t_1)

5.1.3 Types

In the O_2 language, the instances of a type are values and the instances of a class are objects. These properties are offered in Thémis through concrete and abstract types.

Thémis	O_2
Concrete type	type
Abstract type	class

5.1.4 *Subtyping and inheritance*

O_2 and Thémis follow the same subtyping rules:

- An explicit subtyping for abstract types (Thémis) and the classes (O_2).
- An implicit subtyping for concrete types (Thémis) and types (O_2).

5.2 Constraints and transactions

The constraints defined in Thémis are instances of a predefined class "Constraint" in O_2. The transactions are translated into O_2 transactions and compiled by the O_2C compiler.

5.3 Example

In this section, we describe the fonctionalities provided by the O_2integrity precompiler.

The following figure presents our schema in Thémis together with the constraints and the transactions.

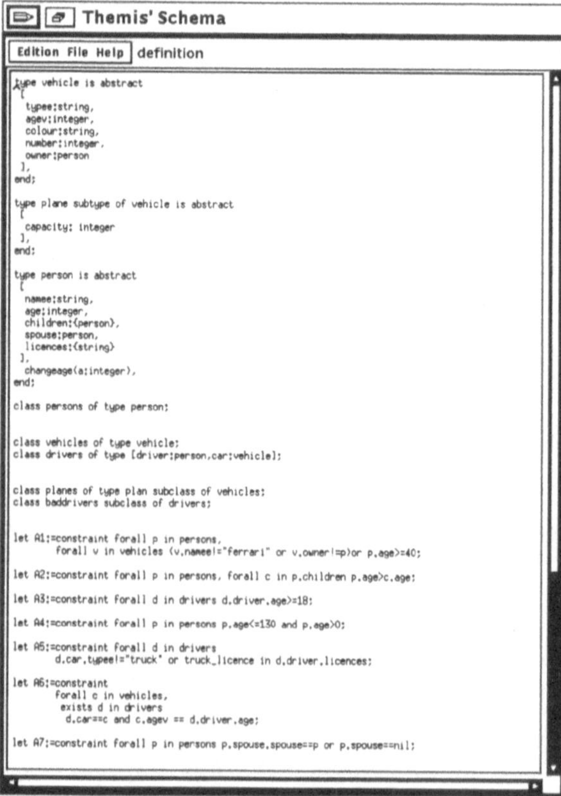

Figure 4 : Schema in Thémis

The various components generated by the precompiler, namely, the constraints, the transactions and the classes are displayed in the Figures 5, 6, 7 and 8.

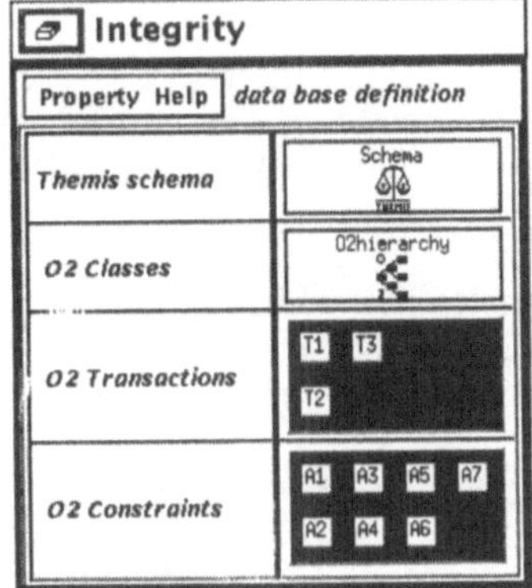

Figure 5 : O_2integrity components

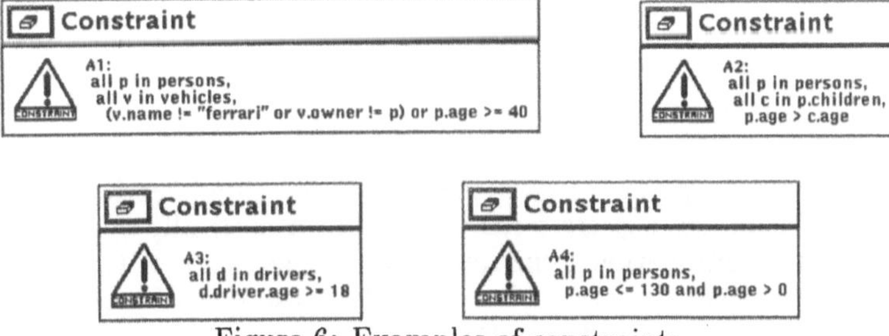

Figure 6: Examples of constraints

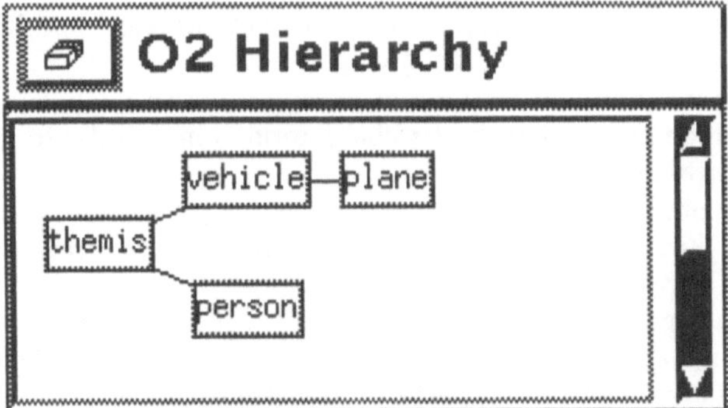

Figure 7: O_2 Classes

```
Transaction

transaction body T2 (
                  p1 : person,
                  p2 : person)  in application constraints_o2
{
 p1->spouse=p2;
 p2->spouse=p1;
};
```

Figure 8: O_2 Transactions

Finally, the set of constraints which might be violated by the transactions of the current schema is represented in Figure 9.

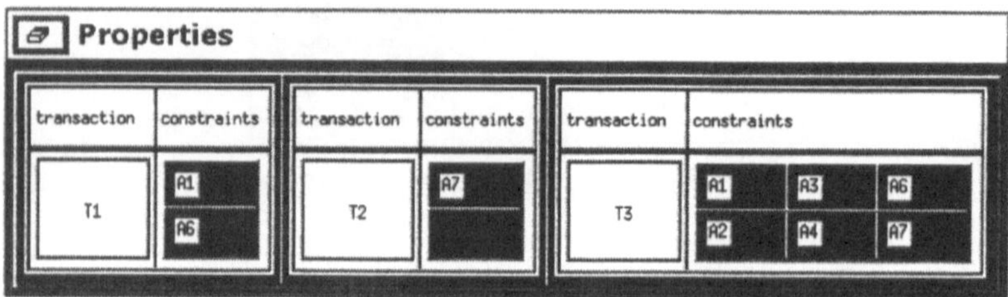

Figure 9: Constraints hit by transactions

6 Conclusion

In this paper, we proposed to extend relational simplification methods in the context of complex objects with identity in a statically typed environment. Using simple compilation techniques, we have shown how to statically reduce the number of constraints to be checked at the end of a given transaction. While adapting the techniques, focus has been devoted to set-structured data types. Unlike other techniques which only consider the constraint prefix, we consider as well the matrix thus refining the relevant sets of objects that could be involved in the process of checking. Finally, we have presented enforcement tests generation techniques.

This work is a preliminary work on the specification of a compiler for the language proposed in [LR90]. In order to get complete specifications, we will extend our techniques in the following directions.

In Sections 2 and 3, we did not consider methods (that is n-ary features). We will extend our work on static characterisation in order to take into account methods as well.

For the optimisation of constraint checking, we shall work in three different directions. First, we will try to extend our result in the case of quantifiers over general set expressions (not only class names). In the present work, we do not consider such complex iterations. Then, we will consider the case of constraints with negation and/or existential quantifiers. Third, we shall refine the checking algorithms in order to avoid performing redundant checks.

In order to be able to estimate the impact of such extensions, we will try, at the same time, to formalise the cost (in time and space) of constraints verifications. Such a formalisation would allow, for example, to make some trade-off between time (verification at the end of a transaction) and space (amount of data collected during the transaction).

Finally, in order to get more results on constraint optimisation, we will continue to compare our work with the more general domain of logic programs compilation. We think that, although the underlying data models and type systems are very different, there are enough commonalities between these two problems to get some more results.

Acknowledgements

This work was initiated when the authors were in the Altaïr group at INRIA together with C. Lécluse and P. Richard. We are thankful to them for helpful advices and for stimulating discussions and ideas. We also would like to thank P.Y. Policella and P. Tronowski who greatly contributed in the implementation of the first Thémis prototype.

References

[BDM88] F. Bry, H. Decker, and R. Manthey. A Uniform Approach to Constraint Satisfaction and Constraint Satisfiability in Deductive Databases. In *EDBT International Conference*, 1988.

[BM86] F. Bry and R. Manthey. Checking Consistency of Database Constraints: A Logical Basis. In *VLDB International Conference*, 1986.

[Car84] L. Cardelli. A Semantics of Multiple Inheritance. In *Semantics of Data Types*. Springer-Verlag, 1984.

[GM79] G. Gardarin and M. Melkanoff. Proving the Consistency of Database Transactions. In *VLDB International Conference*, Rio, Brasil, October 1979.

[HI85] A. Hsu and T. Imielinski. Integrity Checking for Multiple Updates. In *ACM SIGMOD International Conference*, 1985.

[HMS89] R. Hull, R. Morrison, and D. Stemple, editors. *International Workshop on Database Programming Languages*. Morgan Kaufmann, 1989.

[KSS87] R. Kowalski, F. Sadri, and P. Soper. Integrity Checking in Deductive Databases. In *VLDB International Conference*, 1987.

[LR89] C. Lécluse and P. Richard. Modeling Complex Structures in Object-Oriented Databases. In *ACM PODS International Conference*, March 1989.

[LR90] C. Lécluse and P. Richard. Data Base Schemas and Types Systems for DBPLs, a Definition and its Applications. Technical report, GIP Altaïr, June 1990.

[Mar91] H. Martin. *Contrôle de la cohérence dans les bases objets : Une approche par le comportement*. PhD thesis, Université Joseph-Fourier - Grenoble I, 1991.

[Nic79] J.M. Nicolas. Logic for Improving Integrity Checking in Relational Databases. Technical report, ONERA-CERT, 1979.

[SS89] T. Sheard and D. Stemple. Automatic Verification of Database Transaction Safety. *ACM Transactions on Database Systems*, 14(3), September 1989.

[Sto75] M. Stonebraker. Implementation of Integrity Constraints and Views by Query Modification. In *ACM SIGMOD International Conference*, San Jose, California, May 1975.

[WSK83] W. Weber, W. Stugky, and J. Karzt. Integrity Checking in database systems. *Information Systems*, 8(2), 1983.

Bounded Fixpoints for Complex Objects

Dan Suciu
Department of Computer and Information Science
University of Pennsylvania
Philadelphia, USA

Abstract

We investigate a query language for complex-object databases, which is designed to (1) express only tractable queries, and (2) be as expressive over flat relations as first order logic with fixpoints. The language is obtained by extending the *nested relational algebra* $\mathcal{NRA}$, of [9], with a "bounded fixpoint" operator. Extending the flat case [15, 21] , all *PTime* computable queries over *ordered* databases are expressible in this language. The main result consists in proving that this language is a conservative extension of the first order logic with fixpoints, or of the *while*-queries (depending on the interpretation of the bounded fixpoint: inflationary or partial). The proof technique uses indexes, to encode complex objects into flat relations, and is strong enough to allow for the encoding of $\mathcal{NRA}$ with unbounded fixpoints into flat relations. We also define a complex object logic based language with fixpoints and prove that its range restricted fragment is equivalent to $\mathcal{NRA}$ with bounded fixpoints.

1 Introduction

Several query languages for databases with complex objects have been studied in recent years (e.g. [1], [2], [3], [9], [12], [13], [14], [17], [20], [22]). A natural way of designing such a language is to extend first order logic to a logic for hereditary finite sets, and consider only *domain independent* queries, like in the case of first order logic. Abiteboul and Beeri follow this path in [1], define *safe* queries, and show that the resulting language, which they call *the calculus*, can express *powerset*, hence, unlike first order logic, it can express untractable queries. They design an algebraic language equivalent to *the calculus*, called *the algebra*, in which *powerset* is one of the primitives. Searching for a tractable sublanguage, they observe that by removing the powerset from the algebra one gets such a language, and that the same expressive power can be obtained by enforcing stricter safety rules in the calculus (the resulting language is called *the strictly safe calculus*).

Another way, based on an investigation of the primitives associated with the types occurring in complex objects, has been pursued by Breazu-Tannen Buneman and Wong ([9]), who designed a tractable language with the same expressive power as the algebra without powerset. Following established tradition, they called this language the *nested relational algebra* ($\mathcal{NRA}$), and showed that, like in first order logic, all queries expressible in $\mathcal{NRA}$ are in PTIME. We shall adopt their formalism in this paper.

Paredaens and Van Gucht in [17] and Wong in [23] show that $\mathcal{NRA}$, or languages equivalent to it, are conservative extensions of first order logic, meaning that using intermediate results of heigher set complexity does not help us expressing more queries. For example, the transitive closure of a flat relation cannot be computed in these languages, because it cannot be computed in first order logic. In contrast, in [1] it is shown that one can express transitive closure in the *algebra* (which has the same expressive power as $\mathcal{NRA}+powerset$), but in an inefficient way, by using more complex intermediate types. In fact, Hull and Su prove in [13] that the expressive power of this language becomes strictly more powerful as we allow intermediate types of larger set heights.

Transitive closure can be expressed in first order logic *with (inflationary) fixpoints*, a language equivalent to $DATALOG^{\neg}$ (see [6] for a review). Adding fixpoints to first order logic keeps the queries tractable, but adding them to $\mathcal{NRA}$ does not: we show that they are equivalent to *powerset* (see example 2 and proposition 3). It is natural to search for an extension of $\mathcal{NRA}$ which is still tractable and which has at least the expressive power of $DATALOG^{\neg}$. Peter Buneman suggested adding a *bounded fixpoint* and conjectured the conservativity result (theorem 2). When $f : \mathcal{P}(D) \to \mathcal{P}(D)$ is a function, and A is a subset of D, then the *bounded* fixpoint of f is the fixpoint of the function $g(x) \stackrel{\text{def}}{=} f(x) \cap A$. We consider both *inflationary* and *partial* semantics for the (bounded) fixpoints (see e.g. [4], or section 3 of this paper), and we denote them with $bfix_i$ and $bfix_p$. We prove in proposition 5 (section 3) that all queries in $\mathcal{NRA} + bfix_i$ are in $PTime$, and that all queries in $\mathcal{NRA} + bfix_p$ are in $PSpace$.

A further contrast between the fixpoint over flat types and the fixpoint over complex objects is given by proposition 2, which shows that both inflationary and partial fixpoint have the same expressive power over complex objects: Abiteboul and Vianu prove in [7], that the inflationary and partial fixpoint have the same expressive power over first order logic iff $PTime = PSpace$, which most people believe to be false.

We also present a logic based language having the same expressive power as $\mathcal{NRA}+bfix$. Grumbach and Vianu in [12] also present a tractable logic based language which can express recursive queries, but we do not know its precise expressive power, or whether it is closed under *map* (as our language is). We hope to be able to clarify in the future the relationship between our language and that presented in [12]. We remark that the range restriction rules in [12] differ substantially from ours.

The main result of this paper is the conservativity property of $\mathcal{NRA} + bfix$ over first order logic with fixpoints. We emphasize that this result holds for *arbitrary* databases: in fact, in the presence of order, this would be an immediate consequence of Immerman and Vardi's results, that first order logic with fixpoints can express all $PTime$ ($PSpace$) queries over ordered databases ([15], [21]). For the proof, we use a different technique than the ones used in [17] and [23], because it is not clear how to adapt their reduction methods for the bounded fixpoint. It also differs from the proof of conservativity results in [16], because we do not have order. Our approach is of a semantic nature, and splits in two steps the translation of $\mathcal{NRA} + bfix$ into the relational algebra with fixpoints: first, we encode all complex object into flat relations, using indexes from some infinite set I. In fact, this encoding is strong enough to translate even the unbounded fixpoint. We have learned that indexes have been used in a related way by Van den Bussche ([20]) for proving a conservativity result for the nested algebra (without fixpoints). In the second step, we show how to eliminate the indexes when both the input and the output of some relational algebra expression with indexes, are encodings of flat relations. It should be emphasized that, although I has some additional structure, no order relation or additional structure is needed on the other domains. Finally we observe that the bounded fixpoint over flat relations has the same expressive power as the unbounded fixpoint. In fact, by composing the transformations performed in these two steps, we do get a direct translation of $\mathcal{NRA}+bfix$ into the relational algebra (without indexes).

In fact, our result is slightly more general, because it holds also when the language contains *interpreted* function symbols, over base types and flat relations. In that case, $\mathcal{NRA} + bfix$ is a conservative extension of the relational algebra with *bounded* fixpoints, because only in the absence of interpreted function symbols has the bounded fixpoint over flat relations the same expressive power as the unbounded fixpoint.

An immediate consequence of the conservativity result is the fact that, in general, there are queries in *PTime* which are not expressible in $\mathcal{NRA} + bfix$ (e.g. the test whether a flat relation has an even number of elements). But, as in the flat case (see [21] and [15]), we can prove that any *PTime* or *PSpace* database transformation over *ordered* databases is expressible in $\mathcal{NRA} + bfix$.

In [16], Libkin and Wong prove for a query language with arithmetic, order, and bounded fixpoints, that, for any $k \geq 1$, it is a conservative extension of its restriction to types of set height $\leq k$. This result, and our conservativity result, do not imply each other. Our result does not *require* the presence of order and arithmetic (but still holds in the presence of additional interpreted function symbols), however we consider only the case $k = 1$.

In [18] Saraiya shows that *DATALOG* can be simulated with structural recursion on sets, preserving the PTIME complexity, by using as an intermediate step a loop operator which iterates a function a number of times equal to the cardinality of a set. Several complexity-theoretic results for program properties and transformations are then be obtained by recourse to known results for *DATALOG*.

In section 2, we give the basic definitions of $\mathcal{NRA}$. In section 3, we define the unbounded and the bounded fixpoint, state some basic properties, and give a simple proof of the equivalence between the expressive power of the inflationary and partial fixpoint, over complex objects. Section 4 states our main results. Section 5 presents a logic based language called $\mathcal{NRCALC} + fix$, which is equivalent to $\mathcal{NRA} + bfix$. In section 6 we describe the encoding of the nested relational algebra into the relational algebra with indexes, then, we prove in section 7 that indexes can be eliminated, for flat relations. Together, these prove the conservativity extension theorem.

2 The Nested Relational Algebra

We consider a set of base types, like *nat*, *string*, etc., to be given, and define **types** by the grammar $\sigma = b \mid unit \mid \sigma_1 \times \sigma_2 \mid \{\sigma\}$ (b stands for a base type, $unit = \{()\}$, $\sigma_1 \times \sigma_2$ is the product type, and $\{\sigma\}$ contains all finite subsets of σ). For the particular set of base types, we also assume a given collection of external functions to be given, each function p with a specified domain d_p and codomain c_p, written $p : d_p \rightarrow c_p$. Examples are *cardinality* at type σ ($card_\sigma : \{\sigma\} \rightarrow nat$), *addition* ($add : nat \times nat \rightarrow nat$), the constant *zero* ($0 : unit \rightarrow nat$) etc. Note that function symbols of arity $unit \rightarrow b$ play the role of a constant of type b. Let Σ be the set of base types and external functions. Sometimes we restrict Σ to having only base types and constants (i.e. function symbols of type $unit \rightarrow \sigma$): we shall write $\Sigma = \emptyset$ in this case, although Σ is *not* necessarily empty (it may contain base types and constants). Following [9], we define the **nested relational algebra** $\mathcal{NRA}(\Sigma)$ as an algebra of functions over complex objects, without variables. The functions in this language are defined by the following rules:

$$\frac{p \in \Sigma}{p : d_p \rightarrow c_p} \qquad \frac{}{id_\sigma : \sigma \rightarrow \sigma} \qquad \frac{f : \sigma \rightarrow \tau \quad g : \tau \rightarrow \nu}{g \circ f : \sigma \rightarrow \nu}$$

$$\frac{}{\pi_i : \sigma_1 \times \sigma_2 \rightarrow \sigma_i}(i = 1, 2) \qquad \frac{f_i : \sigma \rightarrow \tau_i \ (i = 1, 2)}{(f_1, f_2) : \sigma \rightarrow \tau_1 \times \tau_2}$$

$$\frac{}{\iota_\sigma : \sigma \rightarrow unit}$$

$$\frac{}{\eta_\sigma : \sigma \rightarrow \{\sigma\}} \qquad \frac{}{\mu_\sigma : \{\{\sigma\}\} \rightarrow \{\sigma\}} \qquad \frac{f : \sigma \rightarrow \tau}{map(f) : \{\sigma\} \rightarrow \{\tau\}}$$

$$\frac{}{\rho_{2,(\sigma,\tau)} : \sigma \times \{\tau\} \rightarrow \{\sigma \times \tau\}}$$

$$\frac{}{\emptyset_\sigma : unit \rightarrow \{\sigma\}} \qquad \frac{}{\cup_\sigma : \{\sigma\} \times \{\sigma\} \rightarrow \{\sigma\}}$$

$$\frac{}{not : \{unit\} \rightarrow \{unit\}} \qquad \frac{}{eq_b : b \times b \rightarrow \{unit\}}(b \text{ a base type})$$

We abbreviate $\mathcal{NRA}(\Sigma)$ by $\mathcal{NRA}$ when $\Sigma = \emptyset$ (i.e. Σ contains only base types and constants). The semantics of these operations is fully described in [9]. Here, we briefly sketch it: π_1, π_2 are the projections, $\iota_\sigma(x) \stackrel{\text{def}}{=} ()$, $\eta_\sigma(x) \stackrel{\text{def}}{=} \{x\}$, $\mu_\sigma(\{x_1, \ldots, x_n\}) \stackrel{\text{def}}{=} x_1 \cup \ldots, \cup x_n$, $map(f)(\{x_1, \ldots, x_n\}) \stackrel{\text{def}}{=} \{f(x_1), \ldots, f(x_n)\}$, $\rho_{2,(\sigma,\tau)}(x, \{y_1, \ldots, y_n\}) \stackrel{\text{def}}{=} \{(x, y_1), \ldots, (x, y_n)\}$, $\emptyset_\sigma$ returns the empty set, $\cup_\sigma$ is set union, $not(\emptyset) = \{()\}$ and $not(\{()\}) = \emptyset$, $eq_b(x, x) = \{()\}$ and $eq_b(x, y) = \emptyset$ when $x \neq y$.

Following [9], we use the type $\{unit\}$ as booleans, using the convention that $\emptyset$ stands for *false*, and $\{()\}$ stands for *true*. Then, one can show (see also [9]) that in $\mathcal{NRA}$ we can express equality at all types $eq_\sigma : \sigma \times \sigma \rightarrow \{unit\}$ (*not* is necessary for this), the membership test $member : \sigma \times \{\sigma\} \rightarrow \{unit\}$, the *cartesian product* $\bowtie_{\sigma,\tau}: \{\sigma\} \times \{\tau\} \rightarrow \{\sigma \times \tau\}$[1] ($x \bowtie y \stackrel{\text{def}}{=} \{(a, b) \mid a \in x, b \in y\}$), set difference $- : \{\sigma\} \times \{\sigma\} \rightarrow \{\sigma\}$, intersection $\cap_\sigma : \{\sigma\} \times \{\sigma\} \rightarrow \{\sigma\}$, the conditional *if then else* $: \{unit\} \times \{\sigma\} \times \{\sigma\} \rightarrow \{\sigma\}$, $nest : \{\sigma \times \tau\} \rightarrow$

[1] We use $\bowtie_{\sigma,\tau}$ instead of $\times_{\sigma,\tau}$ to avoid confusion with the bifunctor $\times$, e.g. in expressions like $\times_{\sigma,\tau} \times \times_{\sigma',\tau'}$ (meaning $\bowtie_{\sigma,\tau} \times \bowtie_{\sigma',\tau'}$).

$\{\sigma \times \{\tau\}\}$, $unnest : \{\sigma \times \{\tau\}\} \to \{\sigma \times \tau\}$, the database projections Π_i : $\{\sigma_1 \times \sigma_2\} \to \{\sigma_i\}$ ($\Pi_i \stackrel{\text{def}}{=} map(\pi_i)$, $i = 1, 2$), etc. Also, for $f : \sigma \to \{\tau\}$, one defines $ext(f) : \{\sigma\} \to \{\tau\}$ to be $\mu_\tau \circ map(f)$ (see [9]): the meaning of ext is $ext(f)(\{x_1, \ldots, x_n\}) = f(x_1) \cup \ldots, \cup f(x_n)$. We shall eliminate type indexes, when they are understood from the context, i.e. we shall write μ instead of μ_τ, etc.

In [9] it is shown that all functions expressible in $\mathcal{NRA}(\Sigma)$ are in $PTime$, provided that all functions in Σ are in $PTime$. Moreover, they show that $\mathcal{NRA}$ is equivalent to the *strictly safe calculus* or *the algebra without powerset* in [1]. It is also (almost) equivalent to the *nested algebra* in [17] (see [16]).

Following [13], we define the **set height of a type** σ to be: $sh(b) = sh(unit) = 0$, $sh(\sigma \times \tau) = max(sh(\sigma), sh(\tau))$, $sh(\{\sigma\}) = 1 + sh(\sigma)$. The **set height of a function** $f : \sigma \to \tau$ is $sh(f) \stackrel{\text{def}}{=} max(sh(\sigma), sh(\tau))$.

For $k \geq 0$, we want to define $\mathcal{NRA}_k(\Sigma)$ to be the sublanguage of $\mathcal{NRA}(\Sigma)$ whose types have set height $\leq k$. We encounter, however, the following problem: consider some function $f : \sigma \to \{\tau\}$ in $\mathcal{NRA}_k(\Sigma)$, for which $sh(\sigma) = k - 1$, and $sh(\{\tau\}) \leq k$. We would like $ext(f) : \{\sigma\} \to \{\tau\}$ to be also in $\mathcal{NRA}_k(\Sigma)$, but the latter is defined as $\mu \circ map(f)$, and uses an intermediate type of set height $k + 1$, hence it cannot be expressed in $\mathcal{NRA}_k(\Sigma)$. So, we define $\mathcal{NRA}_k(\Sigma)$ similar to $\mathcal{NRA}(\Sigma)$, with the following change:

- We remove map, μ and ρ_2, and add ext_2, a generalized version of ext:

$$\frac{f : \nu \times \sigma \to \{\tau\}}{ext_2(f) : \nu \times \{\sigma\} \to \{\tau\}}$$

(with the semantics $ext_2(f)(x, \{y_1, \ldots, y_n\}) \stackrel{\text{def}}{=} f(x, y_1) \cup \ldots \cup f(x, y_n)$). Now $ext(f)$ is expressible as $ext(f) \stackrel{\text{def}}{=} ext_2(f \circ \pi_2) \circ (\iota_{\{\sigma\}}, id_{\{\sigma\}})$, $map(f)$ is expressible as $map(f) \stackrel{\text{def}}{=} ext(\eta \circ f)$, μ is expressible as $ext(id)$, and $\rho_2 \stackrel{\text{def}}{=} ext_2(\eta)$.

Fact 1 $\mathcal{NRA}(\Sigma) = \bigcup_{k \geq 0}(\mathcal{NRA}_k(\Sigma))$

Proposition 1 (Combinatorial Completeness) *Let $\mathcal{X}$ be some set of variables, i.e. function symbols of type $x : unit \to t_x$, where t_x is the type of x. Then $\mathcal{NRA}_k(\Sigma \cup \mathcal{X})$ is* **combinatorial complete**, *i.e. for any expression $f : \sigma \to \tau$ and any variable $x : unit \to t$, there is some expression $Kx.f : t \times \sigma \to \tau$ which doesn't contain the variable x*[2]*, such that $f = (Kx.f) \circ (x \circ \iota_\sigma, id_\sigma)$.*

Proof (Sketch) The proof is done by induction on the size of the expression f. All base cases are trivial. When f is of the form $g \circ f$ or (f_1, f_2), then the proof is identical to [9]. It remains to consider the case when $f = ext_2(g)$, where $g : \nu \times \sigma \to \{\tau\}$ and $ext_2(g) : \nu \times \{\sigma\} \to \{\tau\}$. By induction, there is some $Kx.g : t \times (\nu \times \sigma) \to \{\tau\}$. Let $h : (t \times \nu) \times \sigma \to \{\tau\}$ be $Kx.g \circ (\pi_1 \circ \pi_1, (\pi_2 \circ \pi_1, \pi_2))$; then $Kx.ext_2(g) \stackrel{\text{def}}{=} ext_2(h) \circ ((\pi_1, \pi_1 \circ \pi_2), \pi_2 \circ \pi_2)$. To prove the equation for

[2] $Kx.f$ contains all variables in f, except x. The notation is analog to the $\lambda x.f$ syntax.

$Kx.ext_2(g)$ from the one corresponding to $Kx.g$, one uses $ext_2(f \circ (k \circ \pi_1, \pi_2)) = ext_2(f) \circ (k \circ \pi_1, \pi_2)$, for $f : \nu' \times \sigma \rightarrow \{\tau\}$ and $k : \nu \rightarrow \nu'$. □

As a consequence, $\mathcal{NRA}_k(\Sigma)$ can be presented in a friendlier calculus-style language, with variables and lambda-abstractions (see [9] for details), and we shall feel free to use such a language in the sequel. For example, consider some predicate $p : \tau \rightarrow \{unit\}$ in $\mathcal{NRA}(\Sigma)$. We want to define the *selection* associated to p, $\sigma_p : \{\tau\} \rightarrow \{\tau\}$, like this: $\sigma_p \stackrel{\text{def}}{=} \lambda x.\Pi_2(ext(\lambda v.p(v) \bowtie \{v\})(x))$. We can translate this into $\mathcal{NRA}(\Sigma)$, by first introducing variables $v : unit \rightarrow \tau$ and $x : unit \rightarrow \{\tau\}$. Next, we translate expressions of some type ν into functions of type $unit \rightarrow \nu$, and we translate functions of type $\nu \rightarrow \nu'$, into functions of the same type. The definition of σ_p will be translated into: $(Kx.\Pi_2 \circ ext((Kv. \bowtie \circ(p \circ v, \eta \circ v)) \circ (id_\tau, \iota_\tau)) \circ x) \circ (id_{\{\tau\}}, \iota_{\{\tau\}})$.

As shown in [8], $\mathcal{NRA}_1$ is a conservative extension of the relational algebra (because one can see that $\mathcal{NRA}_1$ is equivalent to the language of $\mathcal{E}$'-expressions with free tuple variables and the emptiness test, as defined in [8]).

A natural question arises: can we express more functions using intermediate types of higher set height ? For example, it is known that we cannot express the transitive closure $tc : \{b \times b\} \rightarrow \{b \times b\}$ in $\mathcal{NRA}_1$ (see [19]): can we express it in $\mathcal{NRA}$, by using intermediate results of higher set heights, in some clever way ? The answer is negative:

Theorem 1 *([23], [17])* $\forall k \geq 1$, *if all function symbols in* Σ *have set height* $\leq k$, *then* $\mathcal{NRA}(\Sigma)$ *is a conservative extension of* $\mathcal{NRA}_k(\Sigma)$

The condition imposed on the functions in Σ is obviously necessary. Indeed, suppose that Σ contains the powerset over binary relations $powerset : \{b \times b\} \rightarrow \{\{b \times b\}\}$ (a function of set height 2). Then, using the technique from [1], one can express transitive closure $tc : \{b \times b\} \rightarrow \{b \times b\}$, which cannot be expressed in $\mathcal{NRA}_1(\Sigma)$, where *powerset* cannot be invoked.

As a consequence of this theorem, $\mathcal{NRA}$ is a conservative extension of the relational algebra.

3 Fixpoints

First order logic and the relational algebra have been extended to strictly more expressive languages, like first order logic with inflationary fixpoints (which is equivalent to $DATALOG^{\neg}$ with inflationary semantics), or first order logic with partial fixpoints (which is equivalent to the *while*-queries; see [6] for a review). These two languages can express only queries in *PTime* ($DATALOG^{\neg}$) or in *PSpace* (*while*-queries), and they are in some restricted sense complete for the respective complexity classes, namely they can express *all PTime* or *PSpace* queries over *ordered* databases[3] ([15], [21]).

As a consequence of the conservativity result (theorem 1), $\mathcal{NRA}$ is, over flat relations, only as expressive as first order logic. So we investigate possible extensions, to make it as powerful as first order logic with fixpoints (inflationary or partial). But, by simply adding the obvious generalization of the fixpoints to higher order sets, we get a language whose queries are no longer in *PTime* (or

[3] No query language capable of expressing *exactly* the *PTime* queries is currently known.

PSpace) ! We investigate an alternative fixpoint, the ***bounded fixpoint*** (an idea due to Peter Buneman), with inflationary or partial semantics. The resulting two languages turn out to be conservative extensions of first order logic with inflationary or partial fixpoints, express only queries in *PTime* and *PSpace* respectively, and express *all* queries in these complexity classes, over ordered databases.

Fixpoints cannot be defined at all types, but only at set types and products of set types. So we define a **product of sets type (PS type)** to be either a set type $\{t\}$, or the product $\sigma \times \tau$ of two PS types σ and τ. Examples of PS types are $\{b\}$, $\{b \times \{b\}\} \times \{b\} \times \{b \times b\}$ etc., while b and $b \times \{b\}$ are not PS types. For some PS type τ, we write $\cup, \cap : \tau \times \tau \to \tau$ and $\emptyset : unit \to \tau$, for the union and intersection of the components, and for the tuple of empty sets.

Consider the following fixpoint constructions, in which τ is a PS type[4]:

$$\frac{f : \sigma \times \tau \to \tau}{fix\ f : \sigma \to \tau} \qquad \frac{f : \sigma \times \tau \to \tau \quad g : \sigma \to \tau}{bfix(f \mid g) : \sigma \to \tau}$$

We consider two semantics: the ***partial***, and the ***inflationary*** semantics (see [4]). To distinguish them, we write $fix_p\ f$ and $fix_i\ f$ (respectively $bfix_p(f \mid g)$ and $bfix_i(f \mid g)$). For $x \in \sigma$, define the sequence $y_0 = \emptyset\ (\in \tau)$, $y_{n+1} = f(x, y_n)$; if there is some n for which $y_n = y_{n+1}$, then we define the **partial fixpoint** of f to be $(fix_p\ f)(x) = y_n$. Else, $(fix_p\ f)(x) =$ undefined. The **inflationary fixpoint** is defined to be the partial fixpoint of $f_i(x, y) = y \cup f(x, y)$, or, equivalently, $(fix_i f)(x) = \bigcup_{n \geq 0} y_n$, where $y_0 = \emptyset$, $y_{n+1} = y_n \cup f(x, y_n)$. The **bounded** partial (inflationary) fixpoint of f and g, $bfix(f \mid g)$, is defined to be the partial (inflationary) fixpoint of $f(x, y) \cap g(x)$.

All four resulting languages $\mathcal{NRA}(\Sigma) + fix_p$, $\mathcal{NRA}(\Sigma) + bfix_p$, $\mathcal{NRA}(\Sigma) + fix_i$, $\mathcal{NRA}(\Sigma) + bfix_i$ are combinatorial complete. The first three can express *partial* (as opposed to *total*) queries. When $\Sigma = \emptyset$, then only the first two can express partial queries.

Example 1 *The transitive closure can be computed using the bounded fixpoint: let* $f : \{\sigma \times \sigma\} \times \{\sigma \times \sigma\} \to \{\sigma \times \sigma\}$ *and* $g : \{\sigma \times \sigma\} \to \{\sigma \times \sigma\}$ *be:* $f(x, y) = x \cup (x \circ y)$ *(where* $x \circ y$ *is* relation composition, *which can be easily defined in* $\mathcal{NRA}$*),* $g(x) = (\Pi_1(x) \cup \Pi_2(x)) \bowtie (\Pi_1(x) \cup \Pi_2(x))$*. Then the transitive closure of* x *is given by* $tc(x) = bfix(f \mid g)(x)$*.*

Let fix_p^1, fix_i^1, $bfix_p^1$, $bfix_i^1$ stand for the fixpoint constructions in which the type τ is restricted to having the form $\{t\}$ (i.e. they allow fixpoints over only one set, not over several sets simultaneously). They are as expressive as fix_p, fix_i, $bfix_p$ and $bfix_i$ respectively (this is a straightforward generalization of the proof for flat relations, see e.g. [15]). But, in the presence of complex objects types, we can prove more:

Proposition 2 *Let* $\Omega_\sigma : unit \to \sigma$ *be the (totally) undefined function, and* $\Omega = \{\Omega_\sigma\}_{\sigma \in Types}$*, i.e. we have a symbol for the undefined object at each type* σ *(including complex types). Then*[5]*:* $\mathcal{NRA}_k(\Sigma) + fix_i^1 \subseteq \mathcal{NRA}_k(\Sigma) + fix_p \subseteq$

[4] The presence of the type σ in both definitions is necessary for combinatorial completeness.

[5] For the language $\mathcal{NRA}_k(\Sigma \cup \Omega)$, we consider the conditional *if then else* to be nonstrict in the last two arguments

$\mathcal{NRA}_{k+1}(\Sigma \cup \Omega) + fix_i^1$. As a consequence, by extending $\mathcal{NRA}(\Sigma)$ with any *of fix_i, fix_p, fix_i^1 or fix_p^1 we get, essentially, the same expressive power. Therefore, we shall abbreviate with $\mathcal{NRA}(\Sigma) + fix$ any of them.*

This proposition is in contrast to Abiteboul and Vianu's result in [7], that the inflationary and partial fixpoint have the same expressive power over first order logic iff $PTime = PSpace$.

Proof (Sketch) The partial fixpoint can express the inflationary fixpoint, because $fix_i(f) = fix_p(\lambda(x,y).y \cup f(x,y))$: so $\mathcal{NRA}_k(\Sigma) + fix_i^1 \subseteq \mathcal{NRA}_k(\Sigma) + fix_p^1$. Obviously, $\mathcal{NRA}_k(\Sigma) + fix_p^1 \subseteq \mathcal{NRA}_k(\Sigma) + fix_p$. So we only have to prove that $\mathcal{NRA}_k(\Sigma) + fix_p \subseteq \mathcal{NRA}_{k+1}(\Sigma) + fix_i^1$. Let $f : \sigma \times \tau \rightarrow \tau$. The idea for computing $fix_p(f)$, is to compute iteratively the sets $Y_n = \{y_0, y_1, \ldots, y_{n-1}\}$, where $y_0 = \emptyset$, $y_{k+1} = f(x, y_k)$. For this, define $g : \sigma \times \{\tau\} \rightarrow \{\tau\}$ to be: $g(x,Y) = \{\emptyset\} \cup (map\ \lambda y.f(x,y))(Y)$. Now if f has a partial fixpoint $y_n = fix_p(f)(x)$, then g has an inflationary fixpoint, namely $fix_i^1(g)(x) = \{y_0, y_1, \ldots, y_n\}$. So we start by computing $Y = fix_i^1(g)$. Next, we extract y_n from the set Y, by noticing that y_n is the only object $y \in Y$ having the property that $f(x,y) = y$. The problem is that sometimes $fix_i^1(g)(x)$ exists while $fix_p(f)(x)$ does not. E.g. when $y_4 = y_2$, then $fix_i^1(g)(x) = \{y_0, y_1, y_2, y_3\}$, while $fix_p(f)(x) =$ undefined. In this case, there is no $y \in Y$ s.t. $f(x,y) = y$, and, in order to simulate $fix_p(f)$, we have to return an undefined value - hence the necessity of having the Ω's in the language. So define $(fix_p\ f)(x) = if\ (\exists y \in fix_i^1(g)(x).(f(x,y) = y))\ then\ y\ else\ \Omega$[6]. Returning the unique y with the property that $f(x,y) = y$ may seem a problem: we can compute the singleton set $\{y\}$, but in general there is no way to extract the unique element from a set. In our case this *is* possible, because the type of y is a PS type. E.g. when $\tau = \{\tau_1\} \times \{\tau_2\}$, take $y = (\mu(\Pi_1(\{y\})), \mu(\Pi_2(\{y\})))$, etc. □

In particular, the above proof also implies that all total functions expressible in $\mathcal{NRA}(\Sigma) + fix_p$ are expressible in $\mathcal{NRA}(\Sigma) + fix_i^1$ as well, and that, by extending the definition of the partial fixpoint to a "total" fixpoint in a reasonable way, say by: $fix_t(f)(x) \stackrel{\text{def}}{=} y$ when $fix_p(f)(x)$ is defined and equal to y, and $fix_t(f)(x) \stackrel{\text{def}}{=} \emptyset$ otherwise, we get that $\mathcal{NRA}(\Sigma) + fix_t = \mathcal{NRA}(\Sigma) + fix_i$.

Example 2 *We present three ways to compute the powerset using the (unbounded) fixpoint. Consider the following functions $f_i : \{\sigma\} \times \{\{\sigma\}\} \rightarrow \{\{\sigma\}\}$, $i = 1,2,3$: $f_1(x,Y) \stackrel{\text{def}}{=} \{\emptyset\} \cup map(\eta)(x) \cup map(\lambda(y_1,y_2).y_1 \cup y_2)(Y \bowtie Y)$, $f_2(x,Y) \stackrel{\text{def}}{=} \{\emptyset\} \cup map(\lambda(e,y).ins(e,y))(x \bowtie Y)$, and $f_3(x,Y) \stackrel{\text{def}}{=} \{x\} \cup map(\lambda(e,y).\ del(e,y))(x \bowtie Y)$ (where $ins, del : \sigma \times \{\sigma\} \rightarrow \{\sigma\}$ are: $ins(e,x) \stackrel{\text{def}}{=} \{e\} \cup x$, $del(e,x) \stackrel{\text{def}}{=} x - \{e\}$). Then $fix(f_i) : \{\sigma\} \rightarrow \{\{\sigma\}\}$ computes the powerset, for all $i = 1,2,3$. In the same spirit, we can express the function $even : \{\sigma\} \rightarrow \{unit\}$, with $even(x) = true$ iff $card(x)$ is even, by first computing, using one of the above methods, the function $p : \{\sigma\} \rightarrow \{\{\sigma\} \times \{unit\}\}$, defined by $p(x) = \{(y, even(y)) \mid y \subseteq x\}$. In conjunction with proposition 5, this example shows that the unbounded fixpoint is strictly more powerful at higher types that the bounded fixpoint, even when $\Sigma = \emptyset$.*

[6] In the calculus-style language, Ω_σ is just a constant of type σ, instead of a function of type $unit \rightarrow \sigma$.

In fact, when $\Sigma = \emptyset$, fixpoints are as powerful as powerset. This can be shown using example 2 and the idea from the proof of proposition 2.

Proposition 3 $\mathcal{NRA} + fix = \mathcal{NRA} + powerset$.

Unbounded fixpoints are known to express all "elementary queries":

Proposition 4 *(See [12])* $\mathcal{NRA} + fix =$ *the class of all Kalmar elementary queries, i.e. whose time - or space - complexity is* $exp(k,n)$ *(for some* k*), where* $n =$ *the size of the input, and* $exp(0,n) = n$, $exp(k+1,n) = 2^{exp(k,n)}$. *More, when* $k \geq 1$, $\mathcal{NRA}_{k+1} + fix_i$ *coincides with all queries whose* time *complexity is* $O(exp(k,n^c))$ *(for some* $c > 0$*), while* $\mathcal{NRA}_{k+1} + fix_p$ *coincides with the queries whose* space *complexity is* $O(exp(k,n^c))$ *(for some* $c > 0$*).*

The condition $\Sigma = \emptyset$ is important. Example 3 below shows that, for a certain Σ, $\mathcal{NRA}(\Sigma) + fix$ can express all recursive queries.

Example 3 *Let* Nat *be the signature containing the type* nat *of natural numbers, and the function symbols* $0 : unit \to nat$, $succ : nat \to nat$. *Let* $p : nat \times nat \to \{unit\}$ *be some predicate expressible in* $\mathcal{NRA}(\Sigma) + fix$, *and* $\varphi : nat \to nat$ *be the partial function for which* $\varphi(x) =$ *the smallest number* y *satisfying* $p(x,y) = true$, *i.e.* $\varphi(x) \stackrel{\text{def}}{=} min\{y \mid p(x,y)\}$. *The function* $F(x) = \{0, 1, \ldots, \varphi(x)\}$ *is expressible in* $\mathcal{NRA}(Nat) + fix$, *as* $F(x) \stackrel{\text{def}}{=} fix(f)(x)$, *where* $f(x,y) = if\ ext(\lambda z.p(x,z))(y)\ then\ y\ else\ \{0\} \cup map(succ)(y)$. *Then, we can express* $\eta \circ \varphi : nat \to \{nat\}$ *as* $(\eta \circ \varphi)(x) \stackrel{\text{def}}{=} \{y \mid y \in F(x)\ and\ succ(y) \notin F(x)\}$. *This shows that the class of functions* $\varphi : nat \to nat$ *expressible in* $\mathcal{NRA}(Nat) + fix$ *is closed under the operation of minimization. In fact, we can prove that for any recursive* φ, *the function* $\eta \circ \varphi$ *is expressible in* $\mathcal{NRA}(Nat) + fix$. *This example shows that (1) for certain* Σ, $\mathcal{NRA}(\Sigma) + fix$ *can express more than just elementary queries, and (2) for certain* Σ, $\mathcal{NRA}_1(\Sigma) + fix$ *is more powerful than* $\mathcal{NRA}_1(\Sigma) + bfix$ *(see proposition 5 and lemma 1).*

For the bounded fixpoints, we have immediately:

Proposition 5 $\mathcal{NRA}(\Sigma) + bfix_p \subseteq PSpace$ *and* $\mathcal{NRA}(\Sigma) + bfix_i \subseteq PTime$, *provided that all functions in* Σ *are in* $PSpace$ *or* $PTime$ *respectively.*

Note that, in contrast to Proposition 4, this result holds for any Σ.

4 Main results

The main result of this paper is the following theorem (an extension of theorem 1), and in its corollary:

Theorem 2 *If all function symbols in* Σ *have set height* ≤ 1, *then*

1. $\mathcal{NRA}(\Sigma) + bfix$ *is a conservative extension of* $\mathcal{NRA}_1(\Sigma) + bfix$, *for both inflationary and partial fixpoint semantics. The latter is a conservative extension of the relational algebra with bounded fixpoints* $\mathcal{RA}(\Sigma) + bfix$.

2. *If I is an index type (to be defined), then $\mathcal{NRA}(\Sigma \cup I) + fix$ is a conservative extension of $\mathcal{NRA}_1(\Sigma \cup I) + fix$, which is, in turn, a conservative extension of $\mathcal{RA}(\Sigma \cup I) + fix$.*

The proof is given in sections 6 and 7, and consists essentially in encoding complex objects into flat relations with indexes, and in translating queries over complex objects into queries in the relational algebra extended with a function *pair* defined on the indexes. The translation also suggests a compilation method of complex objects into flat relations. The importance of the second part of the theorem lies in the fact that it shows that this compilation method works for queries with fixpoints as well as for queries with bounded fixpoints.

When $\Sigma = \emptyset$, then the bounded fixpoints and the unbounded fixpoint have the same expressive power over flat relations. More precisely:

Lemma 1 $\mathcal{NRA}_1 + fix_p = \mathcal{NRA}_1 + bfix_p$ *and* $\mathcal{NRA}_1 + fix_i = \mathcal{NRA}_1 + bfix_i$.

As we show in example 3 above, the condition $\Sigma = \emptyset$ is essential for this lemma.

Corollary 1

1. *$\mathcal{NRA} + bfix_p$ is a conservative extension of the relational algebra + partial fixpoint, which is equivalent to the while - queries ([11]), and to $DATALOG^{*\neg}$ ([6]).*

2. *$\mathcal{NRA} + bfix_i$ is a conservative extension of the relational algebra + inflationary fixpoint which is equivalent to $DATALOG^{\neg}$, and to the first order logic with (inflationary or monotone) fixpoints ([4], [6]).*

This result has as a negative consequence the fact that the inclusions from prop 5 are strict: the function *even* : $\{\sigma\} \rightarrow \{unit\}$ which is definable with fix by proposition 4, is not expressible with bounded fixpoints. On the other hand, no database query language capable of capturing *exactly* the *PTime* queries is currently known, so $bfix_i$ and $bfix_p$ seem to offer a reasonable extension to higher types, of the fixpoints in the relational algebra (or, equivalently, first order logic). As in the flat case, we have:

Theorem 3 $\mathcal{NRA} + bfix_p + order = PSpace$ *and* $\mathcal{NRA} + bfix_i + order = PTime$.

The proof goes along the lines of the proofs in [12] and [15], and is omitted.

5 A logic based language

We have two reasons for giving a logic based version of $\mathcal{NRA}(\Sigma) + bfix$. First, we want to gain a greater confidence in its robustness, and secondly, we want to understand how the bounded fixpoint can be expressed through range restriction.

We call our language $\mathcal{NRCALC}(\Sigma) + bfix$. It is strongly inspired by previous work ([1], [12], [13]), but its syntax is kept closer to the algebraic language, to simplify the proof of the conversions. Its main interest consists in the rules for range restriction, especially those connected to the fixpoint construction.

We consider a signature Σ given, as for $\mathcal{NRA}$. There is exactly one **input variable** for each type σ, x^σ, and there are denumerable many **variables** $u^\sigma, v^\sigma, \ldots$ for each type σ. The terms (t) and formulas (φ) are typed, and are defined inductively:

terms The following are terms: () (the empty tuple), x^σ, $u^\sigma, v^\sigma, w^\sigma, \ldots$ (variables), (t_1, t_2) (the tuple), $f(t)$ (where $f \in \Sigma$ is a function symbol), $\pi_i(t)$ (the i's projection, $i = 1, 2$), $\{u^\tau \mid \varphi\}$ where u^τ is a variable and φ is some formula (the type of this term is $\{\tau\}$). u^τ becomes bound in $\{u^\tau \mid \varphi\}$.

formulas The following are formulas: *true*, *false*, $t_1 \in t_2$, $t_1 = t_2$, $\varphi \wedge \psi$, $\varphi \vee \psi$, $\neg\varphi$ (where φ, ψ are formulas and t_1, t_2 are terms), $\exists u^\sigma \in t.\varphi$ (where u^σ is a variable, t is a term of type $\{\sigma\}$, and φ is some formula).

We extend the language with a fixpoint construction:

fixpoint $\mu w^{\{\tau\}}.\{u^\tau \mid \varphi\}$ is a term of type $\{\tau\}$, where $w^{\{\tau\}}$ and u^τ are variables, and φ is a formula. Both $w^{\{\tau\}}$ and u^τ become bound in $\mu w^{\{\tau\}}.\{u^\tau \mid \varphi\}$.

We shall assume that all bounded variables in some term t or formula φ are distinct, and distinct from the free variables[7].

A **query** of type $\sigma \to \tau$ in $\mathcal{NRCALC}(\Sigma)$ or $\mathcal{NRCALC}(\Sigma) + fix$, is simply a term of type τ, having only one free variable, namely x^σ, the input variable of type σ. Note that, although we can write some purely algebraic queries, like $(f(\pi_1(x), \pi_2(x)), g(\pi_2(x)))$, for "real" database queries one has to make use of formulas, like in $unnest : \{\sigma \times \{\tau\}\} \to \{\sigma \times \tau\}$: $unnest \stackrel{\text{def}}{=} \{u \mid \exists v \in x.\exists w \in \pi_2(v).u = (\pi_1(v), w)\}$, or in the following $nest$ query, $\{\sigma \times \tau\} \to \{\sigma \times \{\tau\}\}$, $nest \stackrel{\text{def}}{=} \{u \mid \exists v \in x.u = (\pi_1(v), \{w \mid (\pi_1(v), w) \in x\})\}$.

The values of terms and formulas depend on the values assigned to their free variables. Formulas can be *true*, *false*, or undefined. $\exists u \in t.\varphi$, is interpreted as follows: it is defined iff t is defined, and for all $a \in t$, $\varphi[u/a]$ is defined; in that case, $\exists u \in t.\varphi = true$ iff there is some $a \in t$ s.t. $\varphi[u/a] = true$. The interpretation of the term $\{u \mid \varphi\}$ is the set $\{\alpha \mid \varphi[u/\alpha] = true\}$; it is undefined, if the latter set is infinite[8]. For the fixpoint construction, we consider both inflationary and partial interpretations.

To avoid exponential queries, like the powerset of $x^{\{\sigma\}}$, $\{u^{\{\sigma\}} \mid \forall v^\sigma \in u^{\{\sigma\}}.v^\sigma \in x^{\{\sigma\}}\}$ ($\forall$ is expressed using $\exists$ and $\neg$), or domain dependent queries, like $\{u^\sigma \mid \neg u^\sigma \in x^{\{\sigma\}}\}$, we restrict the language, to the *range restricted* sublanguage $(\mathcal{NRCALC}(\Sigma) + bfix)^{rr}$. For this, let M be a term or a formula: we define certain subterm occurrences t to be range restricted in M - and then we write $\underline{t}$ -, and certain variables v to be range restricted in a subterm or subformula occurrences N of M - then we write $\underbrace{N}_{v}$. The following rules define the range restriction. Recall that the range restriction is a property of a subterm or subformula occurrence N, of some term or formula M.

$$\frac{op(\underline{t_1}, \ldots, \underline{t_m})}{\underline{op(t_1, \ldots, t_m)}} \text{(op is any operation)} \qquad \frac{(t_1, t_2)}{(\underline{t_1}, \underline{t_2})} \qquad \frac{}{\underline{()}}$$

[7] Any term or formula can be converted to an equivalent form, which satisfies this requirement, by renaming the bound variables.

[8] This will be impossible in the range restricted version of $\mathcal{NRCALC}$, to be defined below.

$$\underline{x} \; (x \text{ is the input variable}) \qquad \frac{t_1 \in \underline{t_2}}{\underline{t_1} \in \underline{t_2}} \qquad \frac{\underline{t_1} = t_2}{\underline{t_1} = \underline{t_2}} \qquad \frac{t_1 = \underline{t_2}}{\underline{t_1} = \underline{t_2}}$$

$$\frac{\underline{u}}{\underbrace{u}_{u}} \qquad \frac{\underbrace{u}_{u}}{\underline{u}} \qquad \frac{}{\underbrace{\mathit{false}}_{u}}$$

$$\frac{\underbrace{op(t_1, \ldots, t_m)}_{u}}{op(\underbrace{t_1}_{u}, \ldots, \underbrace{t_m}_{u})} \qquad \frac{op(t_1, \ldots, \underbrace{t_i}_{u}, \ldots, t_m)}{\underbrace{op(t_1, \ldots, t_m)}_{u}}$$

$$\frac{\underbrace{t_1}_{u} \in t_2}{\underbrace{t_1 \in t_2}_{u}} \qquad \frac{\underbrace{t_1 \in t_2}_{u}}{\underbrace{t_1}_{u} \in \underbrace{t_2}_{u}}$$

$$\frac{\underbrace{t_1}_{u} = t_2}{\underbrace{t_1 = t_2}_{u}} \qquad \frac{t_1 = \underbrace{t_2}_{u}}{\underbrace{t_1 = t_2}_{u}} \qquad \frac{\underbrace{t_1 = t_2}_{u}}{\underbrace{t_1}_{u} = \underbrace{t_2}_{u}}$$

$$\frac{\{u \mid \underbrace{\varphi}_{u}\}}{\underline{\{u \mid \varphi\}}} \qquad \frac{\mu w.\{u \mid \underbrace{\varphi}_{u}\}}{\underline{\mu w.\{u \mid \varphi\}}}$$

$$\frac{\exists u \in \underline{t}.\varphi}{\exists u \in \underline{t}.\underbrace{\varphi}_{u}} \qquad \frac{\exists u \in t.\underbrace{\varphi}_{v}}{\underbrace{\exists u \in t.\varphi}_{v}} \qquad \frac{\underbrace{\exists u \in t.\varphi}_{v}}{\exists u \in t.\underbrace{\varphi}_{v}}$$

$$\frac{\underbrace{\varphi}_{u} \wedge \psi}{\underbrace{\varphi \wedge \psi}_{u}} \qquad \frac{\varphi \wedge \underbrace{\psi}_{u}}{\underbrace{\varphi \wedge \psi}_{u}} \qquad \frac{\underbrace{\varphi \wedge \psi}_{u}}{\underbrace{\varphi}_{u} \wedge \underbrace{\psi}_{u}}$$

$$\frac{\underbrace{\varphi}_{u} \vee \underbrace{\psi}_{u}}{\underbrace{\varphi \vee \psi}_{u}} \qquad \frac{\underbrace{\varphi \vee \psi}_{u}}{\underbrace{\varphi}_{u} \vee \underbrace{\psi}_{u}} \qquad \frac{\underbrace{\neg\varphi}_{u}}{\neg \underbrace{\varphi}_{u}}$$

Note that, when a variable u is range restricted in the subformula φ of $\varphi \wedge \psi$, then it is range restricted also in ψ; this does *not* hold for $\vee$. Also, note the rule for the fixpoint (μ): we must be able to prove that u is range restricted, without assuming anything about the fixpoint variable w (which, in fact, may not be range restricted). This is a different approach than in [12].

A query is **range restricted** if it is range restricted as a term, and if all subterms occurring as bounds for quantifiers are range restricted (i.e. the quantifiers are of the form $\exists u \in \underline{t}.\varphi$). The **range restricted** fragment $(\mathcal{NRCALC}(\Sigma) + fix)^{rr}$ of $\mathcal{NRCALC}(\Sigma) + fix$ is defined to contain only the range restricted queries.

Example 4 *nest defined above is range restricted. Indeed:*

$$\{u \mid \exists v \in \underline{x}.u = (\pi_1(v), \{w \mid (\pi_1(v), w) \in \underline{x}\})\}$$

$$\{u \mid \exists v \in x.\underbrace{u = (\pi_1(v), \{w \mid (\pi_1(v), w) \in \underline{x}\})}_{v}\}$$

$$\{u \mid \exists v \in x.u = \underbrace{(\pi_1(v), \{w \mid (\pi_1(v), w) \in \underline{x}\})}_{v}\}$$

$$\{u \mid \exists v \in x.u = (\underbrace{\pi_1(v)}_{v}, \{w \mid (\pi_1(v), w) \in \underline{x}\})\}$$

$$\{u \mid \exists v \in x.u = (\pi_1(\underbrace{v}_{v}), \{w \mid (\pi_1(v), w) \in \underline{x}\})\}$$

$$\{u \mid \exists v \in x.u = (\pi_1(\underline{v}), \{w \mid (\pi_1(v), w) \in \underline{x}\})\}$$

$$\{u \mid \exists v \in x.u = (\underline{\pi_1(v)}, \{w \mid \underline{(\pi_1(v), w)} \in x\})\}$$

$$\{u \mid \exists v \in x.u = (\underline{\pi_1(v)}, \{w \mid (\pi_1(v), \underline{w}) \in x\})\}$$

$$\{u \mid \exists v \in x.u = (\underline{\pi_1(v)}, \{w \mid (\pi_1(v), \underbrace{w}_{w}) \in x\})\}$$

$$\{u \mid \exists v \in x.u = (\underline{\pi_1(v)}, \{w \mid \underbrace{(\pi_1(v), w) \in x}_{w}\})\}$$

$$\{u \mid \exists v \in x.u = (\underline{\pi_1(v)}, \underline{\{w \mid (\pi_1(v), w) \in x\}})\}$$

$$\{u \mid \exists v \in x.\underline{u} = (\pi_1(v), \{w \mid (\pi_1(v), w) \in x\})\}$$

$$\{u \mid \exists v \in x.\underbrace{u}_{u} = (\pi_1(v), \{w \mid (\pi_1(v), w) \in x\})\}$$

$$\{u \mid \underbrace{\exists v \in x.u = (\pi_1(v), \{w \mid (\pi_1(v), w) \in x\})}_{u}\}$$

$$\underline{\{u \mid \exists v \in x.u = (\pi_1(v), \{w \mid (\pi_1(v), w) \in x\})\}}$$

As this example shows, proving range restriction of some term requires us to apply several rules on subterms/subformulas of the same *term or formula.*

Theorem 4 *$(\mathcal{NRCALC}(\Sigma) + fix)^{rr}$ and $\mathcal{NRA}(\Sigma) + bfix$ have the same expressive power.*

6 Encoding of $\mathcal{NRA}(\Sigma)$ $(+fix, +bfix)$ into the relational algebra with indexes

In this section, we present the technique used for proving the conservativity result (theorem 2). The idea is to encode $\mathcal{NRA}(\Sigma) + bfix$ into the relational algebra over the same signature Σ plus indexes: $\mathcal{RA}(\Sigma \cup I) + bfix$.

First we consider the case when all function symbols in Σ have the set height 0. That is, Σ may contain functions like $add : nat \times nat \to nat$ or $zero : unit \to nat$, but not functions like $card : \{b\} \to nat$ or $sum : \{nat\} \to nat$. Later we show how to extend this result to the case when Σ may contain functions of set height ≤ 1. We define the **the relational algebra** $\mathcal{RA}(\Sigma)$ to be a minor extension of the traditional relational algebra, as presented in [19]: its types (called **flat types**) are $\{t\}$ (with $sh(t) = 0$), and $\sigma \times \tau$ (with σ, τ flat types), and its operations contain union ($\cup$), difference ($-$), cartesian product ($\bowtie$), all functions of the form $map(f)$ with f in $\mathcal{NRA}_0(\Sigma)$[9], and all selection functions $\sigma_p : \{t\} \to \{t\}$, where $p : t \to \{unit\}$ is in $\mathcal{NRA}_0(\Sigma)$[10]. In addition, $\mathcal{RA}(\Sigma)$ contains the empty set $\emptyset : \{t\} \to \{t'\}$[11], and not. $\mathcal{RA}(\Sigma) + fix$ and $\mathcal{RA}(\Sigma) + bfix$ are extensions obtained by adding fix or $bfix$.

An **index** set is a base type I together with an injective function $pair : I \times I \to I$ (so I is infinite), and two distinct constants $left, right : unit \to I$. We write $\Sigma \cup I$ for the signature Σ extended with I, $left$, $right$ and $pair$.

The translation of $\mathcal{NRA}(\Sigma)$ ($+fix$ or $+bfix$) into $\mathcal{RA}(\Sigma \cup I)$ ($+fix$ or $+bfix$), begins with the translation of types: each type σ in $\mathcal{NRA}$ is translated into a flat type π_σ in $\mathcal{RA}$. Then, we define an *encoding relation* for each type: $\sim_\sigma \subseteq \sigma \times \pi_\sigma$. When $x \in \sigma$ and $r \in \pi_\sigma$, then $x \sim_\sigma r$ means that "r is an encoding of x": each x has at least one encoding (but it may have several), and it turns out that not every $r \in \pi_\sigma$ is somebody's encoding. However, the encoding is injective ($x \sim_\sigma r$, $x' \sim_\sigma r \Rightarrow x = x'$), and the decoding function $decode_\sigma : \pi_\sigma \to \sigma$ is also injective, expressible in $\mathcal{NRA}$, and is even in $\mathcal{RA}$, when σ is flat. Finally, we define a translation of some function $f : \sigma \to \tau$ in $\mathcal{NRA}(\Sigma)$ ($+fix$ or $+bfix$) into a function $R_f : \pi_\sigma \to \pi_\tau$ in $\mathcal{RA}(\Sigma \cup I) + bfix$, such that the following **soundness** property holds: $x \sim_\sigma r \Rightarrow f(x) \sim_\tau R_f(r)$.

The translation of types and the encoding relation are: $\pi_b \stackrel{\text{def}}{=} \{b\}$ and $\forall x \in b, x \sim_b \{x\}$, $\pi_{\sigma\times\tau} \stackrel{\text{def}}{=} \pi_\sigma \times \pi_\tau$ and $(x, y) \sim_{\sigma\times\tau} (r, q)$ iff $x \sim_\sigma r$ and $y \sim_\tau q$. The difficult part is encoding $\{\sigma\}$. Recall that π_σ is a flat type, and we need to encode finite sets r from π_σ (i.e. $r \in \{\pi_\sigma\}$) also as elements of some flat type. The idea is to encode r as a partial function $\psi : I \Rightarrow \pi_\sigma$ having the range r. The function is *finite*, i.e. it is defined only on a finite subset of I. Suppose π_σ is a set type, say $\pi_\sigma = \{t\}$. A straightforward representation of such a function is as a binary relation of type $\{I \times \{t\}\}$. However, this relation is not flat, and we need a more sophisticated approach, namely we unnest the above relation, to get a relation of type $\{I \times t\}$, and denote this type by $[I \to \pi_\sigma]$. Any relation $R \in [I \to \pi_\sigma]$ encodes some partial, finite function $\psi : I \to \pi_\sigma$, namely

[9] These are generalized projections. E.g. from $\pi_1 : t_1 \times t_2 \to t_1$ is in $\mathcal{NRA}_0(\Sigma)$, we get $\Pi_1 \stackrel{\text{def}}{=} map(\pi_1)$ in $\mathcal{RA}(\Sigma)$.

[10] $\sigma_p \stackrel{\text{def}}{=} ext(\Pi_2 \circ \bowtie \circ (p, \eta))$. E.g. from $p : (b \times b) \times t \to \{unit\}$, $p = eq \circ \pi_1$, we get the selection σ_p, traditionally written as $\sigma_{1=2}$.

[11] Recall that the type $unit$ is not in $\mathcal{RA}(\Sigma)$.

$\forall i \in \Pi_1(R)$, $\psi(i) \stackrel{\text{def}}{=} \Pi_2(\sigma_{1=i}(R))$, and $\forall i \in I - \Pi_1(R)$, $\psi(i) = \text{undefined}$. This is almost what we need, except that we cannot encode functions ψ for which for some $i \in I$, $\psi(i)$ is defined and is $\emptyset$. To take this into account, let $dom(\psi)$ be the finite domain of ψ. We represent ψ by $(dom(\psi), R)$, a relation of type $\{I\} \times [I \rightarrow \pi_\sigma]$: we denote this type by $[I \Rightarrow \pi_\sigma]$. Any finite, partial function $\psi : I \rightarrow \pi_\sigma$ has a representation as a pair of flat relations of type $[I \Rightarrow \pi_\sigma]$, and any such pair (D, R) with the property that $\Pi_1(R) \subseteq D$ represents some function ψ.

Formally, for any flat type $\nu = \{t_1\} \times \ldots \times \{t_n\}$, we define $[I \rightarrow \nu] \stackrel{\text{def}}{=} \{I \times t_1\} \times \ldots \times \{I \times t_n\}$ and $[I \Rightarrow \nu] \stackrel{\text{def}}{=} \{I\} \times [I \rightarrow \nu]$. There is a one to one correspondence between the partial, finite, *nonempty*[12] functions $\psi : I \rightarrow \nu$ and the elements of type $[I \rightarrow \nu]$, and there is a one to one correspondence between the partial finite functions $\psi : I \rightarrow \nu$ and those values $(D, R_1, \ldots, R_n)$ of type $[I \Rightarrow \nu]$ which satisfy $\Pi_1(R_1) \subseteq D, \ldots, \Pi_1(R_n) \subseteq D$: for some partial finite function ψ, we denote $rel(\psi)$ its encoding in $[I \Rightarrow \nu]$.

Returning to our translation of types, we define $\pi_{\{\sigma\}} \stackrel{\text{def}}{=} [I \Rightarrow \pi_\sigma]$ and $x \sim_{\{\sigma\}} r$ iff there are two finite, partial functions $\omega : I \Rightarrow \sigma$ and $\psi : I \Rightarrow \pi_\sigma$, such that $dom(\omega) = dom(\psi)$, $\forall i \in dom(\psi).\omega(i) \sim_\sigma \psi(i)$ and $x = range(\omega)$, $r = rel(\psi)$.

The encoding of the operations $f \rightsquigarrow R_f$ proceeds in two steps. First, one encodes all operations f from $\mathcal{NRA}(\Sigma)$ (i.e. without fixpoints). $\mu : \{\{\sigma\}\} \rightarrow \{\sigma\}$ is translated int $R_\mu : [I \Rightarrow [I \Rightarrow \sigma]] \rightarrow [I \Rightarrow \sigma]$ as follows: first one notes that $[I \Rightarrow [I \Rightarrow \sigma]] = \{I\} \times [I \times I \Rightarrow \sigma]$, so R_μ is defined using $pair : I \times I \rightarrow I$, which extends (via *map*) to a function $[pair \Rightarrow \sigma] : [I \times I \Rightarrow \sigma] \rightarrow [I \Rightarrow \sigma]$. The injectivity of *pair* is used in the proof of the soundness of R_μ. Instead of $\cup$, we encode $doubleton$[13] $: \sigma \times \sigma \rightarrow \{\sigma\}$ by using $left$ and $right$, and use $left \neq right$ for soundness ($\cup$ is defined indirectly, using *doubleton*), $R_{map(f)} \stackrel{\text{def}}{=} [I \Rightarrow R_f]$. η is translated using $left$ (chosen arbitrarily from $left$ and $right$). Some function symbol $f : t_1 \times \ldots \times t_m \rightarrow t$ in Σ, is encoded by $R_f : \{t_1\} \times \ldots \times \{t_m\} \rightarrow \{t\}$, $R_f(r_1, \ldots, r_m) \stackrel{\text{def}}{=} map(f)(r_1 \bowtie \ldots \bowtie r_m)$. The rest of the cases are trivial.

Note that $R_\cup \neq \cup$ and $R_\cap \neq \cap$: both $\cup$ and $\cap$ are derived operations. More, even if σ is a set type and $r, q \in \pi_\sigma$ are valid encodings (of, say, x and y), it is not necessarily the case that $r \cup q$ is a valid encoding[14], because r and q might accidentally use the same index for encoding different elements. Therefore, the encoding of $bfix$ and fix has to be done with some care, and we use different techniques for each of them.

To encode $bfix(f, g)$, we proceed as follows. Suppose $f : \sigma \times \tau \rightarrow \tau$, $g : \sigma \rightarrow \tau$ (τ a PS type), and let R_f, R_g be their translations. Define $Q : \pi_\sigma \times \pi_\tau \rightarrow \pi_\tau$ as follows. To compute $Q(r, q)$, first compute $s \stackrel{\text{def}}{=} R_f(r, q)$ and $t \stackrel{\text{def}}{=} R_g(q)$. Next "decode" s, t to get $u, v \in \tau$. Intersect them, to get $w \stackrel{\text{def}}{=} u \cap v$, and encode w, using the indexes from t: all this can be done in $\mathcal{RA}$. We define the result to be $Q(r, q)$. So, $Q(r, q) \subseteq R_g(q)$ and, whenever $x \sim_\sigma r$, $y \sim_\tau q$, we

[12] I.e. when $\psi(i)$ is defined, then $\psi(i) \neq (\emptyset, \ldots, \emptyset)$.

[13] $doubleton : \sigma \times \sigma \rightarrow \{\sigma\}$ is defined as $\cup \circ (\eta \times \eta)$, with the meaning $doubleton(x, y) = \{x, y\}$. Then $\cup \stackrel{\text{def}}{=} \mu \circ doubleton$.

[14] At first glance, one would expect $r \cup q$ to be an encoding of $x \cup y$.

have $f(x,y) \cap g(x) \sim_\tau Q(r,q)$. Finally, define $R_{bfix(f,g)} \stackrel{\text{def}}{=} bfix(Q, R_g)$. For the partial fixpoint, the soundness of the translation follows immediately, for the inflationary fixpoint we need to observe that $x \sim r$, $y \sim q$, $z \sim s$ and $x \subseteq z$, $y \subseteq z$, $r \subseteq s$, $q \subseteq s$ implies $x \cup y \sim r \cup q$.

To encode $fix(f)$, where $f : \sigma \times \tau \to \tau$, one defines $Q : \pi_\sigma \times \pi_\tau \to \pi_\tau$ as follows. First, compute $s \stackrel{\text{def}}{=} R_f(r,q)$, where R_f is the translation of f, and let s' be the set of "new" values, i.e. which were not in q: more precisely, $s' = R_-(s,q)$, where R_- is the translation of $-$ (minus). As for the bounded fixpoint, decode s and q to get $u, v \in \tau$, compute $w \stackrel{\text{def}}{=} u \cap v$, and encode w using the indexes from q: call the result q'. We would like to define $Q(r,q) \stackrel{\text{def}}{=} s' \cup q'$, but the latter is not necessarily a valid encoding, because s' and q' may accidentally use common indexes. So we repeatedly change all indexes used in s', by replacing each index i with $pair(left, i)$, until none of its indexes occurs in q': an unbounded fixpoint is needed at this stage, and we assume that $(I, pair)$ is freely generated, to make sure that this process halts. Call s'' the result (i.e. both s' and s'' encode the same value, but they may use different indexes). Then define $Q(r,q) \stackrel{\text{def}}{=} s'' \cup q'$. Clearly $R_f(r,q)$ and $Q(r,q)$ are encodings of the same value, but Q ensures that $f(x, y_n) \subseteq y_n$ implies $Q(r, q_n) \subseteq q_n$. Finally, define $R_{fix(f)} \stackrel{\text{def}}{=} fix(Q)$.

This construction is enough to prove that $\mathcal{NRA}(\Sigma \cup I) + fix$, and $\mathcal{NRA}(\Sigma \cup I) + bfix$, are conservative extensions of $\mathcal{RA}(\Sigma \cup I) + fix$, and $\mathcal{RA}(\Sigma \cup I) + bfix$ respectively, and, hence, that all expressions over flat types in $\mathcal{NRA}(\Sigma) + fix$ and $\mathcal{NRA}(\Sigma) + bfix$ are also in $\mathcal{RA}(\Sigma \cup I) + fix$ and $\mathcal{RA}(\Sigma \cup I) + bfix$ respectively. Using this result, it is straightforward to prove that $\mathcal{NRA}(\Sigma \cup I) + fix$ and $\mathcal{NRA}(\Sigma \cup I) + bfix$ are also conservative extensions of $\mathcal{NRA}_1(\Sigma \cup I) + fix$ and $\mathcal{NRA}_1(\Sigma \cup I) + bfix$ respectively. This concludes the proof of the part 2 of theorem 2. For the part 1 however, we need to eliminate the indexes from R_f, when $f : \sigma \to \tau$ is a function over flat types, which is done in the next section.

7 Elimination of indexes for encodings of flat relations

Let σ, τ be flat types, and $f : \sigma \to \tau$ be a function in $\mathcal{NRA}(\Sigma) + bfix$. Compose the function $R_f : \pi_\sigma \to \pi_\tau$ (which is in $\mathcal{RA}(\Sigma \cup I) + bfix$), with $decode_\tau : \pi_\tau \to \tau$ (which is expressible in $\mathcal{RA}$), to get $Q : \pi_\sigma \to \tau$, with the property $x \sim_\sigma r \Rightarrow f(x) = Q(r)$. Then, we use the following:

Lemma 2 *Let $Q : \pi_\sigma \to \tau$ be in $\mathcal{RA}(\Sigma \cup I) + bfix$, such that, for any index I, if $r, r' \in \pi_\sigma$ are encodings of the same $x \in \sigma$, then $Q(r) = Q(r')$. Then there is some function $g : \sigma \to \tau$ in $\mathcal{RA}(\Sigma) + bfix$ (without indexes), such that $x \sim_\sigma r \Rightarrow g(x) = Q(r)$.*

Proof (Sketch) For simplicity, assume $\sigma = \{t_1\} \times \{t_2\}$, where $t_1 = b$ and $t_2 = b \times b$: then $\pi_\sigma = (\{I\} \times \{I \times b\}) \times (\{I\} \times \{I \times b\} \times \{I \times b\})$. In general, there is no function $encode_I : \sigma \to \pi_\sigma$ in $\mathcal{RA}$, with the property: $x \sim_\sigma encode_I(x)$, $\forall x \in \sigma$, simply because such a function would not be *generic*. We consider a particular index set I, namely the smallest set containing the disjoint union $unit_1 \sqcup unit_2 \sqcup t_1 \sqcup t_2$[15], and closed under pairing (i.e. $x, y \in I \Rightarrow (x, y) \in I$). Define $pair(x, y) \stackrel{\text{def}}{=} (x, y)$, $left \stackrel{\text{def}}{=} ()_1$ and $right \stackrel{\text{def}}{=} ()_2$. Then t_1 and t_2 are subtypes of I, so $(\{t_1\} \times \{t_1 \times b\}) \times (\{t_2\} \times \{t_2 \times b\} \times \{t_2 \times b\}) \subseteq \pi_\sigma$, and $\mathcal{RA}$ can express some function $encode : \sigma \rightarrow (\{t_1\} \times \{t_1 \times b\}) \times (\{t_2\} \times \{t_2 \times b\} \times \{t_2 \times b\})$ with the above property (but, of course, with a different type). As defined, I is a disjoint union of scalar types. Now, we look at the syntactic structure of the expression $Q(r)$ as a tree, and label its nodes with their types. In this tree, we replace the lowest occurrences of I (namely in the type π_σ of the input variable r), with the subtypes t_1 and t_2 respectively (π_σ becomes now $(\{t_1\} \times \{t_1 \times b\}) \times (\{t_2\} \times \{t_2 \times b\} \times \{t_2 \times b\})$). Step by step, we transform the tree $Q(r)$ bottom up, into an equivalent expression, such that any occurrence of the type I is replaced by some of its subtypes t. At the same time, each occurrence of the function $pair : I \times I \rightarrow I$, is replaced by the identity $id : t \times t' \rightarrow t \times t'$, for appropriate subtypes $t, t', t \times t'$ of I, while $left$ and $right$ are replaced by $()$. Call $\bar{Q}$ the resulting expression: then take $g(x) \stackrel{\text{def}}{=} \bar{Q}(encode(x))$. $\Box$

We end this section, with a comment about the case when Σ contains function symbols of set height 1, e.g. aggregate functions, like $sum : \{nat\} \rightarrow nat$, or generators like $gen : nat \rightarrow \{nat\}$ ($gen(n) \stackrel{\text{def}}{=} \{0, 1, \ldots, n\}$). Then, we proceed as above, with one exception: to define R_f for function symbols $f \in \Sigma$ whose range is a set, say $\{s\}$, we need index invention. So we add to the definition of an index I, a family of "invention" functions $c_s : \{s\} \rightarrow \{I \times s\}$, for each set type $\{s\}$ which is the range of some function symbol in Σ. These too can be eliminated, like in the proof of lemma 2, by imposing s to be a subtype of I, and replacing c_s with $map(id, id) : \{s\} \rightarrow \{s \times s\}$.

8 Concluding remarks and further research

We have investigated the power of the nested relational algebra enriched with a bounded fixpoint. The language turned out to be still of polynomial time or space complexity - according to the interpretation of the fixpoint: inflationary or partial - and it can express all *PTime* or *PSpace* queries over ordered databases. The main result consists in proving that, over flat relations, the language has the same expressive power as the first order logic with inflationary or partial fixpoints. We also define a logic based language, having the same expressive power.

The method used in the proof of the conservativity result could be used as a compilation technique, for encoding complex objects by flat relations, and for translating queries in $\mathcal{NRA} + bfix$ into queries of the relational algebra extended with a function *pair* and with bounded fixpoints.

Rather than having a fixed interpretation, the function *pair* is more like an oracle, which may be consulted when computing some query: this view is different from that of *interpreted* functions in [1]. By defining $succ(x) \stackrel{\text{def}}{=} pair(x, x)$ and $nat \stackrel{\text{def}}{=} \{left, succ(left), succ^2(left), \ldots\} \subseteq I$, we can express in $\mathcal{NRA}(\Sigma \cup I) + fix$ all partial recursive functions over *nat*: however, unlike [1], the query $p(x) = \{y \mid pair(y, y) = x\}$ is not expressible in this language.

[15] $unit_1 = unit_2 = unit$: we just want, for the moment, to distinguish the two copies in I.

We would like to investigate such "queries with oracles" in the future. For example, it might be useful to redefine the notion of a generic function, such that the p is no longer "generic"; we hope to be able to prove that all generic functions are expressible in $\mathcal{NRA}(\Sigma \cup I) + fix$. We also intend to compare the expressive power of our language with that of $RR - (CALC + IFP)$ and $RR - (CALC + PFP)$, in [12].

Finally, we believe that our methods can be extended to show that, for any $k \geq 1$, $\mathcal{NRA}(\Sigma) + bfix$ is a conservative extension of $\mathcal{NRA}_k(\Sigma) + bfix$, provided that all functions in Σ have set height $\leq k$.

9 Acknowledgements

I wish to give special thanks to Val Breazu-Tannen, for numerous discussions and comments, to Peter Buneman, for his suggestions and encouragement, and to Catriel Beeri, for his careful reading of this paper, and for his many comments and suggestions. I also wish to thank Leonid Libkin and Limsoon Wong, for their help and suggestions.

References

[1] S. Abiteboul, C. Beeri, *On the power of languages for the manipulation of complex objects*, Technical Report 846, INRIA, 1988

[2] S. Abiteboul, S. Grumbach, A. Voisard, E. Waller *An Extensible Rule-Based Language with Complex Objects and Data-Functions*, Proc. DBPL-II Workshop, Oregon, 1989

[3] S. Abiteboul, P. Kanellakis, *Object Identity as a Query Language Primitive*, Proc. of ACM SIGMOD conf, 1989

[4] S. Abiteboul, M. Vardi, V. Vianu, *Fixpoint Logics, Relational Machines, and Computational Complexity*, Proc. Conf. on Structure in Complexity Theory, 1992.

[5] S Abiteboul, V. Vianu, *Fixpoint extensions of first-order logic and Datalog-like languages*, Proc. 4th IEEE Symp. on Logic in Computer Science, pp 71-79, 1989

[6] S. Abiteboul, V. Vianu, *Expressive Power of Query Languages*, Theoretical Studies in Computer Science, ed. J. Ullman, Academic Press, 1991.

[7] S. Abiteboul, V Vianu, *Generic Computation and Its Complexity*, Proc ACM Symposium on Theory of Computing, 1991

[8] V. Breazu-Tannen, P. Buneman, S. Naqvi, *Structural Recursion As A Query Language*, MS-CIS-92-17., University of Pennsylvania

[9] V. Breazu-Tannen, P. Buneman, L. Wong, *Naturally Embedded Query Languages*, in Biskup and Hull, editors, LNCS 646: *Proceedings of the International Conference on Database Theory, Berlin, Germany*, October 1992, Springer-Verlag

[10] A. Chandra, D. Harel, *Computable Queries for Relational Data Bases*, Journal of Computer and System Sciences, 21:156-178, 1980

[11] A. Chandra, D. Harel, *Structure and complexity of relational queries*, Journal of Computer and System Sciences, 25:99-128, 1982

[12] S. Grumbach, V. Vianu, *Tractable Query Languages for Complex Object Databases*, Proc ACM SIGACT-SIGMOD-SIGART Symposium on Principles of Database Systems, 1991

[13] R. Hull, J. Su, *On the Expressive Power of Database Queries with Intermediate Types* Proc 7th Symp. on Principles of Database Systems, 1988

[14] R. Hull, J.Su, *Untyped Sets, Invention and Computable Queries* Proc 8th ACM Symp. on Principles of Database Systems, 1989

[15] N. Immerman, *Relational queries computable in polynomial time*, Information and Control, 68:86-104, 1986

[16] L. Libkin, L. Wong, *Aggregate Functions, Conservative Extension, and Linear Orders*, Proc. 4th International Workshop in Database Programming Languages, 1993 (this volume)

[17] J Paredaens, D Van Gucht, *Converting nested algebra expressions into flat algebra expressions* ACM Transactions on Database Systems, 17(1):65-93, 1992

[18] Yatin Saraiya, *Fixpoints and optimizations in a language based on structural recursion on sets*, Manuscript, December 1992.

[19] J. D. Ullman, *Database and Knowledge-Base Systems*, Vol I and II, Computer Science Press, 1989

[20] J. Van den Bussche, *Complex Object Manipulation through Identifiers - an Algebraic Perspective*, TR 92-41, Universitaire Instelling Antwerpen, Sept. 1992

[21] M. Vardi, *The complexity of relational query languages*, Proc ACM SIGACT Symp. on the Theory of Computing, pp 137-146, 1982

[22] D. Van Gucht, P. Fischer *Multilevel Nested Relational Structures*, Journal of Computer and System Sciences 36, 77-105, 1988

[23] L. Wong, *Normal Forms and Conservative Properties for Query Languages over Collection Types*, to appear in PODS 93

Aggregate Functions, Conservative Extension, and Linear Orders

Leonid Libkin Limsoon Wong

Department of Computer and Information Science
University of Pennsylvania
Philadelphia, PA 19104-6389, USA

1 Summary

Practical database query languages are usually equipped with some aggregate functions. For example, "find mean of column" can be expressed in SQL. However, the manner in which aggregate functions were introduced in these query languages leaves something to be desired. Breazu-Tannen, Buneman, and Wong [3] introduced a nested relational language $\mathcal{NRC}(=)$ based on monads [16, 24] and structural recursion [1, 2]. It was shown in Wong [27] that this language is equivalent to the nested relational algebras of Thomas and Fischer [22], Schek and Scholl [20], and Colby [4]. $\mathcal{NRC}(=)$ enjoys certain advantages over these languages: it is naturally embedded in functional languages, it is readily extensible, and it has a compact equational theory. Therefore, it is used in this report as a basis for investigating aggregate functions.

In section 2, the nested relational calculus $\mathcal{NRC}(=)$ is described. It is then endowed with rational numbers, rational arithmetic, and a summation operator. The augmented language, $\mathcal{NRC}(\mathbb{Q}, +, \cdot, -, \div, \sum, =)$, is able to express a variety of aggregate functions commonly found in real database query languages. The main results of this paper remain valid in a uniform way if any summation-like primitive, such as bounded product, is added to the language. This approach is more disciplined and general than those proposed by Klug [12], Ozsoyoglu, Ozsoyoglu, and Matos [18], and Klausner and Goodman [11].

In section 3, we prove that every function $f : s \to t$ expressible in $\mathcal{NRC}(\mathbb{Q}, +, \cdot, -, \div, \sum, =)$ can be computed without using any intermediate data whose depth of nesting of sets exceeds that of the input and output. This is known as the *conservative extension* property. Conservativity of nested relational query languages in the absence of aggregate functions was studied by Paredaens and Van Gucht [19] and Wong [26]. The former proved that it holds when input and output are flat relations. The latter generalized it to any input and output. Conservativity in the presence of aggregate functions was not previously studied.

In section 4, the conservative extension property is used to demonstrate the somewhat surprising fact that $\mathcal{NRC}(\mathbb{Q}, +, \cdot, -, \div, \sum, =)$ cannot express the usual linear ordering on rational numbers. As linear orders play a central role in fundamental data organization algorithms [14], this calls for special attention. We present a technique for lifting linear order at base types to linear order at all types. This technique yields linear orders that are expressible in $\mathcal{NRC}(\mathbb{Q}, +, \cdot, -, \div, \sum, =, \leq)$, which is the language obtained by augmenting $\mathcal{NRC}(\mathbb{Q}, +, \cdot, -, \div, \sum, =)$ with linear orders at base types. Linear order is known to increase expressive power in the context of database query languages [8, 23]. In our case, this is a major advantage. Queries such as "find maximum of column," "find mode of column" and "test parity of cardinality of a set" are expressible in $\mathcal{NRC}(\mathbb{Q}, +, \cdot, -, \div, \sum, =, \leq)$. More importantly, a function that assigns rank to elements of a set is now expressible.

This rank assignment function is used in section 5 to show that $\mathcal{NRC}(\mathbb{Q}, +, \cdot, -, \div, \sum, =, \leq)$ augmented with any combination of the transitive closure operator *tc*, the bounded fixpoint operator *bfix*, or the powerset operator *powerset* retains the conservative extension property. Hull and Su [7] showed that $\mathcal{NRC}(=, \mathit{powerset})$ is not conservative over flat input and output. This failure of conservativity for $\mathcal{NRC}(=, \mathit{powerset})$ was generalized to all input and output heights by Grumbach and Vianu [6]. In contrast, our result shows that conservativity can be repaired with very little extra. Suciu [21] showed that $\mathcal{NRC}(=, \mathit{bfix})$ is conservative over flat relations. His result is remarkable in that it did not need any arithmetic nor order. Furthermore, it is also valid when bounded fixpoint is replaced by bounded partial fixpoint operator. Our result uses arithmetic but holds for bounded fixpoint operator over any input and output. In fact, our proof of conservative extension holds *uniformly* for $\mathcal{NRC}(\mathbb{Q}, +, \cdot, -, \div, \sum, =, \leq, \prod, \odot, \iota)$ where $\prod$, ι, and $\odot$ are any triple of additional primitives which are in a relationship like that between $\sum$, 0, and $+$.

2 Nested relational calculus with summation

The monad calculus of Breazu-Tannen, Buneman, and Wong [3] is denoted $\mathcal{NRC}$ here. In this section, it is extended with rational numbers, simple arithmetics, and a summation operator. The extended language is able to express many aggregate functions commonly found in commercial relational database query languages such as SQL.

A type in $\mathcal{NRC}$ is either a complex object type or is a function type $s \to t$ where s and t are complex object types. The complex object types are given by the grammar:

$$s, t ::= b \mid \mathbb{B} \mid \mathit{unit} \mid s \times t \mid \{s\}$$

Objects of type $\mathbb{B}$ are the two boolean values *true* and *false*. The unique object of type *unit* is denoted by (). Objects of type $s \times t$ are pairs whose first components are objects of type s and second components are objects of type t. Objects of type $\{s\}$ are finite sets of objects of type s. We also include some uninterpreted base types b.

Expressions of $\mathcal{NRC}$ are constructed using the rules in the figure below. Note that [3] uses $ext(\lambda x^s.e_1)(e_2)$; but here we use the equivalent construct $\bigcup\{e_1 \mid x^s \in e_2\}$ instead. The language also contains some uninterpreted constants c of base type $Type(c)$ and uninterpreted functions p of function type $Type(p)$. The type superscripts are omitted in the rest of the paper because they can be inferred [17, 10]. Throughout this paper we assume the usual convention that variables are distinct and that expressions are well formed.

Lambda Calculus and Products

$$\frac{}{x^s : s} \qquad \frac{e : t}{\lambda x^s.e : s \to t} \qquad \frac{e_1 : s \to t \quad e_2 : s}{e_1\ e_2 : t}$$

$$\frac{}{() : unit} \qquad \frac{e : s \times t}{\pi_1\ e : s \quad \pi_2\ e : t} \qquad \frac{e_1 : s \quad e_2 : t}{(e_1, e_2) : s \times t}$$

Set Monad

$$\frac{}{\{\}^s : \{s\}} \qquad \frac{e : s}{\{e\} : \{s\}} \qquad \frac{e_1 : \{s\} \quad e_2 : \{s\}}{e_1 \cup e_2 : \{s\}} \qquad \frac{e_1 : \{t\} \quad e_2 : \{s\}}{\bigcup\{e_1 \mid x^s \in e_2\} : \{t\}}$$

Booleans

$$\frac{}{true : \mathbb{B}} \qquad \frac{}{false : \mathbb{B}} \qquad \frac{e_1 : \mathbb{B} \quad e_2 : t \quad e_3 : t}{if\ e_1\ then\ e_2\ else\ e_3 : t}$$

The semantics of $\mathcal{NRC}$ was described in [3]. The lambda calculus, product, and boolean constructs are standard. We briefly repeat the meaning of the monad constructs here. $\{\}$ is the empty set. $\{e\}$ is the singleton set containing e. $e_1 \cup e_2$ is the union of sets e_1 and e_2. The construct $\bigcup\{e_1 \mid x \in e_2\}$ denotes the set obtained by first applying the function $\lambda x.e_1$ to elements of the set e_2 and then taking their big union. Hence $\bigcup\{e_1 \mid x \in e_2\} = f(o_1) \cup \ldots \cup f(o_n)$, where f is the function $\lambda x.e_1$ and $\{o_1, \ldots, o_n\}$ is the set e_2. The shorthand $\{o_1, \ldots . o_n\}$ is used to denote $\{o_1\} \cup \ldots \cup \{o_n\}$. It must be stressed that the $x \in e_2$ part in the construct $\bigcup\{e_1 \mid x \in e_2\}$ is not a membership test; it is the introduction of a new variable x whose scope is the subexpression e_1.

As it stands, $\mathcal{NRC}$ can merely express queries that are purely structural. It was shown in [3] that endowing $\mathcal{NRC}$ with equality test $=^s: s \times s \to \mathbb{B}$ at all types s elevates $\mathcal{NRC}$ to a fully fledged nested relational language (which was shown by Wong [27] to be equivalent to classical nested relational algebras of Thomas and Fischer[22], Schek and Scholl [20], and Colby [4]). That is, operations such as nest, membership test, subset test, set intersection, set difference, etc. are expressible in $\mathcal{NRC}(=)$. (We write the additional primitive in brackets to distinguish various extensions of the language.) It should also be remarked that in [3], booleans are simulated by values of type $\{unit\}$ with $\{()\}$ for *true* and $\{\}$ for *false*. However, over the class of functions of type $s \to \{s_1\} \times \cdots \times \{s_n\}$, it does not matter which presentation of booleans is used — the resulting languages have the same expressive power.

Examples. $\bigcup\{\{x, 5 \cdot x\} \mid x \in \{1, 2, 3\}\}$ evaluates to the set $\{1, 2, 3, 5, 10, 15\}$. $\bigcup\{\bigcup\{\{(x, y)\} \mid x \in X\} \mid y \in Y\}$ forms the cartesian product of sets X and Y. $\bigcup\{\bigcup\{\{(\pi_1\ x, y)\} \mid y \in \pi_2\ x\} \mid x \in X\}$ is the unnesting of the set X. $\bigcup\{\{(\pi_1\ x,\ \bigcup\{if\ \pi_1\ x = \pi_1\ y\ then\ \{\pi_2\ y\}\ else\ \{\} \mid y \in X\}\} \mid x \in X\}$ is the relational nesting of X.

Real database query languages frequently have to deal with queries such as "select average from column," "select maximum of column," "select count from column," etc. To handle this kind of queries, additional primitives must be added to $\mathcal{NRC}$. In this paper, we add rational numbers (whose type is denoted by $\mathbb{Q}$) and the following constructs:

$$\frac{e_1 : \mathbb{Q} \quad e_2 : \mathbb{Q}}{e_1 + e_2 : \mathbb{Q}} \qquad \frac{e_1 : \mathbb{Q} \quad e_2 : \mathbb{Q}}{e_1 \cdot e_2 : \mathbb{Q}} \qquad \frac{e_1 : \mathbb{Q} \quad e_2 : \mathbb{Q}}{e_1 \div e_2 : \mathbb{Q}}$$

$$\frac{e_1 : \mathbb{Q} \quad e_2 : \mathbb{Q}}{e_1 - e_2 : \mathbb{Q}} \qquad \frac{e_1 : \mathbb{Q} \quad e_2 : \{s\}}{\sum\{\!|e_1 \mid x^s \in e_2|\!\} : \mathbb{Q}}$$

where $+$, $\cdot$, $-$, and $\div$ are respectively addition, multiplication, subtraction, and division of rational numbers. The summation construct $\sum\{\!|e_1 \mid x^s \in e_2|\!\}$ denotes the rational obtained by first applying the function $\lambda x.e_1$ to every item in the set e_2 and then adding the results up. That is, $\sum\{\!|e_1 \mid x \in X|\!\}$ is $f(o_1) + \ldots + f(o_n)$ if f is the function denoted by $\lambda x.e_1$ and $\{o_1, \ldots o_n\}$, with o_1, ..., o_n all distinct, is the set denoted by X. It should be emphasized that the $\{\!|e_1 \mid x \in e_2|\!\}$ part of the construct $\sum\{\!|e_1 \mid x \in e_2|\!\}$ is not an expression of the language; hence $\sum\{\!|1 \mid x \in \{5,6\}|\!\}$ is 2 and not 1.

The extended language $\mathcal{NRC}(\mathbb{Q}, +, \cdot, -, \div, \sum, =)$ is capable of expressing many aggregate operations found in commercial databases. Here are some examples:

- "Count the number of records in R" is $count(R) \triangleq \sum\{\!|1| \; x \in R|\!\}$.
- "Total the first column of R" is $total(R) \triangleq \sum\{\!|\pi_1 \; x \mid x \in R|\!\}$.
- "Average of the first column in R" is $average(R) \triangleq total(R) \div count(R)$.
- "Variance of the first column of R" is $variance(R) \triangleq (\sum\{\!|sq(\pi_1 \; x) \mid x \in R|\!\} - (sq(\sum\{\!|\pi_1 \; x \mid x \in R|\!\}) \div count(R))) \div count(R)$, where $sq \triangleq \lambda y.y \cdot y$.

Aggregate functions were first introduced into flat relational algebra by Klug [12]. He introduced these functions by repeating them for every column of a relation. That is, $aggregate_1$ is for column 1, $aggregate_2$ is for column 2, and so on. Ozsoyoglu, Ozsoyoglu, and Matos [18] generalized this approach to nested relations. Our use of the summation construct is more general. On the other hand, Klausner and Goodman [11] had "stand-alone" aggregate functions such as $mean : \{\mathbb{Q}\} \to \mathbb{Q}$. However, they had to rely on a notion of hiding to deal correctly with duplicates. Hiding is different from projection. Let $R \triangleq \{(1,2),(2,3),(2,4)\}$. Projecting out the second column of R gives us $R' \triangleq \{1,2\}$. Hiding the second column of R gives us $R'' \triangleq \{(1,[2]),(2,[3]),(2,[4])\}$, where the hidden components are shown between square brackets. Observe that the former "eliminates" duplicates as sets have no duplicate by definition. The latter "retains" the duplicated 2 by virtue of tagging them with different hidden components. Then $mean(R'')$ produces the average of the first column of R, whereas $mean(R')$ does not compute the mean correctly. The use of hiding to retain duplicates is rather clumsy. Our use of the summation construct is simpler.

3 Conservative extension

Let us first define the concept of conservative extension. The set height $ht(s)$ of a type s is defined by induction on the structure of type: $ht(unit) = ht(b) = 0$, $ht(s \times t) = ht(s \to t) = \max(ht(s), ht(t))$, and $ht(\{s\}) = 1 + ht(s)$. Every expression of our language has a unique typing derivation. Hence the set height of expression e is defined as $ht(e) = \max\{ht(s) \mid s$ occurs in the type derivation of $e\}$. Let $\mathcal{L}_{i,o,h}$ denote the class of functions whose input has set height at most i, whose output has set height at most o, and which are definable in the language $\mathcal{L}$ using an expression whose set height is at most $h \geq \max(i, o)$. $\mathcal{L}$ is said to have the *conservative extension property with fixed constant* k if $\mathcal{L}_{i,o,h} = \mathcal{L}_{i,o,h+1}$ for all i, o, and $h \geq \max(i, o, k)$. Note that if $\mathcal{L}$ has the conservative extension property with constant k, then for any additional primitive $p : s \to t$, $\mathcal{L}(p)$ has it with constant at most $\max(ht(p), k) = \max(ht(s \to t), k)$.

In this section, we present a rewrite system for $\mathcal{NRC}(\mathbb{Q}, +, \cdot, -, \div, \sum, =)$ that is strongly normalizing. The normal forms induced by this rewriting are then used to prove that every definable function is definable using operators whose set height is at most the set height of the input/output of the function. The theorem implies that $\mathcal{NRC}(\mathbb{Q}, +, \cdot, -, \div, \sum, =)$ has the conservative extension property with fixed constant 0. Consequently, the class $\mathcal{NRC}(\mathbb{Q}, +, \cdot, -, \div, \sum, =)_{i,o,h}$ is *independent* of h. Hence using intermediate data structure of great height does not increase the horsepower of the language (though it frequently makes programs more elegant).

We proceed using the strategy developed by Wong [26]. First, observe that any equality test $=^s: s \times s \to \mathbb{B}$ can be implemented in terms of equality tests at base types $=^b: b \times b \to \mathbb{B}$. Hence, in the rest of the report, we assume that $=^s$, where s is not a base type, is a syntactic sugar as implemented in the proposition below.

Proposition 3.1 *Any equality test* $=^s: s \times s \to \mathbb{B}$ *can be implemented in terms of equality tests at base types* $=^b: b \times b \to \mathbb{B}$, *using* $\mathcal{NRC}(\mathbb{Q}, +, \cdot, -, \div, \sum, =)$ *as the ambient language.*

Proof. Proceed by induction on s.

- $=^b$ is the given equality test at base type b.
- $x =^{s \times t} y \triangleq \textit{if } \pi_1\, x =^s \pi_1\, y \textit{ then } \pi_2\, x =^t \pi_2\, y \textit{ else false}$
- $X =^{\{s\}} Y \triangleq \textit{if } X \subseteq^s Y \textit{ then } Y \subseteq^s X \textit{ else false}$, where
- $X \subseteq^s Y \triangleq ((\sum\{\!|\textit{if } x \in^s Y \textit{ then } 0 \textit{ else } 1 \mid x \in X|\!\}) =^{\mathbb{Q}} 0)$
- $x \in^s Y \triangleq (\sum\{\!|\textit{if } x =^s y \textit{ then } 1 \textit{ else } 0 \mid y \in Y|\!\}) =^{\mathbb{Q}} 1$. □

The next step toward proving the conservative extension property for $\mathcal{NRC}(\mathbb{Q}, +, \cdot, -, \div, \sum, =)$ is a rewrite system adapted from Wong [26]. Let $e[e'/x]$ stands for the expression obtained by replacing all free occurrences of x in e by e', provided the free variables in e' are not captured during the substitution. Now, consider the rules below.

- $(\lambda x.e)(e') \leadsto e[e'/x]$

- $\pi_i(e_1, e_2) \leadsto e_i$
- $\pi_i(\textit{if } e_1 \textit{ then } e_2 \textit{ else } e_3) \leadsto \textit{if } e_1 \textit{ then } \pi_i\, e_2 \textit{ else } \pi_i\, e_3$
- $\bigcup\{e \mid x \in \{\}\} \leadsto \{\}$
- $\bigcup\{\{\} \mid x \in e\} \leadsto \{\}$
- $\bigcup\{e \mid x \in \{e'\}\} \leadsto e[e'/x]$
- $\bigcup\{e \mid x \in \textit{if } e_1 \textit{ then } e_2 \textit{ else } e_3\}$
  $\leadsto \textit{if } e_1 \textit{ then } \bigcup\{e \mid x \in e_2\} \textit{ else } \bigcup\{e \mid x \in e_3\}$
- $\bigcup\{e_1 \mid x \in \bigcup\{e_2 \mid y \in e_3\}\} \leadsto \bigcup\{\bigcup\{e_1 \mid x \in e_2\} \mid y \in e_3\}$
- $\bigcup\{e \mid x \in e_1 \cup e_2\} \leadsto \bigcup\{e \mid x \in e_1\} \cup \bigcup\{e \mid x \in e_2\}$
- $\sum\{\!|e \mid x \in \{\}|\!\} \leadsto 0$
- $\sum\{\!|e \mid x \in \{e'\}|\!\} \leadsto e[e'/x]$
- $\sum\{\!|e \mid x \in e_1 \cup e_2|\!\} \leadsto \sum\{\!|e \mid x \in e_1|\!\} + \sum\{\!|\textit{if } x \in e_1 \textit{ then } 0 \textit{ else } e \mid x \in e_2|\!\}$
- $\sum\{\!|e \mid x \in \textit{if } e_1 \textit{ then } e_2 \textit{ else } e_3|\!\}$
  $\leadsto \textit{if } e_1 \textit{ then } \sum\{\!|e \mid x \in e_2|\!\} \textit{ else } \sum\{\!|e \mid x \in e_3|\!\}$
- $\sum\{\!|e \mid x \in \bigcup\{e_1 \mid y \in e_2\}|\!\}$
  $\leadsto \sum\{\!|\sum\{\!|(e \div \sum\{\!|\sum\{\!|\textit{if } x = v \textit{ then } 1 \textit{ else } 0 \mid v \in e_1|\!\} \mid y \in e_2|\!\}) \mid x \in e_1|\!\} \mid y \in e_2|\!\}$

This system of rewrite rules preserves the meanings of expressions. The last rule deserves special attention. Consider the incorrect equation: $\sum\{\!|e \mid x \in \bigcup\{e_1 \mid y \in e_2\}|\!\} = \sum\{\!|\sum\{\!|e \mid x \in e_1|\!\} \mid y \in e_2|\!\}$. Suppose e_2 evaluates to a set of two distinct objects $\{o_1, o_2\}$. Suppose $e_1[o_1/y]$ and $e_1[o_2/y]$ both evaluate to $\{o_3\}$. Suppose $e[o_3/x]$ evaluates to 1. Then the left-hand-side of the "equation" returns 1 but the right-hand-side yields 2. The division operation in the last rule is used to handle duplicates properly.

Proposition 3.2 (Soundness) *If $e_1 \leadsto e_2$, then $e_1 = e_2$. That is, $e_1 \leadsto e_2$ implies e_1 and e_2 denote the same value.*

Proof. Straightforward. □

A system of rewrite rules is said to be strongly normalizing if any sequence of applications of these rules is guaranteed to terminate.

Proposition 3.3 (Strong normalization) *The above rewrite system is strongly normalizing.*

Proof. While the last three rules seem to increase the "character count" of expressions, it should be remarked that $\sum\{\!|e \mid x \in e'|\!\}$ is always rewritten by these three rules to an expression that decreases in the e' position. This is the key to the proof. The detail can be found in the appendix of Libkin and Wong [15]. □

Hence every expression can be rewritten to some normal form. These normal forms have the following property:

Theorem 3.4 (Conservative extension) *Let* $e : s$ *be an expression of* $\mathcal{NRC}(\mathbb{Q}, +, \cdot, -, \div, \sum, =)$ *in normal form. Then* $ht(e) \leq \max(\{ht(s)\} \cup \{ht(t) \mid t$ *is the type of a free variable occurring in* $e\})$*. Therefore,* $\mathcal{NRC}(\mathbb{Q}, +, \cdot, -, \div, \sum, =)$ *has the conservative extension property with fixed constant* 0*.*

Proof. By a fairly routine structural induction on e. □

Conservativity for $\mathcal{NRC}(=)$ was studied by Paredaens and Van Gucht [19] and by Wong [26]. The former proved that $\mathcal{NRC}(=)_{i,o,h} = \mathcal{NRC}(=)_{i,o,h+1}$ for $i = o = 1$. The latter generalized it to all i and o. However conservativity in the presence of aggregate functions was not studied. The above theorem implies that $\mathcal{NRC}(\mathbb{Q}, +, \cdot, -, \div, \sum, =)_{i,o,h} = \mathcal{NRC}(\mathbb{Q}, +, \cdot, -, \div, \sum, =)_{i,o,h+1}$ for any i, o, $h \geq \max(i, o)$. Hence we have generalized the results of [19] and [26] to the case where aggregate functions are present.

The theorem has practical significance. Some databases are designed to support nested sets up to a fixed depth of nesting. For example, Jaeschke and Schek [9] designed a statistical database whose relations are those having height at most 2. Another example is the commercially successful SQL which supports just flat relations. Both of these systems have a suitable collection of aggregate functions. "$\mathcal{NRC}(\mathbb{Q}, +, \cdot, -, \div, \sum, =)$ restricted to height 2 or 1" is a natural query language for such databases. But knowing that $\mathcal{NRC}(\mathbb{Q}, +, \cdot, -, \div, \sum, =)$ is conservative at all set heights, one can instead provide the user with the entire language $\mathcal{NRC}(\mathbb{Q}, +, \cdot, -, \div, \sum, =)$ as a more convenient query language for these databases, so long as queries have input/output height not exceeding 2 or 1.

4 Linear ordering on nested relations

The conservative extension property can be used to study many properties of languages (see Libkin and Wong [15] for some examples). In this section, we use it to demonstrate that $\mathcal{NRC}(\mathbb{Q}, +, \cdot, -, \div, \sum, =)$ is incapable of expressing the usual linear ordering $\leq^{\mathbb{Q}}: \mathbb{Q} \times \mathbb{Q} \to \mathbb{B}$ on rational numbers. So we introduce linear order for base types. Then a technique for lifting linear order at base types to all types is presented.

Proposition 4.1 $\mathcal{NRC}(\mathbb{Q}, +, \cdot, -, \div, \sum, =)$ *cannot express* $\leq^{\mathbb{Q}}$*.*

Proof. It is enough to show that the following function cannot be expressed: $g(x) = 0$ if $x \leq 1$ and $g(x) = 1$ if $x > 1$. Observe that $g : \mathbb{Q} \to \mathbb{Q}$ has height 0. By the conservative extension property, it must be definable using an expression of height 0. However, we can prove the following claim:

Claim. Let $g(x) : \mathbb{Q}$ be an expression defined wholely in terms of $+, -, \cdot, \div, =^b$, *if-then-else*, constants, and the variable $x : \mathbb{Q}$. Then there are two polynomials $p(x)$ and $q(x)$ with rational coefficients such that $g(x)$ coincides with $p(x) \div q(x)$ almost everywhere. That is, $g(x) \neq p(x) \div q(x)$ for only finitely many $x \in \mathbb{Q}$.

Now $p(x) \div q(x) = 1$ iff $p(x) - q(x) = 0$. Since $p(x) - q(x) = 0$ is a polynomial equation, it has finitely many roots. Hence $g(x)$ cannot coincide with $p(x) \div q(x)$ almost everywhere. Consequently, g is not expressible. □

Therefore, we propose to augment $\mathcal{NRC}(\mathbb{Q}, +, \cdot, -, \div, \sum, =)$ with a linear order $\leq^b$: $b \times b \to b$ for each base type b. Many important data organization functions such as sorting algorithms and duplicate detection/elimination algorithms rely on linear orders. In the remainder of this section, we show how to lift linear order at base types to linear order at all types. First recall that the Hoare ordering $\sqsubseteq^b$ on the subsets of an ordered set is defined as $X \sqsubseteq^b Y$ iff for every $x \in X$ there is $y \in Y$ such that $x \sqsubseteq y$. Then

Proposition 4.2 *Let $(D, \sqsubseteq)$ be a partially ordered set. Define an order $\lesssim^b$ on the finite subsets of D as follows: $X \lesssim^b Y$ iff either $X \sqsubseteq^b Y$ and $Y \not\sqsubseteq^b X$, or $X \sqsubseteq^b Y$ and $Y \sqsubseteq^b X$ and $X - Y \sqsubseteq^b Y - X$. Then $\lesssim^b$ is a partial order. Moreover, if $\sqsubseteq$ is a linear order, then so is $\lesssim^b$.*

Proof. See Libkin and Wong [15]. □

Kupert, Saake, and Wegner [14] gave three linear orderings on collection types in their study of duplicate detection and elimination. The ordering defined above coincides with one of them and is in fact a particular case of an order well known in universal algebra and combinatorics [13, 25]. An important feature of our technique of lifting linear orders is that the resulting linear orders are readily seen to be computable by our very limited language. Hence in the rest of the report, we assume that $\leq^s$, where s is not a base type, is a syntactic sugar as implemented in the theorem below.

Theorem 4.3 (Linear order) *$\mathcal{NRC}(\mathbb{Q}, +, \cdot, -, \div, \sum, =)$ augmented with linear order $\leq^b$: $b \times b \to b$ at every base type b can express a linear order $\leq^s$: $s \times s \to s$ at every type s.*

Proof. Proceed by induction on s.

- $\leq^b$ is the given linear order on base type b.
- $x \leq^{s \times t} y \triangleq$ *if* $\pi_1\ x \leq^s \pi_1\ y$ *then* (*if* $\pi_1\ x =^s \pi_1\ y$ *then* $\pi_2\ x \leq^t \pi_2\ y$ *else true*) *else false*
- $X \leq^{\{s\}} Y \triangleq$ *if* $X \sqsubseteq^b_s Y$ *then* (*if* $Y \sqsubseteq^b_s X$ *then* $X \lesssim^b_s Y$ *else true*) *else false*
- $X \sqsubseteq^b_s Y \triangleq (\sum\{\!|(if\ (\sum\{\!|(if\ x \leq^s y\ then\ 1\ else\ 0) \mid y \in Y|\!\}) = 0\ then\ 1\ else\ 0) \mid x \in X|\!\}) = 0$
- $X \lesssim^b Y \triangleq (\sum\{\!|if\ x \in^s Y\ then\ 0\ else\ (if\ (\sum\{\!|if\ y \in^s X\ then\ 0\ else\ (if\ x \leq^s y\ then\ 1\ else\ 0) \mid y \in Y|\!\}) = 0\ then\ 1\ else\ 0) \mid x \in X|\!\}) = 0.$ □

Hence we denote the language endowed with linear order at base types by $\mathcal{NRC}(\mathbb{Q}, +, \cdot, -, \div, \sum, =, \leq)$. Several other queries commonly encountered in practical database environments, as well as some unusual ones, are now easily expressed:

- "Rows of R whose first column value is the maximum of the column" is $maxrows(R) \triangleq \bigcup\{if\ (\sum\{\!|if\ \pi_1(x) = \pi_1(y)\ then\ 0\ else\ if\ \pi_1(y) \leq \pi_1(x)\ then\ 1\ else\ 0 \mid x \in R|\!\} = 0)\ then\ \{y\}\ else\ \{\} \mid y \in R\}$.

- "Rows of R whose first column value is the mode of the column" is $moderows(R) \triangleq maxrows(\bigcup\{\{(\sum\{\!|if\ f(y) = f(x)\ then\ 1\ else\ 0 \mid y \in R|\!\},\ x)\} \mid x \in R\})$.

- "Parity of the cardinality of a set R" is $odd(R) \triangleq \bigcup\{if\ \sum\{\!|if\ x \leq y\ then\ 1\ else\ 0 \mid y \in R|\!\} = \sum\{\!|if\ y \leq x\ then\ 1\ else\ 0 \mid y \in R|\!\}\ then\{()\}\ else\ \{\} \mid x \in R\} = \{()\}$.

More significantly, the rank assignment function can be expressed. The rank assignment function leads to a few rather surprising results to be discussed shortly.

Proposition 4.4 *A rank assignment* $sort^s : \{s\} \rightarrow \{s \times \mathbb{Q}\}$ *is the function such that* $sort\{o_1, \ldots, o_n\} = \{(o_1, 1), \ldots, (o_n, n)\}$ *where* $o_1 < \ldots < o_n$. $\mathcal{NRC}(\mathbb{Q}, +, \cdot, -, \div, \sum, =, \leq)$ *can define* $sort^s$.

Proof. $sort(R) \triangleq \bigcup\{\{(x,\ \sum\{\!|if\ y \leq x\ then\ 1\ else\ 0 \mid y \in R|\!\})\} \mid x \in R\}$. □

5 More conservative extension results

The ability to compute a linear order and a rank assignment function at every type proves to be an asset. In this final section, we present a few more conservative extension results. First, let us consider the following primitives:

$$\frac{g : \{s\} \quad f : \{s\} \rightarrow \{s\}}{bfix^s(f, g) : \{s\}}$$

$$\overline{tc^s : \{s \times s\} \rightarrow \{s \times s\}} \qquad \overline{powerset^s : \{s\} \rightarrow \{\{s\}\}}$$

where $tc(R)$ is the transitive closure of R; $bfix(f, g)$ is the bounded fixpoint of f with respect to g; that is, it is the least fixpoint of the equation $f(R) = g \cap (R \cup f(R))$; and $powerset(R)$ is the powerset of R.

Corollary 5.1 *The followings have the conservative extension property:*

- $\mathcal{NRC}(\mathbb{Q}, +, \cdot, -, \div, \sum, =, \leq, tc)$ *with fixed constant* 1.

- $\mathcal{NRC}(\mathbb{Q}, +, \cdot, -, \div, \sum, =, \leq, bfix)$ *with fixed constant* 1.

- $\mathcal{NRC}(\mathbb{Q}, +, \cdot, -, \div, \sum, =, \leq, powerset)$ *with fixed constant* 2.

Proof. We provide the proof for the first one, the other two are straightforward adaptation of the same technique. First observe that $\mathcal{NRC}(\mathbb{Q}, +, \cdot, -, \div, \sum, =, \leq, tc^{\mathbb{Q}})$, where we restrict computation of transitive closure to binary relations of rational numbers, has the conservative extension property with constant 1. Therefore, it suffices for us to show that tc^s is expressible in it for any s. This can be achieved by exploiting the rank assignment function $sort$ by defining

- $tc(R) \triangleq decode(tc^{\mathbb{Q}}(encode(R, sort(dom(R)))), sort(dom(R)))$, where

- $dom(R) \triangleq \bigcup\{\{\pi_1\ x\} \mid x \in R\} \cup \bigcup\{\{\pi_2\ x\} \mid x \in R\}$,
- $encode(R, C) \triangleq \bigcup\{\bigcup\{\bigcup\{$*if* $\pi_1\ x = \pi_1\ y$ *then if* $\pi_2\ x = \pi_1\ z$ *then* $\{(\pi_2\ y, \pi_2\ z)\}$ *else* $\{\}$ *else* $\{\} \mid z \in C\} \mid y \in C\} \mid x \in R\}$, and
- $decode(R, C) \triangleq \bigcup\{\bigcup\{\bigcup\{$*if* $\pi_1\ x = \pi_2\ y$ *then if* $\pi_2\ x = \pi_2\ z$ *then* $\{(\pi_1\ y, \pi_1\ z)\}$ *else* $\{\}$ *else* $\{\} \mid z \in C\} \mid y \in C\} \mid x \in R\}$. □

Conservativity of $\mathcal{NRC}(=, powerset)$ was considered by Hull and Su [7] and Grumbach and Vianu [6]. The former showed that $\mathcal{NRC}(=, powerset)_{i,o,h} \neq \mathcal{NRC}(=, powerset)_{i,o,h+1}$ for any h and $i = o = 1$. This implies the failure of conservative extension for $\mathcal{NRC}(=, powerset)$ with respect to flat relations. The latter generalized this result to any i and o. The corollary above showed that the failure at higher heights can be repaired by augmenting $\mathcal{NRC}(=, powerset)$ with a summation operator.

More recently, Suciu [21] showed, using a technique related to that of Van den Bussche [5], that $\mathcal{NRC}(=, bfix)_{i,o,h} = \mathcal{NRC}(=, bfix)_{i,o,h+1}$ for $i = o = 1$. This is remarkable because he did not need any arithmetic operation. The corollary above showed that the conservativity of bounded fixpoint can be extended to all input and output in the presence of arithmetics.

Immerman [8] showed that first-order logic with least fixpoint and order is equivalent to PTIME. This may imply $\mathcal{NRC}(\mathbb{Q}, +, \cdot, -, \div, \sum, =, \leq, lfp)_{1,1,h} = \mathcal{NRC}(\mathbb{Q}, +, \cdot, -, \div, \sum, =, \leq, lfp)_{1,1,h+1}$. In which case, $\mathcal{NRC}(\mathbb{Q}, +, \cdot, -, \div, \sum, =, \leq, lfp)$ is conservative over flat relations. This should be contrasted with the corollary above. The languages in the corollary do not necessarily give us all PTIME queries over flat relations. Furthermore, conservativity holds for them over any input and output.

The technique used in our proof of conservative extension has an intrinsic uniformity. To illustrate this, let us introduce three partially interpreted primitives ι, $\odot$ and $\prod$ to $\mathcal{NRC}(\mathbb{Q}, +, \cdot, -, \div, \sum, =, \leq)$,

$$\frac{}{\iota : b} \qquad \frac{e_1 : b \quad e_2 : b}{e_1 \odot e_2 : b} \qquad \frac{e_1 : b \quad e_2 : \{s\}}{\prod\{\!|e_1 \mid x^s \in e_2|\!\} : b}$$

where b is some fixed type, $\odot : b \times b \to b$ is a commutative associative binary operation, $\iota : b$ is the identity for $\odot$, and $\prod\{\!|e \mid x^s \in \{o_1, \ldots, o_n\}|\!\} = e[o_1/x^s] \odot \ldots \odot e[o_n/x^s] \odot \iota$ for any set $\{o_1, \ldots, o_n\}$, with o_1, ..., o_n all distinct, of type $\{s\}$. As an example, take $\odot$ to be $\cdot$ and b to be $\mathbb{Q}$, then ι becomes 1 and $\prod$ becomes a sort of bounded product.

Proposition 5.2 *For every i, o, and $h \geq \max(i, o, ht(b))$, $\mathcal{NRC}(\mathbb{B}, \mathbb{Q}, +, \cdot, -, \div, \sum, =, \leq, \odot, \prod, \iota)_{i,o,h} = \mathcal{NRC}(\mathbb{B}, \mathbb{Q}, +, \cdot, -, \div, \sum, =, \leq, \odot, \prod, \iota)_{i,o,h+1}$.*

Proof. It suffices to append the rules below to the rewrite system of section 3. Note the use of the linear ordering $\leq$. (If $\odot$ is also idempotent, simpler rules can be used.)

- $\prod\{\!|e \mid x \in \{\}|\!\} \leadsto \iota$
- $\prod\{\!|e \mid x \in \{e'\}|\!\} \leadsto e[e'/x]$

- $\prod\{\!|e \mid x \in e_1 \cup e_2|\!\} \leadsto \prod\{\!|e \mid x \in e_1|\!\} \odot \prod\{\!|\mathit{if}\ x \in e_1\ \mathit{then}\ \iota\ \mathit{else}\ e \mid x \in e_2|\!\}$

- $\prod\{\!|e \mid x \in \mathit{if}\ e_1\ \mathit{then}\ e_2\ \mathit{else}\ e_3|\!\} newline \leadsto \mathit{if}\ e_1\ \mathit{then}\ \prod\{\!|e \mid x \in e_2|\!\}\ \mathit{else}\ \prod\{\!|e \mid x \in e_3|\!\}$

- $\prod\{\!|e \mid x \in \bigcup\{e_1 \mid y \in e_2\}|\!\} \leadsto \prod\{\!|\prod\{\!|\mathit{if}\ (\sum\{\!|\mathit{if}\ x \in e_1[w/y]\ \mathit{then}\ (\mathit{if}\ w = y\ \mathit{then}\ 0\ \mathit{else}\ (\mathit{if}\ w \leq y\ \mathit{then}\ 1\ \mathit{else}\ 0))\ \mathit{else}\ 0 \mid w \in e_2|\!\}) = 0\ \mathit{then}\ e\ \mathit{else}\ \iota \mid x \in e_1|\!\} \mid y \in e_2|\!\}$. □

6 Conclusion and future work.

The conservative extension property of nested relational calculi is studied in the presence of aggregate functions and linear orders. We showed that this property is retained by the nested relational calculus $\mathcal{NRC}(=)$ when very simple arithmetics and a summation operator are added to the language. We proved also that the presence of linear orders at base types leads to a more uniform and perhaps unexpected demonstration of the conservative extension property of several nested relational calculi. In particular, the well-known failure of conservativity of $\mathcal{NRC}(=, \mathit{powerset})$ is shown to be repairable at higher heights when very simple arithmetics, bounded summation, and linear orders are available. These results have many consequences, including an interesting finite-cofiniteness property of the bag query language of Libkin and Wong [15]; we hope to present them in detail in a future report.

It is known that the presence of a linear order adds power to first-order query languages [8, 23]. Our nested set language has enough power to express a linear order at all types. It is a good framework for investigating the impact of linear orders on nested collections. Also, other kinds of linear orders on nested collections such as those in [14] should be studied.

We were able to demonstrate the conservative extension property for the nested set language with aggregate functions and additional primitives such as transitive closure, bounded fixpoint and powerset by reducing these primitives to the corresponding ones on rational numbers. What is the general property of these primitives that allowed this reduction?

The nested relational language with summation seems to be adequate for statistical databases. Does it have sufficient expressive power for querying databases for other advanced applications such as spatial databases, geographic databases, and genome databases?

Acknowledgements. Discussions with Peter Buneman, Val Breazu-Tannen, and especially Dan Suciu directly resulted in this paper. We thank them for their encouragement and insights. We are also grateful to Anthony Kosky and Paula Ta-Shma for their valuable comments. Support for Leonid Libkin is provided in part by National Science Foundation Grant IRI-90-04137 and a AT&T Doctoral Fellowship. Support for Limsoon Wong is provided in part by National Science Foundation Grant IRI-90-04137 and Army Research Office Grant DAAL03-89-C-0031-PRIME.

References

[1] V. Breazu-Tannen, P. Buneman, and S. Naqvi. Structural recursion as a query language. In *Proceedings of 3rd International Workshop on Database Programming Languages, Naphlion, Greece*, pages 9–19. Morgan Kaufmann, August 1991.

[2] V. Breazu-Tannen and R. Subrahmanyam. Logical and computational aspects of programming with Sets/Bags/Lists. In *LNCS 510: Proceedings of 18th International Colloquium on Automata, Languages, and Programming, Madrid, Spain, July 1991*, pages 60–75. Springer Verlag, 1991.

[3] Val Breazu-Tannen, Peter Buneman, and Limsoon Wong. Naturally embedded query languages. In *LNCS 646: Proceedings of International Conference on Database Theory, Berlin, Germany, October, 1992*, pages 140–154. Springer-Verlag, October 1992.

[4] Latha S. Colby. A recursive algebra for nested relations. *Information Systems*, 15(5):567–582, 1990.

[5] Jan Van den Bussche. Complex object manipulation through identifiers: An algebraic perspective. technical Report 92-41, University of Antwerp, Department of Mathematics and Computer Science, Universiteitsplein 1, B-2610 Antwerp, Belgium, September 1992.

[6] Stephane Grumbach and Victor Vianu. Playing games with objects. In *LNCS 470: 3rd International Conference on Database Theory, Paris, France, December 1990*, pages 25–39. Springer-Verlag, 1990.

[7] Richard Hull and Jianwen Su. On the expressive power of database queries with intermediate types. *Journal of Computer and System Sciences*, 43:219–267, 1991.

[8] Neil Immerman. Relational queries computable in polynomial time. *Information and Control*, 68:86–104, 1986.

[9] G. Jaeschke and H. J. Schek. Remarks on the algebra of nonfirst normal form relations. In *Proceedings ACM Symposium on Principles of Database Systems*, pages 124–138, Los Angeles, California, March 1982.

[10] L. A. Jategaonkar and J. C. Mitchell. ML with extended pattern matching and subtypes. In *Proceedings of ACM Conference on LISP and Functional Programming*, pages 198–211, Snowbird, Utah, July 1988.

[11] Aviel Klausner and Nathan Goodman. Multirelations: Semantics and languages. In *Proceedings of 11th International Conference on Very Large Databases, Stockholm, August 1985*, pages 251–258, Los Altos, CA, August 1985. Morgan Kaufmann.

[12] Anthony Klug. Equivalence of relational algebra and relational calculus query languages having aggregate functions. *Journal of the ACM*, 29(3):699–717, July 1982.

[13] J. B. Kruskal. The theory of well-quasi-ordering: A frequently discovered concept. *Journal of Combinatorial Theory Series A*, 13:297–305, 1972.

[14] K. Kupert, G. Saake, and L. Wegner. Duplicate detection and deletion in the extended NF^2 data model. In *LNCS 367: Foundation of Data Organization and Algorithms*, pages 83–101. Springer-Verlag, June 1989.

[15] Leonid Libkin and Limsoon Wong. Query languages for bags. This volume.

[16] Eugenio Moggi. Notions of computation and monads. *Information and Computation*, 93:55–92, 1991.

[17] A. Ohori, P. Buneman, and V. Breazu-Tannen. Database programming in Machiavelli: A polymorphic language with static type inference. In *Proceedings of ACM International Conference on Management of Data*, pages 46–57, Portland, Oregon, June 1989.

[18] G. Ozsoyoglu, Z. M. Ozsoyoglu, and V. Matos. Extending relational algebra and relational calculus with set-valued attributes and aggregate functions. *ACM Transactions on Database Systems*, 12(4):566–592, December 1987.

[19] Jan Paredaens and Dirk Van Gucht. Converting nested relational algebra expressions into flat algebra expressions. *ACM Transaction on Database Systems*, 17(1):65–93, March 1992.

[20] H.-J. Schek and M. H. Scholl. The relational model with relation-valued attributes. *Information Systems*, 11(2):137–147, 1986.

[21] Dan Suciu. Fixpoints and bounded fixpoints for complex objects. This volume.

[22] S. J. Thomas and P. C. Fischer. Nested relational structures. In *Advances in Computing Research: Theory of Databases*, pages 269–307. JAI Press, 1986.

[23] M. Y. Vardi. The complexity of relational query languages. In *Proceedings of 14th ACM Symposium on Theory of Computing*, pages 137–146, 1982.

[24] Philip Wadler. Comprehending monads. In *Proceedings of ACM Conference on Lisp and Functional Programming*, Nice, June 1990.

[25] W. Wechler. *Universal Algebra for Computer Scientists*, volume 25 of *EATCS Monograph on Theoretical Computer Science*. Springer-Verlag, Berlin, 1992.

[26] Limsoon Wong. Normal forms and conservative properties for query languages over collection types. In *Proceedings of 12th ACM Symposium on Principles of Database Systems*, pages 26–36, Washington, D. C., May 1993.

[27] Limsoon Wong. Query languages over collection types. Manuscript available from Limsoon@Saul.CIS.UPenn.EDU, June 1993.

First-Order Incremental Evaluation of Datalog Queries

(Extended Abstract)

Guozhu Dong*

Department of Computer Science, The University of Melbourne
Parkville, Vic. 3052, Australia

Jianwen Su‡

Department of Computer Science, University of California
Santa Barbara, CA 93106, USA

Abstract

We consider the problem of repeatedly evaluating the same (computationally expensive) query to a database that is being updated between successive query requests. In this situation, it should be possible to use the difference between successive database states and the answer to the query in one state to reduce the cost of evaluating the query in the next state. We use first-order (i.e., nonrecursive) queries to compute the differences, and call this process *first-order incremental query evaluation.*

After formalizing the notion of a first-order incremental query evaluation system (FOIES), we present an earlier result that every regular chain query (which are associated with chain Datalog programs) has a FOIES. We then extend this result to the situations (1) where regular chain queries are *augmented* with binary conjunctive queries with unions, defining nonrecursive predicates, that have "cartesian-closed increment" (CCI), and (2) where insertions for regular queries are unbounded but "cartesian-closed" sets. The notion of CCI is essential in proving (1). We also studied the decision problem for CCI. It is shown that the CCI property is decidable for binary conjunctive queries with unions but undecidable for recursive queries and for relational calculus queries. We also consider a subclass of FOIES, "space-free" FOIES, which use no additional facts in the incremental evaluation. We show that there are queries which have FOIES but not space-free FOIES and that it is undecidable if a Datalog query has a space-free FOIES. Finally, many questions remain open. For example, does there exist a Datalog query which does not have any FOIES?

1 Introduction

The relational query languages have limited power since they cannot express recursive queries [5]. Datalog incorporates recursion but also raises the complex-

*This author gratefully acknowledges support of Australian Research Council through research grants and the Centre for Intelligent Decision Systems.

‡Work by this author supported in part by NSF grants IRI-9109520 and IRI-9117094.

ity of query evaluation. The problem of efficiently computing Datalog queries has attracted a great deal of attention in the database and logic programming communities [6, 8, 12, 14, 16, 17, 22, 23, 24].

In this paper, we consider the problem of repeatedly evaluating the same (computationally expensive) query to a database that is being updated between successive query requests. Such mode of computation is very useful in maintaining materialized views upon updates. In this case, it should be possible to use the difference between successive database states and the answer to the query in one state to reduce the cost of evaluating the query in the next state. We use first-order (i.e., nonrecursive) queries to compute the differences, and call this process "first-order incremental query evaluation."

This optimization approach is analogous to the incremental checking of integrity constraint satisfaction by using (i) database updates and (ii) the fact that the integrity constraints were satisfied prior to the updates [9, 25, 26]. Our task is closely related to the problem of efficiently updating the standard model [2] of a definite or more generally stratified database [4, 23]. It is also closely related to the problem of partially evaluating definite logic programs [24]. When restricted to transitive closure queries, our task can be viewed as solving the incremental transitive closure computation problem for graphs [10, 14, 18, 19].

In general, all these optimization approaches store extra information to reduce the time required for subsequent computations. In our case, we store the answer to the query in one database state (and possibly additional derived facts) to reduce the cost of evaluating the query in subsequent database states.

Informally, the idea of first-order incremental query evaluation is as follows. Let Q be a Datalog query, D an initial database state, $Q(D)$ the answer, and Δ a set of a bounded number of facts to be inserted. Then our approach is to store $Q(D)$ (and possibly some additional derived facts), and compute the answer to Q on the new database $D \cup \Delta$ by a nonrecursive "incremental" program Q' which satisfies

$$Q'(Q(D) \cup \Delta) \cup Q(D) = Q(D \cup \Delta).$$

Using incremental evaluation, the task of evaluating Q is replaced by the task of evaluating the computationally cheaper Q'. Queries that can be incrementally evaluated by nonrecursive queries form a strict generalization of bounded Datalog queries.

Nonrecursive Datalog programs are (roughly) the conjunctive queries with unions, which permit efficient computation [29] and are suitable for parallel computation [3]. For database applications, we believe that nonrecursive Datalog programs are much better than recursive algorithms using elaborate data structures even though the latter might have lower sequential complexity [17]. Indeed, a nonrecursive program has a bounded number of relational join operations, whereas a recursive algorithm has usually an unbounded number of iterations. Furthermore, nonrecursive programs are a subset of relational queries and thus readily programmable in database programming languages, whereas recursive algorithms using elaborate data structures are not easily expressible in usual database languages.

This approach is similar to database programming by structural recursion [7], though we only use first-order queries to compute the increment; and is also related to bounded iteration constructs [27] and the more general treatment of database states and their differences (deltas) [21].

We formally introduce the notion of "first-order incremental evaluation system" (FOIES) and state a result that every regular chain query (which are associated with chain Datalog programs) has a FOIES [15], i.e., can be incrementally evaluated by a nonrecursive program. We extend this result to the situations (1) where regular chain queries are *augmented* with conjunctive queries defining the nonrecursive (binary) predicates having "cartesian-closed increment" (CCI), and (2) where insertions for regular chain queries are unbounded but "cartesian-closed" sets. The notion of CCI is essential in proving (1). Informally, a binary relation p is cartesian closed if it equals to the product of the projections to its two columns, i.e., $p = (\pi_1 p) \times (\pi_2 p)$. A query Q has CCI if $\exists k, \forall D, \Delta$, $Q(D \cup \Delta) - Q(D)$ is a subset of a union of some k cartesian-closed sets contained in $Q(D \cup \Delta)$. We show that the CCI property is decidable for binary conjunctive queries with unions but undecidable for Datalog queries and for first-order (the relational algebra and calculus) queries. Finally, we define and study a subclass of FOIES, "space-free" FOIES, which use no additional facts in the incremental evaluation. We show that there are queries which have FOIES but not space-free FOIES and that it is undecidable if a Datalog query has a space-free FOIES.

Section 2 formalizes the concepts and gives examples, Section 3 reviews the case of regular chain queries; Section 4 contains the results for the extended cases; Section 5 examines the CCI property; Section 6 discusses space-free FOIES; and Section 7 gives some concluding remarks. The detailed proofs are provided in the full paper.

2 First-Order Incremental Evaluation System

After a brief review of definitions of databases, queries and answers, we introduce the central concept of a "first-order incremental evaluation system" (FOIES) and illustrate it with several examples.

We first assume the existence of the following pairwise disjoint and countably infinite sets:

- A set $\mathcal{P}$ of *predicate (names)*;
- A set $\mathcal{U}$ of *constants*; and
- A set $\mathcal{V}$ of *variables.*

A *term* is either a variable in $\mathcal{V}$ or a constant in $\mathcal{U}$. If q is a predicate in $\mathcal{P}$ and $t_1, \ldots, t_k$ are terms then $q(t_1, \ldots, t_k)$ is an *atom*. *Facts* are grounded atoms, i.e., without any variables. The set $\mathcal{P}$ is further divided into two disjoint parts: a set of *extensional database (EDB)* predicates and a set of *intentional database (IDB)* predicates. A *database* D is a finite set of EDB facts (facts over EDB predicates). A *(Datalog) program* Π is a finite set of safe rules of the form

$$A \leftarrow A_1, \ldots, A_n,$$

where A and $A_1, \ldots, A_n$ are atoms without built-in predicates such as equality and A is over an IDB predicate. A *(Datalog) query* Q is a pair (Π, p), where p is an IDB predicate. $\Pi(D)$ denotes the set of IDB facts in the least (Herbrand) model for $\Pi \cup D$ [28]. The *answer* $Q(D)$ of query $Q = (\Pi, p)$ on a database D is the set of facts $\Pi(D)|_p$. (If S is a set of predicates and I a set of facts, define $I|_S = \{p(a_1, \ldots, a_n) \in I \mid p \in S\}$. Let $I|_p$ denote $I|_{\{p\}}$.)

A program is *first-order* or *nonrecursive* if it contains no recursive predicate. First-order programs define unions of conjunctive queries [11], which allow very efficient computations and received extensive earlier attention [29, 3].

To differentiate from new facts in a current state, we use a special predicate q^o to represent facts over q stored or computed in the previous state. (In particular, for each set I of facts, I^o is the set of facts obtained from I by replacing each predicate q with q^o.) These old facts will then be used for computing the new facts in the query answer after the updates.

Definition: A *first-order incremental evaluation system* (or *FOIES*)) *for* a query (Π, p) is a triple $\langle \Pi_p, S, \Pi_\delta \rangle$, where:

- Π_p is an *initial* program such that $\Pi_p(D)|_p = \Pi(D)|_p$ for each database D;
- S is a set of IDB predicates containing p; and
- Π_δ is a nonrecursive, *incremental* program such that

$$\Pi_p(D \cup \Delta)|_S = \Pi_\delta([\Pi_p(D)|_S \cup D]^o \cup \Delta)|_S \cup \Pi_p(D)|_S$$

  for each database D and each set Δ consisting of one EDB fact.

Intuitively we store $\Pi_p(D)|_S$ to reduce the cost of evaluating $\Pi_p(D \cup \Delta)|_S$. This avoids recomputing the facts in $\Pi_p(D)|_S$ after inserting the fact in Δ. The benefits of incremental evaluation depend mostly on the choice of Π_δ, which computes the new facts in the answer on the updated database. To concentrate on efficiency benefit, we require Π_δ to be nonrecursive (or first-order).

Example 2.1: Consider the query $Q = (\Pi, p)$, where

$$\Pi = \left\{ \begin{array}{l} p(x,z) \leftarrow g(x,z) \\ p(x,z) \leftarrow g(x,y), p(y,z) \end{array} \right\}.$$

Then $\langle \Pi_p, S, \Pi_\delta \rangle$ is a FOIES for Q, where $\Pi_p = \Pi, S = \{p\}$, and Π_δ is the program

$$\begin{array}{ll} p(x,z) \leftarrow g(x,z) & p(x,z) \leftarrow g(x,y), p^o(y,z) \\ p(x,z) \leftarrow p^o(x,y), g(y,z) & p(x,z) \leftarrow p^o(x,y_1), g(y_1,y_2), p^o(y_2,z) \end{array}$$

For $D = \{g(1,2), g(3,4)\}$ and $\Delta = \{g(2,3)\}$, $\Pi_p(D) = \{p(1,2), p(3,4)\}$. Predicate g^o (or p^o) in Π_δ denotes the old g (respectively, p) facts:

$$(\Pi_p(D) \cup D)^o = \{\{p^o(1,2), p^o(3,4), g^o(1,2), g^o(3,4)\}.$$

Predicate g (or p) in Π_δ denotes the new g (respectively, p) facts. The only new g fact is $g(2,3)$ from Δ. So, Π_δ computes these new facts $\{p(i,j) \mid i \in \{1,2\}, j \in \{3,4\}\}$. □

Example 2.2: Let $Q = (\Pi, p)$ be a query where Π is the following program

$$\begin{array}{l} p(x) \leftarrow s(x,y,z), p(y) \\ p(x) \leftarrow s(x,y,z), p(z) \\ p(x) \leftarrow q(x) \end{array}$$

It represents the propagation of signals p on wires x, y, z through a network of logical OR gates s with inputs q. Let $S = \{p, t\}$, where $t(x, y)$ if x is "on" whenever y is "on" and

$$\Pi_p = \left\{ \begin{array}{ll} t(x,y) \leftarrow s(x,y,z) & p(x) \leftarrow q(x) \\ t(x,z) \leftarrow s(x,y,z) & p(x) \leftarrow t(x,y), q(y) \\ t(x,z) \leftarrow t(x,y), t(y,z) & \end{array} \right\}$$

$$\Pi_\delta = \left\{ \begin{array}{ll} t(x,y) \leftarrow t_1(x,y) & \\ t(x,z) \leftarrow t^o(x,y), t_1(y,z) & \\ t(x,z) \leftarrow t_1(x,y), t^o(y,z) & \\ t(x,z) \leftarrow t^o(x,y_1), t_1(y_1,y_2), t^o(y_2,z) & \\ t_1(x,y) \leftarrow s(x,y,z) & p(x) \leftarrow q(x) \\ t_1(x,z) \leftarrow s(x,y,z) & p(x) \leftarrow t^o(x,y), q(y) \\ & p(x) \leftarrow t(x,y), q^o(y) \end{array} \right\}$$

Then it can be verified that $\langle \Pi_p, S, \Pi_\delta \rangle$ is a FOIES for Q. We will show in Section 6 that there are no FOIES $\langle \Pi'_p, S', \Pi'_\delta \rangle$ for Q with either $\Pi'_p = \Pi$ or $S' = \{p\}$. □

3 Regular Chain Queries

In this section, we define a subclass of Datalog queries, called "regular chain queries", and state an earlier result reported in [15] in the new framework of FOIES and then discuss associated complexity issues. Extensions of the regular chain queries are given in Section 4.

A *chain program* is a finite set of *chain rules* of the form

$$q(x,z) \leftarrow q_1(x,y_1), q_2(y_1,y_2), \ldots, q_k(y_{k-1},z) \tag{1}$$

where $k \geq 1$ and $x, y_1, \ldots, y_{k-1}$, and z are distinct variables. Chain programs and generalizations allow special optimization techniques [1, 12, 13]. We also explore such possibilities.

For each chain program Π, a query (Π, p) can be associated with a (context-free) grammar constructed as follows. The terminal (nonterminal) symbols are the EDB (respectively, IDB) predicates; the start nonterminal is p; and for each rule in Π of the form (1) there is a production of the form $q \rightarrow q_1 q_2 \cdots q_k$.

Definition: A query (Π, p) is *regular* if Π is a chain program and the associated grammar is right-linear (the only nonterminal in the right hand side of each production is the rightmost symbol).

The edge-path query in Example 2.1 is regular but the same-generation query is not.

Theorem 3.1: (Dong and Topor [15]) Each regular query has a FOIES. Furthermore, there is an algorithm to construct a FOIES for each regular query. □

Example 2.1 presented a FOIES for the edge-path query constructed by the algorithm (omitted here); the following example illustrates this construction on an involved regular chain query.

Example 3.2: Suppose $Q = (\Pi, p)$ is a regular query, whose associated grammar generates the regular expression $E = (qs \cup q^+t)^+$. For each subexpression e containing at least one operation, let p_e be a new IDB predicate. Let $e_1 = qs$, $e_2 = q^+$, $e_3 = e_2 t$, $e_4 = e_1 \cup e_3$, and $e_5 = e_4^+$. Then $\langle \Pi_p, S, \Pi_\delta^q \cup \Pi_\delta^s \cup \Pi_\delta^t \rangle$ is a FOIES for Q, where $S = \{p_{e_i} \mid 1 \leq i \leq 5\}$,

$$\Pi_p = \left\{ \begin{array}{ll} p_{e_1}(x,z) \leftarrow q(x,y), s(y,z) & p_{e_4}(x,z) \leftarrow p_{e_1}(x,z) \\ p_{e_2}(x,z) \leftarrow q(x,z) & p_{e_4}(x,z) \leftarrow p_{e_3}(x,z) \\ p_{e_2}(x,z) \leftarrow q(x,y), p_{e_2}(y,z) & p_{e_5}(x,z) \leftarrow p_{e_4}(x,z) \\ p_{e_3}(x,z) \leftarrow p_{e_2}(x,y), t(y,z) & p_{e_5}(x,z) \leftarrow p_{e_4}(x,y), p_{e_5}(y,z) \end{array} \right\}$$

$$\Pi_\delta^q = \left\{ \begin{array}{l} p_{e_1}(x,z) \leftarrow q(x,y), s^o(y,z) \\ p_{e_2}(x,z) \leftarrow q(x,z) \\ p_{e_2}(x,z) \leftarrow q(x,y), p_{e_2}^o(y,z) \\ p_{e_2}(x,z) \leftarrow p_{e_2}^o(x,y), q(y,z) \\ p_{e_2}(x,z) \leftarrow p_{e_2}^o(x,y_1), q(y_1,y_2), p_{e_2}^o(y_2,z) \\ p_{e_3}(x,z) \leftarrow p_{e_2}(x,y), t^o(y,z) \\ p_{e_4}(x,z) \leftarrow p_{e_1}(x,z) \\ p_{e_4}(x,z) \leftarrow p_{e_3}(x,z) \\ p_{e_5}(x,z) \leftarrow p_{e_4}(x,z) \\ p_{e_5}(x,z) \leftarrow p_{e_5}^o(x,y_1), p_{e_4}(y_1,y_2), p_{e_5}^o(y_2,y_3), p_{e_4}(y_3,y_4), p_{e_5}^o(y_4,z) \\ \qquad\qquad (\text{10 other rules defining } p_{e_5}) \end{array} \right\}$$

There are 12 rules defining p_{e_5}; they correspond to the following predicate sequences: $p_{e_5}, p_{e_5}^o p_{e_4}, p_{e_4} p_{e_5}^o, p_{e_4} p_{e_4}, \cdots$. The sequences are all subsequences of $p_{e_5}^o p_{e_4} p_{e_5}^o p_{e_4} p_{e_5}^o$ which contain at least one p_{e_4} and no consecutive $p_{e_5}^o$. Π_δ^s and Π_δ^t can be constructed similarly. □

The construction is correct because, for each edge $q(a_1, a_2)$, if there is an $L(E)$-path in a graph from b_1 to b_2, then there is such a path in which $q(a_1, a_2)$ occurs at most $\#_q(E)$ times, where $\#_q(E)$ is the number of occurrences of q in the expression E. (An $L(E)$-path is a path whose labels spell a word in $L(E)$.)

We briefly discuss complexity of FOIES. Suppose E is a $\{*, \epsilon, \emptyset\}$-free regular expression for a recursive regular query (Π, p). Then E contains at least one occurrence of $+$. We examine the number of joins in Π_δ^q where q is an EDB predicate in Π.

Proposition 3.3: There exists a FOIES $\langle \Pi_p, S, \Pi_\delta \rangle$ such that the number of joins in Π_δ^q is bounded by the sum of (i) $\sum (k_e - 1)(2^{\#_q(e)} - 1)$ where Σ ranges over E's maximal subexpressions e of the form $e_1 ... e_{k_e}$, and (ii) $2 \sum \#_q(e)(2^{\#_q(e)+2} - 4)$, where Σ ranges over E's subexpressions e with the form e_1^+ for some e_1. □

In Example 2.1, $E = g^+$, Π_δ has four rules and four joins are needed. In Example 3.2, $E = (qs \cup q^+t)^+$. The number of joins needed is 31. In general, Π may require an unbounded number of joins whereas Π_δ only need a bounded number of joins. The worst case time complexity of computing $\Pi_\delta((\Pi(D)|_S \cup D)^o \cup \Delta)$ by using Π_δ^q is n^{2j}, where n is the number of constants in D and j is the number of joins. Hence it cannot compete with incremental graph algorithms in this aspect. However, as was argued earlier, for database applications the number of joins is the desirable measure for efficiency. The most desirable aspect of Π_δ^q is its parallel efficiency. Indeed, membership of facts in the answer to the query can be checked in constant time using Π_δ^q since Π_δ is first-order [3].

4 Weakly Regular Queries

Regular queries are limited to binary predicates and chain rules. In this section we partially remove both of these restrictions by allowing nonrecursive predicates defined as unions of conjunctive queries involving predicates of arbitrary arities. We generalize the FOIES existence result for regular queries to this case and to a special case of unbounded set insertions for regular queries.

Both generalized results are based on a useful key notion of "cartesian-closed increment". A set D of facts over a binary predicate q is *cartesian closed* if $q(a_1, b_2) \in D$ whenever $q(a_1, b_1), q(a_2, b_2) \in D$ for some constants b_1, a_2. (In particular, the singleton set $\{q(a, b)\}$ is cartesian closed.) As we shall see (Lemma 4.3), each cartesian-closed set of facts can be treated as "one fact" in incremental computations. A program is a *single IDB-predicate* program if there is at most one predicate occurring in all of its rule heads(, which can have different variable patterns).

Definition: A single binary IDB-predicate program Π has *k-cartesian-closed increment* (*k-CCI*) if $k \geq 0$ and for each database D and each set Δ of one EDB fact, there exist k cartesian-closed sets $C_1, \ldots, C_k$ such that

$$\Pi(D \cup \Delta) - \Pi(D) \subseteq \cup_{i=1}^k C_i \subseteq \Pi(D \cup \Delta).$$

Π has *cartesian-closed increment* (*CCI*) if it has k-CCI for some k.

The two containments basically say that the increment of Π following the insertion of Δ is "bounded" by the k cartesian-closed sets. Note that each nonrecursive query can be converted into an equivalent nonrecursive single IDB-predicate program. Hence, no generality is lost by considering only single IDB-predicate programs.

Example 4.1: The empty program $\Pi_\emptyset$ has 1-CCI. Program $\Pi_1 = \{p_1(x, y) \leftarrow q_1(x, u, v), q_2'(v, w, z), q_3(z, y)\}$ has 1-CCI. In fact, for each database D and set Δ of one EDB fact, let

$$C = \begin{cases} \{p_1(a, y) \mid \exists w \exists z, q_2'(c, w, z), q_3(z, y) \in D\} & \text{if } \Delta = \{q_1(a, b, c)\} \\ \{p_1(x, y) \mid \exists u, q_1(x, u, a), q_3(c, y) \in D\} & \text{if } \Delta = \{q_2'(a, b, c)\} \\ \{p_1(x, b) \mid \exists u \exists v \exists w, q_1(x, u, v), q_2'(v, w, a) \in D\} & \text{if } \Delta = \{q_3(a, b)\} \end{cases}$$

Then C is cartesian closed and the containments $\Pi_1(D \cup \Delta) - \Pi_1(D) \subseteq C \subseteq \Pi_1(D \cup \Delta)$ hold.

Program $\Pi_2 = \{p_1(x,y) \leftarrow q_1(x,u,v), q_2'(v,u,z), q_3'(z,u,y)\}$ also has 1-CCI. The two rule program $\Pi_1 \cup \Pi_2$ has 2-CCI but not 1-CCI.

Program $\Pi_3 = \{p(x,y) \leftarrow q(x,z_1), q(z_1,y)\}$ has 2-CCI (by Proposition 5.3) but not 1-CCI. If $D = \{q(0,1), q(2,3)\}$ and $\Delta = \{q(1,2)\}$, then $\Pi(D) = \emptyset$ and $\Pi(D \cup \Delta) - \Pi(D) = \Pi(D \cup \Delta) = \{p(0,2), p(1,3)\}$, which is not cartesian closed.

Program $\Pi_4 = \{p_1(x,y) \leftarrow q_1'(x,y), q_2(u,v)\}$ does not have CCI. Indeed, for each $k \geq 0$, suppose D is a set of q_1' facts such that D is not the union of any k cartesian-closed sets. Then $\Pi_4(D \cup \{q_2(a,b)\}) - \Pi_4(D)$ is not bounded by any k cartesian-closed sets in $\Pi_4(D \cup \{q_2(a,b)\})$, violating the two containments in the above definition. Similarly, $\Pi_5 = \{p(x,y) \leftarrow q_1(x,u,v), q_2(z,v), q_3'(z,u,y)\}$ has no CCI. □

We shall generalize the FOIES existence result to queries whose program component are the union of a regular chain program and, for each nonrecursive predicate, one program with CCI defining that nonrecursive predicate.

Definition: A query (Π, p) is *weakly regular* if for each IDB predicate q depended on by p, the set of all rules defining q forms a regular query when q is recursive and forms a (possibly empty) program with CCI when q is nonrecursive.

Example 4.2: The query (Π, p) is weakly regular, where Π has the following three rules:

$$\begin{aligned} r_1: &\quad p(x,y) \leftarrow p_1(x,z), p(z,y) \\ r_2: &\quad p(x,y) \leftarrow p_1(x,y) \\ r_3: &\quad p_1(x,y) \leftarrow q_1(x,u,v), q_2'(v,w,z), q_3(z,y) \end{aligned}$$

$\{r_1, r_2\}$ is a regular chain program and $\{r_3\}$ is Π_1 in Example 4.1 which has CCI. □

Lemma 4.3: Let D be a labelled directed graph, $C \subseteq D$ a cartesian-closed set of edges labelled by q, E a $\{*, \epsilon, \emptyset\}$-free regular expression, and b_1, b_2 two nodes. If there is a path from b_1 to b_2 whose labels spell a word in $L(E)$ in D, then there is such a path in which the number of occurrences of edges from C is at most the number of occurrences of q in E. □

Theorem 4.4: There is a FOIES for each weakly regular query (Π, p).

Proof: (Sketch) For each nonrecursive binary predicate q in Π, let Π_q be the program defining q. Then Π_q has k_q-CCI for some k_q. Let $k = \sum_q k_q$. For an insertion of one EDB fact, we view each of the k cartesian-closed sets derived by Π_q as one "fact" to q. We then use the construction for regular queries to k inserted facts. □

Corollary 4.5: If (Π, p) is a weakly regular query such that the rules for p compute the transitive closure: $\{p(x,y) \leftarrow q(x,y);\ \ p(x,y) \leftarrow q(x,z), p(z,y)\}$, then it has a FOIES. □

Since (Π, p) of Example 4.2 is a weakly regular query, by Theorem 4.4 there is a FOIES for (Π, p). Example 4.6 below shows there is a non-weakly regular query (Π, p) which has a FOIES. It is still open whether there is a non-weakly regular query (Π, p) which does not have a FOIES. However, one can easily verify that the construction given in Theorem 4.4 does not work for the non-weakly regular queries (Π, p), where Π has three rules:

$$\begin{aligned} p_0(x,y) &\leftarrow q_1(u,x,z), q_2(z,v), q_3'(v,u,y) \\ p(x,y) &\leftarrow p_0(x,y) \\ p(x,y) &\leftarrow p_0(x,z), p(z,y) \end{aligned}$$

Example 4.6: Let $\Pi = \{r_1', r_2', r_3'\}$ be a three-rule program shown below. Then $\{r_1', r_2'\}$ is regular, and r_3' defining p_1 does not have CCI (Π_4 in Example 4.1).

$$\begin{aligned} r_1'\!: \; p(x,y) &\leftarrow p_1(x,z), p(z,y) \\ r_2'\!: \; p(x,y) &\leftarrow p_1(x,y) \\ r_3'\!: \; p_1(x,y) &\leftarrow q_1'(x,y), q_2(u,v) \end{aligned}$$

However, (Π, p) is equivalent to (Π', p), where Π' is the following program:

$$\begin{aligned} r_1\!: \; p(x,y) &\leftarrow p_2(x,y), q_2(u,v) \\ r_2\!: \; p_2(x,y) &\leftarrow q_1'(x,y) \\ r_3\!: \; p_2(x,y) &\leftarrow q_1'(x,z), p_2(z,y) \end{aligned}$$

If $\Pi_1 = \{r_2, r_3\}$, there is a FOIES $\langle \Pi_{1p}, S_1, \Pi_{1\delta} \rangle$ for (Π_1, p_2). Let $\Pi_p = \Pi_{1p} \cup \{r_1\}$, $S = S_1 \cup \{p\}$, and $\Pi_\delta = \Pi_{1\delta} \cup \{r_1\}$. Then $\langle \Pi_p, S, \Pi_\delta \rangle$ is a FOIES for (Π, p). □

So far we have limited to FOIES which computes the increment after the insertion of one fact. For a-set-at-a-time insertions, we have the following result:

Theorem 4.7: For each regular query (Π, p), there is a FOIES $\langle \Pi_p, S, \Pi_\delta \rangle$ which computes the increment after each insertion of a cartesian-closed set, i.e.,

$$\Pi_p(D \cup \Delta)|_S = \Pi_\delta([\Pi_p(D)|_S \cup D]^\circ \cup \Delta)|_S \cup \Pi_p(D)|_S$$

for each database D and each cartesian-closed set Δ of EDB facts. □

It is also of interest to extend the results beyond weakly regular queries.

5 Cartesian-Closed Increment Property

The key to the results in Section 4 is the CCI property. Thus, it is of interest to know when a query has CCI. We show that it is undecidable whether a binary Datalog or relational calculus (algebra) query has CCI. Faced with this negative result, we then focus on nonrecursive programs having only binary IDB predicates and completely characterize CCI for nonrecursive one-rule programs, and establish a characterization and the decidability of CCI for multi-rule programs.

We establish the undecidability results by reductions from the halting problem of Turing machines (modified from the reduction in [30]) and from the PCP (modified from the reduction in proving undecidability of satisfiability of relational calculus queries [3]).

Theorem 5.1: It is undecidable if a binary Datalog query has CCI and undecidable if a binary relational calculus (algebra) query has CCI. □

Nonrecursive rules with binary heads are binary conjunctive queries. We present characterizations for conjunctive queries to have CCI according to two cases, depending on whether the two variables in the rule head are the same or not. We first need the following definitions. Two programs Π_1, Π_2 are *equivalent*, denoted $\Pi_1 \equiv \Pi_2$, if $\Pi_1(D) = \Pi_2(D)$ for each database D. A rule $r : A_0 \leftarrow A_1, ..., A_m$ is ***nonredundant*** if, for each $i \in [1..m]$, $\{r\} \not\equiv \{A_0 \leftarrow A_1, ..., A_{i-1}, A_{i+1}, ..., A_m\}$. A program Π is ***nonredundant*** if for each rule r in Π, r is nonredundant and $\Pi \not\equiv \Pi - \{r\}$. In [29] nonredundant is termed "minimal", and a detailed discussion and a method for obtaining minimal equivalent program of a nonrecursive program are given.

Proposition 5.2: A nonredundant conjunctive query $\Pi = \{p(x_1, x_1) \leftarrow A_1, ..., A_m\}$ has CCI iff x_1 occurs in A_i for all $i \in [1..n]$ iff there exists an integer k such that $\Pi(D \cup \Delta) - \Pi(D)$ contains at most k facts for each database D and set Δ of one EDB fact. □

For sets $\mathcal{S}$ and $\mathcal{S}'$ of atoms, variables x and y are $(\mathcal{S}, \mathcal{S}')$-*connected* if there is a sequence $A_1, ..., A_m$ of atoms in $\mathcal{S}$ (repetitions permitted) so that x occurs in A_1, y in A_m, and A_i and A_{i+1} have a common variable not occurring in $\mathcal{S}'$ for each $i \in [1..m-1]$. We write $(\mathcal{S}, A)$-connected for $(\mathcal{S}, \{A\})$-connected. Note that $(\mathcal{S}, \emptyset)$-connectivity reduces to the usual connectivity. For $\mathcal{S} = \{q_1(x, u, v), q_3'(z, u, y)\}$ and $A = q_2(v, z)$, x and y are $(\mathcal{S}, A)$-connected: the sequence $q_1(x, u, v)$, $q_3'(z, u, y)$ is a witness since x occurs in $q_1(x, u, v)$, y in $q_3'(z, u, y)$, and u in both atoms and not in A. In contrast, for $\mathcal{S} = \{q_1(x, u, v), q_3'(z, u, y)\}$ and $A = q_2'(v, u, z)$, x and y are not $(\mathcal{S}, A)$-connected.

Proposition 5.3: A nonredundant conjunctive query $\Pi = \{p(x_1, x_2) \leftarrow A_1, \ldots, A_m\}$ where $x_1 \neq x_2$ has CCI iff for each $i \in [1..m]$, either (1) A_i contains x_1 or x_2, or (2) x_1 and x_2 are not $(\mathcal{S}_i, A_i)$-connected, where $\mathcal{S}_i = \{A_j \mid 1 \leq j \leq m, A_j \neq A_i\}$. □

Propositions 5.2 and 5.3 characterize CCI for one-rule programs. For the multi-rule case, the characterization can be reduced to the one-rule case, and is stated as follows.

Proposition 5.4: A nonredundant union of binary conjunctive queries has CCI if and only if each of its rules has CCI. □

Since a nonredundant equivalent of a nonrecursive, single IDB-predicate program can be constructed [29], we have the following:

Theorem 5.5: It is decidable if a union of binary conjunctive queries has CCI. □

6 Space-Free FOIES

We study a subclass of FOIES that (intuitively) do not use extra "space" during incremental evaluation. We first show that there are queries which have FOIES but do not have any "space-free" FOIES. We then state that the class of queries having space-free FOIES is not decidable. The proof is based on a reduction from Datalog boundedness problem.

Definition: A FOIES $\langle \Pi_p, S, \Pi_\delta \rangle$ for a query (Π, p) is *space-free* if it does not require extra stored predicates, i.e., $S = \{p\}$.

Proposition 6.1: For a single IDB-predicate query (Π, p), there is a FOIES of form $\langle \Pi, S, \Pi_\delta \rangle$ iff there is a FOIES of form $\langle \Pi, \{p\}, \Pi_\delta \rangle$ iff there is a space-free FOIES. □

Recall that the query in Example 2.2 has a FOIES. Also, consider the same-generation query (Π, sg) where Π is the following program:

$$sg(x, x) \leftarrow person(x)$$
$$sg(x, y) \leftarrow par(x, z_1), sg(z_1, z_2), par(y, z_2)$$

Proposition 6.2: There are no space-free FOIES for the query Q in Example 2.2 or for the same-generation query. □

Intuitively, the reason the query Q in Example 2.2 does not have any FOIES is that when s is large and q empty, inserting a q fact may cause the signal to be transitively passed along the network. This is not possible since the transitive closure query is not expressible without recursion. The reason for the same-generation query is similar.

We now consider the class of queries having space-free FOIES. It turns out to be undecidable. This is shown by a reduction from the "predicate boundedness" problem of Datalog programs. Predicate boundedness is a special case of boundedness [20, 17]. A Datalog program Π' is called *p'-bounded*, where p' is a predicate, if there is a nonrecursive Datalog program Π'' such that $\Pi''(D)|_{p'} = \Pi'(D)|_{p'}$ for each database D.

Lemma 6.3: Suppose Π' is a Datalog program and p' is a k-ary IDB predicate occurring in Π'. Then Π' is p'-bounded iff there is a FOIES of the form $\langle \Pi_p, \{p\}, \Pi_\delta \rangle$ for (Π, p), where Π is obtained, for each rule r in Π', by adding $q_0(y)$ to its body and replacing p' with p, and where q_0 is a new EDB predicate, p a new k-ary IDB predicate, and y a variable. □

Note that Example 2.1 showed that there are queries which have FOIES but are not predicate bounded. Combining this with Lemma 6.3, we see that FOIES strictly generalize bounded programs as a means of efficient query computation. Since it is undecidable whether an arbitrary Datalog program is predicate bounded [17], we have:

Theorem 6.4: It is undecidable if a given query (Π, p) has a space-free FOIES. It remains undecidable even if Π is a binary and/or single IDB-predicate program. □

Although there are queries that do not have space-free FOIES, it remains open if every Datalog query (and in particular, the same-generation query) has a FOIES.

7 Conclusions

We formalized the notion of FOIES. Such systems apply an efficient nonrecursive Datalog program to compute the difference in answers to the query between successive database states. Using such systems one only need to use a bounded number of joins to compute the difference after each fact insertion.

FOIES can be constructed for regular and weakly regular queries, which are regular chain programs possibly augmented with nonrecursive rules having the CCI property. FOIES can also be used to compute the increments to query answers after insertions of unbounded, cartesian-closed sets of facts. Queries having FOIES strictly generalize bounded Datalog queries. It is undecidable if, for arbitrary query, there are FOIES which do not need stored relations other than the query answer. Although there are queries that do not have space-free FOIES, it remains open if every Datalog query has a FOIES.

The CCI property is also an interesting and useful one. We gave complete characterizations and decidability results for nonrecursive programs (or unions of conjunctive queries).

Acknowledgment

The authors gratefully thank Rodney Topor and Leo Fegaras for their comments that lead to improvement of the paper.

References

[1] F. Afrati and S.S. Cosmadakis. Expressiveness of restricted recursive queries. In *Proc. ACM SIGACT Symp. on the Theory of Computing*, 113–126, 1989.

[2] K.R.Apt, H.A.Blair, and A.Walker. Towards a theory of declarative knowledge. In J.Minker, editor, *Foundations of Deductive Databases and Logic Programming.* Morgan Kaufmann, 1988.

[3] S. Abiteboul, R. Hull, and V. Vianu. *Foundations of Databases.* Manuscript. 1992.

[4] K. R. Apt and J.-M. Pugin. Maintenance of stratified databases viewed as a belief revision system. In *Proc. 6th ACM Symp. on PODS*, pages 136–145, 1987.

[5] A. Aho and J. Ullman. Universality of data retrieval languages. In *Proc. ACM Symp. on Principles of Programming Languages*, pages 110–120, 1979.

[6] F. Bancilhon. Naive evaluation of recursively defined relations. In M. L. Brodie and J. Mylopoulos, editors, *On Knowledge Base Management Systems: Integrating Artificial Intelligence and Database Technologies*. Springer-Verlag, 1985.

[7] V. Breazu-Tannen, P. Buneman, and L. Wong. Naturally embedded query languages. In *Proc. 1992 Int'l Conference on Database Theory*, pages 140–154, Berlin, Germany, October 1992.

[8] F. Bancilhon, D. Maier, Y. Sagiv, and J. D. Ullman. Magic sets and other strange ways to implement logic programs. In *Proc. 5th ACM Symp. on PODS*, 1–15, 1986.

[9] F. Bry, H. Decker and R. Manthey. A uniform approach to constraint satisfaction and constraint satisfiability in deductive databases. In *Proc. 1st Int. Conf. on EDBT*, 1988.

[10] A.L. Buchsbaum, P.C. Kanellakis and J.S. Vitter. A data structure for arc insertion and regular path finding. In *Proc. ACM-SIAM Symp. on Discrete Algorithms*, 1990.

[11] A. Chandra and P. Merlin. Optimal implementation of conjunctive queries in relational data bases. In *Proc. ACM SIGACT Symp. on the Theory of Computing*, pages 77–90, 1977.

[12] G. Dong. On Datalog linearization of chain queries. In J.D. Ullman, editor, *Theoretical Studies in Computer Science*, pages 181–206. Academic Press, 1991.

[13] G. Dong. Datalog expressiveness of chain queries: Grammar tools and characterizations. In *Proc. Eleventh ACM Symp. on Principles of Database Systems*, pages 81-90, 1992.

[14] G. Dong and J. Su. First-order on-line computation of transitive closure queries. In *Proc. of 16th Australian Computer Science Conference*, pages 721–729, 1993.

[15] G. Dong and R. Topor. Incremental evaluation of Datalog queries. In *Proc. Int'l Conference on Database Theory*, pages 282–296, Berlin, Germany, October 1992.

[16] A. Gupta, D. Katiyar, and I. S. Mumick. Counting solutions to the view maintenance problem. In K. Ramamohanarao, J. Harland, and G. Dong, editors, *Proceedings of the JICSLP Workshop on Deductive Databases, Washington DC, November 1992.*

[17] G. G. Hillerbrand, P. C. Kanellakis, H. G. Mairson, and M. Y. Vardi. Tools for Datalog boundedness. In *Proc. 10th ACM Symp. on PODS*, pages 1–12, 1991.

[18] T. Ibaraki and N. Katoh. On-line computation of transitive closure of graphs. *Information Processing Letters*, 16:95-97, 1983.

[19] G.F. Italiano. Amortized efficiency of a path retrieval data structure. *Theoretical Computer Science*, 48:273-281, 1986.

[20] Y. Ioannidis. A time bound on the materialization of some recursively defined views. In *Proc. of International Conference on Very Large Data Bases*, 1985.

[21] D. Jacobs and R. Hull. Database programming with delayed updates. In *Proc. 3rd Int'l Workshop on Database Programming Languages*, pages 416–428, 1991.

[22] H. Jakobsson. On materializing views and on-line queries. In *Proc. Int'l Conference on Database Theory*, pages 407–420, Berlin, Germany, October 1992.

[23] V. Küchenhoff. On the efficient computation of the difference between consecutive database states. In C. Delobel, M. Kifer, and Y. Masunaga, editors, *Proc. 2nd Int. Conf. on DOOD*, Lecture Notes in Computer Science 566, 478–502. Springer-Verlag, 1991.

[24] J. W. Lloyd and J. C. Shepherdson. Partial evaluation in logic programming. *Journal of Logic Programming*, 11:217–242, 1991.

[25] J. W. Lloyd, E. A. Sonenberg, and R. W. Topor. Integrity constraint checking in stratified databases. *Journal of Logic Programming*, 4(4):331–343, 1987.

[26] J-M. Nicolas. Logic for improving integrity checking in relational data bases. *Acta Informatica*, 18(3):227–253, 1982.

[27] X. Qian. On the expressive power of the bounded iteration construct. In *Proc. 2nd Int'l Workshop on Database Programming Languages*, pages 411–421, 1989.

[28] M. H. van Emden and R. A. Kowalski. The semantics of predicate logic as a programming language. *Journal of the ACM*, 23(4):733–742, 1976.

[29] J. D. Ullman. *Principles of Database and Knowledge-base Systems, Vols I and II.* 1989, Computer Science Press.

[30] M. Vardi. Decidability and undecidability results for boundedness of linear recursive programs. In *Proc. of the ACM Symposium on Principles of Database Systems*, pages 341–351, 1988.

Database Programming in Transaction Logic

Anthony J. Bonner*
University of Toronto
Department of Computer Science
Toronto, Ontario M5S 1A4, Canada
bonner@db.toronto.edu

Michael Kifer†
SUNY at Stony Brook
Department of Computer Science
Stony Brook, NY 11790, U.S.A.
kifer@cs.sunysb.edu

Mariano Consens
University of Toronto
Department of Computer Science
Toronto, Ontario M5S 1A4, Canada
consens@db.toronto.edu

Abstract

This paper presents database applications of the recently proposed *Transaction Logic*—an extension of classical predicate logic that accounts in a clean and declarative fashion for the phenomenon of state changes in logic programs and databases. It has a natural model theory and a sound and complete proof theory, but, unlike many other logics, it allows users to *program transactions*. In addition, the semantics leads naturally to features whose amalgamation in a single logic has proved elusive in the past. Finally, Transaction Logic holds promise as a logical model of hitherto non-logical phenomena, including so-called *procedural knowledge* in AI, and the *behavior* of object-oriented databases, especially methods with side effects. This paper focuses on the applications of $\mathcal{TR}$ to database systems, including transaction definition and execution, nested transactions, view updates, consistency maintenance, bulk updates, non-determinism, sampling, active databases, dynamic integrity-constraints, hypothetical reasoning, and imperative-style programming.

---

*Work supported in part by an Operating Grant from the Natural Sciences and Engineering Research Council of Canada and by a Connaught Grant from the University of Toronto.

†Supported in part by NSF grant CCR-9102159 and a grant from New York Science and Technology Foundation. Work done during sabbatical year at the University of Toronto. Support of Computer Systems Research Institute of University of Toronto is gratefully acknowledged.

1 Introduction

Transaction Logic (abbreviated $\mathcal{TR}$) accounts in a clean, declarative fashion for the phenomenon of updating arbitrary logical theories, most notably, databases and logic programs. Unlike most logics of action, $\mathcal{TR}$ is a declarative formalism for specifying and executing procedures that update and permanently change a database, a logic program or, more generally, a logical theory. As a special case, transactions can be defined as logic programs. This is possible because, like classical logic, $\mathcal{TR}$ has a "Horn" version that has *both* a procedural and a declarative semantics, as well as an efficient SLD-style proof procedure. Since the formal aspects of $\mathcal{TR}$ can be found in [12, 10, 11], this paper focuses on the applications of $\mathcal{TR}$ to database systems.

$\mathcal{TR}$ was designed with several applications in mind, especially in databases, logic programming, and AI. It was therefore developed as a general logic, so that it could solve a wide range of update-related problems. Individual applications can be carved out of different fragments of the logic. These applications, both practical and theoretical, are discussed in great detail in [10]. For instance, in logic programming, $\mathcal{TR}$ leads to a clean, logical treatment of the *assert* and *retract* operators in Prolog, which effectively extends the theory of logic programming to include updates as well as queries. In object-oriented databases, $\mathcal{TR}$ can be combined with object-oriented logics, such as F-logic [23], to provide a logical account of *methods*—procedures hidden inside objects that manipulate these objects' internal states. Thus, while F-logic covers the structural aspect of object-oriented databases, its combination with $\mathcal{TR}$ would account for the behavioral aspect as well. In AI, $\mathcal{TR}$ suggests a logical account of planning. STRIPS-like actions,[1] for instance, and many aspects of hierarchical and non-linear planning are easily expressed in $\mathcal{TR}$. In spite of the previous efforts to give these phenomena declarative semantics, until now there has been no unifying *logical* framework to account for all of them.

On the surface, there would seem to be many other candidates for a logic of transactions, since many logics reason about updates or about the related phenomena of time and action. However, despite a plethora of action logics, researchers continue to complain that there is no clear declarative semantics for updates, whether in databases or in logic programming [7, 5, 28]. In fact—in stark contrast to classical logic—no action logic has ever become a core of databases or logic-programming, in theory or in practice. There appear to be a few simple reasons for this unsuitability of existing action logics. These reasons are discussed at length in [10], and we discuss some of them briefly here.

First, most logics of time or action are *hypothetical*. For instance, some systems can infer that if action A precedes B, and B precedes C, then A must precede C. Others can infer that if a student took history 400, then he could graduate. Such systems were intended to be observers of action, not participants. They are therefore useful for reasoning about alternatives, or for analyzing programs and plans; but they are not very useful for defining procedures that actually *accomplish* state changes being reasoned about. In $\mathcal{TR}$, actions can be carried out hypothetically or they can be executed and have a permanent effect on the database, depending on one's desire. Furthermore, the proof theory of $\mathcal{TR}$ is not only a verifier of truth, but also an *executor* of

[1] STRIPS was an early AI planning system that simulated the actions of a robot arm.

transactions.

Second, many logics make a clear distinction between queries and updates. However, this distinction is blurred in object-oriented systems, where both queries and updates are special cases of a single idea: method invocation. In such systems, an update can be thought of as a query with side effects. We would like to model this behavior and thereby provide a logical foundation for object-oriented databases. $\mathcal{TR}$ achieves this by allowing every logical formula to have not only a truth value, but also a "side effect" on the database. In this way, one can account for the *behavior* of object-oriented databases—something that most formalisms do not do. By integrating $\mathcal{TR}$ with F-logic [23], the structural aspect of object-oriented systems can be accounted for as well.

The system that comes closest in *spirit* to $\mathcal{TR}$ is Prolog. Unfortunately, updates in Prolog are non-logical operations and, as a result, state-changing procedures are often the most awkward of Prolog programs, and the most difficult to understand, debug, and maintain. $\mathcal{TR}$ provides a general solution to the aforementioned limitations, both of Prolog and of action logics.

2 Overview of Transaction Logic

$\mathcal{TR}$ is an extension of first-order logic, both syntactically and semantically. It also has a natural model theory and a sound-and-complete proof theory. This section gives an overview of the syntax and the model theory. A complete development of $\mathcal{TR}$, including proof theory, can be found in [10] (and to some extent in [12]).

Like classical logic, $\mathcal{TR}$ has a "Horn" version that is of particular interest for deductive databases. In Horn $\mathcal{TR}$, a transaction is defined by Datalog-style rules in which the premise specifies a *sequence* of queries and updates. Horn $\mathcal{TR}$ is thus a logical language for programming database transactions, just as Datalog is a logical language for programming queries. Furthermore, Horn $\mathcal{TR}$ has an efficient SLD-style proof procedure and also a dual, bottom-up procedure [12, 10]. These proof procedures answer queries, execute transactions, *and* update the database. Because of its importance, much of this paper focuses on applications of Horn $\mathcal{TR}$, but first we describe full $\mathcal{TR}$, without the Horn restriction.

2.1 Syntax

The syntax of $\mathcal{TR}$ distinguishes two kinds of formulas: *transaction formulas* and *elementary transitions*. The former define composite transactions, and the latter define elementary updates.

Transaction formulas are used to define transactions and formulate queries. Transaction formulas extend first-order formulas with a new connective, $\otimes$, called *serial conjunction*. Formally, transaction formulas are defined recursively as follows. An *atomic* transaction formula is an expression of the form $p(t_1, \ldots, t_n)$, where p is a predicate symbol, and $t_1, \ldots, t_n$ are terms (as in classical predicate calculus). If ϕ and ψ are transaction formulas, then so are $\phi \vee \psi$, $\phi \wedge \psi$, $\phi \otimes \psi$, $\neg\phi$, $(\forall X)\phi$, and $(\exists X)\phi$, where X is a variable. Thus, the expression $a(X) \vee \neg[b(X) \otimes c(X, Y)]$ is a transaction formula. Informally,

$\psi \otimes \phi$ says, "Do ψ and then do ϕ." A dual connective, *serial disjunction*, is also useful (Section 3.8): $\psi \oplus \phi$ is equivalent to $\neg(\neg\phi \otimes \neg\psi)$.

Serial conjunction provides a basic way to *sequence* transactions, where $\phi\otimes\psi$ means "do ϕ then do ψ." In contrast, classical conjunction, "$\wedge$", constrains the non-determinism of a transaction. For instance, $\phi \wedge \psi$ means, "do ϕ in a way compatible with doing ψ." This use of "$\wedge$" is further discussed in Section 3.8. Apart from this, "$\wedge$" also has the traditional role of forming logic programs: in $\mathcal{TR}$, as in classical logic, any finite set of rules is equivalent to a conjunction of all the rules in the set. In $\mathcal{TR}$, such a set of transaction formulas is called a *transaction base*.

A transaction base defines complex formulas in terms of simpler ones. However, we also need a way to specify *elementary changes* to a database. One way to define such transitions is to build them into the semantics as in [25, 27, 16, 2]. A problem with this approach is that adding new kinds of elementary transitions leads to a redefinition of the very notion of a model and thus to an overhaul of the entire proof theory. This is a serious drawback since there appears to be no small, single set of elementary transitions that is best for all purposes [10]. Indeed, Sections 3.3 and 3.4 introduce two new kinds of elementary update. Thus, rather than committing $\mathcal{TR}$ to a fixed set of elementary transitions, we have chosen to treat the elementary transitions as a *parameter* of $\mathcal{TR}$. Each set of elementary transitions thus gives rise to a different version of the logic. To achieve this, elementary transitions are defined by logical axioms.

Elementary transitions are formulas of the form $\langle\phi, \psi\rangle u$, where ϕ, ψ are (sets of) closed first-order formulas and u is an atomic formula, called the *name* of the transition. Intuitively, this formula says that u is an update that transforms database ϕ into database ψ. For instance, if the atoms $ins{:}q(t)$ and $del{:}q(t)$ stand for the insertion and deletion of atom $q(t)$, then they would be defined by an enumerable set of elementary transitions consisting of the following formulas:

$$\langle \mathbf{D}, \mathbf{D} + \{q(t)\}\rangle\, ins{:}q(t) \qquad\qquad \langle \mathbf{D}, \mathbf{D} - \{q(t)\}\rangle\, del{:}q(t)$$

for every relational database $\mathbf{D}$.[2] Enumerable sets of elementary transitions are called *transition bases*. In practice, these formulas would not be materialized all at once, but would be generated on demand by an algorithm. The reader is referred to [10] for a more detailed discussion of transition bases.

As seen from the above syntax, there is no strict distinction in $\mathcal{TR}$ between predicates that query the database and predicates that update it. As in classical logic, every predicate has a truth value, but in addition, every predicate may have a side effect by changing the state of the database. This uniformity of representation is important for modeling *methods* in object-oriented databases, where one generally does not distinguish between information-retrieving and state-changing methods. Nevertheless, if desired, $\mathcal{TR}$ can make such a distinction by using different sorts of predicates, one for updates and one for queries. For instance, it may be a good programming practice to reserve a special set of predicates for certain basic updates. This paper uses just such a convention:

[2]For relational databases, the operators $+$ and $-$ can be thought of as union and set-difference. However, if $\mathbf{D}$ is a general first-order formula, then defining insertion and deletion is more involved [22].

for each predicate symbol p, we use another predicate symbol, $ins{:}p$, to represent insertions of tuples into p. Likewise, we represent deletions from p by the predicate $del{:}p$. Thus the formula $ins{:}p(a) \otimes ins{:}p(b) \otimes ins{:}p(c)$ represents an updating transaction that inserts $p(a)$ into the database, then $p(b)$, and then $p(c)$.

2.2 An Example

This section gives a simple example of a transaction base. The body of each rule is a sequence of atomic formulas, some of which are queries and some of which are updates. The example shows how updates can be combined with queries to define complex transactions. It also illustrates the use of transaction subroutines (or nested transactions), and shows how $\mathcal{TR}$ improves upon Prolog's update operators.

Example 2.1 (Financial Transactions) Suppose the balance of a bank account is given by the relation $balance(Acct, Amt)$. To modify this relation, we are provided with a pair of elementary update operations: $del{:}balance(Acct, Amt)$ to delete a tuple from the relation; and $ins{:}balance(Acct, Amt)$, which inserts a tuple into the relation. Using these two updates, we define four transactions: $change{:}balance(Acct, Bal1, Bal2)$ to change the balance of an account from one amount to another; $withdraw(Amt, Acct)$ to withdraw an amount from an account; $deposit(Amt, Acct)$ to deposit an amount into an account; and $transfer(Amt, Acct1, Acct2)$ to transfer an amount from one account to another. These transactions are defined by the following four rules, which form a transaction base:

$$
\begin{array}{lll}
transfer(Amt, Acct1, Acct2) & \leftarrow & withdraw(Amt, Acct1) \otimes deposit(Amt, Acct2) \\
withdraw(Amt, Acct) & \leftarrow & balance(Acct, Bal) \otimes Bal \geq Amt \\
 & & \quad \otimes change{:}balance(Acct, Bal, Bal - Amt) \\
deposit(Amt, Acct) & \leftarrow & balance(Acct, Bal) \\
 & & \quad \otimes change{:}balance(Acct, Bal, Bal + Amt) \\
change{:}balance(Acct, Bal1, Bal2) & \leftarrow & del{:}balance(Acct, Bal1) \\
 & & \quad \otimes ins{:}balance(Acct, Bal2)
\end{array}
$$

In each rule, the premises are evaluated from left to right—an evaluation order imposed by the serial conjunction, $\otimes$. For instance, the first rule says: to transfer an amount from $Acct1$ to $Acct2$, first withdraw the amount from $Acct1$ and, if the withdrawal succeeds, deposit the amount in $Acct2$. Likewise, the second rule is interpreted thus: to withdraw an amount, Amt, from an account, $Acct$, first retrieve the balance of the account; then check that the account will not be overdrawn by the transaction; if all is well, change the balance from Bal to $Bal - Amt$. Notice that the atom $balance(Acct, Bal)$ is a query that retrieves the balance of the specified account and $Bal \geq Amt$ is a test. All other atoms in this example are updates. The fourth rule changes the balance of an account by deleting the old balance and then inserting the new balance. Unlike the other rules, this rule is defined in terms of built-in, elementary updates, *del:balance* and *ins:balance*. □

Observe that the rules in Example 2.1 can easily be rewritten in Prolog, by replacing "$\otimes$" with "," and replacing the elementary transitions, *ins:balance* and *del:balance*, with *assert* and *retract*, respectively. However, the resulting, apparently innocuous, Prolog program will not execute correctly! The problem is that Prolog does not undo updates during backtracking. As an example, consider a transaction involving two transfers, defined as follows:

$$?-\ transfer(Fee, Client, Broker) \otimes transfer(Cost, Client, Seller)$$

That is, a fee is transferred from a client to a broker, and then a cost is transferred from the client to a seller. Because this is intended to be transaction, it must behave atomically; that is, it must execute entirely or not at all. Thus, if the second transfer fails, then the first one must be rolled back. In this respect, $\mathcal{TR}$ behaves correctly. Prolog, however, does not, since it commits updates immediately and does not undo partially executed transactions. Thus, if the second transfer above were to fail (say, because the client's account would be overdrawn by the transaction), then Prolog would *not* undo the first one, thus leaving the database in an inconsistent state.

Getting around this problem takes much out of the simplicity of Prolog programming. In fact, the non-logical behavior of Prolog updates is notorious for making Prolog programs cumbersome and heavily dependent on Prolog's backtracking strategy. $\mathcal{TR}$ fixes this problem by providing a simple logical semantics for database updates.

2.3 Model Theory

This section discusses the model theory of $\mathcal{TR}$. For easy reference, some details are given in Appendix A; the reader is referred to [10] for a full treatment.

Just as the syntax of $\mathcal{TR}$ is based on two basic ideas—serial conjunction and elementary transitions—semantics is also based on a few fundamental principles:

- *Transaction Execution Paths*: A transaction causes a sequence of database state changes;
- *Database States*: A database state is a *set* of (classical) first-order semantic structures;
- *Executional Entailment*: Transaction execution corresponds to truth over a sequence of states.

Transaction Execution Paths: When the user executes a transaction, the database may change, going from some initial state to some final state. In doing so, the database may pass through any number of intermediate states. For example, execution of the transaction $ins{:}a \otimes ins{:}b \otimes ins{:}c$ takes the database from an initial state, $\mathbf{D}$, through the intermediate states $\mathbf{D}+\{a\}$ and $\mathbf{D}+\{a,b\}$, to the final state $\mathbf{D}+\{a,b,c\}$. This idea of a sequence of states is central to our semantics of transactions. It also allows us to model a wide range of constraints. For example, we may require that every intermediate state satisfy some condition, or we may forbid certain sequences of states.

To model transactions, we start with a modal-like semantics, where each state represents a database, and each elementary update causes a transition from one state to another, thereby changing the database. At this point, however, modal logic and Transaction Logic begin to part company. The first major difference is that truth in $\mathcal{TR}$ structures does not hinge on a set of arcs between states. Instead, we focus on *paths*, that is, on sequences of states. (This focus on paths is related to the version of Process Logic in [20], but the two logics are fundamentally different [10].) Because of the emphasis on paths, we refer to semantic structures in $\mathcal{TR}$ as *path structures*. Second, truth in path structures is defined on paths, not states. For example, we would say that the path $\mathbf{D}$, $\mathbf{D}+\{a\}$, $\mathbf{D}+\{a,b\}$ satisfies the formula $ins{:}a \otimes ins{:}b$, since it represents an insertion of a followed by an insertion of b. A path of length 1 corresponds to a single database state. In this way, one model-theoretic device, paths, accounts for databases, updates, queries and more general transactions.

Other logical connectives are also interpreted on paths, *i.e.*, in terms of action. For instance, $\phi \vee \psi$ is true on a path iff ϕ is true or ψ is true. This gives rise to non-deterministic actions, since intuitively, $\phi \vee \psi$ means, "Do ϕ or do ϕ." Section 3.4 illustrates this idea. Likewise, $\phi \wedge \psi$ is true on a path iff ϕ and ψ are both true. This provides a way of constraining non-deterministic actions. For instance, $\phi \wedge \neg\psi$ intuitively means, "Do ϕ but without doing ψ in the process." Section 3.8 illustrates this idea. Finally, note that $\otimes$ and $\wedge$ are identical on paths of length 1. Thus, on states, $\mathcal{TR}$ reduces to classical logic.

Database States: Another difference between modal logic and Transaction Logic is in the nature of states. In modal logic, a state is basically a first-order semantic structure, since each state specifies the truth of a set of ground atomic formulas. Such structures are adequate for representing relational databases, but not for representing more general theories, like indefinite databases or general logic programs. We therefore take a more general approach. Since a database is a first-order formula, which has a *set* of first-order models, we define a state to be a *set* of first-order semantic structures. Each database thus corresponds to a particular state—the state consisting of all the models of the database.

This approach to states provides a lot of flexibility when defining elementary updates. Such flexibility is needed since, for general databases, the semantics of elementary updates is not obvious, not even for relatively simple updates like insert and delete. For example, what does it mean to insert an atom b into a database that entails $\neg b$, especially if $\neg b$ itself is not explicitly present in the database? There is no simple answer to this question, and many solutions have been proposed (see [22] for a comprehensive discussion). For these reasons, we take a general approach to elementary updates. For us, an elementary update is a mapping that takes each database $\mathbf{D}_1$ to some other database $\mathbf{D}_2$, where a database is any first-order formula. More generally, an elementary update may be non-deterministic, so it is not just a mapping, but a *binary relation* on databases.

3 Database Applications

A wide variety of interesting and useful formulas can be constructed in $\mathcal{TR}$, formulas that capture many of the novel and important features of database and knowledge-base systems. These features include transaction definition and execution, ad hoc queries, view updates, consistency maintenance, bulk updates, non-determinism, sampling, dynamic integrity-constraints, invented values, and more. This section describes some of these applications; more can be found in [10]. We shall also see that the semantics of $\mathcal{TR}$ allows the easy introduction of a modal necessity operator, $\Box$, which captures a whole new range of applications. These applications include hypothetical reasoning, imperative programming constructs, active databases, software verification, and more. $\mathcal{TR}$ thus provides a wide range of features whose amalgamation in a single declarative formalism has proved elusive in the past. Furthermore, these features all follow naturally from $\mathcal{TR}$'s path-based semantics.

3.1 Consistency Maintenance

Updating one relation often entails the need for additional updates to other relations in order to maintain the semantic consistency of the database. In such cases, updates to a relation can be done through special procedures that handle the details of consistency maintenance. Such procedures are easily defined in $\mathcal{TR}$.

For example, suppose a university has a database of students, courses, and professors. This database includes the following four base relations:

- *takes(Stud,Crs,Sec)*, which records the students enrolled in each section of each course.
- *enrolled(Crs,N)*, which records the total number of students, N, enrolled in a course.
- *instructs(Prof,Crs,Sec)*, which records the professors who teach each section of each course.
- *load(Prof,N)*, which records each professor's course load, N, *i.e.*, the total number of classes that he teaches.

Per the convention adopted in this paper, we assume that for each base relation, p, the transition base underlying the database system defines two elementary update predicates, *ins:p* and *del:p*, for inserting and deleting tuples from relation p.

Using these elementary updates, we define two update-procedures by which students drop courses and professors are relieved from teaching sections of a course. These procedures ensure database consistency by decrementing the enrollment total when a student drops a course, and by decrementing a professor's course load when he is relieved from teaching a course.

$$\begin{array}{rcl}
drop(Stud, Crs, Sec) & \leftarrow & takes(Stud, Crs, Sec) \otimes del{:}takes(Stud, Crs, Sec) \\
 & & \quad \otimes\ decr_enrolled(Crs) \\
relieve(Prof, Crs, Sec) & \leftarrow & instructs(Prof, Crs, Sec) \otimes \\
 & & \quad del{:}instructs(Prof, Crs, Sec) \otimes decr_load(Prof) \\
decr_enrolled(Crs) & \leftarrow & enrolled(Crs, N) \otimes del{:}enrolled(Crs, N) \otimes \\
 & & \quad ins{:}enrolled(Crs, N-1). \\
decr_load(Prof) & \leftarrow & load(Prof, N) \otimes del{:}load(Prof, N) \otimes \\
 & & \quad ins{:}load(Prof, N-1)
\end{array}$$

The last two rules define procedures for decrementing the enrollment of a course and the teaching load of a professor, respectively.

3.2 View Updates

Updating a view is often an ill-defined or non-deterministic process, since changes to a view may not uniquely determine the corresponding changes to the underlying stored database. To illustrate the problems and some solutions, consider the university database of Section 3.1 to which we add the following view definition that indicates which professors teach which courses to which students:

$$
\begin{aligned}
teaches(Prof, Stud, Crs) \leftarrow\ & takes(Stud, Crs, Sec) \\
& \otimes instructs(Prof, Crs, Sec)
\end{aligned}
$$

Since *teaches* is not a base predicate, the transition base does not provide update-procedures for it. The problem is that such updates are underspecified, since an update to *teaches* must be carried out in terms of updates to the base predicates *takes* and *instructs*. For instance, a deletion from *teaches* requires either a deletion from *takes* or a deletion from *instructs*. Since there are two choices, this view update is non-deterministic.

$\mathcal{TR}$ offers two solutions to this problem. The first one is to define a distinct procedure for each allowed way of deleting a tuple from a view. The second solution is based on defining a non deterministic transaction for removing tuples from a view.

To illustrate the first approach, we define a procedure called *rem_student* that allows a user of the view to remove a student from a course. Likewise, we define a procedure called *rem_prof* that allows a user to remove a professor from a course. These two procedures are defined as follows:

$$
\begin{aligned}
rem\_student(Prof, Stud, Crs) \leftarrow\ & takes(Stud, Crs, Sec) \\
& \otimes drop(Stud, Crs, Sec) \\
rem\_prof(Prof, Stud, Crs) \leftarrow\ & takes(Stud, Crs, Sec) \\
& \otimes relieve(Prof, Crs, Sec)
\end{aligned}
$$

In this way, a user can do view deletions without knowing what section of a course a student takes or a prof teaches, and without being given direct access to the transactions *drop* and *relieve*. This approach to view updates is similar to that advocated for object-oriented databases, in which a different update method is programmed for each allowed view update [1, 6].

The second approach to the above problem is to define a non-deterministic update-procedure, *rem_teaches*, by combining the above definitions of *rem_student* and *rem_prof*:

$$
\begin{aligned}
rem\_teaches(Prof, Stud, Crs) \leftarrow\ & takes(Stud, Crs, Sec) \\
& \otimes drop(Stud, Crs, Sec) \\
rem\_teaches(Prof, Stud, Crs) \leftarrow\ & takes(Stud, Crs, Sec) \\
& \otimes relieve(Prof, Crs, Sec)
\end{aligned}
$$

To delete the fact that a professor teaches a course to a certain student, the system can perform one of two actions: (*i*) it can drop the student from the course, or (*ii*) it can relieve the professor from the course. This choice is non-deterministic and is made by the system at run time.

Of course, a user will not usually want to leave such choices entirely to the database system. In such cases, the user can constrain the system's choice, to ensure, for instance, that a deletion from the *teaches* relation does not relieve a professor from a course. To do this, he could specify the following transaction:

$$?- \ load(alberto, N) \ \otimes \ rem\_teaches(alberto, mariano, cs100) \\ \otimes \ load(alberto, N)$$

This transaction removes $teaches(alberto, mariano, cs100)$ from the view, but only if Alberto's course-load remains the same after the update. Thus, the path in which Mariano drops *cs100* will be chosen. Alternatively, the user might want to ensure that the transaction does *not* drop Mariano from the course. In this case, he would write:

$$?- \ enrollment(cs100, N) \ \otimes \ rem\_teaches(alberto, mariano, cs100) \\ \otimes \ enrollment(cs100, N)$$

This transaction succeeds only if the enrollment in the course remains the same after the transaction execution. Thus, the path in which Alberto is relieved from teaching $cs100$ will be chosen. By such means, we can constrain the way in which view updates are carried out. More generally, we can constrain the way in which any transaction is carried out, and without having to reprogram the transaction. Section 3.8 considers more sophisticated kinds of constraints.

3.3 Bulk Updates

The ability to perform bulk updates is one of the cornerstones of database languages. It is routine in such database *lingua franca* as SQL or QUEL. For example, inserting a set of tuples into a relation is a basic SQL operation, as is deleting a set of tuples from a relation. Yet, bulk updates like these are conspicuously absent from most logic-based proposals for updating logic programs. The few exceptions are [13, 16, 27, 2], which are discussed in Section 4. The unusual difficulty with this kind of update seems to arise because most logical formulations of updates are based on the insertion and deletion of *single* tuples. This is not how SQL works, however. SQL first computes a query and then inserts the resulting *set* of tuples into a relation. Deletion is handled in a similar fashion.

To capture such behavior, it appears that we need an elementary state transition that accomplishes bulk updates at the lowest level. In this section, we consider *relational assignment*, which copies the contents of one relation into another relation. Just as variable assignment is a basic operation of procedural programming languages, relational assignment can be used as a basic operation of procedural database languages [14, 15]. The rest of this section shows how to express and use relational assignment in $\mathcal{TR}$.

Unlike [25, 27, 16], specific elementary transitions are not built into the semantics of $\mathcal{TR}$. Relational assignment can therefore be added to $\mathcal{TR}$ by simply adding appropriate formulas to the transition base. To see how, consider a $\mathcal{TR}$ language, $\mathcal{L}$. For every pair of predicate symbols, r and q, of the same arity, let $\mathcal{L}$ contain a propositional constant, denoted $[r := q]$. For simplicity, we restrict our attention to deductive databases in which r is an extensional (*i.e.*, non-derived) predicate. If $\mathbf{D}$ is such a database, then let $\mathbf{D}'$ be the database derived from $\mathbf{D}$ by deleting all r-facts and replacing them by the set $\{r(t_1, \ldots, t_n) \mid \mathbf{D} \models q(t_1, \ldots, t_n)\}$ (*i.e.*, first delete the contents of relation r, and then copy the contents of relation q into r.) Finally, let the transition base, $\mathcal{B}$, contain the formula $\langle \mathbf{D}, \mathbf{D}' \rangle [r := q]$ for every such pair of databases. Thus, the transition base contains the following formulas (among many others):

$$\langle \{q(a), q(b)\}, \quad \{q(a), q(b), r(a), r(b)\} \rangle \; [r := q]$$
$$\langle \{q(a), q(b), r(c)\}, \quad \{q(a), q(b), r(a), r(b)\} \rangle \; [r := q]$$
$$\langle \{q(a), q(b), r(c), r(d)\}, \quad \{q(a), q(b), r(a), r(b)\} \rangle \; [r := q]$$

Note that, by definition, the extent of r after executing the elementary state transition $[r := q]$ is determined entirely by the current database state. This has the following important implication: if q is defined by a set of rules where some of the rules are in the database and some are in the transaction base, then only the tuples contributed by the rules in the database will be assigned to r.

Having defined relational assignment, we can easily define bulk inserts and deletes. Suppose we wanted to add to r all tuples satisfying some condition ϕ and delete from s all tuples satisfying ψ. To do so, for each of these operations, we first define two derived relations, $q1$ for the insertion into r, and $q2$ for the deletion from s, as follows:

$$\begin{aligned} q1(X) &\longleftarrow r(X) \\ q1(X) &\longleftarrow \phi(X) \\ q2(X) &\longleftarrow s(X) \wedge \neg\psi(X) \end{aligned} \tag{1}$$

Note that the extension of $q1$ is $r \cup \phi$, and the extension of $q2$ is $s - \psi$. To actually perform the updates, we use the elementary transitions $[r := q1]$ and $[s := q2]$, which effectively insert the tuples satisfying ϕ into r, and delete the tuples satisfying ψ from s. In this way, relational assignment captures the update behavior of SQL, including the use of existential subqueries to perform bulk deletion. It should be clear from an earlier remark that the above rules must all be in $\mathbf{D}$ for the relational assignment to work as intended.

More-complex transactions are also easy to express. For example, consider the transaction, "*Raise the salary of all managers by 7%, and then retrieve all employees whose salary is greater than 100K.*" This transaction can be expressed as follows:

$$\begin{aligned} &empl2(E, Sal * 1.07, mngr) \longleftarrow empl(E, Sal, mngr) \\ &empl2(E, Sal, Rank) \longleftarrow empl(E, Sal, Rank) \wedge Rank \neq mngr \\ &result(E) \longleftarrow [empl := empl2] \otimes query(E) \\ &query(E) \longleftarrow empl(E, Sal, Rank) \otimes Sal > 100K \\ &query(\mathtt{null}) \longleftarrow \end{aligned} \tag{2}$$

The new contents of the employee relation is computed by the first two rules and is held in the relation *empl2*. As explained above, both these rules must be in the database, $\mathbf{D}$, in order for the assignment $[empl := empl2]$ in the third rule to work as intended. The query $?-\ result(E)$ changes the database state *and* returns all suitable employees as the answer. If no employee earns in excess of 100K after the update, the update is performed anyway, but the only answer to be returned is some specifically designated value, `null`. Observe also that this transaction simultaneously involves deletion of some tuples with old salaries *and* insertion of tuples with new salaries. Of course, this combined transaction could have been expressed following the methodology for deletions and insertions described earlier, in (1). However, this would have required two relational assignments instead of one. In the above example, we defined the temporary relation *empl*2 in such a way that only one relational assignment is needed.

We should also note that when the auxiliary predicates (such as $q1$, $q2$, *empl*2 above) are non-recursive, it is possible to do away with these predicates and their defining rules. To this end, we can define the following, more general, form of relational assignment: $[q := (\bar{X}).\phi]$. Here ϕ is a first-order formula all of whose predicates are in $\mathbf{D}$ and $(\bar{X})$ is a list of all free variables in ϕ (with possible repetitions). We assume that the length of $\bar{X}$ equals the arity of q. This elementary state transition has the effect of assigning q the relation $\{\bar{x} \mid \phi[\bar{x}] \text{ is true}\}$ — the set of all tuples that when substituted for $\bar{X}$ makes ϕ true.[3] We can now rewrite rulebase (2) as follows:

$$\begin{array}{l} result(E) \longleftarrow [empl := (E, Sal, Rank).\phi] \otimes query(E) \\ query(E) \longleftarrow empl(E, Sal, Rank) \otimes Sal > 100K \\ query(\mathtt{null}) \longleftarrow \end{array}$$

where ϕ is the following first-order formula:

$$\begin{array}{l} \exists S[empl(E, S, mngr) \;\wedge\; Sal = 1.07 * S] \\ \vee[empl(E, Sal, Rank) \;\wedge\; Rank \neq mngr] \end{array}$$

These generalized bulk updates have all the power of bulk updates in SQL, including subqueries. This is because a generalized bulk update computes an arbitrary first-order query, ϕ, and assigns its output to a base relation, q. As a special case, a bulk update can change the value of q to $q \cup \phi$, thereby expressing arbitrary SQL insertions. Likewise, a bulk update can change the value of q to $q - \phi$, thereby expressing arbitrary SQL deletions.

Finally, it is worth noting that the use of generalized bulk updates in $\mathcal{TR}$ closely parallels the embedding of SQL in procedural programming languages. In both cases, bulk updates are elementary operations invoked from a host language. And in both cases, these bulk updates can have free variables (parameters) that are bound at run time. Furthermore, in an update like $[q := (\bar{X})\phi]$, the base relation q can play the role of a *cursor*. Using the methods introduced in Section 3.6, one can iterate over the relation q one tuple at a time, just like an SQL cursor. $\mathcal{TR}$ can thus be seen as a formal basis for embedded SQL.

3.4 Non-Deterministic Sampling

In [24], Krishnamurthy and Naqvi proposed the so-called *choice*-operator. They argued that non-deterministic choice is needed to write queries such as, "Pro-

[3] If ϕ is a disjunction of existentially quantified conjuncts of positive literals then "truth" can be taken to mean truth in all models of ϕ. Otherwise, if literals can be negative, truth should be viewed with respect to a perfect model of ϕ. See [10] for more details.

duce a sample of one employee from each department." The idea was to introduce a special construct, $choice((\bar{X}),(\bar{Y}))$, that selects those instantiations of the variables $\bar{X}$ and $\bar{Y}$ that satisfy the functional dependency (abbr., FD) $\bar{X} \rightarrow \bar{Y}$.

In $\mathcal{TR}$, the *choice*-operator can be represented as another kind of elementary bulk update, one closely related to the relational assignment operator of the previous section. For example, consider the following query: *For each department with over 100 employees, choose an employee earning less than \$20K.* We can represent this query in $\mathcal{TR}$ using a pair of rules, as follows:

$$\begin{aligned} eligible(D,E) &\longleftarrow dept(E,D) \;\wedge\; size(D,N) \;\wedge\; N > 100 \\ &\qquad\qquad \wedge\; salary(E,S) \;\wedge\; S < 20K \\ answer(D,E) &\longleftarrow [sample \overset{1\rightarrow 2}{:=} eligible] \otimes sample(D,E) \end{aligned} \tag{3}$$

The first rule produces a set of candidate answers, by selecting *all* eligible employees from the appropriate departments. The second rule then samples the set of candidates, selecting *one* eligible employee per department. The heart of this rule is a new type of elementary update, $[sample \overset{1\rightarrow 2}{:=} eligible]$, that sets the extent of relation *sample* to be a subset of relation *eligible*. Any subset will do as long as it has the following two properties:

- it satisfies the specified FD, $1 \rightarrow 2$; and
- $sample[1] = eligible[1]$, i.e., the projections of *sample* and *eligible* on the first attribute are equal (and thus every department is represented in the sample).

In general, we introduce an elementary update, called *sampling assignment*, denoted $[p \overset{fd}{:=} q]$, where fd is an FD, and p and q are predicate symbols of the same arity (where p is an extensional predicate). Given a database, $\mathbf{D}$, the assignment updates relation p non-deterministically. In particular, it sets the extent of p to be some subset, *rel*, of the relation $\{\, \bar{x} \mid \mathbf{D} \models q(\bar{x}) \,\}$ that satisfies the following two properties:

1. *rel* satisfies the functional dependency fd; and
2. *rel* is a *maximal* subrelation of $\{\bar{x} \mid \mathbf{D} \models q(\bar{x})\}$ having property 1.

As with bulk updates, sampling assignments are defined in the transition base. For instance, to define $[p \overset{1\rightarrow 2}{:=} q]$, we add the following entries to the transition base (among many others):

$$\langle \{q(a,b), q(a,c), q(a,d)\},\quad \{q(a,b), q(a,c), q(a,d), p(a,b)\}\rangle\ [p \overset{1\rightarrow 2}{:=} q]$$

$$\langle \{q(a,b), q(a,c), q(a,d)\},\quad \{q(a,b), q(a,c), q(a,d), p(a,c)\}\rangle\ [p \overset{1\rightarrow 2}{:=} q]$$

$$\langle \{q(a,b), q(a,c), q(a,d)\},\quad \{q(a,b), q(a,c), q(a,d), p(a,d)\}\rangle\ [p \overset{1\rightarrow 2}{:=} q]$$

In practice, this transition base would probably be enumerated by a special procedure written in a language like C. The important point here is that the semantics of $\mathcal{TR}$ allows such procedures. Thus we do not have to explicitly construct a choice operator, unlike in [24, 30]. Instead, it falls out naturally from the semantics of $\mathcal{TR}$ as a special case.

3.5 Hypothetical Reasoning

Hypothetical queries play an important role in reasoning about knowledge [9]. Because of such queries, it is often necessary to perform hypothetical updates as well as actual ones. For instance, a game-playing program may reason as follows: After performing some given series of actions, α, does the opponent's situation improve? Observe that the actions mentioned in this query are purely hypothetical and are *not* committed. If the answer to the query is "no," then the program would perform action α, at which point the action *is* committed. Otherwise, the program would do further depth analysis and perform the most favourable move that it finds. By distinguishing between real and hypothetical actions, this program combines reasoning about action (planning, exploration of alternatives, etc) with actual execution of actions (committing itself to a particular course of action). $\mathcal{TR}$ is the only logic we are aware of that can do *both* these things.

To represent hypothetical actions, we extend the syntax of $\mathcal{TR}$. Formally, a *hypothetical formula* is an expression of the form $\Diamond\phi$ or $\Box\phi$, where ϕ is a transaction formula or a hypothetical transaction formula. Hypothetical operators can thus be nested. In modal terms, $\Diamond\phi$ means that the execution of ϕ is *possible* starting at the present state, and $\Box\phi$ means that the execution of ϕ is *necessary* at the present state. Necessity means that ϕ is executable along *every* path leaving the current state, **D**. Likewise, possibility means that ϕ is executable along *some* path leaving the current state. Hypotheticals hold immediately, *i.e.*, over paths of length 1, and so they do not cause any real state transitions. The formal meaning of hypothetical formulas is given in the appendix. As shown in [10], these formulas cannot be be expressed in the version of $\mathcal{TR}$ presented so far. Thus they strictly increase the power of the language.

The next two sections explore some non-trivial application of hypothetical operators. Other applications of hypotheticals as well as a sound-and-complete proof theory for them are developed in [10].

3.6 Imperative Programming Constructs

Perhaps, one of the most interesting bonuses provided by the hypothetical operators in $\mathcal{TR}$ is the ability to express standard imperative constructs, such as **if-then-else** and **while-do** in a simple, declarative way. For instance, the following rules express an **if-then-else** statement:

$$\begin{array}{l} if\_a\_b\_c \longleftarrow (\Diamond a) \otimes b \\ if\_a\_b\_c \longleftarrow (\Box\neg a) \otimes c \end{array} \tag{4}$$

Intuitively, the query $?\!-\ if\_a\_b\_c$ says, "if it is possible to do a, then do b, else do c." We shall therefore write **if** $\Diamond a$ **then** b **else** c **fi** as an abbreviation for the proposition $if\_a\_b\_c$, provided that $if\_a\_b\_c$ does not occur in the head of any other rule. (Alternatively, it could abbreviate the formula $(\Diamond a \otimes b) \vee (\Box\neg a \otimes c)$, which combines the bodies of the two rules above.) Because a can be an action that changes the state of the database, the use of the hypotheticals is crucial to the proper formulation of this imperative statement. Furthermore, the negation in "$\Box\neg a$" is of the negation-by-failure variety. In [10], we present the perfect-model semantics for this negation, an adaptation from [29].

In imperative programming, it is often the case that the **else**-part is omitted, which corresponds to "**else** do nothing." To capture this, we simply remove action c from (4), Thus, the statement **if** $\Diamond a$ **then** b **fi** can be expressed as follows:

$$\begin{array}{l} if\_a\_b \longleftarrow (\Diamond a) \otimes b \\ if\_a\_b \longleftarrow \Box\neg a \end{array} \quad (5)$$

Similarly, the following rules express a **while-do** statement:

$$\begin{array}{l} while\_a\_b \longleftarrow (\Diamond a) \otimes b \otimes while\_a\_b \\ while\_a\_b \longleftarrow \Box\neg a \end{array} \quad (6)$$

Intuitively, $?-\ while\_a\_b$ says, "while it is possible to do a, do b." Here, $while\_a\_b$ is a new proposition whose definition is *recursive*, which is what achieves the iterative effect. Notice, again, the role of "$\Box\neg a$" in the second clause of (6). Here it says that if a cannot be executed, then do nothing, which effectively terminates the loop. As with the **if-then-else** construct, it is suggestive to write **while** $\Diamond a$ **do** b **od** for proposition $while\_a\_b$, provided that $while\_a\_b$ does not occur in the head of any other rule.

Note that if b cannot be executed during an iteration, then the entire loop fails, so all previous iterations are undone. This is a form of automatic error recovery. In many cases, however, it may be desirable to not undo previous iterations, but to proceed with the loop either by ignoring the failed execution of b or by invoking a designated *error-handling* routine. In $\mathcal{TR}$, this can be expressed thus:

while $\Diamond a$ **do**
  if b **then do nothing else** *error-handler* **fi**
od

Here, if b fails during any iteration, then the error-handling transaction is executed. The if statement itself denotes an atom, if_b, defined by the following rules:

$$\begin{array}{l} if\_b \longleftarrow \Diamond a \\ if\_b \longleftarrow (\Box\neg a) \otimes error\text{-}handler \end{array} \quad (7)$$

3.7 Active Databases

This section shows how active database systems can be represented as transaction bases in $\mathcal{TR}$. This representation captures several sides of the problem: (*i*) specifying an application using so-called active rules, (*ii*) detecting events, and (*iii*) specifying the algorithmic internals of the active database system, i.e., the policy for executing triggered actions. Because of space limitations, we consider a fairly simple system, one in which actions are triggered by the invocation of transactions, which sets no priorities on the triggered actions, and which executes triggered actions immediately. It is not hard to program more sophisticated systems.

The use of database programming languages to model active database systems has been discussed in [21, 32]. In those attempts, the underlying semantics is denotational. There are two main reasons for using $\mathcal{TR}$ to specify active database features and implementations. First, $\mathcal{TR}$ provides a complete formalization (including a model and a proof theory) for the behavior of the system. Second, $\mathcal{TR}$ has one underlying notation and semantics, which can describe behavior procedurally and in detail, or declaratively and at a high level.

We shall use the notation for active rules[4] suggested in Starburst [33]:[5]

$$\begin{array}{l}\textbf{define active rule } a\_rule \\ \textbf{when } event \\ \textbf{if } condition \\ \textbf{then } action\end{array} \tag{8}$$

We consider these active rules to be part of the transaction base. This particular active rule is given the name *a_rule*, and its intended meaning is that when the given *event* occurs, and provided that *condition* is true at that moment, the system should automatically execute *action*. This policy is known as *immediate coupling* of conditions and actions [26]. Later, we show how active rules like these can be programmed in $\mathcal{TR}$.

In this paper, we limit our attention to two kinds of events: commencement of a transaction and termination of a transaction. For each named transaction, $trans(X)$, these two events are represented by two atomic formulas: $trans\_start(X)$ and $trans\_done(X)$, respectively. Active rules that are triggered by such events will be executed just before *trans* starts or just after it terminates. Events specified in this way generalize those supported in actual systems [31, 34, 18], and are analogous to the idea of method invocation and method termination proposed in [8].

An Example

Consider an active database system that enforces the following constraint: after any salary increase or a salary cut, no staff member should earn more than 120% of his manager's salary. Whenever this constraint is violated, the company policy is as follows: repeatedly increase the manager's salary by 2% while simultaneously decreasing the staff member's salary by 1%, until the constraint is satisfied.

We shall first represent this salary control policy informally, using $\mathcal{TR}$ syntax mixed with Starburst-style notation for active rules. After this, we describe a general mechanism for implementing active rules in $\mathcal{TR}$.

Let us assume that the appropriate way to raise or cut a salary by a given percent is by executing transactions $raise(Empl, Percent)$ and $cut(Empl, Percent)$. (The exact definition of these transaction is immaterial for the present discussion.) These transactions can be invoked by the user explicitly, or they may be subtransactions of some other transaction that is explicitly invoked.

To enforce the salary policy for staff members, we add a pair of active rules to the transaction base. For clarity, we use deductive rules to define conditions

---

[4] We use the qualifier *active* to emphasize the differences between active database rules and (unqualified) deductive database rules.

[5] Our motive for separating the condition from the action in an active rule is simply a concession to existing approaches. In $\mathcal{TR}$, however, there is no intrinsic need to make such a distinction.

and actions. The active rule and the deductive rules are all added to the transaction base.

$$\begin{array}{l} \textbf{define active rule } \ raise\_policy \\ \textbf{when } \ raise\_done(E,P) \\ \textbf{if } \ salary\_condition(E,M) \\ \textbf{then } \ cut(E,1) \end{array} \tag{9}$$

$$\begin{array}{l} \textbf{define active rule } \ cut\_policy \\ \textbf{when } \ cut\_done(E,P) \\ \textbf{if } \ salary\_condition(E,M) \\ \textbf{then } \ raise(E,2) \end{array} \tag{10}$$

$$\begin{array}{rcl} salary\_condition(E,M) & \leftarrow & staff(E) \wedge manages(M,E) \wedge salary(E,S_{emp}) \\ & & \wedge\, salary(M,S_{mngr}) \wedge S_{emp} > 1.2 \times S_{mngr} \end{array}$$

Thus, after each invocation of the transaction $raise(E,P)$, rule (9) checks if the employee, E, is a staff member, and whether his new salary, S_{emp}, is too high relative to his manager's salary, S_{mngr}. If this condition is satisfied, the staff member's salary is lowered by 1%. This, in turn, may trigger a raise of a manager's salary by 2%.

Since rule (9) invokes the transaction *cut*, we have an implicit recursion: raising a salary triggers rule (9), which can cause salary cut, triggering rule (10). The latter may cause salary raise again, and so on. In this way, the manager's salary is repeatedly increased, and the staff member's salary is repeatedly cut, until the constraints on their salaries are satisfied.

Implementing Triggers in $\mathcal{TR}$

We now show how an active rule of the form (8) can be represented in $\mathcal{TR}$. Recall that the events associated with named transactions, *e.g.*, $trans(X)$, are represented by a pair of atoms, $trans\_start(X)$ and $trans\_done(X)$, which denote the start and end of transaction execution. The idea is to define these events as transactions that invoke the appropriate active rules just before and just after the execution of $trans(X)$.

Implementing these ideas in $\mathcal{TR}$ involves three steps. The first step is to associate the transaction, *trans*, with the events *trans_start* and *trans_done*. This is accomplished by replacing each occurrence of $trans(X)$ in the transaction base by the following formula:

$$trans\_start(X) \otimes trans(X) \otimes trans\_done(X) \tag{11}$$

This idea is common in active systems, as it makes events easy to detect.

The second step is to associate each event with the active rules that it triggers. In addition, we must specify the order (or orders) in which the active rules may fire. Let $event(X)$ denote an arbitrary event, i.e., either $trans\_start(X)$ or $trans\_done(X)$. Using rules like the following, $event(X)$ executes a sequence of active rules of the form (8):

$$\begin{array}{l} event(X) \leftarrow a\_rule_1(X) \otimes a\_rule_2(X) \otimes \cdots \otimes a\_rule_n(X) \\ \quad \ddots \\ event(X) \leftarrow a\_rule_n(X) \otimes a\_rule_{n-1}(X) \otimes \cdots \otimes a\_rule_1(X) \end{array} \tag{12}$$

Each of these rules specifies a set of active rules and an order in which they may execute. If the order of the active rules is immaterial, then the definition of $event(X)$ will have one rule for each permutation of the active rules. By selecting a particular subset of all permutations, one can specify the *conflict resolution* strategy employed by the system [34, 3]. (The reader should not be frightened by the prospect of having to write $n!$ rules. First, this can be done automatically. Second, $\mathcal{TR}$ has an operator, called *shuffle*, which makes this tiresome encoding much more succinct. Furthermore, the number of rules does not increase the cost of executing $event(X)$, since $\mathcal{TR}$'s proof theory selects just one rule non-deterministically.)

The third, and final, step in implementing the triggering mechanism is to represent each active rule as a $\mathcal{TR}$-rule. The Starburst-style rule (8) is then represented as follows:

$$a\_rule \leftarrow \textbf{if } condition \textbf{ then } action \textbf{ fi} \tag{13}$$

Note that the use of the **if-then** imperative construct from Section 3.6 is important for the correctness of our encoding of active rules in $\mathcal{TR}$. It ensures that if *condition* fails, then *a_rule* still succeeds but leaves the database unchanged. Although it is tempting to define *a_rule* using a simpler rule,

$$a\_rule \leftarrow condition \otimes action$$

this representation is incorrect. Indeed, *a_rule* thus defined would fail if *condition* fails. As a consequence, the *event*-transaction in (12) would fail too. This in turn would cause the entire transaction in (11) to fail. Obviously, this is not what is required of a trigger. In contrast, by defining *a_rule* as in (13), we achieve the effect that whenever a pre-condition of an active rule fails, the rule simply does not fire, but the *event*-transaction succeeds anyway.

The Example, Continued:

Returning to our example, each occurrence of $raise(E,P)$ in the transaction base is thus replaced by the following formula:

$$raise\_start(E,P) \otimes raise(E,P) \otimes raise\_done(E,P)$$

The start of a *raise* transaction triggers no actions; so the event $raise\_start(E,P)$ is defined by the following rule, which does nothing and always succeeds:

$$raise\_start(E,P) \longleftarrow$$

A similar transformation is done for the *cut* transaction. The completion of a *raise* or a *cut* transaction is more complex since it does trigger actions. We represent *raise_done* and *cut_done* as follows:

$$\begin{aligned} raise\_done(E,P) &\longleftarrow raise\_policy(E,P) \\ cut\_done(E,P) &\longleftarrow cut\_policy(E,P) \end{aligned}$$

To represent the active rules themselves, we use the following $\mathcal{TR}$ rules:

$$\begin{aligned} raise\_policy(E,P) &\longleftarrow \textbf{if } salary\_condition(E,M) \textbf{ then } cut(E,1) \textbf{ fi} \\ cut\_policy(E,P) &\longleftarrow \textbf{if } salary\_condition(E,M) \textbf{ then } raise(M,2) \textbf{ fi} \end{aligned}$$

3.8 Dynamic Constraints on Transaction Execution

Because transactions are defined on paths, it is possible to express a large variety of constraints on the way they execute. For instance, we can place conditions on the state of the database during transaction execution, or we may forbid certain sequences of states. We refer to such conditions as *path constraints*, or *dynamic constraints*. Such constraints are particularly well suited to areas such as planning and design, where it is common to place constraints on the way things are done. This section illustrates a variety of dynamic constraints expressible in $\mathcal{TR}$. These include temporal constraints in the style of James Allen [4], such as, "immediately after," "some time after," "during," "at the start of," and "at the end of."

There are several important problems related to constraints. One such problem, and the main subject of this section, is *constraint satisfaction*. That is, given a transaction and a constraint, we want to execute the transaction in such a way that it satisfies the constraint. For example, we might ask a robot to carry out a task while not entering restricted areas and not executing certain undesirable or dangerous sequences of action. In general, starting from the current database, we want to find *some* way of executing a transaction while satisfying constraints.

Constraint satisfaction problems are particularly easy to express in $\mathcal{TR}$ because they correspond to classical conjunction. That is, if ψ and ϕ are transaction formulas, then the formula $\psi \wedge \phi$ means, "Do transaction ψ in such a way that ϕ is satisfied along the entire execution path." The formula ϕ thus constrains the way in which ψ executes.

Constraints Based on Serial Conjunction:

Two types of path constraint naturally arise in $\mathcal{TR}$: those based on serial conjunction, and those based on serial implication. The former specify that something must be true *somewhere* on a path, and the latter specify that something must be true *everywhere* on a path. These two types of path constraint correspond roughly to two types of database integrity constraint: those based on existential quantification, and those based on universal quantification, respectively. This section gives examples of the former type of constraint. For instance, the following formula requests a robot to go to room A, passing through rooms A_1, A_2 and A_3 along the way:
$goto(roomA) \wedge go\_thru(roomA_1) \wedge go\_thru(roomA_2) \wedge go\_thru(roomA_3)$
where $go\_thru(X)$ is defined in terms of serial conjunction. The full paper elaborates on this idea.

Constraints Based on Serial Implication:

This section considers constraints based on the binary connectives "$\Leftarrow$" and "$\Rightarrow$", called *left serial implication* and *right serial implication*. These connectives are defined in terms of serial disjunction, $\oplus$, which is the dual of $\otimes$. In particular, the formula $\psi \Leftarrow \phi$ is defined to be $\psi \oplus \neg\phi$, and $\phi \Rightarrow \psi$ is defined to be $\neg\phi \oplus \psi$. Intuitively, the formula $\phi \Rightarrow \psi$ means that transaction ψ must come immediately after transaction ϕ; or more precisely, *whenever* ϕ occurs, then ψ occurs just *after* it. The formula $\psi \Leftarrow \phi$ is a kind of dual. It says that *whenever* ϕ occurs, then ψ must have occurred just *before* it.

Constraints based on serial implication constrain a transaction during every moment of its execution. For instance, we might want a robot to remain inside a particular region while executing a task. We can also put constraints on specific actions that the robot might take. For instance, we might request a robot to perform a series of actions subject to the following constraints: (*i*) Before leaving a room, turn off all the lights; (*ii*) After entering a room, turn on all the lights; (*iii*) Unlock the rifle before firing it; (*iv*) Lock and reload the rifle after firing it. In these examples, "before" and "after" mean "immediately before" and "immediately after," respectively. Serial implication expresses these two relations. For example, constraints (*iii*) and (*iv*) are expressed by the following two formulas, respectively:

$$unlock \Leftarrow shoot \qquad\qquad shoot \Rightarrow lock \otimes load$$

In addition to the temporal relations "immediately before" and "immediately after," $\mathcal{TR}$ can express many other temporal relations in the style of James Allen's theory of time intervals [4]. These relations include "some time before," "some time after," "during," "at the start of," "at the end of," etc. The full paper elaborates on these ideas.

4 Comparison with Other Works

As far as databases are concerned, we are not aware of any other declarative approach to updates that is as comprehensive as $\mathcal{TR}$. In particular, none of the works discussed below is capable of expressing constraints on the execution of complex transactions. Likewise, none of them can *seamlessly* accommodate hypothetical state transitions with transitions that actually commit; and, with the exception of [22], all of the works are limited to updating sets of ground atomic facts. A much more extensive comparison can be found in [10].

Winslett [35] did foundational work on the meaning of updates to general logical theories. Later, Grahne, Katsuno and Mendelzon [22, 19] axiomatized various theories of state transition and studied tractable cases of what we call "elementary state transitions." Our approach to state transitions is inspired by these results.

Manchanda and Warren [25] introduce Dynamic Prolog—a logic system where update transactions "work right," *i.e.*, when failed, they do not leave a residue in the database. Like $\mathcal{TR}$, their logic can be used to update views, and transactions can be nondeterministic. However, they distinguish between update predicates and query predicates—a drawback if we keep an eye on object-oriented applications, as explained in the introduction. Furthermore, bulk updates, constraints on transaction execution, and the insertion and deletion of rules cannot be expressed, due to the chosen semantics. In addition, the proof theory for Dynamic Prolog is impractical for carrying out updates, since one must know the final database state *before* inference begins. Apparently, realizing this drawback, Manchanda and Warren developed an interpreter for "executing" transactions. However, this interpreter is incomplete with respect to the model theory and, furthermore, it is not based on the proof theory of Dynamic Prolog. To a certain extent, it can be said that Manchanda and Warren have managed to formalize their intuition procedurally, but not as an inference system.

Naqvi and Krishnamurthy [27] extended Datalog with update operators, which were later incorporated in the LDL language. Since LDL is geared towards database applications, this extension has bulk updates, for which an operational semantics exists. Unfortunately, the model theory presented in [27] is somewhat limited. First, it matches the proposed execution model only in the propositional case, and so it does not cover bulk updates. Second, it is only defined for update-programs in which commutativity of elementary updates can be assumed. For sequences of updates in which this does not hold, the semantics turns out to be rather tricky and certainly does not qualify as "model theoretic." Third, the definition of "legal" programs in [27] is highly restrictive, making it difficult to build complex transactions out of simpler ones.

Abiteboul and Vianu developed a family of declarative update languages [2], including impressive results on complexity and expressibility. However, these languages lack several features that are present in $\mathcal{TR}$. First, they apply only to relational databases, not to arbitrary sets of first-order formulas. Thus, it is not possible to insert or delete rules from a deductive database. Second, there is no facility for constraining transaction execution. Indeed, transaction output is the only concern. Third, these languages are not part of a full-blown *logic*: arbitrary logical formulas cannot be constructed, and although there is an operational semantics, there is no model theory and no logical inference system. It is therefore unlikely that these languages have the flexibility to find applications in other domains, such as AI. Finally, these languages do not support transaction subroutines. This lack of subroutines is reflected in the data complexity of some of the languages: they are in PSPACE, whereas recursive subroutines require EXPTIME.

The works [28, 17] are related to [2] in that they all borrow much of their syntax from deductive databases and yet their semantics is operational (although inspired by logical model theory). As such, these languages are in a different league than $\mathcal{TR}$; they are also unsuitable for defining transaction subroutines, nested transactions, constraints, and for reasoning about actions.

Acknowledgments: Alberto Mendelzon provided us with many insights regarding updates of logic theories. Thanks to Ray Reiter for commenting on various aspects of $\mathcal{TR}$, especially on the issues related to the frame problem. Discussions with Gösta Grahne, Peter Revesz, Fangzhen Lin, Javier Pinto, Dimitris Lagouvardos, Jan Van den Bussche, and Roel Wieringa are also gratefully acknowledged.

References

[1] S. Abiteboul and A.J. Bonner. Objects and views. In *ACM SIGMOD Conference on Management of Data*, pages 238–247, Denver, Colorado, May 29–31 1991.

[2] S. Abiteboul and V. Vianu. Procedural and declarative database update languages. In *ACM SIGACT-SIGMOD-SIGART Symposium on Principles of Database Systems (PODS)*, pages 240–250, 1988.

[3] R. Agrawal, R. Cochrane, and B. Lindsay. On maintaining priorities in a production rule system. In *Intl. Conference on Very Large Data Bases (VLDB)*, pages 479–487, 1991.

[4] J.F. Allen. Towards a general theory of action and time. *Artificial Intelligence*, 23:123–154, July 1984.

[5] F. Bancilhon. A logic-programming/Object-oriented cocktail. *SIGMOD Record*, 15(3):11–21, September 1986.

[6] T. Barsalou, N. Siambela, A.M. Keller, and G. Wiederhold. Updating relational databases through object-based views. In *ACM SIGMOD Conference on Management of Data*, pages 248–257, Denver, Colorado, May 29–31 1991.

[7] C. Beeri. New data models and languages—The challenge. In *ACM SIGACT-SIGMOD-SIGART Symposium on Principles of Database Systems (PODS)*, pages 1–15, San Diego, CA, June 1992.

[8] C. Beeri and T. Milo. A model for active object-oriented database. In *Intl. Conference on Very Large Data Bases (VLDB)*, pages 337–349, 1991.

[9] A.J. Bonner. Hypothetical datalog: Complexity and expressibility. *Theoretical Computer Science*, 76:3–51, 1990.

[10] A.J. Bonner and M. Kifer. Transaction logic programming (or a logic of declarative and procedural knowledge). Technical Report CSRI-270, University of Toronto, April 1992. Revised: August 1993. Available in *csri-technical-reports/270/report.ps* by anonymous ftp to *csri.toronto.edu*.

[11] A.J. Bonner and M. Kifer. Transaction logic: An (early) exposé. In V.S. Alagar, L.V.S. Lakshmanan, and F. Sadri, editors, *Proceedings of the Workshop on Formal Methods in Databases and Software Engineering*, Workshops in Computing, pages 1–23. Springer Verlag, 1993. Keynote address. Workshop held 15–16 May, 1992, Montreal, Canada.

[12] A.J. Bonner and M. Kifer. Transaction logic programming. In *Intl. Conference on Logic Programming (ICLP)*, Budapest, Hungary, June 1993.

[13] F. Bry. Intensional updates: Abduction via deduction. In *Intl. Conference on Logic Programming (ICLP)*, Jerusalem, Israel, June 1990.

[14] A.K. Chandra and D. Harel. Computable queries for relational databases. *Journal of Computer and System Sciences*, 21(2):156–178, 1980.

[15] A.K. Chandra and D. Harel. Structure and complexity of relational queries. *Journal of Computer and System Sciences*, 25(1):99–128, 1982.

[16] W. Chen. Declarative specification and evaluation of database updates. In *Intl. Conference on Deductive and Object-Oriented Databases (DOOD)*, volume 566 of *Lecture Notes in Computer Science*, pages 147–166. Springer Verlag, December 1991.

[17] C. de Maindreville and E. Simon. Non-deterministic queries and updates in deductive databases. In *Intl. Conference on Very Large Data Bases (VLDB)*, 1988.

[18] N. Gehani and V. Jagadish. ODE as an active database: Constraints and triggers. In *Intl. Conference on Very Large Data Bases (VLDB)*, pages 327–336, 1991.

[19] G. Grahne and A.O. Mendelzon. Updates and subjunctive queries. Technical Report KRR-TR-91-4, CSRI, University of Toronto, July 1991.

[20] D. Harel, D. Kozen, and R. Parikh. Process Logic: Expressiveness, decidability, completeness. *Journal of Computer and System Sciences*, 25(2):144–170, October 1982.

[21] R. Hull and D. Jacobs. Language constructs for programming active databases. In *Intl. Conference on Very Large Data Bases (VLDB)*, pages 455–467, 1991.

[22] H. Katsuno and A.O. Mendelzon. On the difference between updating a knowledge database and revising it. In *Proceedings of the International Conference on Knowledge Representation and Reasoning (KR)*, pages 387–394, Boston, Mass., April 1991.

[23] M. Kifer, G. Lausen, and J. Wu. Logical foundations of object-oriented and frame-based languages. Technical Report 93/06, Department of Computer Science, SUNY at Stony Brook, April 1993. To appear in J. of ACM.

[24] R. Krishnamurthy and S. Naqvi. Non-deterministic choice in datalog. In *Proceedings of the 3-d Intl. Conference on Data and Knowledge Bases*, pages 416–424. Morgan-Kaufmann Publ., 1988.

[25] S. Manchanda and D.S. Warren. A logic-based language for database updates. In J. Minker, editor, *Foundations of Deductive Databases and Logic Programming*, pages 363–394. Morgan-Kaufmann, Los Altos, CA, 1988.

[26] D.R. McCarthy and U. Dayal. The architecture of an active database management system. In *ACM SIGMOD Conference on Management of Data*, pages 215–224, 1989.

[27] S. Naqvi and R. Krishnamurthy. Database updates in logic programming. In *ACM SIGACT-SIGMOD-SIGART Symposium on Principles of Database Systems (PODS)*, pages 251–262, March 1988.

[28] G. Phipps, M.A. Derr, and K.A. Ross. Glue-Nail: A deductive database system. In *ACM SIGMOD Conference on Management of Data*, pages 308–317, 1991.

[29] T.C. Przymusinski. On the declarative semantics of deductive databases and logic programs. In J. Minker, editor, *Foundations of Deductive Databases and Logic Programming*, pages 193–216. Morgan Kaufmann, Los Altos, CA, 1988.

[30] D. Sacca and C. Zaniolo. Stable models and non-determinism in logic programs with negation. In *ACM SIGACT-SIGMOD-SIGART Symposium on Principles of Database Systems (PODS)*, pages 205–217, April 1990.

[31] M. Stonebraker, A. Jhingran, J. Goh, and S. Potamianos. On rules, procedures, caching and views in data base systems. In *ACM SIGMOD Conference on Management of Data*, pages 281–290, 1990.

[32] J. Widom. A denotational semantics for the starbust production rule language. *ACM SIGMOD Record*, 21(3):4–9, 1992.

[33] J. Widom, R.J. Cochrane, and B.G. Lindsay. Implementing set-oriented production rules as an extension to starbust. In *Intl. Conference on Very Large Data Bases (VLDB)*, pages 275–285, 1991.

[34] J. Widom and S.J. Finkelstein. Set-oriented production rules in relational database systems. In *ACM SIGMOD Conference on Management of Data*, pages 259–270, 1990.

[35] M. Winslett. A model based approach to updating databases with incomplete information. *ACM Transactions on Database Systems*, 13(2):167–196, 1988.

A Appendix: Model Theory

This section makes the discussion in Section 2.3 precise.

A.1 Path Structures

In the definitions below, each path structure has a domain of objects and an interpretation for all function symbols, which are used to interpret formulas on every path in the structure.

Definition A.1 (Path Structures) Let $\mathcal{L}$ be a first-order language with function symbols in $\mathcal{F}$ and predicate symbols in $\mathcal{P}$. A *path structure*, $\mathbf{M}$, over $\mathcal{L}$ is a quadruple $\langle U, I_{\mathcal{F}}, N, I_{path} \rangle$ where

- U is the *domain* of $\mathbf{M}$.
- $I_{\mathcal{F}}$ is an interpretation of function symbols in $\mathcal{L}$. It assigns a function $U^n \longmapsto U$ to every n-ary function symbol in $\mathcal{F}$.

  We shall use $Struct(U, I_{\mathcal{F}})$ to denote the set of all usual first-order semantic structures over $\mathcal{L}$ of the form $\langle U, I_{\mathcal{F}}, I_{\mathcal{P}} \rangle$, where $I_{\mathcal{P}}$ is some mapping that interprets predicate symbols in $\mathcal{P}$ by relations on U.
- N is a non-empty set of *states,* where each state is a non-empty subset of $Struct(U, I_{\mathcal{F}})$. An element of N is called a state of the path structure, $\mathbf{M}$.

  A *path* of length k in $\mathbf{M}$ is any finite sequence of states, $\langle s_1, \ldots, s_k \rangle$ where $k \geq 1$ and $s_i \in N$.
- I_{path} is a mapping that assigns to every path in $\mathbf{M}$ a first-order semantic structure in $Struct(U, I_{\mathcal{F}})$, subject to the restriction that $I_{path}(\langle s \rangle) \in s$ for every state s. (Recall that s is a *set* of semantic structures.) □

The mapping I_{path} serves as a semantic link between transactions and paths: Given a path and a transaction formula, I_{path} determines whether the formula is true on the path (Definition A.2, below). The restriction that $I_{path}(\langle s \rangle) \in s$ guarantees that any path of length 1 (*i.e.*, a view of the database state) is a model of the underlying database. Note that for an arbitrary path, π, the semantic structure $I_{path}(\pi)$ is independent of the subpaths of π. Intuitively, this means that we know nothing about the relationship between transactions and their subtransactions. Such knowledge, when it exists, is encoded in the transaction base. It is therefore in the definition of satisfaction that paths and subpaths are related.

Before defining satisfaction, it is convenient to define path *splits*. Given a path, $\langle s_1, ..., s_n \rangle$, any state, s_i, on the path defines a split of the path into two parts, $\langle s_1, ..., s_i \rangle$ and $\langle s_i, ..., s_n \rangle$. If path π is split into parts γ and δ, then we write $\pi = \gamma \circ \delta$. Thus, γ is a prefix of π, and δ is a suffix of π.

As in classical logic, in order to define satisfaction for quantified formulas and open formulas, it is convenient to introduce variable assignments. A *variable assignment*, ν, is a mapping, $\mathcal{V} \longmapsto U$, that takes a variable as input, and returns a domain element as output. We extend the mapping from variables to terms in the usual way, *i.e.*, $\nu(f(t_1, \ldots, t_n)) = I_{\mathcal{F}}(f)(\nu(t_1), \ldots, \nu(t_n))$.

Definition A.2 (Satisfaction) Let $\mathbf{M} = \langle U, I_{\mathcal{F}}, N, I_{path} \rangle$ be a path structure, let π be a path in $\mathbf{M}$, and let ν be a variable assignment. Then:

1. $\mathbf{M}, \pi \models_\nu p(t_1, \ldots, t_n)$ if and only if $I_{path}(\pi) \models^c_\nu p(t_1, \ldots, t_n)$, for any atomic formula $p(t_1, \ldots, t_n)$, where "$\models^c_\nu$" denotes classical satisfaction in first-order predicate calculus.

2. $\mathbf{M}, \pi \models_\nu \neg\phi$ if and only if it is not the case that $\mathbf{M}, \pi \models_\nu \phi$.

3. $\mathbf{M}, \pi \models_\nu \phi \vee \psi$ if and only if $\mathbf{M}, \pi \models_\nu \phi$ or $\mathbf{M}, \pi \models_\nu \psi$.

4. $\mathbf{M}, \pi \models_\nu \phi \wedge \psi$ if and only if $\mathbf{M}, \pi \models_\nu \phi$ and $\mathbf{M}, \pi \models_\nu \psi$.

5. $\mathbf{M}, \pi \models_\nu \phi \otimes \psi$ if and only if $\mathbf{M}, \gamma \models_\nu \phi$ and $\mathbf{M}, \delta \models_\nu \psi$ for *some* split $\gamma \circ \delta$ of path π.

6. $\mathbf{M}, \pi \models_\nu \phi \oplus \psi$ if and only if $\mathbf{M}, \gamma \models_\nu \phi$ or $\mathbf{M}, \delta \models_\nu \psi$ for *every* split $\gamma \circ \delta$ of path π.

7. $\mathbf{M}, \pi \models_\nu (\exists X)\phi$ if and only if $\mathbf{M}, \pi \models_\mu \phi$ for *some* variable assignment μ that agrees with ν everywhere except on X.

8. $\mathbf{M}, \pi \models_\nu (\forall X)\phi$ if and only if $\mathbf{M}, \pi \models_\mu \phi$ for *every* variable assignment μ that agrees with ν everywhere except on X.

To do hypothetical reasoning, we add the following two items, where $\langle s \rangle$ is a path of length 1 containing state s:

9. $\mathbf{M}, \langle s \rangle \models_\nu \Diamond\phi$ if and only if there is a path, π, starting at state s, such that $\mathbf{M}, \pi \models_\nu \phi$ holds.

10. $\mathbf{M}, \langle s \rangle \models_\nu \Box\phi$ if and only if for every path, π, starting at state s, it is the case that $\mathbf{M}, \pi \models_\nu \phi$.

As in classical logic, the mention of variable assignment can be omitted for *sentences*, *i.e.*, for formulas with no free variables. From now on, we will deal only with sentences, unless explicitly stated otherwise. □

In $\mathcal{TR}$, atoms like $p(t_1, \ldots, t_n)$ play the role of "subroutine calling sequences" in programming-language parlance. Intuitively, executing the subroutine corresponds to finding a path on which $p(t_1, \ldots, t_n)$ is true. Items 5 and 6 establish a relationship between a path and its subpaths, which corresponds to the relationship between a transaction and its subtransactions. In particular, an atom, p, may be true on a path but false on all proper subpaths (and vice-versa). Intuitively, this means that transaction p does not call itself recursively.

Definition A.3 (Models of Transaction Formulas) A path structure, $\mathbf{M}$, is a *model* of a $\mathcal{TR}$-formula ϕ, denoted $\mathbf{M} \models \phi$, if and only if $\mathbf{M}, \pi \models \phi$ for every path π in $\mathbf{M}$. A path structure is a model of a set of formulas if and only if it is a model of every formula in the set. □

As usual in first-order logic, we define $\phi \leftarrow \psi$ and $\psi \rightarrow \phi$ to mean $\phi \vee \neg\psi$, and $\phi \leftrightarrow \psi$ to mean $(\phi \leftarrow \psi) \wedge (\phi \rightarrow \psi)$. By replacing $\vee$ with $\oplus$ (the dual of $\otimes$), we obtain another interesting pair of serial connectives: *left serial implication*, $\psi \Leftarrow \phi$, standing for $\psi \oplus \neg\phi$, and *right* serial implication, $\phi \Rightarrow \psi$, standing for $\neg\phi \oplus \psi$. Intuitively, these formulas say that, "action ϕ must be immediately preceded (resp., followed) by action ψ." Unlike "$\leftarrow$" and "$\rightarrow$", these connectives are not identical, *i.e.*, $\phi \Leftarrow \psi$ is *not* equivalent to $\psi \Rightarrow \phi$; rather, $\phi \Leftarrow \psi$ is equivalent to $\neg\phi \Rightarrow \neg\psi$. It is easy to verify that the following formulas, analogous to De Morgan's laws, are tautologies:

$$
\begin{array}{rcl}
\neg(\phi \oplus \psi) & \leftrightarrow & \neg\phi \otimes \neg\psi \\
\neg(\phi \otimes \psi) & \leftrightarrow & \neg\phi \oplus \neg\psi \\
(\phi \vee \psi) \otimes \eta & \leftrightarrow & (\phi \otimes \eta) \vee (\psi \otimes \eta) \\
(\phi \wedge \psi) \oplus \eta & \leftrightarrow & (\phi \oplus \eta) \wedge (\psi \oplus \eta) \\
(\phi \wedge \psi) \otimes \eta & \rightarrow & (\phi \otimes \eta) \wedge (\psi \otimes \eta) \\
(\phi \vee \psi) \oplus \eta & \leftarrow & (\phi \oplus \eta) \vee (\psi \oplus \eta)
\end{array}
\tag{14}
$$

Definition A.3 tells us what it means for a path structure to be a model of a transaction formula ϕ. Such formulas are used to define complex transactions in terms of simpler ones. In addition, we must define what it means to be a model of an elementary state transition, $\langle \mathbf{D}_1, \mathbf{D}_2 \rangle u$. Informally, this transition states that u is an update that changes database $\mathbf{D}_1$ into database $\mathbf{D}_2$. The next two definitions make this idea precise.

Definition A.4 (Correspondence) Let $\mathbf{M} = \langle U, \mathcal{F}, N, I_{path} \rangle$ be a path structure. For each first-order formula $\mathbf{D}$, the expression $\mathbf{D} \rightsquigarrow s$ means, "s is the set of *all* (first-order) models of $\mathbf{D}$ in *Struct*$(U, I_{\mathcal{F}})$." We say that s *corresponds* to database $\mathbf{D}$. □

Note that the meaning of $\mathbf{D} \rightsquigarrow s$ depends on the path structure $\mathbf{M}$ (*i.e.*, on its domain and its interpretation of function symbols). This structure will always be clear from the context.

Definition A.5 (Models of Transition Bases) Let $\mathbf{M}$ be a path structure, let $\langle \mathbf{D}_1, \mathbf{D}_2 \rangle u$ be an elementary state transition, and suppose that $\mathbf{D}_1 \rightsquigarrow s_1$ and $\mathbf{D}_2 \rightsquigarrow s_2$. Then, the transition is *satisfied* in $\mathbf{M}$, denoted $\mathbf{M} \models \langle \mathbf{D}_1, \mathbf{D}_2 \rangle u$, if and only if s_1 and s_2 are states of $\mathbf{M}$ and $\mathbf{M}, \langle s_1, s_2 \rangle \models u$. □

In this definition, $\langle s_1, s_2 \rangle$ is a path of length 2, and the entailment relation "$\models$" is from Definition A.2. Informally, the statement $\mathbf{M} \models \langle \mathbf{D}_1, \mathbf{D}_2 \rangle u$ means that u is true on the arc from s_1 to s_2 in $\mathbf{M}$. Note that unlike transaction formulas, which are true on paths, truth of an elementary transition is determined with respect to the entire path structure. We say that $\mathbf{M}$ is a *model* of a transition base $\mathcal{B}$ if and only if $\mathbf{M}$ satisfies every elementary state transition in $\mathcal{B}$.

A.2 Execution as Entailment

We are now ready to define *executional entailment*, a concept that connects the model theory with transaction execution. Informally, execution of formulas corresponds to truth on a path.

A $\mathcal{TR}$ program consists of three distinct parts: a transaction base $\mathbf{P}$, a database $\mathbf{D}$, and a transition base $\mathcal{B}$. Each of these parts plays a distinct role in defining executional entailment. Of these three parts, only the database is updatable. The other two parts specify transactions that update the database and/or answer queries. The transition base defines elementary updates (state transitions), and the transaction base contains logical rules that define complex queries and transactions. The transaction base will normally be composed of formulas containing the serial connectives $\otimes$ or $\oplus$, though classical first-order formulas are also allowed. In contrast, the database consists entirely of classical first-order formulas.

Definition A.6 (Executional Entailment) Let $\mathcal{B}$ be a transition base, and $\mathbf{P}$ be a transaction base. Let ϕ be a transaction formula, and let $\mathbf{D}_0, \mathbf{D}_1, \ldots, \mathbf{D}_n$ be a sequence of databases (first-order formulas). Then, the following statement

$$\mathcal{B}, \mathbf{P}, \mathbf{D}_0, \mathbf{D}_1, \ldots, \mathbf{D}_n \models \phi \qquad (15)$$

is true if and only if for every model, $\mathbf{M}$, of $\mathcal{B}$ and $\mathbf{P}$, there is a path $\langle s_0, s_1, \ldots, s_n \rangle$ in $\mathbf{M}$ such that $\mathbf{D}_i \rightsquigarrow s_i$, for $i = 0, 1, \ldots, n$, and $\mathbf{M}, \langle s_0, s_1, \ldots, s_n \rangle \models \phi$. Related to this are the following statements:

$$\mathcal{B}, \mathbf{P}, \mathbf{D}_0 \text{---} \models \phi \qquad (16)$$

$$\mathcal{B}, \mathbf{P}, \mathbf{D}_0 \text{---} \mathbf{D}_n \models \phi \qquad (17)$$

$$\mathcal{B}, \mathbf{P}, \text{---} \mathbf{D}_n \models \phi \qquad (18)$$

which are true if and only if there is a sequence of databases $\mathbf{D}_0, \mathbf{D}_1, \ldots, \mathbf{D}_n$ such that Statement (15) is true. □

Informally, Statement (15) says that a successful execution of transaction ϕ can change the database from state $\mathbf{D}_0$ to $\mathbf{D}_1$ ... to $\mathbf{D}_n$. Formally, it means that every model of $\mathcal{B}$ and $\mathbf{P}$ has a path corresponding to $\mathbf{D}_0, \mathbf{D}_1, \ldots, \mathbf{D}_n$ that satisfies formula ϕ. The statement is read as follows: "Under transition base $\mathcal{B}$ and transaction base $\mathbf{P}$, transaction ϕ may transform database $\mathbf{D}_0$ into database $\mathbf{D}_n$ by passing through intermediate states $\mathbf{D}_1, \ldots, \mathbf{D}_{n-1}$."

Normally, users issuing transactions know only the initial database state, $\mathbf{D}_0$; so defining transaction execution via (15) is not quite appropriate. To account for this situation, the version of entailment in (16) allows us to omit the intermediate and the final database states. Intuitively, Statement (16) says that transaction ϕ can execute successfully starting from database $\mathbf{D}_0$. Formally, this statement is read as follows: "Under transition base $\mathcal{B}$ and transaction base $\mathbf{P}$, transaction ϕ succeeds from database $\mathbf{D}$." When the context is clear, we simply say that transaction ϕ *succeeds*. Likewise, when statement (16) is not true, we say that transaction ϕ *fails*. In [12, 10], we present an inference system that allows us to actually *find* a database sequence $\mathbf{D}_1, \ldots, \mathbf{D}_n$ (in fact, to enumerate all sequences) that satisfy Statement (15) whenever a transaction succeeds.

Statement (18) is the dual of (16). Informally, it says that ϕ can execute successfully *terminating* at state $\mathbf{D}_n$. This is discussed more fully in [10]. Statement (17) is also a useful abbreviation. Intuitively, it says that ϕ can execute successfully starting at state $\mathbf{D}_0$ and ending at state $\mathbf{D}_n$.

The following lemma lists some straightforward consequences of Definition A.6.

Lemma A.1 (Basic Properties of Executional Entailment) *For any transition base $\mathcal{B}$, any transaction base* $\mathbf{P}$, *any database sequence* $\mathbf{D}_0, \ldots, \mathbf{D}_n$, *and any transaction formulas α and β, the following statements are all true:*

1. *If* $\mathcal{B}, \mathbf{P}, \mathbf{D}_0, \ldots, \mathbf{D}_n \models \alpha$ *and* $\mathcal{B}, \mathbf{P}, \mathbf{D}_0, \ldots, \mathbf{D}_n \models \beta$ *then* $\mathcal{B}, \mathbf{P}, \mathbf{D}_0, \ldots, \mathbf{D}_n \models \alpha \wedge \beta$.

2. *If* $\mathcal{B}, \mathbf{P}, \mathbf{D}_0, \ldots, \mathbf{D}_i \models \alpha$ *and* $\mathcal{B}, \mathbf{P}, \mathbf{D}_i, \ldots, \mathbf{D}_n \models \beta$ *then* $\mathcal{B}, \mathbf{P}, \mathbf{D}_0, \ldots, \mathbf{D}_n \models \alpha \otimes \beta$.

3. *If* $\alpha \leftarrow \beta$ *is in* $\mathbf{P}$ *and* $\mathcal{B}, \mathbf{P}, \mathbf{D}_0, \ldots, \mathbf{D}_n \models \beta$ *then* $\mathcal{B}, \mathbf{P}, \mathbf{D}_0, \ldots, \mathbf{D}_n \models \alpha$.

4. *If* $\langle \mathbf{D}_0, \mathbf{D}_1 \rangle \alpha$ *is in* $\mathcal{B}$, *then* $\mathcal{B}, \mathbf{P}, \mathbf{D}_0, \mathbf{D}_1 \models \alpha$.

5. *If* $\mathbf{D}_0 \models^c \psi$ *then* $\mathcal{B}, \mathbf{P}, \mathbf{D}_0 \models \psi$, *where ψ is a first-order formula, and $\models^c$ denotes classical entailment.*

Note that assertions in Lemma A.1 deal with inference of two kinds of true statements. On the one hand, items 4 and 5 infer truth directly from the transition base and the database. Specifically, item 4 deals with elementary updates, and item 5 handles database queries. On the other hand, items 1, 2 and 3 combine existing entailments to infer new truths. Specifically, item 1 infers classical conjunctions; item 2 infers serial conjunctions; and item 3 infers defined transactions. Items 2–5 anticipate the proof procedures given in [12, 10], and indeed, they form the model-theoretic basis of the procedures. Item 1 is the basis for a wide class of dynamic constraints, such as those in Section 3.8.

In Lemma A.1, $n = 0$ corresponds to the special case in which a transaction does not affect a database, *i.e.*, in which it acts as a query. In this case, classical and serial conjunction are identical. This is reflected by the following two rules, which are special cases of items 1 and 2, above, respectively:

1b. If $\mathcal{B}, \mathbf{P}, \mathbf{D}_0 \models \alpha$ *and* $\mathcal{B}, \mathbf{P}, \mathbf{D}_0 \models \beta$ *then* $\mathcal{B}, \mathbf{P}, \mathbf{D}_0 \models \alpha \wedge \beta$.

2b. If $\mathcal{B}, \mathbf{P}, \mathbf{D}_0 \models \alpha$ *and* $\mathcal{B}, \mathbf{P}, \mathbf{D}_0 \models \beta$ *then* $\mathcal{B}, \mathbf{P}, \mathbf{D}_0 \models \alpha \otimes \beta$.

In fact, we have the following lemma, which follows directly from the definitions. Informally, this lemma says that the result of evaluating a conjunctive query is the same whether the conjuncts are evaluated sequentially or in parallel.

Lemma A.2 (Conjunctive Queries) *For any transition base $\mathcal{B}$, any transaction base* $\mathbf{P}$, *any database* $\mathbf{D}$, *and any transaction formulas α and β,*

$$\mathcal{B}, \mathbf{P}, \mathbf{D} \models \alpha \wedge \beta \quad \textit{if and only if} \quad \mathcal{B}, \mathbf{P}, \mathbf{D} \models \alpha \otimes \beta$$

$F_{\leq}^{\&}$: integrating parametric and "ad hoc" second order polymorphism

(extended abstract)

Giuseppe Castagna*
LIENS(CNRS)-DMI, 45 rue d'Ulm
75005 Paris. FRANCE

Abstract

In the last years several object-oriented database systems have come to life. However among them there is a lack of statically strongly typed languages. This is a very important deficiency especially for languages, as the database programming languages, which are designed for complex applications of large size and that evolve in time.

The absence of such a type discipline is justified by the complexity of the problem and of the structures it has to be applied to. Therefore we think that only a fundamental study, which were able to capture the essential features of the system, would lead to a typeful object-oriented programming. Thus we define an extension of $F_{\leq}$ [CG92] to which we add functions that dispatch on different terms according to the type they receive as argument. In other words, we enrich the explicit parametric polymorphism of $F_{\leq}$ by an explicit "ad hoc" polymorphism (according to the classification of [Str67]). We prove that the calculus we obtain, called $F_{\leq}^{\&}$, enjoys the properties of Church-Rosser and Subject Reduction.

This extension constitutes our paradigmatic language for the foundation of object-oriented programming: the connections between $F_{\leq}^{\&}$ and object-oriented languages are widely stressed, and the modeling by $F_{\leq}^{\&}$ of some features of the object-oriented style is described.

1 Introduction

System F is a language that allows to write functions that take types as inputs; however these functions depend on their input in a very strict way: different input types affect just the type of the result, not its value. The practical counterpart of this observation is given by the fact that types are thrown away during the computation which is then performed on the *erasures* of the terms. $F_{\leq}$ is a conservative extension of F, which allows to specify bounds on the types that are passed to a function; the type-checker uses this further information to type the body of the function. Though the functions of $F_{\leq}$ still have the same kind of dependence as in System F, since types again disappear during the computation. Here we want to extend $F_{\leq}$ by a type dependency also affecting the computation. We want to have functions that dispatch on different codes according to the type passed as argument. As a side effect we obtain that types will no longer be erasable at runtime.

*E-mail: castagna@dmi.ens.fr. The author was supported by the grant n. 203.01.56 of the Consiglio Nazionale delle Ricerche - Comitato Nazionale delle Scienze Matematiche

This research fits into a larger framework: In language theory, polymorphism has two orthogonal classifications: "parametric vs. *ad hoc*" (see [Str67]) and "explicit vs. implicit". Parametric polymorphism, i.e. the capability of performing the same code on different types, has been widely studied, both in the explicit form (where types participate directly in the syntax; e.g. System F) and in the implicit one (where types participate via the terms they type; e.g. ML). "Ad hoc" polymorphism, i.e. the capability of performing a different code for each different type, has not received the same attention. In [CGL92], with the definition of the $\lambda\&$-calculus, we started a theoretical analysis of implicit "ad hoc" polymorphism (on the line of some ideas in [Ghe91]). In this paper we tackle the *explicit* counterpart, by defining $F^{\&}_{\leq}$ a calculus with subtyping, which integrates parametric and "ad hoc" explicit polymorphism.

Object-oriented programming

This extension has not a mere logical interest: its main motivations lie in the research of a model for object-oriented languages and of a definition of a flexible type discipline to type-check them. Indeed in the last decade a considerable effort has been done to overcome the limitations of the data models available on commercial data base management systems. New data models have been been proposed and among them one of the most promising is the object-oriented one. In the last six years several object-oriented database systems have come to life; either as brand new systems (e.g. [BDe92]) or by extending existing object-oriented languages by mechanisms to model databases (e.g. [Ont]), foremost persistence. However among them there is a lack of statically strongly typed languages, i.e. languages with a type discipline which assure the absence of type errors (in this specific case the absence of the exception "message not understood") and whose correction can be verified at compile time (even if some efforts in that direction has been performed in the previous DBPL meetings). This is a very important deficiency, especially for languages, as the database programming languages, which are designed for complex applications of large size and that evolve in time; furthermore a suitable type system could be very useful in the conceptual modeling of a database since it could be used as a first specification language for the conceptual schema (as shown by Galileo [AGOO88]).

The absence of such a type discipline is justified by the complexity of the problem and of the structures it has to be applied to. Therefore we think that only a fundamental study, which were able to capture the essential features of the system, would lead to a typeful object-oriented programming. We do not believe that there is a unique way to model the essential features of object-oriented programming, as well as there is not a unique way to decide *which* are these essential features. Here we propose a possible solution, which is based on our intuition of some object-oriented systems.

Let us try to be more specific. In object-oriented languages the computation evolves on objects. Objects are programming items grouped in *classes* and possessing an internal state that is modified by sending messages to the object. When an object receives a message it invokes the method (i.e. code or procedure) associated to that message. The association between methods and messages is described by the class the object belongs to. Now, there are two possible ways to implement message-passing: the first is to consider objects as records that associate to each message a method. Thus messages are labels of a record, methods are the values in the fields and message passing corresponds to field selection. This implementation has been extensively studied and corresponds to the "objects as records" analogy of [Car88]. The second way is to consider messages as (identifiers of) special functions which take an object as argument and are able to dispatch on different codes according to the class of that argument (this is done in CLOS: [DG87]). This is the approach taken in [CGL92] where classes are used to type objects and messages are thus overloaded functions, i.e. functions that dispatch on different codes according to the type (the class) of their arguments. There, an overloaded function is a finite collection of ordinary functions (λ-abstractions) that are grouped together to form the different branches, and its type is the set of the types of its branches. More precisely the different branches are glued together by means of "&" (whence the name of λ&-calculus); thus

$$m = (a_1 \& a_2 \& \ldots \& a_n)$$

is an overloaded function with n branches $a_1 \ldots a_n$. If $a_i : C_i \to T_i$ then type of m is

$$m : \{C_1 \to T_1, \ldots, C_n \to T_n\}$$

In object-oriented terms, this means that the "message" m has been associated to a method in the "classes" $C_1, .., C_n$, each method returning the type T_i respectively. If we apply m to a value b of type C_j (i.e. if we pass the message m to an object b of class C_j) then the branch (method) a_j is selected and $a_j(b)$ is executed.

Inheriting methods

In this calculus a subtyping relation is defined on types. Thus in the example above it may happen that the type C of b does not exactly match one of the C_i's but it is a subtype of one of them. In this case the selected branch is the one that best approximates the type of the argument, i.e. the branch j such that $C_j = \min_{i=1..n}\{C_i | C \leq C_i\}$. On this selection of the minimum relies the mechanism of inheritance, and it corresponds to the usual method look-up of object-oriented languages: in object-oriented terms if we send the message m to the object b of class C then the method defined in the class $C_j = \min_{i=1..n}\{C_i | C \leq C_i\}$ is executed: if this minimum is exactly C, this means that the receiver b uses the method that has been defined in its class; otherwise, that is if this minimum is strictly greater than C, the receiver uses the method that its class, C, has *inherited* from the class C_j, which is the least super-class of C in which the message m has been (re)defined.

The problem of loss of information

Suppose to have a message m' which modifies the internal state of a class C_1. Since we are in a functional approach the method in C_1 returns a *new* object of class C_1. Thus $m' : \{..., C_1 \to C_1, ...\}$. Let C_2 be a subclass of C_1 from which it inherits the method at issue. If we pass the message m' to an object of C_2 then the branch defined in C_1 is selected. Since this branch has type $C_1 \to C_1$, the result of message passing has type C_1, rather than C_2 as it would be natural. This problem was already pointed out for the record-based model in [Car88] and it is known as the "loss of information problem";

there the solution adopted was to pass to a second order formalism. This yielded the definition of Fun in [CW85], which was further developed by many other authors (a non exhaustive list includes [CCH+89, Ghe90, CHC90, CL91, CMMS91, BTCGS91, Bru92, PT93]) and, in particular, which gave raise to the definition of $F_{\leq}$ in [CG92].

Here we adopt the same solution w.r.t. the $\lambda\&$-calculus, and we pass to a second order formalism to avoid the problem of loss of information. The idea is to have a type system which types the previous m' in the following way:

$$m' : \{..., \forall X{\leq}C_1.X \rightarrow X, ...\}$$

For this reason in this paper we define $F_{\leq}^{\&}$ where this type dependency is dealt with in an explicit way[1].

Type dependency

In a programming language a function which performs a dispatch on a type passed as argument would be probably written as:

```
Fun(X:*) =>
      if X<T1 then exp1 else if X<T2 then exp2 ... else if X<Tn then exp_n
```

This function executes exp_1 if we pass to it a type less than or equal to T_1, exp_2 if it is less than or equal to T_2 and so on. If there is more than one candidate we select among them the branch with the least bound. In $F_{\leq}^{\&}$ this function is denoted by:

$$(\Lambda X{\leq}T_1.exp_1 \ \& \ \Lambda X{\leq}T_2.exp_2 \ \& \ldots \& \ \Lambda X{\leq}T_n.exp_n)$$

and its type is $\forall X\{T_1.S_1, T_2.S_2, \ldots, T_n.S_n\}$ (where $exp_i : S_i$). However this type is a rough approximation yet. Indeed, to obtain a coherent and expressive system, we need strong restrictions on the T_i's and the S_i's.

First of all note that the selected branch may change during the computation. For example take a function f of type $\forall X\{T_1.S_1, T_2.S_2\}$ with $T_2{\leq}T_1$. Consider now the expression $(\Lambda Y{\leq}T_1.f[Y])$. Since $Y{\leq}T_1$ we guess that the branch selected for $f[Y]$ will be the one associated to T_1 and thus the type of this expression will be $\forall(X{\leq}T_1)S_1$ (more precisely, $\forall(Y{\leq}T_1)S_1[X := Y]$). But if we pass to the function above the type T_2 then, as Y is bound to T_2, the selected branch will be the second one and the result will have type S_2. System F and $F_{\leq}$ satisfy the subject reduction property, i.e. types are preserved under reductions. If we want reductions to preserve the type also in the new system we must require S_2 to be the same type as S_1. Though, it turns out that this is too strong a condition to model object-oriented languages (see the examples in section 5). Thus we adopt a less restrictive discipline, according to which types are allowed to decrease during computation. Thus in the example above it must be possible to deduce $X{\leq}T_2 \vdash S_2{\leq}S_1$. Summing up, the first restriction we impose on an overloaded type $\forall X\{T_i.S_i\}$ is that if $\vdash T_i{\leq}T_j$ then $X{\leq}T_i \vdash S_i{\leq}S_j$ (we call it the *covariance condition*, since it accounts for a longstanding debate on covariance vs. contravariance in the subtyping of the arrow types: see more on it in [CGL92]). Note the use of sequents: the premise records the subtyping relation on the type variables; we call it a type constraint system.

[1]The other solution is to deal with it in an implicit way by introducing type schemas *à la* ML, with bounds on the generic variables.

Definition 1.1 $\emptyset$ is a type constraint systems (tcs); $dom(\emptyset)=\emptyset$. If C is a tcs, $X \notin dom(C)$ and for every $Y \in FV(T)$, $Y \in dom(C)$ then $C \cup \{X \leq T\}$ is a type constraint system and $dom(C \cup \{X \leq T\})=dom(C) \cup \{X\}$. □

Sometimes we will use the notation $C(X)$ to denote the bound associated to X in C. By the definition above for a given tcs C and a type variable $X \in dom(C)$ there always exists a least non variable type T greater than X. We denote it by $\mathcal{B}(X)_C$ (the $\mathcal{B}$ stands for *bound*). More precisely we have the following definition.

Definition 1.2 Let C be a tcs and T a (raw) type such that $FV(T) \subseteq dom(C)$ then

1. $\mathcal{B}(T)_C = T$ if T is not a type variable.
2. $\mathcal{B}(T)_C = \mathcal{B}(C(T))_C$ otherwise. □

In the rest of the paper we will omit the subscript C in $\mathcal{B}(T)_C$ whenever it results clear from the context.

We limit our study to the case where the bounds of an overloaded function range over basic types (e.g. Bool, Int, Real ...). Indeed, the use of arrow types in the bounds poses many non-trivial problems, due to the contravariance of the left argument in the subtyping relation.

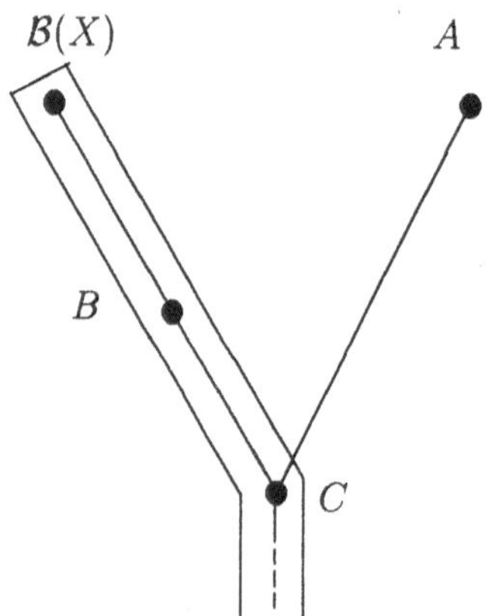

Therefore the second restriction we impose is that $\forall X\{T_i.S_i\}_{i\in I}$ is well-formed only if for every $i \in I$ $\mathcal{B}(T_i)$ is a basic type[2]. Thus every bound T_i must be an atomic type, i.e. either a basic type or a type variable. When the bound is a type variable, say X, the basic type $\mathcal{B}(X)$ plays an important role, since the set of its subtypes (denoted by $\mathcal{P}(\mathcal{B}(X))$) is the range of X. When we apply a type to an overloaded function, a selection rule picks the branch to execute. As we already said, this rule selects the branches with a bound provably larger than or equal to the type passed as argument, and among them it chooses the one with the least bound. Some conditions are required to assure that this minimum exists.

In λ&-calculus this existence was assured by requiring that the bounds had to form a partial downward semi-lattice.[3] But there we had only closed types. Now with type variables this restriction no longer suffices: consider the example of the figure above; it is clear that X and A have no common lower bound. Nevertheless if X takes the value B, it can enter in conflict with A since they have a common lower bound C. Thus if a variable X appears in an overloaded type as a bound then conflicts must be checked taking into account every type in $\mathcal{P}(\mathcal{B}(X))$. To this purpose we require that every set of bounds satisfies the property of $\cap$-*closure*, defined as follows:

[2]The major drawback of this restriction is that we cannot obtain the quantification of System F as a special case of the overloaded one and thus we will be obliged to add it explicitly. See also sections 5.3 and 6

[3]A set S is a partial downward semi-lattice iff for all $a, b \in S$ if $a \Downarrow b$ then $a \cap b \in S$. Where $a \Downarrow b$ means that a and b have a common lower bound (in S) and $a \cap b$ denotes their greatest lower bound.

Definition 1.3 Let C be a type constraint system. Given a set of atomic types $\{A_i\}_{i\in I}$ we write $C \vdash \{A_i\}_{i\in I}\cap$-closed iff for all $i, j \in I$ if $\mathcal{B}(A_i)_C \Downarrow \mathcal{B}(A_j)_C$ then there exists $h \in I$ such that $C \vdash A_h = A_i \cap A_j$. □

Here $C \vdash A_h = A_i \cap A_j$ means that from C it is provable that A_h is the g.l.b. of A_i and A_j, and $B_1 \Downarrow B_2$ that B_1 and B_2 have a common lower bound.

Note that $\cap$-closure is quite a draconian restriction. Indeed $\cap$-closed sets of bounds have a very precise form (see proposition 2.4): they are partial downward semi-lattices, i.e. formed by disjoint unions of downward semi-lattices. These semi-lattices are divided in two parts: the upper part is a semi-lattice formed only by basic types; the lower part is formed by a chain of type variables starting from the least element of a semi-lattice of basic types. Any of these two parts may be missing. A pictorial representation of the situation is the following one:

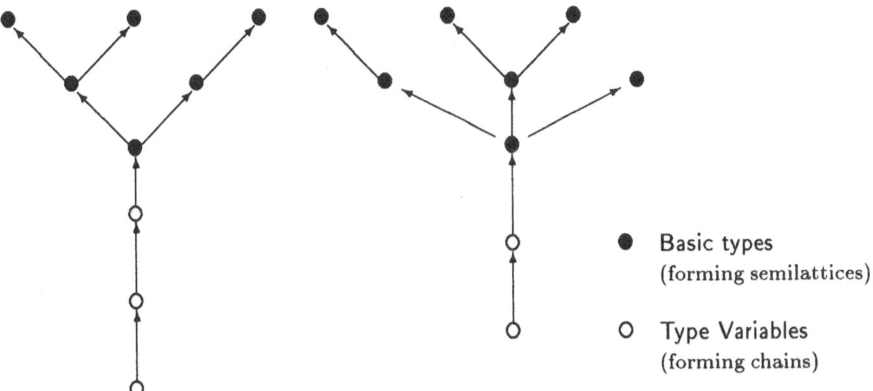

2 Type system

In this section we describe the type system. We first define the raw types. Among them we select the types, i.e. those raw types that do not contain overloaded types not satisfying the three rules we hinted in the introduction. In other terms $\forall X\{A_i.T_i\}_{i\in I}$ must:

1. have bounds ranging over basic types, i.e. for each $i\in I$ $\mathcal{B}(A_i)$ must be a basic type.

2. have a $\cap$-closed set of bounds.

3. satisfy covariance, i.e. if $A_i \leq A_j$ then $X\leq A_i \vdash T_i\leq T_j$

We suppose to have a predefined ordering on basic types which must form a partial lattice. This partial order is extended to higher types by a set of subtyping rules that are mutually recursive with those selecting the types.

Raw Types

$$A \quad ::= \quad X \mid B \qquad \text{(atomic types [}B\text{ basic types])}$$

$$\begin{array}{rcl} T & ::= & A \mid \mathsf{Top} \\ & \mid & T \to T \\ & \mid & \forall (X{\leq}T)T \\ & \mid & \forall X\{A_1.T_1, \ldots, A_n.T_n\} \end{array}$$

(raw $F_{\leq}^{\&}$ types)

(also denoted by $\forall X\{A_i.T_i\}_{i=1..n}$)

Judgments
We have three kinds of judgment: for type formation ($C \vdash T$ type), for the subtyping relation ($C \vdash T{\leq}T'$) and for the typing relation ($C \vdash a{:}T$). We call the first two kinds of judgments *type judgments.* Along the paper we also use some informal judgements: for example "$C \vdash T = \min_{i\in I}\{T_i\}$" stands for "$T \in \{T_i\}_{i\in I}$ and for all $i{\in}I$ $C \vdash T \leq T_i$".

Types

(Basic$_{type}$) $$C \vdash B \text{ type}$$

(Top$_{type}$) $$C \vdash \mathsf{Top} \text{ type}$$

(Vars$_{type}$) $$\frac{C \vdash T \text{ type}}{C \cup \{X{\leq}T\} \vdash X \text{ type}}$$ (*)

($\to_{type}$) $$\frac{C \vdash T \text{ type} \qquad C \vdash T' \text{ type}}{C \vdash T \to T' \text{ type}}$$

($\forall_{type}$) $$\frac{C \cup \{X{\leq}T\} \vdash T' \text{ type} \qquad C \vdash T \text{ type}}{C \vdash \forall(X{\leq}T)T' \text{ type}}$$ (*)

($\{\}_{type}$) $$\frac{\begin{array}{c} C \vdash A_i \text{ type} \\ C \vdash \{A_i\}_{i=1..n}\ \cap\text{-closed} \\ C \cup \{X{\leq}A_i\} \vdash T_i \text{ type} \\ \text{if } C \vdash A_i \leq A_j \text{ then } C \cup \{X{\leq}A_i\} \vdash T_i{\leq}T_j \end{array}}{C \vdash \forall X\{A_1.T_1, \ldots, A_n.T_n\} \text{ type}}$$ (*) $\mathcal{B}(A_i)_C$ basic for $i, j \in [1..n]$

Subtyping

(refl) $$\frac{C \vdash T \text{ type}}{C \vdash T{\leq}T}$$

(trans) $$\frac{C \vdash T_1 \leq T_2 \qquad C \vdash T_2 \leq T_3}{C \vdash T_1 \leq T_3}$$

(taut) $$\frac{C \vdash T \text{ type}}{C \cup \{X{\leq}T\} \vdash X{\leq}T}$$ (*)

$$\text{(Top)} \qquad \frac{C \vdash T \text{ type}}{C \vdash T \leq \mathsf{Top}}$$

$$(\rightarrow) \qquad \frac{C \vdash T_1' \leq T_1 \qquad C \vdash T_2 \leq T_2'}{C \vdash T_1 \rightarrow T_2 \leq T_1' \rightarrow T_2'}$$

$$(\forall) \qquad \frac{C \vdash T_1' \leq T_1 \quad C \cup \{X \leq T_1'\} \vdash T_2 \leq T_2' \quad C \vdash \forall(X \leq T_1)T_2 \text{ type}}{C \vdash \forall(X \leq T_1)T_2 \leq \forall(X \leq T_1')T_2'} \qquad (*)$$

$$(\{\}) \qquad \frac{\begin{array}{c} C \vdash \forall X\{A_j.T_j\}_{j\in J} \text{ type} \quad C \vdash \forall X\{A_i'.T_i'\}_{i\in I} \text{ type} \\ \text{for all } i \in I \text{ exists } j \in J \text{ s.t.} C \vdash A_i' \leq A_j \quad C \cup \{X \leq A_i'\} \vdash T_j \leq T_i' \end{array}}{C \vdash \forall X\{A_j.T_j\}_{j\in J} \leq \forall X\{A_i'.T_i'\}_{i\in I}} \qquad (*)$$

Where (*) denote the condition $X \notin dom(C)$

2.1 Some useful results

Theorem 2.1 *If* $C \vdash T \leq T'$ *then* $C \vdash T$ type *and* $C \vdash T'$ type

Proposition 2.2 *Let* $C \vdash T_1 \leq T_2$. *Then*
1. If T_1 *is not a variable then* T_2 *either is* Top *or it has the same shape as* T_1
2. If T_2 *is not* Top *then* T_2 *either is a variable or it has the same shape as* T_1

Proposition 2.3 *If* $C \vdash T_1 \leq T_2$ *then* $C \vdash \mathcal{B}(T_1)_C \leq \mathcal{B}(T_2)_C$

The following proposition describes the the form of the $\cap$-closed set of types:

Proposition 2.4 *If* $C \vdash \{A_i\}_{i\in I}\cap$*-closed then for any pair of elements* A_i *and* A_j *such that* $\mathcal{B}(A_i)_C \Downarrow \mathcal{B}(A_j)_C$ *one of this cases must hold:*

1. $\mathcal{B}(A_i)_C$ *and* $\mathcal{B}(A_j)_C$ *are unrelated,* A_i *and* A_j *are both basic types and their g.l.b. is in* $\{A_i\}_{i\in I}$
2. $\mathcal{B}(A_i)_C \leq \mathcal{B}(A_j)_C$ *and both* A_i *and* A_j *are basic types.*
3. $\mathcal{B}(A_i)_C \leq \mathcal{B}(A_j)_C$, A_i *is a variable and* A_j *is a basic type.*
4. $\mathcal{B}(A_i)_C \leq \mathcal{B}(A_j)_C$, A_i *and* A_j *are both variables and* $C \vdash A_i \leq A_j$.

The rules of subtyping given above do not describe a deterministic algorithm: a subtyping judgment does not univocally determine neither the rule to apply to prove it nor the parameters that such a rule must have. In particular the non-determinism is introduced in the system by the rules (refl) and (trans). The difficult rule is (trans) since it introduces a deeper form of non-determinism quite hard to eliminate. Indeed, the (trans) rule does not respect the so-called "sub-formula property", according to which all the types appearing at the premises of a rule must appear in its consequence, too. When proving $T_1 \leq T_3$ by transitivity, a new level of non-determinism is introduced by the choice of the *intermediate type* T_2 such that $T_1 \leq T_2$ and $T_2 \leq T_3$.

The reader will have recognized in it a cut elimination problem. Indeed, transitivity elimination in subtyping systems corresponds to cut elimination in Gentzen's sequent calculus for the first order logic. Both of them lead to a coherence result of the corresponding proof system, by returning a canonical derivation for each provable judgment. The resemblance is even stronger since we can use the Gentzen's technique for cut elimination to prove also transitivity elimination. Namely, one can define a weakly normalizing rewriting system on the derivations of subtyping judgments. This system will push the transitivity rules towards the leaves of the derivation. The derivations in normal form will have all the (trans) rules applied to a leaf of the derivation tree. Actually it can be proved that $F_{\leq}^{\&}$ enjoys the transitivity elimination property. Indeed let denote by $\vdash_{\mathcal{A}}$ the system obtained by replacing (refl) and (trans) by the following two rules:

$$C \vdash_{\mathcal{A}} X \leq X \qquad\qquad \frac{C \vdash_{\mathcal{A}} C(X) \leq T}{C \vdash_{\mathcal{A}} X \leq T}$$

Then the system $\vdash_{\mathcal{A}}$ defines a deterministic algorithm which is sound and complete w.r.t. the previous formulation.[4]

Theorem 2.5 $C \vdash_{\mathcal{A}} \Delta \Longleftrightarrow C \vdash \Delta$

Of course, in this short abstract we have not enough space to include the proof; the interested reader can examine [CG92] to see the technique to be used.

3 Terms

In this section we describe the terms of the language. We start by the definition of the *raw terms*, among which we distinguish the *terms*, i.e. those raw terms that possess a type. Roughly speaking, (raw) terms are divided in three classes: terms of the simply typed λ-calculus, terms for parametric polymorphism and terms for overloading. Overloaded functions are built in a list fashion, starting by an *empty* overloaded function ε and concatenating new branches by &. The &'s are indexed by a list of (pairs of) types which is used to type the term and to perform the selection of the branch.

Indexes

$$I ::= [A_1.T_1 \parallel \ldots \parallel A_n.T_n]$$

Raw Terms

$$\begin{array}{rcll} a & ::= & x^T \mid (\lambda x^T.a) \mid a(a) & \text{simply typed } \lambda\text{-calc} \\ & \mid & \mathsf{top} \mid \Lambda X{\leq}T.a \mid a(T) & F_{\leq} \\ & \mid & \varepsilon \mid (a\&^I a) \mid a[A] & \text{overloading} \end{array}$$

We required that the bounds of an overloaded function range over constant types. Therefore the argument of an overloaded function can be restricted to be an atomic type ($a[A]$) since a term of the form, say, $a[S \to T]$ would be surely rejected by the type checker.

[4] It is well known that type checking in $F_{\leq}$ is only semidecidable [Pie93]; this is inherited by $F_{\leq}^{\&}$, therefore the algorithm above describes only a semidecision procedure

Terms

We use two meta notations: $a[x := b]$, $a[X := S]$, $T[X := S]$ for substitutions and $\cup$ for set-theoretic union. Also we use $C \vdash a\colon S \leq T$ to denote that $C \vdash a\colon S$ and $C \vdash S \leq T$. Type substitutions are performed on indexes, too. Terms are selected by the rules below; since term variables are indexed by their type, the rules do not need assumptions of the form $(x\colon T)$

[VARS] $$C \vdash x^T\colon T \qquad C \vdash T \text{ type}$$

[→INTRO] $$\frac{C \vdash a\colon T'}{C \vdash (\lambda x^T.a)\colon T \to T'} \qquad C \vdash T \text{ type}$$

[→ELIM] $$\frac{C \vdash a\colon T' \qquad C \vdash b\colon S' \leq S}{C \vdash a(b)\colon T} \qquad \mathcal{B}(T')_C = S \to T$$

[TOP] $$C \vdash \mathsf{top}\colon \mathsf{Top}$$

[∀INTRO] $$\frac{C \cup \{X \leq T\} \vdash a\colon T'}{C \vdash \Lambda X \leq T.a\colon \forall(X \leq T)T'} \qquad C \vdash T \text{ type}$$

[∀ELIM] $$\frac{C \vdash a\colon T' \qquad C \vdash S' \leq S}{C \vdash a(S')\colon T[X := S']} \qquad \mathcal{B}(T')_C = \forall(X \leq S)T$$

[ε] $$C \vdash \varepsilon\colon \forall X\{\}$$

[{}INTRO] $$\frac{C \vdash a\colon T_1 \leq \forall X\{A_i.T_i\}_{i \leq n} \quad C \vdash b\colon T_2 \leq \forall(X \leq A)T}{C \vdash (a \&^{[A_1.T_1 \| \ldots \| A_n.T_n \| A.T]} b)\colon \forall X(\{A_i.T_i\}_{i \leq n} \cup \{A.T\})}$$
$$C \vdash \forall X(\{A_i.T_i\}_{i \leq n} \cup \{A.T\}) \text{ type}$$

[{}ELIM] $$\frac{C \vdash a\colon T \qquad C \vdash A_j = min_{i \in I}\{A_i | C \vdash A \leq A_i\}}{C \vdash a[A]\colon T_j[X := A]}$$
$$\mathcal{B}(T)_C = \forall X\{A_i.T_i\}_{i \in I}$$

Note the form of the premises in the rule [{}INTRO]; we cannot require that the components of an & must have the same type as the one specified in the index: since it is possible to reduce inside an & then the types of the components may decrease (see the subject reduction theorem 4.6), thus one cannot fix them (the index does not change with the reduction).

Theorem 3.1 *If $C \vdash a\colon T$ then $C \vdash T$* type

An important theorem for this system is the one that states that every well typed term has a unique type:

Theorem 3.2 *If $C \vdash a\colon T_1$ and $C \vdash a\colon T_2$ then and $T_1 \equiv T_2$*

Thanks to the theorem 2.5 we can associate to every provable judgment a canonical derivation.

Theorem 3.3 *Let Π_1 and Π_2 be two derivations for the same judgment $C \vdash a{:}T$. Let $(\Pi_i)^*$ $(i = 1,2)$ denote the derivation Π_i in which every (sub-)derivation of a subtyping judgment has been replaced by its canonical form. Then $\Pi_1 \equiv \Pi_2$.*

By combining the result of this two theorems we obtain that every well typed term has a canonical derivation for its type.

Thus one would expect that it is possible to define a type-checking algorithm for the raw terms. This is the cases, indeed: if in the system above you replace every subtyping judgment $C \vdash S{\leq}T$ by $C \vdash_{\mathcal{A}} S{\leq}T$ you have a type-checking algorithm that can be easily proved sound and complete w.r.t. the original system.

4 Reduction

In this section we give the equational theory of the terms of $F^{\&}_{\leq}$. We present it under the form of reduction rules. We suppose to work modulo α-conversion for term variables; note that no clash is possible for type variables because of the definition of tcs

Notions of reduction

(β) $C \vdash (\lambda x^T.a)(b) \rhd a[x^T := b]$

$(\beta_\forall)$ $C \vdash (\Lambda X{\leq}T.a)(T') \rhd a[X := T']$

$(\beta_{\{\}})$ If $A, A_1 \dots, A_n$ are closed then

$$C \vdash (a\&^{[A_1.T_1\|\dots\|A_n.T_n]}b)[A] \rhd \begin{cases} b(A) & \text{if } A_n = min_{1\leq i\leq n}\{A_i \mid C \vdash A{\leq}A_i\} \\ a[A] & \text{else} \end{cases}$$

Besides these rules there are the usual rules for the context closure; among these the only one that deserves a note is the rule for Λ, for it changes the tcs of the reduction:

$$\frac{C \cup \{X{\leq}T\} \vdash a \rhd a'}{C \vdash (\Lambda X{\leq}T.a) \rhd (\Lambda X{\leq}T.a')}$$

For what it concerns the rules note that in $\beta_{\{\}}$ we require that the types involved in the selection of a branch are closed. In this way we always select the most precise branch (i.e. the one with the smallest possible bound). This correspond in object-oriented programming to the implementation of the *dynamic binding* (for a wider discussion on this topic see [CGL93].)

4.1 The encoding of records

In this section we show how to encode in $F^{\&}_{\leq}$ updatable records. Records will be used in section 5. Updatable records are constructed starting from an empty record value, denoted by $\langle\ \rangle$, and two elementary operations:

- *Overwriting* $\langle r \leftarrow \ell_i = M\rangle$; if ℓ_i is not present in r, then it adds a field of label ℓ_i and value M to the record r; otherwise replaces the value of the field with label ℓ_i by the value M, provided that M has the same type as the type of the value it replaces.
- *Extraction* $r.\ell_i$; extracts the value corresponding the label ℓ_i, provided that a field having that label is present.

The type of a record r is $\langle\!\langle \ell_1 : T_1, \ldots, \ell_n : T_n \rangle\!\rangle$ where $\ell_1 \ldots \ell_n$ are the labels of all the fields of r and $T_1 \ldots T_n$ their respective types. [5] We encode these records in the following way:

Definition 4.1 Let $L_1, L_2, \ldots$ be an infinite list of basic types. Assume that they are isolated (i.e., for every type T, if $L_i \leq T$ or $T \leq L_i$, then $L_i = T$). Then set

$$\langle\!\langle \ell_1 : T_1, \ldots, \ell_n : T_n \rangle\!\rangle \stackrel{def}{\equiv} \forall X\{L_1.T_1, \ldots, L_n.T_n\} \quad X \notin \cup_{i=1..n} FV(T_i)$$

$$\langle\,\rangle \stackrel{def}{\equiv} \varepsilon$$

$$\langle r \leftarrow \ell_i = M\rangle \stackrel{def}{\equiv} (r \& \Lambda X{\leq} L_i.M)$$

$$r.\ell_i \stackrel{def}{\equiv} r[L_i]$$

□

Note that both the conditions in *Overwriting* and *Extraction* are enforced statically by the encoding. Also note that the usual rules to subtype simple record types and to type record values are obtained as the special case of the encoding, i.e. when the input types are isolated. For example, it is easy to check that if L_i's are isolated then $\forall X\{L_i.T_i\}_{i\in I} \leq \forall X\{L_i.T_i'\}_{i\in J}$ if and only if $J \subseteq I$ and $\forall i{\in}J\ T_i \leq T_i'$.[6] The same holds for the reduction rules, too.

4.2 Subject Reduction

In this section we prove that the type-checking system of $F_{\leq}^{\&}$ well behaves w.r.t. the reduction rules. More precisely we prove that every (well-typed) term rewrites to another (well-typed) term, whose type is smaller than or equal to the type of the former; therefore the correctness w.r.t. types of a program can be verified at compile time (static type-checking). We can give but the statements of the various lemmas since the proofs require twice the space we dispose here. First we need some notation:

Notation 4.2 *Let $C \cup \{X{\leq}T\}$ be a tcs. Define $(C \cup \{X{\leq}T\})[Y{:=}S]$ as $(C[Y{:=}S] \cup \{X{\leq}T[Y{:=}S]\})$ and $\emptyset[X{:=}S]$ as $\emptyset$. Let $C \vdash \Delta$ be a type judgment. Then $C \vdash \Delta[X{:=}S]$ is defined as $C \vdash T[X{:=}S]$* type *if $\Delta{\equiv}T$* type, *as $C \vdash T_1[X{:=}S] \leq T_2[X{:=}S]$ if $\Delta{\equiv}T_1{\leq}T_2$.*

[5] This calculus of records is very close to the one in [Wan87], which is, though, less constrictive than ours since it does not have any conditions on types in *Overwriting*.

[6] Note that even if we have the power of the calculus on the values in [Wan87], we have not the same power for the types: for example we cannot have an operation of updating that returns a record whose type is a type variable, since we do not have variables for indexes (just indexes containing variables). However it is possible to use the encoding of extensible records defined in [Car92] for $F_{\leq}$ which have different characteristics from the records described above.

The proof of subject reduction requires three technical lemmas:

Lemma 4.3 (main lemma) *If* $C \cup \{X \leq S\} \vdash \Delta$ *is a provable type judgment,* $X \notin FV(S')$ *and* $C[X := S'] \vdash S' \leq S$ *is provable, then* $C[X := S'] \vdash \Delta[X := S']$ *is provable, too.*

Lemma 4.4 (term substitution) *If* $C \vdash b : T' \leq T$ *and* $C \vdash a : S$ *then* $C \vdash a[x^T := b] : S' \leq S$.

Lemma 4.5 (type substitution) *If* $C \cup \{X \leq S\} \vdash a : T$, $C[X := S'] \vdash S' \leq S$ *and* $X \notin FV(S')$ *then* $C[X := S'] \vdash a[X := S'] : T' \leq T[X := S']$

Lemmas 4.3 and 4.5 constitute the hard part of the proof. The main difficulty resides in proving that $\cap$-closure is preserved by (feasible) substitutions. It is then rather straightforward to prove the theorem of subject reduction by using the same technique of [CGL92].

Theorem 4.6 (subject reduction) *If* $C \vdash a : T$ *and* $C \vdash a \rhd b$ *then* $C \vdash b : T'$ *and* $C \vdash T' \leq T$

4.3 Church-Rosser

By the property of transitivity elimination we proved the syntactic coherence of the *proof system* of $F_{\leq}^{\&}$. In this section we prove the syntactic coherence of the *reduction system* of $F_{\leq}^{\&}$, i.e. the Church-Rosser property (**CR**).

The Church-Rosser property states that every reduction strategy leads to the same result, if any[7]. Since there are many possible strategies this result leads the way for query optimizations.

In the reductions that follow we omit the tcs. Again for space reasons we omit the proofs. To prove the Church-Rosser property we use a method of Hindley [Hin64] and Rosen [Ros73]:

Lemma 4.7 (Hindley-Rosen) *Let* R_1, R_2 *be two notions of reduction. If* R_1, R_2 *are* **CR** *and* $\rhd^*_{R_1}$ *commutes with* $\rhd^*_{R_2}$ *then* $R_1 \cup R_2$ *is* **CR**.

Set now $R_1 \equiv \beta_{\{\}}$ and $R_2 \equiv \beta \cup \beta_{\forall}$; if we prove that these notions of reduction satisfy the hypotheses of the lemma above then we proved **CR**. It is easy to prove that $\beta \cup \beta_{\forall}$ is **CR**: indeed in [Ghe90] it is proved that $\beta \cup \beta_{\forall}$ is terminating; by a simple check of the conflicts it is possible to prove that it is also locally confluent; applying the Newman's Lemma ([New42]) we obtain **CR**.

Lemma 4.8 $\beta_{\{\}}$ *is* **CR**.

To prove that the two notions of reduction commute we need three technical lemmas:

Lemma 4.9 *If* $a \rhd_{\beta_{\{\}}} a'$ *then* $a[x := b] \rhd^*_{\beta_{\{\}}} a'[x := b]$

Lemma 4.10 *If* $a \rhd_{\beta_{\{\}}} a'$ *then* $a[x := T] \rhd^*_{\beta_{\{\}}} a'[x := T]$

[7] We conjecture that $F_{\leq}^{\&}$ is strongly normalizing

Lemma 4.11 *If* $b \triangleright_{\beta_{\{\}}} b'$ *then* $a[x{:}= b] \triangleright^*_{\beta_{\{\}}} a[x{:}= b']$

These lemmas can be proved by a straightforward use of induction (on $a \triangleright_{\beta_{\{\}}} a'$ for the first two and on a for the third). Just for the proof of the second, note that in $\beta_{\{\}}$ $A, A_1, \ldots, A_n$ are required to be closed. We can now prove that the two notions of reduction commute.

Lemma 4.12 *If* $a \triangleright_{\beta\cup\beta_\forall} a_1$ *and* $a \triangleright_{\beta_{\{\}}} a_2$ *then there exists* a_3 *such that* $a_1 \triangleright^*_{\beta_{\{\}}} a_3$ *and* $a_2 \triangleright_{\beta\cup\beta_\forall} a_3$. *Pictorially:*

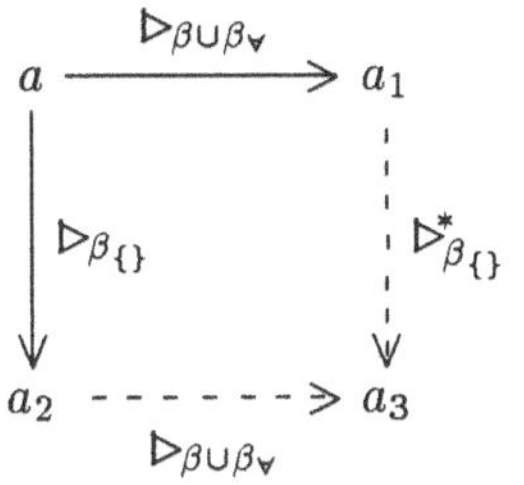

$$\begin{array}{ccc}
a & \xrightarrow{\triangleright_{\beta\cup\beta_\forall}} & a_1 \\
\Big\downarrow \triangleright_{\beta_{\{\}}} & & \vdots\ \triangleright^*_{\beta_{\{\}}} \\
a_2 & \dashrightarrow_{\triangleright_{\beta\cup\beta_\forall}} & a_3
\end{array}$$

(Where full arrows are used for the hypotheses and dashed arrows for the theses.)

Corollary 4.13 $\triangleright^*_{\beta_{\{\}}}$ *commutes with* $\triangleright^*_{\beta\cup\beta_\forall}$

Thus all the hypotheses of lemma 4.7 are satisfied, and we can conclude that $F^{\&}_{\leq}$ is **CR**.

5 Object-oriented programming

From the examples given in the introduction it should be clear that we use the name of a class to type the objects of that class. A message then is (an identifier of) an overloaded function whose branches are the methods associated to that message. The method to be executed is selected according to the type (the class-name) passed as argument which will be the class of the object the message is sent to. Thus the sending of a message *mesg* to an object a of class A will be modeled by $(mesg[A])a$.

Class-names are *basic types*. We want to associate to each basic type a *representation type*; in particular we want to associate to each class(-name) the type of the internal state of its objects (i.e. the type of the instances variables). The way to formalize it does not concern the subject of this paper (this is done in [Cas93]); thus here we follow the rudimentary approach of [CGL92]: we suppose that a program (a $F^{\&}_{\leq}$-term) may be preceded by a declaration of *class types*: a *class type* is a basic type, that is associated by its declaration to a unique *representation type*, which is a record type. Two class types are in subtyping relation if this relation has been explicitly declared and it is *feasible*, in the sense that the respective representation types are in subtyping relation too. There is an operation $\_^{classType}$ to transform a record value $r{:}\,R$ into a class type value $r^{classType}$ of type *classType*, provided that the representation type of *classType* is R.

We use *italics* to distinguish class types from the usual types, and $\doteq$ to declare a class type and to give it a name; we will use $\equiv$ to associate a name to a value (e.g. to a function). For example we can declare the following class types:
$\mathit{2DPoint} \doteq \langle\!\langle x : \mathrm{Int}; y : \mathrm{Int} \rangle\!\rangle$
$\mathit{3DPoint} \doteq \langle\!\langle x : \mathrm{Int}; y : \mathrm{Int}; z : \mathrm{Int} \rangle\!\rangle$
and then impose on them that $\mathit{3DPoint} \leq \mathit{2DPoint}$ (which is feasible since it respects the ordering of the record types these class types are associated to). We can define a message *Norm* working on these class types[8]:

$$\begin{aligned} \mathit{Norm} \equiv\ &(\ \Lambda \mathit{MyType} \leq \mathit{2DPoint}\ .\lambda \mathit{self}^{\,\mathit{MyType}}.\sqrt{\mathit{self}.x^2 + \mathit{self}.y^2} \\ &\ \&\, \Lambda \mathit{MyType} \leq \mathit{3DPoint}\ .\lambda \mathit{self}^{\,\mathit{MyType}}.\sqrt{\mathit{self}.x^2 + \mathit{self}.y^2 + \mathit{self}.z^2} \\ &\ ) \end{aligned}$$

whose type is

$$\forall \mathit{MyType}.\{\mathit{2DPoint}.\mathit{MyType} \to \mathrm{Real}, \mathit{3DPoint}.\mathit{MyType} \to \mathrm{Real}\}$$

We have used the variable *self* to denote the receiver of the message and, following the notation of [Bru92], the type variable *MyType* to denote the type of the receiver. Note however that we do not need, as in [Bru92], recursion for these features since they are just parameters of the message.

Let us consider the meaning of the covariance condition of section 2 in this framework. Define the message *Erase* that set to zero the internal state of an object

$$\begin{aligned} \mathit{Erase} \equiv\ &(\ \Lambda \mathit{MyType} \leq \mathit{2DPoint}.\lambda \mathit{self}^{\,\mathit{MyType}}.\langle \mathit{self} \leftarrow x = 0, y = 0 \rangle^{\mathit{2DPoint}} \\ &\ \&\, \Lambda \mathit{MyType} \leq \mathit{3DPoint}.\lambda \mathit{self}^{\,\mathit{MyType}}.\langle \mathit{self} \leftarrow x = 0, y = 0, z = 0 \rangle^{\mathit{MyType}} \\ &\ ) \end{aligned}$$

it has type

$$\forall \mathit{MyType}.\{\mathit{2DPoint}.\mathit{MyType} \to \mathit{2DPoint}, \mathit{3DPoint}.\mathit{MyType} \to \mathit{MyType}\}$$

Since $\mathit{3DPoint} \leq \mathit{2DPoint}$ we check that the covariance condition is satisfied:

$$\{\mathit{MyType} \leq \mathit{3DPoint}\} \vdash \mathit{MyType} \to \mathit{MyType} \leq \mathit{MyType} \to \mathit{2DPoint}$$

In general if a method has been defined for the message m in the classes B_i for $i \in I$ then its type is of the form $\forall \mathit{MyType}.\{B_i.\mathit{MyType} \to T_i\}_{i \in I}$. If $B_h \leq B_k$ that means that the method defined for m in the class B_h overrides the one defined in B_k. Since *MyType* is the same in both branches then the covariance condition reduces to prove that

$$\{\mathit{MyType} \leq B_h\} \vdash T_k \leq T_h$$

In other terms the covariance condition requires that an overriding method returns a type smaller than or equal to the type returned by the overridden one. Note that if a method returns a result of type *MyType* then a method that overrides it has to return *MyType* too and it is not allowed to return say the class-name of the class in which the method has been defined (since, by inheritance, this could be a type larger then the actual value of *MyType*)[9].

Suppose now that *3DColoredPoint* is a subclass of *3DPoint* from which it inherits the method for *Erase*; then the definition of *Erase* persists unchanged.

[8] In the examples we will omit ε and the indexes of &

[9] Of course in the previous example it would have been more reasonable that *Erase* returned *MyType* rather than *2DPoint*.

If an object b of type *3DColoredPoint* receives the message *Erase* then the method selected is the one for *3DPoint*; but since $Erase[3DColoredPoint](b)$: *3DColoredPoint* the loss of information is avoided.

In this framework bounds are always basic types (more precisely class-names); thus the $\cap$-closure reduces to impose that if a message has type $\forall X.\{B_i.T_i\}_{i \in I}$ and there exists $h, k \in I$ such that B_h and B_k have a common subclass then there must be a method defined for the message, in the class that is the g.l.b. of B_h and B_k. In other terms, in a class defined by multiple inheritance if two common ancestors can respond to a same message, then the method for that message cannot be inherited but must be explicitly redefined, as in [CGL92].

5.1 Extending classes

Inheritance is not the only way to specialize classes: if every time we have to add a method to a class we were obliged to define a new class, the existing objects of the old class could not use the new method. The same is worth also in the case that a method of a class must be redefined: *overriding* would not suffice. For this reason some object-oriented languages such as Objective-C [NeX91], Dylan [App92] and CLOS [DG87] offer the capability to add new methods to existing classes or to redefine the old ones. The extension of the set of the methods of a class affects all its subclasses, in the sense that when a class is extended with a method then that method is available to the objects of every subclass. For example in Dylan the following expression

```
(define-method isOrigin (self <2DPoint>)
    (and (zero? self.x) (zero? self.y)))
```

adds to the class *2DPoint* a method responding to the message *isOrigin*[10]. If a method for that message has already been defined in the class then it is replaced by the new one.

This can be implemented in our system by adding a new branch to the overloaded function denoted by the message at issue:

$$\textbf{let } isOrigin = (isOrigin \;\&\; \Lambda MyType{\leq}2DPoint.\; \lambda self^{MyType}.(self.x = 0) \wedge (self.y = 0))$$

Remark that by this construction one does not define a new class but only new methods; in other terms one does not modify the existing types but only (the environment of) the expressions. This is possible in our system since the type of an object is not bound to the procedures that can work on it (and for this reason it differs from abstract data types and from the "objects as records" approach). Of course this flexibility is paid by a minor protection. For that reason for example Dylan has a function **freeze-methods** which prevents certain methods associated to a message to be replaced or removed.

5.2 First class messages

In this model messages are identifiers of overloaded functions. Since overloaded functions have first class citizenship, then also messages are first class. Thus it

[10]This is not the standard Dylan's syntax where record (slot) selection of the field x of self is written `(x self)`

is possible to model functions that take as parameter a message, or functions whose result is a message. A trivial example of its use is the implementation of a super-like function: suppose that in the definition of a method you want to send a message to *self* but that the method selected must be the one defined for the objects of a certain class C. This can be obtained by the following function:

$$\textbf{let}\ \text{super\_C} = \lambda m^{\forall X\{C.T\}}.m[C]self$$

This function takes a message m accepting objects of class C and sends it to *self* but selecting the method defined for the object of class C (of course this function is well typed if $MyType \leq C$).

5.3 Multiple dispatch

In this paper we have studied a very kernel calculus. A simple extension of this calculus allows us to model multiple dispatch, i.e. a mechanism of selection of methods (in this case called multi-methods) based not only on the class of the receiver but also on the class of further parameters. The simplest extension of $F_{\leq}^{\&}$ to obtain multiple-dispatch consists in allowing as bounds of an overloaded function products of basic types. Thus we redefine atomic types in the following way

$$A \quad ::= \quad X \mid B \mid B \times \ldots \times B \qquad \text{(atomic types [}B\text{ basic types])}$$

we modify the condition in the rule of good formation for overloaded types by precising that "$\mathcal{B}(A_i)_C$ basic type or $A_i = B_1 \times \ldots \times B_m$", and of course we add tuples to terms:

$$a ::=< a, \ldots, a >$$

It is then very easy to check that this extension enjoys all the properties we have already proved for $F_{\leq}^{\&}$.

One example of use of multiple dispatch is the method *Equal*: you want to extend the class *2DPoint* with a method that compares two points and to redefine it for *3DPoint*; furthermore you want that in comparing a *2DPoint* with a *3DPoint* the method for *2DPoint* is used. In $\lambda\&$ we had that a function *Equal* of type $\{2DPoint \to 2DPoint \to Bool, 3DPoint \to 3DPoint \to Bool\}$ would not have a well-formed type since covariance is not respected. So in $\lambda\&$ we defined

$$Equal : \{(2DPoint \times 2DPoint) \to Bool, (3DPoint \times 3DPoint) \to Bool\}$$

obtaining in this way multiple dispatch[11]. When applied to *2DPoint* and a *3DPoint* or viceversa it executes the first branch. In $F_{\leq}^{\&}$ the difference is subtler: indeed $\forall X\{2DPoint.X \to X \to Bool, 3DPoint.X \to X \to Bool\}$ is well formed. However to select the right branch you have to pass to a function of this type the greater of the types of the two actual parameters. This is not what one would like to have: one would like to pass to the function both the types and leave to the system the task to select the right branch. This can be done by using multi-methods and defining *Equal* with the following type:

$$\forall X\{2DPoint \times 2DPoint.X \to Bool, 3DPoint \times 3DPoint.X \to Bool\}$$

A possible implementation of *Equal* is then

[11]Note that this is impossible in the "objects as records" models

$$
\begin{aligned}
Equal \equiv (\Lambda X \leq & 2DPoint \times 2DPoint\,.\,\lambda p^X.\\
& (\pi_1(p).x = \pi_2(p).x) \wedge (\pi_1(p).y = \pi_2(p).y)\\
\&\ \Lambda X \leq & 3DPoint \times 3DPoint\,.\,\lambda p^X.\\
& (\pi_1(p).x = \pi_2(p).x) \wedge (\pi_1(p).y = \pi_2(p).y) \wedge (\pi_1(p).z = \pi_2(p).z)\\
)\quad &
\end{aligned}
$$

$F^{\&}_{\leq}$ is not the mere formal version of an object-oriented languages. For many aspects it is less powerful than object-oriented languages, but it possesses some features that existing object-oriented languages have not. Thus one can imagine to enrich object-oriented languages by these features suggested by the model; for example one could design new object-oriented languages that handle parametricity and overloading, in which classes (class-names) could be passed as arguments to functions; these functions would also be able to dispatch to different codes according to class-name received as argument. It is possible to imagine many applications of this blend of parametric polymorphism and explicit overloading; for example suppose that you have to write a general installation routine for software products working on various machines. Suppose that you distinguish your software products between graphic software and mathematical software, and the machines between b/w and color machines. Then you would probably have the following classes: *GraphSW*, *MathSW* $\leq$ *Software* and *Color*, *B&W* $\leq$ *Machine* and your general installation routine would have type

$$install : \forall(M \leq Machine)\forall(S \leq Software)(M \times S) \to \ldots$$

The body of this routine would include some parts common for all kinds of machines and software, and then some parts specialized according to the kinds of the parameters. This specialization could be obtained by using functions of type

$$
\begin{aligned}
\forall X\{&Software \times Machine.\ \ldots,\\
&GraphSW \times B\&W.\ \ldots,\\
&GraphSW \times Color.\ \ldots,\\
&MathSW \times B\&W.\ \ldots,\\
&MathSW \times Color.\ \ldots\}
\end{aligned}
$$

6 Future work

In this paper we defined and studied $F^{\&}_{\leq}$ and we sketched how it can be used to model object-oriented features. We showed that it accounts for many features of object-oriented programming and that it also suggests new features to add to the existing paradigms. However there are some features that are not easily handled (e.g. the keyword *super*; see at this purpose [Cas93]).

The major restriction is that meet-closure allows overloading only on atomic types. In the last section we showed how to weaken this condition to model multiple dispatching; though also this definition still prevents us to model the generic classes of Eiffel [Mey88]. A generic class is a class parameterized by a type variable. For example if X is a type variable, one would like to define a class *Stack*$[X]$ with methods *pop*: X and *push*: $X \to ()$, and then obtain a stack of integers by instantiating the type variable X in the following way:

`new(Stack[Int])`. We believe that it is not difficult to further weaken meet-closure to allow among the bounds of an overloaded function, monotonic type constructors. But we are at a loss to think how to allow non monotonic type constructors. In the same way it should be possible to extend meet-closure to closed types and to add recursive types to implement recursive objects (even if we think that recursive types are not indispensable: see [PT93]).

Meet closure constitutes an even more serious limitation from a proof-theoretical point of view. It would be very interesting to let bounds range over all the types; this would require a suitable definition of $\cap$-closure assuring consistency also for higher order bounds. Note that the proof theory would be greatly complicated since a new level of impredicativity would be added. However this would correspond to a major increase of the expressive power. In that case indeed, by a slight weakening of the $\beta_{\{\}}$ rule, it would be possible to obtain parametric functions as a special case of overloaded functions with only one branch.

Acknowledgments
I am very grateful to Martín Abadi and Florian Matthes for their valuable suggestions on a earlier draft. I want also to thank Giuseppe Longo for his constant advice, for his patient in reading the proofs and ... a lot more.

References

[AGOO88] A. Albano, G. Ghelli, M.E. Occhiuto, and R. Orsini. *Galileo reference Manual Version 2.0.* Servizio editoriale universitario di Pisa, Febbraio 1988.

[App92] Apple Computer Inc., Eastern Research and Technology. *Dylan: an object-oriented dynamic language*, April 1992.

[BDe92] F. Bancilhon, C. Delobel, and P. Kanellakis (eds.). *Implementing an Object-Oriented database system: The story of O_2.* Morgan Kaufmann, 1992.

[Bru92] K.B. Bruce. A paradigmatic object-oriented programming language: Design, static typing and semantics. Technical Report CS-92-01, Williams College, Williamstown, MA 01267, January 1992.

[BTCGS91] V. Breazu-Tannen, T. Coquand, C. Gunter, and A. Scedrov. Inheritance as implicit coercion. *Information and Computation*, 93(1):172–221, July 1991.

[Car88] Luca Cardelli. A semantics of multiple inheritance. *Information and Computation*, 76:138–164, 1988. A previous version can be found in Semantics of Data Types, LNCS 173, 51-67, Springer-Verlag, 1984.

[Car92] Luca Cardelli. Extensible records in a pure calculus of subtyping. Research report 81, DEC Systems Research Center, January 1992. To appear in [GM93].

[Cas93] G. Castagna. A meta-language for typed object-oriented languages. In R.K. Shyamasundar, editor, *13th Conference on the Foundations of Software Technology and Theoretical Computer Science*, LNCS, Bombay, India, December 1993. Springer-Verlag.

[CCH+89] P.S. Canning, W.R. Cook, W.L. Hill, J. Mitchell, and W.G. Orthoff. F-bounded quantification for object-oriented programming. In *ACM Conference on Functional Programming and Computer Architecture*, September 1989.

[CG92] P. L. Curien and G. Ghelli. Coherence of subsumption, minimum typing and the type checking in $F_{\leq}$. *Mathematical Structures in Computer Science*, 2(1), 1992.

[CGL92] G. Castagna, G. Ghelli, and G. Longo. A calculus for overloaded functions with subtyping, 1992. To appear in *Information and Computation*. An extended abstract has appeared in the proceedings of the *ACM Conference on LISP and Functional Programming*, pp.182-192; San Francisco, June 1992.

[CGL93] G. Castagna, G. Ghelli, and G. Longo. A semantics for λ&-*early*: a calculus with overloading and early binding. In M. Bezem and J.F. Groote, editors, *International Conference on Typed Lambda Calculi and Applications*, number 664 in LNCS, pages 107–123, Utrecht, The Netherlands, March 1993. Springer-Verlag. TLCA'93.

[CHC90] W.R. Cook, W.L. Hill, and P.S. Canning. Inheritance is not subtyping. *17th Ann. ACM Symp. on Principles of Programming Languages*, January 1990.

[CL91] L. Cardelli and G. Longo. A semantic basis for Quest. *Journal of Functional Programming*, 1(4):417–458, 1991.

[CMMS91] L. Cardelli, S. Martini, J.C. Mitchell, and A. Scedrov. An extension of system F with subtyping. In T. Ito and A.R. Meyer, editors, *Theoretical Aspects of Computer Software*, pages 750–771. Springer-Verlag, September 1991. LNCS 526 (preliminary version). To appear in Information and Computation.

[CW85] L. Cardelli and P. Wegner. On understanding types, data abstraction, and polymorphism. *Computing Surveys*, 17(4):471–522, December 1985.

[DG87] L.G. DeMichiel and R.P. Gabriel. Common lisp object system overview. In Bézivin, Hullot, Cointe, and Lieberman, editors, *Proc. of ECOOP '87 European Conference on Object-Oriented Programming*, number 276 in LNCS, pages 151–170, Paris, France, June 1987. Springer-Verlag.

[Ghe90] G. Ghelli. *Proof Theoretic Studies about a Minimal Type System Integrating Inclusion and Parametric Polymorphism*. PhD thesis, Dipartimento di Informatica, Università di Pisa, March 1990. Tech. Rep. TD-6/90.

[Ghe91] G. Ghelli. A static type system for message passing. In *Proc. of OOPSLA '91*, 1991.

[GM93] Carl A. Gunter and John C. Mitchell. *Theoretical Aspects of Object-Oriented Programming: Types, Semantics, and Language Design.* The MIT Press, 1993. To appear.

[Hin64] R. Hindley. The Church-Rosser property and a result of combinatory logic. Dissertation, 1964. University of Newcastle-upon-Tyne.

[Mey88] Bertrand Meyer. *Object-Oriented Software Construction.* Prentice-Hall International Series, 1988.

[New42] M.H.A. Newman. On theories with a combinatorial definition of "equivalence". *Annals of Math.*, 43(2):223–243, 1942.

[NeX91] NeXT Computer Inc. *NeXTstep-concepts. Chapter 3: Object-Oriented Programming and Objective-C*, 2.0 edition, 1991.

[Ont] Ontologic Inc., 47 Manning Rd., Billerica , MA 01821. *Vbase+: object database for C++.*

[Pie93] B.C. Pierce. Bounded quantification is undecidable. In *20th Ann. ACM Symp. on Principles of Programming Languages.* ACM-Press, 1993.

[PT93] B.C. Pierce and D.N. Turner. Simple type-theoretic foundations for object-oriented programming. *Journal of Functional Programming*, 1993. To appear; a preliminary version appeared in Principles of Programming Languages, 1993, and as University of Edinburgh technical report ECS-LFCS-92-225, under the title "Object-Oriented Programming Without Recursive Types".

[Ros73] B. K. Rosen. Tree manipulation systems and Church-Rosser theorems. *Journal of ACM*, 20:160–187, 1973.

[Str67] C. Strachey. Fundamental concepts in programming languages. Lecture notes for International Summer School in Computer Programming, Copenhagen, August 1967.

[Wan87] Mitchell Wand. Complete type inference for simple objects. In *2nd Ann. Symp. on Logic in Computer Science*, 1987.

Building an Integrated Persistent Application

Dag Sjøberg*
Malcolm Atkinson
João Lopes
Phil Trinder

Computing Science Department, University of Glasgow
Glasgow, Scotland

{sjoberg,mpa,jlopes,trinder}@dcs.glasgow.ac.uk

Abstract

The major motivation for database programming language (DBPL) research is to facilitate the construction and maintenance of large data-intensive applications. To fully benefit from DBPLs, supporting methodologies and tools are needed. This paper describes the construction of a multi-author, multi-level thesaurus application (TA). Some tools and methodologies were used in the TA construction, and requirements for other tools and methodologies are identified as the result of our experiences. Although built in a specific language (Napier88), the principles discovered apply to other DBPLs.

The TA comprises several loosely-integrated components constructed by different programmers. The components were themselves implemented using general purpose sub-components, including libraries. A principle result is that a realistic application could be constructed quickly in a DBPL. Rapid construction was facilitated by the use of libraries, code reuse and an incremental construction methodology supported by the persistent store. Language features such as a polymorphic type system and structural type equivalence were important. Nevertheless, some problems were encountered with code reuse, with integrating independently constructed components, with the lack of concurrency and with build management such as installation and recompilation. Our experiences lead us to suggest several improvements, including models, methodologies and supporting tools for persistent application construction and maintenance.

1 Introduction

The major motivation for database programming language (DBPL) research is the belief that such languages will facilitate the construction of large, long-lived

*Current address: Department of Informatics, University of Oslo, NORWAY (dagsj@ifi.uio.no)

data-intensive applications. Most database programming language research has been directed towards constructing new languages and object stores. There are relatively few reports of experience using these facilities to construct and maintain persistent applications. Non-trivial DBPL applications are also rare because many languages and stores are experimental prototypes. However, Napier88 [MBCD89] is a new persistent programming language (PPL) that is sufficiently well-engineered to support the construction of non-trivial applications.

The following sections describe experience gained in constructing the Thesaurus Application (TA) in Napier88. Although built in a specific language, many of the principles discovered apply to any DBPL where code is accumulated in a single repository, for example object-oriented DBPLs. One impact of a single repository of code is that programs are no longer constructed as large discrete units. Instead, a typical program is a small unit that retrieves and reuses code already in the repository.

Although small, around 14000 lines of code, TA has an interesting external and internal architecture. The first external feature is that, like many much larger applications, it was *multi-authored*. That is, each of the three components was constructed by a different programmer. Secondly, the application is not a close-knit product, such as might be delivered to a "user". Instead the architecture is more open, or extensible. Indeed it appears that, in a persistent world, programs from several sources are accreted to manipulate and interrogate the thesauri.

The TA internal architecture is *multi-level*, i.e., the three components are implemented using several general-purpose sub-components, namely the WIN and Maps libraries [CDK90, ALPR91] and the Ringad comprehension translator [ATW93]. Some sub-components are used in more than one component; Section 3 describes the architecture in detail. Moreover, some subsidiary components were constructed by non-TA authors, and some originate from a remote site. A second implementation feature is the degree of reuse in the internal architecture. Both the Thesaurus-based Software Information Tool (TSIT) and the Ringad comprehension translator reuse parts of the St Andrews Napier88 compiler.

The TA construction started using the tools and methodologies available in 1990. Because DBPL research is advancing, better tools and methodologies are now available. We are, however, constrained to report our experiences with the tools and methodologies used during the development.

We found that a realistic, i.e. multi-author and multi-level, application could be constructed quickly in a DBPL. All three programmers, although experienced in other languages, were novice Napier88 programmers. Despite our inexperience, the TA was constructed in less than eight person-months work. The rapid construction was facilitated by the use of libraries, code reuse and an incremental construction methodology.

As detailed in Section 4, the TA project benefited from the powerful type system of Napier88. Useful libraries existed and proved easy to use. Reuse of code, even foreign-site code, was possible, although some difficulties were encountered. In particular, locating all of the source code of a sub-component is hard. Separately developed sub-components can be integrated by inserting them into the same store, but discovering an *installation-order*, i.e., a permissible order for installing sub-components, proved very difficult. Lack of concurrency[1] complicated both multiple-author cooperation and software maintenance.

As described in Section 5, our experiences lead us to propose several improvements. Many of these issues are even now being addressed by the Napier88 community. A well-developed methodology would facilitate construction and maintenance of large applications. Several tools would also have been useful, particularly tools that provide cross-referencing and consistency checking, determine installation-order and perform partial recompilation when a small part of an application changes.

The remainder of the paper is structured as follows. Section 2 describes the external TA structure. Section 3 describes the internal implementation structure. Section 4 is a discussion of the experience we gained from writing the application. Section 5 describes the improvements we recommend. Section 6 concludes.

1.1 Enabling Technology

Napier88 is a persistent programming language, that is, it conforms to the principles of orthogonal persistence [ABC+83]. Napier88 is a strongly typed language with some type inference. It provides labelled Cartesian product (structures), labelled disjoint sums (variants) and explicit parametric polymorphism. Existential polymorphism is used to implement ADTs. Napier88 is a store-based language that combines persistence, higher-order procedures [AM85] and L-value and R-value binding [MBDA90].

During the TA development we adhered to a programming methodology based on L-values bound to named persistent locations [Dea87, Mem90, Con91, DCC92]. A stub for a procedure or another kind of value is initially inserted into a new location to which other programs can then bind. For each stub a template program is created that inserts a meaningful value into the location. Incremental development is supported in that the template program can be edited and the location correspondingly updated with a new value without the need for editing, recompilation or re-execution of the other programs using the value.

Currently most Napier88 applications are components of what may be called a Napier88 programming environment which includes a callable compiler [Cut93a], a window manager (WIN), browsers [Kir93, FDK+92], a hyper-programming environment [KCC+92], a Maps library and both model and schema editors [Zhe92]. TA enhances the Napier88 programming environment even further, and this paper demonstrates how TA was built by *using* the Maps and WIN libraries, *reusing* components of a Napier88 compiler and browser and *integrating* existing components (TSIT, ShTh, Utility Queries).

2 External Thesaurus Application Structure

The Thesaurus Application (TA) assists persistent programmers in keeping track of the structure of the programs and other data in the persistent store.

[1] The latest versions of Napier88 have multi-threading.

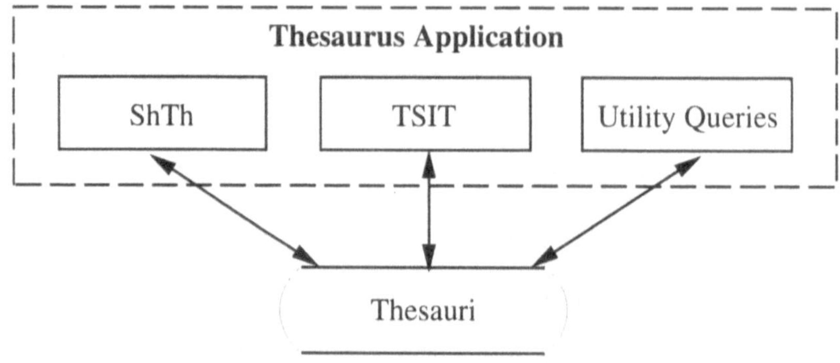

Figure 1: TA structure

It is a meta-application in that its universe of discourse is applications themselves. TA provides answers to questions like the following: Which environments, types, procedures, etc. exist? In which programs or environments are they defined or used? Which places may be affected by changes to them? etc. The need for such a tool has often been experienced by persistent programmers.

The fundamental component of TA is the collection of thesauri (Figure 1). For each application registered with TSIT there is an associated thesaurus holding information about names in the source programs and names denoting name-type-value-constancy bindings in a persistent store [ABC+83, MBDA88]. The thesaurus is automatically updated by TSIT at times specified by the user, for example daily at 02:00. A thesaurus update can also be initiated at any time.

As the interface to the thesaurus and the query facilities provided by TSIT are rather primitive, a need was felt for a more convenient window-based interface with enhanced query possibilities. The ShTh component was then developed by using WIN and provides a graphical interface to one or more thesauri [Lop93]. ShTh also includes a simple query language for operations on the thesauri. Complex queries (involving recursion), however, cannot be expressed. To meet this deficiency another software component, the comprehension query language, was constructed. Queries and their results can be saved in the persistent store.

2.1 A Thesaurus-based Software Information Tool

The heart of the Thesaurus-based Software Information Tool (TSIT) is the thesaurus which keeps track of identifiers of all kinds (denoting types, structures, (polymorphic) procedures, ADTs, etc.).

Names are the focus of attention of the thesaurus since they are central to programmers' and system builders' thinking and thus influence the way software is organised. The meanings attached to names are relatively stable when dealing with concepts at an abstract level — even though the detailed semantics and interpretation may vary between people and between contexts. This contrasts with all changes in physical software implementations [Sjø93a].

The most important information held by a thesaurus entry is as follows:

- name (a textual form of an identifier in a source program or of a binding in a persistent store)
- container (file or environment)
- line number (if container is a file)
- kind — base type (integer, real, string, etc.) or constructed type (structure, procedure, etc.)
- constancy (constant or variable)
- usage (informs whether the name occurs as a declaration or use of a type identifier, or as a declaration, left context or right context of a value identifier)
- context (declaring use of binding in the store, declaring type parameter, procedure parameter, structure field, variant tag, etc., inserting into or dropping binding from persistent store, dereferencing structure field, projecting variant tag, etc.)

There are two categories of thesauri:

1. The *master-thesauri* contain automatically generated data reflecting the state of the source code and persistent store of an application at the time of the analysis.
2. The *derived-thesauri* are generated from the master-thesauri via queries.

TSIT is the tool responsible for creation and update of the master-thesauri. Initially one thesaurus is created for each application registered with TSIT. A thesaurus is populated by an analyser component of TSIT that scans all the source files and the persistent store of the application being analysed. Each time a name occurrence is encountered associated information is stored in the thesaurus. To ensure correctness and consistency of the master-thesauri, entries cannot be inserted, modified or removed interactively or by any program that is not part of TSIT. A more detailed description can be found in [Sjø92].

TSIT provides primitive search facilities and simple consistency checks via a textual interface. A thesaurus created by ShTh or Utility Queries is typically a result of a query on a master-thesauri. Such derived-thesauri may, in turn, be the subject of new queries.

2.2 Show Thesaurus User Interface

The ShTh user interface was implemented in order to provide an easy way of filtering the (potentially) huge amount of information contained in a thesaurus [Lop93]. ShTh provides menu-driven facilities that help the user to query a thesaurus and visualise the result of query application. It also provides facilities to store and retrieve queries and thesauri; thesauri may also be imported or exported via text files.

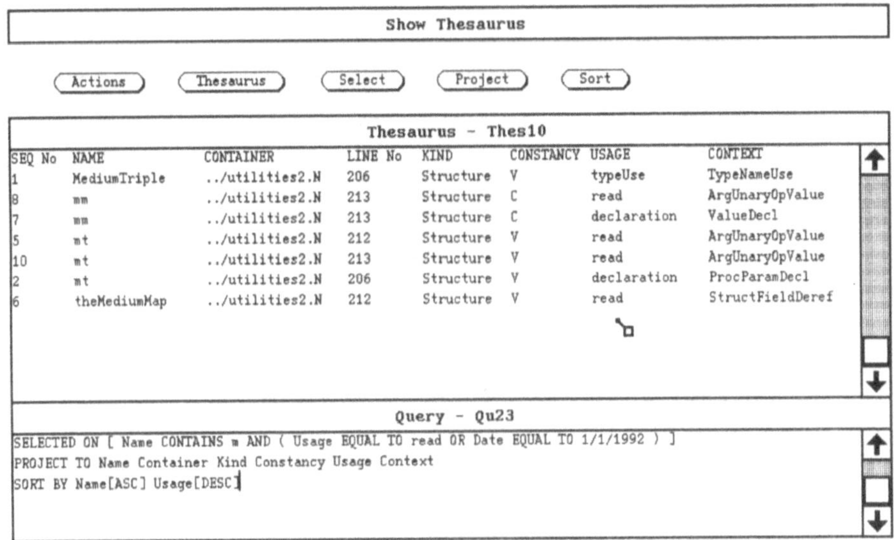

Figure 2: ShTh Interface

Figure 2 presents the ShTh interface; the top menu line gives a broad idea of its functionality. In the "Actions" menu the user has options to load, close, save, save as, delete, revert, and run queries; it also has undo and quit. The "Select", "Project" and "Sort" menus are used to build a query. Queries and thesauri may be stored, retrieved and visualised using this interface. In the same figure, part of the display of a thesaurus can be seen. The user can also perform a union of two thesauri or renumber a thesaurus to compact the sequential key.

By using pull-down menus from the menu line, the user can incrementally build a query to be run against the current thesaurus. Figure 2 shows an example of a query and the corresponding results. The notation used to visualise the query is a subset[2] of ASTRID[3]. The query consists of a selection, a projection over domains and a display order specified by a nested sort clause.

2.3 Utility Queries

Typical data-intensive applications often use a powerful, and usually embedded, query language for three reasons. First, although interactive query languages, like those provided by TSIT and ShTh, may be used by naïve users, they lack the computational power to express some useful queries. A TA query that requires a powerful query language is to generate a call-graph or procedure explosion. An explosion discovers all of the procedures that are called by a given procedure, and all of the procedures they in turn call. An explosion can be used to split off a subsystem within a larger system. Another TA query requiring power implodes a procedure to find all procedures that call it, and

[2] Note that there is no join as there is only one thesaurus at a time.

[3] ASTRID is a generalised relational algebra [Gra84].

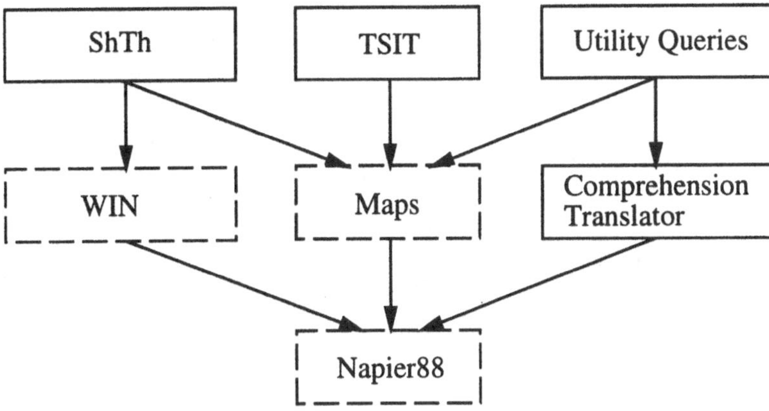

Figure 3: Implementation levels

any procedure that calls the caller.

The second reason for using a powerful, non-interactive query language is for "canned" queries. These are queries or reports that are run regularly (end-of-day, end-of-month, etc.). Primarily to avoid errors such queries are stored, i.e. canned. Storing a query may also aid efficiency and ensure that the information is always provided in the same format. A typical TA canned query is to find type or value identifiers defined but not used. Third, many TA users will have a high degree of computing skill and be able to use a powerful query notation themselves to extract information of interest about their programs. Incidentally, for any naïve users, the utility queries could easily be packaged into a menu.

3 Internal Thesaurus Application Structure

Figure 3 presents the implementation levels of the TA application. Each component usage is represented by an arrow; the solid boxes indicate work done by the TA authors. The authors were using libraries and other software components that they had not written themselves: the WIN Library and the Napier88 compiler were developed in St Andrews; the Maps library in Glasgow.

The first level comprises the three components already described: TSIT, ShTh and Utility Queries. The second level has add-on libraries of Napier88 procedures implementing the WIN windowing system, the Maps bulk data types and the translator from comprehension programs to Napier88 programs. All these components were entirely written in Napier88.

Table 1 illustrates the size of the (sub-)components in terms of lines of code and number of name occurrences. The table also shows the distribution of value identifiers occurring in declarations, right contexts and left contexts, respectively. The measurements were collected by TSIT itself [Sjø92].

(Sub-)component	*Lines of code*	*Name occ.*	*% Declaration*	*% R-Context*	*% L-Context*
ShTh	4986	9934	26	67	7
TSIT	8356	14626	31	64	5
Utility Queries	360	943	11	88	1
Total Components	13702	25503	23	73	4
WIN	24053	37546	28	68	4
Maps	4844	9479	32	63	5
Compr. Translator	1018	1555	22	69	9
Total Sub-comp.	29915	48580	27	67	6
Total TA	43617	74083	25	70	5

Table 1: Measurements of the (sub-)components

3.1 Components

Utility queries are typically small programs written to extract specific information from the thesaurus. Queries are written in Napier88 with comprehensions. Although "Utility Queries" is currently the smallest component, additional queries can be written.

The Shth interface was built in Napier88 and by using the Maps and WIN libraries. Napier88 provides linguistic support for two graphical types: *pic* and *image*. Using pic, pictures are constructed as line drawings in two dimensions of an infinite real space. Pictures may be combined with the operations of join, concatenate, shift, scale, rotate, colour and text [MBDA86]. Images are simply arrays of pixels. Maps were used to provide the storage and retrieval facilities, sets, indexes and stored finite partial functions. WIN provided the user interface building blocks.

The component of TSIT that processes Napier88 source programs is based on the Napier88-in-Napier88 (NinN) compiler developed at St Andrews [Cut93a]. The lexical and syntax analyser of the compiler have been adjusted to conform to special information needs of TSIT. Instead of generating code, the TSIT analyser extracts various information during the analysis and inserts it into the thesaurus.

The thesaurus also contains information about the contents of the persistent store. The code for scanning the store was implemented by reusing low-level procedures used in the implementation of the Napier88 browser [KD90]. These procedures are not type-safe and are thus not available in standard Napier88. Instead of using the low-level procedures reflection could have been used, but that alternative might have impaired the performance [Kir93]. The Maps library is heavily used in the implementation of TSIT (Figure 3). In particular, each thesaurus is stored as a map.

3.2 Sub-Components

WIN

WIN is a library of procedures providing a set of generators of the most common user interface objects: windows, editors, dialogue boxes, window managers, icon managers, menus, light buttons and check boxes.

In WIN actions take place after the occurrence of some *event*. Events are generated by the mouse or the keyboard. An interactive program is built upon a number of sub-programs that perform an action in response to some event. These programs are *applications* which are packed together in a *notifier*'s list. The application part of notifiers (*distributeEvent*) can also be an application inside other notifiers. This allows hierarchies to be built as multi-level notifiers. WIN also allows dynamic reconfiguration of notifiers by adding or removing applications from a notifier list. An *event monitor* will send events to the top most notifier which will route that event through the notifier's list of applications to the first application that accepts it. Each window has encapsulated in it an application that processes input events received by the window and an image on which raster operations are performed.

Maps Bulk Data Types

Maps constitute an add-on bulk data type language implemented as a library of polymorphic Napier88 procedures [ALPR91]. Formally, maps are extensional functions from a domain of type A to a range of type Z, with A and Z being any Napier88 data type. Values of this type constructor denote a stored finite mutable function and may be considered as a set of tuples. The operations provided include iterations (e.g. *for each*); insert, find and remove entries; copy, union, intersection, difference, filter and size, among others. A map may be arbitrarily large, and in TA the thesauri are maps.

Ringad Comprehension Translator

Both WIN and Maps are libraries of procedures. In contrast, the comprehension translator is a language processor. It is a preprocessor that translates Napier88 programs with embedded Ringad comprehensions into standard Napier88. A comprehension is translated into several recursive polymorphic functions. The translator reuses the lexical analyser, error handling and utility components of the St Andrews Napier88 compiler [Cut93a].

Ringad comprehensions are a general purpose query language. In particular they can be defined over several different bulk types, e.g. maps, lists, ordered sets and vectors in Napier88. Comprehension queries are both powerful and easily optimised [Tri91]. Because the utility queries access thesauri, which are maps, they use procedures out of the Maps library.

4 Construction and Cooperation Experience

4.1 Napier88 Language

Almost all DBPLs are experimental languages and hence far from robust. In contrast, Napier88 is well engineered. Moreover, the polymorphic type system provided by Napier88 was crucial to the implementation of the comprehension translator. A generic translator that permits queries over lists, maps, vectors and sets could not have been constructed in a language without polymorphism, e.g. PS-algol [ACC82], an early persistent language. However, if Napier88 had supported bounded parametric polymorphism, the translator would have been further simplified. In summary, the most important observation we make is that very few other DBPLs are sufficiently robust and simultaneously possess a sufficiently rich type system to permit the construction of a complex application like TA. Built-in support of graphical types and first class procedures packaged together with the related objects and parameterised types proved useful in the ShTh implementation.

4.2 Napier88 Libraries

Because Napier88 is a robust and stable language platform, useful libraries of software have been constructed, and more are under construction [ABJP93]. Again this contrasts favourable with many other DBPLs. The Maps and standard libraries are used by all of the TA sub-components; the WIN library is used by ShTh. These libraries proved very useful, and due to persistence accessing them was straightforward. More complete documentation of some of these libraries would have made them easier to use.

4.3 Reuse

In a large-scale software development project one should aim at software reuse [Kru92]. The success of reuse depends heavily on the availability and quality of the information about the existing software.

As described in Section 3.1, the TSIT analyser is a based on a modified version of the NinN compiler developed at St Andrews [Cut93a]. Similarly, the comprehension translator reuses the lexical analysis, printing and some utility components of NinN.

The code for extracting information from the persistent store into the thesaurus was implemented by directly reusing low-level procedures used in the implementation of the Napier88 browser. Implementing the code proved easy due to good documentation [KD90].

Reusing the syntax analyser was not straightforward. The compiler is one-pass, i.e., the parsing and code generation are inter-twined which means that detecting all program parts concerned with code generation is difficult. The documentation and some structuring principles alleviated the problem but were not sufficient for easy modification of the software to the needs of TSIT. In spite of this problem we heavily benefited from reusing the compiler components — developing TSIT would have been very much harder without reusing NinN. In order to simplify reuse, work is in progress to identify substitutable generation interfaces [Cut93b].

When installing bindings, including environments and procedures, into a persistent store, the installation-order is significant. That is, a binding must be inserted before it can be used. For example, an environment must be created before it can be populated, a location must be created for a procedure before its L-value can be updated, etc. It was a hard task to install the modified compiler components from St Andrews into the store of the TSIT author. The original Unix Makefiles [Fel79] could not be used since they had not been updated in accordance with the changes to the Napier88 code. Since the author did not fully understand the structure of the compiler components and their interaction with the persistent store, the installation-order was determined by trial-and-error.

Whereas TSIT uses most of the NinN compiler, the comprehension translator uses primarily the lexical analyser. Discovering which environments and procedures are required by the lexical analyser is difficult. The difficulty arises because the lexical analyser code extracts environments containing procedures and other values. Discovering the name of the program that inserted those values may also be hard, but is necessary in order to locate the source code. The problem is exacerbated in an application with several levels of directory structure.

4.4 Integration

The code necessary for integrating ShTh and Utility Queries with TSIT (including the master-thesauri) is quite simple. There is one environment for each of the three components. All procedures and data structures local to these applications are contained in their respective environments. That is, the persistence paradigm enhances extensibility and integration.

The collection of type definitions in a Napier88 application approximately corresponds to the schema in a conventional database. The source of such type definitions may be contained in *type-programs* which consist exclusively of type definitions; the compiled form is stored in persistent environments. A few cases of naming conflicts were experienced when the type definitions of the sub-components were integrated. In addition to resolution of naming conflicts, integrating persistent software components also requires removal of duplicates, determination of dependencies among type definitions, etc. This is equivalent to the problem of schema integration in conventional databases [BLN86].

4.5 Multiple Authors — Cooperation

A severe problem of Napier88 (in use at the time of this experiment) is that it does not provide concurrent and distributed access to a persistent store implying that the software components had to be developed separately in the private store of each author. Eventually the components were integrated by re-installing ShTh and Utility Queries in the store of the thesaurus and TSIT tool. However, maintenance is complicated as long as no concurrency is provided. Another consequence of the lack of concurrency is that libraries have to be installed into each of the private stores of the users, raising well-known problems with keeping multiple copies of software consistent. A partial solution to this problem can be envisaged by using Munro's store-to-store copying facilities [Mun93].

5 Proposed Improvements

To simplify and improve large-scale application development, which typically involves integrating separately developed components, comprehensive construction and maintenance methodologies are needed. Appropriate supporting tools are also essential. From, *inter alia*, our experience with the TA project they should provide the following functionality:

Cross-referencing Information about where and how things are defined and used should be provided. This includes for example finding the corresponding source file of a procedure in the persistent store.

Recompilation and re-execution In addition to recompiling every changed program there are some special cases to be considered. If a type definition is changed, the dependent programs need to be recompiled. Moreover, if there are dependencies between several type-programs, a compilation order must be determined. After program modifications programs that change the contents of the persistent store (e.g. updating a procedure value) should be re-executed.

Installation Determining the installation-order for programs that insert bindings into the persistent store may be a non-trivial task for medium or large applications and should therefore be automated.

Consistency checking Constraints like the following should be checked: "all declared bindings in a program should be used within that program," "a binding inserted into the store, not intended for export, should be used somewhere within the application," "there should be exactly one program updating a procedure (or another kind of value) bound to a persistent location initialised with a stub (cf. methodology of Section 1.1)," etc. Such constraints are part of a proposed model for persistent application systems [Sjø93b].

Indeed our experiences of constructing the TA application have confirmed the need for TA itself — one of the purposes of building TA was to provide a foundation for tools that tackle the deficiencies described in the previous section. TA keeps track of all the names denoting identifiers in source code or bindings in the persistent store of an application. Extensive cross-referencing is also supported.

At present, many Napier88 programmers use Make [Fel79] to help rebuild the application after change. The programmers, however, have to manually specify compilation and execution dependencies. Similarly, Make and sometimes Unix shell-scripts are used to install software into the persistent store. A correct installation-order, however, has to be determined and typed in manually into a Makefile or a script.These problems are addressed by EnvMake [Sjø93b] — another thesaurus-based tool that automatically infers the necessary dependencies from the thesaurus and initiates (re)compilation and (re-)execution. If installation is requested, EnvMake installs components in correct order (if such an order exists[4]) into the persistent store. EnvMake thus relieves the programmers from the burden of maintaining Makefiles and scripts.

In addition to replacing the use of Make, EnvMake provides additional functionality tailored for persistent application development such as checking a whole range of constraints that the application should adhere to. Among other things, inconsistencies between the programs and data in the persistent store of an application will be detected.

[4] If components cyclically refer to each other, installation is impossible.

6 Conclusions

At first sight application development appears more complicated in a database programming language context than in a traditional context. The reason is that issues that earlier were dealt with by the operating system or DBMS, and not made explicit, are now dealt with within the programming language itself.

The main purpose of DBPLs is to facilitate the construction of large long-lived data-intensive applications. A conclusion from the TA project is that realistic applications can be constructed quickly in a DBPL. (The three TA programmers, all inexperienced in Napier88, needed only eight person-months in total to develop the TA.) Our experiences fall into two categories: those specific to Napier88 and those relevant to any DBPL with a code repository.

Several of the issues specific to Napier88 are known and are being addressed. As there were several authors, we felt the lack of concurrency [Mun93]. Bounded parametric polymorphism would have simplified the implementation of the Ringad comprehension translator.

Several issues arise in any DBPL where code resides in a repository. In a typical object-oriented DBPL, for example, a class definition with its methods may also be preserved in the database. In contrast, in a conventional programming environment code resides in a file system. Keeping code in a repository gives several advantages. Programs are no longer large discrete units; instead they are smaller and typically extract and use sub-programs from the repository. Under this model libraries are easy to use, and large applications can be constructed incrementally [Mem90, Con91, DCC92]. Code reuse would be easy with suitable tools, but without the tools proposed in Section 5 we had some difficulties.

Many of the potential benefits of storing the code in a repository rather than in a file system are not realised because of transitional problems. There are many tools available to support application development using file-based code, e.g. *make*, *rcs* and *grep*. Analogous tools are required to operate on code in a repository. Potentially these tools can be superior to those operating on byte-stream files because a repository is coherent, transactional, structured and typed. Such tools were not available to us during the TA construction, but some are now being constructed [Sjø93b].

Similarly, guidelines or design principles were developed for traditional programming languages where programs communicate via data files, e.g. structured programming [DDH72, Jac75] or modularisation where a high degree of cohesion and a low degree of coupling among software components should be pursued [CY79]. Such guidelines would also apply to a DBPL, but due to more sophistication and communication via a strongly typed repository more comprehensive programming methodologies are needed to fully benefit from the new technology. Currently such methodologies are rudimentary, although they are being developed [Atk93, Sjø93b]. Comparing file-based program construction methodologies with those based on persistent stores, we observe that in the persistent store case all possible data structures (e.g. Maps) and their types are accommodated and preserved when data is stored for later use or passed between programs. Typically file-based program composition has little support from the type system and thus loses structural information as data is mapped to a sequence of bytes. Although persistence leads to more sophisticated interfaces between program parts using arbitrary modules, we believe it will ultimately yield benefits because of the significant structural information that is conveyed between programs.

Acknowledgements

Paul Philbrow co-authored the Maps libraries. Ray Welland made several useful comments on the paper. The St Andrews development team, in particular Quintin Cutts and Graham Kirby, provided robust software for us to reuse.

Dag Sjøberg's work was supported by the Research Council of Norway, Division NAVF. Malcolm Atkinson's work was supported by FIDE (ESPRIT BRA 3070). João Lopes's work was supported by the Portuguese National Council for Science and Technology Research (JNICT, "Programa Ciência", scholarship BD/1310/91–IA). Phil Trinder's work was supported by the SERC Bulk Data Type Constructors (project GR/F28953).

References

[ABC+83] M.P. Atkinson, P.J. Bailey, K.J. Chisholm, W.P. Cockshott, and R. Morrison. An approach to persistent programming. *The Computer Journal*, 26(4):360–365, November 1983.

[ABJP93] M.P. Atkinson, P.J. Bailey, N. Jackson, and P.C. Philbrow. Napier88 libraries. Technical report, in preparation, Department of Computing Science, University of Glasgow, 1993.

[ACC82] M.P. Atkinson, K.J. Chisholm, and W.P. Cockshott. PS-algol: An algol with a persistent heap. *ACM SIGPLAN Notices*, 17(7):24–31, July 1982.

[ALPR91] M.P. Atkinson, C. Lécluse, P.C. Philbrow, and P. Richard. Maps as bulk types for data base programming languages. In *Proceedings of the Annual Esprit Conference (1991)*, 1991.

[AM85] M.P. Atkinson and R. Morrison. Procedures as persistent data objects. *ACM Transactions on Programming Languages and Systems*, 4(7):539–559, October 1985.

[Atk93] M.P. Atkinson. Lecture notes in Napier88 programming. Department of Computing Science, University of Glasgow, 1993.

[ATW93] M.P. Atkinson, P.W. Trinder, and D.A. Watt. Bulk type constructors. Technical Report FIDE/93/61, ESPRIT Basic Research Action, Project Number 3070—FIDE, 1993.

[BLN86] C. Batini, M Lenzerini, and S.B. Navathe. A comparative analysis of methodologies for database schema integration. *ACM Computing Surveys*, 18(4):323–364, April 1986.

[CDK90] Q.I. Cutts, A. Dearle, and G.N. Kirby. WIN programmers' manual. Technical Report CS/90/17, Department of Computational Science, University of St Andrews, 1990.

[Con91] R.C.H. Connor. *Types and Polymorphism in Persistent Programming Systems.* PhD thesis, Department of Computational Science, University of St Andrews, 1991.

[Cut93a] Q.I. Cutts. *Delivering the Benefits of Persistence to System Construction and Execution.* PhD thesis, Department of Computational Science, University of St Andrews, 1993.

[Cut93b] Q.I. Cutts. Private communication, 1993.

[CY79] L.L. Constantine and E. Yourdon. *Structured Design.* Englewood Cliffs, NJ, 1979.

[DCC92] A. Dearle, Q.I. Cutts, and R.C.H. Connor. An application architecture using type-safe incremental linking. Technical Report FIDE/92/56, ESPRIT Basic Research Action, Project Number 6309—FIDE$_2$, 1992.

[DDH72] O.J. Dahl, E.W. Dijkstra, and C.A.R. Hoare. *Structured Programming.* Number 8 in A.P.I.C. Studies in Data Processing. Academic Press, 1972.

[Dea87] A. Dearle. Constructing compilers in a persistent environment. In R. Carrick and R.L. Cooper, editors, *Proceedings of the Second International Workshop on Persistent Object Systems: Their Design, Implementation and Use (Appin, Scotland, 25th–28th August 1987)*, pages 443–455, 1987. Technical Report PPRR-44-87, Universities of Glasgow and St Andrews.

[FDK+92] A. Farkas, A. Dearle, G. Kirby, Q. Cutts, R. Morrison, and R. Connor. Persistent program construction trough browsing and user gesture with some typing. In A. Albano and R. Morrison, editors, *Fifth International Workshop on Persistent Object Systems. Design, Implementation and Use (San Miniato, Italy, 1st-4th September 1992)*, Workshops in Computing. Springer-Verlag in collaboration with the British Computer Society, 1992.

[Fel79] S.I. Feldman. Make — a program for maintaining computer programs. *Software Practice and Experience*, 9(4):255–265, April 1979.

[Gra84] Peter Gray. *Logic, Algebra and Databases.* Ellis Horwood Limited, Chichester, 1984.

[Jac75] M.A. Jackson. *Principles of Program Design.* Number 12 in A.P.I.C. Studies in Data Processing. Academic Press, 1975.

[KCC+92] G. Kirby, R. Connor, Q. Cutts, A. Dearle, A. Farkas, and R. Morrison. Persistent hyper-programs. In A. Albano and R. Morrison, editors, *Fifth International Workshop on Persistent Object Systems. Design, Implementation and Use (San Miniato, Italy, 1st-4th September 1992)*, Workshops in Computing. Springer-Verlag in collaboration with the British Computer Society, 1992.

[KD90] G.N.C. Kirby and A. Dearle. An adaptive graphical browser for Napier88. Technical Report CS/90/16, Department of Computational Science, University of St Andrews, 1990.

[Kir93] G.N.C. Kirby. *Reflection and Hyper-Programming in Persistent Programming Systems.* PhD thesis, Department of Computational Science, University of St Andrews, 1993.

[Kru92] C.W. Krueger. Software reuse. *ACM Computing Surveys*, 24(2):131–183, June 1992.

[Lop93] J.C. Lopes. ShTH — Show Thesaurus User Interface. Technical Report FIDE/93/76, ESPRIT Basic Research Action, Project Number 6309—FIDE$_2$, 1993.

[MBCD89] R. Morrison, F. Brown, R. Connor, and A. Dearle. The Napier88 reference manual. Technical Report PPRR-77-89, Universities of Glasgow and St Andrews, June 1989.

[MBDA86] R. Morrison, A.L. Brown, A. Dearle, and M.P. Atkinson. An integrated graphics programming environment. *Computer Graphics Forum*, 5(2):147–157, June 1986. Also available as PPRR-14-86.

[MBDA88] R. Morrison, A.L. Brown, A. Dearle, and M.P. Atkinson. Flexible incremental binding in a persistent object store. *ACM SIGPLAN Notices*, 23(4):27–34, April 1988.

[MBDA90] R. Morrison, A.L. Brown, A. Dearle, and M.P. Atkinson. On the classification of binding mechanisms. *Information Processing Letters*, 34:51–55, February 1990.

[Mem90] Members of the FIDE types club with M.P. Atkinson and P. Richard as editors. Types for large scale systems. Club report of meeting in Pisa, 5th–6th July 1990. Technical Report FIDE/90/1, ESPRIT Basic Research Action, Project Number 3070—FIDE, October 1990.

[Mun93] D. Munro. *On the Integration of Persistence, Concurrency and Distribution.* PhD thesis, submited, Department of Computational Science, University of St Andrews, 1993.

[Sjø92] D. Sjøberg. Measuring name and identifier usage in Napier88 applications. Technical Report FIDE/92/37, ESPRIT Basic Research Action, Project Number 3070—FIDE, 1992.

[Sjø93a] D. Sjøberg. Quantifying schema evolution. *Information and Software Technology*, 35(1):35–44, January 1993.

[Sjø93b] D. Sjøberg. *Thesaurus-Based Methodologies and Tools for Maintaining Persistent Application Systems.* PhD thesis, Department of Computing Science, University of Glasgow, 1993.

[Tri91] P.W. Trinder. Comprehensions, a query notation for DBPLs. In P. Kanellakis and J.W. Schmidt, editors, *Proceedings of the Third*

International Workshop on Database Programming Languages (Nafplion, Greece, 27th-30th August 1991). San Mateo, CA: Morgan Kaufmann Publishers, 1991.

[Zhe92] Qin Zhenzhou. Second year report. Department of Computing Science, University of Glasgow, 1992.

A Moose and a Fox Can Aid Scientists with Data Management Problems *

Janet L. Wiener
Yannis E. Ioannidis
Dept. of Computer Sciences, University of Wisconsin-Madison
1210 W. Dayton St., Madison, WI 53706 U.S.A.
{wiener,yannis}@cs.wisc.edu

Abstract

Fox (Finding Objects of eXperiments) is the declarative query language for Moose (Modeling Objects Of Scientific Experiments), an object-oriented data model at the core of a scientific experiment management system (EMS) being developed at Wisconsin. The goal of the EMS is to support scientists in managing their experimental studies and the data that are generated from them.

Moose is unique among object-oriented data models in permitting sets to have relationships to classes other than their elements' class, in providing a construct for indexing collections by other collections, such as time series, and in distinguishing structural relationships from non-structural ones.

Fox contains several new features necessary to manage experiments, such as support for associative element retrieval from (indexed) sets and highly expressive path expressions. Fox path expressions can traverse any relationship in the schema graph, including inheritance relationships, and in either direction of the relationship, which makes many queries more concise. Fox also supports a new form of deep equality based on structural information and a new, concise, description of periodic data, e.g., time series. Finally, Fox offers the only object-oriented bulk-loading facility of which we are aware, for loading data from a file.

1 Introduction

Scientific databases are expected to play an important role in enabling scientists from any discipline to study complex phenomena and systems of interest. We are currently involved in the development of a desktop *Experiment Management System (EMS)*, whose primary goal is to support individual (or small teams of) scientists in managing their experimental studies and the data that are generated from them [IL92, ILH+93].

As one of its components, the EMS under development includes an Object-Oriented Database Management System (OO-DBMS). Due to the special needs of many experimental sciences, we have developed our own data model, Moose

*This work has been partially supported by the National Science Foundation under Grants IRI-9224741 and IRI-9147368 (PYI Award) and by grants from DEC, IBM, HP, and AT&T.

(Modeling Objects Of Scientific Experiments), and declarative query language, Fox (Finding Objects of eXperiments). In this paper, we briefly describe the salient features of Moose and then focus on the most interesting aspects of Fox. More details on Moose and Fox are available elsewhere [WI93], as are descriptions of earlier versions of Moose [IL89, IL92].

Several characteristics of the data expected to be found in scientific experiments and of the ways scientists are expected to interact with an EMS led us to develop Moose and Fox. Specifically, a new data model was desirable because of the following:

- In many experimental studies, object collections (e.g., sets or multisets) are reused several times during the course of the study. In addition, they are often associated with other pieces of information, which may or may not depend on the contents on the collection, e.g., the number of objects in the collection or a name given to the collection. To serve these needs, Moose collections are individual objects that may be directly associated with objects besides their elements.
- Distinguishing the structural components (parts) of a complex object from any other objects with which it is associated is important to scientists. Such distinction captures the semantics of experiments, or any other type of information, more naturally [MF91, WCH87]. The additional semantics expressed by this distinction can be used in several ways. First, the structural components of a complex object may be seen as defining its scope, which determines certain properties of the object. For example, object comparisons may be made based only on the objects' structural components, and immutability of an object's relationships may be recursively propagated along structural components only. Second, incompletely specified path expressions in the query language may be disambiguated based on the differences in the two types of relationships [Las93].
- Scientists often need to represent collections that are indexed by other, arbitrary, collections, e.g., indexed by time series. Arrays (indexed by the set of consecutive integers $\{1, \ldots, n\}$, for some n) are the only special case of indexed collections supported by existing OO data models. Moose provides a direct construct to support arbitrary indexing.

Nowadays computation is part of many experimental studies, and most scientists (or at least their graduate students!) feel comfortable using some programming language, usually Fortran. The ability to use declarative queries for data retrieval and simple computations on the retrieved data is very appealing to many of them. Fox is the declarative query language that we developed for Moose; we also plan to develop an equivalent graphical query language, which we believe will be even more intuitive to use. Because Fox is completely declarative, queries are simple to write and have much optimization potential. Fox supports several interesting features that were motivated by the novel features of Moose and the needs of experimental scientists for interacting with the database. These needs include the following:

- Scientists need to access experimental data in ad-hoc ways. Most current OO query languages impose restrictions on how object relationships may be traversed in query path expressions, for instance, only allowing traversal in one direction [BCG+87, CDV88, DGJ92, FBC+90, NO92]. This restriction is too strict for queries in an EMS environment, because it forces scientists to start most queries with the root of the schema graph. Fox allows arbitrary path expressions that may traverse all types of relationships in both directions. As an important special case, path expressions in Fox may involve inheritance (is-a) relationships. This allows the user to restrict the classes involved in the path expression to specific subclasses. It also provides both explicit specification of inherited relationships and a mechanism for dealing with multiple inheritence.

- To support Moose collections indexed by other, arbitrary collections, Fox provides an indexing mechanism intuitively derived from array indexing. Any (or all) element(s) of the indexing collection may be used to access elements of the indexed collection.

- Many scientific experiments involve time series or spatial data. Most often, these sets are periodic in all their dimensions, e.g., the time instances in a time series are equally spaced. In most other OO query languages, such sets must be explicitly specified, which may be very cumbersome. Fox provides support for concise descriptions of such sets of arbitrary dimensions.

- Much data generated by scientific computations are initially stored in flat files. Although connecting the EMS directly to the computations is one of our goals, in many instances it is necessary for this data to be explicitly loaded into the system after it has already been generated and written into a file. Although all relational languages offer such a bulk-loading facility, we are aware of no OO language that does. Fox provides such a facility to create new objects based on the contents of files. The new objects may reference both other new objects specified in the file and pre-existing objects in the database.

In this paper, we describe the salient features of Moose and then focus on Fox. The Moose data model is overviewed in Section 2 and Section 3 details the Fox query language. Section 4 explains the data modification commands of Fox, including the bulk loader. We conclude in Section 5.

2 The Moose Data Model

Moose is an OO data model that supports complex objects, object identity, classes, and (multiple) inheritance. In Moose, real world entities are modeled by objects with unique object identifiers (OIDs) [KC86]. Objects are grouped together by uniquely named *classes*, which capture the objects' common properties. Every class maintains a class extent, stored in the database, to allow subobjects to exist independently of top level objects. For example, in an experimental study of plant growth, objects representing new species of plants may be stored even though they are not yet part of a top level experiment object. Binary *relationships* describe the connections between objects in the schema classes.

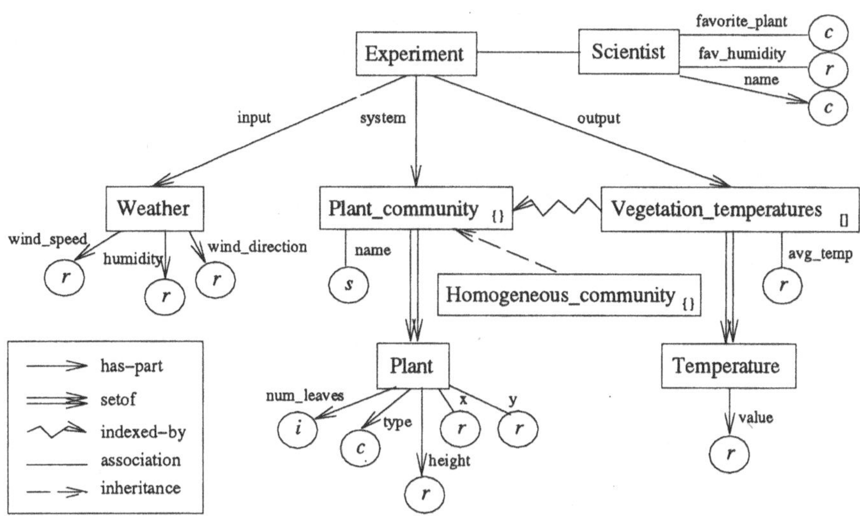

Figure 1: A simple Moose schema showing a soil science experiment to measure plant temperatures under various weather conditions.

Our convention is to represent the schema as a graph: each class is a node (rectangle or oval) and each relationship is an edge in the graph. Each relationship has a label in each direction, which if unspecified, is equal to the name of the target class of the relationship in that direction. For example, the default label of the relationship from Experiment to Scientist is *Scientist*. A simple Moose schema is shown in Figure 1, representing a (simplified) soil science study of how various weather characteristics affect the temperatures of different types of plants. Each experiment is modeled as a complex object, with subobjects representing the experimental system, *Plant_community*, the input parameters, *Weather*, and the output results, *Vegetation_temperatures* for each plant. In addition, each experiment is associated with an object from the *Scientist* class, representing the scientist who conducted the study. More details on the graph representation of Moose will be given along with the descriptions of the corresponding features.

2.1 Object classes in Moose

Each class has a *kind*, which describes the class's basic structure. There are three kinds of classes in Moose: *primitive*, *tuple*, and *collection*. The primitive classes are built into Moose and are currently *Integer*, *Real*, *Boolean*, and *Character String*; in Figure 1, they are represented by ovals and abbreviated *i*, *r*, *b*, and *c*, respectively. (The same primitive class is sometimes represented by multiple ovals for ease of display.)

Objects in tuple classes consist of a prespecified number of other objects, called *parts*, usually from several different classes. Each part is identified by a labeled relationship; labels are unique among relationships of a given class.

Objects in collection classes consist of an arbitrary number of other objects, all from a single class, called the *elements* class. Moose has four specializations of collection classes: *set*, *multiset* (bag), *sequenced-set* (list or array), and *indexed-set*. An indexed-set is a generalization of a sequenced-set. Whereas the members of a sequenced-set are indexed by the set of consecutive integers $\{1, \ldots, n\}$, for some n, the elements of an indexed-set are indexed by (the elements of) an arbitrary collection object. This collection object is called the *keyset* for the indexed-set, because its elements provide indexing *keys* into the indexed-set. (We also say that the collection object's class is the keyset for the indexed-set class.) Each element in the keyset uniquely identifies an element in the indexed-set.[1] In Figure 1, Plant_community is a set class, and serves as the keyset for Vegetation_temperatures, which is an indexed-set class.

2.2 Object relationships in Moose

Like many other semantic and OO data models [HK87, BCG+87, CDV88, Deu90, ISK+93, NO92, SKL88], Moose provides two major categories of relationships between classes: *connection* relationships and *inheritance* relationships.[2]

2.2.1 Connection relationships

Many data models only provide one form of connection relationship [Che76, Deu90, FBC+90]. A major contribution of Moose is to provide different kinds of connection relationships, to reflect the different ways that objects may be related and capture additional semantics implied by these ways. Moose has four kinds of connection relationships: *tuple-composition, collection-membership, collection-indexing*, and *association*. In general, each kind of a relationship may be interpreted in two different ways, from the perspective of each of the two classes it connects. In each interpretation, one of the two related classes plays the role of the *source* class and the other plays the *target* class, thus imposing a direction in the interpreted relationship. Table 1 lists each of the four kinds of relationships, the edge types used in Figure 1 to identify each relationship, and a brief description of their semantics. Table 2 shows their directed interpretations and any constraints on the kinds of the corresponding source and target classes.

Note that associations have the exact same interpretation in both directions (they are *isotropic*), while the remaining three kinds of relationships have a different interpretation in each direction (they are *non-isotropic*). For example, in Figure 1, Experiment *has-part* Weather, but Weather *is-part-of* Experiment. For the non-isotropic relationships, we believe that one of their directed interpretations is dominant, i.e., has-part, (is-)set-of, and (is-)indexed-by are dominant for tuple-composition, collection-elements, and collection-indexing

---

[1]The analogy between sequenced-sets and indexed-sets is even clearer in the query language. An integer is used to retrieve a sequenced-set element in typical array fashion, e.g., my_sset[5]. A keyset element is used in the same way to retrieve an indexed-set element, e.g., my_iset[my_key_elt].

[2]Connection relationships are related to *aggregation* relationships proposed in other semantic and OO data models [SS77, SKL88]. Not all connection relationships, however, represent aggregations of simpler to more complex objects, hence the different term.

Relationship Kind	Edge Type	Description
tuple-composition	single directed	Connects a tuple class to one of its part classes
collection-membership	double directed	Connects a collection class to the class of its elements
collection-indexing	zigzag directed	Connects an indexed-set class to its keyset collection class
association	undirected	Connects two classes that are mutually associated

Table 1. Kinds of relationships in Moose.

Relationship Kind	Directed Interpretation	Source Kind	Target Kind
tuple-composition	has-part	tuple	
	is-part-of		tuple
collection-membership	is-set-of	collection	
	is-element-of		collection
collection-indexing	is-indexed-by	indexed-set	collection
	indexes	collection	indexed-set
association	is-associated-with		
	is-associated-with		

Table 2. Constraints on relationships in Moose.

relationships, respectively. Often, we will draw non-isotropic relationships as directed edges from the source to the target class of their dominant directed interpretations, as we have done in Figure 1.

Non-isotropic relationships are *structural*: they define the structure of their dominant source class. There are constraints on the kinds and number of structural relationships that a class may have, as indicated in Table 1. Association relationships are not structural and therefore are not constrained. Associations connect objects in two arbitrary classes (including collection classes). For example, the average temperature of a set of temperatures may most naturally be associated with the corresponding collection class, as in Figure 1. In other data models, collection objects cannot be associated with other objects. To capture the above examples, one would have to create artificial tuple classes containing both the sets and the associated attributes.

2.2.2 Properties of connection relationships

Moose also provides several dimensions of flexibility for connection relationships, which are orthogonal to the kind of the relationship and may take different values for each of its two directed interpretations. The provided choices along these dimensions represent the various properties a connection relationship may have. Mutability constraints determine whether the source object in a relationship must always be related to the same target object. A cardinality ratio determines the number of other objects to which a given object may be related via a relationship. If null objects are permitted, the target object of a relationship may be the *"does not exist"* null defined in GEM [Zan83]. The chosen combination of mutability constraints and null permissions also determines complex object existence dependencies: if a relationship is immutable or does not allow a null target object, then the source object is deleted whenever the target is.

2.2.3 Derived connection relationships

Independently of the dimensions of structure, mutability, cardinality ratio, and null object permissions, each relationship may optionally be *derived* in one direction. In that case, given an object of the source class, the corresponding target object is specified by a rule (often a query). When a query is not sufficient to express a rule, an arbitrarily complex procedure in a programming language, e.g., C++, may be used. Most aggregate characteristics of collections (e.g., sum, max, min, avg, count) will be derived. For example, the average temperature for a set of temperatures may be a derived relationship from the set of temperatures to a real number. Since scientists are often interested in the statistical properties of some phenomenon, it is extremely useful to be able to implicitly compute aggregates and other analytic results. Derived relationships may also be used in more general ways; for example, the output of the experiment in Figure 1 is dependent on the experiment input and system and is essentially derived by running the experiment. For a simulation experiment, a derivation rule for the output relationship could actually compute the output from the input by invoking the simulator.

2.2.4 Inheritance relationships

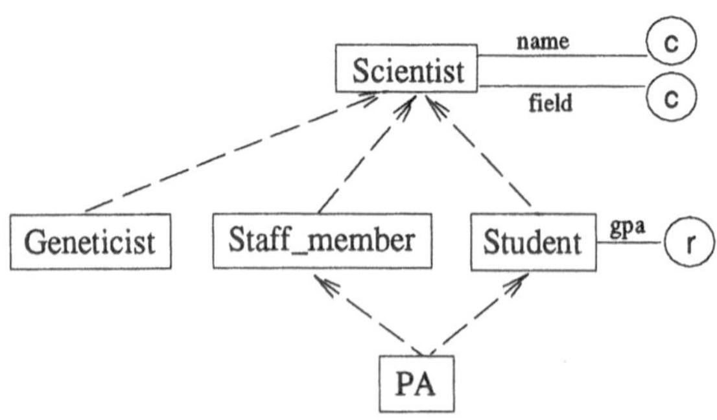

Figure 2: An inheritance hierarchy.

Suppose that the schema in Figure 1 is enhanced so that a scientist may be classified as a Geneticist, Staff member, Student, or Project Assistant (PA).

The relevant subschema is shown in Figure 2, using dashed directed edges to capture the *inheritance* relationships. An inheritance relationship is a directed relationship between two classes, called the *superclass* and the *subclass*. Moose defines inheritance in terms of *inclusion inheritance* and *specialization inheritance*. Inclusion inheritance means that all objects in the subclass are also instances of the superclass. Specialization inheritance means that the subclass inherits all of the relationships of the superclass. In Figure 2, the subclass Student inherits the relationships labeled *name* and *field* from Scientist, and additionally has a relationship labeled *gpa*, which is only applicable to Student objects.

Relationships inherited from a superclass may be refined by the subclass, i.e., a new target class may be specified, which will be a subclass of the original target class. When this happens, the new relationship overrides the old relationship. Derived relationships may additionally be refined by specifying a new derivation rule for the subclass, without changing the target class. A subclass may also create a relationship having the same label as a superclass relationship that is not intended to override the latter. In this case, the subclass can access either relationship by using the appropriate Fox path expression.[3] Moose supports multiple inheritance and resolves name conflicts between inherited relationships by making both relationships available via their inheritance path. Inheritance is important for scientific experiments because it allows the scientist to gradually refine a highly complex experimental schema over the course of a study. This flexibility permits the scientist to retain a core schema, although the specific details for each study may vary.

2.2.5 Derived subclasses

Moose supports *derived* subclasses, which are defined using *constraint* inheritance [ABD+89]. The class extent of a subclass is computed intensionally from the extent of the superclass using a rule. In Figure 2, Geneticist is a derived subclass of Person, defined as those persons whose field equals "Genetics". The extents of derived subclasses are automatically maintained by the system. Derived subclasses are particularly useful when the scientist discovers that certain experiments with interesting characteristics have special behaviors. For example, in the experiments represented by Figure 1, it may turn out that plant communities whose plants all have the same type exhibit certain temperature patterns. The user could then create a derived subclass of Plant_community, Homogeneous_community (also shown in Figure 1), to keep closer track of those communities and the experiments that use them. Encore [SZ89] supports derived subclasses whose rule is a predicate.

3 Fox: the query language for Moose

Fox (Finding Objects of eXperiments) is the declarative query and data modification language for Moose. In addition to the novel features mentioned in the introduction, Fox has the following useful characteristics. It allows arbitrary object construction; it provides closure [ASL89], so that query results

[3]We expect many scientific schemas to contain hundreds of classes. It is quite easy to forget what names have already been used for relationships.

can be used in later queries; it provides optional persistence of query results, so that query results can be stored when needed later, but need not clutter the database; and it supports queries based on both named objects and class extents.

There are several other declarative query languages that have been proposed for OO data models, namely O2query [BCD89], Extra/Excess [CDV88], CQL++ [DGJ92], COQL [NO92], OQL [ASL89], IQL [AK89], XSQL [KKS92], Ontos's OSQL [Ont92], and the Orion query language [Kim89], as well as the Equal query algebra [SZ89]. Fox differs from them in several aspects. The two most prominent ones are its ability to use complex path expressions to navigate any path in the schema graph in any direction, even through inheritance relationships, and its ability to associatively retrieve individual elements of an indexed-set given the corresponding elements of its keyset. The power of Fox in these two aspects is discussed in more detail in the appropriate subsections below. We compare Fox to other languages directly in Section 3.3, primarily to O2query [BCD89].

3.1 Structure of a query

The basic structure of a Fox query is derived directly from SQL. A Fox query has the form

> **for** <range-binding-list>
> **select** <projection-list>
> **where** <qualification>
> **as** <name>;

The following subsections explain the various clauses. First, we describe object naming, because names for objects play central roles in the other clauses.

3.1.1 Object naming

Any Moose object may be *named.* A name acts as a surrogate object identifier for the object, one that is user-generated and likely to be mnemonic (in contrast to system OIDs, which are system-generated and would have no particular meaning to a user). Named objects serve two important purposes: they allow users to access and reuse query results easily, and they provide users with a quick handle to special or frequently used objects.

Each (sub)query has an optional *naming* clause, "**as** <name>", which attaches <name> to the query result object. These names must be unique throughout the database, and may subsequently be used to identify the object. Class extents are essentially special cases of named objects: the name of the class is automatically attached to the class extent when the class is created.

3.1.2 Object variables and path expressions

In the **for** clause of Fox, *object variables* may be bound to the members of class extents or collection objects described by path expressions. At any point, the object variable represents a single member of the collection and can be used as if it were a name for the object. More than one object variable may be bound in the **for** clause, and the object variables may be dependent on each other. The scope of the object variable bindings includes all subqueries that do not rebind the variable, as well the **select** and **where** clauses. Fox's object variables are similar to tuple variables in SQL [DW89], iteration variables in Orion [BKK88], reference variables in Daplex [Shi81], and range variables in CQL++ [DGJ92]. The names of all named objects used in the query must also appear in the **for** clause. The following is an example **for** clause that binds three object variables and indicates the use of a named (Scientist) object Jo.

for e **in** Experiment, p **in** e.system.Plant, s **in** Scientist, Jo

Path expressions are the primary mechanism of specifying what information to retrieve. A path expression corresponds to a path in the schema graph. A path expression starts with the name of an object or an object variable, called the *path expression root*, and continues by traversing relationships. Fox path expressions are more expressive than those of other languages because they can traverse both connection and inheritance relationships in both directions. OQL "contexts" [ASL89] are similar to Fox path expressions and can indicate paths through any relationships. However, OQL contexts are only used to restrict the results (which are sub-databases) and do not directly evaluate to objects. In some OO models, such as ObjectStore [LLOW91], Versant [Ver91], and Objectivity [Obj91], it is possible to define an inverse relationship, which can then be used to traverse the relationship "in reverse." However, these inverse relationships must be explicitly declared.

The syntax of a path expression begins with the path expression root object, which is specified either by an object variable or by a named object. Then, for each relationship traversed, the path expression contains a symbol corresponding to the type of relationship and the relationship label. Inheritance relationships use the symbol '@' (pronounced "as"). Connection relationships use the symbol '.' (pronounced "dot"). Some sample path expressions are: *s.Experiment.input.humidity*, *e.system@Homogeneous_community.Plant*, and *p.Plant_community.Experiment.input*. The first path expression indicates the humidity of the input of some experiment run by the scientists. The second expression traverses an inheritance indicates all plant objects that are members of a homogeneous community that is the system for some experiment *e*. The third expression, which traverses some relationships in their non-dominant direction, indicates the input of all experiments run using a plant community containing the plant *p*.

The result of evaluating a path expression is all objects reachable from the path expression root. If all relationships traversed are single-valued, the result is a single object. If any relationship is multi-valued (a set-of relationship), then the result is potentially many objects and these objects must become the elements of a collection, specified implicitly or explicitly by the query. If the path expression traverses multiple set-of relationships, then the effect is that of unioning the innermost collection elements [BNPS92, KKS92, HM81]. If two path expressions begin with the same prefix, then they are implicitly joined by their common prefix when they are evaluated.

A complete path expression to an inherited relationship (such as the *name* relationship of the Student class) always traverses the inheritance relationships involved. This solves any name conflict problems, including those caused by multiple inheritance. The PA class in Figure 2 has two relationships labeled dept, but their path expressions are different: *PA@Student.dept* and *PA@Instructor.dept*. A path through an inheritance relationship toward a subclass restricts the class of the result object, by requiring that it be an instance of the subclass.

Path compression techniques may be used to permit the specification of incomplete paths. That is, PA.salary may be expanded by the system to PA@instructor.salary. We are investigating ways of efficiently determining the correct complete path, since there may be more than one possible completion [Las93].

*3.1.3 Object retrieval (**select** clause)*

Fox supports query results that include arbitrary projections on objects and arbitrary joins between objects, which frequently lead to new objects being created by the query. While projections and joins are a fundamental part of relational DBMSs, many OO systems have chosen to allow only the retrieval of existing objects from their declarative query languages, not the creation of new ones. (In order to create new objects in these systems, the programming language must be invoked.) For example, Orion's query language only returns the OIDs of existing objects [BKK88], Ontos's OSQL returns relations [Ont92], and O2query results are values (not objects) [BCD89].

Fox allows the user to explicitly specify the structure of the result of a query. The **select** clause specifies not only what to retrieve, but also exactly what the resulting objects should look like. For each binding specified in the **for** clause, an object is produced. The object has a connection relationship to the objects produced by evaluating each component (path expression or subquery) in the **select** clause, and the object's kind is given by one of the keywords **tuple**, **set**, **multiset**, **sequencedset**, and **indexedset**. If the new object would have only one relationship, the user may instead directly project that component by omitting the kind keyword. The final result is a single object, which is a multiset containing all the objects produced.

When a query creates new objects of a given structure, it also creates a corresponding class, outside the persistent class hierarchy, to which the new objects belong. The query below returns a multiset of new tuple objects, each having a humidity and fav_humidity. The query also implicitly creates the new multiset and tuple classes.

for e **in** experiment
select tuple e.input.humidity, e.scientist.fav_humidity;

The type of a connection relationship optionally may be given, preceding the path expression or subquery. The keywords **haspart**, **assoc** or **association**, **setof** and **indexedby** are used. A connection relationship is exclusive, immutable, and allows null values in both directions by default. The cardinality ratio property is determined by evaluating the component. In the example query below, each object in the result is a set object which is associated with the name of the plant community and whose elements are plant types.

for p **in** Plant_community
select set p.name, **setof** p.plant.type;

Individual elements may be retrieved from a sequenced-set or indexed-set according to their position or indexing element. Sequenced-set element retrieval looks just like list element retrieval in O2query [BCD89], and like array element retrieval in many programming languages, e.g., C and Pascal. If Plant_community in Figure 1 were a sequenced-set, the following query would retrieve the first plant in each experiment's system.

for e **in** Experiment
select e.system[1];

The query syntax to retrieve indexed-set elements is a natural extension: instead of identifying the position of the indexed-set elements, its indexing element is specified. However, since Moose is unique in providing an associative connection from a set to an indexed-set, Fox is unique in providing associative retrieval. The next query retrieves the height of each plant in each experiment, and the temperature value that was associated with it in that experiment.

for e **in** Experiment, p **in** e.system.Plant
select tuple p.height, e.output[p].value

If the indexing element were a single, named object, its name could be used in place of the object variable *p* inside the brackets.

Other options in the **select** clause include relabeling the relationships of the new objects, using the **unique** keyword to eliminate shallow-equal duplicate objects in the result, and using the **the** or **any** keyword to extract a single object a collection, usually from the result multiset. The **the** keyword extracts the sole element from a singleton collection, while the **any** keyword extracts a random element from an arbitrary collection. Further details are in the extended version of this paper [WI93].

*3.1.4 Selection of result objects (**where** clause)*

The qualification in the **where** clause is a single boolean expression, which is evaluated for each potential object in the result. Fox supports object comparisons by identity, shallow equality, and deep equality, using the operators **is**, =, and ==, respectively. We extend earlier definitions of shallow and deep equality [BNPS92, SZ89] to differentiate a complex object from its associations: only the has-part, set-of, and keyset relationships of the objects are compared, directly for shallow equality and recursively for deep equality. Fox also provides comparison operators for comparing scalars to collections and collections to collections by membership. All membership tests are by object identity. In addition to the operators provided by other languages [KKS92, BNPS92], Fox adds the **disjoint** and **overlaps** operators for comparing two collections (although they may be simulated using set intersection and an (in)equality comparison with the empty set). Collection objects may also be combined with set-theoretic union, intersection, and difference, and additive union [VD91]. Note that shallow equality for collection objects is the same as a membership test for equality.

As an example, the following query finds the input parameters of all experiments using a system that Jo used.

```
for e in Experiment
select tuple e.input.wind_speed, e.input.humidity,
        e.input.wind_direction
where e.system in (for s in Scientist
                   select s.Experiment.system
                   where s.name = "Jo");
```

3.1.5 Constants and periodic data

Constants may be used in queries wherever an object is needed, e.g., in the **for** clause or for comparisons. When a collection is expected, a constant may be specified as a series of element values inside {}'s. In addition, Fox provides a special construct for creating set constants for periodic data, such as a time series. Consider the set {5, 10, 15, 20, 25}. Explicitly typing out the elements of the set may be very tedious, especially when the set contains tens or hundreds of elements. Fox supports the construct "(**from** <start> **to** <finish> **step** <interval>)", which can be used to represent the set {<start>, <start> + <interval>, ..., <finish>}. For example, the above set may then be specified as (**from** 5 **to** 25 **step** 5). We expect this construct to be used often to intensionally specify the members of periodic sets, in combination with a derived **setof** relationship. Similar functionality could be obtained using a looping construct provided by a programming language, but that would require mixing the programming language and query language statements. By keeping all the constructs inside the declarative query language, Fox permits optimization of the whole query by the query optimizer. It also prevents crossing the boundary between the query language and the programming language at run time, which is generally quite time-consuming. The following query example generates a time series that includes all weekdays in the eighth through twelfth weeks of the semester.

```
for w in (from 8 to 12 step 1), d in (from 2 to 6 step 1)
select tuple week = w, day = d
as my_time_series;
```

3.1.6 Ordering, grouping, and aggregate functions

Any set result may be ordered, making it a sequenced-set. Ordering is specified by an optional **order by** clause as in SQL. There is no **group by** clause in Fox. The effects of grouping can be accomplished with subqueries that include a join on the grouping attributes [DW89]. Aggregate functions, which are expressed in an unintuitive manner in SQL, operate on a subquery in Fox. This more intuitive syntax was first proposed for SQL/NF [RKB87]. Group qualifications are expressed in the **where** clause for the query, instead of in a **having** clause. If the subquery is needed twice, e.g., for two aggregate functions or for the **where** clause, the result of the subquery may be named and the name used instead of repeating the subquery. The following query will print the name of each experiment's system and the average height of all the plants in that system, when the average height exceeds 60 inches.

```
for e in Experiment
select tuple e.system.name, avg(for p in e.system.plant
                                 select p.height
                                 as heights)
where avg(heights) > 60.0;
```

3.2 Persistence of results

Moose supports three levels of persistence for query results: *transient*, *temporary*, and *persistent*. These levels apply to both the result class and the result objects. Transient results exist only for the duration of a query. All query results are transient by default. If a query result is named by the query, it becomes temporary, along with all the other objects created by that query and the name itself. Temporary results persist until the user exits the current session with the database. Transient and temporary classes are not part of the persistent class hierarchy. To make query results persistent, the user must use the **insert** statement to explicitly store the objects in an existing class in the database. Names attached to persistent objects are also persistent.

Temporary results provide flexibility by allowing the user to examine and perhaps refine a result before deciding whether to make it persistent. If all results were persistent, the database would quickly become cluttered with objects the user does not want to see again. For example, scientists often generate tens or hundreds of graphs plotting various points, when they only want to choose one or two for a paper or talk. Making the graphs temporary would allow the scientist to make a final selection before inserting the most useful ones into the database for future use. CQL++ also supports temporary results [DGJ92].

3.3 Comparison with other query languages

The major differences between Fox and other query languages lie in the expressiveness of Fox's path expressions and the ability to have associative indexing. In this section, we give examples of Fox queries with their corresponding (more complicated) equivalents in O2query [BCD89]. We also show queries that cannot be expressed in O2query, or any other declarative query language besides Fox. We chose O2query because it is one of the most expressive declarative query languages, and also the language most similar to Fox.

Traversing relationships in non-dominant directions Consider the following Fox query on a plant object named *tall_corn*.

```
for tall_corn
select tall_corn.Plant_community.Experiment;
```

This query retrieves all experiments that used the plant *tall_corn*. It is a simple query because the **select** path expression can navigate directly from *tall_corn* to the experiments, along the non-dominant direction of the relationships between Experiment and Plant_community and between Plant_community and Plant. The equivalent O2query query follows. (Since O2query syntax is similar to Fox syntax, we show the O2query syntax.)

```
select e
from e in Experiment, p in e.system.Plant
where p is tall_corn;
```

In the above query, it is necessary to first indicate looping through all experiment objects, and then through all the plant objects of each experiment, to see if any of them are the object *tall_corn*. The O2query query requires much more effort to write, since it is necessary to introduce variables for all the collections in the path to the corn object, instead of only one, and to introduce a **where** clause that is unnecessary in Fox. In the general case, the O2query query would require an extra object variable and an extra conjunct in the **where** clause for every collection in the path expression, greatly increasing the complexity of formulating it.

Traversing inheritance relationships Path expressions through inheritance relationships can be used in Fox to restrict which objects belong to the query result. The following query retrieves plant objects that are members of a homogeneous community used as the system for some experiment. The inheritance relationship restricts the Plant_community objects to only Homogeneous_community objects, and thus additionally restricts the Plant objects to only members of a Homogeneous_community.

```
for e in Experiment
select e.system@Homogeneous_community.Plant;
```

To get the same result without traversing an inheritance relationship, a join between the Plant_community objects and Homogeneous_community objects is required. This also necessitates an object variable ranging over the Homogeneous_community objects, which is not necessary in the above Fox query. The following is the equivalent query in O2query[4].

```
select e.system.Plant
from e in Experiment, h in Homogeneous_community
where e.system is h;
```

Path expresssions may also traverse inheritance relationships in the direction toward the superclass, to resolve potential name conflicts that arise from multiple inheritance. That is, although two superclasses of the same class may each have a relationship labeled L, both L relationships are accessible. The desired L is specified by including the inheritance relationship to the correct superclass in the path expression. In O2query and all other languages we know, it is not possible to traverse the inheritance relationship, and so one of the L relationships is lost.

Indexed element retrieval One of the most novel constructs in Moose is indexed-sets. Accordingly, the query facilities that deal with indexed-sets are the most novel part of Fox, and the most difficult (if not impossible) to mimic in any other query language.

[4]XSQL [KKS92] provides a simple syntax for expressing the join in the path expression, although it still requires the extra object variable.

In O2, it would be possible to model the indexed-set Vegetation_temperatures as a list. If Plant_community were also a list, rather than a set as in Figure 1, then a correlation could be maintained between the elements of the two lists. (This is a variation of parallel arrays.) However, the user would need to maintain the correlation explicitly, and we know of no way to associatively retrieve the elements of Vegetation_temperatures. Given a particular Plant_community element, there is no way in O2query to find out its position, and hence no way to retrieve the corresponding Vegetation_temperatures element. Also, although it would be possible to retrieve the corresponding elements for a given position (by specifying the position), there is no way to iterate through all the possible positions. O2query's iteration mechanism treats lists as sets, and ignores position.

It would also be possible in O2 to model the indexed-set Vegetation_temperatures as a tuple with three parts: one each for the plant, the temperature, and the experiment. However, this would result in a lot of redundancy inside the database. For each plant in a given experiment, the experiment would be repeatedly stored. For each experiment that used the same plant community, the plants would be repeatedly stored. Also, the additional tuple classes would add complexity to the schema, when the single indexing relationship suffices in Moose.

Deep equality Fox's deep equality is similar to that of other languages, in that it recursively traverses the relationships of two objects to compare them. The objects are deep equal if and only if the same object is found along each relationship path. However, the deep equality of other languages traverses all relationships. Because Moose distinguishes structural and non-structural relationships, Fox's deep equality is able to traverse only structural relationships, resulting in more meaningful comparisons. For example, when comparing two Experiment objects of the schema in Figure 1, the associated Scientist object should not affect the result. The Experiments are deep equal if they used the same input parameters, plants with the same characteristics, and produced the same collection of temperature values. It does not matter whether the same scientist ran both experiments or not.

Queries in other languages would need to explicitly compare the input, output, and system of the Experiment object. Although a function could be written specifically for Experiment, a different function would be necessary for each class, since the other models do not distinguish structural relationships. (Even if a model did distinguish structural relationships, we know of no way to test whether a relationship is structural or not, inside a user-defined function.)

4 Data Modification

Fox's data modification statements are closely integrated with its query language. There are four such statements: **insert**, **update**, **delete**, and **load**. We only describe **insert** and **load** below, since **update** and **delete** in Fox are very similar to the same commands in SQL. However, we have extended **update** to allow multiple relationships of the same object to be updated in one statement.

4.1 Insert

The **insert** statement adds new objects to the database. There are two forms of **insert**: in the first one, the objects related to the new object via the appropriate relationships are explicitly specified, whereas in the second one, they are obtained by a query. For explicit specification, **insert** uses the keyword **instance**, followed by the list of related objects in parentheses. Like Iris [FBC+90], we have extended **insert** to allow multiple object insertions in one statement and we allow the objects to be named when they are created. Each instance is followed by an optional naming clause. The following query creates three new corn plants, and attaches the name "tall_corn" to the second one.

```
insert into plant(num_leaves, type, height, x, y)
      instance(3, "corn", 2.3, 0.2, 1.2),
      instance(8, "corn", 5.0, 0.8, 1.4) as tall_corn,
      instance(4, "corn", 3.7, 1.2, 2.2);
```

Insert can also use an arbitrary query to create objects and insert them into a class. Although each **insert** statement inserts objects into exactly one class, we have extended **insert** to allow nested insertions. This extension permits insertions into multiple classes in the same statement. For example, the entire experiment input may be specified in one statement. The result of an **insert** statement is a multiset containing the inserted objects. The multiset may optionally be named to facilitate using the collection of new objects in later queries.

An **insert** statement may be nested. A nested **insert** statement is needed to make a temporary object into a persistent one when the object is related to other temporary objects, since they must also be inserted. Nested **insert** statements also have the advantage of allowing the user to mostly copy a complex object, but make a few changes. For example, when creating a new simulation experiment the scientist often wants to use almost the same input as the last experiment, with a few modifications. The following example creates new experiments based on those that used a system named "Nebraska," but increases the humidity of each experiment by 5%. Each new experiment is associated with the Scientist object *Sally*, and will have a null output object until it has been run.

```
insert into Experiment(Scientist, system, input)
for e in Experiment
select tuple Sally, e.system,
          (insert into Weather(wind_speed, humidity, wind_direction)
          select tuple e.input.wind_speed,
                    e.input.humidity * 1.05, e.input.wind_direction)
where e.system.name = "Nebraska";
```

4.2 Load

The **load** command is for bulk insertion of data from a file, generally into multiple classes at once. Many scientific experiments have input and output parameters that number in the hundreds and thousands, and must be loaded into the EMS for each experiment. There needs to be an easier and less time-consuming way to store the new data in the EMS than using multiple **insert** statements (or "new" statements in a programming language), the only method available in many other OO systems. The **load** command provides an easy way to load the new data: the scientist generates one text file containing all the data in the load format and calls **load**. The system can then optimize the loading process for the specified new objects, while multiple insert or new statements would be executed in the (probably non-optimal) order they were specified. Additionally, the ability to load data that already exists in flat files or notebooks is critical to providing an effective new environment for scientists with ongoing experiments. By writing small programs to transform the old flat file data into the load file format, a scientist can easily load old data into a Moose database.

Load facilities exist in most relational DBMS, but in almost no OODBMS. In a relational DBMS, there is no cross-referencing between tuples and therefore data is easily represented in a file. In OO data models, the use of OIDs makes the representation of bulk data harder. We address the problem in Moose by allowing the user to generate surrogate OIDs for the objects. One of the relationships of the objects may be used as a surrogate OID if it uniquely identifies objects [PG88]; otherwise an arbitrary identifier may be used, e.g., meaningful strings or integers automatically generated by a counter in the program generating the data. Surrogate OIDs may be assigned to new objects created in the file, and also to already existing objects in the database by using queries (either before calling **load** or inside the file) to name them.

The following example is a sample data file for part of the schema of Figure 1. Within the text file, objects are grouped together by class, although a given class may appear more than once in the file and the order of the classes is not important. Each class is described by its name, labels for the relationships for which target objects will be given, and a surrogate key type. If a relationship of the class is not specified, then new objects get a null target object for that relationship. Next, the objects in the class are listed. Each object begins with a surrogate key (possibly one of its target objects, as in Plant_community below), continues with a comma-separated list of its (other) target objects, and ends with a semicolon. The target objects for a **setof** relationship are listed inside curly brackets. Strings are surrounded by quotes, have no maximum length, and may contain any characters.

```
Weather<wind_speed, humidity, wind_direction> key string
{
"hot&dry": 5.2, 0.08, 35.0;
"damp": 15.5, 0.73, 186.0;
"sticky": 12.0, 0.89, 320.0
}

Plant_community<name, Plant> key name
{
"tall", {"corn2", "corn6", "rye1"};
"corn", {"corn5", "corn2", "corn6", "corn7"};
}
```

```
Plant<num_leaves, type, height, x, y> key string
{
"corn2": 24, "corn", 62.2, 14.2, 3.3;
"corn5": 10, "corn", 33.5, 24.3, 22.8;
"corn6": 38, "corn", 64.8, 16.6, 4.7;
"corn7": 14, "corn", 42.0, 2.6, 18.7;
"rye1": 50, "rye", 70.2, 34.5, 5.6;
"wheat8": 9, "wheat", 20.6, 89.3, 17.2;
}

Experiment<input, system> key integer
{
1: "hot&dry", "corn";
2: "damp", "corn";
3: "sticky", "corn";
}
```

There are several features worth noting in the above example. The surrogate keys for Plant_community objects are the (string) target objects of its *name* relationship. They are listed only once, as the first target relationship, and there is no surrogate key field in the object description. For Experiment objects, the target objects for the *input* relationship are the surrogate identifiers of the Weather objects, and the new Experiment objects will have a null Scientist target object. Also, there are new Plant and Plant_community objects which are not used in any Experiment.

5 Conclusions

In this paper, we have presented a new declarative query language, Fox, for the Moose data model, which has been designed specifically for the needs of an Experiment Management System. We have completed a preliminary implemention of Moose and Fox on top of the Exodus storage manager [CDG+90]. The implementation is limited in that it only processes the **select** clause. However, it is the foundation for our current efforts to add more processing capabilities. We are also designing a query algebra to correspond to the expressive power of Fox, and investigating various techniques for efficient query processing.

6 Acknowledgements

We would like to thank Miron Livny and the rest of the Zoo project members (Eben Haber, Renée Miller, and Odysseas Tsatalos) for generating a stimulating environment in which many of the ideas presented in this paper were conceived. We would also like to thank Sophie Cluet, Mark McAuliffe, Scott Vandenberg, and the anonymous reviewers from Brown University whose comments improved many aspects of this paper.

References

[ABD$^+$89] M. Atkinson, F. Bancilhon, D. DeWitt, K. Dittrich, D. Maier, and S. Zdonik. The Object-Oriented Database System Manifesto. In *Proceedings of the International Conference on Deductive and Object-Oriented Databases*, pages 223–240, Kyoto, Japan, December 1989.

[AK89] S. Abiteboul and P. Kanellakis. Object Identity as a Query Language Primitive. In *Proceedings of the ACM SIGMOD International Conference on Management of Data*, pages 159–173, Portland, OR, June 1989.

[ASL89] A. M. Alashqur, S. Y. W. Su, and H. Lam. OQL: A Query Language for Manipulating Object-0riented Databases. In *Proceedings of the International Conference on Very Large Data Bases*, pages 433–442, Amsterdam, The Netherlands, August 1989.

[BCD89] F. Bancilhon, S. Cluet, and C. Delobel. A Query Language for the O2 Object-Oriented Database System. In R. Hull, R. Morrison, and D. Stemple, editors, *Proceedings of the International Workshop on Database Programming Languages*, pages 122–138. Morgan-Kaufman, Inc., San Mateo, CA, 1989.

[BCG$^+$87] J. Banerjee, H. T. Chou, J. Garza, W. Kim, D. Woelk, N. Ballou, and H. J. Kim. Data model issues for object-oriented applications. *ACM Transactions on Office Information Systems*, 5(1):3–26, January 1987.

[BKK88] J. Banerjee, W. Kim, and K. C. Kim. Queries in Object-Oriented Databases. In *IEEE Conference on Data Engineering*, pages 31–38, Los Angeles, CA, February 1988.

[BNPS92] E. Bertino, M. Negri, G. Pelagatti, and L. Sbattella. Object-Oriented Query Languages: The Notion and the Issues. *IEEE Transactions on Knowledge and Data Engineering*, 4(3):223–237, June 1992.

[CDG$^+$90] M. J. Carey, D. J. DeWitt, G. Graefe, D. M. Haight, J. E. Richardson, D. T. Schuh, E. J. Shekita, and S. L. Vandenberg. The EXODUS Extensible DBMS Project: An Overview. In Stanley B. Zdonik and David Maier, editors, *Readings in Object-Oriented Database Systems*, pages 474–499. Morgan Kaufmann Publishers, Inc., San Mateo, CA, 1990.

[CDV88] M. Carey, D. DeWitt, and S. Vandenberg. A Data Model and Query Language for Exodus. In *Proceedings of the ACM SIGMOD International Conference on Management of Data*, pages 413–423, Chicago, IL, June 1988.

[Che76] P. P. Chen. The Entity-Relationship Model — Towards a Unified View of Data. *ACM Transactions on Database Systems*, 1(1):9–36, March 1976.

[Deu90] O. Deux. The Story of O2. *IEEE Transactions on Knowledge and Data Engineering*, 2(1):91–108, March 1990.

[DGJ92] S. Dar, N. H. Gehani, and H. V. Jagadish. CQL++: A SQL for a C++ Based Object-Oriented DBMS. In *Proceedings of the International Conference on Extending Database Technology*, pages 201–216, Vienna, Austria, April 1992.

[DW89] C. J. Date and C. J. White. *A Guide to DB2*. Addison Wesley, Reading, MA, 3rd edition, 1989.

[FBC+90] D.H. Fishman, D. Beech, H.P. Cate, E. C. Chow, T. Connors, J. W. Davis, N. Derrett, C. G. Hoch, W. Kent, P. Lyngbaek, B. Mahbod, M. A. Neimat, T.A. Ryan, and M. C. Shan. Iris: An Object-Oriented Database Management System. In S. B. Zdonik and D. Maier, editors, *Readings in Object-Oriented Database Systems*, pages 216–226. Morgan-Kaufman, Inc., San Mateo, CA, 1990.

[HK87] R. Hull and R. King. Semantic Database Modeling: Survey, Applications, and Research Issues. *ACM Computing Surveys*, 19(3):201–260, September 1987.

[HM81] M. Hammer and D. McLeod. Database Description with SDM: A Semantic Database Model. *ACM Transactions on Database Systems*, 6(3):351–386, September 1981.

[IL89] Y. Ioannidis and M. Livny. Moose: Modeling Objects in a Simulation Environment. In *Proc. IFIP 1989, 11th World Computer Congress*, pages 821–826, San Francisco, CA, August 1989.

[IL92] Y. Ioannidis and M. Livny. Conceptual Schemas: Multi-Faceted Tools for Desktop Scientific Experiment Management. *International Journal of Intelligent and Cooperative Information Systems*, 1(3):451–474, December 1992.

[ILH+93] Y. Ioannidis, M. Livny, E. Haber, R. Miller, O. Tsatalos, and J. Wiener. Desktop Experiment Management. *IEEE Data Engineering Bulletin*, 16(1):19–23, March 1993.

[ISK+93] H. Ishikawa, F. Suzuki, F. Kozakura, A. Makinouchi, M. Miyagishima, Y. Izumida, M. Aoshima, and Y. Yamane. The Model, Language, and Implementation of an Object-Oriented Multimedia Knowledge Base Management System. *ACM Transactions on Database Systems*, 18(1):1–50, March 1993.

[KC86] S. Khoshafian and G. Copeland. Object Identity. In *Proceedings the International Conference on Object-Oriented Programming Systems, Languages, and Applications*, pages 406–416, 1986.

[Kim89] W. Kim. A Model of Queries for Object-Oriented Databases. In *Proceedings of the International Conference on Very Large Data Bases*, pages 423–432, Amsterdam, The Netherlands, 1989.

[KKS92] M. Kifer, W. Kim, and Y. Sagiv. Querying Object-Oriented Databases. In M. Stonebreaker, editor, *Proceedings of the ACM SIGMOD International Conference on Management of Data*, pages 393–402, San Diego, CA, June 1992.

[Las93] Y. Lashkari. Domain Independent Disambiguation of Vague Query Specifications. Technical Report 1181, Department of Computer Sciences, University of Wisconsin-Madison, October 1993. Master's Thesis.

[LLOW91] C. Lamb, G. Landis, J. Orenstein, and D. Weinreb. The Object-Store Database System. *Communications of the ACM*, 34(10):50–63, October 1991.

[MF91] G. Miller and C. Fellbaum. Semantic Networks of English. *Cognition*, 41(1-3):197–229, 1991.

[NO92] M. Nabil and S. L. Osborn. COQL: A Query Language for an Object-Oriented Database System. Unpublished manuscript, May 1992.

[Obj91] Objectivity, Inc. *Objectivity/DB Documentation Vol. 1*, 1991.

[Ont92] Ontos. *Ontos Object SQL Guide*, 2.2 edition, February 1992.

[PG88] N. W. Paton and P. M. D. Gray. Identification of Database Objects by Key. In K. R. Dittrich, editor, *Advances in Object-Oriented Database Systems: 2nd International Workshop on Object-Oriented Database Systems*, pages 280–285, Berlin, Germany, September 1988. Springer-Verlag.

[RKB87] M. A. Roth, H. F. Korth, and D. S. Batory. SQL/NF: A Query Language for ¬1NF Relational Databases. *Information Systems*, 12(1):99–114, January 1987.

[Shi81] D. W. Shipman. The Functional Data Model and the Data Language DAPLEX. *ACM Transactions on Database Systems*, 6(1):140–173, March 1981.

[SKL88] S. Su, V. Krishnamurthy, and H. Lam. An Object-oriented Semantic Association Model (OSAM). In S. Kumara, A. L. Soyster, and R. L. Kashyap, editors, *A.I. in Industrial Engineering and Manufacturing: Theoretical Issues and Applications*, chapter 17, pages 463–494. American Institute of Industrial Engineering, 1988.

[SS77] J. M. Smith and D. C. P. Smith. Database abstractions: Aggregation and generalization. *ACM Transactions on Database Systems*, 2(2):105–133, June 1977.

[SZ89] G. M. Shaw and S. B. Zdonik. An Object-Oriented Query Algebra. In R. Hull, R. Morrison, and D. Stemple, editors, *Proceedings of the International Workshop on Database Programming Languages*, pages 103–112, San Mateo, CA, 1989. Morgan-Kaufman, Inc.

[VD91] S.L. Vandenberg and D.J. DeWitt. Algebraic Support for Complex Objects with Arrays, Identity and Inheritance. In *Proceedings of the ACM SIGMOD International Conference on Management of Data*, pages 158–167, Denver, CO, May 1991.

[Ver91] Versant Object Technology. *VERSANT System Reference Manual, Release 1.6*, 1991.

[WCH87] M. Winston, R. Chaffin, and D. Herrmann. A Taxonomy of Part-Whole Relations. *Cognitive Science*, 11:417–444, 1987.

[WI93] J. L. Wiener and Y. Ioannidis. A Moose and a Fox Can Aid Scientists with Data Management Problems. Technical Report 1182, Department of Computer Sciences, University of Wisconsin-Madison, October 1993.

[Zan83] C. Zaniolo. The Database Language GEM. In *Proceedings of the ACM SIGMOD International Conference on Management of Data*, pages 207–218, San Jose, CA, May 1983.

InterSQL: A Multidatabase Transaction Programming Language*

James G. Mullen and Ahmed K. Elmagarmid

Department of Computer Sciences
Purdue University
West Lafayette, IN 47907

Abstract

This paper presents the InterSQL transaction programming language used in the InterBase-Star multidatabase system. InterBase-Star supports the atomic execution of transactions over heterogeneous, autonomous, and distributed component database systems. The component systems may use a variety of commitment methods, including ones recently developed specifically for multidatabase systems. Some of these new methods require the specification of semantic actions (e.g. compensating actions that semantically undo the effects of a subtransaction), and it is possible that multiple commitment methods may be used. Therefore, one requires the ability to specify which commitment methods may be used, and, for certain methods, semantic actions that are used to effect commitment. InterSQL is an object-oriented SQL-based transaction programming language that supports the specification of multidatabase transactions whose subtransactions may use various and multiple commitment methods.

1 Introduction

Multidatabase systems combine autonomous and heterogeneous component (or local) database systems into a global database system. Transactions represent logical units of work in database systems, and in multidatabase systems there are two types of transactions: global transactions and local transaction. Global transactions are divided into subtransactions, with one subtransaction per local system that the global transaction accesses. Local transactions execute at a single local database system. Global transactions are submitted to the multidatabase system, and local transactions are submitted directly to local database systems. A conceptual view of a multidatabase system is shown in

*This research was funded by a PYI Award from NSF under grant IRI-8857952, a grant from the Software Engineering Research Center at Purdue University (a National Science Foundation Industry/University Cooperative Research Center — NSF Grant No. ECD-8913133), and a Graduate Student Researchers Program Grant from NASA.

Figure 1. A global transaction G_i, and its decomposition into subtransactions $G_{i,1}$, $G_{i,2}$, ..., $G_{i,n}$ is shown. Also, a local transaction $L_{j,1}$ that executes at $LDBS_1$, and a local transaction $L_{k,n}$ that executes at $LDBS_n$, are shown.

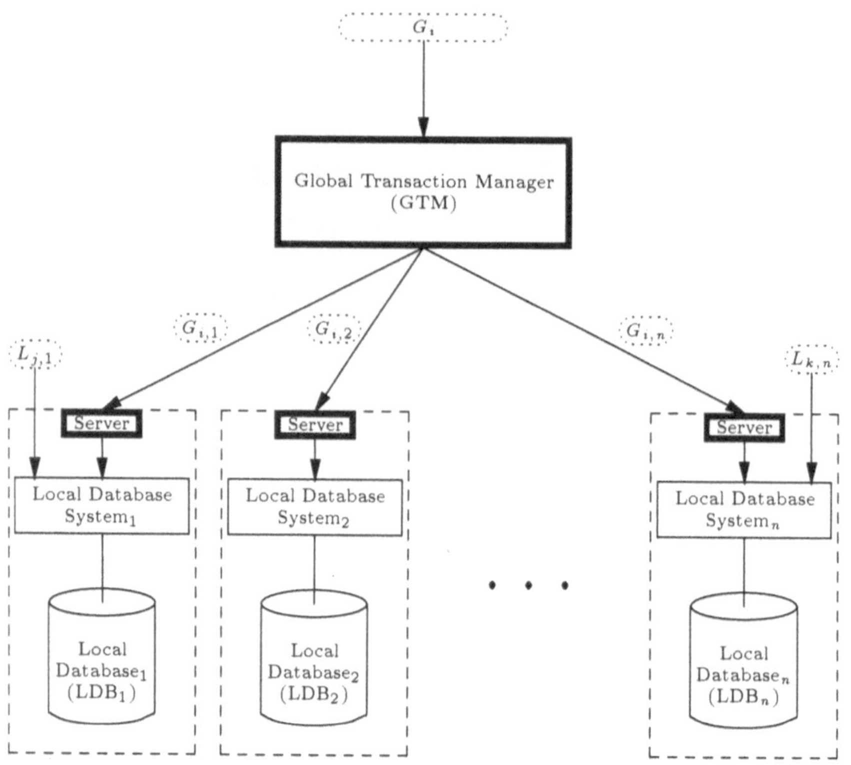

Figure 1: Conceptual Multidatabase Architecture.

Because of component system autonomy, traditional commitment methods (e.g. two phase commitment) are not generally applicable to multidatabase systems. As a result, much theoretical work has been done recently on atomic commitment protocols for multidatabase systems (e.g. [BÖ91], [BST90], [BST92], [Geo91], [MRB+92], [MR91], [PRR91], [SKS91], [WV90]). Many of these protocols are presented from the point of view of all component systems supporting the given approach, however, it should be expected, due to the heterogeneous and autonomous nature of multidatabase systems, that different component systems will be able to support different commitment methods. In addition, some of these new commitment methods require the specification of semantic actions for use in the commitment process. Therefore, it is necessary for multidatabase systems that supports multiple commitment protocols to provide support for the specification of multiple commitment methods and their associated semantic actions (if any).

In this paper, we present the InterSQL language, which is our method for supporting the specification of transactions that use multiple commitment methods. InterSQL is an object-oriented SQL-based transaction programming language that is used in the InterBase* (or InterBase-Star) multidatabase system. InterBase* supports the atomic execution of transactions over heterogeneous, autonomous, and distributed component database systems. The component systems may use a variety of (and multiple) commitment methods, including ones recently developed specifically for multidatabase systems.

The remainder of this paper is organized as follows. Section 2 discusses the InterBase-Star system which supports the InterSQL language. Section 3 discusses the InterSQL language. And, Section 4 presents our conclusions.

2 The InterBase-Star System

In this section we will briefly describe the InterBase* system, which is the environment in which InterSQL is used. InterBase* is a loosely coupled multidatabase system that integrates heterogeneous database systems.

Components. InterBase* Systems consist of four types of components:

1. **InterBase* Servers.** These servers maintain the data dictionary and are responsible for processing InterSQL queries.
2. **InterBase* Clients.** These clients connect to InterBase* servers and are used to issue InterSQL queries. Each InterBase* server may have multiple clients.
3. **Component Database Systems (CDBSs).** These are the heterogeneous systems that are integrated into the multidatabase. In general, it is assumed that local transactions may be submitted directly to CDBSs.
4. **Component System Interfaces (CSIs).** These components act as an interface for the InterBase* servers to heterogeneous component database systems. The CSIs are responsible for translating InterSQL queries to the native query language, and translating data from the native format to the InterSQL format.

Figure 2 shows the overall system architecture for InterBase*. Physical system boundaries are not shown in the figure, but the following rules apply:

- Clients of an InterBase* server do not have to be on the same physical system as the server, but it is generally expected that they are, or at least on the same LAN.
- There is one component system interface per component system integrated, and it will reside on the same physical system as the component system.

Data Dictionary. In general, InterBase* stores data dictionary information in system relations so that this information can be accessed in the same manner as normal relations. The data dictionary is divided into the following four parts:

1. **Directory.** Describes the remote systems with which the system is familiar.

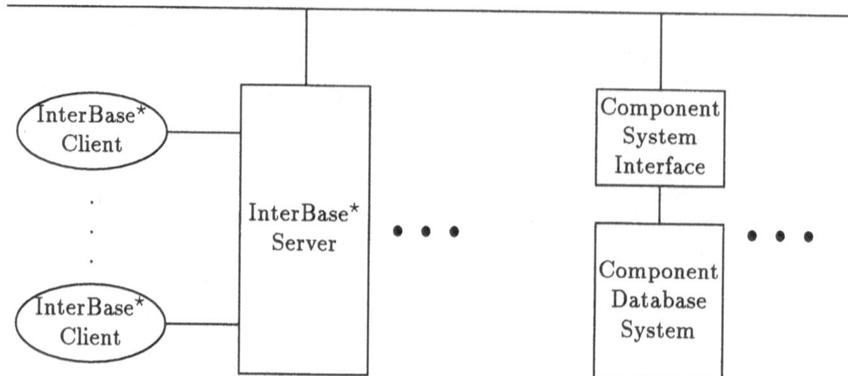

Figure 2: InterBase* System Architecture.

2. **Private Schema.** Describes the data of the system.

3. **Import Schema.** Describes the data at remote systems of which the system has knowledge.

4. **Export Schema.** Describes the data that the system is willing to share with remote systems.

Note that, in general, the data dictionary information is *not* considered to be replicated. Each InterBase* server is considered to have its own view of the global system, which may well vary from that of other servers. This is essentially the federated architecture presented in [HM85]. However, there are a couple of differences. First, in InterBase* the directory is distributed instead of being centralized as it is in [HM85]. Second, not all systems in the multidatabase have all of the data dictionary information or can process distributed InterSQL transactions. Specifically, the heterogeneous component systems will generally only provide an export schema to the multidatabase system; they will not support an import schema or handle the processing of distributed transactions. This is due to the local autonomy of the heterogeneous component systems. In general, it would require system modification to provide these features.

Transactions. In InterBase*, transactions consist of one or more subtransactions. Each subtransaction accesses exactly one database, which can be the database of an InterBase* server, or the database of a (heterogeneous) component database system. Each transaction may have at most one subtransaction per database system.

An InterBase* transaction may not have cyclic value dependencies between any two of its subtransactions. That is, they cannot have two subtransactions that read from each other. Non-cyclic reads are allowed. This decision was made for the following reasons:

- **Ease of Implementation.** Allowing cyclic value dependencies makes implementation harder for a number of reasons. For example, communication becomes more difficult because the global transaction manager may have to send several messages back and forth to a component system to retrieve data from, and send data to, the subtransaction. In our case, all data is sent before subtransaction execution begins, and all results are retrieved after execution is complete. The determination of the committability, and the commitment, of subtransactions also becomes more difficult. Several commitment approaches proposed for multidatabase systems use a "redo" approach where failed subtransactions are redone (or re-executed) until they commit. Allowing cyclic value-dependencies can lead to problems of intra-transactional non-recoverable executions. In other words, it can lead to problems where the values read from a subtransaction (by another subtransaction belonging to the same global transaction) are for an execution that ultimately fails, and the (re)execution that actually commits would have provided different values. As long as one has no cyclic value dependencies, one can simply commit a subtransaction before allowing other subtransaction in the same global transaction to read from it.

- **Lack of Component System Support.** Allowing cyclic value dependencies requires that component system support the partial execution of a transaction. That is, one must be able to split up a subtransaction into parts and be able to retrieve intermediate results. This, however, is not possible in many cases. Some database systems do not have a commit operator, and, in effect, require the entire subtransaction to be submitted at once (e.g. University Ingres [Sto86]). Also, we are interested in integrating non-database systems. Often in such systems, the only way to guarantee the atomicity of a subtransaction executing there is to submit the entire subtransaction as a unit. Therefore, the lack of transaction support for cyclic value dependencies may not really be much of a restriction, since the functionality of component systems may prevent it anyway.

As is standard in transaction processing systems, no direct communication is allowed between subtransactions belonging to *different* global transactions. All communication between such subtransactions must occur solely through data in component database systems.

One of the key features of the InterBase* transactions is that they may use various and multiple commitment methods. Commitment in InterBase* is specified at the subtransaction level. That is, each subtransaction may use various and multiple commitment methods, and the commitment methods of the subtransactions of a given transaction do not have to be equivalent.

The three basic approaches allowed are:

- **Prepare.** The subtransaction is executed to a prepare-to-commit state, where it is guaranteed to be committable, but can still be aborted. This method of commitment would be provided by component systems that provide a visible prepare-to-commit state. Two phase commitment (2PC) uses such an approach for each of its subtransactions. If all subtransactions successfully reach the prepare-to-commit state, 2PC will decide to commit the transaction, and a commit message will be sent to each subtransaction's component system. Otherwise, an abort message is sent to each subtransaction's component system that successfully reached the prepare-to-commit state.

- **Reservation (Redo).** In this case the subtransaction is essentially redone (or re-executed) until it successfully commits. In general, this approach will not be successful unless the re-execution is guaranteed to be eventually successful. One approach to achieve this is to use an explicit reservation step. Another approach is to construct the system in such a way that the subtransaction will by default be guaranteed to succeed eventually, which we refer to as implicit reservation. If a transaction contained only reservable subtransactions, the explicit reservations would be attempted. If all of them succeeded, each of the subtransactions would be re-executed until they all committed. Otherwise the transaction would be aborted.

- **Compensation (Undo).** In this approach, the subtransaction is committed independently of the global transaction, and if the global transaction ultimately aborts, the subtransaction is undone. It may be that in order for the compensating action to be guaranteed to succeed, a reservation step is required. If a transaction contained only compensatable subtransactions, its subtransactions would be committed according to the order specified in the transaction program. If all the subtransactions committed, the transaction would be considered committed. If one of the subtransactions aborted, the subtransactions that committed would be compensated (undone), and the transaction would be considered aborted.

It is possible that no commitment method is available for a subtransaction. In certain cases, as long as there is only one such subtransaction, the commitment of the transaction can still be guaranteed. If there is more than one, then it cannot. A detailed and formal discussion of what types of global transactions are, and are not, committable is provided in [EM93].

InterBase* supports a flexible transaction model similar to the one in InterBase [ELLR90]. The transaction model is flexible in the sense that multiple execution plans can be specified for transactions. If any one of the execution plans can be completed successfully, the transaction can be committed. For example, a transaction program may have three different subtransactions that each reserve a different hotel. The execution plan of the transaction may be specified so that only one of the hotel reservation subtransactions must commit for the transaction to commit.

3 InterSQL

InterSQL is the query/transaction specification language of InterBase*. InterSQL combines the transaction and execution specification abilities of InterBase's IPL [BCC+92] with the unified common query language approach of FSQL used in FBASE [Mul92], and adds high-level support for atomic commitment. One may use InterSQL to write ad-hoc transactions, or to define standard subtransactions. A system may define standard subtransactions and place them in a library for use by other transactions. InterSQL allows one to define various and multiple commitment approaches for subtransactions.

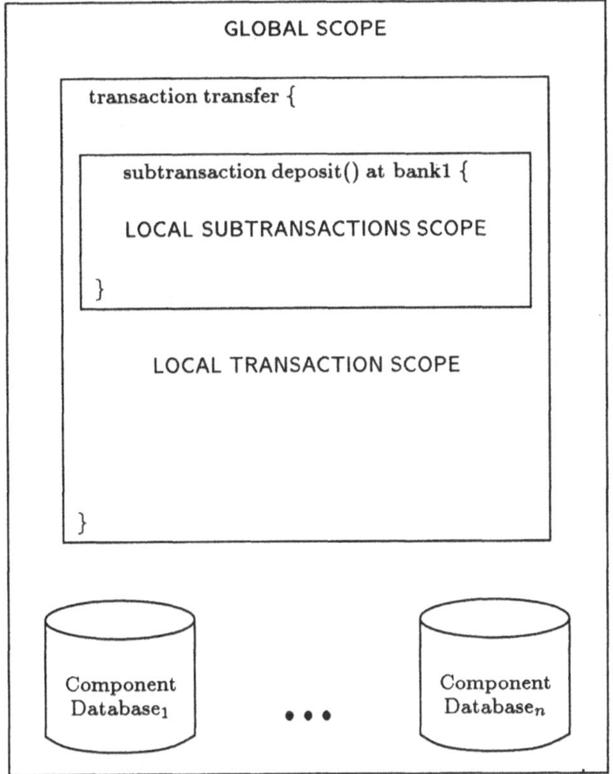

Figure 3: InterSQL Data Scopes.

3.1 InterSQL Annotated Partial Syntax

In this section we discuss the main constructs of the InterSQL language.

Data Scope. In InterSQL programs there are three basic data scopes:

- **Global Scope.** Data that is global to all transactions. This is the data that is stored in the component database systems that make up the multidatabase system.
- **Local Transaction Scope.** Data local to a transaction that can be accessed by the commands in the transaction that are not in a subtransaction.
- **Local Subtransaction Scope.** Data declared in a subtransaction that can only be accessed by that subtransaction.

Programs. An InterSQL program consists of either a transaction program specification, or a single command that accesses or modifies data at the local InterSQL server:

< *program* > ::= **transaction** < *transaction_name* > {
< *subtransaction_list* >
< *reservation_list* >
< *command_list* >
}
| < *command* >

A transaction program consists of two parts: a subtransaction definition part, and an execution part (represented above by < *reservation_list* > and < *command_list* >), which specifies what the transaction does and can reference previously defined subtransactions. Single commands are provided for convenience reasons, and are ultimately converted to transaction programs.

The subtransaction list of the transaction program defines subtransactions that the transaction can use. In addition, the transaction may use subtransactions defined in system libraries. The reservation list represents explicit reservation actions to be taken in an attempt to ensure that the transaction can be committed. The command list of the transaction specifies the execution plan of the transaction. One may specify multiple acceptable execution plans. Each plan specifies which subtransactions are executed, and the order of their execution (including in parallel). We will refer to the reservation and transaction command lists as the "main program" of the transaction.

The data and subtransactions that are accessible to the transaction command list are:

- local data declared within the transaction (which can be passed as arguments to subtransactions)
- subtransactions declared within the transaction
- subtransactions in system libraries

The transaction command list cannot access any database data directly; its goal is to describe the execution plan of the transaction, i.e., which subtransactions will be executed and in which order.

A very simple program is listed below. In this example the transaction contains no subtransaction list or reservation list. It has one command in its command list that prints the message "Hello World."

```
transaction very_simple {
   print("Hello World.");
}
```

Subtransaction Lists. Subtransaction lists contain a set of subtransaction definitions. Each subtransaction definition must specify the name of the subtransaction, the system at which it executes, a list of subtransaction argument declarations, a list of commands to be executed, and the specification of commitment methods that can be used to commit the subtransaction.

< *subtransaction_list* > ::= ϵ | < *subtransaction_list* > < *subtransaction* >

< *subtransaction* > ::= **subtransaction** < *name* >
(< *arg_declaration_list* >)
at < *system_name* >
{ < *command_list* > < *commit_list* > }

Each subtransaction in a given transaction must have a unique name. Also, there may be no more than one subtransaction specified per system. The reason for this is that concurrency control is not maintainable when a single transaction has multiple subtransactions at the same component system. For example, suppose a global transaction has two subtransactions $G1$ and $G1'$ that execute at the same component system. A non-serializable order such as $G1 \rightarrow L \rightarrow G1'$ could result. The global transaction manager, which has no direct knowledge or control of local transactions, cannot prevent such a situation from occurring. The system name "local" is reserved and specifies the local database system. In other words, this subtransaction would access the database of the InterBase* server to which it was submitted.

Each subtransaction may only access the following data:

- (global) data stored in the database at the system where the subtransaction executes.
- its arguments (which could be set by other subtransactions).
- local data declared within the subtransaction.

An example is listed below. In this example the transaction contains one subtransaction definition in its subtransaction list. The subtransaction executes at system "db1" and displays the relation "employees" stored in the database at system "db1."

```
transaction simple {
   subtransaction s() at db1 {
      select * from employees;
   }

   s();
}
```

The main program in this case has no reservation list, and the command list consists of one subtransaction call "s()."

Argument Declaration Lists. Subtransaction arguments may be scalar or tables:

$$
\begin{aligned}
< arg\_delcaration\_list > ::= \;& \epsilon \\
\mid\;& < arg\_declaration > , \\
& < arg\_declaration\_list >
\end{aligned}
$$

$$
\begin{aligned}
< arg\_declaration > ::= \;& < at\_identifier > < attribute\_type > \\
\mid\;& < at\_identifier > \textbf{table} \; (< definition\_list >)
\end{aligned}
$$

Arguments are used to pass data to subtransactions and to return results from subtransactions. Since one must be able to modify the actual arguments in order to return results, copy-restore is used. Arguments are the sole means of passing data between subtransactions belonging to the same transaction.

Below is an example subtransaction with two arguments. The first argument, "@salary," is a scalar integer argument that is used as an input argument.

The second argument, "@names," is a table argument with one attribute named "name" of type integer. This argument is used as an output argument, specifically to return the names of all the employees that earn more than "@salary."

```
subtransaction s(@salary integer, @names table (name varcharacter))
at db1 {
    @names := select * from employee where employee.salary > @salary;
}
```

Commit List. The commit list specifies the possible ways a given subtransaction can be committed. Reservation can be specified, compensation can be specified (either with or without reservation), or prepare can be specified. And, any combination of the three basic methods or no method can be specified. It is illegal to have more than one of the same options specified in a given subtransaction. In addition, either both the "reservation" and "unreservation" options must be specified or neither specified. Either both the "compensation reservation" and "compensation unreservation" options must be specified or neither, and, furthermore, they must only be used if the "compensation" option has been specified.

< *commit_list* > ::= ϵ | < *commit_list* > < *commit* >

< *commit* > ::= **reservation** { < *command_list* > }
| **unreservation** { < *command_list* > }
| **compensation** { < *command_list* > }
| **compensation reservation** { < *command_list* > }
| **compensation unreservation** { < *command_list* > }
| **prepare**

The meanings of each of the commitment specifications is explained in more detail below.

- **reservation:** commands that, if executed successfully, guarantee that the subtransaction will eventually commit if re-executed when it fails. Using an explicit reservation action can support the reservation commitment method in [MJSA93]. An implicit reservation (a reservation with an empty command list) would be used for data-partitioning redo[1] approaches, such as in [BST90], [BST92], [MRB$^+$92], and [WV90], and for methods that reroute local transactions through an agent of the multidatabase system, such as [MR91] and in [SKS91]. An implicit reservation could also be used for component systems that allow the multidatabase system exclusive access after failures, so that subtransactions can be redone (e.g. [BÖ91] and [Geo91]).
- **unreservation:** commands that undo the effects of a reservation's commands.

[1] In these approaches data is partitioned into locally and globally updatable sets in such a way that the re-execution of the subtransaction is guaranteed to succeed eventually.

- **compensation:** commands that will undo the effects of the subtransaction. Obviously, this would be used for compensation methods. An implicit compensation (a compensation with an empty command list) could be used for subtransactions with certain semantic properties, such as read-only subtransactions, and for approaches that provide a general way of undoing subtransactions, such as in [MR91] and [PRR91]. These approaches assume a mechanism is available for preventing local transaction from accessing global transactions whose commitment decision is still undecided.

- **compensation reservation:** commands that, if executed successfully, guarantee that the compensation for the subtransaction will succeed. This construct could be used to specify subtransactions using the undo approach in [MJSA93]. An example of such an action would be one that would ensure that an account does not go below $100, so that a deposit of $100 dollars can be compensated by withdrawing $100. Without the reservation action, the compensation action could abort indefinitely. Methods for implementing such actions in a multidatabase environment are covered in [MJSA93].

- **compensation unreservation:** commands that undo the effects of a compensation reservation.

- **prepare:** statement that indicates that a visible prepare-to-commit state is available for this subtransaction. That is, the subtransaction can be executed to a prepare-to-commit state where it is guaranteed to be committable, but can still be aborted.

Below is a simple example where the subtransaction is read-only and has two commitment specifications: an implicit reservation and an implicit compensation. In general, read-only subtransactions can be considered to be both implicitly reservable and implicitly compensatable.

```
subtransaction read_only {
    select * from employee;
    reservation { }
    compensation { }
}
```

A subtransaction with an explicit reservation (or compensation) would have commands within the brackets after "reservation" ("compensation") to carry out the reservation (compensation).

Reservation Lists. Reservation lists are optional and are used to represent explicit reservation actions. Reservation lists have the following form:

< *reservation_list* > ::= **reservation** {
< *command_list* >
}

Reservation lists are needed for explicit reservations that have arguments. With compensations, one can simply use the argument's value used by the subtransaction call. However, reservations occur *before* the subtransaction call, so the transaction manager needs a method for knowing what arguments to use for the reservation. It is not possible, in general, to determine what argument values a subtransaction will be called with in advance. The command list for a reservation can consist of normal commands and reservation commands:

< *reservation_list_command* > ::=
  < *sql_command* >
 | **reserve** < *subtransaction_name* > (< *arg_list* >) ;
 | **reserve compensation for** < *subtransaction_name* >
  (< *arg_list* >) ;

For an example reservation list, see Figure 4.

Commands. The standard SQL commands are provided, as well as additional commands to increase functionality:

< *command_list* > ::= ϵ | < *command_list* > < *command* >

< *command* > ::= [< *system_name* > :] < *procedure_name* > (< *arg_list* >) ;
 | **execute in parallel** < *command_list* >
 | **execute one of** < *command_list* >
 | < *sql_commands* >

The procedure invocation command is used to invoke procedures. If a procedure is invoked in the main program, it represents the invocation of a subtransaction. The subtransaction must either be defined in the transaction program, or defined in a system library. To specify a system library subtransaction, the system name of the library is prepended to the subtransaction name, for example:

```
bank1:withdraw(101, 1000);
```

The above example represents a withdraw subtransaction at system "bank1" that withdraws $1000 from account number 101. If a procedure is invoked within a subtransaction it refers to a database method (or function). The database method must have been previously defined at the system that is accessed. A subtransaction cannot invoke another subtransaction.

The "execute one of" command is included for the purpose of allowing alternate possible execution paths to achieve global commitment. For example, a user may want to reserve a room at only one of three hotels, and write the following in the main program:

```
execute one of {
    reserve_hotel1();
    reserve_hotel2();
    reserve_hotel3();
}
```

The "execute one of" statement here says to execute (in this case commit) only one of the subtransaction calls listed, and to abort the transaction if none of them can be committed.

Listing subtransaction invocations sequentially, for example:

```
s1(); s2(); s3();
```

means that "s1()," "s2()," and "s3()" should all be committed, and they should be committed in sequential order. And, that if any of them cannot be committed, the global transaction should be aborted.

The "execute in parallel" statement has the same effect as listing subtransaction invocations sequentially, except that the subtransactions may be executed in any order, including in parallel. So all the subtransaction invocations listed in an "execute in parallel" statement must be committed for the transaction to succeed.

The "execute one of" and "execute in parallel" commands can be arbitrarily nested. Clearly, any combination of acceptable goals can be specified, although it is illegal to specify an execution plan that would execute the same subtransaction twice.

Object-Oriented Extensions. The object-oriented extensions of InterSQL are motivated by the desire to facilitate the integration of heterogeneous systems. Many consider the object-oriented approach well suited for this purpose (see, for example, [BEM92]). For example, object-oriented languages are typically very rich in semantic expressiveness, and it is beneficial from an integration standpoint to have the common query language be a superset (at least semantically, if not syntactically) of the native languages of the component systems. This way, one can map all the features of the component systems' languages to constructs in InterSQL.

The object-oriented extensions to InterSQL were taken from object-oriented extensions to SQL of FBASE's FSQL [Mul92]. FSQL was based on SQL2, which did not provide object-oriented features. Now, however, a new SQL standard has been developed (SQL3) which provides object-oriented features (see, for example, [Gal92]). We may investigate using these extensions in the future. In any event, the object-oriented features of InterSQL are as described below.

In InterBase*, each component system, as well as the data in the component system's database, are viewed as objects. Therefore, one can define methods for both the component system and its data. In the InterSQL data model, data are organized into relations; relations represent the instances of a class. Therefore, the InterSQL data model can be viewed as either an extended relational model, or an object-oriented model. And, structurally, the InterSQL data model supports the nested relation model because an attribute may be defined to be a collection of objects of a single type (i.e., a relation). Again, the purpose of this model is to facilitate integration, and not to study advanced data models per se.

The specific object-oriented features of InterSQL are as follows:

- modeling of aggregation/decomposition and subobject referencing
- inheritance
- method definition and invocation

Identifiers. Identifiers in InterSQL are of two general types: local identifiers, and global identifiers. Local identifiers represent relations, scalar variables, and subtransaction arguments that are local to the transaction. Global identifiers represent relations in database systems that can be accessed by all transactions and are, therefore, global relative to the transactions. In InterSQL, local identifiers start with the "@" symbol, whereas global identifiers start with a letter or underscore. The "@" is used to disambiguate identifiers, and is primarily for the benefit of people reading the program. From the system point of view, it could be determined whether an identifier refers to local or global data, or is ambiguous, without the "@" naming convention. However, we feel that it is useful from the user's perspective to be able to distinguish easily between commands that access local data, and commands that access data actually stored in a database.

Comments. Comments in InterSQL are indicated by a "//." Text after a "//" until the end of the line is considered to be a comment.

3.2 InterSQL Example

In this section we present an InterSQL transaction program example. A bank transfer transaction example is shown in Figure 4. The transaction program in this example has two subtransaction: "withdraw" and "deposit." The transaction withdraws money from one account, and, in effect, deposits that money in another account.

Subtransaction "withdraw" has two arguments: the account number from which to withdraw, and the amount of money to withdraw. This subtransaction uses reservation as its commitment method. It executes its reservation step, which if successful will guarantee that the subtransaction can eventually be committed. The unreservation step undoes the effects of the reservation. In this case, it is assumed that each account has a lower limit below which the balance of the account may not go. The reservation first checks to see if there is enough money in the account to make the withdrawal. If there is not enough the reservation aborts and the subtransaction's commitment cannot be guaranteed. If there is enough money, the lower limit is increased by the amount that will be withdrawn to ensure that there will be enough money in the account for the withdrawal to succeed.

Subtransaction "deposit" has the same arguments as subtransaction "withdraw," but uses compensation as its commitment method. The compensating action simply withdraws the amount that was deposited.

In this example, the transaction program was written as an ad-hoc transaction where the subtransactions are defined in the transaction program. However, the withdraw and deposit subtransactions could have been pre-defined and included in a system library, so the user would only have to write the main program portion of the transaction. In general, the subtransaction library approach works well if the access to the component system is restricted in functionality. For example, if a banking system only allows access in the form of withdrawals, deposits, and balance listings.

Another approach would be for the system to provide database methods that the subtransactions could access. The withdraw subtransaction might then look as shown in Figure 5.

```
transaction transfer {
  subtransaction withdraw (@account_number integer, @amount integer)
  at bank1 {
    update account set balance = balance - @amount
        where account.number = @account_number;
    reservation {
        create variable @lower_limit integer;
        create variable @balance integer;
        @lower_limit := select account.lower_limit from account
            where account.number = @account_number;
        @balance := select account.balance from account
            where account.number = @account_number;
        if (@balance - @lower_limit < @amount) abort;
        update account set lower_limit = lower_limit + @amount
            where account.number = @account_number;
    }
    unreservation {
        update account set lower_limit = lower_limit - @amount
            where account.number = @account_number;
    }
  }

  subtransaction deposit (@account_number integer, @amount integer)
  at bank2 {
    update account set balance = balance + @amount
        where account.number = @account_number;
    compensation {
        update account set balance = balance - @amount
            where account.number = @account_number;
    }
  }

  reservation {
    create variable @from_account integer;
    create variable @to_account integer;
    create variable @amount integer;
    input("Enter from account number:  ", @from_account);
    input("Enter to account number:  ", @to_account);
    input("Enter amount:  ", @amount);
    reserve withdraw(@from_account, @amount);
  }
  deposit(@to_account, @amount);
  withdraw(@from_account, @amount);
}
```

Figure 4: InterSQL Bank Transfer Example.

```
transaction transfer {
  subtransaction withdraw (@account_number integer, @amount integer)
  at bank1 {
    db_withdraw(@account_number, @amount);
    reservation {
        db_reserve_withdraw(@account_number, @amount);
    }
    unreservation {
        db_unreserve_withdraw(@account_number, @amount);
    }
  }
  ...
}
```

Figure 5: InterSQL Database Method Example.

4 Conclusions

This paper has presented the InterSQL language used by the InterBase* multidatabase system. The combination of features provided by InterSQL is unique as far as we know, and can be summarized as follows:

- Specification of distributed multidatabase transactions.
- SQL based common query language (with object-oriented extensions).
- High-level specification of multiple multidatabase atomic commitment methods for subtransactions that includes: reservation, compensation, reservation-compensation, and prepare-to-commit.

InterSQL provides heterogeneity transparency in regard to its transaction programming language, since a single language is used for all systems. However, InterSQL does not provide distribution transparency, which could be considered a disadvantage. And, the commitment protocol is not completely transparent in InterSQL. Users have to specify argument values for explicit reservations, and completely ad-hoc transaction programs must specify the semantic actions of reservations and compensations. However, library subtransactions and database methods can be used, which can hide the details of the commitment protocol to the user. In addition, the user does not need to worry about writing committable transactions, as InterBase* will automatically check the committability of each transaction, and will not execute a transaction whose atomicity cannot be guaranteed.

Significant implementation progress has been made, and an initial version of InterBase* has been completed that supports all of the atomic commitment features described in this paper. An area for future investigation is the construction of a higher-level interface built on top of InterSQL that support a greater degree of distribution and/or commitment transparency.

References

[BCC+92] O. Bukhres, Jiansan Chen, Jindong Chen, A. Elmagarmid, Yungho Leu, and Gang Zhu. IPL: The InterBase Parallel Language. In *Proc. of the 2nd International Workshop on Research Issues on Data Engineering : Transaction and Query Processing*, pages 69–76, Tempe, AZ, 1992.

[BEM92] Omran A. Bukhres, Ahmed K. Elmagarmid, and James G. Mullen. Object-oriented multidatabases: Systems and research overview. In *Proceedings of the International Conference on Information and Knowledge Management*, pages 27–34, Baltimore, Maryland, USA, November 1992.

[BÖ91] K. Barker and M.T. Özsu. Reliable transaction execution in multidatabase systems. In *Proceedings of the First International Workshop on Interoperability in Multidatabase Systems*, pages 344–347, Kobe, Japan, April 1991.

[BST90] Y. Breitbart, A. Silberschatz, and G. Thompson. Reliable Transaction Management in a Multidatabase System. In *Proceedings of the ACM SIGMOD Conference on Management of Data*, pages 215–224, May 1990.

[BST92] Yuri Breitbart, Avi Silberschatz, and Glenn R. Thompson. Transaction managemnet issues in a failure-prone multidatabase system environment. *VLDB Journal*, 1(1):1–39, July 1992.

[ELLR90] A. K. Elmagarmid, Y. Leu, W. Litwin, and M. Rusinkiewicz. A Multidatabase Transaction Model for InterBase. In *Proceedings of the 16th International Conference on Very Large Data Bases*, pages 507–581, Brisbane, Australia, August 1990.

[EM93] Ahmed K. Elmagarmid and James G. Mullen. Multidatabase atomic commitment protocols: A taxonomy and unified approach. Technical Report CSD-TR-93-018, Purdue University, March 1993.

[Gal92] Leonard J. Gallagher. SQL: Language extensions for object data management. In *Proceedings of the International Conference on Information and Knowledge Management*, pages 17–26, Baltimore, Maryland, USA, November 1992.

[Geo91] D. Georgakopoulos. Multidatabase recoverability and recovery. In *Proceedings of the First International Workshop on Interoperability in Multidatabase Systems*, pages 348–355, Kobe, Japan, April 1991.

[HM85] D. Heimbigner and D. McLeod. A Federated Architecture for Information Management. *ACM Transaction on Office Information Systems*, 3(3), July 1985.

[MJSA93] James G. Mullen, Jin Jing, and Jamshid Sharif-Askary. Reservation commitment and its use in multidatabase systems. In *Proceedings of the Fourth IEEE International Conference on Database and Expert Systems Applications (DEXA)*, pages 116–121, Prague, Czech Republic, September 1993.

[MR91] P. Muth and T.C. Rakow. Atomic commitment for integrated database systems. In *Proceedings of the 7th Intl. Conf. on Data Engineering*, pages 296–304, Kobe, Japan, April 1991.

[MRB+92] S. Mehrotra, R. Rastogi, Y. Breitbart, H. F. Korth, and A. Silberschatz. Ensuring transaction atomicity in multidatabase systems. Technical Report TR-92-12, University of Texas at Austin Department of Computer Science, 1992.

[Mul92] James G. Mullen. FBASE: A Federated Objectbase System. *International Journal of Computer Systems Science and Engineering*, 7(2):91–99, April 1992.

[PRR91] William Perrizo, Joseph Rajkumar, and Prabhu Ram. HYDRO: a heterogeneous distributed database system. In *Proceedings of the ACM SIGMOD International Conference on Management of Data*, pages 32–39, Denver, Colorado, USA, May 1991.

[SKS91] Nandit Soparkar, Henry F. Korth, and Abraham Siberschatz. Failure-resilient transaction management in multidatabases. *IEEE Computer*, 24(12):28–36, December 1991.

[Sto86] Michael Stonebraker, editor. *The INGRES Papers: Anatomy of a Relational Database System.* Addison-Wesley, 1986.

[WV90] A. Wolski and J. Veijalainen. 2PC Agent method: Achieving serializability in presence of failures in a heterogeneous multidatabase. In *Proceedings of PARBASE-90*, Miami Beach, Florida, 1990.

The Joy of Sets

Richard Connor, Malcolm Atkinson†, Sonia Berman‡, Quintin Cutts, Graham Kirby and Ron Morrison

Department of Mathematical and Computational Science,
University of St Andrews, St Andrews, KY16 9SS, Scotland

†Department of Computer Science, University of Glasgow,
Glasgow G12 8QQ, Scotland

‡Department of Computer Science, University of Capetown, South Africa.

{richard, quintin, graham, ron}@dcs.st-and.ac.uk
mpa@dcs.glasgow.ac.uk
sonia@cs.uct.ac.za

Abstract

The semantics of many bulk data models depends on user-defined attributes such as definitions of element equality, ordering, and other domain predicates. While these attributes are an intrinsic part of the data model, they are not normally treated as part of the static type description. This leads to the occurrence of data modelling errors which are not statically detectable, such as a union operator accidentally being applied to two sets which have different equality semantics.

Here we introduce a model of bulk types which includes such attributes as part of the type definition, along with a typechecking scheme which is statically decidable. The model relies upon the value dependencies being manifest to the typechecker; one neat way of achieving this is through the new paradigm of hyper-programming. For cases where the static typechecking introduced is unnecessarily restrictive a polymorphism scheme which provides controlled flexibility is introduced.

1 Introduction

The semantics of many bulk data models depends on user-defined attributes such as definitions of element equality, ordering, and other domain predicates. While these attributes are an intrinsic part of the data model, they are not normally treated as part of the type description. This may lead to the occurrence of data modelling errors such as a union operator accidentally being applied to two sets which have different semantics for the equality of their elements.

Attributes such as the definition of element equality are typically held with instances of bulk data types, rather than with their type [ALP+91]. When a function such as union is applied, an arbitrary choice is made between the two possible equality functions. The chosen equality is used not only as an attribute of the newly constructed bulk value, but also to implement the application of the union function itself, as this depends upon the definition of element equality. Thus the semantics of union and similar set functions is compromised as, among other reasons, commutivity is lost.

By including these attributes as part of the type, however, it should be possible to define function types over bulk values such that the functions they describe are limited in application to bulk values where the element domain attributes are the same. Any attempt to apply these functions to bulk values with different attributes will be detected by the type system and the execution will be disallowed. A dynamically typed system will generate a type error or exception when the operator is erroneously applied, and a statically typed system will detect such errors before the program which contains them starts to execute.

A directory of Scottish names is used as an example of the inclusion of element attributes in the type. People may take a different view as to whether the names "MacFarlane", "Macfarlane", and "McFarlane" are really different names, but their owners are usually protective of their different forms. If they are used to retrieve data however it is likely that the retriever will not wish to distinguish between them. A telephone company's applications may require a number of directories, some of which distinguish between different spellings and some of which do not. For example a printed version of a telephone directory may distinguish between them whereas an electronic version used by an operator enquiry service may not. These directories are characterised in the system by bulk data dictionaries; whether different spellings are distinguished or not is characterised by different domain equality rules in these dictionaries.

Bulk operators such as union and intersection over directories whose elements have different equality rules are undefined and should be considered as an error. If such errors are not detected, and an arbitrary choice of equality is used, then no further mechanical error will result and the program will appear to execute correctly. The only way of detecting that an error has occurred is by analysing the directory which results. By including the equality definition in the type the error will be detected earlier in a strongly typed system, ideally during the program's typechecking.

Figure 1 shows a possible syntax for type definitions where domain equality attributes are described as a part of the type. The types *customerDirectory* and *operatorDirectory* are defined as specialisations of the type operator *Dictionary*, which has been previously defined. The structural attributes of the two dictionary types are the same, but different domain equality rules are associated with the types.

These different rules for domain equality mean that the types *customerDirectory* and *operatorDirectory* are not equivalent types within this system.

```
type customerDirectory is Dictionary[ string, phoneNo ] with
        ! simple (system-defined) equality
        domainEq = proc( a,b : string -> bool ) ; a = b

type operatorDirectory is Dictionary[ string, phoneNo ] with
        ! some complex equality rules
        domainEq = proc( a,b : string -> bool ) ; ...
```

Figure 1 Attributes associated with type

This restriction of bulk type equivalence must be carefully introduced to avoid losing flexibility within the programming system. The telephone company software may include a procedure *printDirectory*, which has a single operand of type *customerDirectory*. The application of *printDirectory* to a value of type *operatorDirectory* is an error, and the inequivalence of these types will lead to the reporting of a type error in such circumstances. However, there is also a large class of functions which may be correctly applied to bulk data values with any equality rule, such as a membership test. Figure 2 shows examples of such typings.

```
printDirectory( aCustomerDirectory )                    ! typing is correct
printDirectory( anOperatorDirectory )                   ! typing is incorrect

let x = member( "McPhee",aCustomerDirectory )   ! typing is correct
let y = member( "McPhee",anOperatorDirectory )  ! typing is also correct
```

Figure 2 Correct typing of different functions

The importance of the examples is that they demonstrate not only the importance of treating domain equality as an attribute of type in some circumstances, but also the importance of an appropriate form of polymorphism to allow abstraction over domain equality where it is not required. In fact the type of the functions union and intersection also requires polymorphism over element equality: the correct restriction is that the operands must have the same definition of equality, but the functions are applicable to any such pair of bulk values.

Equality of elements is not the only value that might be associated with bulk types; for instance some bulk types require order, others may require a characteristic function that restricts the values in the domain. The rest of this paper considers in detail the example of a set with an associated element equality function only; the mechanisms outlined are sufficiently general to extend easily to other examples of bulk types that depend on function values.

2 Name and structural equivalence

In general, the equivalence of types may be defined either by name or by structure. In name equivalence regimes two types are considered to be the same if and only if they share the same instance of a definition. Thus in the above example *customerDirectory* and *operatorDirectory* are de facto different types irrespective of the particular equality semantics defined.

Name equivalence thus gives a trivial solution to the requirement that sets with different element equality rules should be regarded as different types. However there are a number of problems in the use of a strict name equivalence regime in the context of database programming languages; these may be solved, but only by the use of structural equivalence testing in some circumstances [CBC+90]. In particular, the ability to abstract over part of the type definition, as required in the typing of functions such as *member*, can not be achieved without the use of structural equivalence.

The structural type equivalence of bulk types whose specification includes attributes such as domain equality requires the following to be true:

- the two bulk constructors are the same,
- the element types are the same, and
- the two equality tests are the same.

Traditional type checking takes care of the first two but the final test is problematic, and is the subject of this paper. The first obvious problem is the definition of "sameness" over values which in this case are function types. The second problem is that to achieve static typechecking the particular instances of the values must be available to the typechecker during its analysis of the program text.

Thus to achieve the static structural checking of these types in the most general context it is necessary to solve two well known intractable problems: the equality of functions and the static checking of dependent types. However, the careful introduction of certain restrictions may be used to allow partial solutions to both problems. The good news is that these restrictions may be easily explained to a programmer and give a useful programming algebra which allows precisely the desired static typechecking over bulk types with value dependencies.

3 Decidable Static Checking

There are two major problems with the decidable static typechecking of types which depend upon function values. The first is that dependent types in general pose difficulties with decidable static checking; the second is that function values in general do not have a good decidable notion of equality.[1]

An angle of attack is outlined here which provides partial solutions to both of these problems. The conjunction of these partial solutions gives a useful degree of static checking over dependent set types.

3.1 Dependent Types

For dependent types to be structurally equivalent it is necessary for the values upon which they depend to be equal. For the equivalence of dependent types to be statically decidable it is therefore necessary for the values upon which the types depend to be statically available to the typechecker. For some simple examples this is not a problem. For example, array types in Pascal are dependent upon their bounds; as these values are constrained to being manifest constants, the values are available to the typechecker and their equality is statically decidable.

For types which are dependent on more complex values statically decidable typechecking causes more difficulties. There are however two circumstances in which static typechecking can be maintained: either when a manifest constant binding is set up between the types and the values upon which they depend , or else when the system can arrange for the values upon which the type depends to be available to the typechecker during static analysis. The first of these is of limited use in the context of database programming languages, as will be shown; the second is more useful, however, and may be provided by systems which support incremental compilation or hyper-programming.

3.1.1 Value equality deduced by constant binding

Where the full equivalence of dependent types is not statically decidable, a syntactic rule may be introduced to constrain the use of dependent types to contexts where a more restrictive rule is statically enforceable. This mechanism relies upon the use of values being constrained to contexts where their equality is a consequence of that

---

[1]To avoid confusion the term *equality* will be used to mean the usual equivalence relation as defined over values, and *equivalence* will be used to mean the usual equivalence relation as defined over types.

context. Such a mechanism is commonly used to constrain a value dependency which arises with existentially quantified types [MP88].

One way of enforcing this with bulk types is to allow type definitions only to use functions referred to by identifiers with constant bindings. This allows identity to be used to determine that the equality functions are the same. Figure 3 shows an example of equivalent set type definitions which have associated equality functions. Because the identifier *stringEq* is a constant binding, it is possible to deduce statically that any other set type which defines equality as the same binding will also share the same procedure. Notice that this is a different consideration from the procedure itself being manifest; *stringEq* may be bound to the result of an arbitrary computation.

```
let stringEq = proc( a,b : string -> bool ) ; ...
        !** = means constant binding **!

type dictType1 is set[ string ] with stringEq
type dictType2 is set[ string ] with stringEq
```

Figure 3 Dependent set type definitions

That sound static typing can be achieved here is clear; however such a system is of limited use. The main problem is that only a subset of the desired equivalence semantics is achieved. Figure 4 shows a program where equivalent types cannot be determined statically.

```
let dictStringEq = if caseSensitive() then stringEq else
ignoreCase

type dictType1 is set[ string ] with stringEq
type dictType2 is set[ string ] with dictStringEq
```

Figure 4 Correct typechecking not statically decidable

This may be of limited consequence within a single program; a programmer would most likely use a single definition for all set types which share equality semantics, thus avoiding in any case the problems of structural type equivalence. The real limitation of this mechanism becomes apparent when separate compilation and the merging of independently prepared subsystems are considered; the ability to share a constant binding does not exist in these cases. To achieve correct type equivalence it is necessary to make the values available to the typechecker.

3.1.2 Values available to typechecker

Some programming language environments allow for the possibility of values of non-trivial types to be available in the typechecking domain. For example, the incremental compilation strategy of languages such as ML [MTH89] and Galileo mean that structured values are potentially available to the compiler at typechecking time. The hyper-programming system of Napier88 [MBC+89] allows arbitrary bindings to be performed at composition time, thus making the values potentially available to the typechecker. If all values upon which the types depend are available before the compilation of a program, and the typechecker has the ability to perform the required equality tests over them, then static typechecking may be achieved. An essential part of this mechanism is that, once references to dependent values are made, the system preserves these for the lifetime of the programs; that is, the system guarantees referential integrity.

The essential requirement is that any values upon which a type depends are evaluated before any equivalence testing is performed upon the type. This restriction of the general type description can be enforced in incremental compilation systems by restricting the stated dependencies to free identifiers which are resolved in the external environment, and in a hyper-programming system by restricting the dependencies to being hyper-links.

Figure 5 shows how the program shown in Figure 4 may be adapted for use in an incremental compilation system. Representing the same text as two compilation/evaluation sessions meets the requirement that the type dependencies appear as free identifiers with respect to the compilation unit. The point is that in this case, the function value *dictStringEq* has been evaluated, as has the value *stringEq*, before the compilation of the second program. The typechecker can therefore access these values during the static analysis of the program fragment and perform the necessary equality testing on them whenever a structural comparison of the two types is required.

```
let dictStringEq = if caseSensitive() then stringEq else
ignoreCase
```

```
type dictionary1 is set[ string ] with stringEq
type dictionary2 is set[ string ] with dictStringEq
```

Figure 5 Correct typechecking statically decidable by incremental compilation

The same technique may be used in a hyper-programming system where type dependencies are constrained to being represented as hyper-links; this guarantees in a subtly different manner that the required values have been evaluated before typechecking time. This will be explained in more detail later. There are two other situations discussed later where such values may be available at compilation time: these are where the value is a manifest literal, and where compile-time linguistic reflection [SSS+92] is used.

There are two major advantages of this solution over that of constant binding. Firstly it allows a fully general type equivalence check, rather than a restricted subset of it. The second is a consequence of this particularly important in database programming languages: it is possible to merge independently constructed subsystems whilst preserving the type equivalence semantics.

The problem of how to determine whether two functions have the same behaviour as each other is now examined.

3.2 Functional Equality

The most general notion of functional equality is that, for any two functions, they are equal if they produce an equal result for any equal operands. It is well known that there exists no decidable algorithm which tests this notion for any given pair of functions. As a consequence, many programming languages provide no notion of equality over values of function type.

There are however other less general equivalence relations which may be usefully defined over functions. In some languages for example the concept of identity may be defined for functions; the identity of a function is created when its closure is formed [MBC+89]. Another possibility is that the code, perhaps normalised according to some semantics preserving rule, is equal, and the bindings from that code are equal [DD85]. The point here is that there do exist a number of equivalence relations which may be tested by fully decidable algorithms and which are sub-partitions of the most general relation defined by functional equality. Thus although it is not possible in general to determine the equivalent behaviour of arbitrary functions, it is possible to determine the equivalent behaviour of particular subsets of functions. Figure 6 shows three pairs of equal functions, the detection of whose equality is of varying complexity.

Without further elaboration we define a notion of weak functional equality, which will detect that both the second and third pair of functions are equal. The important attribute of this equality over simple identity is that it does not preclude the equality of pairs of functions which are independently constructed in different environments. The usefulness of this weak notion of equality may be seen in two situations: the merging of sub-systems, and the copying of values between persistent environments.

```
let first = proc( a : int -> int ) ; if a = 0 then 1 else 37
let second = proc( x : int -> int )
begin
        let res := 37
        if x = 0 do res := 1
        res
end

let difficultToDecide = ( first = second )
```

```
let first = proc( a : int -> int ) ; if a = 0 then 1 else 37
let second = first

let easyToDecide = ( first = second )
```

```
let first = proc( a : int -> int ) ; if a = 0 then 1 else 37
let second = proc( x : int -> int ) ; if x = 0 then 1 else 37

let quiteEasyToDecide = ( first = second )
```

Figure 6 Varying degrees of complexity for functional equality testing

The merging of sub-systems, including the merging of independently prepared program and data, may only be sensibly achieved in cases where the type of the data has been agreed beforehand. In the case of dependent set types, the type includes the description of the element equality function. The importance of weak equality in this context is that as long as the equality is agreed beforehand, different instances of the same equality function may be prepared in the sub-systems, and then mechanically detected as equal during the system merge.

Copying values between typed object stores is really a special case of merging. In a typed object store every object must have a strong association with a representation of its type, to allow the typechecking of programs which bind to it. When values are copied between stores their associated type representations must also be copied. The importance of weak equality over identity in this case is that the equality of functions is preserved over copying, thereby preserving type equivalence over values independently propagated from a common source.

4 Hyper-programming interface and examples

Hyper-programming is a new style of programming made possible when source code representations are stored inside a typed persistent store. A hyper-program is a source representation which contains, in addition to the normal linear text, embedded links to other values in the store. Since the linked values can be accessed by scanning the hyper-program, they are available to the compiler. If the language definition allows the values on which types depend to be denoted by links, those values will be accessible by the typechecker for static checking. This may only be allowed in cases where the links are known to refer to immutable values, so that a constant binding is maintained from type to value as above.

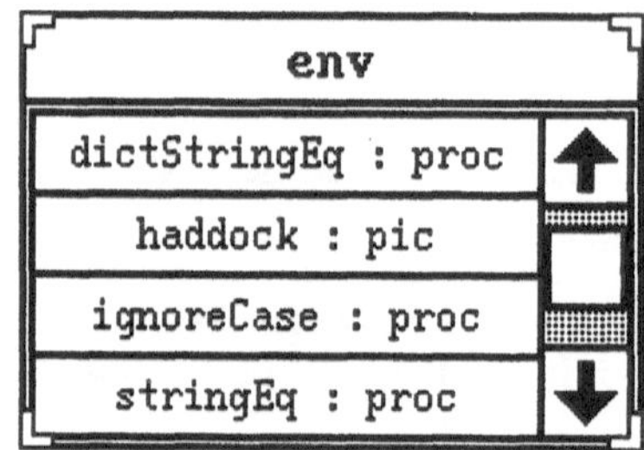

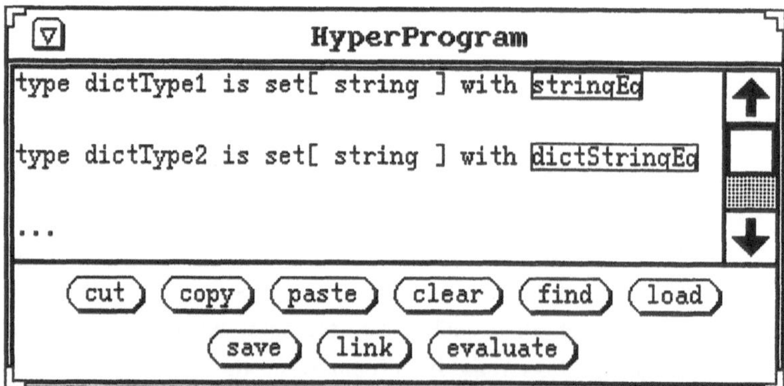

Figure 7 An example hyper-program

Figure 7 shows the programmer's view of a simple hyper-program in which dependent set types may be checked statically. The values on which they depend are denoted by light-buttons which represent direct links to values already present in the persistent store. Although it is not possible to tell from the text of the program whether the types are the same, the typechecker is able to follow the links into the persistent store and perform arbitrary computation over the values in their closure.

Although the example above serves to illustrate the mechanism, it is unlikely to be used in practice since the programmer would not normally write separate equivalent type definitions within a single program. Figure 8 shows two separate compilation units using equivalent dependent types. They may be compiled in entirely separate environments, or in the same environment, so long as the function values are already present in the compilation environment.

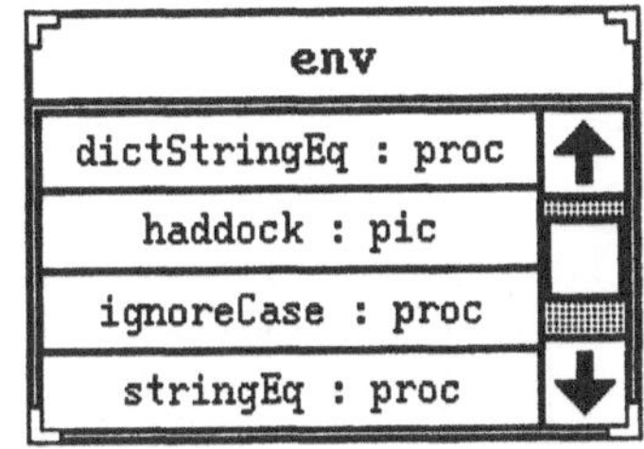

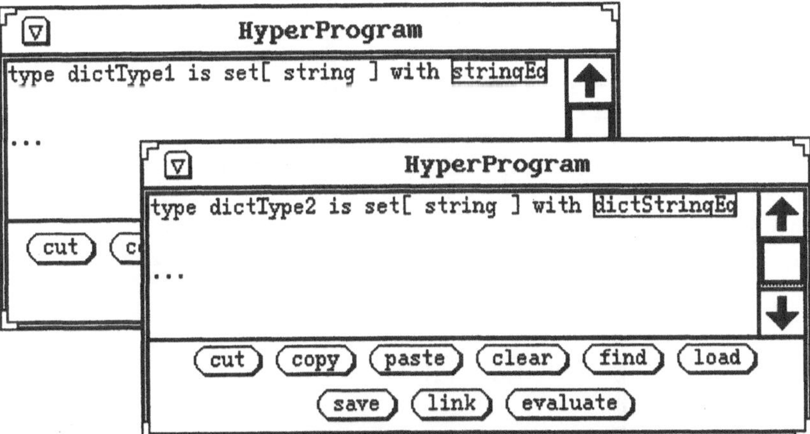

Figure 8 Separate compilation units

If the types declared in the programs above are equivalent to each other, then data of these types which is created and placed in the persistent store will be seen to be typed equivalently in later use. Figure 9 shows an example of a hyper-program which applies the union operator to two values created by the programs in Figure 8. Note that these are typed set values whose type equivalence is checked at compilation time. It is not possible to see whether this program is typed correctly by a simple examination of the program text; however the typechecker is again able to access the closure of the embedded hyper-links, which contains the necessary information. It perhaps should be pointed out that in a hyper-programming system the programmer should also be given this ability!

One further point to make is that the light buttons named as *d1* and *d2* may refer to locations, rather than instances of the bulk types. After the program has been compiled it is possible for these locations to be updated with other values of the same type; however the program will work correctly with the new versions since their types, including dependencies, must be the same as the old versions. The significance of this in database terms is that the programs may be typechecked after the schema has been defined, rather than after it has been populated.

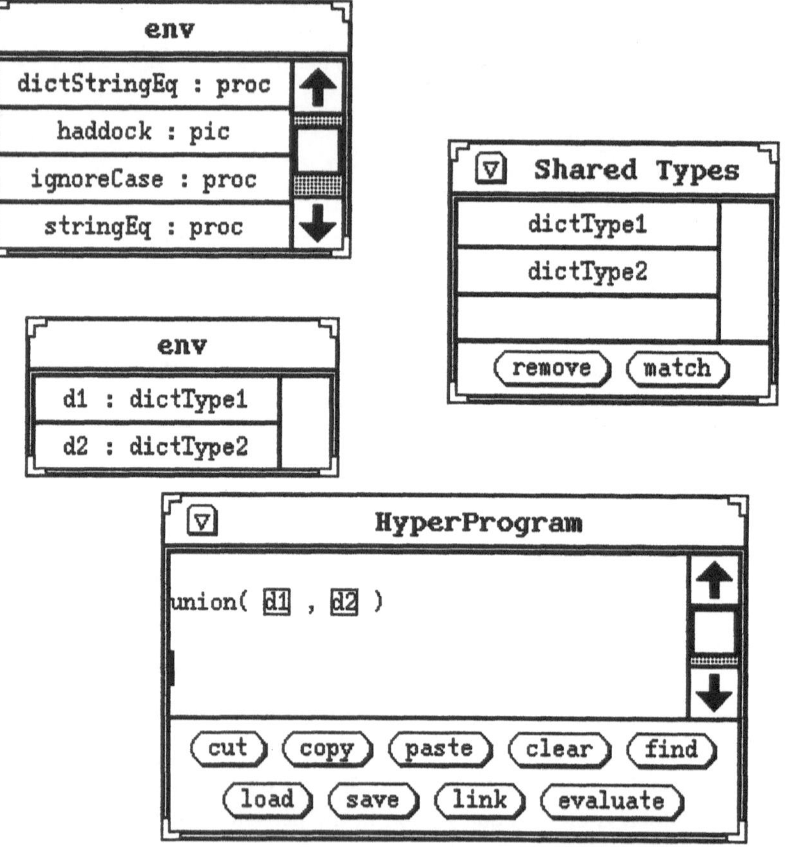

Figure 9 Statically checkable union application

5 Polymorphism

The main motivation for introducing value dependencies to bulk data types is to make a class of errors statically detectable. As always, however, the restriction introduced decreases the class of correct programs, as well as the class of incorrect ones. Polymorphic forms are required to re-introduce some of the lost flexibility in a controlled manner.

The notation used here for polymorphism is deliberately verbose in order to expose all of the concepts being introduced. It is expected that a programming language with these concepts would elide much of the unnecessary information to reduce noise. The notation will be introduced by example in the style of Napier88 polymorphic forms. Figure 10 shows a polymorphic procedure in Napier88, and a call to that procedure. Notice that the parametric form of the polymorphism is made explicit, and that the type parameter is explicitly supplied at the call.

```
let id = proc[ T ]( x : T -> T ) ; x

let three = id[ int ]( 3 )
```

Figure 10 The polymorphic identity procedure in Napier88

To help understanding, formal identifiers are introduced within the square brackets for every type, and aspect of type, which is being abstracted over. To abstract over a set type, a notation must therefore introduce formal parameters for the type of the element, and the value of the equality function. Figure 11 shows a possible notation for the type of the procedure *cardinality*. This type should be read as: "a procedure which, for every type *T*, and for every type *S* which is a set with element type *T* and equality value *e*, takes a parameter of type *S* and returns an integer."

The only new concept introduced here is that the formal parameter *e* stands for a value; as this value is part of the type, however, it is included in the universal quantification. The value denoted by *e* must be locally accessible, as it is required to check any insertion into a value of the set type; there is no reason why *e* should not be used as a value within the procedure body.

```
cardinality : proc[ T, S : set[ T ] with e ]( S -> int )
```

Figure 11 The polymorphic *cardinality* procedure type

Figure 12 shows a call to the *cardinality* procedure. Notice that although the set type including the equality value is passed explicitly in this example, this could be inferred according to the type of the set parameter.

```
let x = cardinality[ string, set[ string ] with ignoreCase ](
mySet )
```

Figure 12 A call of cardinality

Enough abstraction has been introduced to write some different forms of the set union operation. Figure 13 shows a union procedure for sets with the same equality.

```
let union = proc[ T, S : set[ T ] with e ]( a , b : S -> S )
begin
        let new = createSet[ T , S ]()
        for i in a do new := insert[ T, S ]( new , i )
        for i in b do new := insert[ T, S ]( new, i )
        new
end
```

Figure 13 A set union implementation

It is also useful to consider the case where the operand sets have different models of equality. Typically where equality is not part of the type information and is instead associated with the bulk type instances one or other function is chosen arbitrarily, or the programmer may supply a new equality function. Each of these may be programmed using the notations introduced; the difference is that the programmer has fine control over the outcome, and must specify the static types involved at each stage.

```
let union = proc[ T , S1 : set[ T ] with e1 , S2 : set[ T ] with e2 ]
                    ( a : S1 ; b : S2 -> set[ T ] with
                              proc( a,b : T -> bool ) ;
                                      e1( a , b ) and e2( a , b ) )
begin
    type resType is set[ T ] with proc( a,b : T -> bool ) ;
                                      e1( a , b ) and e2( a , b )
    let new = createSet[ T, resType ]()
    for i in a do new := insert[ T, resType ]( new , i )
    for i in b do new := insert[ T, resType ]( new, i )
    new
end
```

Figure 14 A more interesting union operator

One further possibility is that the type of the result may be constructed in terms of the equality functions used for the operands. This requires relaxing the rules for the construction of set types to allow the use of manifest literals as well as constant hyper-links. Figure 14 shows a union procedure in which the type of the result uses an equality relation which is the conjunction of those of the operand types, and which is still statically checkable. Successive calls to this procedure with equivalent operand types will result in equivalent result types, and the result type can be determined statically.

This typing relies upon the recursive application of weak equality over function values. Notice that the example does not introduce general value dependencies, as the definition of the equality function relies only upon values which are part of type parameters to the procedure, rather than value parameters. The use of arbitrary values within the body of the function would preclude the static checking which is possible here as the functional equality could not be determined statically.

6 Conclusions and further work

This paper has outlined how bulk data types that depend upon value based attributes may be statically type checked. The technique depends upon the equality relation over the value based attributes being decidable statically. One way of achieving this is by hyper-programming, a programming technique that allows links to persistent objects to be part of the source representation of a program. These links are available to the type checker and therefore can be used as part of the type equivalence relation for bulk types. To restore the flexibilty that has been lost by the introduction of static type checking, a polymorphic abstraction mechanism is introduced over these value dependent bulk types.

One expected result not discussed in this paper is that major efficiency gains may be made by using static knowledge of these functions in the implementation of the bulk values.

7 Acknowledgements

The title of this paper derives from an inspiration by Fred Curtis of Sydney University whilst on a chance visit to St Andrews, and is in no way connected with the authors' knowledge of literature [Deu90]. Dave Stemple of the University of Massachusetts at Amherst is to be thanked for his constructive comments on the paper. This work was supported by Esprit III Basic Research Action 6309 - FIDE 2, and Richard Connor is supported by SERC Postdoctoral Fellowship B/91/RFH/9078.

8 References

[ACO85] Albano, A., Cardelli, L. & Orsini, R. "Galileo: a Strongly Typed, Interactive Conceptual Language". ACM Transactions on Database Systems 10, 2 (1985) pp 230-260.

[ALP+91] Atkinson, M.P., Lécluse, C., Philbrow, P. & Richard, P. "Design Issues in a Map Language". In **Bulk Types & Persistent Data**, Kanellakis, P. & Schmidt, J.W. (ed), Morgan Kaufmann (1991) pp 20-32.

[BL84] Burstall, R. & Lampson, B. "A Kernel Language for Abstract Data Types and Modules" Proc. International Symposium on theSemantics of Data Types, LNCS Vol. 173, Springer-Verlag (1984).

[CBC+90] Connor, R.C.H., Brown, A.L., Cutts, Q.I., Dearle, A.,Morrison, R. & Rosenberg J. "Type Equivalence Checking in Persistent Object Stores". In **Implementing Persistent Object Bases - Principles and Practice**, Morgan - Kaufmann, pp 154-170.

[DD85] Donahue, J. & Demers, A. "Data Types are Values". ACM Transactions on Programming Languages and Systems 7, 3 (1985) pp 421-445.

[Deu90] Deux, O.O. "The Story of O_2". IEEE Transactions on Knowledge and Data Engineering 2, 1 (1990).

[KCC+92] Kirby, G.N.C., Connor, R.C.H., Cutts, Q.I., Dearle, A., Farkas, A.M. & Morrison, R. "Persistent Hyper-Programs". In Proc. 5th International Workshop on Persistent Object Systems, San Miniato, Italy (1992) pp 73-95.

[MBC+89] Morrison, R., Brown, A.L., Connor, R.C.H. & Dearle, A. "The Napier88 Reference Manual". University of St Andrews Technical Report PPRR-77-89 (1989).

[MP88] Mitchell, J.C. & Plotkin, G.D. "Abstract Types have Existential Type". ACM Transactions on Programming Languages and Systems 10, 3 (1988) pp 470-502.

[MTH89] Milner, R., Tofte, M. & Harper, R. **The Definition of Standard ML**. MIT Press, Cambridge, Massachusetts (1989).

[SSS+92] Stemple, D., Stanton, R.B., Sheard, T., Philbrow, P., Morrison, R., Kirby, G.N.C., Fegaras, L., Cooper, R.L., Connor, R.C.H., Atkinson, M.P. & Alagic, S. "Type-Safe Linguistic Reflection: A Generator Technology". ESPRIT BRA Project 3070 FIDE Technical Report FIDE/92/49 (1992).

[Tur36] Turing, A. "On Computable Numbers with an Application to the Entscheidungs-problem". Proceedings of the London Mathematical Society 42 (1936) pp 230-265.

Author Index

Published in 1990–92

AI and Cognitive Science '89, Dublin City University, Eire, 14–15 September 1989
A. F. Smeaton and G. McDermott (Eds.)

Specification and Verification of Concurrent Systems, University of Stirling, Scotland, 6–8 July 1988
C. Rattray (Ed.)

Semantics for Concurrency, Proceedings of the International BCS-FACS Workshop, Sponsored by Logic for IT (S.E.R.C.), University of Leicester, UK, 23–25 July 1990
M. Z. Kwiatkowska, M. W. Shields and R. M. Thomas (Eds.)

Functional Programming, Glasgow 1989
Proceedings of the 1989 Glasgow Workshop, Fraserburgh, Scotland, 21–23 August 1989
K. Davis and J. Hughes (Eds.)

Persistent Object Systems, Proceedings of the Third International Workshop, Newcastle, Australia, 10–13 January 1989
J. Rosenberg and D. Koch (Eds.)

Z User Workshop, Oxford 1989, Proceedings of the Fourth Annual Z User Meeting, Oxford, 15 December 1989
J. E. Nicholls (Ed.)

Formal Methods for Trustworthy Computer Systems (FM89), Halifax, Canada, 23–27 July 1989
Dan Craigen (Editor) and Karen Summerskill (Assistant Editor)

Security and Persistence, Proceedings of the International Workshop on Computer Architecture to Support Security and Persistence of Information, Bremen, West Germany, 8–11 May 1990
John Rosenberg and J. Leslie Keedy (Eds.)

Women into Computing: Selected Papers 1988–1990
Gillian Lovegrove and Barbara Segal (Eds.)

3rd Refinement Workshop (organised by BCS-FACS, and sponsored by IBM UK Laboratories, Hursley Park and the Programming Research Group, University of Oxford), Hursley Park, 9–11 January 1990
Carroll Morgan and J. C. P. Woodcock (Eds.)

Designing Correct Circuits, Workshop jointly organised by the Universities of Oxford and Glasgow, Oxford, 26–28 September 1990
Geraint Jones and Mary Sheeran (Eds.)

Functional Programming, Glasgow 1990
Proceedings of the 1990 Glasgow Workshop on Functional Programming, Ullapool, Scotland, 13–15 August 1990
Simon L. Peyton Jones, Graham Hutton and Carsten Kehler Holst (Eds.)

4th Refinement Workshop, Proceedings of the 4th Refinement Workshop, organised by BCS-FACS, Cambridge, 9–11 January 1991
Joseph M. Morris and Roger C. Shaw (Eds.)

AI and Cognitive Science '90, University of Ulster at Jordanstown, 20–21 September 1990
Michael F. McTear and Norman Creaney (Eds.)

Software Re-use, Utrecht 1989, Proceedings of the Software Re-use Workshop, Utrecht, The Netherlands, 23–24 November 1989
Liesbeth Dusink and Patrick Hall (Eds.)

Z User Workshop, 1990, Proceedings of the Fifth Annual Z User Meeting, Oxford, 17–18 December 1990
J.E. Nicholls (Ed.)

IV Higher Order Workshop, Banff 1990
Proceedings of the IV Higher Order Workshop, Banff, Alberta, Canada, 10–14 September 1990
Graham Birtwistle (Ed.)

ALPUK91, Proceedings of the 3rd UK Annual Conference on Logic Programming, Edinburgh, 10–12 April 1991
Geraint A.Wiggins, Chris Mellish and Tim Duncan (Eds.)

Specifications of Database Systems
International Workshop on Specifications of Database Systems, Glasgow, 3–5 July 1991
David J. Harper and Moira C. Norrie (Eds.)

7th UK Computer and Telecommunications Performance Engineering Workshop
Edinburgh, 22–23 July 1991
J. Hillston, P.J.B. King and R.J. Pooley (Eds.)

Logic Program Synthesis and Transformation
Proceedings of the LOPSTR 91, International Workshop on Logic Program Synthesis and Transformation, University of Manchester, 4–5 July 1991
T.P. Clement and K.-K. Lau (Eds.)

Declarative Programming, Sasbachwalden 1991
PHOENIX Seminar and Workshop on Declarative Programming, Sasbachwalden, Black Forest, Germany, 18–22 November 1991
John Darlington and Roland Dietrich (Eds.)

Building Interactive Systems: Architectures and Tools
Philip Gray and Roger Took (Eds.)

Functional Programming, Glasgow 1991
Proceedings of the 1991 Glasgow Workshop on Functional Programming, Portree, Isle of Skye, 12–14 August 1991
Rogardt Heldal, Carsten Kehler Holst and Philip Wadler (Eds.)

Object Orientation in Z
Susan Stepney, Rosalind Barden and David Cooper (Eds.)

Code Generation – Concepts, Tool, Techniques
Proceedings of the International Workshop on Code Generation, Dagstuhl, Germany, 20–24 May 1991
Robert Giegerich and Susan L. Graham (Eds.)

Z User Workshop, York 1991, Proceedings of the Sixth Annual Z User Meeting, York, 16–17 December 1991
J.E. Nicholls (Ed.)